BATTLES LOST AND WON

Great Campaigns of World War II

BATTLES LOST AND WON

Great Campaigns of World War II

Hanson Baldwin

This edition published in 1995 by Smithmark Publishers,
a division of U.S. Media Holdings, Inc., 16 East 32nd Street,
New York, NY 10016.

SMITHMARK books are available for bulk purchase for
sales promotion and premium use. For details write or call
the manager of special sales, SMITHMARK Publishers, Inc.,
16 East 32nd Street, New York, NY 10016; (212) 532-6600.

This edition published by special arrangement
with W.S. Konecky Associates, Inc., 156 Fifth Avenue,
New York, NY 10010.

ISBN: 0-8317-6706-5

Printed in the United States of America

10 9 8 7 6 5 4 3 2

The quotations from General Eisenhower (each identified by footnotes
in various chapters) are from Crusade in Europe,
by Dwight D. Eisenhower. Copyright, 1948 by Doubleday and Company, Inc.
Reprinted by permission of the publisher.

The lyrics on page 92 are from the song "Beer Barrel Polka"
Copyright 1934 and 1939 by Shapiro, Bernstein & Co., Inc.
Copyright Renewed and Assigned by Shapiro, Bernstein & Co., Inc.
Used by permission.

The lyrics on page 342 are © Copyright 1942 Irving Berlin
© Copyright assigned to Gene Tunney, A. L. Berman and Ralph J. Bunche
as Trustees God Bless America Fund.
Reprinted by Permission of Irving Berlin Music Corporation.

Maps by John Tremblay

CONTENTS

MAPS

A NOTE FOR THE READER

Plan of the Book

For every generation of man the drums of war have broken the cadence of peace.

Battle—between man and man, tribe and tribe, village, city, state and nation—regarded by the unthinking as the abnormal or aberrant in human behavior, has been, historically, the norm.

What has changed since the warriors' weapons were spear and bow has been the scope of war. Politically, the growth of integrated nation-states with immense economic and industrial power, and technically, the revolution of the last half-century which has bridged continents and oceans and has produced weapons of cataclysmic power, have made modern war staggering in extent.

War today is total; no corner of our world can escape its effects; millions march in its train.

World War II, with its forty million dead, was, by far, the greatest conflict in man's history.

Like all wars it produced for all belligerents its great victories and its great defeats, its battles lost and won, its turning points, its brilliant plans and its lost opportunities, its tactical successes and its technical failures, its great leaders and those who were tried and found wanting, its horror and its heroism, its human drama.

Yet World War II is already fading into the past; several generations now know of it, not through personal experience but solely as a dark and dangerous but exciting thundercloud across the dim yesterdays. To those born since World War II the heroes and the knaves—the household names of those tremendous years—live only as ghosts, as half-forgotten figures of history.

World War II was names and dates and battles—the tide of history rolling to the flood; yet above all it was human history, personalized narrative, the history of the tens of millions who fought or served, who conquered or who lost.

Military history is often written and read simply as chronology or tactical narrative with little accent on the human drama. War is the greatest tragedy presented on the stage of Man; in its modern immensity, the individual tragedies, the detailed dramas which comprise the whole, can be easily lost.

Military history and drama are compatible; in fact, they are inseparable; one without the other is incomplete. This book has been written with such a concept as a guideline. An effort has been made to present not only the facts of World War II but the drama as well; to make history readable, interesting, viable and accurate.

The eleven selected battles present a cross-section of the world's greatest war—from the Polish campaign, where blitzkrieg was born, to Okinawa, "the last battle," where the kamikaze portended the coming menace of the missile. Some chapters deliberately emphasize particular aspects of the battle upon which the whole depended—viz., the struggle of planes versus ships at Okinawa; most attempt to provide an over-all view of the campaign. Each battle was, in fact, more than a battle; each was so extensive in time and space [some more than others] and comprised so many separate episodes of struggle that each transcended the older meaning of the word "battle" and was, in essence, a campaign. Yet each was an entity; many were turning points; upon some, the scales of history rested.

Though tailored to the general reader, the author hopes that this book may also offer fact and opinion interesting to the military specialist and to the student.

It has, indeed, been written for that purpose.

Each chapter describes the narrative of battle; each draws the lessons of conflict, summarizes the results and attempts to place the campaign in perspective in the war and in history. Each account is supplemented by extensive notes and bibliographies, which provide a large amount of additional information to the interested reader. Thus, each chapter presents (1) a Narrative of Battle; (2) the Results of Battle; (3) a Critique of Battle; and (4), in the back of the book, extensive Supplementary Notes and background material about each campaign in particular and World War II in general. Maps, and an appendix which provides a breakdown of World War II casualties by countries, supplement the text.

Thus, each chapter stands alone, complete; yet each supplements the others; collectively, the book is a military panorama of World War II.

There are certain to be errors in any work with the scope of this one—all the more so since the writing of military history is an inexact art. The battlefield gets dressed up overnight. Every effort has been made to avoid error. This book has drawn heavily upon a wide variety of works, particularly upon the meticulously prepared official histories. Nearly all of the chapters have been read and checked by experts in the campaigns described. But the errors that remain—as well as the lessons deduced and judgments drawn—are mine alone.

The mistakes described, the personality or other differences portrayed, that seem so stark, so clear today—decades later—were not, it should be remembered, so obvious during the "red hell of the fight." This book is an attempt to combine the emotional and dramatic immediacy of many of the war's moments of truth with the retrospective knowledge and wisdom of after-years.

It represents, for me, a labor of love for my family, who lived and suffered with me through these campaigns, and my own tribute to the world's fighting men—particularly to the soldiers, sailors, marines and airmen of the United States who, in World War II, scaled the ramparts of glory and descended to the abyss of defeat.

HANSON W. BALDWIN

CHAPTER 1

"WE WANT WAR!" THE BEGINNING—
THE POLISH CAMPAIGN

September 1–October 6, 1939

"*. . . We want war!*"—JOACHIM VON RIBBENTROP, AUGUST 11, 1939

"*Our enemies are little worms. . . . Close your hearts to pity!*
Act brutally! . . . The stronger man is right!"—ADOLF HITLER,
AUGUST 22, 1939[1]

Blood and iron was Bismarck's doctrine, but the Second World War was started twenty-five years ago with an added ingredient: a cynical ruthlessness which would have shocked even the Iron Chancellor.

On the night of August 31, 1939—the last day of peace [in the world that was]—Hans-Walter Zech-Nenntwich and his fellow members of a German "choral society" cast off their bogus masks in the Free City of Danzig, doffed their civilian clothes and donned the jack boots and black uniforms of the Nazi SS (Elite Guard).

And at about 8 P.M. near the little town of Gleiwitz in German Silesia near the Polish border a group of nervous men suddenly invaded the local radio station, slugged two German employees, seized the transmitter, broadcast a fiery, aggressive speech in Polish and raced away toward the frontier, leaving near the station's doorstep, dying and bullet-riddled, a man whose name may be forever unknown to fame.

Alfred Helmut Naujocks, son of a Kiel grocer, member of the Nazi SS, led the "raiders" in the Gleiwitz incident, a faked attack on a German border town, arranged to provide Hitler with an excuse for war against Poland. This mock Polish "provocation" was buttressed by a bleeding body, one of Naujock's men—shot and killed apparently by accident—later described as a Polish "raider."[2]

Gleiwitz, one of several staged "incidents" along the frontier, was the last step in Adolf Hitler's march toward World War II. The die was already cast; the troops were moving when Polish phrases stuttered from the Gleiwitz transmitter. The incident was merely camouflage, frosting, deception—Hitler's cynical concession to history's demand for justification.

World War II festered for a quarter of a century, growing out of the ashes of a Europe devastated by World War I.

The defeat of the Central Powers and the Versailles Treaty, with its emphasis upon the self-determination of peoples, had changed the map of Europe. Alsace and Lorraine were returned to France. A Polish corridor, carved out of what had been Germany, gave Warsaw access to the Baltic and separated East Prussia from Berlin. Danzig was established as a free city under the League of Nations with a League Commissioner, but, despite its Germanic population, with Polish control over customs and foreign affairs. The seeds of irredentism thus were sown while the gun barrels still were hot. . . .

The brave new world, safe for democracy, soon, it became apparent, was to be the same old world with patches on it. Washington rejected the vision of its wartime President, Woodrow Wilson, and refused to join the League of Nations, and Europe commenced to stew in the bitter juices of devastation, disillusion and depression.[3]

Germany's brief experiment in democracy—the Weimar Republic—was beset with a host of problems.

It was identified by the strong and influential Nationalists with the "stab-in-the-back" legends which excused and extenuated the collapse of the German armies and the loss of World War I. Large segments of the German population blamed the government of the short-lived Republic for having signed the Versailles Treaty, for saddling their country with a war-guilt psychology, for having "given away" Alsace-Lorraine, a large part of Prussia and part of Silesia, and for having accepted a staggering reparations commitment and reduction of the once-proud Imperial Army and Navy to the status of a 100,000-man police force, with neither tanks nor aircraft, and a 15,000-man coastal patrol force.

A runaway inflation and incipient anarchy were succeeded, after a few brief years, by major unemployment—the product of the great world depression that started in 1929. Left-wing and right-wing extremists—Communists and Brown Shirts—battled in the streets for dominance, and in 1933 Adolf Hitler came to power, opening one of the darkest periods in the modern history of man.

From the beginning Hitler was dedicated to dominance—to a Master Race, to expansionism by subtlety and guile and ruthless power. He rearmed openly and moved his armed forces into the Rhineland (in 1936) despite the restrictions of the Versailles Treaty, reassured his potential enemies publicly while excoriating them privately, signed a nonaggression pact with Poland in order to have a free hand against Czechoslovakia and Austria, and started the construction of the West Wall—a fortified zone opposite France and Belgium.

Paris and London equivocated, hesitated, but did nothing; the United States was preoccupied with its own economic problems and the social revolution led by Roosevelt; and the League of Nations proved to be a debating society, powerless to halt or even influence Mussolini's rape of Ethiopia.

Germany's techniques for conquest—economic barter deals, political infiltration, psychological terror—and Hitler's recipe for repression—concentration camps, Nuremberg rallies, emotional flagellation and the "Big Lie" of Goebbels, the Nazi Propaganda Minister—became familiar prescriptions. Nazi "Fifth Columns," boring from within, and "quislings," or traitors—Seyss-Inquart in Austria, Konrad Henlein in the Sudetenland, Josef Tiso in Slovakia and Vikdun Quisling (for whom the tribe was named) in Norway[4]—were the puppets of Nazi hegemony.

The year 1938 saw the tide of the Third Reich of Adolf Hitler, that was to last a thousand years, rolling to the flood. German tanks moved into Austria; Hitler threatened war against Czechoslovakia. Hastily, in a conference whose name is now forever synonymous with appeasement, the leaders of Europe convened at Munich to dismember a nation, Czechoslovakia, not even represented at the conference.[5] Hitler got the Sudetenland and the Czech fortifications; and Poland and Hungary, like vultures, tore off pieces of the dying rump state. London and Paris hailed Munich with cheers of relief as "peace in our time."

Before the year was out Hitler was looking toward new horizons; Joachim von Ribbentrop, Nazi Foreign Minister, acting for his master, suggested to Warsaw the return of Danzig to Germany.

And so the stage was set. . . .

The year of Doomsday—1939—opened with the brass tongue of propaganda loud throughout the world. Hitler insisted upon the return of Danzig and upon German control of a 15-mile connecting strip across the Corridor. Strident charges and countercharges echoed from the

Corridor and the German-Polish frontiers; in the Free City of Danzig Nazis agitated and harangued. In mid-March what was left of Czechoslovakia ceased to exist as a sovereign state; German troops moved into Bohemia, Moravia and Slovakia; Poland was now outflanked from the south as well as from the north. One week later, Lithuania, with the iron fist of Nazi might as an inducement, surrendered Memelland, former German territory, to Hitler. Even Rumania, which had been, along with Poland and vanished Czechoslovakia, a French ally, signed an agreement with Berlin promising most of her oil output to Germany. And on March 28 the long siege of Madrid ended and the forces of Francisco Franco, aided by Germans and Italians, won the Spanish Civil War.

But now at last in London the blinders were almost off. The students who signed the Oxford Oath—never again to go to war—and the columnists and intellectuals who asked, "Who wants to die for Danzig?" were almost silenced, along with the politicians of appeasement and the Cliveden set.[6]

Hitler's absorption of Czechoslovakia, with its preponderant non-Germanic population, went far beyond his stated aims of rectifying the injustices of the Versailles Treaty; even Chamberlain now saw Czechoslovakia and Poland not as far-distant lands for which no Englishman should shed his blood but as symbols of Hitler's insatiable appetite for world conquest. On the last day of March, 1939, the British Prime Minister told the House of Commons that if Poland were attacked, Britain and France would "feel themselves bound at once to lend the Polish Government all support in their power."[7]

Britain, with French concurrence, extended her mantle of moral protection to Greece and Rumania, and Britain, France and Turkey signed formal agreements for mutual assistance in the Mediterranean.

Hitler was furious ("I'll cook them a stew that they'll choke on"[8]), the more so since it was becoming obvious in Berlin that Poland couldn't be bluffed. Warsaw called up reservists after Hitler's triumphant entry into Memel, and Beck, the Polish Foreign Minister, answered Ribbentrop's threats in kind.

In early April the strutting Mussolini, aping the long-dead Caesars and jealous of Germanic power, sent his legions into Albania in search of a quick and easy conquest.

Unknown to the world, Hitler gave oral instructions to his military commanders to prepare for war against Poland by the end of August and followed up, on April 3, with written orders—a part of the OKW's (Oberkommando der Wehrmacht, or Supreme Command of the Armed Forces) "Directive for the Armed Forces, 1939-40."

Plan Weiss, labeled "Top Secret," drafted by Hitler himself, stated that "the present attitude of Poland requires . . . the initiation of military preparations to remove, if necessary, any threat from this direction forever. . . . Preparations must be made in such a way that the operation can be carried out at any time from September 1, 1939, onward."[9]

At the end of April Hitler abrogated the Polish-German nonaggression pact of 1934 and simultaneously repudiated the Anglo-German naval agreement of 1935 which had limited the tonnage of the German Fleet to 35 percent of the British.

The summer of 1939 witnessed a steady march toward war.

ITEM: Directives to Army Group North and Army Group South, charged with the attack upon Poland, were issued in May; in June eight divisions were assigned to the Polish frontier for "entrenchment" work, and were gradually built up during the summer from peace to war strength.[10]

ITEM: On May 22 a Fascist "Axis"—Rome-Berlin—was forged in the so-called "Pact of Steel" when the Fuehrer and the Duce signed a military alliance.

ITEM: Leaders of Hungary, Yugoslavia and Bulgaria came to Berlin to pay obeisance to Hitler; each was greeted with a display of Germany's military might. The German armed forces were "formidable," though their strength had been "exaggerated."[11] The Army was probably the best trained and best equipped in Europe; the Air Force the most modern though not so large as then publicly pictured; the Navy small but already including fifty-seven submarines.

ITEM: Reluctantly, hesitatingly, Britain and France put pressure on Poland to compromise on the Corridor and sent envoys to Moscow to attempt to establish a unified front against Hitler. But the German dictator had more to offer, and Stalin was obviously anxious to avoid war.

ITEM: A militarized German "Freikorps" infiltrated into Danzig; the German Gauleiter Albert Forster openly proclaimed his intention of incorporating the Free City into Hitler's Reich.

Disorders increased; the League administration virtually broke down; the Polish Corridor was tense.

ITEM: German military concentrations, camouflaged as "maneuvers," increased in East Prussia and opposite the Corridor throughout August.

ITEM: Count Galeazzo Ciano, Italian Foreign Minister and son-in-law of Mussolini, noted in his diary entry of August 12 that "Hitler is very cordial, but implacable in his decision. . . . I realize immediately there is no longer anything that can be done. He has decided to strike, and strike he will . . . the great war must be fought while he and the Duce are still young."[12]

ITEM: General Franz Halder, Chief of the German Army General

Staff, recorded in his diary entry of August 14 the belief of Hitler that England and France did not want to fight.

"The men I met in Munich will not start a new world war." And on August 15 the German Under Secretary of State echoed his master: "Chamberlain and Halifax [British Foreign Secretary] in particular wish to avoid bloodshed. America is markedly reserved."[13]

ITEM: On August 17 the Wehrmacht was ordered to supply Reinhard Heydrich, the deputy to Heinrich Himmler, with Polish uniforms—the objective, "a simulated raid . . . organized by Himmler . . . against Gleiwitz."[14]

ITEM: On August 21 the pocket battleship *Graf Spee* sortied from her closely guarded harbor and headed toward the South Atlantic, under orders, when war started, to harry Allied shipping.

ITEM: On August 22 Hitler held a conference at Obersalzberg with service chiefs—a "rambling monologue lasting for hours . . . the time was ripe to resolve German differences with Poland by war and to test the Reich's new military machine."[15]

"Be steeled," the Fuehrer said, "against all signs of compassion! Whoever has pondered over this world order knows that its meaning lies in the success of the best by means of force."[16]

. . . Stalin and I are the only ones that see only the future. So I shall shake hands with Stalin within a few weeks on the common German-Russian border and undertake with him a new distribution of the world. . . .

My pact with Poland was only meant to stall for time. . . . After Stalin's death . . . we shall crush the Soviet Union. . . .

I have only one fear and that is that Chamberlain or such another dirty swine comes to me with propositions or a change of mind. He will be thrown downstairs. And even if I must personally kick him in the belly before the eyes of all the photographers . . .

. . . The invasion and extermination of Poland begins on Saturday morning, August 26. I will have a few companies in Polish uniform attack in Upper Silesia or in the Protectorate. Whether the world believes it doesn't mean a damn to me. The world believes only in success.

Be hard. . . . Be without mercy. The citizens of Western Europe must quiver in horror.[17]

ITEM: A cryptic code word—*"Befehlsübernehmen"* ("Assume Command")—was dispatched from the OKH (Oberkommando des Heeres, the High Command of the Army), and on August 23 Army Groups North and South, on the Polish frontiers, and Army Group C, on the French-Belgian frontier, become operational.

Another German submarine shaped course toward the North Atlantic.

ITEM: The scene: the Kremlin, the night of August 23–24. The characters: the archconspirators Stalin and Ribbentrop. With many

toasts in vodka and much conviviality, the sworn enemies of Right and
Left signed a nonaggression pact, with a secret protocol which gave
Russia a free hand in Finland, Estonia, Latvia, Poland east of the Narev,
Vistula and San rivers, and in Rumanian Bessarabia. Hitler and Stalin,
the most ruthless cynics of their era, were now virtual allies; Poland was
doomed, the West checkmated.[18] Hitler smirked and gloated, and set Y-
day, the date for the attack upon Poland, as August 26.

On August 24 the National Socialist leader, Albert Forster, was
appointed "Head of the State" by the German-dominated Danzig Senate;
the bank rate was raised in England and in Eire; frontier guards were
increased and mobilization started in Belgium, Holland and Switzerland.
The West reeled under the shock of the Nazi-Communist pact, but the
House of Commons passed a special Emergency Powers Act in one day;
President Roosevelt addressed a personal appeal for peace first to King
Victor Emmanuel of Italy, then to Germany and Poland; and Pope Pius
XII raised his voice "for the force of reason and not . . . of arms."

Yet Mussolini temporized; his army was in a "pitiful state"; Italy
was not ready for war. And, in the Foreign Office in London, the British,
with that peculiar tenacity of a race which achieves the magnificent when
faced with the hopeless, put in writing, in a formal United Kingdom–
Poland mutual assistance pact, their determination to give Poland "all
the support and assistance in its power."

Hitler hesitated; Mussolini's fearfulness and the unexpected British
and French firmness prompted him to defer Y-day. The German Army,
with "everything in order"[19] and some units already moving toward the
frontier, was halted in place.

On August 26, the original Y-day, there was some local shooting in
Upper Silesia in front of von Reichenau's Tenth Army. "K-men," special
counterintelligence units under the direct control of the High Command,
skirmished with Polish border guards.

The British and French ambassadors in Berlin—Sir Nevile Henderson and Robert Coulondre—had repeated audiences with Ribbentrop or
Hitler to re-emphasize their countries' determination to assist Poland, to
urge negotiations. The approaches were conciliatory but firm. The
French were stringing barbed wire along the frontier; French garrison
troops and reservists, the so-called "shellfish of the forts," moved into the
"impregnable" casemates of the Maginot Line. All Europe mobilized.

At 7:30 P.M. on August 28 there was a conference in the Reich
Chancellery with Hitler, Heinrich Himmler, SS Major General Reinhard
Heydrich, Joseph Paul Goebbels, Martin Bormann, Halder and other
high Nazis. Halder recorded his personal impression of Hitler in his
diary: "Lacks sleep, haggard, voice brittle, preoccupied . . ." Later:
"Hitler—'If things come to the worst I shall even fight a war on two
fronts.' "[20]

On August 29, as the bells tolled for a dying Europe, Sir Nevile Henderson was received by Ribbentrop and a ranting Hitler, who demanded the return of Danzig and the Corridor, but agreed to enter into direct negotiations with Poland. But a Polish emissary must arrive in Berlin on Wednesday, August 30—the following day—almost a physical impossibility.

The time limit, Henderson said, *"hatte den Klang eines Ulti-matums"* ("sounds like an ultimatum"). And he added later: "I left the Reich Chancellery that evening filled with the gloomiest forebodings."[21]

THE LAST DAY OF PEACE—AUGUST 31

Berlin: 12:01 a.m.

Henderson's "forebodings" are justified about midnight, August 30–31, in an audience with Ribbentrop,

whose reception of me was . . . one of intense hostility, which increased in violence as I made each communication in turn.

He kept jumping to his feet in a state of great excitement, folding his arms across his chest and asking if I had anything more to say. . . .

After I had finished making my various communications to him, he produced a lengthy document which he read out to me in German or rather gabbled through to me as fast as he could in a tone of the utmost scorn and annoyance.[22]

The document incorporates Germany's 16 demands, or conditions for peace, but it is already, Ribbentrop contemptuously says, academic, or *"überholt"* ("out of date"), since no Polish emissary has reached Berlin.

As Ribbentrop says, the German demands are already out of date.

At 0030—half an hour after midnight—the Reich Chancellery issues the code word to carry out "Case White"—the attack against Poland.[23]

Berlin: 2:00 a.m.

Sir Nevile Henderson receives the Polish Ambassador to Germany, Josef Lipski, and transmits to him the gist of the stormy Ribbentrop interview.

Berlin: 6:30 a.m.

Captain Houser, Cavalry, aide to General Halder, Chief of the Army General Staff, transmits orders from the Reich Chancellery: Y-day will be

September 1 (the next day); H-hour, 0445. Halder does some figuring and enters it in his journal: Germany now has mobilized some 2,600,000 men (including 155,000 militarized laborers working on the West Wall fortifications). Of these slightly more than 1,000,000—some 34 divisions, mostly reserve divisions—are deployed in the west; the rest—some 1,500,000 men—more than 50 divisions (including six Panzer or tank divisions) are poised against Poland.

London: 7:00 a.m.

Sandbags are piled against the House of Commons, "the Mother of Parliaments," and the stations are crowded as the evacuation of 3,000,000 children, women, invalids and old men from London and 28 other British cities starts—a mass movement unprecedented in modern history. The shadow of air power, the fear of bombs, already looms heavily over the world.

Berlin: 9:00 a.m.

The Italian Ambassador to Berlin, Bernardo Attolico, advises Rome the situation is "desperate . . . war in a few hours."[24]

Rome: 11:00 a.m.

Palazzo Venezia. Ciano and the Duce agree "Italy can intervene with Hitler only if [Mussolini] brings a fat prize: Danzig."[25]
Ciano so informs Halifax.

Berlin: Noon

". . . an eerie atmosphere . . . everyone . . . going around in a daze . . ."[26]

Oslo

Representatives of the Scandinavian powers—Norway, Sweden, Denmark, Finland—issue their "customary" declaration of neutrality.

Warsaw

Farm cars, wagons, trains and trucks are loaded with men no longer young, as all reserve classes are called up to join younger men already in uniform.

The North Sea

Three Polish destroyers stand out of the narrow straits between the Baltic and the North Sea and shape course toward the British Isles. Not far behind, German submarines head out beyond soundings into deep water and submerge.

Berlin: 12:30 p.m.

Hitler signs "Directive No. 1 for the Conduct of the War"—a "solution by force." Göring, arrogant, asks later: "What am I supposed to do with this *dumf?* I've known all this for ages."[27]

New York: 1:00 p.m.

The 7th Cavalry Brigade, Mechanized—the only armored unit of the United States Army—parades in wind-whipped rain through the city's streets to a sodden camp site in the "World of Tomorrow"—the New York World's Fair. Its 110 tanks and armored cars—virtually the total armored might of the United States Army—are more symbolic of the world to come than all the Fair's glittering dreams.

Berlin: 5:00 p.m.

A kind of "Mad-Hatter's" tea party is held with Field Marshal Göring and Ambassador Henderson as the principals, and one Birger Dahlerus, a Swedish businessman who has tried to act as an unofficial mediator, as a go-between. Göring talks "for the best part of two hours of the iniquities of the Poles and of Hitler's and his own desire for friendship with England. . . .

"It was," Henderson later noted, "a conversation which led nowhere. . . . I augured the worst . . . he could scarcely have afforded at such a moment to spare time in conversation, if it did not mean that everything, down to the last detail, was now ready for action."[28]

Göring: "If the Poles should not give in, Germany would crush them like lice, and if Britain should decide to declare war, I would regret it greatly but it would be most imprudent of Britain."[29]

Berlin: 6:15 p.m.

The Polish Ambassador Lipski, under orders from Warsaw which in turn is pressed by London, seeks out Ribbentrop. It is one of the shortest interviews on record. Lipski says his government is favorably considering the British proposal for direct negotiations, but that he himself has no authority to negotiate. Ribbentrop dismisses him; back at his embassy, Lipski finds his communications to Warsaw have been cut.[30]

Rome: 8:20 p.m.

Ciano is informed by the telephone central office that London has cut its communications with Italy. The Duce says: "This is war but tomorrow we shall declare in the Grand Council that we are not marching."[31]

Berlin: 9:00 p.m.

At long last the text of Hitler's 16 conditions about Poland are broadcast over the Berlin radio, and a few minutes later Henderson receives for the first time a copy of the proposals which were "gabbled" at him by Ribbentrop the night before. It is more window dressing; Army Groups North and South are already moving. Later Hitler confesses it:

"I needed an alibi, especially with the German people, to show them that I had done everything to maintain peace. That explains my generous offer about the settlement of Danzig and the Corridor."[32]

Europe: Midnight

As the last day of peace ends, France is mobilized, Europe stands to arms. In Berlin and Warsaw, London and Paris and Rome the lights are out again for the second time in a quarter of a century. . . .

At 4:40 A.M. on September 1, 1939, the Luftwaffe bombed Polish airfields all over the country; the old German battleship *Schleswig-Holstein,* on a "friendly" visit to Danzig Harbor, shelled the Polish fortress of Westerplatte; the Nazi SS took over Danzig; German tanks rolled across the frontiers from north and south and west—and the blitzkrieg (lightning war) was born.

While Polish cavalrymen charged German tanks, Hitler justified his aggression to the Reichstag at 10 A.M., September 1. He characterized the German assault as a "counterattack," and declared "this night [*sic*] for the first time Polish regulars fired on our own territory . . . from now on bombs will be met with bombs."

He said he had no quarrel with France and England, but later in the morning when Göring and Dahlerus, the Swedish businessman, saw him in the Chancellery, he shouted: "If England wants to fight for a year, I shall fight for a year; if England wants to fight for two years, I shall fight two years. . . . If England wants to fight for three years, I shall fight for three years. . . . *Und wenn es erforderlich ist will ich zehn Jahre kämpfen* (and if it is necessary I will fight for ten years)."[33]

At 3 P.M. in Rome, the Duce addressed the Council of Ministers and announced "nonintervention."

"September 2 was a day of suspense."[34] Poles were dying under German bombs and guns. The French Cabinet was split and Georges Bonnet, the French Foreign Minister, grasped at a straw. The straw was a belated attempt by Mussolini to mediate. The capitals of Europe sought for hope. Ambassadors in Rome, Berlin, London came and went; messages and answers streamed in and out of the foreign offices of Europe, but it was all in vain. The British Cabinet insisted as a condition to acceptance of Mussolini's offer that German troops be withdrawn from Poland. Ciano knew it was to Hitler an impossible condition.

Sunday, September 3, in Berlin was "a lovely end-of-the-summer day."[35] It was also the end of an era.

About 9 A.M. Sir Nevile Henderson delivered to Ribbentrop's office a communication from Lord Halifax: "I have . . . the honor to inform you," it read in the stilted language of diplomacy, that as of 11 A.M. (British summer time) "a state of war will exist between" England and Germany.[36]

France, her Cabinet beset by doubts, her leaders by anxiety, delayed joining Britain until 5 P.M.

By then the world had heard a sad King—George VI—speak with a halting voice to his people in England and overseas:

"For the second time in the lives of most of us, we are at war. . . ."

Hope flared briefly at Warsaw, but it was not to be. The war declarations of Britain and France, the realists knew, could bring no succor to the reeling Poles. The Germans had protected their southern flank with the West Wall fortifications (still incomplete), and some 34 divisions—most of them low-category units—guarded the French frontiers. More important, France was riven by divisive political factions[37]—among them some staunch admirers of Hitler—and the French Army was wedded to the defensive and to the supposed security of its great fortress system. The Baltic was a German lake, and the offensive against Poland had been well prepared.

Poland, with a population in 1939 of almost 35,000,000 people (only 22,000,000 of them ethnic Poles), was primarily an agricultural country—a land of great estates and a wealthy few; a land of horses and of herds, of wayside shrines and many churches; a land epitomized by Warsaw, the capital, where Eastern and Western Europe—Slav and German, French culture and Russian backwardness—met in confusion, a city with many cobbled and dirt streets.

Poland was in a hopeless strategic position, virtually surrounded—

west, north and south—by German territory, and bordered to the east by the despised and hated Russian colossus.

The Polish armed forces, like the Polish state, were a strange mixture of past and present (mostly past) and gestures to the future. The Army included some of the most magnificent horsemen in the world. Near Warsaw the cavalrymen of Pilsudski's Own Regiment, which held the *Bunczuk* (trophy) for excellence, were accustomed to giving military observers colorful demonstrations of their skill with lance and saber, and of machine-gun fire from little carts (troikas) pulled by three horses at full gallop.

The Polish Army was large in numbers, short in most of the other ingredients of warfare, save courage. Thirty infantry divisions organized in ten corps, plus an extraordinary amount of horsed cavalry, and an incomplete mechanized cavalry brigade, totaled at peacetime strength about 280,000 men.[38]

There were more than 1,500,000 reservists—men 24 to 42 years old—who had received military training, and on paper there were at least 15 additional reserve divisions and many smaller units. But equipment was short; it required about 30 to 60 days to mobilize fully, and Warsaw did not initiate general mobilization until August 30. By then it was too late. On September 1, when the blow fell, there was apparently a grand total of between 800,000 and 1,000,000 men, including all the newly mobilized reservists and men en route to their units—many of them with their requisitioned farm carts and horses, many still in civilian clothes.

These were grouped at the start of the campaign into six so-called armies, or groups of small and uneven strength, designated the Narev Group (from Lomza to Lithuania along the East Prussian border); the Modlin Army; the Pomorze Army in the Corridor: the Poznań Army; the Lódź Army; the Cracow Army; and the Carpathian Army in the south.[39] A special coastal defense zone, under a Navy admiral, covered the seaward approaches to Danzig, Gdynia and the Corridor. Concentration areas for general reserve groupings to back up these armies were scattered throughout the country—the strongest south, northeast and west of Warsaw. The grand total actually mobilized approximated 27 to 30 divisions or their equivalent. In effect the Poles attempted a discontinuous cordon defense of their indefensible 1,750 miles of frontier with Germany.

The Army was supported by two air divisions—less than 1,000 aircraft, only about half of them combat types and a large number obsolete.[40]

The Navy was minuscule—about 3,100 men—a few destroyers, submarines, gunboats and river craft.

There were some—but discontinuous and isolated—concrete and

steel fortifications and strong posts. Permanent fortifications, some of them more than a quarter-century old, were sited in various parts of the country—near Bydgoszcz, Lódź, Częstochowa, Katowice, Cracow, Mlawa, Poznań, along the Narev River, and in the Hel Peninsula and at the Baltic approaches to Danzig and Gdynia. But field fortifications were primitive and poorly prepared—a few trenches, barbed wire and easily evaded tank traps. Even the weather—it had been a hot, very dry summer—deserted the defenders; the normal September rains did not fall. The Vistula and other Polish rivers were at low water, the San was "a trickling rivulet," all were easily fordable in many places. The ground was hard and dry and Poland's famed "General Mud" played no part in the campaign.[41]

And the Poles were victims, too, of their hopeless geographic position and their own ambivalent attitudes. They respected and feared the Germans, despised and feared the Russians. Beck, the Foreign Minister, had been, until the year of crisis, anti-French and friendly to Berlin. Rydz-Smigly once said: "With the Germans we risk losing our freedom. With the Russians we shall lose our soul."[42]

The new Reich of Adolf Hitler had a population of about 80,000,000 people and produced more than 22,000,000 tons of steel annually, some 15 times the Polish production.

In a few short years, the disciplined, homogeneous German people, under the lash of the Nazis' virulent nationalism, had produced the strongest military machine in the world. Germany was well prepared for a short war though her armed forces had major deficiencies. Hitler originally had not anticipated general war for several years ("at the latest," he said, by 1943–1945). Many of the Wehrmacht's tanks were undergunned and too light; its surface Navy was far inferior to Britain's; the Luftwaffe needed more maintenance and repair facilities and spare parts, and there were shortages of gasoline and ammunition.

But the Luftwaffe, with some 4,300 operational aircraft, most of them modern combat types, was a powerful instrument of policy— particularly in air operations involving the support of ground armies. The Navy, though small, compensated in quality for what it lacked in quantity; its ingenious pocket battleships (armored cruisers), the 26,000-ton battleships *Scharnhorst* and *Gneisenau* and its 57 U-boats were dangerous threats to British commerce.

The German Army had benefited from the defeat of 1918 and the restrictive clauses of the Versailles Treaty. Its equipment was new, its tactical concepts and policies were uncluttered by obsolescent ideas, and its "hard core" of noncoms and officers were true military professionals, masters of their art. Mobilization plans contemplated the ultimate call-up of more than 100 divisions in categories, or "waves," with a total strength of several million men.

Against Poland, in September, 1939, Berlin hurled more than 50 divisions, 4 brigades and several SS regiments,[43] plus 2 air fleets and some naval forces, a total of considerably more than 1,500,000 men. The campaign was keyed to speed; all of Germany's four light divisions (a mixture of motorized infantry and tanks), four motorized and six Panzer divisions were used.

The German plan of campaign was essentially simple, adapted to take advantage of the impossible problems of Poland's geography. Strategically, it was conceived as nothing less than a gigantic Cannae—a battle of annihilation, a double envelopment of Polish Army units west of the Vistula, and then of Warsaw and the remaining Polish forces.

The Poznań bulge, where the Polish frontier extended deep into Germany, was held only lightly with frontier guard units and reservists backed by a fortified area along the Oder River. The Germans intended to remain on the defensive in this central area. The strongest German forces were concentrated in the south, grouped in Army Group South, under General Karl Gerd von Rundstedt. Under Rundstedt, three armies—the Fourteenth (General Wilhelm List), the Tenth (General Walther von Reichenau) and the Eighth (General Johannes Blaskowitz) —comprising 34 divisions, crossed the frontier from Silesia-Moravia and Slovakia.

The mission of the Tenth Army was to break through to the Vistula and to occupy the Polish capital. The Eighth Army, its units echeloned in a bent-back or "refused" flank toward the German frontier, provided flank protection against any Polish threat from the Poznań salient. The Fourteenth Army, in the extreme south, debouched out of the Beskid Mountains toward the San and the Bug rivers in Galicia.

Army Group North, General Fedor von Bock commanding, was split by the Polish Corridor. The Fourth Army (General Gunther von Kluge) operated from Pomerania, the Third Army (General Georg von Küchler) from East Prussia, with a total of 21 divisions and other smaller units.

The Fourth Army was to force a crossing of the Vistula between Toruń and Grudziadz and then to establish contact with the left (northern) flank of Army Group South, hopefully trapping, in the process, thousands of Polish troops. The Third Army, advancing southward out of East Prussia, was to envelop Warsaw in a wide sweep to the east.

The major army groups were supported by Luftflotten 1 and 4, with more than 1,600 aircraft. Naval Command East in the Baltic, centered around the old training battleship *Schleswig-Holstein* anchored in Danzig Bay, included several destroyers, some submarines and a number of smaller surface craft.

To meet this formidable offensive, the partially mobilized Polish forces (many units disorganized and underequipped) tried to hold everything, and as a result lost everything. The Silesian coal fields and the Polish industrial areas were in the vulnerable western part of the country. Warsaw attempted to hold these as well as the indefensible Corridor, instead of establishing a concentrated defense behind the Vistula and the San rivers. The Poles, like the French, had an unwarranted faith in fortifications and in the defensive—a heritage of the trench stalemate of World War I. They were proud and overconfident, living in the past. Many Polish soldiers, infected with the martial spirit of their people and their traditional hatred for the Germans, spoke and dreamed of "the march to Berlin." One of their songs portrayed their hopes:

> . . . *dressed in steel and mail,*
> *Under the leadership of Rydz-Smigly,*
> *We shall march to the Rhine. . . .*[44]

But the Poles, like the rest of the world, had never before witnessed the tactics of "blitzkrieg."

Despite the threats and warnings the Germans achieved tactical surprise; many Polish reservists were still en route to their units, and many units were still moving to concentration points or assigned positions when the Luftwaffe dropped the first bombs at 0440 on September 1.

All over the country, at Warsaw, Cracow, Lódź and some nine other principal Polish air bases, and at 75 dirt strips and smaller fields, the crump of bombs heralded the start of war. In a few hours most of the infant Polish Air Force died on the ground, its wings never stretched in combat.

The citizens of the "Free City of Danzig" awoke to the thunder of the guns to find themselves "free citizens" no longer; black-uniformed SS troops patrolled the streets of the city and the swastika flew above the City Hall, as the *Schleswig-Holstein* bombarded Polish coastal positions. Only along the Hel Peninsula and the Westerplatte, where the Poles had erected formidable concrete emplacements with coast defense and light guns, were the German attacks repulsed; elsewhere German forces moved rapidly across the frontiers, brushing aside light opposition—"all divisions advancing according to plan."

But Poland—in the first few days—was undaunted. Warsaw had confidence in the promises of its allies; England and France would attack in the west. ". . . the public spirit at the moment of mobilization was magnificent."[45]

In cities, towns and villages the martial strains of Poland's national anthem stirred the blood:

. . . as long as we live,
Poland shall not perish.

Courage was not rare. Here and there, amid the constant air raids, the burning houses, there were successes; here and there—but rarely—Polish 37 mm. AT guns disabled German light tanks.

But the German flood of conquest was irresistible.

On many parts of the front, a heavy ground fog, which limited close air support and hampered observed artillery fire, delayed the Germans more than Polish opposition.

The lack of combat experience of the German troops and some deficiencies in leadership—inevitable in any army until hardened in battle—also caused delays, in most cases speedily overcome by the intervention of a few tough professionals.

General Heinz Guderian, commanding the XIX Corps, recorded a holdup at the Brahe River when a regimental commander allowed his unit to bog down. A young Panzer lieutenant approached Guderian:

. . . his shirt sleeves were rolled up and his arms black with powder.

"Herr General," he said, "I've just come from the Brahe. The enemy forces on the far bank are weak. The Poles set fire to the bridge at Hammermühle, but I put the fire out from my tank. The bridge is crossable. The advance has only stopped because there's no one to lead it. You must go there yourself, sir."

Guderian "went there himself," found some "idiotic" panicky firing going on, stopped the unnecessary bombardment, put a battalion in rubber boats, established a bridgehead and took prisoner a Polish bicycle company—sole defenders of that sector of the river.

"Casualties," Guderian noted, "were negligible."[46]

The advance went on—but not without alarms and some brief checks.

There was a large gap between the northern flank of Eighth Army (a unit Field Marshal von Rundstedt was later to describe as "always my problem child") and Army Group North, and the Polish forces in the Poznań bulge were expected to attack southward to bite into the exposed flank of Army Group South. Obligingly, most of them retreated instead to the east and destruction.

From the first hours the movements of the Polish forces had been impeded by "crowds of refugees, their belongings piled on all manner of vehicles . . . driving their cattle ahead of them," who clogged the roads. "Military communications became almost impossible. The shadow of disaster . . . loomed."[47]

To foreigners, as well as to Poles, the sudden thunderclap of war and the rapid advance of the German armies seemed incredible, not to be believed.

The baroque architecture of Cracow became curiously weightless by moonlight. . . . I had the impression of something at the same time near and beyond the world: a dream or a set for *Don Giovanni*. Then abruptly a voice yelled: . . . "Uwaga! Uwaga! Uwaga!" and the sirens screeched. It was a raid-warning. . . . Soon after dawn the sound of heavy artillery was plain. . . .

I noticed the strange calm of the Jews. Others screamed and the din of antiaircraft guns seemed to break one's eardrums; but the Jews, with their great beards and black coats, went about the streets with dignity.[48]

In the Polish town of Bydgoszcz the population fled in disorderly panic early in the morning of September 3, as guns started firing "burst after burst" in the city's streets. "Military baggage wagons were being driven off as fast as the horses could gallop; cars and lorries were crowding on one another, all making for the bridge over the Brda."

But it was not the German Panzers, but what the Poles called "diversionists"—German-Poles with Nazi sympathies, or Germans who had infiltrated into Poland to act as a "Fifth Column" in the days immediately preceding war.

The Bydgoszcz Poles forgot their panic, turned against the enemy in their midst, and in sharp street battles—typical of other skirmishes near the German frontier—won back their town, administering as they mopped up the summary justice of the firing squad to any captured "diversionists."

But it was brief triumph. The German tanks, slightly behind schedule, rumbled into the evacuated town of Bydgoszcz on September 4.[49]

By September 3, Halder noted "good progress on the whole. . . ."

The German victory in Poland was the victory of the "Big Battalions," of present over past, of strength over weakness, but the speed of the triumph was the result of new tactics—the tactics of massed tanks and screaming dive bombers, the mental product of an obstreperous German general named Heinz Guderian, who in turn borrowed many of his ideas from an unknown French officer named de Gaulle and from two English veterans of World War I, Major General J. F. C. Fuller and Captain B. H. Liddell Hart.

Three thousand tanks debouched across the dry Polish plains, bypassed strong points, sliced deep into rear areas, and whistled up the fear-inspiring Stukas, which dove like falcons at their prey.

The Poles fought and died. From north and west and south, from the sandy beaches of the Baltic, the lake regions of East Prussia, the flat plains of Pomerania, to the Jablunka Pass and the high slopes of the

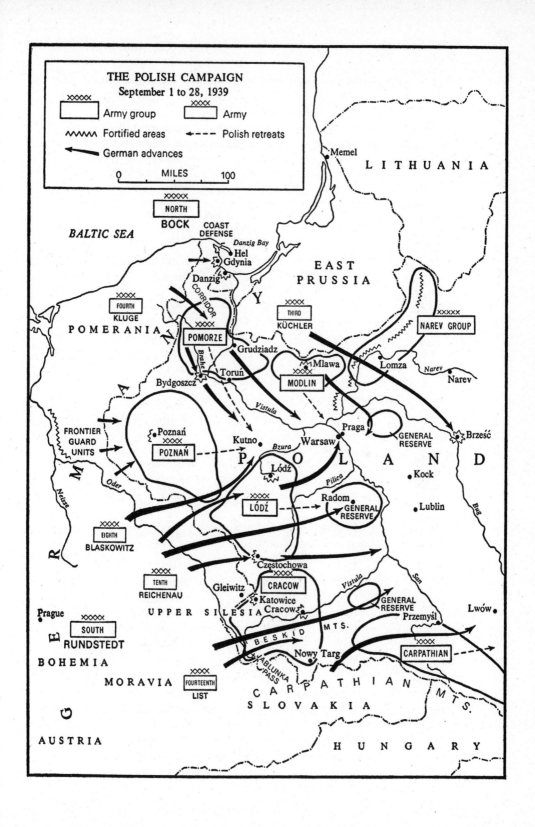

THE POLISH CAMPAIGN
September 1 to 28, 1939

xxxxx ☐ Army group   xxxx ☐ Army
ꟺꟺ Fortified areas   ◄- - - Polish retreats
◄━━ German advances

0   MILES   100

BALTIC SEA

LITHUANIA

Memel

NORTH
BOCK

COAST
DEFENSE

Danzig Bay
Hel
Gdynia

Danzig

CORRIDOR

EAST
PRUSSIA

FOURTH
KLUGE

POMERANIA

Brahe

POMORZE

Grudziadz

Toruń

Bydgoszcz

THIRD
KÜCHLER

Mlawa

MODLIN

Lomza

NAREV GROUP

Narev

Narev

FRONTIER
GUARD
UNITS

Poznań

POZNAŃ

Kutno

Vistula

Bzura

Łódź

Warsaw

Praga

GENERAL
RESERVE

Brześć

Kock

Oder

Neisse

EIGHTH
BLASKOWITZ

LÓDŹ

Pilica

Radom

GENERAL
RESERVE

Lublin

Bug

TENTH
REICHENAU

Częstochowa

Gleiwitz

CRACOW

Katowice
Cracow

Vistula

San

GENERAL
RESERVE

Lwów

Przemyśl

UPPER SILESIA

Prague

SOUTH
RUNDSTEDT

BESKID   MTS.

BOHEMIA

MORAVIA

FOURTEENTH
LIST

JABLUNKA
PASS

Nowy Targ

CARPATHIAN

SLOVAKIA

CARPATHIAN   MTS.

AUSTRIA

HUNGARY

Carpathians the German legions swept across Poland. Only in the extreme north on the shores of the Baltic where heavy fortifications defied the rain of shells and bombs did the Poles hold.

In the disputed Corridor, impossible to hold, two Polish infantry divisions and the Pomorze cavalry brigade trying to hold it were cut off by the German XIX Corps of the Fourth Army, which had sliced across the base of the Corridor to East Prussia. On September 2—one day after war started—these units were almost wiped out. The magnificent horsemen, with their lances lowered to the charge and their saddle leather creaking, died with their steeds in droves with the drumbeat of hoofs at the gallop in their ears. They pitted man and animal and courage time and again against tanks and gunfire, and it was no contest. . . .

The Third (East Prussia) and Fourth (Pomerania) Armies of Army Group North were completely linked by September 3; the Corridor, except at its northern end, was eliminated. The stubborn, though brief, defense of the Mlawa concrete and steel forts and antitank guns was outflanked, and Third Army's advance on Warsaw continued.

The Jablunka Pass was forced on September 1 against fierce but ineffective resistance of Polish mountain troops, and Army Group South units moved as much as 15 miles the first day, brushing aside Polish resistance, or by-passing it to be left to the following infantry. Long columns of mules and men wound through the mountains and hills into the heart of Poland.

Blown bridges, cratered roads, mined culverts and felled trees slowed but did not halt the German advance. The engineers moved in, removed obstacles, built bridges, repaired the railroads and behind the combat legions moved in steady procession the petrol and the powder and the food—the stuff of war.

The moving front was marked by a smudged line of dissolution; "a dark mist of smoke from the burning villages and from gunfire hovered low over the ground."[50]

Częstochowa fell on September 3. Tenth Army units from Army Group South crossed the Pilica River and turned northwest toward Warsaw on September 5, and Halder recorded in his diary: "Enemy as good as beaten." On the sixth, the Fourteenth Army captured the ancient city of Cracow, with its proud records of the days of Poland's greatness, its medieval buildings and its heritage of tradition. "Our tanks proved very good," Halder noted.

Polish AT rifles fail to pierce our armor. . . .

Cracow taken, Poznań has fallen. . . . Polish government leaves Warsaw during night. . . .

Of the total Polish forces, five divisions [can] be considered annihilated; ten . . . still "completely intact"; the rest suffered severely in combat and march movements.

The German Luftwaffe ruled the air; Polish railroads and roads were under continuous attack; Polish troop concentrations were never completed. Here and there, the Polish fliers claimed their debts of blood; here and there, flying from dispersed and makeshift fields, they had brief moments of glory. At Nowy Targ on September 3, light bombers of the 31st Squadron wrote their footnote to history. The single-engined, three-man planes, with three machine guns and 600 kilograms of bombs, roared above a road

simply crammed with motor transport along its entire length—a perfect target. . . .

The first bombs were very well aimed—they struck the middle of the road. A petrol tanker was burning with a blue flame. Two tanks which got direct hits turned over and smoke poured from their torn steel plates. They blocked the road.

Our gunners fired on the Germans who ran about trying to escape.

Although the Germans had been fully surprised their panic did not last long and soon there was strong opposition from the ground. . . .

White tracer trails sliced the air just behind our tails, by the wings, in front. . . . One [of the Polish bombers] was hit and on fire.[51]

But such successes were sporadic, small, unimportant. The Polish Air Force, outnumbered originally at least four or five to one, was chivvied and harried; its few surviving planes moved constantly from sun-baked strip or meadow to new "fields"; its planes crashed or failed; radios blacked out; in a short time it was reduced to one- or two-plane "raids" with 12-kilogram bombs. "In three days (by September 3) the Luftwaffe had driven the Polish Air Force from the skies, destroyed most of its bases on the ground, and crippled aircraft repair and production facilities."[52]

The Poles, though they retreated rapidly, were continuously out-flanked, their front pierced or strong points by-passed, and thousands of them, scattered and disorganized, were left in the ruck of the German advance to be mopped up at leisure.

Fifth Columnists and German spies and saboteurs played their roles in the degeneration of a nation into chaos. Outside of Warsaw, where Polish artillery batteries were emplaced in a copse of trees, a civilian was caught red-handed, firing rockets to mark the spot for German dive bombers. He was equipped with a suitcase with a false bottom, the rockets stacked in neat rows, like wine bottles.[53]

But the enemy from without—the enemy of tanks and planes and blitzkrieg—rather than the enemy from within toppled the Polish state.

The Polish High Command, under the personal direction of Marshal Rydz-Smigly, attempted after the first few days to reorganize the defense and to concentrate the many dispersed elements of the original scattered army groupings into three main armies—one north of Warsaw and the

Vistula, one south of Warsaw to the San River and one in the extreme south. But German air attacks time and again dispersed Polish units and destroyed bridges—and the Poles moved by foot and horse, the German spearheads by tanks and trucks. The Nazis moved too fast, and the uncoordinated defense by scattered elements of six so-called armies continued.

By September 8 the 4th Panzer Division reached the suburbs of Warsaw, and some tanks penetrated the city's streets on the ninth but were driven out in a fierce five-hour fight. The capital city was a prize stoutly held.

The German shelling of Warsaw, crowded with thousands of refugees, started—methodically, deliberately, persistently—on the eighth, and a six-hour air raid against the eastern suburb of Praga, across the Vistula, set raging fires.

On September 9 the Lord Mayor of Warsaw, Stefan Starzynski, indefatigable and indomitable, appealed for volunteers; 150,000 men and women dug trenches and built street barricades.

By the tenth the city's slow crucifixion had well started:

All about us buildings lie in ruins. The fire at the Transfiguration Hospital, with its several hundred wounded, was a ghastly business. I saw a soldier with both legs amputated crawling from the building on his elbows; other wounded jumped out of windows on to the pavement.[54]

The German Panzers now swept in a second pincers toward the east.[55] Behind them lay chaos—disorganized remnants, hidden in forests or swamps; groups of squad, platoon, company or battalion strength, which sortied from their coverts to fight briefly or with hands held high surrendered to the "Master Race."

A German soldier, named Wilhelm Prüller, noted in a diary later to become famous, that "We're moving at a terrific pace. The roads are simply beyond description. And the Polish dead every foot. The dust is at least a foot deep."

And later: "Everywhere it was the same picture: Houses which had been hit by our artillery and set on fire. Homeless families, weeping women and children, who face the future with nothing."[56]

There were checks for the Germans; above the Hel Peninsula the Polish flag still flew, and further south near Kutno the German 30th Infantry Division of the Eighth Army suffered "heavy losses" when its overextended open flank and wide front were attacked by several Polish divisions.[57]

But General Halder noted cheerfully in his diary on September 10: "Troops everywhere in good shape . . . performance of troops is marvelous," and forecast the looming horrors to come: "SS artillery of the Armd. Corps herded Jews into a church and massacred them. . . ."

By the tenth Hitler had given permission for the Luftwaffe to extend its reconnaissance flights across the Franco-German frontier, and Halder noted that British soldiers had arrived at Perl (near the French-Luxembourg border). The Army conference at 1600 on September 10 was already concerned with the details of the administration of the conquered Polish territories and with the transfer of troops to the Western Front.

The Poles fought on, but by now the bright high hopes of victory had faded. Everywhere it was the same—the endless marches, the retreats and skirmishes, the constant air attacks, the slow bloodletting. By September 13 the 11th Polish Infantry Division near Przemyśl had been reduced to

barely six battalions, each numbering not more than 300 men. . . .

The German aeroplanes raided us at frequent intervals. There was no shelter anywhere: nothing but the accursed plain. The soldiers rushed off the road, trying to take cover in the furrows, but the horses were in a worse plight. After one of the raids we counted 35 dead horses, and a few days later the divisional artillery lost 87 horses in a single raid. Such a march was not like the march of an army; it was more like the flight of some Biblical people, driven onward by the wrath of Heaven, and dissolving in the wilderness.[58]

There were few communications between the scattered Polish armies; radios had failed or had been lost; land lines were disrupted. Control was impossible, but it was attempted—as in Napoleon's time—by couriers and by orders dropped from light unarmed liaison aircraft.

In the beleaguered capital city of Warsaw confusion spread.

"Even in the presence of the enemy, bureaucrats will remain bureaucrats—inefficient, stupid," an eyewitness remarked acidly.[59] Under the horrible whistling of the shells and the crump of bombs, the organized life of the city degenerated rapidly; only the voice of the Mayor, calm and indomitable, broadcasting each evening, rallied the terror-stricken.

By mid-September the Polish campaign had become a series of disconnected battles of encirclement and annihilation. The two fortress cities of Warsaw and Modlin were surrounded and under air and artillery bombardment.

In Warsaw the Jewish quarter—Nalewski—has been bloodily bombed; water mains were ruptured by shellfire; food was scarce. Some 700 horses, among them prize Polish thoroughbreds, were slaughtered daily for meat; "Twenty years of Polish horsebreeding must have gone to waste in this war." The German shelling continued, implacable, incessant: two shells every minute. Many buildings collapsed; the Royal Castle was hit, the electrical power plant wrecked—the city left in darkness, shrouded in the fine dust of wind-blown rubble and the smoke of myriad fires. The devout died at their devotions; a shell hit St. John's Cathedral during mass.[60]

A huge milling mass, the remnants of 12 Polish divisions and three cavalry brigades, fought desperately against a closing ring north of the Bzura River near Kutno. General Waadyslaw Bortnowski, commander of this Polish force, made two major attempts to break out of the *Kessel* (pocket) on September 12 and September 16; but the ring slowly contracted and on the seventeenth Luftwaffe units attacking Warsaw shifted their targets to the Kutno area and the Poles collapsed. At least 40,000 prisoners were captured and thousands of others killed.

Much further to the east, where the roads "push out white and whiter trails of packed dust,"[61] the town of Brześć (Brest-Litovsk) on the Bug River was reached by the 10th Panzer Division on September 14, but Polish courage won short respite. The defenders, when the city's outer fortifications were penetrated, withdrew into the stout-walled citadel and blocked the entrance gate with an old tank. The Poles held out with a small force until September 17.

But it was brief solace. Guderian, personification of the blitzkrieg concept, had proved the theories he had helped to develop. It was his XIX Corps—the 10th and 3rd Panzer Divisions and the 2nd and 20th Motorized Infantry Divisions—that had swept deep into eastern Poland and taken Brześć. Its fast-moving armored units, with motorized infantry following the spearheads, had taken off "into the blue," under radio control only, its left flank "in the air," as it raced southward. Strong points were left to be mopped up at leisure. The speed and mobility and power of the German drive disrupted all Polish attempts to form a continuous front; Guderian's drive set a pattern for deep armored penetrations in later campaigns.

By September 11 another encircled Polish force at Radom—remnants of five divisions and a cavalry brigade—had been destroyed by Army Group South and 60,000 prisoners taken. By September 17 Tenth Army units were fighting in the streets of Lublin, amid "acres of ruins."

Far to the south, a task force of the German 1st Mountain Division under a colonel, later to be known to fame as Field Marshal Ferdinand Schörner,[62] reached Lwów on September 12. It was the Poles' last citadel; the government and High Command had established headquarters there a few days before to rally a vain hope. Lwów was quickly encircled, but its stubborn defenders fought to the death, despite the fall on September 15 of a strong Polish position at Przemyśl, further to the west. . . .

Suddenly, on September 17, like a global thunderclap, strong Russian Red Army forces (about 35 divisions and nine tank brigades) invaded Poland from the east. It was a *coup de grâce* to a dying nation, prearranged by Hitler, though unknown until the event to most German soldiers. It was Poland's fourth partitionment in her long history of tragedy.

The Russian entry into eastern Poland against inconsequential and scattered resistance (elements of about two divisions and two cavalry brigades) from a Polish Army already beaten produced some confusion between the forces of the two totalitarian allies. Some wild Russian air attacks killed and wounded German soldiers, and there were numerous sporadic shooting incidents with casualties to both armies as the suspicious soldiery of Poland's two traditional enemies met east of the Bug and the San rivers.[63]

The rest was anticlimax: Marshal Rydz-Smigly, the Polish President, Ignacy Mościcki and other government leaders fled (on September 18) to Rumania;[64] stragglers and small units holed up in swamps and forest, or filtered across the frontiers, and OKW (the Supreme Command) commenced to shift forces to the Western Front.

Lwów abruptly surrendered on September 21.

Warsaw was dying.

Shells and bombs obliterated the work of man; thousands of victims were buried in the rubble or in hastily dug graves in the city's parks. The remaining diplomats were evacuated on September 21; the Poles strung more barbed wire.

On September 22 the pumping station was finally destroyed, the water mains sundered in many places; the Poles struggled to put out incendiary bombs with sand, but fire fighters on the rooftops were strafed by German planes.

On September 23 the dead lay unburied in the streets; houses toppled; Warsaw at midday was dark with dust and smoke; the Art Gallery and the French Embassy were afire.

By September 24 the City Hall was in ruins, the sewers were destroyed, the city's few remaining wells besieged by long queues who braved death by shellfire for water. Pestilence stalked the streets—and hunger; still quivering flesh was stripped from a horse's bones as soon as the animal was hit by shellfire; the merciless bombardment continued.[65]

Morale broke.

"Today [September 24th] for the first time, we heard women scoffing at our army. . . . 'Perhaps we are going to fight the tanks with bows and arrows like the Abyssinians,' " one remarked bitterly.[66]

With ruthless determination, the German Third and Tenth Armies slowly wore down the Warsaw defenders with sustained artillery fire and air attacks, and on September 26, as 137 large fires flamed in the city, the Eighth Army, which had relieved the Tenth, commenced an assault from the south.

The Polish capital, burning, battered, bloody but unbowed, has endured the first of several Calvaries the war was to bring to its ancient streets. The German Panzers drew fire from cellars, and gasoline-filled bottles, thrown from high windows and basement shelters, flared down upon the invaders.[67] Warsaw's buildings were gutted or ruined, many of its dead unburied, as the Warsaw radio broadcast plaintive appeals for aid followed by its famous electronic "signature"—the first delicate notes of Chopin's "Polonaise." London and Paris watched the siege with helpless horror and with tense pride. But the hope was forlorn.

By 1400 on September 27 General Juliuscz Rommel, former commander of the Łódź Army, senior officer in Warsaw, surrendered 140,000 Polish troops.

It was time—and high time. The city had endured 27 days of bombing, 19 of shellfire. It was chaos and holocaust. No one—combatant or noncombatant, man or woman or child, Pole or German prisoner of war—had been immune to death or mutilation. The city was a shambles, the hospitals an inferno.

Each day, "wheel barrows full of corpses looking in the morning sun like piles of wax dummies" were trundled to mass graves. The wounded lay untended—"tables and floors covered with moaning humanity."[68] Hospitals had been bombed; they blazed and belched fire and smoke as the wounded died with their nurses, screaming.

In one hospital, as the shellfire ceased and an eerie silence descended on the battered city, a literal "river of blood was flowing down the corridor . . . with its rows of shattered bodies."[69]

Some 16,000 of the garrison had been wounded, there were uncounted civilian dead, the city's water supply had been cut off for five days and an epidemic of typhoid "appeared imminent."[70]

And yet, to the starving Poles of Warsaw, the sudden silence of the afternoon of September 27, 1939, was "the worst day of the whole siege, the most alarming."[71] It meant capitulation; it meant the end of hope.

Modlin and its forts held out a few days longer—until September 29; when his water supply was severed, General Wiktor Thomme surrendered 24,000 troops, 4,000 of them wounded, to the German Third and Eighth Armies. The fortified, sandy peninsula of Hel in the Baltic, which had defied for so long the guns of the *Schleswig-Holstein* and the bombs of the Stukas, was almost the last to go.

Rear Admiral J. Unrug surrendered with 5,000 of his men on October 1.

The last organized stand by the Polish Army was made at Kock, where heavy fighting raged from 4 to 6 October. Panzer and motorized infantry units of Tenth Army ended this last Polish resistance, and the Kock force surrendered on 6 October, adding 17,000 more to the total of prisoners taken by the Germans. The Polish campaign was over, though sporadic fighting was to continue in some of the more remote areas for a considerable period.[72]

The Polish conquest stunned the world. A campaign involving more than two million men was virtually decided within less than a week, its major battles fought within two weeks, a nation destroyed in a month. The German tactics of speed and mobility and armored spearheads driving recklessly into the heart of an enemy country, supported by heavy and persistent air attacks and the traitorous cooperation of Fifth Columnists,[73] were keyed to the mass use of tanks and Stuka dive bombers and ruthless power. They were tactics long discussed but never before tried in war. A new word was coined—"blitzkrieg," or lightning war—the war of movement and maneuver and mobility, utilizing the internal combustion engine in the tank on the ground and in the plane in the air.

The Polish campaign was studied by all the staff colleges of the world. It was obvious that the trench stalemate of World War I and the fortified zones represented by the Maginot Line belonged to history; as Lieutenant General Mieczyslaw Norwid-Neugebauer commented shortly afterward, "It seems that the wars of continuous fronts are definitely a thing of the past."[74] The tank and the plane were the new queens of the battlefield, and mobility had returned to war. The spearheads of the German Army had fought their way 200 to 400 miles across Poland in two to three weeks. Particularly impressive was the performance of Guderian's XIX Corps (with two Panzer divisions), which had swept around Brześć (Brest-Litovsk). Poland was a highly successful proving ground for the armored theorists, who believed that tanks should be used en masse, as an arm of assault, penetration and exploitation.

Even to the layman, it was apparent that a new and powerful form of offensive had been developed, and that the Anglo-French faith in the defensive and in the concept of static positions and fixed fortifications in linear positions was open to doubt.

The Nazis did not hesitate to gild the lily, even though the statistics of the Polish defeat were impressive without embellishment. Berlin claimed some 700,000 Polish prisoners; more than 100,000 other Poles had been killed, driven into Russian hands, or had fled into Rumania or Hungary or into hiding in the swamps and forests of their native lands. (Perhaps 80,000 escaped across neutral frontiers.[75]) The Germans captured a whole arsenal of war—more than 3,200 field guns, machine guns numbered in five figures, some 1,700 mortars and great quantities of ammunition. Only about five out of some 77 light units of the Polish Navy escaped to Britain. The Polish Air Force was wiped out, though a few pilots escaped to serve in the Battle of Britain. The conquered territories, after the Germans pulled back from that part of eastern Poland which Hitler had agreed to turn over to the tender mercies of the Russians, brought more than 22,000,000 people under the Nazi yoke, less than a million of them ethnic Germans.

The victory was not won without loss: 40,389 total casualties for the

German Army (killed, wounded and missing), plus very light casualties (about 5,500) for the Air Force and Navy. More than 10,500 German officers and men of all services were killed in 36 days.[76]

The triumph was real and impressive.

Winston Churchill called the Polish campaign:

A perfect specimen of the modern Blitzkrieg; the close interaction on the battlefield of army and air force; the violent bombardment of all communications and of any town that seemed an attractive target; the arming of an active Fifth Column; the free use of spies and parachutists; and above all, the irresistible forward thrusts of great masses of armor.[77]

The German Army was well trained, and on the whole well organized. Its military traditions and the long-term, highly trained officers and noncoms who had served in the 100,000-man army of the Weimar Republic gave it skilled leadership. Its homogeneity—ethnically it was entirely German—provided strength. Its tactical organization was simple and lent itself to the flexible demands of modern war. The so-called *"Einheit"* system eased the problem of tailoring a task force to the form and dimensions required by its mission; one unitary building block could easily be added to another, the requisite amount of artillery, engineers and so on added until the force was fashioned.

The German Army of World War II originated the modern task force; in fact, in later fighting many of its units, decimated by casualties, were grouped into task forces (or Kampfgruppen—i.e., "battle groups") usually called by the names of their commanders. To those who studied the campaign closely, Poland demonstrated that the Army of the Nazi Reich was manned by soldiers with much tactical or battlefield initiative.

B. H. Liddell Hart has commented on the "initiative and flexibility . . . in the best vein of the old tradition," that were demonstrated by the German commanders in Poland. But as Hart also states, the victory in Poland had an "intoxicating effect on Hitler."[78]

He became more and more self-assured. He assumed, after the Polish campaign, more and more of the role of Commander in Chief: he did not propose; he disposed. In the Polish campaign, which Hitler considered a kind of police action, the Supreme Command did not function as such. Hitler was more or less content with an active observer's role; he followed the campaign with a very small and inactive staff, from his headquarters aboard a train, the Fuehrer Special, which was generally stationed near a military training area in Pomerania. Hitler toured the front visiting army and corps headquarters; he made suggestions but gave no orders. The Polish campaign was really run by the Army High Command (Von Brauchitsch, Commander in Chief, and Halder, Chief of Staff). But Poland was an exception. Hitler always yearned for more and more power, and he exercised it in increasing measure as the war went on. He made it clear during the campaign in the Low Countries (May, 1940) that he was "now determined to direct operations himself."[79] As long as victory crowned his legions this had no major ill effect, but when stalemate or defeat withered the laurel wreaths he became more and more dogmatic and assumed tighter and tighter control. Later in the war, particularly after the Battle of Moscow, the Nazi strategy was dominated by Hitler; far too often, as at Stalingrad, it was inflexible and small defeats became big ones. But the *tactics* of the German Army, until almost the end, were flexible; its soldiers retained initiative until half-trained replacements and impressed or defected citizens from all the races and nations of Europe fleshed out the huge gaps in its ranks caused by the unlimited ambitions and grandiose aims of Hitler.

For much of the Western world, imbued with the propaganda that Germans were automata, marching solely to the tune of Hitler's whims, this was hard to accept. In fact, the myth that the German Army was a rigid, inflexible organization that carried out orders to the letter but did not think for itself died hard; Poland did not end it—except to the few who closely studied its lessons. The idea was still prevalent, even in the American Army, when the United States entered the war, three years later; it died, as many Americans died, on the battlefield.

Poland stamped the Wehrmacht as the best "short-war" army in the world. But Hitler and Goebbels not only advertised it to the full; they exaggerated the German strengths, minimized the Polish weaknesses. The Polish Army was strong in men—many, if not all, stout of heart—but its strategy was incompetent, its higher leadership weak, its tactics obsolete. Above all, its equipment was no match for that of the Germans; it dated back to another war. And planes and tanks destroyed the inadequate communications of Poland so thoroughly and so quickly that a concerted defense, after the first few days, was impossible.

Western commentators emphasized the tank spearheads and the screaming terror of the Stukas, but overlooked what later became in the vast Russian spaces a major weakness: the largely horse-drawn supply trains of the German infantry, the lack of effective heavy tanks, of armored personnel carriers, of communications units, of specialized support and logistics troops, and of well-trained reserves.[80]

But these weaknesses were overmatched by strengths. The German emphasis on artillery was fully justified; the 88 mm. antiaircraft gun proved its versatility against ground targets and began to earn its accolade of the "best gun" of World War II; it matched in time the well-deserved world-wide fame enjoyed by the French 75 in World War I. The light divisions were too light, tactically a military hermaphrodite; they were reorganized as Panzer divisions later. There were many other lessons; from them Germany profited more than France or England. The Reichswehr remedied its weak points and led from strength both in its global propaganda offensive, based on its Polish victory, and—months later—on the battlefield when its Panzers conquered France.

Berlin dubbed the Polish campaign *"Der Feldzug der Achtzehn Tage"* ("The Campaign of the Eighteen Days"[81]), and combat motion pictures of the Nazi war machine rolling across the plains of Poland— shown at the German Embassy in Washington, sent to Rome, leaked to Paris and to London, exhibited all over the world—deeply impressed the neutrals and the waverers, encouraged the appeasers, sowed the seeds of doubt and cultivated a harvest of fear.

"Deutschland über alles"—"Tomorrow the world."[82]

But Poland was for Hitler a hollow victory, for it marked not the short and local war he wanted but the start of World War II, a long, exhausting total conflict, which was to engulf the world. For when Hitler's Panzers were checked at the gates of Moscow many lives later and the United States entered the war, the blitzkrieg became a war of attrition—a many-front war, which, like World War I, Germany could not win.

With his Polish victory, Hitler's megalomania reached a new crescendo. He was to go on to new and far greater victories; his war machine swept across Europe, darkened the skies above England, engulfed all of western Russia, severed the Mediterranean, drove deep into Egypt—only to recoil in blood and defeat at Stalingrad and El Alamein, and to end in the shattered ruins of Berlin.

What Hitler started on September 1, 1939, grew, with Japan's attack on Pearl Harbor on December 7, 1941, into the century's second Total War—a war immeasurably larger in geographic scope than the First World War and even more sanguinary. Some 16,000,000 men in uniform from 53 nations, countries and dominions were killed or died; probably 24,000,000 civilians died from bombs or guns, hunger or disease or, in the concentration camps, from man's inhumanity to man.[83]

World War II, like World War I, convulsed civilization, upset empires, destroyed nations, and with catholic impartiality scythed down by the millions the mean and the petty, the brave and the best.[84]

CHAPTER 2

THE BATTLE OF BRITAIN

July–September, 1940

"Never in the field of human conflict was so much owed by so many to so few."—WINSTON CHURCHILL, AUGUST 20, 1940

England faced defeat.

The stark tragedy of Dunkirk had ended, and the people of Britain had been rallied by the indomitable voice of Winston Churchill:

"We shall not flag or fail. We shall go on to the end. . . . We shall fight on the seas and oceans, we shall fight . . . in the air . . . we shall fight on the beaches, we shall fight on the landing grounds, we shall fight on the fields and in the streets, we shall fight in the hills; we shall never surrender."

The manic ambitions of Adolf Hitler, the megalomaniac chauvinism and ruthless anti-Semitism that swept the German people under his leadership, the world depression of the thirties, the weak and hesitant diplomacy of Britain and France in the appeasement era—these and a host of other factors fashioned the web of fate that entrapped the nations of Europe in World War II.

The preparations for the new Armageddon, veiled in the secrecy with which Man always hides his plans to slaughter other men, had started years before the Wehrmacht crossed the Polish frontier in September, 1939, and a King, in hesitant speech and with agony of soul, told the empire upon which the sun never set that Britain was at war.

In Germany a curious triumvirate directed the prewar renaissance of the Luftwaffe. Fat and decadent Hermann Göring, Commander in Chief of the German Air Force, Air Minister, veteran of the famous "Richthofen Circus" of World War I, archapostle of Hitlerism, taker of drugs and lover of fine food and wines and gorgeous uniforms, dilettante in art, a man of great brilliance and charm but no balance, a man of rages and polished calm, was the political and psychological leader of Germany's reborn air power.

Ernst Udet, speed pilot, glider enthusiast, aircraft designer, fighter pilot in World War I, "cosmopolitan, amusing, *bon vivant*," presided as the technical midwife at the birth of Hitler's Luftwaffe. To him, and others, the German Air Force owed its concentration upon a single-engined fighter design; he personally flew in 1937 the Me-109, destined to play a large role in the Battle of Britain. His bias, plus Hitler's need to build an air force in a hurry and the German strategic conception of air power largely in a ground support role, committed Germany to the dive bomber and to light and medium two-engined bombers during the early years of the war.[1]

Erhard Milch, deputy of Göring, Quartermaster General of the Luftwaffe, disciplinarian, politician, cruel and dynamic, was the organizer and personnel expert.

As early as 1936 the handwriting was on the wall for all to see; the Legion Kondor—200 Nazi aircraft—was sent to Spain under General Hugo Sperrle, whose name history was to record again during the darkest days of Britain's Calvary. The laboratory of blood of Spain's Civil War forecast the tactics of a greater conflict:

Troop transport: 10,000 Moors of General Francisco Franco crossed the Straits of Gibraltar in Junkers 52's.

Ground support: Heinkels and Henschels strafed and bombed near Madrid, Toledo, Santander.

Bombing: The ancient sun-baked towns with musical names—Malaga, Cartagena, Alicante—felt the weight of German bombs in the dress rehearsal of 1936–1939.

In Britain, too, coming events cast their shadows long before. . . .

The Royal Air Force, much impressed by the German attempts at strategic bombing in World War I, and influenced by Trenchard's belief that the plane was essentially an offensive, not a defensive, weapon, had a "bomber obsession," fed, too, in the postwar years by the heady wine of Giulio Douhet, the Italian prophet of air power. Thus, even until Munich a blind and hesitant England—to whom Churchill was an objectionable man—was reluctant to provide enough funds for both air offense and air defense.[2]

There had been authorizations in plenty; as early as 1934, a year after "British agents in Germany reported that Hitler was rearming in defiance of the Versailles Treaty," the Cabinet initiated a five-year plan to strengthen British air power, a plan subsequently revised upward, but there were delays and discouragements; Germany had a head start.

But some men were far-seeing, among them a strange composite of a man, with Calvinistic, dour thoroughness and forbidding personality, which earned him his nickname, "Stuffy": "Stuffy" Dowding, Air Marshal, RAF, who was to become Commander in Chief, Fighter Command, and would preside over the destiny of nations in Britain's darkest hour.

And that technical foresight and inventive genius which have always characterized British development since the industrial revolution had not deserted the descendants of Nelson and Wellington. As early as 1934 the Air Ministry, under Dowding's spur, had formulated design characteristics for a fighter with eight machine guns and a speed of more than 300 miles an hour. In February, 1935, Robert Watson-Watt, "bounced" radio waves off a plane in flight eight miles away and triumphantly traced the electronic reflection of the target. Radar was born, and by 1936 work had started on "the first operational radar system [installed] anywhere in the world"—a chain of electronic sentinels that guarded the east and southeast coasts of England 24 hours a day from Easter, 1939—approach of crisis—until the end of World War II.[3]

And yet after Dunkirk the opponents seemed ill-matched—David against Goliath.

Munich, synonym for appeasement, had been for the RAF and the British armed forces a blessing in disguise; it had given them time— much-needed time.

In March, 1938, the British Joint Chiefs of Staff unanimously and categorically urged the then Prime Minister, Neville Chamberlain, to avoid war until Britain was better prepared. In a long and written report to Mr. Chamberlain,

they stated, without making any qualifications, that the country was not ready for war, that no measures of force, whether alone or in alliance with other European countries, could now stop Germany from inflicting a crushing defeat on Czechoslovakia, and that any involvement in war with Germany at this stage could well lead to an ultimate defeat. . . .

. . . no matter what the cost, war must be averted until the rearmament program began to bear substantial fruit.[4]

And a few days before Munich, Leslie Hore-Belisha, then British Secretary of State for War, entered in his diary:

The P.M. [Chamberlain] yesterday spoke to us of the horrors of war, of German bombers over London and of his horror in allowing our people to suffer all the miseries of war in our present state. No one is more conscious than I am of our present deficiencies. Chiefs of Staff view—to take offensive against Germany now would be like "a man attacking a tiger before he has loaded his gun."[5]

To the applauding throngs who greeted Prime Minister Chamberlain and his umbrella, Munich might have meant "peace in our time," but the RAF knew better; it was the next step to war, a diplomatic delaying action to gain time.

At the time of Munich, "Stuffy" Dowding had 406 aircraft organized in 29 squadrons, with only 160 in reserve and a production output of 35 fighters monthly. His force had only a few eight-gun Hurricanes, none of the new Spitfires; and the Germans already were operating the deadly Me-109's.

Between Munich and the outbreak of war in September, 1939, the RAF had increased its total first-line home strength (including Dowding's Fighter Command) to 1,476 planes and 118,000 regulars. But the Luftwaffe disposed of approximately 4,300 operational aircraft (including 540 transports) and a half-million men. Only in one significant statistic was Britain approximately equal to Germany—in aircraft production. Britain was turning out almost 800 planes a month when Warsaw was bombed in September, 1939; Germany, which expected a war of blitzkrieg and never mobilized her full production strength in World War II until much too late, was producing only slightly more. (The figures for GAF production in 1939: fighters, 1,856; bombers, 2,877; transports, 1,037: trainers, 1,112; others, 1,413; total, 8,295).

But the world did not know this then; estimates of German aircraft production were enormous, and when the war started, London expected a blitz from the air.

But the blitz came on land: Poland was overrun; then, later, Denmark, Norway, Holland, Belgium, France. Hitler danced his little obscene jig of joy beside the historic railway car at Compiègne where he received the French surrender, and Britain was on her own, alone against the conqueror.

But long before France died, in fact soon after war started in 1939, the idea of invasion was born. "Operation Sea Lion" the Nazis called it; like Napoleon they looked across the misty waters of the Channel toward the chalk cliffs of England. "Sea Lion" slumbered as the German legions moved across Poland, into Copenhagen and Oslo, The Hague and Brussels and Paris. . . . But on July 2, 1940, with the Channel ports safely in German hands and their enemies on the continent routed, Supreme Headquarters issued its first directive:

The Fuehrer and Supreme Commander has decided: that a landing in England is possible, providing that (1) air superiority can be attained and certain other necessary conditions fulfilled. . . .

And two weeks later:

Since England, in spite of her militarily hopeless position, shows no sign of coming to terms, I have decided to prepare a landing operation against England, and if necessary to carry it out. . . . The preparations for the entire operation must be completed by mid-August.[6]

Little time, indeed, to prepare to invade a land sacrosanct against assault since the days of the Norman invasion; little time—one short month—to program the most difficult operation known to war: amphibious invasion!

Britain reeled under staggering defeats, but her courage did not falter. She had sustained huge losses at Dunkirk, an evacuation which was at best a limited moral victory paid for heavily in physical terms. The Royal Navy had saved more than half a million fighting men from the debacles in Norway and France in about a month, but they were more a rabble than an army, nearly all heavy equipment lost, units disorganized, survirors tired, wounded and groggy.[7] Twenty-two tanks out of 704 sent to France came home; there was little artillery, less ammunition, insufficient rifles, not enough uniforms. The Royal Navy, too, was sorely hurt; "more than half the destroyers in home waters had been put out of action," some 16 sunk and 42 damaged in two months. Heavy naval losses had been suffered in covering the evacuation from Dunkirk, and British naval armament at that time was grossly inadequate in AA guns.

For many weeks in that fateful summer of 1940, "an invading force of 150,000 picked men might have created mortal havoc in our midst," Churchill was later to tell Parliament.

"Stuffy" Dowding, too, had suffered: 463 planes, 284 pilots lost in one month in the battles of the Low Countries and France; his operational strength after Dunkirk (466 operational aircraft on June 5) was not much more than it had been at the ill-fated time of Munich.[8]

The Germans, in answer to Hitler's directive to prepare for the invasion of England, worked with great energy but little conviction. On July 31 the tentative date for invasion was set for September 15. But neither the German Admiralty, which had a hearty respect for the British Fleet and understood fully the difficulties of so extensive an amphibious operation, nor the German Army was enthusiastic about "Sea Lion." Hitler himself saw it as an "exceptionally bold and daring undertaking," with at least four prerequisites for success: Luftwaffe air superiority over the Strait and landing beaches; successful use of long-range guns

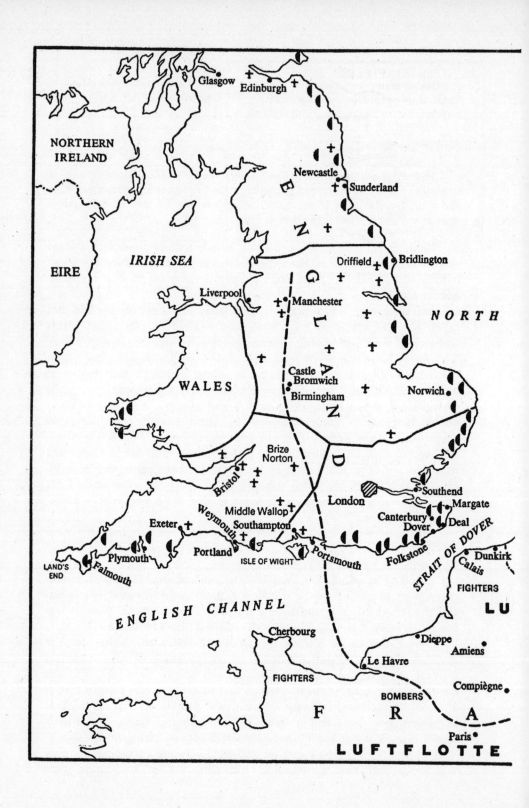

NORTHERN IRELAND

EIRE

IRISH SEA

Glasgow
Edinburgh

NORTHERN IRELAND

Newcastle
Sunderland

Driffield
Bridlington

Liverpool

Manchester

NORTH

WALES

Castle Bromwich
Birmingham

Norwich

Brize Norton

Bristol

Middle Wallop

London
Southend
Margate
Canterbury
Dover
Deal
Folkstone

Exeter
Weymouth
Southampton
Portland
ISLE OF WIGHT
Portsmouth

Plymouth
Falmouth
LAND'S END

STRAIT OF DOVER

Dunkirk
Calais
FIGHTERS
LU

ENGLISH CHANNEL

Cherbourg

Dieppe
Amiens

Le Havre

FIGHTERS

Compiègne

BOMBERS

F R A

Paris

LUFTFLOTTE

FIGHTER AIRFIELDS
in London area

Stanmore
North Weald
Northolt
Uxbridge
London
Hornchurch
Croyden
Kenley
Biggin Hill
West Malling
Gosport
Manston
Hawkinge
Lympne
Thorney I.
ISLE OF WIGHT
ENGLISH CHANNEL
FRANCE

LUFTFLOTTE 5
NORWAY AND DENMARK

DENMARK

SYLT
Hörnum

Brunsbüttel

SEA

Wilhelmshaven

The Hague
NETHERLANDS
Rotterdam

Flushing
Ostend
STUKAS

Brussels

BELGIUM

FTFLOTTE 2

STUKAS

GERMANY

LUXEMBOURG

BOMBERS

N   C   E

THE BATTLE OF BRITAIN
July and August, 1940

——— R A F Group boundaries
+ Fighter airfields
(Radar stations
- - - Luftflotte boundary

0   MILES   100

3

mounted on the Channel coast opposite Dover (to provide long-range artillery support for the landings and to fight off British men-of-war); a heavy belt of mine fields cordoning off the transport lanes to hold out the British Fleet; and—good weather.

The plans and marshaling preparations went on as beleaguered England watched Hitler's continent gird for the trial by fire. By the beginning of September, 1940, the German Admiralty had acquired 168 transports of more than 700,000 tons, 1,910 barges, 419 tugs and trawlers and 1,600 motorboats, and had commenced moving them southward toward the Channel ports from Rotterdam to Le Havre. After many bickerings and sharp exchanges between the German armed services, Hitler directed a compromise plan—landings on a broad front between Folkstone and Bognor were to be made by a first assault of 90,000 men. The Sixteenth, Ninth and Sixth Armies—13 divisions in attack, 12 in reserve—were to span the Channel, assault the beaches, conquer England!

In Berlin, the Nazis were singing:

> *Heute gehert uns Deutschland,*
> *Und Morgen, die ganze Welt!*
>
> (Today Germany belongs to us,
> And tomorrow, the whole world!)

As German shipping was marshaled and the German armies prepared, the Luftwaffe mustered its forces for the *Adlerangriff*. The "Eagle Attack" was to launch, some four to six weeks before the approximate date of invasion, the knockout blow against the Royal Air Force. Preliminary operations started in June and increased in intensity during July; there was no real hiatus between the Battle of France and the Battle of Britain. In July the ports of Falmouth, Plymouth, Portland, Weymouth, Dover, and Channel convoys were among the targets; on July 10 Fighter Command flew more than 600 daylight sorties. But the attacks were sporadic and ill-planned, in five weeks from 10 July to 12 August only 30,000 tons of shipping were sunk between Land's End and the Nore, and the old ports of England worked the clock round, despite the crump of bombs. The Luftwaffe effort was too small and too dispersed, but it did increase the strain on Fighter Command.

The Germans did not schedule the full weight of their great air onslaught until August, though soon after the middle of July the swastika-marked squadrons assumed "full readiness." But the British estimated that the great air battle began its build-up phase on July 10, though the preliminary attacks during that month were minor compared with what was to come.

The main battle opened, according to various reckonings between August 8 and 13. The British were ready, their courage stoked by Winston Churchill's immortal words:

The Battle of Britain is about to begin. . . . The whole fury and might of the enemy must very soon be turned on us. Hitler knows that he will have to break us in this island or lose the war. . . . Let us therefore brace ourselves to our duties, and so bear ourselves that, if the British Empire and its Common- wealth last for a thousand years, man will say, "This was their finest hour."[9]

"Stuffy" Dowding had 704 "operationally serviceable" aircraft on August 11, 1940—620 of them eight-gunned Hurricanes and Spitfires.[10] He had 289 planes in reserve. Britain had used the two months' respite after Dunkirk well.

British factories under the spur of Lord Beaverbrook had built 1,665 planes during July, almost 500 of them fighters.[11] Main radar cover—to 15,000 feet supplemented by the eyes and ears of the Observer Corps— extended from Southampton around the southern and eastern and northern coasts of Great Britain; in the Strait of Dover and Channel area the magic eye of British radar could actually "watch" the enemy planes across the water take off from their coastal airfields.

But there were great weaknesses. There were not enough trained pilots; Dowding's squadrons had been augmented by pilots from the Fleet Air Arm, a Canadian squadron and Polish and Czech fliers. Britain had only one-quarter of the antiaircraft guns she needed. Balloon barrages and a Rube Goldberg device known as the "PAC" (parachute and cable)—rockets carrying cables suspended from parachutes for use against low-flying raiders—protected aircraft factories. Thousands of British women and children had been evacuated from London. And so England waited as "Stuffy" Dowding, the keeper of the gates, scanned the battleground, a large-scale map of England in Fighter Command HQ at Stanmore. . . .

Three German air fleets were mustered for the battle: Luftflotte 2, Field Marshal Albert Kesselring commanding, based in Holland, Bel- gium and northeast France; Luftflotte 3, Field Marshal Hugo Sperrle commanding, based in France; Luftflotte 5, Colonel General Hans- Jürgen Stumpff commanding, based in Norway and Denmark. Their total strength approximated 3,350 aircraft, but only about 75 percent of these were operationally serviceable, and almost the entire brunt of the battle was borne, in any case, by Luftflotten 2 and 3. The Germans used against Britain about 900 to 1,000 fighters—chiefly single-engined Mes- serschmitt 109's, with later a few ME-110's; and about 1,000 Heinkel 111's, Dornier 17's and Junkers 88's, with 300 Ju-87's (the famous Stukas).

THE OPENING PHASE

The German plan contemplates a series of initial attacks chiefly by daylight and gradually mounting in intensity against British radar stations, airfields and aircraft factories, supplemented by strong secondary attacks against ports and Channel shipping—the objectives which had been the principal targets during the two-months' "warm-up" between Dunkirk and the opening phase of the Battle of Britain.

Early on the eighth of August, the map board at HQ of No. 11 Group at Uxbridge shows sixty bogies approaching the Isle of Wight. No. 11 Group, "on which our [Britain's] fate largely depended," covers the heart of England—London and the counties of Essex, Kent, Sussex, Hampshire and Dorset. Hurricanes and "Spits" rise in angry haste to take on the Stukas and the Ju-88's and the south coast of England has a grandstand view of the battle in the skies. A convoy is the German objective; the morning battle ends with two ships sunk. But the Germans strike again in the afternoon, and squadrons from No. 10 Group (covering the southwest) come barreling to the rescue. The surface ships scatter as the cloud fight shrills above them; four ships are sunk, six damaged.

Pilot Officer D. M. Crook of 609 Squadron takes off in a Spitfire, with five companions, from Middle Wallop; he sees a "big number of enemy fighters circling above the [convoy] looking exactly like a swarm of flies buzzing round a pot of jam." Crook spots an Me-109 below him; the German is a "sitting target," but before the "Spit" can get him, a Hurricane appears and shoots him down in flames. Crook is "annoyed."

On the eleventh the ancient ports feel the wrath from the skies; Portland and Weymouth and convoys in the Thames estuary and off Norwich are bombed.

The tempo mounts; on August 12 the Huns come again in great strength; convoys and fleets of Stukas and Ju-88's and Heinkels, covered by Me-109's, roar above the white cliffs of Dover, and strike in the hundreds in five or six major raids against radar stations and airfields, and Portsmouth and a convoy in the Thames.

The radar stations are unmistakable targets; their steel masts 360-foot-high tower on crags and headlands and coastal hills, modern replicas of the beacon fires which five centuries before had warned of the Spanish Armada. The station at Ventnor on the Isle of Wight is completely clobbered—out of action until replaced by another station on August 23; five others take minor damage, and German bombs salvo upon Manston airfield, Lympne and Hawkinge, cratering the runways. But not without loss: No. 10 and 11 Groups exact tribute from the invader; the Stuka proves vulnerable; 31 flaming Nazi aircraft crash on British soil or in bordering waters; the RAF loses 22.

On the thirteenth, favored by cloudy skies, they come hard again; 1,400 aircraft fly against Britain. It was, for the Germans, the opening of their great attack—"Eagle Day." But the radar eyes of England picked them out, gaining altitude above Amiens, moving north from Dieppe and Cherbourg. And No. 11 Group is ready again; from many of the airfields of the south counties "Spits" and Hurricanes and two-seater Defiants have scrambled to meet the enemy at the sky gates of England. Bombs roil Southampton water that day, and from Margate to Southend over the estuary of the Thames, the sound of battle echoes in the heavens.

"It is a 'boiling summer's day,'" and the British fly in their shirt sleeves, but they are "absolutely soaked in sweat" as they dive upon the Nazi aircraft. Pilot Officer Crook works off his "annoyance" of a few days before. He gets into quite a "party" (200 Huns) over the Isle of Wight:

"There was the whole German air force, bar Göring!"

Crook dives "straight down into the middle" of a German circle of fighters, blazes away with his eight guns for a few seconds, sees his deflection is wrong, narrowly misses a collision with another fighter, pulls out above the sea in the long, shuddering blackout of "terrific speed," sees a flaming Messerschmitt "fall past within 200 yards" and gets back to Middle Wallop to drink a pint of iced Pimm's and feel better.

But Crook and his mates cannot prevent damage.

Kesselring and Sperrle have sent their bombers against a dozen RAF airfields and stations; two they have damaged heavily; seven others—including stations with historic names, Middle Wallop, Thorney Island—hear the wailing shriek of falling bombs, the siren and the "All Clear," but escape serious damage. The price: 45 Nazi aircraft. The RAF loses 13.

But Colonel General Franz Halder notes optimistically in his diary: "Results very good . . . Eight major air bases have been virtually destroyed."

That night there is a more ominous development. The Germans open—with a bull's-eye—nightly attacks on British aircraft plants. Bombing Gruppe 100, specially trained in night operations hits the factory at Castle Bromwich, producing the vital "Spits," with 11 HE bombs.

The fourteenth is the calm before the storm; German bombs fall on widely scattered parts of England; eight RAF stations feel the lightning from the skies, but the strikes are piecemeal, small, and at Manston ME-110's (two-seater, two-engined fighters) carrying bombs replace the vulnerable Stukas.

On the fifteenth Göring, arrogant, confident, launches his greatest attack.[12] Luftflotte 5 from Scandinavian bases is flung into the fight;

widespread raids approach Britain from Norway to France. If "Stuffy" Dowding strips the north to stiffen up the defenses of the "heart," Tyneside and Yorkshire will suffer. Saturation raids will confuse the British radar and exhaust the British pilots.

At 1129 this day sixty Stukas with fifty 109's cross the coast south of Dover; Nos. 54 and 501 Squadrons of No. 11 Group intercept; Lympne airfield is damaged. At noon, far to the north, the "ops" table mapboard of No. 13 Group, charged with the defense of the north country, shows "its first plot of German aircraft"—65 Heinkels and 34 110's, 100 miles off the Firth of Forth. No. 72 Squadron, on patrol, is vectored to intercept; later Nos. 79, 41, 605 and 607 Squadrons join in and then the Tyneside AA guns take over. The Germans are hectored and chivvied about the skies; the twin-engined Me-110's, the only German fighters with enough range to fly across the North Sea, are "very unhappy" in the presence of "Spits" and "Hurries." Twenty-four houses are destroyed in Sunderland, but not a single factory or airfield is hit; the German raiders are mauled.

Another raid from Scandinavia has better luck; it encounters and outdistances makeshift Blenheim fighters, detonates an ammo dump near Bridlington in a cascading inferno of smoke and flame and badly roughs up the airdrome at Driffield, where the British lose ten planes on the ground.

But the results for Luftflotte 5 are unhappy; never again during the Battle of Britain will Stumpff attempt a daylight raid against the northeast coasts; German bombers without Me-109 cover are too vulnerable.

But the day is not done. In the southeast No. 11 Group is hardpressed. Hundred-plane raids come in north of the Thames estuary, over Folkstone and Deal, and late in the day 200 to 300 aircraft approach Hampshire and Dorset. All over the southern skies this day, the fierce straggling battle rages; the great formations break up into detachments and dogfights; spent bullets drop near the British land girls in their fields; contrails line the upper heavens, and smoke, arching across the sky, is the ephemeral wind-blown monument to pilots, dead in combat, graves unknown. This day almost 1,800 enemy planes attack Britain—more than 500 bombers, almost 1,300 fighters. Two aircraft factories are badly hit, some damage is done to airfields, but the British are jubilant; they claim 182 enemy definitely destroyed, 53 probables, against losses of 34. The headlines blazon forth: it is the greatest "kill" since the battle opened; the Germans are "routed." But the claims are inflated. The Germans admit only 32 aircraft destroyed; actually, they lose 75—far less than the RAF claims, but nevertheless the largest single toll on any one day of the battle.

At his Prussian country seat, the corpulent Göring feeds his prize stallions, holds a conference with Kesselring, Sperrle, Stumpff.

"Until further orders," the Reich Marshal directs, "operations are to be directed exclusively against the enemy air force." But—fatal mistake—"it is doubtful whether there is any point in continuing the attacks on radar sites, in view of the fact that not one of those attacked has so far been put out of operation."

On the sixteenth the bandits swarm over Britain like bees about a hive—1,700 aircraft, but only 400 are bombers—tacit tribute to the toughness of the British defense. The enemy scores heavily—"the biggest single success of the whole battle"—when two Ju-88's, diving out of the low overcast, destroy 46 aircraft in their hangars at Brize Norton. But German intelligence is poor; only three of eight airfields attacked this day are used by "Stuffy" Dowding's boys.

Flight Lieutenant J. B. Nicholson of 249 Squadron wins the V.C. (Victoria Cross) in a melee this day over Gosport. His Hurricane fighter— "hotly engaged with the enemy"—is struck by four 20 mm. cannon shells; Nicholson is wounded; the petrol tank is touched off; flames pour into the cockpit. The pilot is about to bail out when he sees a twin-engined Me-110 in his sights; Nicholson stays with his burning ship and pours a cone of fire into the enemy. Only then, burned, bloody and gasping, does he take to his chute. As he lands he is shot in the buttocks by an excited Home Guard volunteer.

The seventeenth is a day of surcease—blessed interval of small-scale action, few alarums.

But on the eighteenth the Germans come again and draw blood. They destroy most of the hangars at Kenley, important sector station of No. 11 Group, get four Hurricanes on the ground, crater the runways, damage communications. Croydon, Biggin Hill, West Malling, Gosport, Thorney Island and Poling radar stations are also hit. The RAF claims 155 "certains"; the Germans admit 36 and actually lose 71 aircraft— second heaviest toll of the battle. The famous Stukas are decimated; Göring withdraws most of them from the battle.

THE ONSLAUGHT

For five days there is respite; scattered raids harass Britain but they are in small force; heavy clouds hold off the great armadas. The RAF takes stock. The enemy had lost almost 400 aircraft since the first week in August (the British claims, accepted then, are almost twice that number); Fighter Command, 213. But "Stuffy" Dowding already had started eating into his reserve; the bombed factories had not been able to replace the losses in Hurricanes and Spitfires, the backbone of the defense. And 154

British pilots are dead or wounded; only 63 new ones have been trained; the veteran survivors are red-eyed, tense.

The large-scale raids start again on August 24, and from then through September 6 Kesselring and Sperrle send an average of almost 1,000 planes daily against Britain. The fundamental objective is No. 11 Group, guardian of the heartland of Britain—its inland airfields, communications centers, hangars, repair depots, sector commands. This is the pay-off: "We have reached," Göring says, "the decisive period of the air war against England."

Kenley and Biggin Hill, Hornchurch, North Weald and Northolt—sector command "CP's," airfield sentinels for London—are attacked again and again and again. Manston, its buildings wrecked, its runway cratered and its field pocked with delayed action or unexploded bombs, is abandoned. Day after day the great enemy armadas roar above the green fields of England; Dowding's boys, high in the heavens, are vectored toward the enemy, shout out their "Tallyho!" as they sight him, put their sticks forward, dive with screaming guns. Day after day the crump of bombs rocks the English countryside; day after day the cumulative damage of attrition wears down the stout defense.

The young men of England rise to flaming fight: the legless pilot, Douglas Bader, known to the Canadians he leads as "Tin-Legs"; the South African "Sailor" Malan; a company of youngsters whose names are written imperishably in the hearts of Englishmen everywhere.

Day after day the red-eyed pilots—the few to whom the many owe so much—scramble their planes, rise to fight, perhaps to die, and, if they live, to fight again. Day after day the pilot officers and the flight lieutenants, the mechanics and the WAAF's (those young women in their helmets with such English names—Corporal Elspeth Henderson, Assistant Section Officer Felicity Hanbury) "carry on" in the dogged British way; some even find time in the few off-duty moments in the pubs near the fields to join the chorus of "Waltzing Matilda."

But there is no surcease for the outnumbered. They fly and fight, land to refuel and reload, eat by their aircraft, wait in restless readiness.

"Two-forty-two Squadron scramble! Bogies fifteen, North Weald."

Off the runway, wheels still spinning, the squadron leader reports "Airborne," and over his radio hears the voice of the controller on the ground: "Vector one nine zero. Buster [full throttle]. Seventy plus bandits approaching North Weald."

Far above England, the squadron sights the enemy—a glint of sun, another—"and in seconds, a mass of little dots."

"Bandits—ten o'clock level."

The Hurricanes split up; one section takes on "the top lot" of the Germans; six dive on a swarm of 70 Dorniers; both formations break up into a swirl of individual dogfights. The sky blooms with flaming bullets; fire and smoke suddenly blossom at wing roots and in cockpits; sudden death is in the skies. In a few seconds it is all over—another mission ended, so many more to come. . . .

On August 31 Fighter Command suffers its heaviest losses: 39 planes shot down, 14 pilots killed. The Germans lose 41 aircraft in the same 24-hour period.

The attacks are so numerous that on one day—September 4—the plotboard in Fighter Command is "saturated" with raids; the Vickers factory at Brooklands (Weybridge) is hit without warning; casualties are heavy and production of the Wellington, heavyweight of the RAF bomber fleet, is reduced. Hawker's also is damaged, source of half of England's supply of Hurricanes. . . .

The RAF Fighter Command is hard hit: in August 300 pilots are casualties; there are only 260 replacements; the command is "literally wasting away."[13]

"It was at this stage," says Dennis Richards, "when the German efforts were straining our defenses to the utmost that Hitler . . . once more came to our aid."[14]

During the early stages of the Battle for Britain, in fact, long before the battle starts, the Bomber Command of the RAF has not been idle. The first British air raids against Germany—the objective the German fleet at the naval bases of Wilhelmshaven and Brunsbüttel—are staged in small force soon after Britain enters the war on September 4, 1939, as the German Wehrmacht gives Poland its death blow.

British bombers drop some bombs by accident on the island of Heligoland on December 3, but no casualties are caused.

On March 16, 1940, German aircraft—their objective the British Fleet at Scapa Flow—loose stray bombs on nearby islands. The Royal Air Force immediately retaliates by a night attack—described somewhat inadequately in the British official history as the "first ever delivered by Bomber Command against a land target"—against the German seaplane base of Hörnum, on the island of Sylt.[15]

In early May, 1940, nine Whitleys attack "roads, railways and bridges in and near four German towns on the enemy's route to southern Holland." And ever since May of 1940 Bomber Command has been sending its day bombers against German objectives, chiefly aircraft factories and communications.[16] On August 25–26, "the night after London had been unintentionally attacked by German bombers," British night bombers raid Berlin.[17]

These are the first raids for both capitals, and in Berlin the moral effect is, to use Shirer's word, "tremendous." Like the German bombardment of London in World War I, the military effects achieved in these initial RAF raids against Berlin are slight, but the traumatic effects are major.[18] Bomber Command strikes again and again at Berlin and other German objectives in the closing days of August and the opening days of September as the Luftwaffe builds up to climax its onslaught against "Stuffy" Dowding's airfields of No. 11 Group.

On September 4 Hitler rages in a public speech:

"The British drop their bombs indiscriminately and without plan on civilian residential quarters and farms and villages. . . . For three months I did not reply. . . . The British will know that we are now giving our answer night after night. . . . If they attack our cities, we will rub out [exterminate] their cities from the map. . . . The hour will come when one of us two will break and it will not be Nazi Germany."[19]

The day before, unknown to the British, Hitler, still undecided, had designated the tentative date for the invasion of Britain as September 21. But he was to reserve decision until September 10–11.

And "three days later the Luftwaffe [abandons] its offensive against the sector stations and [begins] its assault on London," an attack intended not only as reprisal but to force RAF Fighter Command to commit its dwindling resources to definitive battle.

THE CRISIS

On September 7, 1940, London's trial by blood and fire begins. The Germans are confident; Luftwaffe intelligence thinks the British have only 350 fighters left. They actually have about 650.

The day starts ominously for Britain. Photoreconnaissance shows the invasion ports are filling up with Nazi shipping; there were 18 barges in Ostend on August 31; there are 205 on September 6; Flushing is crowded with barges and motorboats; in the past two days 34 more barges are photographed at Dunkirk, 53 additional ones at Calais. Four German spies are captured; they indicate Hitler's preparations for invasion are about complete.

And in the afternoon the blitz starts. Almost 400 bombers, escorted by more than 600 fighters, converge on London.

Hard-pressed No. 11 Group, still holding the heartland, rises to do battle; it is reinforced by three squadrons from No. 12 Group, which covers the Midlands. In late afternoon the air over Kent is roiled with dogfights. On the ground the many who owe so much hear the faint roar of scores of engines; the rataplan of machine guns "like the sound made by a small boy in the next street when he runs a stick along a stretch of iron railings"; the distant crump of bombs; and the occasional thunder of a falling plane, flaming to its destruction.

The RAF does execution, but the Germans are canny; they have "beefed up" their fighter cover, and their 109's are now in and among, below and above, the Dorniers and the Heinkels. The enemy cruises in stepped-up formation—"like looking up the escalator at Piccadilly Circus"; the sky battles rage from 12,000 to 30,000 feet.

The raiders break through, and London suffers. Woolwich is pocked with bomb smoke and flame; the docks at West Ham burn. By nightfall Thames Haven is an inferno, and all along the Thames the "roar of burning warehouses mingles . . . with the grey dust of humble homes."

At 8:07 P.M. that night, as German night bombers return to the scene of daytime carnage, GHQ Home Forces sends out the code word: "Cromwell—Invasion Imminent."[20] And through the long night, as German bombers high in the night sky cross and recross the Channel, the men and women of Britain stand to arms on headlands, chalk cliffs and guarded beaches. Two hundred and fifty Nazi bombers maintain "a slow, agonizing procession over the capital" from 8 P.M. to 4 A.M.; only one is shot down.

Sunday, the eighth, the smoke of burning London forms beacon and funeral pall, towering high in the still sky as omen and monument. The daylight raiders come again, but in small strength; the beleaguered fortress cheers as the opening salvo from four 3.7-inch AA guns plucks the three leading planes of a *"Geschwader"* of 15 Dornier 17's out of the sky south of the Thames. But the enemy comes again that night; the East End suffers and again the docks; the railway stations are hit, and the poor and the mighty huddle deep in subways.

By Monday morning civil defense is hard-pressed; fires rage unchecked, walls topple, streets are debris, uncounted bodies lie in the ruins of humble homes.

On the ninth, the eleventh, the twelfth, the thirteenth, by day and by night they come, but still No. 11 Group fights back. (And on the tenth Hitler, still uneasy, postpones the hard decision on invasion until the fourteenth.) Most of the daylight raids are turned back or broken up; bombing is intermittent and inaccurate, but by night the barrage of the ground guns is the chief—and weak—defense. Downing Street and Trafalgar Square are hit, and even Buckingham Palace.

But England fights back. Bomber Command, the Royal Navy and the British long-range artillery on the cliffs of Dover have intensified their strikes since the "Cromwell—Invasion Imminent" warning of September 7. The invasion ports are bombed and shelled; British MTB's roam the Channel. On September 12 the German headquarters of Naval Group West reports to Berlin:

Interruptions caused by the enemy's air force, long-range artillery and light naval forces have for the first time assumed major significance. The harbours at

Ostend, Dunkerque, Calais and Boulogne cannot be used as night anchorages for shipping because of the danger of English bombing and shelling. Units of the British fleet are now able to operate almost unmolested in the Channel. Owing to these difficulties, further delays are expected in the assembly of the invasion fleet.[21]

On September 14 Hitler agrees that "Sea Lion" "is not yet practicable"; the necessary degree of air supremacy "has not yet been attained." However, the Fuehrer is confident: "The air attacks have been very effective and would have been more so if the weather had been good."

The fifteenth of September is the day of climax. Hermann Göring, prodigal of men and blood, throws a thousand aircraft against London, five fighters escorting every bomber. The formation is meticulous, the assembly careful. British radar picks up the swarm far out over the Channel; No. 11 Group has ample time. The Canadians vault into the sky; the bitter Poles climb high into the sun; reinforcing squadrons come from Nos. 10 and 12 Groups.

All over southern England this day, the air fights rage. The machine guns chatter, and in the earphones sound the sightings: "Tallyho!," "Bandits! Twelve o'clock high," or, in guttural tones: *"Achtung—Schpitfeuer!"*

The day is bright and clear; there are light cumulus clouds at 2,000 or 3,000 feet as the battle swirls over the south counties.

The intercepting fighters bore into the German formations; the ordered squadrons break up into swirling dogfights; "Spits" dive through Heinkel squadrons, guns blazing; yellow-nosed Messerschmitts scream down out of the sun—it is a "terrific scrum," a "bedlam of machines." And burning wreckage falls out of the skies from the sea to Stanmore. A Dornier 17 crashes just outside Victoria Station. It is the victim of Sergeant R. T. Holmes of 504 Squadron. But Holmes, his Hurricane in a spin, bails out of his disabled plane and lands on a roof and rolls into a dustbin in Chelsea. Stricken planes fall in the green fields of Kent, on the cliffs of Dover, on the sands of the South Coast. The crumpled Prussian cross, the twisted swastika, the flaring blaze, mark the funeral pyre of many a German pilot; the British win the day battle.

The German comes again at night in the greatest attack of the month, the bombers limned against a full moon. One hundred and eighty-one aircraft punish London; hundreds of civilians die;[22] railway stations are put out of action, others are damaged; conflagrations flame and flare. But it is insensate destruction; most of Fighter Command pilots rest by night and gird to hold the daytime air.

The fifteenth of September, "the fiercest, most confused and most widespread struggle of the whole battle," stands as a day of glory for

"Stuffy" Dowding's boys. They claim the largest toll of the battle: 185 enemy aircraft destroyed. The Germans admit 43, actually lose 60. The bombing is militarily ineffective; even Göring's five-to-one fighter-bomber ratio has not kept off the "Hurries" and the "Spits."

And now, for Hermann Göring, time is running out. London has felt the steel and shard and still the British people are unbowed. The RAF still fights. The mists of fall are drawing in, and the short winter days, and the Channel lop is up. . . .

That night, and the next, British Bomber Command is out in force; by the twenty-first about 12.5 percent of the transports and barges in the Channel ports have been sunk or damaged.

At Hitler's conference on the seventeenth the facts, at last, are faced. The possibility of a landing in October is to be kept in mind. But: "The enemy air force is still by no means defeated; on the contrary it shows increasing activity. The weather situation as a whole does not permit us to expect a period of calm. . . . The Fuehrer, therefore, decides to postpone 'Sea Lion' indefinitely."[23]

British recon aircraft confirm the decision; by September 23 the concentration of invasion shipping in the Channel ports has been sharply reduced.

The rest was anticlimax. The air battles continued. Luftflotten 2 and 3 drove again against London in daylight raids, and against aircraft factories elsewhere in southern England. September 27 was another day of heavy combat; the Germans lost 55 aircraft, the British 28. And on the thirtieth of September the enemy made his final daylight medium-bomber raids against London; during October Messerschmitt fighter-bombers took up the burden. The night raids continued, were long to continue; the life of London for nearly all the years of war centered around the burst of high explosive, the flaring fire, shattered walls and broken bodies.

But Reich Marshal Hermann Göring had done his worst—and it was not enough.

On October 4 Churchill cabled President Roosevelt:

"The gent has taken off his clothes and put on his bathing suit, but the water is getting colder and there is an autumn nip in the air."

October twelfth was the death knell of "Sea Lion"; the German invasion forces were told it would be postponed "until spring" (of 1941). On the headlands of England the sentries stood easy, and the coasts that had been inviolate since the days of Harold of Hastings were still secure.

And by the spring of 1941 the fatal appetite for conquest had turned the Fuehrer's hopes to wider horizons to the East. . . . England had been saved.

RETROSPECT

In retrospect, the Battle of Britain looms as one of the decisive battles of World War II. The repulse of the German Luftwaffe was neither clear-cut nor complete and sharp; nevertheless it was the first check Hitler had received. It was the first battle in history in which air power had played the principal role.

The battle both exposed and created many myths. One of these postwar myths was that the Germans had actually tried invasion and had been beaten back. This story stemmed from the discovery of the bodies of some 40 German soldiers along the southern coast of England. Actually, these troops were killed when British bombers and/or stormy seas sank their invasion barges as the Germans were practicing embarkations and landings along the French coast. As Churchill notes in *Their Finest Hour,* the British encouraged the world for psychological reasons to believe that an invasion attempt had been defeated.

Another myth stemming from the battle was the carefully nurtured public concept of the immaculate nature of the British bombing effort. Actually, both sides had contemplated well before the war, the British to a far greater extent than the Germans, the bombardment of enemy cities, industries and communications.

But there was, indeed, a curious irony in the actual development of strategic bombardment. As Major Raymond H. Fredette, USAF, has shown in a comprehensive study, *Sky On Fire—The First Battle of Britain,* the Germans originated strategic air warfare in World War I with their Zeppelin and Gotha and Giant raids upon British cities. Long before Douhet or Trenchard or Billy Mitchell became prophets of victory through air power, the Germans struck directly at the peoples, the urban centers, supply and industrial areas and the national will to resist. The results, minor in terms of total war, were disappointing to the Germans but unforgettable to the British. The memories of the bombings of World War I, continuously fed by a spate of lurid and exaggerated books published between the wars, very definitely affected British policy and British planning. Britain anticipated tremendous bombing raids upon London and other British cities at the start of World War II; the anticipation influenced materially British policy at Munich and led to the belated emphasis upon the development of Fighter Command. Conversely, it encouraged the growth of the heavy bomber in Britain. Anachronistically, the Nazis concentrated in the prewar and early war years upon single-engined and two-engined bombers, and dive bombers— most of them designed for a tactical role in support of surface power. The originators of strategic bombing in World War I rejected the concept in World War II until it was too late.[24] In the opening months of the war, both sides refrained from so-called "strategic" or city raids against the other. The Germans did use their aircraft against Warsaw (in attacks against what Kesselring euphemistically calls "military targets"), and they undertook the famous terror raid against Rotterdam.[25]

But their first bombs on British soil fell on the Orkneys on March 16, 1940, when Nazi bombers attacked the Home Fleet's base at Scapa Flow. Some civilians were killed on the bordering island of Hoy, and the British retaliated with raids against German bases at Sylt and Hörnum. But much earlier in the war, in September, 1939, British bombers had bombed German naval bases at Brunsbüttel and Wilhelmshaven, Sylt, Heligoland and other objectives. And about May 10–11, 1940, a couple of days after some German bombs fell near Canterbury, British bombers started a systematic attack, which did not stop until war's end, on communications and industries in Germany itself.[26]

The case of who bombed whom first is therefore the case of the pot calling the kettle black; both sides gradually intensified bombing, first against "purely military" objectives, then less and less discriminately, and finally in openly avowed area and urban attacks. Thus the climactic German raids against London in September, 1940, could be viewed, from the Reich's point of view, as reprisal for the prior British raids against Berlin. On the other hand, the British felt, with some justification, that no holds were barred after Warsaw and Rotterdam.

Still another myth of the battle concerned the combat claims advanced by both sides. The British claimed—and supported their claims with arguments which convinced themselves and much of the neutral world, and so sincerely believed—that they had destroyed far more German aircraft than they actually did during the battle. The RAF official estimate of German losses in the entire Battle of Britain from July 10, the start of the warm-up, through October 31, including the daylight bombing of London, was 2,698. The Germans actually lost 1,733 aircraft (221 brought down by AA fire) and admitted the loss of only 896. Another 643 were damaged. The Germans claimed the destruction of 3,058 planes and actually destroyed 915. The Nazis, like the British, believed some of their own statistics and thought the RAF was much more worn down than it actually was.

The Battle of Britain demonstrated the limitations of air power as well as its capabilities. Both sides, prior to the war, had grossly overestimated the effects of bombing upon industrial production and civilian morale; both had grossly underestimated the air strength required to achieve important results. The bomber was supposed to have been supreme, but the battle demonstrated that it was the fighter which dominated the skies.

The British were perhaps slightly less wrong than the Germans in their pre-evaluation of the role of the fighter in air warfare. All the airmen of that day, including most particularly U.S. Army Air Force officers, had endowed the bomber with omnipotence and had grossly underestimated the numbers of bombers required to make even a minor impression upon a determined nation.

Sir John Slessor, pioneer British airman, Commander in Chief Coastal Command, RAF, during the war, and postwar Chief of Air Staff, has written (in an afterword to Major Fredette's book):

Where we were very wrong in 1939 . . . was in a gross under-estimate of the weight of explosive and the technical efficiency of the means of delivery necessary to achieve decisive results; and in an almost equally serious under-estimate of the capacity of civilian populations to stand up to the scale of attack available before the advent of nuclear explosives.

Professor William R. Emerson, then of Yale University, in a Harmon Memorial Lecture—"Operation Pointblank"—to the U.S. Air Force Academy on March 27, 1962, summed up the general lack of prescience succinctly. His remarks were specifically applied to United States airmen, but his careful exploration of global air power developments prior to World War II make it clear that his comments can be applied, with but few variations, to the British and the Germans.

It cannot be said that American air commanders saw at all clearly the character that air war would assume or that they weighed at all accurately what its demands would be. In particular, they failed completely to grasp the essential meaning of air superiority . . . if American airmen made mistakes, certainly they made fewer than did the airmen of any other nation . . . every salient belief of prewar . . . air doctrine was either overthrown or drastically modified by the experience of war. Germany proved not at all vulnerable to strategic bombing . . . the German Air Force was never truly destroyed. It was defeated in battle, partly by the heavy bomber missions which forced it, as the RAF in 1940 had not been forced, to defend its homeland, partly by the American day fighters who struck not only at its matériel, as the bombers did, but at other factors no less important to an air force—its leadership, its veteran pilots, its command structure, its morale, its hopes. . . . Despite the visions of its pro-tagonists of prewar days, the air war during the Second World War, no less than the fighting on the ground and at sea, was attrition war. It did not supplant the operations of conventional forces; it complemented them.[27]

To which it must be added that Bomber Command contributed powerfully to the German reverses in the Battle of Britain by the bombardment of Berlin and the direct effects this had upon German bombing strategy, and by the heavy attacks upon the German invasion ports, which destroyed large numbers of barges, ships and stores.

In retrospect the Battle of Britain was won by the British, aided by the Germans.

The Nazis' planning was faulty, weakened by the bombast of Göring and the hesitations of Hitler. Their air strength was inadequate, their shifts in objectives fatal; they were too little and too late.

The postwar claim that the RAF alone saved Britain from invasion will not withstand examination. The RAF was a dominant factor, but so, too, were German mistakes, the geographical fact of the English Channel (a major psychological as well as a physical barrier to the Germans) and the presence of the Royal Navy. The "fleet in being" inspired hearty respect in the minds of the German admirals. Most important factor, perhaps, was Hitler's indecision and the lukewarm approach to Operation Sea Lion by the German Navy (particularly) and the Army. Hitler believed after Dunkirk that England would make peace—on his terms; he hesitated when he should have struck. The German surface services had no such confidence in Göring as the Reich Marshal had in himself; the Navy especially respected the power of the British Fleet and the width of the English Channel. There was friction between the services, and inchoate planning; General Jodl remarked caustically after the war that "our arrangements were much the same as those of Julius Caesar."

Kesselring wrote after the war that "I am forced to agree with the opinion of the British military historian [Major General J. F. C.] Fuller when he writes that Sea Lion was often contemplated, but never planned."[28]

And Rear Admiral Walter Ansel has written that "Hitler fought not a battle of arms but a war of nerves in which both Eagle and Sea Lion were threatening gestures lacking conviction." "More than any other single factor," he adds, "Adolf Hitler rendered invasion impossible."[29]

The "if's" of history remain. It seems probable that if the Germans had tried an invasion soon after the Battle of France (tied to a bold and comprehensive plan, which was always lacking) they might well have succeeded, despite the stout resistance of the RAF.[30] The price would have been very high. But after Dunkirk Britain was weakened and vulnerable. She had virtually no defense against airborne attack. At night a large airborne and amphibious force might have spanned the Strait of Dover and the Channel and probably could have forced a landing on British soil despite the intervention of the British Navy and the RAF. The Germans did not try.

It is entirely conceivable, too, that the Germans could have won a localized air superiority over the invasion area—the only kind that mattered. As Kesselring remarks in his book, *A Soldier's Record:*

In an invasion the German combat air forces would have done their job if the invasion planners had taken the necessary step to gain only a qualified air superiority, if all dissipation of strength had been avoided and if the whole Luftwaffe had been available on zero day fully refurbished—conditions which could perfectly well have been fulfilled.[31]

There were many technical reasons for the failure of the German Air Force to achieve the decisive result Göring anticipated. Its single-seater fighter—the Me-109—was better than the Hurricane, as good as or better than the Spitfire, particularly in rate of climb and at high altitude. But it was short-legged; it had only sufficient range to penetrate to the London area and return to base. The Germans lost numerous Me-109's during the battle because they ran out of gas before they could return to their bases. The Me-110 twin-engined twin-seater was long-ranged and capable of operating from Norway or Denmark, but it was no match for the Hurricane or Spitfire. This meant, in effect, that the German attack was concentrated upon southeastern England; the rest of the country was not seriously threatened in daylight raids.

After the climactic August 15 battle Luftflotte 5, based in Norway and Denmark, played virtually no part in the day battle. Its Me-110's were no match for the British interceptors; in fact, the German twin-seaters required protection themselves. This meant that there was, after the fifteenth, virtually no German flank threat to the north, and that only part of the German Air Force was engaged in the onslaught. Many of the Luftflotte 5's bombers, and some of its fighters, were transferred southward to the Low Countries in late August in preparation for the anticipated invasion. From August 24 onward Luftflotte 2 (Kesselring) in the Pas-de-Calais area shouldered the main burden of the day attacks. The British were, therefore, able to concentrate their strength in defense, not disperse it.

England had other advantages. The British fighters had pilot armor; the German fighters and bombers were originally unarmored and were hastily armored during the battle. The German bombers were inadequate to their task. No four-engined bomber was then available to the GAF, and the Stuka dive bomber, useful on the battlefield, was particularly slow and vulnerable when used in strategic bombing. The Heinkels and Dorniers were good, workable machines, but their defensive armament was weak. Their bomb loads were too small for the job assigned. Their range and armament, and the training of the GAF, were inadequate for effective attack upon the Royal Navy, which should have been one of the principal targets.

The tremendous British advantage in radar detection and in fighter control from the ground was a major (probably the principal) factor in the battle. The Germans had no such comparable electronic aids.[32] German air intelligence was inadequate. In short, the Germans undertook a task which the Luftwaffe was not large enough to carry out and one for which it had not been trained or equipped.

Nevertheless, the German Air Force came fairly close to success and might have changed the course of history if Hitler, Göring and their marshals had not violated a fundamental principle of war. In military parlance this is called the principle of the objective. In other words, the Germans took their eye off the ball. For Hitler had only one eye on England; even before the battle started he was looking toward the east.

The great lesson of those months of crisis in the summer and early fall of 1940 is the importance of a clear-cut objective. The German air attacks upon England and the plans for amphibious invasion were never linked to a lucid political and military objective. The German Air Force fought its own war with but tenuous liaison—until too late—with the invasion plans of the other services.

The Germans opened the battle with desultory, widespread operations against a variety of targets. On August 8 they concentrated upon convoys, ports, radar stations, airfields and coastal targets. From August 24 to September 6 they pushed their attacks against the inner and vital ring of British airfields around London, and the master sector stations which controlled the operations of No. 11 Group. On September 7 they switched their main effort to assaults against London.

Their proper objective from first to last should have been the British Fighter Command—specifically No. 11 Group, that segment of Fighter Command which could interfere most with their planned invasion. The establishment of a localized air superiority over the Channel and the invasion beaches should have had first priority.

Their secondary objective was Bomber Command, obviously a major invasion foe, and the British Fleet. But had Fighter Command been put out of business, or greatly weakened, these secondary objectives could have been assailed at leisure. Radar stations, peculiarly vulnerable to assault because exposed; airfields and communications; fighters in the air and on the ground and aircraft factories were the proper targets for the Germans.

When Hitler concentrated upon these, he was winning the battle. By September 6 the RAF was reeling; Fighter Command was declining in strength and effectiveness. Churchill notes (*Their Finest Hour*) that "the scales had tilted against Fighter Command" between August 24 and September 6. During this period Dowding had lost 103 pilots killed, 128 seriously wounded and out of action; 286 "Spits" and Hurricanes destroyed; and a large number of fighter fields and sector headquarters badly "knocked about." About one-quarter of the total fighter pilot strength had been lost, and only 260 "new, ardent, but inexperienced pilots drawn from training units, in many cases before their full courses were complete" had replaced them. The airfield bombing had affected the morale of the labor gangs or works repair depots, who filled in bomb craters and repaired buildings. "Often during an air raid a gang would retire to the shelters and refuse to budge. They claimed that they were not going to do the job if it was dangerous."[33] *Royal Air Force,* Volume I, notes that "not only was there very considerable damage to the ground organization" of Fighter Command during this period, "but the British losses in fighters so greatly exceeded the output from production that in three more weeks of activity on the same scale—if the Germans could have stood three more weeks—the fighter reserves would have been completely exhausted."[34]

A poignant memoir by Air Commander E. M. Donaldson, RAF, published in the London *Daily Telegraph* and the (U.S.) *National Observer,* a quarter-century after the battle, records that

when I relinquished command of the famous No. 151 Fighter Squadron in August 1940, on promotion to wing commander, I was convinced that we were beaten, that we had lost the battle.

I was fantastically tired and utterly depressed. My squadron had been in heavy fighting since May without a break. I left it, I thought, a very depleted and thoroughly beaten fighting unit.[35]

And Dowding himself commented later that the situation was critical. Pilots were withdrawn from Bomber and Coastal Commands and from the Fleet Air Arm. The majority of the Fighter Command squadrons had been reduced to the status of training units.

But on September 7, with potential victory in sight, Hitler vented his fury and London replaced Fighter Command as the principal target. This decision, in retrospect, put the seal on British victory. It was one of the great miscalculations of history. The bombing of London gave Fighter Command a chance to recuperate, and it forced the Luftwaffe to a deeper penetration and thus exposed the bombers and short-legged fighters to greater loss. It antagonized world public opinion, mobilized global sentiment in support of Britain, stiffened English resolution and helped to lead to Germany's loss of the war.

But for this epochal result, "Stuffy" Dowding's boys, the few to whom the many owed so much, deserve a major share of credit. They did not "win" the battle, but they prevented the enemy from winning it.[36] Four hundred and two British airmen, 5 Belgians, 7 Czechoslovakians, 29 Poles, 3 Canadians and 3 New Zealanders died from July 10 to October 31 in the air defense of Britain. To those lighthearted young extroverts, who sang and grinned their way to death—men who loved a party, a fight and a joke; to "Tin-Legs" Bader, "Sailor" Malan, Stanford Tuck and sensitive Hillary, Flight Lieutenant Nicholson, V.C., Sergeant Holmes, who landed in a dustbin, for Calvinistic, dour "Stuffy" Dowding, and the thousand pilots who kept the sky gates of England, history owes the shining accolade:

"This was their finest hour."

CHAPTER 3

CRETE—THE WINGED INVASION

May 20–31, 1941

The island, with its carapace of brown mountain ridges, was once again, after so many centuries, the focus of history in that May of 1941.

Crete, ancient land of the bull dancers, site of the great Minoan civilization which once, so long ago, held so much of the Levant in fief, was the island from which in mythology Daedalus and Icarus flew. Now, in the third year and second spring of the world's greatest war, Crete, for so many centuries slumbering in the shade of history, was for a few brief weeks to be the stage again for great events—the first airborne conquest in warfare. Yet, like ill-fated Icarus, many, borne on fragile wings, were to drop from the skies to death on land or sea.

Crete, like all island fortresses, owed its ancient greatness to geographic position. A long and narrow land mass, it lies squarely athwart the approaches to the Aegean Sea. The island is about 160 miles long, stretching from east to west; about 40 miles wide at its widest point. Its northern coast, sloping gently to the blue seas, harbors Suda Bay, perhaps the finest natural ship haven in the eastern Mediterranean. Along the southern coast rise sheer and stark the spiked peaks and sere, eroded mountains of the 8,000-foot Leoka Ori (White Mountains), the Psiloritis, the Lasithi, and the Setia ranges, their rocky escarpments, sharp defiles and deep gorges at once a sanctuary of the primitive gods and a fortress of the long-dead Cretan kings.

Crete owed its ancient strength to geographic position and to maritime power. It was sited more or less at the center of the ancient Mediterranean world, immune—as an island—to land invasion, large enough to sustain a vigorous society, rugged enough to offer major terrain obstacles to roving predators, and capable of nourishing a sea power formidable for its day. To ancient Crete, kings and kingdoms offered tribute and the propitiation of human victims for sacrifice to the Minoan gods.

But that Mediterranean world of long ago was of small compass, and Crete stood astride it. By the spring of 1941 man had conquered what Icarus assayed, and in the world of steamships and of air power the map was foreshortened, the old empiric facts of geography foresworn, and Crete had become an island dependency in the backwash of history. It was, in 1941, an undeveloped base of limited strategic importance.

Yet over and around and on the island was fought perhaps the most dramatic battle of World War II.

War came to Crete fortuitously, as much by accident as by design, by mistaken judgment rather than well-laid plan.

The popular impression that war is a planned, a rational process, that logic dominates strategy, has no better refutation than the Battle of Crete.

Adolf Hitler and his tough young paratroopers were drawn to Crete, step by step, unintentionally, even unwillingly, by Mussolini's arrogance, Göring's brashness and a process of elimination. Hitler's eyes were on more distant horizons, more grandiose ambitions—the invasion of Russia; he was uninterested in a Mediterranean campaign. Britain, too, became involved in the island by a kind of inexorable circumstance, a web of fate—in part unplanned, at best but hazily envisaged. Her strategic concepts were murky, her implementation best described as "off-ag'in-on-ag'in-Finnigan."

In the waning winter of 1941 England still stood alone against the conquering legions of Hitler. The Battle of Britain had been barely won, but England still shuddered under the ravishment of the bombs. Hitler had shelved Operation Sea Lion—the projected invasion of Britain—and as early as March 27, 1940 (*prior* to the conquest of France), he had stated that "he was keeping the situation in the East under the closest observation."[1] On July 29, 1940, with France conquered but the Battle of Britain barely joined, General Alfred Jodl, Chief of the Operations Staff of the OKW, disclosed to four members of his staff that "Hitler had decided to rid the world 'once and for all' of the danger of Bolshevism by a surprise attack on Soviet Russia to be carried out at the earliest possible moment, i.e., in May, 1941."[2]

The first, secret, generalized directive pointing to "Operation Barbarossa"—the invasion of Russia—was dated in August, 1940, and from then on, culminating with the Fuehrer Directive No. 21, issued December 18, 1940, Hitler's ambitions were focused on the East, and on a campaign that he viewed as a "collision between two different ideologies."[3]

But Hitler's secret preparations for a massive invasion of the U.S.S.R. were complicated by Balkan instability and by the strutting pride of an ally, Benito Mussolini, dictator of Fascist Italy.

Russia had occupied Rumanian Bessarabia in the summer of 1940. Hitler, worried about his oil supplies—then drawn largely from Rumanian wells—and preparing for his *"Drang nach Osten,"* moved planes and troops into Rumania in the summer and fall of 1940, as King Carol, his red-haired mistress, Magda Lupescu, and an entourage and baggage train formidable in size fled to the sunshine and gambling tables of Portugal. Cause created effect, and a dictator's jealousy of another's triumphs and German-Italian rivalry in the Balkans led to a bald ultimatum and a change in the course of history.

Italy had entered the war belatedly in June of 1940, in an infamous "stab-in-the-back," as President Roosevelt described it, against an already defeated France. But the French campaign had brought few spoils to Rome, and in 1940–41 Mussolini was looking for easy conquests. Italy's lackadaisical divisions invaded Greece, with no prior warning to Berlin, in late October, 1940, and, after brief progress, bogged down in reversal and defeat in the harsh mountains and bitter winter. (Prophetically, just six days after the Italian invasion, units of the Royal Air Force arrived in Greece at the invitation of Athens, and in accordance with the Anglo-Greek treaty of 1939.) By March, 1941, the Italians had been soundly whipped; Mussolini, furious, was the laughingstock of Europe. To compound humiliation, the Italian armies had been ejected from Cyrenaica with great loss; in a 62-day campaign General Sir Archibald Wavell drove deep into Cyrenaica, and captured 133,000 Italian prisoners at a total cost in casualties of 3,000—one of the most lopsided victories in warfare.

Germany was committed. Hitler had foreseen the need; as early as December 13, 1940, he had issued secretly War Directive No. 20—"Operation Marita"—anticipating the German invasion of Greece, to rescue Mussolini and to protect the Rumanian oil fields from the prospect of future British bombing from Balkan bases. Early in January, 1941, after the fall of Bardia in North Africa, Hitler ordered German Luftwaffe units established in Sicily and German forces sent to North Africa. But

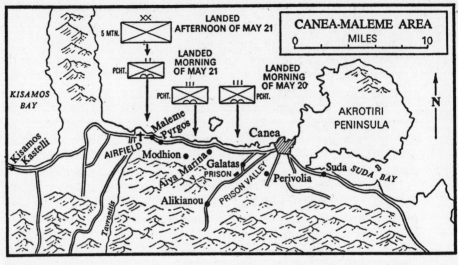

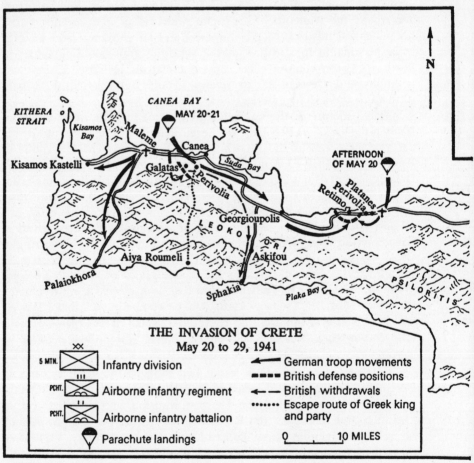

CANEA-MALEME AREA

5 MTN. — LANDED AFTERNOON OF MAY 21

PCHT. — LANDED MORNING OF MAY 21

PCHT. — LANDED MORNING OF MAY 20

MILES 0 — 10

KISAMOS BAY

AKROTIRI PENINSULA

N

Kisamos Kastelli

Maleme Pyrgos

Canea

AIRFIELD

Modhion

Aiya Marina

Galatas PRISON

Alikianou

PRISON VALLEY

Perivolia

Suda SUDA BAY

Tavronitis

KITHERA STRAIT

Kisamos Bay

CANEA BAY MAY 20-21

Maleme

Canea

Suda Bay

AFTERNOON OF MAY 20

Kisamos Kastelli

Galatas

Perivolia

Platanes

Retimo

Perivolia

Georgioupolis

L E U K A   O R I

Aiya Roumeli

Askifou

Palaiokhora

Sphakia

Plaka Bay

PSILORITIS

N

THE INVASION OF CRETE
May 20 to 29, 1941

5 MTN. — Infantry division

PCHT. — Airborne infantry regiment

PCHT. — Airborne infantry battalion

⬤ Parachute landings

← German troop movements

◄- - - British defense positions

◄— · — British withdrawals

········ Escape route of Greek king and party

0 ——— 10 MILES

THE
EASTERN MEDITERRANEAN

✝ German airfields
🔨 British warships sunk

0   MILES   150

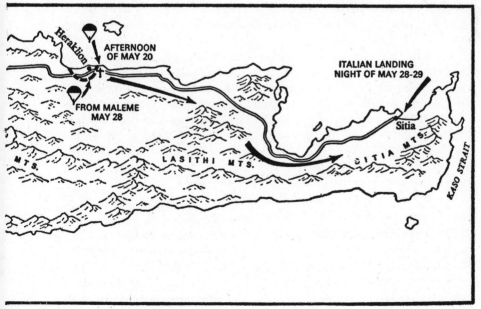

despite the strategic aspirations of the German Navy in the Mediterranean, the Balkans and North Africa were a side show to Hitler, an operation of relief and succor only. May 15, 1941, had been set as the date when all preparations were to be completed for the invasion of Russia; the wheat fields of the Ukraine and the oil wells of the Caucasus were Hitler's distant goal.

But the German intervention in the Mediterranean-Balkan theater immediately changed the complexion of the conflict. Malta early in 1941 commenced to endure the Calvary of bombardment; the direct sea route through the Mediterranean became hazardous and even the Suez Canal was mined by German bombers.

A general named Erwin Rommel reached Tripoli on February 12, followed two days later by the first units of the Deutsches Afrika Korps.[4] Rommel wasted no time. By the end of March he was moving to the offensive against a British force weakened in the moment of triumph.

For just at this moment the thin red line of empire stretched to the breaking point. After a somewhat fatuous mission by Anthony Eden, British Foreign Secretary, to the eastern Mediterranean area in February and March,[5] and repeated discussions (punctuated by alarums of German invasion) with the Greek Government, a British Expeditionary Force was sent to Greece.

At this juncture, with the direct route through the Mediterranean at best a maritime Via Dolorosa for the British, with shortages of all save courage, and the entire British Empire at bay, the gesture was politically and morally sublime—and militarily ridiculous. Like the charge of the Light Brigade at Balaklava, the British expedition to Greece was magnificent but it was not war.

General Sir Archibald Wavell, General Officer Commander in Chief, the Middle East, robbed Peter to pay Paul. He was a commander with many crises but few resources. To the south the Ethiopian and Somaliland operations were still unfinished. In the Levant the Vichy French in Syria and an incipient German-sponsored rebellion in Iraq threatened disaster to the carefully built Middle Eastern fief of the British Raj. With Rommel and his Germans in North Africa, Egypt, the linchpin of the British position, and the Suez Canal, the sea link of empire, appeared threatened by a pincer offensive.

So Wavell, in answer to a Cabinet decision, sent the 6th Australian Division, the New Zealand Division and one armored brigade, plus attachments—some 58,000 men—from Africa to Greece in March.

The British Expeditionary Force never even got into final positions. An anti-German Yugoslav coup in late March forced Hitler's hand, and on April 6 the Nazi legions rumbled into Yugoslavia and Greece. It was a walkover: Yugoslav resistance collapsed; the Nazis quickly broke through the thin, tired line of the Greeks; and the British, outflanked, fought a series of desperate rear-guard actions to an equally desperate evacuation.

About April 27, shortly after the British destroyer *Defender* cleared Kalamata, with 250 soldiers and "the Yugoslav crown jewels in cases," the Germans entered Athens, and Athens radio messaged:

"Closing down for the last time, hoping for happier days. God be with you and for you."[6]

The British Expeditionary Force to Greece accomplished nothing. Britain had come to the aid of an ancient ally at the request of Greece, a request which London had done much to inspire, and in answer to a pledge dated by events.

As Christopher Buckley has written, "Just as William Pitt had conquered Canada on the plains of Germany, so Greece might have been aided best by victory in the desert of Libya."[7]

And it had come to naught—save disaster. In the Greek campaign the British lost more than 12,000 men, "at least 8,000 vehicles," most of the equipment, 209 planes, 6 Royal Navy ships, and more than a score of merchantmen.[8] Worse, Wavell's weakened legions in Africa almost lost Egypt.

The Greeks lost their country. The German losses were trifling. And so history turned to Crete.

On November 3, 1940, Prime Minister Winston Churchill noted in two "minutes" or memoranda that Suda Bay and Crete ought to become a "second Scapa," a "permanent war fortress."[9]

Easier said than done. Scapa Flow in the Orkneys just north of Scotland had been a Royal Navy base for decades. Crete, undeveloped, primitive, flew the flag of another land and was 3,000 miles from England. And Britain was spread thin.

The geography of Crete militated against the British. Its harbors, its only major road, its principal towns—Canea and Heraklion—most of its more than 400,000 people and its three airfields were on the north coast, close to German air bases in Greece, the Greek islands and the Dodecanese (the nearest but 50 miles away), but 300 to 400 air miles from Egypt (420 to 480 miles by sea from Alexandria to Suda Bay), a long haul for fighter planes of that day. British convoys and men-of-war approaching the northern ports had to run the gantlet of two narrow straits—Kithira to the west and Kaso, between Crete and the Italian Dodecanese, to the east.

And, once the perilous transit had been made, shipping found few port aids. Capacious Suda Bay had one unloading jetty capable of handling two small ships; Heraklion could berth four; at Canea and Retimo ships discharged into lighters.

Nevertheless, the British considered Crete, in enemy hands, as a potential threat to their sea communications in the eastern Mediterranean. Under their control it could serve, they thought, as a naval refueling station and an advanced base from which His Majesty's ships and planes might harry the Germans in the Aegean.

With vigorous implementation this British strategic concept, though oversimplified, might have become cogent. But from the fall of 1940 until Crete's moment of truth in May the British made haste slowly, despite constant proddings and numerous detailed suggestions from Churchill and the British Chiefs of Staff.

Small numbers of troops were sent to the island; shipping facilities were slightly improved; some—by no means enough—antiaircraft guns were set up and airstrips built or extended.

The laggard pace was in part understandable.

Crete had a low strategic priority. As late as April 18 the British Chiefs of Staff told General Wavell, "Victory in Libya counts first; evacuation of troops from Greece second; Tobruk shipping, unless indispensable to victory, must be fitted in as convenient; Iraq can be ignored and Crete worked up later."[10]

There was never enough to go around. But clear-cut purpose and vigorous drive were lacking. In the period from November to April 30, Crete had seven different British commanders; it was to be an air base, but it had few planes and fewer air support facilities; it was to be a naval base, but its port facilities were primitive, its harbors open to bombing and unguarded by nets.

Crete's vulnerability was dramatically emphasized on March 26 when six Italian high-speed motorboats penetrated Suda Bay in a daring attack and crippled the cruiser *York*.[11]

For the Germans, Crete was an afterthought to Greece. The final decision to attack the island—not made until April 25—appears to have stemmed in part from Field Marshal Göring's urge for glory, his interest in a Mediterranean campaign and his desire to show what the airborne troops of the Luftwaffe could do. An airborne attack on Malta had been studied, but numerous objections had been raised, so Crete was enthusiastically accepted as a substitute by the Luftwaffe.[12]

General Kurt Student, commander of Fliegerkorps XI, hoped that an airborne conquest of Crete would be the first steppingstone to the Suez Canal, with Cyprus the second conquest.

But Hitler's eyes were still on Russia; he envisaged the Cretan operation as a finale to the Balkan campaign. He did not neglect the potential importance of the "Arab freedom movement," as he called it, in Iraq and the Middle East. But his Middle Eastern policy—if it can, indeed, be called a policy—was purely secondary, diversionary and opportunistic. Russia was the main goal.

"Whether, and in what way, it may later be possible to wreck finally the English position between the Mediterranean and the Persian Gulf, in conjunction with an offensive against the Suez Canal, is still in the lap of the Gods," he said in a Directive.[13]

Crete, in German possession, would seal off the Aegean, help to insure Turkish neutrality, protect the Rumanian oil fields and weaken still further the Royal Navy's tenuous control over maritime routes in the eastern Mediterranean.

THE PREPARATIONS

There had never been before in warfare, there was never to be again, forces and combatants so dissimilar, so polyglot, so curiously contrasted. It was as if the God of War had matched in the coliseum of Crete a warrior with trident and net against a foe with shield and sword. History had fashioned its own web of fate drawing together, as in *The Bridge of San Luis Rey*, from disparate parts of the world, men of different colors and varying patrimony, strangers in name, in tongue, in time, to fulfill their common rendezvous in battle on Crete.

To this struggle on, in and around the Cretan hills and seas came men and women from continents far removed. There were the wild Cretan hill folk, fiercely independent, proudly courageous and—to the German surprise—intensely anti-German. There were Maoris from New Zealand, tough little men who felt a native kinship to the mountain folk of another world. There were big, carousing Australians, singing "Waltzing Matilda." There were Royal Marines and units from some of Britain's ancient regiments, conscious of their tradition. There were 16,000 Italian prisoners, Greek soldiers evacuated from the mainland, Palestinians and Cypriotes and a whole scraggle of units and parts of units evacuated from Greece in haste—"gunners who had lost their guns, sappers who had lost their tools and . . . drivers who had lost their cars."[14]

And, facing them across the narrow waters, where Darius and Xerxes and conquerors of the past had so often sailed, were the Germans, fresh from their recent kills, confident in triumph.

It was, from the first, German air power against British sea power and, on the ground, the men of the British Empire against the soldiers of the Third Reich.

On the last day of April as the last units of the British Expeditionary Force were being evacuated from the Peloponnesos, General Wavell visited Crete. It was high time. The British anticipated an attack upon the island within three weeks, yet in Crete all was confusion.

The island had been flooded with evacuees from the mainland, many of them with no equipment, little discipline, poor morale.

"It was not unusual to find that the men had no arms or equipment, no plates, knives, forks or spoons, and that they ate and drank from bully beef or cigarette tins. There was no unit transport and no tools for most of the battalions. The morale of some of the odds and ends was low."[15]

Some of the men wandered off into the hills, foraging and looting and drinking the heavy, resin-tasting Greek wine. Many slept beneath the olive groves with no tentage and no blankets.

Many of them, exhausted and drained by the ordeal of Greece, lazed in the hot sun or watched the natives dance the Cretan national dance, the *Pentozali*. Few of them understood the folk songs, but those who did thought one verse prophetic:

The youth who never has aspired to ride the clouds unfurled,
Of what use is his life to him, of what use is the world?[16]

In addition to artillery and support forces, there were only three British infantry battalions in Crete (exclusive of the units that had been evacuated from Greece) at the beginning of May. Two more arrived from Egypt before the fighting started. The total of fresh troops, reasonably well equipped and with unit integrity, was about 8,700, all from the United Kingdom. About 27,000 British Empire troops had been evacuated to Crete from Greece. Almost 10,000 of these were stragglers, or without arms, or Palestinian or Cypriote labor troops, or sick, wounded or battle-fatigued. Rifles and equipment were brought in for some of these; many were shipped to Egypt prior to the attack upon Crete.

The Greek military and paramilitary forces totaled almost 15,000— 11,000 army, almost 3,000 armed gendarmes, the balance cadets from the Greek military and air force academies. These were organized in about 11 rifle battalions with no heavy equipment and limited ammunition (an average of less than 30 rounds per man). Their strength, however, was reinforced by Cretan irregulars, mountain folk, armed with swords, fowling pieces and fierce pride.

Thus the island's defense totaled more than 42,000 men—more than 17,000 British, 6,500 Australians, 7,700 New Zealanders, 10,000 to 12,000 Greek regulars plus an uncertain number of irregulars and paramilitary forces. In numbers, the defense appeared formidable; there were considerably more military "bodies" in Crete than German intelligence calculated.[17]

But the deficiencies and shortages were stark and ominous. Many of the men, particularly the Greeks, were without rifles or small arms. There was very little motor transport; some units had none. There was a handful of tanks, most of them obsolescent and in bad condition.[18] Artillery was inadequate and ammunition limited. Only about half of the number of antiaircraft guns required were available. There were two (initially—later three) airstrips and, at a maximum (at any one time in May), some 36 planes, many of them "beaten up" from the Greek operations, only about half of them serviceable. The Royal Navy was immensely superior to the available small units of the Italian Fleet, but Axis bases were only a few hours of sea darkness away from Crete. And the fleet of Admiral Sir Andrew B. Cunningham (Commander in Chief, Mediterranean) was licking its numerous wounds incurred in the Greek evacuation and in the preceding weary months of war. There was only one aircraft carrier, with four planes aboard, in the eastern Mediterranean, and all naval units that operated north of Crete had to run the gantlet of the Kithera and Kaso channels and were subject to incessant air attack from nearby German bases.

To add the last straw to the enormous burdens, the defenders were encumbered with some 16,000 Italian prisoners (only the officers were shifted to Egypt before the invasion) and burdened with the responsibility of royalty, for the Greek king—King George II of the Hellenes— and his Cabinet were in residence near Canea.

Suda Bay and the north coast ports and airstrips were already, on April 30, under frequent air attacks; a tanker, bombed and beached, lay flaming at the entrance to Suda Bay, a funeral pall of black smoke billowing skyward, and bodies floated in the harbor, a grim portent of tomorrow.

To make order out of this chaos in a race against time, General Wavell cut the Gordian knot of command by cooperation and coordination,[19] and on April 30 appointed a famed New Zealander, General Bernard C. Freyberg, V.C., to command "Creforce." Freyberg, with his World War I reputation as a fighter, was a born combat soldier and a favorite of Churchill's.[20] He was ordered to "deny to the enemy the use of air bases in Crete," but was told simultaneously that a combined German air and sea attack upon the island was imminent and that it was very unlikely, because of Britain's shortage of fighters, that any air reinforcements could be expected.

The Germans, too, had their problems. The attack upon Crete was "laid on" so late, and it had to be accomplished so quickly (because of the forthcoming Russian campaign), that there was inadequate time to plan and prepare for "Operation Merkur."

German parachute troops had been used to seize the Corinth Canal and its crossings on April 26; the same transport aircraft used for this operation had to be employed over Crete. Several hundred Ju-52 transport aircraft were flown back to the Vienna area for overhaul, new engines and reconditioning, and then flown back in haste to advanced airfields around Athens.

In the Greek campaign the British had been "handicapped by the lack of airfields."[21] But the German planes were better adapted to improvised fields, and German engineers and construction units using conscripted Greek labor showed tremendous energy and initiative in improving or building new strips. The Germans seized Melos Island on May 10; a landing strip was ready in three days. At Molaoi a strip was built in a week. Scarpanto, Corinth, Argos, the Athens fields, Salonika, Rhodes, Bulgarian airfields, Megara, Phaleron, Eleusis, Tatoi, Topolia, Araxos, Kithira—a whole semicircle of airstrips, the nearest only some fifty miles away, ringed Crete.[22]

Many of the fields utilized, among them Topolia and Megara, were auxiliary fields somewhat hastily built—

. . . no more than large plains located between mountain ranges. . . .

Very poor soil conditions presented great difficulties. Both fields were sandy wastes, and the heavily loaded airplanes sank up to their axles in powdery sand. During take-off or landing operations the airplanes became wrapped in a dense cloud which rose straight into the air to a height of over 1,000 m. [sic—meters]. Due to the dry air, the extremely high temperature, and the complete absence of winds, this cloud lingered over the valley for a particularly long time. . . .

The airplane motors sucked up this granular dust."[23]

Roads and railroads in Greece and the Balkans were damaged, bridges were blown up; much of the fuel and many of the supplies had to be brought in by sea. Distribution of fuel and supplies to the scattered makeshift airfields presented other problems, and pumping facilities were primitive. At many strips fuel was pumped into the airplanes by hand from barrels. Logistic preparations for the Russian campaign complicated the supply problem. The "strained line of communication from Rumania"[24] prevented the transfer of the 22nd Infantry (Air Landing) Division, so that the 5th Mountain Division, already in Greece after participation in the campaign on the mainland, had to be substituted. The 7th Air Division, however, moved to Greece from Germany. The Germans overcame immense logistic difficulties; indeed, their capability to mount so formidable an operation as the airborne invasion of Crete less than three weeks after the conquest of Greece and Yugoslavia— indeed, while mopping up was still continuing—was one of the most amazingly efficient supply operations of the war.

But their usual thoroughness in planning was considerably less noteworthy.

Haste was one reason; only a month intervened between the decision to attack Crete and the actual assault. Overconfidence was another reason; England was despised by the Nazis, and until Crete wherever Germans and Englishmen had met on field of battle, the Nazis had triumphed with relative ease. Inadequate reconnaissance and incomplete intelligence led to underestimation of the strength of the defenders. And there was pressure from the top: from Hitler for a speedy conquest, from Göring for glory for the Luftwaffe. The army and the General Staff had nothing to do with the planning. It was an Air Force operation, and some German fliers—Göring among them—believed that air power unaided could win battles. And an airborne invasion was a new form of use.

Colonel General Alexander Löhr, commanding the 4th Air Fleet, which had supported the army in the Yugoslavian and Greek campaigns, had recommended occupation of Crete as a means of protecting the Ploesti oil fields. General Kurt Student, Commander of the XI Air Corps (subordinate to the 4th Air Fleet), which included the 7th Air Division (parachutists), conceived the airborne invasion and worked out the main details in conferences with Lieutenant General Wilhelm Süssmann, the commander of the parachute division.

General Löhr was in over-all command. Luftflotte 4 included Fliegerkorps VIII (General Wolfram Freiherr von Richthofen commanding) and Fliegerkorps XI (General Student commanding). A number of additional aircraft from Fliegerkorps X and ground units of the Twelfth Army (including the 6th Mountain Division) were available (or "on call") if needed.

The combat aircraft, grouped in Fliegerkorps VIII, included about 280 Ju-88, He-111, and Do-17 bombers; more than 150 of the famous Stuka Ju-87 dive bombers; more than 100 Me-109 single-engined fighters; and another 100 Me-110 twin-engined fighters; and some 50 reconnaissance aircraft.[25] A total of more than 500 of these were reported operational on May 17, and others joined the battle later.

General Student's Fliegerkorps XI included 500 transport aircraft— the reliable Ju-52—more than 70 gliders, and all the troops, including those to be transported by sea, earmarked for the operation. These numbered about 22,750: the 7th Air Division of three parachute rifle regiments and supporting troops totaling 13,000; a special Assault Regiment of three battalions of parachute troops and one of glider-borne infantry; two regiments of the 5th Mountain Division and one of the 6th Mountain Division, and a Panzer battalion, a motorcyclist battalion and attached antiaircraft units. The rest of the 6th Mountain Division was "on call," if needed, and in the event, some of it was used. Available for sea transportation were a number (apparently about 63) of motorized Greek caïques,[26] some 7 small interisland steamers, and 7 Italian destroyers, 12 torpedo boats, motorboats and patrol and mine-sweeping craft.

These were organized into two groups of the caïques and two steamship flotillas, under *Admiral Southeast* (a German admiral in command in the Aegean Sea), each prepared to land troops on the coast of Crete.

Thus the Germans, with an overwhelming air superiority—about thirty to one in combat aircraft—but with virtually no naval strength, planned to conquer an island 100 miles from the Greek mainland defended by more than 40,000 troops with some 22,750 men—750 of them to be landed by glider, 10,000 by parachute, 5,000 by planes, 7,000 by sea.[27]

Freyberg, who alternately blew hot and cold in his assessments of Crete's defensive capabilities, urged Wavell (while reassuring Churchill) to provide more planes, artillery, entrenching tools (some men had to dig trenches and foxholes with their steel helmets) and supplies of all sorts.

"I fully realize," Wavell wrote in reply, "the difficulties and dangers of your situation."[28]

But he could do little about it; in the entire eastern Mediterranean–Middle East theater, the Royal Air Force had at the end of April less than 15 bombers and single-engined fighters and not all of these were serviceable.[29]

Freyberg, aware of the threat of sea-borne, as well as airborne, landings, with little or no motor transport and hence with the mobility of his reserves limited, in effect established a series of four separate "insular" or independent commands, each responsible for the defense of a specific area. There were three usable airstrips (one almost finished by the British just before the invasion) on the island; the British knew these would be primary German objectives, and Suda Bay was an obvious prize. Accordingly, the defending forces were divided into four main groupings. To the east the town of Heraklion and its airstrip (so-called "Buttercup Field") were defended by the 14th Brigade: three British battalions, an Australian battalion, a regiment of artillery, organized and armed as infantry, antiaircraft and other units, six tanks, various "bits and pieces" and three Greek "regiments" (each of about battalion size), Brigadier B. H. Chappel commanding. Around Retimo and its airstrip— more than 30 miles to the west of Heraklion—was Brigadier G. A. Vasey's 19th Australian Brigade, with two to three Greek battalions and an Australian machine-gun company. The Retimo sector defense covered two good beaches—one five miles to the east of Retimo, one 12 miles to the west; thus the defenders were strung out for more than 20 miles. And there were no antiaircraft guns available to cover the airfield. The Suda Bay–Canea sector was defended by a composite force of Royal Marines, an antitank regiment armed with rifles, more than 2,000 Australians, a

Greek battalion and a heavy concentration of AA guns, all under Major General E. C. Weston, Royal Marines. This sector was more than ten miles northwest of the Retimo "island." Another ten miles to the westward was the recently constructed airfield of Maleme, defended— along with the village of Galatas and beaches stretching eastward to Canea—by Brigadier Edward Puttick's New Zealanders, an incomplete New Zealand division plus British and Greek units, supported by some antiaircraft. A Greek regiment took up positions around Kastelli and Kisamos, covering Kisamos Bay on the extreme western end of Crete, and there were small Greek covering forces in the eastern portion of the island.

General Freyberg, with a scratch staff and inadequate communications, established his headquarters in dugouts near Canea. His four main defensive sectors, each (and particularly Retimo) spread thin, were stretched along some 70 miles of northern coast, connected only by one inadequate road. "Creforce" reserves—really part of the Suda and Maleme defenses—amounted to one understrength New Zealand brigade and a British battalion. Two I tanks covered each airfield. But some Greek units had only three rounds per man of ammunition to fit their rifles, many of them had had only two weeks' training and some Cypriote and Palestinian troops had no arms at all. There was very little mobile field artillery, except a few captured Italian pieces, some French guns, a few howitzers and some immobile coast defense and antiaircraft guns. And none of the "insular" defense sectors could support the others.

So Freyberg faced his fate.

The German plans contemplated the capture of all three airfields on the first day of the assault. Generals Löhr and Student assigned Maleme to the Assault Regiment (minus two glider companies); the 7th Air Division was to capture Canea, Retimo and Heraklion, with about one parachute rifle regiment allotted to each objective, plus—in the case of Canea—two glider companies of the Assault Regiment. Maleme and Canea were to be attacked in the morning, Retimo and Heraklion in the afternoon. Sea-borne convoys with heavy equipment of the air division elements of the 5th Mountain Division and a few Italian Marines were embarked to land follow-up troops at Maleme and Heraklion, originally on the first night of the attack but later postponed to the second and third nights.

The Germans hoped to place their airborne troops in areas left uncovered by the defenders. Three major task forces were assigned objectives as follows:

Task Force Mars: Center Group (General Süssmann commanding, consisting of the bulk of the Air Division and some glider troops—the capture of Canea and Galatas, of Retimo and the airstrip.

Task Force Komet: Western Group (Major General Eugen Meindl commanding), consisting of the Assault Regiment—the capture of Maleme airfield and its approaches.

Task Force Orion: Eastern Group (Colonel Hans Brauer, commanding initially; General Ringel was scheduled to take command later), consisting of one parachute regiment and one mountain regiment—the capture of the town and airfield at Heraklion.

General Löhr, with his subordinate commanders, established his CP in Athens. D-day was set for May 20; long before this, the British knew the hour of trial was at hand.

The bombing started slowly in early May; the Dorniers and the Junkers, high in the sky, overflew Crete hour after hour, as "the May days drifted by . . . in brilliant sunshine and cloudless skies, and the slender sickle of the moon swelled nightly towards the full circle."[30] Docks and shipping were the first targets: by May 20 there were some 13 damaged or wrecked ships in Suda Harbor.[31] Palls of black smoke hung over the bay from roaring oil fires; the helpless cruiser *York* was bombed repeatedly as the Germans attempted to destroy her antiaircraft batteries. Between May 1 and 20 "more than half the RE (Royal Engineer) stores . . . were sunk en route or in harbor."[32] Civilian stevedores deserted the bombed docks; 400 Aussie and New Zealand volunteers, soldiers who had worked as "dockers" in civilian life, were organized into shifts. Ships dashed into Suda Bay in the night hours, were hastily unloaded and left again to seek sanctuary in the open seas before dawn. These soldier-stevedores kept the stuff of life flowing into Crete; 500 to 600 tons nightly, despite the bombing, were unloaded in the weeks before the attack.

But it was not enough. Starting May 14, Fliegerkorps VIII intensified its attacks and broadened its bombing objectives to include airfields and antiaircraft positions. Day after day for a week, implacable, relentless, the bombing continued, joined by the screaming Stukas.

The pattern of the attacks made it clear that British intelligence, which had warned that invasion was imminent, was correct. On May 18 two downed German airmen were pulled out of the sea, and they told their Cretan captors that *Der Tag* was May 20. General Freyberg was so informed.[33]

A handful of single-engined Hurricanes and obsolete Gladiator biplanes opposed the German bombers fitfully from the Cretan fields, but not for long. The odds were too great. There was not enough of anything—fuel, spare parts, services. Some planes were cannibalized that others might fly. Pilots were gaunt with fatigue and strain. The Royal Air Force claimed 23 enemy aircraft prior to May 19, but by that date there were four operable Hurricanes and three Gladiators left on all Crete. These had become a liability, not an asset. For this handful of planes the defense had to provide a field and a ground staff to service it. On May 19 the remaining planes were flown to Egypt. The Germans had won the air battle.[34]

General Freyberg wished to mine or destroy the airfields and make them useless. But it was too late.[35]

MAY 20

At dawn, the men of "Creforce" stood to beneath the twisted olive trees. The sky was cloudless, the air clear and still. Over the sea, as in so many mornings past, the hum of aircraft engines grew from a dull drone, like bees buzzing far away, to a tonal immensity that seemed to fill the heavens. As the first bombs fell with whine and thud, Aussies, New Zealanders, British and Greeks took cover in trenches and foxholes. There was nothing—at first—to distinguish the attack from others that had preceded it; Freyberg, perhaps doubting the word of the rescued German fliers, had not warned his command that Tuesday, May 20, might be *Der Tag*.

But within an hour the pattern was clear. This was it. From Suda Bay and Canea to Maleme the skies were filled with German aircraft— dropping sticks of bombs, peeling off in long, shuddering dives to bomb and strafe antiaircraft positions.[36] The heavy guns around Suda Bay, which had fired repeatedly in the preceding weeks in attempts to protect shipping, had been pinpointed; soon the bombing and strafing left gun positions wrecked, crews decimated. Roads and trails were attacked, and Maleme airfield; great clouds of dust mushroomed from the dry soil of Crete, and smoke and haze obscured the gunners' sights.

Before we knew what was happening the skies were full of German planes [an eyewitness reported]. . . . There seemed to be hundreds of them, diving, zooming and criss-crossing. . . . Then a flight of large silvery machines passed low down over our heads. . . . They passed as silently as ghosts . . . and their wings were very long and tapering.[37]

The soft sibilance of the wind over the long, tapering wings of the gliders was the prologue to the invasion of Crete; 750 Germans of the glider battalion of the elite Assault Regiment swooped down from the skies toward Maleme and Canea. Hard behind them came the Ju-52 troop carriers—"huge black beasts with yellow noses,"[38] each carrying a "stick" (plane load) of 13 to 15 German paratroopers.

General Freyberg, watching on a hill behind Canea, was

enthralled by the magnitude of the operation . . . hundreds of planes, tier upon tier coming towards us. . . .

We watched them circle counter-clockwise over Maleme aerodromes and then, when they were only a few hundred feet above the ground, as if by magic white specks mixed with other colors suddenly appeared beneath them as clouds of parachutists floated slowly to earth.[39]

"The whole air throbbed" with the noise of engines, the whine of diving planes and the crunch of bombs; the German fighters "strafed the ground so heavily that it was almost impossible to move except in short starts and rushes."[40] The bombardment severed telephone wires early in the day; Brigadier Puttick, near Canea, knew little of what was happening, Freyberg even less.

In the German CP in Athens first news seemed good; the operation had started as planned. General Student was confident; his men were the elite of the elite—young, proud, well trained, thoroughly indoctrinated. Some of them were veterans of the air drop in Holland in the opening phase of the war, and of the assault upon the Belgian fortress of Eben Emael; some had dropped at the Corinth Canal. They believed what they were taught in the "Ten Commandments of the Parachutist":

"You are the chosen ones of the German Army. . . .

"To you death or victory must be a point of honor. . . .

"Be as nimble as a greyhound, as tough as leather, as hard as Krupp steel, and so you shall be the German warrior incarnate."[41]

The parachutists wore round rimless crash helmets and mottled uniforms, some with special leather coats, camouflage capes and high boots. Their uniforms were heavily padded at the joints. A few carried Schmeisers, or grenades; most carried only pistols and knives as they dropped—their weapons came down in separate containers.

The parachutists were lightly armed: many Schmeiser tommy guns and automatic rifles; a few Mausers with telescopic sights for snipers; their rations—thirst quenchers and a type of Benzedrine energy tablet; Wittler (dried) bread; chocolate; hypodermic syringes with ampoules for the injection of "caffein-sodium salicylate" to compensate for fatigue.[42]

They were in fine fettle on take-off; the night before D-day the paratroopers were issued beer and brandy and they sang the old, proudful, threnodic German songs.

Lieutenant Colonel von der Heydte, CO of 1st Battalion, 3rd Paratrooper Regiment, a German officer with a poet's eye, told Max Schmeling, the German boxer who was one of his men, when Schmeling complained of a bad case of diarrhea, that "you can report sick, my dear fellow, when we get to Crete. Our medical staff is flying with us."[43]

In the troop carriers, flying over the blue Aegean, the young faces were tense, determined. In some of the Ju-52's the sticks of 13 to 15 men sang the "Song of the Paratroops":

> *Fly on this day against the enemy!*
> *Into the planes, into the planes!*
> *Comrades, there is no going back!*

Over Crete, the orders came: "Prepare to jump."

The men hooked their rip cords over the static lines running the length of the fuselages and moved to the door.

"The shadows of our planes swept like ghostly hands over the sun-drenched houses."[44]

The paratroopers jumped from very low altitudes—300 to 400 feet. The sky blossomed with multicolored chutes—black for enlisted men, violet or pink for officers, white for weapons and ammunition, yellow for medical supplies.

It was an inchoate battle, a wild melee of small units, of man against man, with little control by either side.

The sight of the little dangling figures beneath the blossoming chutes was "inexpressibly sinister."

For each man dangling carried a death, his own, if not another's.

Even as they dropped they were within range and the crackle of rifle fire and Bren guns rose to a crescendo. Wildly waving their legs, some already firing their Schmeisers, the parachutists came down, in the terraced vineyards, crashing through the peaceful olive boughs, in the yards of houses, on roofs, in the open fields where the short barley hid them. Many found graves where they found earth.[45]

The sun-drenched arena to these young men of many races was exotic: " . . . groves of lemon, olive, orange . . . Hedgerows of grey-green agaves—grotesquely-shaped, head-high cacti . . . Mountains, goats and sheep. Spiky dry grass thistles, spurge and prickly broom, clusters of Aleppo pines, stone oaks and gnarled olive trees."[46]

And so the battle was joined.

The world did not fully know it then, but a glider and parachute landing operation always produces in battle a mad melee and hours of "wildest confusion" on both sides. For friend and foe vertical envelopment means there are no flanks, no rear; the enemy may be everywhere, the "front" circumferential. In the first hours of any landing ordered control is almost impossible; command devolves on small unit leaders; the fighting is bitter—no quarter asked or given.

So it was in Crete.

The gliders whispered down at about 8:15 to 8:45 A.M. to crash landings, some 45 to 50 of them near the Maleme airstrip, most of them in the dry river bed of the Tavronitis, others scattered to the east. Some of them met disaster; one, on its last approach, became a flaming airborne torch; another was hit by a Bofors gun as it skidded to a stop; others were sieved with machine-gun fire and became coffins for their men, but many of the great square-fuselaged birds, their wings knocked askew by olive trees, some with holes ripped in their fuselages, disgorged heavily armed men with motorbikes, flame throwers, mortars.[47] The Assault Regiment accomplished two of its objectives immediately: it captured the Bofors (40 mm.) antiaircraft battery sited at the mouth of the Tavronitis (the gunners had rifles but no rifle ammunition) and the bridge over the river with some positions on the western edge of the airstrip.

But a glider detachment assigned to capture the dominating terrain feature—Hill (or Point) 107, about 300 meters high, commanding the airstrip—suffered heavy casualties from the 22nd New Zealand Battalion and failed completely. Before the fighting was many hours old most of the German detachment commanders had been killed or wounded.

Amid the smoke and dust and noise of battle, the Ju-52's came in below the angle of fire of the heavy AA guns, and spilled out their sticks of parachutists. Some of them, flying in tight formation, were "sitting ducks" for the Bofors gunners.

"You could actually see the shot breaking up the aircraft and the bodies falling out like potato sacks."[48]

The parachutists came down in, around and among the New Zealand and Greek positions—some of them close to their assigned drop zones, others, in the confusion of battle, far from their objectives.

The eastern part of the German pincer, which had been intended to clamp a vise on Maleme airfield, dropped far out of position, and most of these paratroopers landed amongst the New Zealanders, or within easy range of their guns.

"Suddenly they came amongst us . . . a pair of feet appeared through a nearby olive tree. They were right on top of us. Around me rifles were cracking. I had a Tommy gun and it was just like duck shooting."[49]

There was "terrible havoc." One New Zealand battalion commander personally killed five Germans in a few minutes from his headquarters; the battalion adjutant shot two "without getting up from his packing-case desk."

Near and around Modhion, where the New Zealanders had established a field punishment center, parachutists landed in scores. Lieutenant W. J. G. Roach, the CO of the center, issued what rifles he had to his prisoners and took them out hunting. They killed Germans and supplemented their arms with captured Nazi weapons. Around the houses on the outskirts of Modhion, where the Germans landed on the flat roofs and in the dirt streets, the Greeks, as well as the New Zealanders, harried them—"women, children and even dogs; those Cretans would use any weapons, flintlock rifles captured from the Turks a hundred years ago, axes and even spades."[50] Their armament was considerably improved before the day was old when Ju-52's, on a resupply mission, dropped quantities of German arms squarely into the hands of the defenders.

One artillery battery commander reported:

One Hun is only about 25 yds. away in grape vines. A few rounds are fired but he may be lying "doggo." Gnr. [Gunner] McDonald sets our anxiety at rest by coming up from opposite direction walking straight up to Hun and saying, "You'd look at me, like that, you bastard, would you?" with appropriate action. Another poor devil gets his on the wing. His 'chute catches in an olive tree and he finishes up by leaning on a rock wall, head on hands almost as if he had been meditating by the wall when death caught up to him. Dead Germans everywhere—'chutes caught in trees and still fluttering in the wind . . .[51]

The eastern German pincer against Maleme was broken before noon. There were scattered groups of Germans, holed up in houses, gone to ground in ravines or bush or hiding in the drains, all the way from Modhion to the airstrip, but they had no unit integrity, there was no control. The threat was to the west of the Tavronitis, where some of the Assault Regiment had landed intact and still clung to the western edge of the airfield.

The parachutists of the German Center, or Mars Task Force, dropped widely dispersed around Canea, with concentrations in the Galatas–Prison Valley area along the road to Alikianou, and on the Akrotiri Peninsula (commanding Suda Bay) and south of Canea. This assault started with bad omen. General Süssmann, the 7th Air Division and Center Task Force Commander, and his personal staff were killed on the island of Aiyina, "in full view of Athens," when the wings of his glider tore off in flight.

The main parachute assault in this area started almost an hour after the first wave had "hit the silk" near Maleme. The principal British military hospital in Crete, No. 7 General, was sited in tents on a promontory near the coast, and down among the bed patients and the walking sick and wounded who had taken refuge in slit trenches floated a company of the parachutists. But the Germans won brief triumph. Before the day had ended, the captive patients—those who had not been killed—were freed by New Zealand troops, the promontory had been recaptured with the aid of some light tanks, and most of the German company was wiped out.

Similarly, the threat to the rocky Akrotiri Peninsula was quickly contained. The Germans landed widely scattered; four of 15 gliders came down in the sea, and the attackers suffered a loss of about half their force in the first few hours. They were contained and beleaguered until remnants, weak from hunger or thirst, surrendered to the British two days later.

Many German parachutists died in their harnesses; Lieutenant Colonel von der Heydte reported that "from my aircraft . . . only three men reached the ground unhurt."

It was, in some localities, like a shooting gallery. Incendiaries set some of the silk 'chutes on fire; the Germans fell in a blazing trail of fire to break their legs or backs. Other dangling figures jerked like puppets on strings as British bullets found their marks. The limp figures jerked convulsively, then went limp.

"An untidy battle . . . a series of isolated fights—raged all day around Galatas," and along the road between Canea and Alikianou.[52]

The results were indecisive. Colonel Richard Heidrich, who suc- ceeded Süssmann as CO of the 7th Airborne Division, had succeeded in establishing a fairly heavy concentration in so-called Prison Valley and he took the high ground south of Galatas dominating the area. But one of the three battalions of his parachute rifle regiment was destroyed or scattered; the other two had suffered heavy casualties.[53]

Makeshift dressing stations were full of groaning men, deep in shock or delirious with pain. Von der Heydte noted the "grey" faces of the wounded in a gulley; he brushed back the "blonde hair" from the forehead of a young and badly wounded English soldier, and recorded of another patient that "morphine does not always help. . . . Kept scream- ing with pain. His screams chilled the spine; it was like the cry of a wounded animal."[54]

Suda Bay and Canea were still solidly controlled by the British. And the issue was in doubt.

But not for King George II of the Hellenes, and his peripatetic government. German parachutists dropped within half a mile of the royal residence (at the home of his Cretan Prime Minister, M. Tsouderas, south of Perivolia). At the advice of the British military attaché, the royal party—the King, Prince Peter, the Prime Minister and others—escorted by British and Cretan troops, quickly took to the hills, climbing under a hot sun up the mountains toward the south coast. The King wore a "beribboned tunic," as German aircraft flying overhead commanded what had been Greek skies.[55]

As the day wore on, cloudless and hot, the Germans threw in the second phase of their attack.

In the still afternoon, Retimo and Heraklion felt the thunderbolt of attack from the skies.

At Retimo heavy bombing of defense positions started at 4:15 P.M., but much of the German effort was expended on dummy positions. And the paratroopers came in straggling. . . . The Germans had lost only seven aircraft of the more than 500 Ju-52's employed as troop carriers in the morning's attacks on Maleme and Canea-Suda, but the primitive refueling facilities back on the Greek mainland fields and the heavy dust clouds stirred up by the whirling propellers delayed take-offs. It took more than half an hour for the successive echelons of aircraft to spew out their loads. Again, as in the morning, "the sky was raining falling petals."[56] Again the result was confusion compounded; in some areas the Germans landed on their planned drop zones, in others they were widely scattered. The attackers drove to a dominating hill and the east edge of the airfield and captured two British tanks. But they suffered heavy loss; one Australian battalion buried 400 Germans on May 21. And the Greeks, initially shaky, rallied.

At Heraklion, in the late afternoon the Germans attacked with four paratroop battalions, but again timing was off. The transport aircraft straggled; some 600 of the paratroops had to be left behind in Greece as the schedule became more and more attenuated, and the German fighters could not linger long enough to provide cover for the late-arriving troop carriers.[57]

The British AA guns, silent during the preparatory bombardment, opened up as the troop carriers flew in low, and some 10 to 15 Ju-52's were shot down in the air.

I saw planes burst into flames, then the men inside feverishly leaping out like plums spilled from a burst bag. Some were burning as they dropped to earth. I saw one aircraft flying out to sea with six men trailing from it in the cords of their 'chutes. . . . The pilot was bucketing the plane about in an effort to dislodge them.[58]

Just east of Heraklion "some Germans took refuge in a field of barley.

"Let's set the bloody barley on fire, boys," a soldier cried. . . .
The barley was fairly dry and flared up as matches were touched to it . . . hidden Germans jumped and ran like rabbits smoked out of their burrows. They were machine-gunned and picked off with rifles as they ran.[59]

Some drops near Heraklion were three hours behind schedule, and again the German casualties were heavy; two companies were reduced by dark to some 60 to 70 men; three others, counterattacked as soon as they landed by the Black Watch and tanks, were almost wiped out. Nevertheless, the Germans consolidated the high ground to the east of the airstrip, and in the town of Heraklion itself German paratroopers stalking Greeks, Aussies, Black Watch and Yorks and Lancs during the night, fought their way in a series of brief fire fights to the edge of the harbor.

To General Freyberg, as the New Zealand official history puts it, in a masterpiece of reserve, "the day had been anxious." The confusion and the misleading and false reports inevitable in any airborne attack made assessment difficult. Complete interruption of communications to some sectors, and, at best, sporadic and intermittent reports over inadequate radios, prevented any accurate evaluation of the situation. The prowling German fighters and Stukas who had the skies to themselves had, in many places, virtually inhibited any British movement on the roads in the daytime, and made it difficult to organize even cross-country counter-attacks. Freyberg had one advantage: he read that night a translated copy of a captured operation order of 3rd Parachute Regiment, which summarized the entire enemy plan for the attack on Crete. The order verified what Freyberg had already assumed, that follow-up punches were to come by air and sea. But it also revealed the German hopes for a quick conquest—Maleme, Canea, Retimo on the first day. Nowhere, as far as Freyberg knew, had the enemy been successful, yet his report to Wavell was a sober one: "The day had been hard but so far as was known the defense still held Maleme, Heraklion and Retimo aerodromes and the two harbors, though by a bare margin."[60]

But Freyberg did not know. Even as he wrote his message, a fatal decision had been made that confirmed for the Germans the first of their major objectives—the capture of Maleme airfield.

Lieutenant Colonel L. W. Andrew, CO of 22nd New Zealand Battalion, which held Maleme airfield, was increasingly anxious as the day wore on. His communications with his companies were as intermittent and unsatisfactory as his own with higher headquarters. He knew the German glider troops were well established along the Tavronitis and on the western edge of the field. He still held the high ground; time after time he had tried without result, with flares and signal flags, to get 23rd New Zealand Battalion to the east to come to his support. He thought he could depend, with certainty, upon only two of his five companies; the others were out of communication, or paratroopers had been seen to land in their midst, and their losses were known to be high. Most of his mortars and machine guns were out of action.[61] At 5 P.M. Andrew asked his brigade commander to order 23rd Battalion to make a planned counterattack and was told this was impossible; 23rd Battalion was itself too heavily engaged.

Colonel Andrew then committed his last reserve; he felt he could wait no longer to allow the enemy to build up undisturbed west of the

Tavronitis; he had, he thought, to strengthen his positions that night; tomorrow would be too late. He ordered his two I tanks, supported by a provisional platoon of New Zealand infantrymen and antiaircraft artillerymen grouped as infantry, to counterattack from the western edge of Maleme airstrip toward the Tavronitis bridge.

Almost at once, the second tank found that its two-pounder ammunition would not fit the breech block and that its turret was not traversing properly. It therefore withdrew. The leading tank . . . bellied down in the rough bed of the river and, its turret having jammed, was abandoned by its crew.

The following infantrymen met "withering fire from the front and from the left." Eight or nine men, most of them wounded—all that were left—dragged themselves back to the New Zealand lines.[62] Fiasco!

After dark, Andrew made his decision. He had warned his brigadier he might have to make a limited withdrawal and was told to do so if he had to. He pulled back the two companies he could reach from the Tavronitis and the edge of the airfield to Hill 107, and a ridge behind it. But he was still disturbed. When day came his men, exposed on the bare ridges, would be immobilized by German strafing and bombing attacks. Andrew decided to withdraw what was left of his battalion still further east to link up before daylight with 21st and 23rd New Zealand Battalions. Hill 107, dominating the airstrip, was abandoned except for an isolated and surrounded remnant. The Germans were well on the way to winning their first airstrip on Crete. It was a key decision.

Back in the Grande Bretagne Hotel in Athens on the night of May 20, "the situation had not seemed encouraging" to General Student and General Löhr. It was now obvious, belatedly, that the British had greater strength in Crete than the Germans had estimated. The death of General Süssmann was known; later Student was to discover that General Meindl had been seriously wounded and that many of his task unit or battalion commanders had been killed; casualties had been very heavy. No communications had been established with some of the German airheads and not a single airfield had been captured.

To Student, the German forces on the Tavronitis and along the western edge of the Maleme airstrip and those under Colonel Heidrich in Prison Valley southwest of Canea appeared to be the only coherent and organized units in Crete. The sea-borne landings were not planned until May 21 and May 22, at Maleme and Heraklion respectively. The Germans had to have an airstrip to bring in transport aircraft with much needed ammunition and heavy equipment.

The flexibility of German military doctrine and—contrary to popular impression—of German staff processes enabled Löhr and Student to make a major change in their plans. They determined to reinforce success and to concentrate all available effort at Maleme.

"I decided," Student wrote later, "the whole bulk of the reserve of the parachutists would be put into action at the aerodrome of Maleme."[63]

His phraseology—"the whole bulk of the reserve of the parachutists" —was grandiloquent; Student had available at that time only about four and a half more companies of paratroop infantry and an antitank unit. The German decision: to stake everything on the Maleme *Schwerpunkt;* at first light on the twenty-first to fly in ammunition to the Assault Regiment and the troops along the Tavronitis, then to drop the rest of the parachutists and then to land a battalion of the 5th Mountain Division on Maleme airstrip as soon as it was secured. Meantime, the 1st Motor Sailing Flotilla, which was lying up at the island of Melos on the night of the twentieth, would push on to Crete on the twenty-first with heavy equipment and more mountain troops. The Italian Fleet, bloodied and limping after the Battle of Cape Matapan, had refused to put to sea, and the Luftflotte 4 reconnaissance had reported British men-of-war southeast and southwest of Crete. But the chance had to be taken; speed was vital. . . .

Student, Löhr and the German High Command sweated out the rest of that night in their CP in the Grande Bretagne, waiting for the anticipated counterattack against the thin line of exhausted Germans holding the Tavronitis and the western edge of Maleme. But it never came. . . .

MAY 21

It had been a quiet night at sea; His Majesty's light forces, patrolling in the darkness north of Crete, had a hit-and-run brush with some Italian motor torpedo boats, but that was all.

But on Crete itself darkness had brought no surcease. Battle had been joined under the starlit Mediterranean sky; the two combatants were locked in a death grip; there could be no cessation until one or the other had triumphed.

While the sky was still dark to the west, a Ju-52 set down daringly on the beach, west of the Tavronitis—the first of several. One picked up the wounded General Meindl on its return flight. Even before the resupply missions came roaring in, the Assault Regiment extended its lines to the west to include virtually all of the Maleme strip and the high ground to the south dominating it—mopping up cut-off British remnants. At 8:10— despite the fire of four French 75's, three Italian 75's and two British 3.7 mountain howitzers, a Ju-52 landed on Maleme strip—a portent of ultimate British defeat.[64]

The strip and the beaches east of it—though not those to the west—were still commanded by British artillery and mortars, but the

Germans braved the fire. Some planes lost the gamble and were wrecked or hit, but most won; throughout the day single aircraft swooped in, landed, took off—to provide the transfusions of resupply.

> The airplanes had to land . . . on virtually a postage stamp—a 600 m strip close to the coast [a German report noted]. They were hampered by strong cross-winds and subjected to the most intense enemy artillery and machine-gun fire. An enemy battery that had not yet been taken by German forces, fired on the airfield at intervals of nearly one round per minute. . . . Burning aircraft on the only landing and take-off strip prevented the landing of circling Ju-52's. Supply operations could only be carried out by starting and landing airplanes on the beach on either side of the airfield regardless of losses.[65]

Except for the crump of mortars, the rapid voice of the machine gun and the louder roar of artillery, the early morning was relatively quiet; both sides licked their wounds and waited.

But about 8 A.M. the sky blossomed out in mushrooms of silk once again, as Ju-52's dropped about two and a half companies of paratroopers west of the Tavronitis to join the Assault Regiment. They landed safely, well out of range of British guns, and immediately beefed up the push to the east.

About 3 P.M. under the hot Cretan sun, German Stukas and fighters bombed and strafed, roaring down in ear-splitting dives—their objectives the villages of Maleme and Pyrgos and positions of 23rd New Zealand Battalion to the west of the airstrip. As the Assault Regiment attacked from the west, two more companies of paratroopers were dropped along the coast to the east of Maleme.

But once again German intelligence had miscalculated; the paratroopers dropped squarely on New Zealand positions—the result: free-for-all pot-shooting and wild scrimmage.

> Officers—cooks—bottle-washers—all were in it . . . a Hun dropped not ten feet away . . . I let him have it while he was still on the ground . . . I had hardly got over the shock when another came down almost on top of me and I plugged him too while he was untangling himself. Not cricket, I know, but there it is.[66]

The Maoris tracked down the Germans relentlessly and shot or bayoneted them.

By dusk most of the two companies were dead or wounded; about 80 survivors worked their way into the outskirts of Pyrgos to link up with the German attack from the west. And the Assault Regiment, after taking Pyrgos and Maleme, stalled, leaving in the high tide of the attack some 200 German dead in front of the 23rd Battalion positions.

Nevertheless, relentlessly, inexorably, the Ju-52's came in, taxied to a halt amidst burning wreckage, disgorged their men or cargo, propellers still whirling, and took off with engines laboring. At 5 P.M. a battalion and a regimental headquarters of the 5th Mountain Division started to land at Maleme and the beaches near it. And Colonel Bernhard Ramcke assumed command of the Assault Regiment (replacing the wounded Meindl) and of the entire German western task force. Within two hours his plans were made; tomorrow he would attack again. . . .

For the British it was approaching the point of no return. With Maleme now in use by the Germans and an air ferry to Greece shuttling in men and supplies, the airstrip had to be retaken. Brigadier General Edward Puttick, who commanded the New Zealand Division, his brigadiers and Freyberg made plans to attack.

At Retimo and Heraklion both the defenders and the attackers fought, on May 21, wild and vicious little battles—battalion and company fire fights—actions that lapped and eddied out from the main current of history. . . . At both Retimo and Heraklion the fighting was self-contained, isolated; attack and defense fought in a kind of vacuum, with the main effort of both sides focused on Maleme. The Germans gave their tattered battalions just enough air support and resupply to keep them going—no more. The British and Greeks were cut off, by distance, by the constantly prowling predators of the German-held air and by German positions (seized the first day), from any but indirect communication with the Suda Bay–Canea–Maleme area. The skies belonged to Germany; the falcons with the swastikas on their wings dipped and soared the day through, pouncing with tearing talons and rending beaks on any prey that moved. . . .

At Retimo the Australians scored some indecisive successes. On second try an Australian battalion, after fierce fighting, regained the heights dominating the airstrip to the east, and another hill to the west was also recaptured with greater ease. The commander of the 2nd Parachute Regiment was captured by the Aussies in the afternoon, and things were looking up—but briefly, for the Germans with dogged stubbornness held their positions in the little town of Platanes and around Perivolia. The attackers around Retimo were scattered to east and west of the airstrip, but the British and Greeks in turn were cut off from Suda. And ammunition was scarce. . . .

At Heraklion, the ding-dong battle ended in stand-off at day's end. Here, too, the Germans were split—east and west; their tenuous grip on the airstrip was prized loose during the daylight hours, but they still held the heights to the southeast and some of them infiltrated down to the harbor.

The British reserves on Crete—what there were of them—were pinned down on the twenty-first by German air power constantly prowling the skies, and by a threat of sea-borne invasion. British reconnaissance aircraft had sighted German convoys at sea late on the twenty-first, and Freyberg and his brigadiers believed "early seaborne attack in area Canea likely."[67]

Their information was good.

1st Motor Sailing Flotilla—a collection of spitkits and jerricans—had put out of the island of Melos in full daylight, its orders to land its 2,331 troops (3rd Battalion, 100th Mountain Regiment: heavy weapons units, and part of 2 AA Regiment) near Maleme, if possible before dark on the twenty-first. The little caïques, crowded with men and equipment, were "navigated" and controlled in convoy by lieutenants with pocket compasses and homemade megaphones.[68] The Italian torpedo boat *Lupo* rode shotgun, the only protection the convoy had.

It was a brave gesture, a calculated, even a desperate, gamble, but the Germans believed their Stukas and bombers would keep the British Fleet at bay.

Indeed, there was good reason to suppose so. For the bloody battering the Royal Navy was to receive in the battle of Crete—the worst ordeal that any fleet had to endure until the kamikazes at Okinawa—had already started.

Admiral Cunningham had divided his fleet into light and covering forces. The light forces—Force D (cruisers *Dido, Orion* and *Ajax,* and destroyers *Kimberley, Isis, Imperial* and *Janus*) and Force C (cruisers *Naiad* and *Perth;* destroyers *Kandahar, Nubian, Kingston* and *Juno*)—had patrolled off the north coast of Crete on the night of May 20, and early on the twenty-first moved southward through Kaso and Antikithera straits. Cruising west of Crete to provide cover if the Italian Fleet ventured from its lair were battleships *Warspite* and *Valiant* and six destroyers, under Rear Admiral H. B. Rawlings, with other ships, south of Kaso or steaming hard to join.

The trial by bombs started before noon on the twenty-first. High-level bombers approached in the sun's glare and, though the cottony puffs of bursting ack-ack blossomed around them, they laid their patterns accurately near the speeding, violently twisting British ships.

Destroyer *Juno*'s vitals were laid open; another bomb detonated her magazine and she went down, a blazing pyre, in a few seconds. Shocked, dazed and oil-soaked men—6 officers and 91 ratings—were rescued from the sea, and the battle went on. Ju-87's and 88's joined the assault; dive bombers, low-level attackers, torpedo bombers drove in against the ships. Cruiser *Ajax* was damaged by a near-miss. All through the day, relentless, persistent, incessant, almost demonic, the bombers came; all through the day the ships fought back.

"There is no spot more naked under heaven than the deck of a destroyer as a stick of bombs falls slanting towards it." Near misses "lift the ship as if a giant had kicked her, wrenching the steering gear, straining frames and plates."[69]

Darkness brought surcease, and the light ships steamed through Kaso and Antikithera into the dangerous Aegean to patrol the north coast of Crete. Sometime before midnight, some 18 to 20 miles north of Canea, 1st Motor Sailing Flotilla, slowed by alarms, false starts and head winds in its passage from Melos toward Maleme, met its fate. Rear Admiral I. G. Glennie, with Force D—*Dido, Orion, Ajax* and four destroyers—intercepted the first German sea-borne convoy to Crete. It was wild melee, with the troop-crowded caïques easy prey for guns and ramming in the beams of the searchlights.[70] The convoy scattered and little *Lupo,* a 679-ton Italian destroyer dashing around valiantly, did her best to herd and protect her vulnerable charges. *Lupo* laid a smoke screen and boldly traded punches with the far superior British force. She launched torpedos from 800 yards, fired her guns and machine guns, snaked through the British formation, and though hit 18 times by British shells she survived to fight again.[71] Her audacity saved most of the convoy, but her best was not good enough; the convoy was turned back, shattered; 320 German soldiers drowned.

Force C—Rear Admiral E. L. S. King—had its chance soon after first light on the twenty-second. King's force sank a lone caïque and then intercepted a convoy of 30 small ships bound for Crete just as the convoy, in answer to orders from *Admiral Southeast,* turned back toward Greece. The sole escort, the small Italian destroyer *Sagittario,* rivaled *Lupo's* gallantry. While his convoy scattered behind a smoke screen, *Sagittario* charged the British formation, launched torpedoes and, careening heavily in answer to violent course changes, chased the shell splashes of the enemy salvos. *Sagittario* escaped damage, and so did the British; perhaps one or two caïques were sunk but most escaped.[72]

The British Fleet had not been neutralized; the problem of supplying heavy equipment to the Germans on Crete had not been solved. The German attempt to reinforce by sea had been frustrated.

MAY 22

But for the Royal Navy the trial by bomb had just commenced. King's Force C, which had been reinforced by the antiaircraft cruisers *Calcutta* and *Carlisle,* had steamed deep into the Aegean in pursuit of the scattered caïques. Above him for mile on endless mile, the German Stukas ruled the air. His squadron speed was limited, his AA ammunition low. He turned back, the enemy in sight, abjuring Nelson's dictum that no captain could do wrong if he laid his ship alongside an enemy's.[73]

Force C steamed hard for Kithera Channel to clear the dangerous Aegean; from west and south Rear Admiral Rawlings with battleships of sonorous names—*Warspite* and *Valiant*—and Glennie's Force D closed toward him in support.

It was too late. For hour after hour that long clear day, under skies of startling brilliance, the ships of the British Navy fought the good fight and died. Their battle ensigns strained and flapped in the wind of their passing; puffs of bursting AA shells pocked the skies above them, but for endless minute on minute the planes came swooping and the bombs dropped with the whistling screams that curdled thought.

Naiad took it first; huge bombs burst close aboard and lifted and racked her; her beauty was forever marred. *Carlisle* was hit, her captain killed. Destroyer *Greyhound* took two hits squarely, broke up and went down in a few minutes. *Gloucester*, with *Fiji* in company, was steaming hard for safety, the frothing bow wave curling back from her cutwater, when the bombs sieved her; she shuddered, slowed to a stop, afire, her "upper deck a shamble."[74] Slowly she died, her captain with her; his body, "recognizable by his uniform monkey jacket and the signals in his pocket, came ashore to the west of Mersa Matruh [North Africa] about four weeks later. It was a long way to come home."[75]

Fiji did not last much longer. The light cruiser, which had endured 20 bombing attacks in some four hours and was now defending herself with practice ammunition, succumbed to one plane. She rolled over and sank at 8:15 that night, but not until after *Valiant* had been hit by two bombs and *Warspite*'s 4- and 6-inch starboard batteries had been put out of action.

May 22 was a black day for the British Navy; they had lost much to stop the Germans' sea-borne invasion. But the Germans might come again, and ashore the turn of fate still focused on Maleme.

For the British at Maleme it was do or die. Freyberg, Puttick and his officers had conferred late on May 21. The counterattack against the airdrome must jump off at night; the hours of darkness would provide cover against the circling German sky hawks. Two battalions—one from as far away as Canea (which was to be relieved in turn by an Australian battalion at Georgioupolis 18 miles further to the east)—were to attack along the coastal road to the west toward the village of Pyrgos and the airstrip; time of jump-off, 0400 22 May.

From the beginning it was fiasco. The relieving Australians were bombed on the road and arrived late; one of the attacking battalions straggled along to the start line in bits and pieces, and when the assault finally started two and a half hours late, there was little darkness left and it was mounted with about one and a half battalions instead of two. It was daylight long before the village of Pyrgos was even reached, and the advancing New Zealanders, stumbling through the dark hours, had already encountered pockets of Germans who had resisted stubbornly.

"My impression was," a captain reported, "that we could not accomplish much with the attack from then on—because of the strafing from the air that was going on. Situation seemed unstable and unsatisfactory."[76]

The company actually penetrated to the edge of the Maleme airstrip with "stacks of German aircraft" on it; "some crashed, some not,"[77] but there, under intense mortar and machine-gun fire, it stalled. And German planes were landing, under fire, and disgorging fresh troops directly into battle.

The Maori battalion, with its "ancestral fighting urge," used hand grenades and cold steel as they hacked their way forward, "crying Ah! Ah! and firing at the hip."[78]

But courage was not enough. Along the coastal road and in the shattered rack of Pyrgos, the bloody fighting sputtered and died; to the north, where the high ground commanding the airfield beckoned to conquest, another New Zealand battalion assayed a flanking movement and stalled in midmorning as the German hawks swooped down upon them and German machine-gun fire mounted; they broke into retreat by midafternoon of that hot May day. The thing was done, the chance was lost; the counterattack had failed.

"The counter-attacks toward Maleme had gained no vital ground."[79]

As the winded and weakened British slacked and slowed, the Germans, like Antaeus hurled to earth, gained in strength.

In Athens General Student was anxious to fly to Crete and take command, but General Löhr refused permission, and General Julius Ringel, commanding 5th Mountain Division, was sent instead—his orders being to clear the Maleme-Suda-Canea area and to assume command of all ground operations in Crete.

Through the twenty-second, the troop carriers roared into Maleme and the beaches near it with two infantry battalions of 5th Mountain Division, an engineer battalion and a parachute artillery battery. The landing strip "littered with burning and broken-down aircraft was cleared again and again with the help of captured tanks."[80]

But the British counterattack, though it made no major gains, had frustrated German offensive plans; it was not until the sun was westering low that the Germans pressed forward, retook the ground they had lost and pushed farther to the east. General Ringel landed on the beach west of Maleme about 8 P.M. with British shells still bursting on the airstrip, and immediately planned operations to extend his perimeter and secure the field completely the next day.

Far from the main *Schwerpunkt* around Maleme, vicious, swirling fighting ebbed and flowed throughout the day—in the Galatas–Prison Valley area, around Heraklion and at Retimo. There was little centralized direction; for both the British and the Germans these sectors were cut off, isolated, each fighting its own violent battle—not a battle according to plan, but a struggle for survival.

For the British and Greeks "the problems of transport and communication could not be solved";[81] the Germans ruled the air, and the dispersed nature of an airborne operation meant there were no clear-cut front lines, but rather pockets of German troops scattered everywhere, across the roads, in the olive groves, along the seacoast.

With inadequate wireless equipment, telephone lines destroyed by bomb attack or cut by enemy paratroopers, and no kind of vehicle which could be spared to carry a message, all that remained was the runner. . . . On one occasion a runner was sent with a message from Retimo to Suda Bay. The distance was 45 miles. The messenger had to run the gauntlet of spasmodic fighting on the road, had to pass through enemy positions, wriggling through bushes on his stomach and sniped at if he dared to raise his head. He got through in the end. But it took him—just six days.[82]

In the Prison Valley–Galatas area the day ended more or less as it began—in stalemate, with no substantial changes in the positions of either side. But men had died to make it so. At about 7 in the evening, when the German paratroopers had captured a hill north of Galatas, and the situation looked bad to the New Zealanders, "over an open space in the trees near Galatas came running, bounding and yelling like Red Indians" as motley and strange a crew as Crete had yet seen. It was a charge the like of which is rare in war.

Out of the trees came Captain (Michael) Forrester of the Buffs [a "young blond Englishman of the Queen's Regiment" attached to the Greek military mission, who had assumed command of some Greek stragglers] clad in shorts, a long yellow army jersey reaching down almost to the bottom of the shorts, brass polished and gleaming, web belt in place, and waving his revolver in his right hand. He was tall, thin-faced, fair-haired, with no tin hat—the very opposite of a soldier here; as if he had just stepped on to the parade ground. He looked like . . . a Wodehouse character. . . . Forrester was at the head of a crowd of disorderly Greeks, including women; one Greek had a shot gun with a serrated-edge bread knife tied on like a bayonet, others had ancient weapons—all sorts. Without hesitation this uncouth group, with Forrester right out in front, went over the top of a parapet and headlong at the crest of the hill. The enemy fled.[83]

At Retimo the British held firmly to the airstrip, but their attacks on German positions made no headway. Neither side was reinforced; neither side could be. At Heraklion, where German transports dropped in ammunition and light guns (like "manna," most of it fell in British lines), the British, Australians and Greeks made piecemeal gains west and south of the town, captured and mopped up, but the Germans clung stubbornly to the high ground to the east where their guns enfiladed the airstrip.

That night, the twenty-second, King George of the Hellenes and his party—many of his Cabinet, British diplomats, attachés, the flotsam of disaster—said their last farewell to Greece. For three days the King and his companions had made their way on foot, and on donkey and mule back, over tortuous, rocky trails high into the spine of the southern mountains and then down again, precipitously, to the south coast. They had slept in caves and crevices; the King had stripped off his general's blouse with its gold braid and rows of medals. They had seen the last battle for Crete from high above the northern coastal plain—"the red earth and the fields of ripening corn . . . flecked and spattered with innumerable parachutes—white like patches of snow, sometimes red like patches of blood." At 7,000 feet, they had cleared the snow from the rocky ridges and roasted a lean mountain sheep over the flames, and then gone on, with ripped and tattered boots and "blistered, bleeding feet," to a rendezvous at the little village of Ayla Roumeli on the south coast. Lady Palairet, wife of the British Minister, Sir Michael Palairet, cooked the King his last meal on Grecian soil, and in the deep dark of the night of May 22–23 the King of Greece and his distinguished party boarded HMS *Decoy* and sailed for Egypt. It was high time.[84]

The day ended in last blood for the English. Fifth Destroyer Flotilla, Lord Louis Mountbatten commanding, had just joined up from Malta, and in a high-speed sweep in the darkness inside Canea and Kisamos bays four of the destroyers damaged or set fire to two caïques loaded with troops, and bombarded the airstrip at Maleme. They then withdrew, steaming hard for Kithera Channel to escape the circling hawks before the day had come.

Ironically, that very night, with Maleme lost and the British sore-pressed, transport *Glenroy* sailed from Alexandria for Crete with 900 men of the Queen's Royal Regiment aboard.

MAY 23

Full daylight on the twenty-third found the tired British lines to the eastward of Maleme in full withdrawal. The New Zealanders who had tried so hard the day before were ordered to pull back toward Canea to build up a stronger defensive line. The decision had been made the previous night. Freyberg had wanted to counterattack again, but before it could be mounted Brigadier Puttick learned that the coast road—the main line of communications between his two brigades—had been cut by the Germans; he feared his forward battalions would be destroyed. So the order went out before daylight on the twenty-third: "Retreat" to a new line two and a half miles further to the east. The German hold on Maleme was consolidated; the British were now seven miles away from the airstrip; from then on the build-up would be uninterrupted.[85]

The enemy followed hard—so fast that the British had to spike and abandon seven guns. And before the day was over, British brigadiers were coming to see that a "further withdrawal was inevitable."[86]

For Ramcke's parachutists were driving hard to the east along the coastal road; the 5th Mountain troopers were moving southward and eastward over the hills to outflank the retiring New Zealanders, and from the south in the Prison Valley–Galatas area Heidrich's 3rd Para Regiment, though short of ammunition, was maintaining containment pressure, and a detachment had been sent toward Aiyina Marina to try to cut the coastal road *behind* the retiring British.

It was a melancholy day—how melancholy the fighting men around Suda and Canea did not yet know. They knew they had hurt the Germans though the enemy's losses had been exaggerated, and the troops fighting in the western portion of Crete thought the other German footholds at Retimo and Heraklion had been wiped out. And they had faith in the RAF and the British Navy. That afternoon an RAF bomber attacked Maleme strip, followed soon by others; the tired New Zealanders heard the crump of the bomb explosions, saw smoke and fire and cheered.[87] But it was a pygmy effort, too little and too late; unceasingly that day and thereafter, the German transports roared into Maleme with men, ammunition and supplies. The Germans now had firm hold on a Cretan airstrip a few miles from Suda Bay, the only port capable of supplying British forces in the island. And Suda Bay was

a melancholy sight. Besides H.M.S. *York*, there were also two destroyers, half a dozen merchantmen, and ten or twelve other craft, big or small, in a more or less disabled condition. Some of them were burning furiously and sending tall columns of black and white smoke up into the sky.[88]

At Retimo and Heraklion defenders and attackers each succeeded in containing the other; each fought a desperate fight far from the main battle. The dead and wounded littered the ground east of Retimo; a one-hour truce permitted succor, and the Aussies brought in 70 German wounded to their aid station.

At Heraklion, despite German machine-gun fire across the airstrip, an Egyptian-based Hurricane fighter landed in the afternoon to the cheers of the British;[89] later six Hurricanes tried to break up a German bombing raid, and four damaged fighters sought refuge on the fire-swept strip. There were far too few against too many. Slowly at first but faster as the hours passed, the odds against the British lengthened. . . .

It was, too, a grim day at sea. A mistake in signals had led Cunningham to believe *Warspite* and *Valiant* were virtually out of ammunition; all ships had been ordered back to Alexandria to replenish. But dawn of the twenty-third caught 5th Destroyer Flotilla, which had carried out a sweep north of Crete during the dark hours, only a short distance south of the island. Four Dorniers harried them first; heeling and surging through the blue waters, in answer to violent helm, the destroyers dodged the sticks of bombs. Before eight bells in the morning watch, 24 Stukas roared out of the north and, peeling off, dove one by one against their prey. *Kashmir*, rolling and prancing, dodged the first half-dozen bombs; then fate took her. She sank in two minutes, but not before Ordinary Seaman Ian D. Rhodes, Royal Australian Naval Volunteer Reserve, climbed over the wreckage of his half-submerged Oerlikon to another gun and shot down a Ju-87 as his ship died under him.

Kelly, the flagship, got it next with a 1,000-pounder. She was doing 30 knots with full starboard rudder. Mountbatten shouted, "Keep all the guns firing; we've been hit!" But *Kelly* had had it. She simply turned bottom up in white water, her propellers still turning, her guns firing to the last, and, after a time, went under.

On the Carley floats and rafts, the oil-soaked, shocked and wounded survivors answered with a roar to Mountbatten's "Give her a cheer, lads," as *Kelly* went under. Then, awaiting rescue or death, a sailor struck up a feeble tune:

> *Roll out the barrel;*
> *Let's have a barrel of fun. . . .*[90]

Kipling closed—throttles wide open—evaded bombs, and picked up the survivors, among them Lord Louis Mountbatten, the future C-in-C. Between 8:20 A.M. and 1 P.M. *Kipling*, crowded with oil-grimed, shocked survivors, endured 40 air attacks, 83 bombs, before she found safety off Alexandria.[91]

It was the final straw. Admiral Cunningham, after consulting Wavell, messaged the *Glenroy* with the 900 reinforcements aboard, to turn back to Egypt.[92]

At "Creforce" that Friday, May 23, Freyberg received a cable from Churchill:

"The whole world watches your splendid battle on which great things turn."[93]

But Freyberg was worried about supplies, and—he was to write later—the "situation was rapidly deteriorating in the Maleme sector."[94]

London was peremptory. To Wavell the orders: Crete must be held; send reinforcements.

DEFEAT AND EVACUATION

It was a pipe dream; the defense of Crete was doomed—had been doomed since Maleme fell.

For the British the battle was now all downhill, and day by day, hour by hour, the image of hopelessness sharpened, the aura of defeat darkened, for "Aussie" and for Greek, for Maori and for Englishman.

On 24th May, the Commanders-in-Chief, replying to a request by the Chiefs of Staff for an appreciation, were obliged to say that the scale of air attack made it no longer possible for the Navy to operate in the Aegean or near Crete by day. Admiral Cunningham could not guarantee to prevent sea-borne landings without suffering such further losses as would very seriously prejudice the British command of the Eastern Mediterranean. Reinforcements and supplies could only be run in to Crete by night in fast warships.[95]

It was the end, on May 24, for the brave defense of Kastelli, a little port on the extreme western end of the island, which had been defended by the 1st Greek Regiment, a motley collection of wild Cretan home guards, and a small New Zealand training detachment. On May 20 a 72-man detachment of German parachutists had attempted to seize the town, and thus secure the western flank of the German attack on Maleme. But they had been roughly handled—all were killed, wounded or captured. The Germans wanted a port quickly; on the twenty-fourth a task force, moving west from Maleme, overran the defenses and Kastelli fell. But fierce Cretan guerrillas harassed the invaders for days to come.[96]

Over Crete, the grim hawks with the swastikas on their wings circled and swooped; the weight of air attack was far greater than Freyberg had ever imagined possible. This day, the twenty-fourth, the requiem for Canea was the continuous crump of bombs, the flash of explosions. Hour after hour from squadron after squadron the black bombs dropped in perfect precision; the pattern of death crisscrossed the narrow streets and turned the town into an inferno of flames and smoke and rubble.

Ironically, that night mine layer *Abdiel* succeeded in landing 200 men of a Commando group in Suda; the rest of the 800-man force, embarked in destroyers, turned back to Egypt.

It was again too little and too late; throughout the day the Germans were steadily reinforced.

Sunday, May 25, the sixth day of battle, General Student, eager for action, flew in from Athens to Ringel's headquarters near Maleme. It was a day of fierce fighting and, for the British, ever-crumbling hopes. A German three-pronged attack—toward Alikianou to cut the British line of retreat to the south coast, and thence on eastward of Canea to sever the coast road between Suda and Retimo, and from Prison Valley and Maleme toward Galatas—was mounted in fury and executed with driving determination. Soon, from the British lines, there was a "trickle of stragglers, a sinister symptom. . . .

"Suddenly the trickle of stragglers turned to a stream, many of them on the verge of panic." Colonel H. K. Kippenberger "walked in among them, shouting 'Stand for New Zealand!' and everything else I could think of."[97]

It was a near thing, but the British held—to retire winded, heavily hurt, but in order. It was a day of attack and fierce and piecemeal counterattack. Galatas fell to the German drive, but not for long. Bits and pieces of shattered New Zealand companies, with two light tanks, charged into the ruins of the town, and took it with the bayonet before the Germans could reorganize:

Those which rose against us fell to our bayonets, and bayonets with their eighteen inches of steel entering throats and chests with the same . . . hesitant ease as when we had used them on the straw-packed dummies. . . . One of the boys just behind me lurched heavily against me and fell at my feet, clutching his stomach. His restraint burbled in his throat for half a second as he fought against it, but stomach wounds are painful beyond human power of control and his screams soon rose above all the others. The Hun seemed in full flight.[98]

But it was brief glory.

The British were decimated; that night they pulled back to a shorter line, and Galatas with its bodies and its ruins was left to the Germans.

And while attackers and attacked at Retimo and Heraklion played to mutual checkmate, Freyberg reported to Wavell late on the twenty-fifth: "The line is gone, and we are trying to stabilize. . . . I am apprehensive.[99]

But Wavell, in Egypt, who had just returned from Iraq, and the British Government in London, were hopelessly dated; they were still talking of "greater risks" by the Navy, more air support and of a "costly defeat" for the enemy.

Later, Wavell was to describe Monday, May 26, as the "critical day," but the critical day had long since passed, when Maleme had been lost.

But the twenty-sixth was the day when all hope, even that tenuous thread which kept men to their duty, had gone. The German air attacks on forward positions and rear areas, on supply dumps and lines of retreat, were unrelenting, continuous, heavy; the nerves screamed with unending fear as the Stukas dived and the bombs exploded. The line was falling back, and dock workers and supply and base personnel had been ordered to make their own way across the cruel mountains toward Sphakia, a fishing village on the south coast. Rumors abounded; the discipline which keeps men fighting to the end was strained; some stragglers from combat units made no efforts to rejoin, but streamed away, broken and weaponless.

The dikes were about to break, and Freyberg knew it. At 9:30 A.M. on May 26, after predawn conferences, the doughty New Zealander conceded defeat. In a message to Wavell he said:

I regret to have to report that in my opinion the limit of endurance has been reached by the troops under my command here at Suda Bay. No matter what decision is taken by the Commanders-in-Chief from a military point of view our position here is hopeless . . . the difficulties of extricating this force in full are now insuperable. Provided a decision is reached at once a certain proportion of the force might be embarked.[100]

And so the retreat began. . . .

That night the rest of the Commando force was landed, daringly, in *Abdiel* and two destroyers at Suda Bay, and these fresh troops helped to form the rear guard for the long and bitter trail of defeat across the sere and rugged mountains to the south coast.

The next day, the twenty-seventh, Wavell and London finally accepted the inevitable, but not until after Churchill had cabled Wavell early in the morning that "victory was essential and that he must keep hurling in reenforcements."[101] But Churchill was far behind events, and later that day he understood that once again Britain had tasted the bitterest dregs of war. Evacuate. Save men if not guns. Once again the Royal Navy, so bitterly tested, so sorely tried at Dunkirk, Greece and now Crete, must brave the gantlet of fire to rescue what might be saved.

The end came fast. The German tide lapped high; the dikes of defense broke, now here, now there. Hopelessness and the endless bombing took their toll. Dissolution spread like gangrene; defeat and retreat for many units turned into rout.

The road and trail—winding ever upward from the north coast from Suda and Canea, ever upward into the hills and mountains—was a black and teeming ant trail full of stumbling, exhausted, broken men—here and there "units sticking together and marching with their weapons . . . but in the main a disorganized rabble. . . . Somehow or other the word Sphakia got out and many of these people had taken a flying start in any available transport they could steal and which they later left abandoned."[102]

Rifles, tunics, gas masks, hand grenades and rifled suitcases littered the ditches.[103]

Sun-blistered, haggard men, men with stubbled beards, hobbling wounded, all moved persistently, instinctively—to scatter and cower as German planes roared overhead—on the road to what they hoped would be salvation.

On this same day, the twenty-seventh, the Germans broke through a screen of "Creforce" reserve into the smoldering ash heap of Canea.

The Germans pushed forward past abandoned British positions, dead bodies "with skin going yellow." They attacked as the birds sang "a joyous tremolo"; they moved ahead through the "slightly sweet nauseating stench of decomposing corpses."

In Canea the streets were strewn with debris, the stench of the dead, the acrid odor of smoke, mixed with the resinous smell of olive oil and wine.[104] Rats, "hitherto absolute autocrat[s] of the ruins," fled before the advancing Germans.

Of 1,200 Britishers in Force Reserve only 150 escaped death or capture.

That same day the rest of the 5th Mountain Division and a battalion of the 6th landed at Maleme.

The fight was over; now all that remained was to reduce the toll of defeat.

It was again the Navy's turn, with courage and with hasty improvisation instead of careful plan, to save an army.

Another evacuation under the wings of the Luftwaffe for a fleet already decimated and strained to the limit appeared to be asking the impossible, even of men nurtured in the tradition of Nelson. But Admiral Cunningham was that *rara avis,* a Nelsonian traditionalist.

"It takes the Navy," he said, "three years to build a new ship. It will take 300 years to build a new tradition. The evacuation (that is, rescue) must go on."[105]

Sphakia, the tiny south coast fishing village, was to be the evacuation point for as many men from Suda-Canea-Maleme as could reach there; Retimo's defenders, it was hoped, might straggle across the spiny mountains to Plaka Bay, and Heraklion's 4,000 men would be lifted by the Navy directly from the harbor.

It was a braw plan, but it was hit-or-miss, and the German Air Force was circling the skies to see that it did not work.

By the morning of Wednesday, May 28, Freyberg, and what remained of his staff, had straggled across the mountains to Sphakia, and with a patchwork communications system—one RAF radio, the only one available, operated from a cave—was trying to arrange an evacuation schedule. Freyberg's report was desperate: only 2,000 men with 3 guns, 140 rounds of artillery ammunition and 3 light tanks fit to fight; ultimate limit of resistance the night of May 31–June 1.

Behind Freyberg on that rocky, blood-spattered Via Dolorosa that wound through gullies and ravines, up and down hills and mountains past a plateau at Askifou called "the saucer," up and over spiny ridges, moved an unending trail of the defeated, some of them gallant still. They were singing, some of them, the song of the retreat: the irrepressible Australian war song, "Waltzing Matilda." Not many, to be sure; the sun was blistering, the heat in daylight extreme; one needed to save one's breath, and throats were parched for water.

Most of the men learned to climb by night, when it was cooler and there were no German planes to chivvy them. But others, desperate with the fear of prison, braved sun and bombs. Captain Peter McIntyre, New Zealand war artist, later wrote:

As far as one could see, a long straggly line of men trudged up the mountains, and all along the roadside men lay exhausted. The planes were circling now, so we left the road and clambered up from the floor of the ravine below, where the rocks and trees gave some sort of cover. Single file, the endless line climbed up and up. Men lay asleep or done up across the track, but the others just stepped over them and on. . . .

Sometimes down the face from the rock the wreckage of army trucks would be strewn where they had plunged headlong off the road when attacked by bombers. . . .

Still the ravine wound up and up. Legs were like lead now, and you trudged in a foggy coma, conscious only of aching feet and the raw patch on your hip where the rifle chafed. The sweat ran down your face and stung your cracked lips. Sometimes a creaking wisecrack would come from somewhere down the column. . . . The line of men would move up and up, and then the planes would come and the line of khaki would melt into the rocks. The crash of bombs echoed through the mountains. Huge clouds of smoke and dust belched upwards from the passes. . . .

The will to live, the instinct for survival, seems to rise in aid of a man when most needed and becomes the dominating thought and driving force.[106]

The will to live, the concentration of German air and ground power against Heraklion and Retimo and the Royal Navy helped to make possible the escape of many of the defenders of Maleme and Suda.

The Germans miscalculated. The German command knew the trail to Sphakia ended above the high bluffs on the south coast; they did not believe the British would attempt evacuation from so difficult a locality. Major German strength pushed on to the east along the north coast toward Retimo; only the 1st Mountain Regiment and a few attached troops drove on across the mountains toward Sphakia.[107]

Behind the long column of stragglers, Commandos and Australian and New Zealand troops, leapfrogging each other, threw up roadblocks, held off the eager scrambling Germans in short, brief fire fights.

The German mountain troops, though few in number, followed hard across rocky escarpments, by goat tracks and down defiles, constantly outflanking the British rear guards.

"In their heavy uniforms the mountain soldiers withstood days of scorching heat with temperatures rising up to 130 degrees F. and nights when the mountain air at altitudes ranging up to 7,000 feet was so cold that they were unable to sleep."[108]

That first night, May 28–29, four destroyers, *Napier, Nizam, Kelvin* and *Kandahar,* took off more than 1,000 men from Sphakia, some 230 of them walking wounded. It was slow business; ships' boats were too few, and desperate men not included in the evacuation roster attempted to force their way into the boats. That first night, the destroyers with their human cargo got clean away from the south coast of the embattled island, but behind them they left a disturbed ant heap of boiling, struggling men, crawling over goat trails for the final two miles of the terrible hike, slipping, sliding, falling down a 500-foot cliff to water's edge.

That same night a sea-borne force of Italians from Rhodes landed unopposed at Seteia on Crete's north coast near the eastern end of the island, too late to play any role in history. And some Italian motor torpedo boats cruised into Suda Bay on the twenty-eighth to find the victorious Germans at the end of valor.

The Navy, that night of May 28–29, concentrated its main effort at Heraklion, where Brigadier B. H. Chappel's beleaguered force had kept to the end its tenuous grip on the airstrip. The Germans, on the twenty-eighth, dropped fresh men and supplies around Heraklion. The strip was fire-swept; nevertheless two Hurricanes from Egypt landed to refuel; one was damaged when it tried to take off. But clearly the gallant defense of Heraklion was ending. From Alexandria, at break of day, sailed cruisers *Ajax, Orion* and *Dido,* and destroyers *Hotspur, Decoy, Kimberley, Hereward, Jackal* and *Imperial,* to brave 25-mile Kaso Strait and the circling Luftwaffe and take off 4,000 men.

To make the rendezvous at Heraklion in hours of darkness, the ships had to approach Kaso in hours of light; from 5 P.M. onward until the late sunset the bombers came. *Imperial* shuddered from a near-miss but seemingly was unhurt; *Ajax* was damaged and ordered back to Alex. But the rest pushed on, steamed into Heraklion harbor at 11:30, and in about three and a half hours took off 4,000 men.

The shattered town was "one large stench of decomposing dead, debris from destroyed dwelling places, roads were wet and running from burst water pipes, hungry dogs were scavenging among the dead. There was a stench of sulphur, smouldering fires and pollution of broken sewers."[109] It was a Wagnerian finale. Left behind were the dead and wounded and a forlorn rear guard. But now the trial began.

The ships cleared Heraklion at 29 knots at 3 A.M., still in the full dark. Three-quarters of an hour later *Imperial*'s steering gear suddenly jammed and could not be cleared. There was no time for delay. Admiral Rawlings, in command, ordered troops and crew transferred from *Imperial* to *Hotspur*, and *Imperial* was abandoned and sunk. An hour later *Hotspur*, with 900 passengers aboard, rejoined the main fleet, but the sun was coming up, and it was almost full day when the squadron, one and a half hours behind schedule, steamed into the dreaded Kaso Strait.

The Junkers were pitiless; like hawks against a dying prey they dove and tore at the crowded ships below. *Hereward* was first to go. She took a bomb and lost headway. Rawlings steeled his heart; the fleet pushed on—the interests of the many took priority over the lives of a few. *Hereward*, when last seen, was limping slowly toward the shores of Crete, five miles away, all guns blazing skyward. She died slowly beneath a cloudless sky, but most of her men struggled ashore into captivity or were picked up by Italian torpedo boats and other craft which, ironically, had screened on the twenty-eighth the first sea-borne landing of Italian troops on Crete's easternmost point.

From 6 A.M. to 3 P.M. it was unmitigated horror. Long-range British fighters from Egypt, pitifully few in number, were to have screened the fleet's retirement, but the fleet was late, the rendezvous failed; not until noon did two naval Fulmars fly nearby.

Decoy took a close miss; engine casings were damaged, the speed of the squadron reduced to 25 knots. Soldiers on all the weather decks joined the fleet's pom-pom and AA gunners, with their Brens and Lewis' guns to greet the screaming Stukas with bands of fire.

Orion took a close miss, her speed dropped to 21; *Dido* was hit, *Orion* hit again and flamed and flared.

Rawlings was wounded; Captain G. R. B. Back, flag captain of *Orion*, was mortally wounded by a machine-gun bullet at 7:35. He died slowly, semiconscious; a couple of hours later, as the ship "was convulsed by several near misses, he came back to consciousness and attempted to sit up, calling on everyone to 'Keep steady!' "

When the attack was finished, he shouted, 'It's all right, men—that one's over,' and died."[110]

There was no surcease. German planes occasionally were knocked out of the sky to die in flaming majesty in the blue, blue sea, but they came on and on, implacable, determined. Wounded *Orion*, her fires extinguished, her hurt cared for, took it again—and horribly—when a clutch of Ju-87's dove, shrieking, upon her.

One large bomb penetrated the cruiser's bridge and burst below in the stokers' mess deck, crowded with soldiers.

"The results . . . were indescribably terrible."

Before noon *Orion*, dead, dying and wounded littering her decks, with three boiler rooms damaged, her steering gear gone, her engine-room telegraphs out of order, three of her five engineer officers dead, and with a heavy list to starboard and only one shaft turning, seemed all but done for.

But, spewing from her stacks and sieved upper works great clouds of yellow and black smoke, she limped into Alexandria with her damaged consorts at 8 P.M. on May 29, with two rounds of main battery ammunition and ten tons of fuel oil remaining.

Something like 800 of the 4,000 troops evacuated from Heraklion had been lost—"killed, wounded or captured *after leaving Crete*. . . . If losses were to be on this scale it might be fairer to order the remaining troops to surrender."[111]

But the Navy persisted. The night of the 29th–30th was scheduled for the greatest sea lift. *Glengyle* with her landing craft, *Perth, Calcutta, Coventry*, and six destroyers were ordered to Sphakia. They got home, with 6,000 soldiers, almost scot-free; *Perth* alone took a bomb in her forward boiler room; a few RAF fighters proved the difference between success and disaster.

But ashore on Crete it was the eleventh hour. The little garrison at Retimo, so long encircled, was almost out of food and ammunition; German strength was growing. Freyberg had tried to reach them; so had Middle East headquarters, but communications were out between Retimo and Canea, Heraklion and "Creforce"; the Retimo defenders were fighting in a vacuum. Indeed, the news of what was going on elsewhere in Crete came chiefly from British Broadcasting Company broadcasts; it was not until May 28 that Lieutenant Colonel I. R. Campbell, the Australian commander, heard, via the BBC, that "the situation in Crete is extremely precarious."[112]

May 30 was the end for Retimo. The orders for the little garrison to try to retreat southward to Plaka Bay on the south coast had never gotten through, and on the thirtieth the defenders saw German Army trucks, tanks and field guns moving eastward from the Canea area. Colonel Campbell drew the proper conclusion: Canea–Suda Bay had been overrun; his position was hopeless. Ammunition was almost expended; there were no more rations after that day. Campbell "drank the bitterest cup of war . . . he walked forward under a white flag and gave in his surrender."[113]

General Freyberg, on orders from Egypt, was evacuated that night at about 8:45 P.M., together with some of his brigadiers and key men of various units, in Sunderland flying boats. He left behind him, under

Major General Weston, Royal Marines, a tattered rear guard, still trying desperately to stave off the enemy on the heights above Sphakia, and milling, exhausted remnants on beaches, in caves and hills.

The savage Cretans used their ancient cunning and knowledge of the mountains to harass the advancing Germans. They showed little mercy to the wounded enemy who fell into their hands, and bodies of German dead were found hacked and mutilated.[114]

Four destroyers had been earmarked to take off more troops from Sphakia the night of May 30–31; one broke down and had to limp back to Alexandria; *Kelvin* was damaged by a bomb's near-miss and also turned back. But the two remaining ships, *Napier* and *Nizam,* crowded in almost 1,500 troops and got clean away.

May 31, the twelfth day of battle, was the last day of organized resistance on Crete. "Aussies," a few light tanks, Royal Marines and Commandos held the final rear-guard positions in the passes and on the heights, but the German mountain troops had started flanking movements toward the beaches and time was fast running out. Besides, the RAF air cover for the fleet was desperately needed at beleaguered Tobruk; the night of May 31–June 1 was to be the final evacuation. Weston and his aides knew that at least 5,500 men would have to be left behind. The troops were "desperately hungry"; German patrols had penetrated almost to "Creforce" headquarters in the caves above the beach; it was a day of unmitigated anxiety.

That night was the final formal scene. Cruiser *Phoebe,* mine layer *Abdiel,* destroyers *Jackal, Kimberley* and *Hotspur* hove to off the dark beach. They embarked 4,000 men in 3 hours and 40 minutes and sailed for Egypt.

But the Germans got last blood. Antiaircraft cruisers *Coventry* and *Calcutta* were to cover the evacuating force on its return passage. Within 85 miles of Alexandria two bombs from a Ju-88 hit the *Calcutta;* she died in a few minutes with many of her crew.

General Weston, under orders, was flown out in a flying boat that night, and the next day, June 1, an Australian, Lieutenant Colonel T. G. Walker, the senior battalion commander, acting on written orders, offered a formal capitulation to an Austrian officer of the 100th Mountain Regiment. It was over. . . .

The rest was mop-up—escape, evasion, the roundup of desperate, disorganized, hungry men from hills and mountains and refuge in Cretan mountain shacks. Some of the soldiers left behind said, like one "Aussie," "The bastards are not laying hands on me. I'm for the hills."

Some took to the sea, in abandoned landing craft, fishing boats, by any means; about 600 reached North Africa in this way, many after great hardship. Some roamed the mountains for weeks or months; some formed the nucleus of a Cretan underground. Many waved white flags quickly;

for almost all, freedom was short-lived; the Germans, with exemplary thoroughness, combed the villages and beaches, scoured the mountain fastnesses and took into captivity the men of many races from round the world who had assembled under British battle flags for the defense of Crete.

And the spotlight of history left Crete in the shadows once again and turned toward Russia.

THE COSTS

Crete, by any standards, was a bloody battle.

At the battle's close, the Mediterranean Fleet had only 2 battleships, 2 cruisers and some 13 destroyers fit for service; the Italian Fleet, which had remained in harbor during the struggle, still disposed—at least on paper—of 4 battleships and at least 11 serviceable cruisers.

The Royal Navy lost 1,828 dead, 183 wounded; 3 cruisers and 6 destroyers sunk; 1 aircraft carrier, 3 battleships, 6 cruisers and 7 destroyers damaged—many of them severely.

In addition, more than 300,000 tons of British and Allied merchant shipping were sunk or badly damaged in the Greek and Crete campaigns in March, April and May.[115]

The Royal Air Force lost 46 planes, most of them in a futile attempt to turn the tide of German air power over Crete.[116]

British personnel casualties—killed, wounded, prisoners and missing —totaled almost 48 percent of the approximately 32,000 British troops in the island. The detailed figures:

Unit	Killed or Missing	Wounded	Prisoners
British Army	612	224	5,315
Royal Marines	114	30	1,035
Royal Air Force	71	9	226
Australians	274	507	3,079
New Zealanders	671	967	2,180
Totals	1,742	1,737	11,835[117]

In addition, some 400 Palestinian and Cypriote laborers were captured, and the 10,000 to 15,000 Greek military and paramilitary units were completely dissolved by death in battle, wounds, capture,[118] or by fading away into the civilian population. Some 2,600 of these were killed.[119] Greek civilian deaths are unknown, but were probably numbered in four figures.

For their victory the Germans paid a heavy toll, though not nearly so heavy as the British claimed at the time and for years thereafter. Though the British Navy effectively prevented sea-borne landings until the battle for Crete had been lost to airborne troops, the losses suffered in the interception of the caïque convoys was nowhere near so great as was once thought. General Freyberg in his report estimated the Germans had lost 4,000 killed, 2,000 drowned and 11,000 wounded—a total of 17,000—almost a threefold exaggeration. Actually, only about 324 Germans were lost at sea. The detailed figures:

Unit	Killed	Wounded	Missing	Total
7th Air Division and Assault				
Regiment	1,520	1,500	1,502	4,522
Mountain Troops	395	504	257	1,156
Fliegerkorps XI	56	90	129	275
Fliegerkorps VIII	19	37	107	163
	1,990	2,131	1,995	6,116[120]

The Germans lost 147 aircraft and 64 damaged in the fighting, plus another 73 lost in operational accidents.

But they had Crete—for what it was worth—and once again, as so often before in World War II, British troops had fought, died and been overrun by Hitler's juggernaut of war.

CRITIQUE

Crete was a battle the like of which was never to be seen again.

Never again in World War II did the Germans use airborne troops en masse; never again, before or since, has an island been conquered by air.

To the Germans victory was not much to crow about. It had been a near thing, and the elite paratroops and the Assault Regiment had been badly mauled. More than 25 percent casualties of some 25,000 troops landed, including many of the most senior and skilled commanders, was for that stage of World War II a high toll (though small compared with what was to come). Neither Hitler nor Göring was pleased; henceforth throughout the war, except for small specialized tasks, the paratroopers fought as elite infantry units.

Crete showed the Germans to be human—fallible. They made mistakes.

Their intelligence estimates of British strengths and dispositions both before and during the battle were grossly inaccurate despite their air superiority.

Partly because of the pressure of time—readiness by May 15 for the start of Operation Barbarossa, the invasion of Russia, was the implementing date—reconnaissance was "wholly inadequate and led to serious mistakes"[121] about enemy positions, strengths and terrain.

Partly because of the interservice and personal politics in the Third Reich, the internal struggle for power which at different times and in varying ways racks every form of government, the German planning and preparations for the conquest of Crete were too hasty and too improvised.

General Field Marshal Albert Kesselring was later to comment that "the special characteristic of [Crete] was its improvisation. . . . The landings were planned and carried out in such a way that they bore within themselves the seeds of failure."[122]

And Davin, succinctly summing up the German mistakes, said that he

overestimated the sympathy of Crete's civil population . . . underestimated the strength and sturdiness of the garrison. Worse still, he failed to locate its concentrations. . . .

His plan of attack can hardly avoid disparagement. For it should surely have been assumed that the points which he most wanted to seize were those most likely to be defended. Yet he chose to land his striking force directly on top of them, and thus lost his finest troops on a scale which would not have been necessary had he chosen areas farther away from the airfields. . . .

Again, he chose to try and bring across under feeble convoy his two invasion flotillas by night. So complete was his control of the sky that he could have brought them across by day under an umbrella of aircraft, and Cunningham's ships would have been unable to interfere or at least unable to survive the attempt to do so.[123]

German ground force commanders later complained, with some reason, that in Crete, as in other German airborne operations in World War II, the Luftwaffe was in command, and neither ground force commanders involved nor the OKH "had anything to do with the preparations."[124]

The differences extended to the concept itself. General Student preferred what he called "oil spot tactics"—the initial landing at many different places of paratroop and glider troops to create small airheads without any "definite point of main effort." The airheads would then spread out, like oil spots, as they were reinforced from the air, until they overlapped. General Meindl, however, believed that a *Schwerpunkt*, or point of main effort, must be built up from the start. He was more right than Student. In the event, the initial widely scattered German air landings at five main and several subsidiary areas could not all be supported adequately by the German Air Force; "there were heavy losses and no definitive successes."

"At one time the whole operation was within a hair's breadth of disaster because the airheads, which were too weak and too far from each other, were being narrowed down."[125]

Kesselring later remarked that "exceptionally unfavorable landing conditions [in Crete] should . . . have induced them [the German command] to land in mass outside the occupied objectives and the effective defense fire, and to capture the decisive points (airport and seaport) and secure their possession in a subsequent, clear-cut attack at the point of main effort."[126]

The many landing areas *did* have an inhibiting effect upon the mobility of the defense; the widely scattered airheads *did* tie down British troops and force Freyberg to withhold commitment of reserves until he determined the point of major danger. But the same result might have been achieved and the military principle of concentration of force might have been applied from the beginning had the Germans understood the natural dispersion that would result incident to any airborne landing. The widely scattered paratroopers were bound to create confusion, even if they had been concentrated initially in a major effort against a single point. Moreover, the British without command of the air and fearing a sea-borne landing, could not have moved reserves against the threatened point until they were certain additional landings elsewhere would not take place. A more major concentration of force in the beginning against Maleme might have saved the Germans many unnecessary casualties.

However, in the event, the German command reacted vigorously and promptly to crisis. Student and Löhr wisely chose to reinforce success, and after initial stalemate and partial repulse they concentrated all available power in the one area—Maleme—where the initial operations had had some success. German planning was deficient, but in execution the Germans showed customary flexibility and initiative.

Crete provided many technical lessons. Airborne troops had never before faced such a challenge; in some respects techniques, equipment and weapons were deficient.[127] The parachutists who landed in Crete brought down with them only pistols and hand grenades; their heavy weapons were dropped in separate containers. This left them vulnerable to enemy small-arms fire at the critical moment of landing.

"After the Crete operation this was changed." In the German Army, as in airborne units of other armies, parachutists in later years of World War II carried their rifles with them when they jumped.[128]

The Germans had also developed within a year after Crete, two calibers of recoilless rifles to substitute, in the initial airborne assault, for artillery, and a small-caliber, high-velocity antitank gun. Other types of special, or modified, equipment were also developed, but few were used in combat.

Thus the Germans learned the hard lessons of battle. They won a victory in 12 days of battle—far more rapidly than the British had believed possible, but far slower than the Germans had planned. Instead of capturing Canea on the first day of battle, it was theirs seven days and almost 7,000 casualties later.

Student later was to call Crete "the grave of the German para-chutist," a somewhat melodramatic and oversimplified phrase.[129] There is little doubt that the heavy losses in Crete prejudiced Hitler against further massive airborne employment, not only because of the losses—other conventional units suffered far higher losses later in Russia—but because of the expense and logistical difficulties of training and main-taining large airborne forces. There was general agreement, after Crete, that early link-ups between airheads established behind enemy lines and more heavily armed conventional forces would be necessary if extremely heavy casualties among airborne troops were to be avoided.

The vast spaces and tremendous manpower of Russia, the factors (logistics and supply and weather) that particularly restrict airborne operations, and the great expense of maintaining these specialized units militated, after Crete, against their use en masse. "Only 'the rich man' can afford such forces."[130] In the event, neither the Germans nor the Russians used airborne troops in numbers. The Germans mounted two battalion-sized airborne operations—against Leros in the Aegean and in the Ardennes fighting later in the war. But that was all.

After Crete, Hitler had come to the conclusion "that only airborne operations which came as a complete surprise could lead to success."[131]

And he had never been persuaded, as Student had urged, "of the need to go further than Crete; and his general treatment of the North African front does not suggest that he ever discerned its true impor-tance. . . .

"The victory of our [the British] defeat," as Davin puts it, "was that never again, against Cyprus or elsewhere, were the parachutists launched from the air en masse to gain victory at the cost of crippling losses."[132]

It was left to the United States and Britain to develop to the full the art of vertical envelopment, of conquest from the skies.

But, though the Germans made mistakes, the British erred even more grievously.

Winston Churchill, with his bulldog jaw outthrust, had boasted early in May that "we intend to defend to the death, without thought of retirement, both Crete and Tobruk. . . . Let there be no thought of cutting our losses."

Yet the battle then was already lost before it was even joined. For in Crete Britain had been muddling through. There was no clear-cut plan for the island's development as a naval base, no well-thought-out scheme of defense.

As the Australian history shows it,

Plans and preparations to defend Crete against a major attack were not initiated until the middle of April. Much that could have been done . . . reconnaissance, shipping of vehicles, improvement of roads and harbors, the equipment and training of Greek forces, and the establishment of effective liaison with them—remained undone. The responsibility rests not with the succession of local commanders . . . but higher up.[133]

Churchill himself later wrote: "There had been . . . neither plan nor drive." The blame, he felt correctly, should be apportioned "between Cairo and Whitehall."[134]

Even more than the German attack, the British defense was improvised. It was an improvisation doomed to failure, for with Wavell everywhere beset and the British lion at bay—north, south, east and west—it would have been impossible with the best of plans to provide the men, the guns, the ships, the planes—above all the planes—which alone might have made the defense of Crete possible.

Air power shaped the victory for Germany in the skies over and around Crete; air inferiority doomed the British.

Even so, the resolution typified by Churchill's defiant speech was not translated into effective action, either in plans and preparations or in execution. Long before the battle, and almost to its end, too many tried to command too few. Churchill himself, with his dunning cables, which sometimes by-passed the chain of command, the British Chiefs of Staff in London, and the Commanders in Chief, Middle East, all had ideas about how to fight Freyberg's battle. Sometimes the orders of responsible commanders were "second-guessed" or countermanded from 3,000 miles away; Cunningham has some caustic remarks about this practice in his memoirs, *A Sailor's Odyssey*.[135]

Wavell especially, who was in Churchill's black book well before the battle, was mercilessly heckled from London prior to and during the fighting. Field Marshal Sir John Dill, Chief of the Imperial General Staff, had repeatedly told Churchill, "Back him or sack him," but Churchill did neither.

He continued to send peremptory and exhortatory messages. Major General Sir John Kennedy, director of military operations of the general staff, recorded that at the time of Crete "interference in the details" of Wavell's command had "become intolerable," and added the remark that later became famous: "I don't see how we can win the war without Winston, but on the other hand, I don't see how we can win it with him."[136]

Crete did little to enhance the reputations of the higher British commanders concerned. Wavell won no laurels and showed little prescience, strength or drive, and Freyberg, though faced before the event with almost certain defeat, was somewhat less than precise in his reports to his superiors, and demonstrated as a supreme commander too little of the aggressive and resolute certainty which had earlier won him fame in lesser posts. Only Cunningham with his doughty sailor's toughness and his moral courage—he was never fazed by Churchill—emerged not only as a resolute leader but as a keen strategist who appreciated the meaning of sea power as modified by air power. Cunningham was keenly aware that heavy British naval losses might alter the maritime balance of power in the Mediterranean; he demonstrated a far greater appreciation of the possible strategic consequences than did London. In the event, Britain risked her superiority at sea—and nearly lost it—in the Crete defeat.

Freyberg's brigadiers, charged with the responsibility for the defense of the Maleme-Canea area, showed far too little aggressiveness. As in Freyberg's case, their appreciation of the actual situation lagged behind events. Yet today's critic must always remember yesterday's limitations; we now know, in retrospect, far more than those embattled commanders then knew. Their inadequate information was in part due to poor communications and the German mastery of the air, in part to the placement of their headquarters and their attempt to fight the battle from their CP's. A vigorous counterattack that first night against the German positions around Maleme might well have delayed defeat.

"Only the fact that the defenders of the island limited themselves to purely defensive measures and did not immediately and energetically attack the first troops landed saved the latter from destruction in an extremely dangerous situation," was the German appraisal, at the time and after the war.[137]

Other German critics have commented on the "passivity" of the British leadership in the crucial first hours near Maleme.

But even so, vigorous counterattack probably could not have averted ultimate defeat, no matter how temporarily successful it might have been. For the Germans were not solely dependent for resupply upon the airfields.

Later, British officers reported that they felt a major "mistake was made" in not destroying the airstrips before the invasion started. Demolitions and cratering of the strips would certainly have rendered them at least temporarily unusable; German engineers would have had considerable work to do after capture before the transports could come roaring in. Indeed, Freyberg had planned to make the airfields useless, but it was not until May 19, when the last British aircraft left Crete, that an order to destroy one of the strips (Maleme) was apparently given. It was too late, for the Germans attacked next day. And, in the event, even after battle had been joined, unrealistic planning envisaged the ultimate use of Heraklion by aircraft flown in from Egypt. (A few actually landed there, most of them never to take off again.)

The Germans showed a remarkable capability to land their rugged transports on nearly any level, relatively smooth area. Many landed on the beaches near Maleme; at the end German reinforcements were being air-landed, out of range of British guns, on beaches adjacent to Heraklion. Thus, though the early capture of Maleme sealed Crete's fate, its successful defense would not have insured a British triumph.

Despite their air inferiority the British knew much about German plans and preparations. The excellence of the defenders' intelligence was undoubtedly due, in part, to their agent network in Greece and Crete.

Crete was a triumph of the British soldier rather than of the high command. It was a platoon, company and battalion commander's fight, and these junior officers, their noncoms and their men demonstrated in the hot and dusty hills and primitive villages of Crete the magnificent *élan*, the good humor, the tenacity and the courage which has made the men of British stock a "thin red line of 'eroes" throughout the world.

To both sides and to the world Crete—strategically, tactically, technically—was a forecast of the new order, an amazing demonstration of the power of the plane. Offense and defense—ground, sea and air—were revolutionized. The world would henceforth be different in war and peace. For if seas could be bridged by aerial armadas, terrain barriers no longer had their ancient meaning; war forever after would be three-dimensional.

Crete proved beyond doubt—though no such sanguinary demonstration should have been needed—that surface men-of-war could not operate, without air cover, within close range of strong enemy air power, without unacceptable losses. The cover of night gave the British Fleet a few hours of protection from unending attack, but the presence of a few British fighters in the skies above the Royal Navy provided greater insurance than the hours of darkness. After Crete it was, or should have been, clear that sea power henceforth also meant air power, that control of the sea could not be assured by surface ships alone.

Yet it is hard to avoid the conclusion that for both the Germans and the British Crete was the wrong battle in the wrong place at the wrong time. The island was not worth strategically the costs of attack and defense. Its loss by the British did not, in the event, alter basically the Mediterranean–Middle East situation; its capture by the Germans proved to be of little strategic value for the rest of World War II.

For the British, given the proximity of the Greek islands and the Italian positions in the Dodecanese and the German conquest of the

Balkans, Crete could never have been a useful base or even an advance position of any importance. It was too close to enemy positions and hence too exposed to an overwhelming concentration of force; the British simply could not have afforded the terrible drain in continuing ship and plane losses that a foothold on Crete would have meant. Unlike Malta, Crete was too large an island to be a fortress. Once Greece was gone, Crete was useless to the British, and this should have been clearly understood.[138]

To the Germans Crete proved after conquest a defensive drain rather than an offensive springboard. It had a certain inherent usefulness as flanking threat to British shipping routes in the eastern Mediterranean and as a bomber and mine-laying base against the Suez Canal. Yet both missions could be, and in the event were, carried out from mainland bases, which were easier to supply and to maintain than was Crete. Crete, as a steppingstone to Cyprus (Student's ambition) and the Levant, could have formed part of an eastern Mediterranean strategic pattern. But Hitler's eyes were on Russia, and in any case the major route to the Levant was in North Africa, where Rommel had already scored his initial victories. In the Crete campaign the Germans did not reinforce success but added to the great dispersion of their forces. Had Hitler put first things first, Malta, not Crete, would have been the scene of a German airborne conquest. For Malta was the key to the central Mediterranean and to that narrow bottleneck of sea across which must pass all British east-west traffic, and all German-Italian, north-south supply routes. Rommel and the Afrika Korps depended primarily upon sea supply. In the final analysis, it was British ships, planes and submarines operating from Malta (as well as North Africa) that spelled the very narrow difference between Rommel in the Nile Delta and on the banks of the Suez Canal, and Rommel in full retreat to Tunisia.

Toward the end in North Africa the Germans were utilizing all kinds of futile expedients, including specially designed convoy flak craft, to try to protect their convoys to Tunisia. Even in 1941, in the first five months prior to and during the Crete campaign, the Italians and the Germans lost 31 ships, totaling more than 100,000 tons sunk in or en route to Italian–North African ports. Surface ships, submarines and aircraft, and mines laid by all three types, wrought the destruction, and Malta harbored many of the wasps that were slowly to cause the defeat of Rommel.

Malta unquestionably was the proper objective for the German airborne forces. Indeed, Colonel General Hans Jeschonnek, Chief of Staff of the Luftwaffe, proposed that the reduction of Malta was the most urgent task for the X Air Corps in a conference with Hitler on February 3, 1941. As a result plans were prepared for its capture and completed in mid-March, with the Navy vigorously favoring them. The plans anticipated the use of the major units later used in Crete, with minor assistance from the Italian Fleet. The 1st Stuka Wing, operating from Sicily, did, indeed, carry out neutralizing attacks upon Malta in early 1941, until it was suddenly transferred to Greece, after the Crete battle started, to reinforce German air units there.

General Walter Warlimont, Chief of the National Defense Section (Deputy Chief of Operations) of the Supreme Command (Oberkommando der Wehrmacht-Wehrmachtführungsstal), recalls that

while the Balkan campaign was in progress, Section L had to produce an appreciation to show whether it was more important for future strategy in the Mediterranean to occupy Crete or Malta.

All officers of the section, together with myself, voted unanimously for the capture of Malta since this seemed to be the only way to secure permanently the sea-route to North Africa.

Our views were, however, overtaken by events even before they reached Jodl [Colonel General Alfred Jodl, Chief of OKW, or operations staff of the Supreme Command]. Hitler was determined that Crete should not remain in the hands of the British because of the danger of air attacks on the Rumanian oil fields and he had further agreed with the Luftwaffe that from a base in Crete there were far-reaching possibilities for offensive action in the eastern Mediterranean.[139]

Warlimont, Jeschonnek, the Navy and the Wehrmacht professionals were undercut by Göring and Student, who inflamed Hitler's imagination with prospects of an easy victory in Crete. Jodl, as usual, went along with Hitler's desires; he was a catalyst, a middleman, not a planner.

So the decision was to capture Crete rather than Malta, the key strategic objective in the Mediterranean. Perhaps, therefore, Crete—the wrong battle in the wrong place at the wrong time—was, in a negative sense, decisive; it may have saved Egypt.[140]

There remains only the overriding question: did Crete (or the Balkan campaign) delay the start of Operation Barbarossa? The German armies were to have been completely ready for the invasion of Russia by May 15; in the event, they did not cross the Soviet frontier until June 22. Did the month's delay save Russia? Was it just enough—five months later, with Hitler's legions so near to and yet so far from the onion-shaped domes of Moscow—to allow the deep cold of a Russian winter to aid fresh Siberian divisions in turning back Hitler's massive thrust and in transforming what had been for the Germans a triumphant war of blitzkrieg into the slow death of attrition?

It has been popular to answer these questions in the affirmative; indeed, British historians have tended to dredge from the debacle of the Greece-Crete campaign the consoling thought that these brave defeats represented delaying actions of such importance that they ultimately led to the defeat of Germany.

There is some historical support for this argument; Warlimont says flatly in his book that "because of the campaign in the Balkans the attack on Russia had to be postponed from the middle of May to 22 June."[141] Other German generals have agreed that the Balkan campaign caused a delay in "Barbarossa"; in fact, as early as March 28 after the Yugoslav coup, Army General Staff planners had agreed Barbarossa would have to be postponed for four weeks.

The most prominent and emphatic advocate of the contention that the Balkan campaign ultimately cost Germany the war was Anthony Eden, who as British Foreign Minister was to a considerable degree responsible for the British campaign in Greece and Crete. In his postwar memoirs he wrote that the delay in the invasion of Russia "justifie[d] the sufferings of Greeks and Yugoslavs, British and Dominion troops. . . . Karl Ritter, German Foreign Office liaison officer with the [German] High Command . . . summed up the consequences of the postponement in these words: 'This delay cost the Germans the winter battle before Moscow and it was there the war was lost.' "[142]

But the great bulk of historical evidence is overwhelmingly opposed to such a contention.

Warlimont himself in interrogations after the war stated flatly that the attack on Crete *did not* delay the Russian campaign, though it diverted some aircraft—particularly troop carriers—to Greece from the Russian front. He said that the *Greek* and *Yugoslav* invasions *did* delay "Barbarossa," but immediately qualified this assertion by adding that "it was questionable whether a start could have been made on 15 May due to the floods and the belated mud period following the severe winter in Russia."[143]

Brigadier General Hermann Burkhart Müller-Hillebrand, in a special postwar study of the German campaigns in the Balkans, points out that

theoretically, 15 May, 1941 was the earliest day for the start of the campaign against Russia, for this was the date set for the completion of all preparations.

However, another prerequisite for the beginning of this great offensive was the subsidence of the Russian spring floods caused by the melting of the snow. . . .

The unexpected campaign against Yugoslavia delayed the completion of the Barbarossa concentration by approximately six weeks, from May 15 to June 23 [*sic;* the invasion started June 22]. However it must be borne in mind that a postponement . . . from 15 May to some later date was necessitated in any case by the fact that Spring set in comparatively late. Even as late as the middle of June there were still heavy floods in the Polish-Russian river areas. It is therefore safe to state that, even without the operation against Yugoslavia, the Russian campaign would have been started only one or two weeks earlier than was actually the case."[144]

Charles von Luttichau, of the Office of the Chief of Military History, declares that "historical evidence does not support [the] assumption . . . that Moscow was saved at Athens, Belgrade and on Crete." He points out that May 15 was a "tentative date" for the Russian invasion, that "the spring of 1941 was unusually wet and abnormally heavy" with "widespread flooding," and that "the weather . . . more than anything else, prevented a start of the Russian campaign before 22 June."[145]

May 15 was the date when operational readiness for "Barbarossa" was to be completed, but even when it was set, it was understood that the date for actual invasion could not be established until nature itself had countersigned the feeble plans of man. For the blitzkrieg tactics Hitler intended to employ—he hoped to break the back of Russian resistance in about four months—there had to be tranquil rivers and firm footing for his tanks.

In the event, the spring of 1941 opened on a western Russia drowned in melting snow and seas of mud. The great rivers were in spate in May; whether or not "Barbarossa" had been officially postponed, it would have been impossible to strike with the speed and fury Hitler's plans demanded. The German Army would have been bogged down, waterlogged on the Russian frontiers, and the mobilization of "Mother Russia" would have started.

It is, therefore, impossible to conclude that the Balkan campaign and the stout defense of Crete in themselves delayed the invasion of Russia. Whether or not these battles had been fought, nature would have enforced delay. Nature, which in the spring of 1941 and again as fall gave way to early bitter winter five months after the invasion started, was Russia's greatest ally. This, rather than British courage, was the key factor in enforcing delay.

So Crete had no great influence upon the ultimate outcome of World War II. But those few days of wild melee forever altered the nature of warfare and left an imperishable record of the valor of Man.

CHAPTER 4

"THE ROCK"

THE FALL OF CORREGIDOR

December, 1941–May 6, 1942

MAY 6 (1942), 4:15 P.M.—PHILIPPINE

THEATRE:

THE WAR DEPARTMENT RECEIVED A MESSAGE FROM CORREGIDOR AD-
VISING THAT RESISTANCE OF OUR TROOPS HAS BEEN OVERCOME.
FIGHTING HAS CEASED.

Corregidor and Bataan will forever be, in American memory, synonymous with painful pride—pain in the worst defeat ever inflicted upon
American arms, pride in the courage of the men who fought and suffered
and died in the first campaign of the war in the Pacific.

To the United States in 1941, Manila Bay—as it was in the War
with Spain—was the nexus of our Western Pacific strategy. It was the
finest harbor under the U.S. flag in the Western Pacific, and it commanded the north-south shipping routes from Japan through the South
China Sea. It was the focus of U.S. power in the Orient; all of the Orange
(War with Japan) war plans emphasized the importance of Manila Bay.

The coming war with Japan was always envisaged, in the twenties
and thirties, as a naval campaign. But almost until the start of war there

were many U.S. naval strategists who still thought in terms of the Jutland-type fleet engagement and who foresaw after the war's start a move by the U.S. Fleet through, or past, the spiderweb of Japanese bases in the Mandated Islands (the Marshalls, Carolines and Gilberts) to the Philippines. Somewhere in this area—perhaps in the vicinity of the powerful and mysterious Japanese base at Truk—a fleet engagement would take place which would determine the course of the war. Japanese defeat at sea would permit the relief of the Philippines and the re-establishment of a U.S. base in Manila Bay, from which mop-up operations could be conducted.

The success of any such plan seemed to depend in considerable measure upon the availability of a protected fleet anchorage in Manila Bay. Our Philippine defenses were built around this concept. If U.S. and Filipino forces could hold Bataan Peninsula and the fortified islands at the entrance to Manila Bay, thus denying its use to an enemy for a period of three to six months, the fleet would be able, it was thought, to fight its way westward from Pearl Harbor and relieve and reinforce the defenses.

Nothing was said [Morton notes] in WPO-3 (War Plan—Orange—3) about what was to happen after the defenses on Bataan crumbled. Presumably by that time, estimated at six months, the U.S. Pacific Fleet would have fought its way across the Pacific, won a victory over the Combined [Japanese] Fleet, and made secure the line of communications. . . . The Philippine garrison, thus reenforced, could then counterattack and drive the enemy into the sea.[1]

The validity of such a concept in the age of air power was always open to much doubt. The mutually supporting network of Japanese sea and air bases throughout the Western Pacific, which stretched like a shield across all the maritime approaches to the Philippines, and the tremendous strength of Japan, which had been grossly underestimated, made the hope of relief for the Philippines a chimera. In fact, long before Pearl Harbor the original concept had been completely modified.

In late 1940 and early 1941, despite the unwritten hopes of WPO-3, there was at least a tacit understanding between the Army and Navy in Washington that if the Japanese struck, the Philippines were doomed; nothing we could do, short of two or more years of war, could relieve them.

"The Philippines had been virtually written off as indefensible in a war with Japan."[2]

Washington had already agreed in staff talks with the British (the U.S.-British Commonwealth Joint Basic War Plan, March, 1941) that the main enemy was Germany; until the Nazis were defeated the Pacific was to be a secondary theater.

This attitude suddenly changed in the summer and fall of 1941. The infectious and misplaced optimism and dynamism of General Mac-Arthur, who at the end of July was appointed Commander, U.S. Army Forces in the Far East, a post which would include under its control forces of the Philippine Commonwealth, was largely responsible for the change in *emphasis* in the war plans. MacArthur believed the United States should, and in time could, hold the entire Philippine Archipelago, and the War Department caught his enthusiasm. When he was recalled to active duty to assume his new post, MacArthur was Military Adviser to the Philippine Commonwealth, with the rank of field marshal and "a scrambled egg" hat of his own design.

As an adviser he had developed plans for the defense of the Philippines, which were still chiefly on paper when crisis came. But their theoretical nature had not prevented MacArthur, in sweeping overstatements typical of many of his pronouncements, from predicting a strong defense which could turn away any enemy, or at least make conquest of the islands not worth the price. He became an enthusiast about the Philippine military potential. But in the summer of 1941, a few short months before catastrophe, the Philippine Army existed chiefly in his dreams. Barracks, camp sites, training facilities and equipment, and, above all, the hard core of any army—trained officers—were conspicuously lacking.

When war came not a single division had been completely mobilized and not one of the units was at full strength. . . . Discipline . . . left much to be desired. . . . There was a serious shortage in almost all types of equipment. . . . The enlisted men seemed . . . to be proficient in only two things: "One, when an officer appeared, to yell attention in a loud voice, jump up and salute; the other, to demand three meals per day."[3]

Throughout his career MacArthur was cast, in his own mind and in his view of history, as a man of destiny; he never doubted the validity of his own views, and wherever he served should be, he felt, the focus of American efforts. He had an ability, too, to dramatize, to communicate and to persuade; his powerful personality, his charm and his military seniority mesmerized some of his Army subordinates, both in Manila and in Washington.

But the change in emphasis in U.S. war plans in the summer of 1941 was not wholly due to MacArthur's persuasiveness.

General George C. Marshall, Army Chief of Staff, told his staff on August 1 that "it was the policy of the United States to defend the Philippines," and plans for reinforcing the islands—a complete reversal of past policy—were put in hand. Philippine political pressures, public opinion and, particularly, miscalculations in Washington helped to lead to this change and to the subsequent but futile reinforcement.

A major overassessment of the capabilities of air power—the product of the persuasiveness and propaganda of General "Hap" Arnold (Major General Henry H. Arnold, Chief of the Army Air Forces) and of the bright young officers he had selected to create and to "sell" the new form of warfare—was in part responsible. A heavy air reinforcement of the islands was started in midsummer, 1941, and under the new and optimistic plans the War Department hoped to have a strength of 165 heavy bombers in the islands by March, 1942.

The doctrines of Giulio Douhet, the Italian prophet of victory through air power, and of Alexander de Seversky were exciting stimuli in the summer of 1941, and the theorists of strategic air warfare found ready markets for their views. Even professional judgment and long military experience were not immune to the new-found enthusiasm. General Marshall, in a background secret press briefing for some seven Washington correspondents on November 15, 1941 (three weeks before the Pearl Harbor attack), epitomized the misjudgments of the time.

He noted that war with Japan was imminent, but he felt the U.S. position in the Philippines was highly favorable. Our strength in the islands, he said, was far larger than the Japanese imagined. We were preparing not only to defend the Philippines but to conduct an aerial offensive from these islands against Japan. Thirty-five B-17 Flying Fortresses were based in the Philippines—*the greatest concentration of heavy bomber strength anywhere in the world* (italics the author's). More planes were being sent to the islands; so were tanks and guns; the Philippines were being reinforced daily. If war did start, the B-17's would immediately attack the enemy's naval bases and would set the "paper" cities of Japan on fire. Although the B-17 did not have enough range to reach Japan and return to Philippine bases, General Marshall, with a political naïveté characteristic of many of our military men at the time, said optimistically that the bombers could continue on to Russian Vladivostok and would carry out shuttle bombing raids frrom Vladivostok and Philippine territory.

The new Convair B-24 bombers would soon be in production, General Marshall said, and these planes would be able to *fly higher than any Japanese interceptors* (italics the author's).

The General summed up the then current Army optimism in one of the most amazingly mistaken appraisals of history. By about mid-December, he said, the War Department would feel rather secure in the Philippines. Flying weather over Japan was good; our high-flying bombers could quickly wreak havoc. If a Pacific war started, *there would not be much need for our Navy;* the U.S. bombers could spearhead a victory offensive virtually singlehanded, or, to paraphrase General Marshall's words, *without the use of our shipping* (italics the author's). Our own Pacific Fleet would stay out of range of Japanese air power in Hawaii.[4]

General Marshall's optimism, in turn induced by MacArthur's and

"Hap" Arnold's enthusiasm, grew, too, from the fertile soil of ignorance
—an ignorance then generally shared in the Army: the ignorance of what
air power meant, a lack of understanding of maritime power and an
astigmatic appreciation of the Japanese.

Yet it was already too little and too late. When the Japanese struck
on December 7, 1941, there were only two operational radar sets in the
Philippine Islands, 35 heavy bombers, and probably no more than 60
operational first-line fighters. The ten reserve divisions of the Philippine
Army had been partially mobilized. There were more than 100,000
Filipinos in some kind of uniform, but most of them knew little and
cared less about the mechanics of warfare. U.S. Army troops numbered
31,095 on November 30, including almost 12,000 Philippine Scouts, an
elite and well-trained special part of the Regular Army (Philippine
enlisted men, officered chiefly by Americans).[5]

But the Navy Department, which did not share the War Department's optimism about the defensibility of the Philippines, could promise
no reinforcements for the Asiatic Fleet, and as late as November 20
ordered Admiral Thomas C. Hart, its "small, taut, wiry and irascible"[6]
commander, to carry out the preplanned deployment of his fleet southward, as the war plan required, rather than concentrate in Manila Bay,
as Admiral Hart had suggested.

Admiral Hart knew, as did General MacArthur, that no relief was
anticipated for the Philippines until the U.S. Pacific Fleet had made a
step-by-step advance through the Caroline and Marshall islands and had
seized an advanced base at Truk. This concept was embodied in the
Rainbow 5 plan, a global plan worked out in conformity with the
British, anticipating war by the United States against both Germany and
Japan, thus updating the obsolescent Orange 1 ocean-war plan. But
Rainbow 5, which grew out of staff talks between the United States and
Britain in January, February and March, 1941, and which was completed
shortly before Pearl Harbor, clearly called for a defensive strategy in the
Pacific and implicitly, at least, "accepted . . . the loss of the Philippines,
Guam and Wake."[7] It stated initially that the United States did not
expect to add to its military strength in the Far East, but a revision in
November, 1941, the product of the new and optimistic Army attitude in
Washington and Manila, authorized offensive air operations "in further-
ance of the strategic defensive."

Both the Orange war plans and Rainbow 5 contemplated concentration of Philippine defenses around the entrance to Manila Bay, but
General MacArthur's Philippine Commonwealth plans envisaged a defense of the entire archipelago—even though the plans would not be
fully effective until 1946, when the Philippines had been scheduled to
become politically independent.

To the Japanese, the conquest of the Philippines represented a fractional segment of an ambitious program of conquest, which was to make the island empire predominant in the Western Pacific and in Asia. The oil and rubber and potential wealth of Malaya and the Indonesian archipelago were the economic goals and major objectives. The U.S. Pacific Fleet was to be immobilized by the surprise attack on Pearl Harbor, its island outposts at Guam and Wake seized, and simultaneous attacks upon U.S., British and Dutch positions were to be launched. Earmarked for the invasion of the Philippines was the Fourteenth Army, Lieutenant General Masaharu Homma commanding, consisting (initially) of the 16th and 48th Divisions and the 65th Brigade. It was supported by the 5th Air Group (Japanese Army); Eleventh Air Fleet (Japanese Navy), and the Japanese Third Fleet.

Air strikes, aided by preliminary landings to seize air bases, were to destroy U.S. air power in the islands. Major landings at Lamon Bay and along Lingayen Gulf on Luzon and at Davao in Mindanao would lead to rapid conquest, Tokyo believed. U.S. forces on Luzon were expected to make their main and last stand around Manila.

"Imperial General Headquarters . . . expected General Homma to complete his mission in about fifty days; at the end of that time, approximately half of the 14th Army were to leave the Philippines [for other more vital areas]. . . . Little difficulty was expected."[8]

But war never goes, for either victor or vanquished, "according to plan."

The scope, speed, power and intensity of the Japanese surprise assaults astounded the world. The attack upon Pearl Harbor wrecked many of the battleships of the U.S. Pacific Fleet, and stunned and unified the nation.

In the Western Pacific "during the early morning hours of the 8th (7th of December east longitude), Japanese naval and air forces struck almost simultaneously at Kota Bharu in British Malaya (0140), Singora, just across the border in Thailand (0305), Singapore (0610), Guam (0805), Hong Kong (0900), Wake, and the Philippines."[9]

To the Japanese, Malaya, Singapore and Indonesia were the No. 1 objectives, with the Philippines secondary to these goals. The enemy had been somewhat alarmed by the build-up of American air strength in the islands. They had been informed that the United States had 900 planes in the islands, but a Japanese photoreconnaissance plane, apparently flying at such a height that it was never detected, really won the Philippine campaign for Japan in the late days of November before a shot was fired. The enemy plane photographed carefully and spotted our principal plane concentrations in the islands, and as a result the Japanese revised their estimates of our air strength downward to 300 planes and made careful plans for destroying our aircraft on the ground in early morning December 8 (December 7, Pearl Harbor time). Bad weather intervened, and the first actual bombing attacks were made between noon and 1 P.M., December 8 (hours after Pearl Harbor) instead of at dawn. But 192 planes, all long-range naval planes based on Formosa, participated and the result was still the same—surprise and unprecedented execution among our "sitting ducks." Other determined raids from Formosa, eventually bolstered by short-range Japanese Army planes based at other landing fields captured in the first invasions, quickly followed up the enemy's initial advantage.

The Japanese successes—products of surprise, careful training and their foes' overconfidence—were astounding. In the first day of war U.S. air power in the Philippines, upon which so many hopes had been airborne, was mortally hurt. By the end of the first week U.S. air power in the islands had been virtually destroyed at a cost to the Japanese of 30 planes; the naval stations at Cavite, Mariveles and Olongapo (Subic Bay) had been bombed; most of the remaining mobile units of the Asiatic Fleet had fled to the south; and the Japanese dominated the air and the sea.

Land invasions quickly followed the air blows. Orders for the invasion had reached Lieutenant General Homma on Formosa, on November 20, 1941, 18 days before Pearl Harbor, but Japanese Formosan forces had actually commenced training for the invasion in March, 1941.

The Japanese Second Fleet, under Vice Admiral Nobutake Kondo, earmarked for support of the Southwestern Pacific operations, rendezvoused in the Inland Sea about the middle of November, sortied on the twenty-third, and proceeded to Formosa, where it received word of D-day. This fleet (fleet organization in the Japanese Navy was flexible and strengths varied greatly) originally consisted of the battleships *Haruna* and *Kongo,* and the heavy cruisers *Takao, Atago, Chokai* and *Maya,* but it was reinforced for the operation by other cruisers and light vessels. The main body, which acted only in general support, consisted of the two battleships, two heavy cruisers and four destroyers. The Philippine Island group, divided into four task forces for close support, transport protection and other duties, consisted of 6 heavy cruisers, 3 light cruisers, 46 destroyers and auxiliary vessels. The Eleventh Air Fleet, with headquarters in Takao, Formosa, supported the Philippine operation with about 300 planes, land-based on Formosa. About 150 Japanese Army planes, based on Formosa, also supported the Philippine operations, but until air bases in the Philippines were seized, the range of the Army planes did not permit them to operate over central Luzon or the Manila-Bataan area. After the invasion, Army air units from Formosa moved to Laoag and Vigan, but the fields were unusable and the Japanese planes were subsequently based on captured Clark and Nichols Fields.

JAPAN

CHINA

EAST CHINA SEA

RYUKYU ISLANDS · · OKINAWA

FORMOSA

HONG KONG
DECEMBER 8

DECEMBER 10

Laoag
Vigan · Aparri
LUZON

INDOCHINA

THAILAND

Bangkok

SOUTH CHINA SEA

Manila

DECEMBER 12

Saigon

Legaspi PHILIPPINE ISLANDS

Singora

DECEMBER 8

Kota Bharu

NORTH BORNEO
BRUNEI

PANAY
NEGROS

SAMAR

MINDANAO

MALAY STATES

DECEMBER 16

SARAWAK

Davao

DECEMBER 20

SUMATRA

Singapore

FEBRUARY 14

BORNEO

CELEBES

NETHERLANDS EAST INDIES

NEW GUINEA

Batavia

JAVA SEA

BANDA SEA

FEBRUARY 28

JAVA

TIMOR

FEBRUARY 19

Darwin

INDIAN OCEAN

THE WAR WITH JAPAN
December, 1941, to February, 1942
Dates shown are those of first Japanese attacks

0   MILES   1000

AUSTRALIA

The Japanese Third Fleet, which consisted of the actual transports, supply ships (about 60 in number), mine sweepers, invasion forces and supporting naval craft (cruisers, destroyers and submarines), with the heavy cruiser *Ashigara* as flagship, was based on Formosa and Palau. That section of it which conducted the invasion of northwestern Luzon sortied from Formosa early December 10 and made its first landing at Aparri the same day. Another landing at Vigan quickly followed. There was virtually no opposition, except for sporadic attacks by a few American planes, which cost the Aparri force one mine sweeper sunk and one damaged, and the Vigan force one subchaser and one transport sunk.

The United States quickly claimed that Captain Colin Kelly, Jr. in a B-17 bomber had sunk the Japanese battleship *Haruna,* and Kelly was subsequently awarded posthumously a Distinguished Service Cross. But the *Haruna,* actually sunk three years later at the war's end at Kure, Japan, was not even attacked; she was in the support force of the Second Fleet far from the Philippine coastline. Kelly may have bombed the heavy cruiser *Ashigara,* but she was not damaged.

Forces from Palau conducted the invasions of southeastern Luzon (the Japanese landed at Legaspi December 11) and of Mindanao, and on December 22 the largest Japanese landing took place, as expected, at Lingayen Gulf.

The American forces were woefully inadequate in number, equipment and training for defense of the vast Luzon coastline. Many of the enemy landing places had been anticipated, but the number of them and their timing, and the pincer movement of the enemy from north and south, put the small American forces in a hopeless strategic position. This was particularly true since the defense of the Philippines had been based primarily upon the Philippine Army, large on numbers but short on quality. Most of its men had had only five and a half months' training; most of its units were still being mobilized when the Japanese attacks came; officers were insufficient in number and quality; equipment was lacking; and the Philippine idea of discipline was rudimentary. Most of the Japanese landings were virtually unopposed, and many of the Filipino "divisions" from which so much had been hoped virtually melted away into the hills (some of them to become guerrillas, most to return to their homes) soon after the first shots were fired.

By Christmas the principal Japanese landings had been easily made good against weak and badly organized opposition; no supplies or reinforcements had reached the Philippines, and MacArthur and his polyglot forces were cut off in a widening sea of Japanese conquest. And on Luzon General MacArthur, at last convinced by the poor fighting qualities of the Philippine Army, had already ordered a withdrawal into Bataan.

It was a disorderly but successful withdrawal, save for those Philippine Army units that simply disappeared into the bush. But the hard core of U.S. regulars and the highly trained and intensely loyal Philippine Scouts wrote a brief chapter of glory in retreat as the hard-pressed forces of the United States converged on Bataan Peninsula.

Corregidor, the tadpole-shaped island off the peninsula of Bataan at the entrance of Manila Bay, became the headquarters of all U.S. and Philippine forces in the archipelago, and of President Manuel L. Quezon of the Philippine Commonwealth and High Commissioner Francis B. Sayre. Men, supplies, equipment and food moved in a sporadic, hasty stream from Manila and elsewhere on Luzon by sea and land to Bataan and Corregidor. By the end of the first week of the year 1942, Manila, long-time capital of the Philippines, pride of American power in the Orient, had been captured, and all organized U.S. forces in Luzon were holed up in Bataan Peninsula and in the fortified islands at the entrance to Manila Bay.

The embattled garrisons did not know it then, but already all hope of relief had gone. Everywhere the Japanese were triumphant; everywhere the Allies were on the defensive; everywhere there was too little. United States naval and air power was stretched thin. There were, in a world at war, far more vital areas than the Philippines. The few but precious resources, of ships, of planes, of men, of guns, could not be risked in a vain hope. The islands, once the pride of American "manifest destiny," were written off.

And so the long trial started, complicated for the defenders by the sudden changes in war plans in the prewar months and by the very increments of "strength"—the Philippine Army—which had proved so insubstantial and unreliable in the first weeks of war.

Eighty thousand troops plus 26,000 civilian refugees—most of them Filipinos—crowded into Bataan;[10] original plans had contemplated 43,000. Instead of supplies for six months cached in the peninsula, dumps of food and equipment had been shifted to the invasion beaches and other points on Luzon to support MacArthur's last-minute plan to defend all of the Philippines.

For years our "Orange" war plans had envisaged withdrawal into Bataan and the fortified islands at the entrance to Manila Bay; yet in December, 1941, there were not even field fortifications on the peninsula and the section naval base at Mariveles, near its tip, was far from finished. Although the Philippines lie close to the greatest quinine-producing areas in the world, there was a grossly inadequate supply of that drug in the Army's stores on Luzon. There were no mosquito nets, shelter halves or blankets; uniforms, clothing and shoes were in short supply. The Philippine recruits looked like "Cox's Army."

The consequences were decisive and catastrophic. There was only enough food for 20 to 50 days (depending on the item; i.e., 20 days of rice, 50 days of canned meat and fish, etc.). Gasoline had to be carefully rationed; there was not enough of anything.

The shortage of supplies of all types, and especially of food, had a greater effect on the outcome of the siege of Bataan than any other single factor. "Each day's combat, each day's output of physical energy," wrote one officer in his diary, "took its toll of the human body—a toll which could not be repaired. . . ." When this fact is understood, he added, the story of Bataan is told.[11]

Corregidor, which had long been the site of a permanent garrison and was manned by coast artillery, headquarters and service troops, had long been stocked with food. This supply was augmented just before Christmas by supplies transported from Manila—enough, theoretically, to feed 10,000 men for six months. Even so, "The Rock's" military and paramilitary population was immensely swollen by a whole series of high-echelon headquarters—Army, Navy, Philippine Government and U.S. High Commissioner—and by QM troops and other units evacuated from Manila. The same Churchillian paraphrase that later was applied to the Allied headquarters in North Africa—"Never in the course of human history have so few been commanded by so many"—might have been applied to USAFFE (United States Army Forces in the Far East) and Corregidor. The addition of a stout combat increment—the only infantry "The Rock" had—the 4th Marine Regiment, Colonel Samuel Howard commanding, which had been evacuated from Shanghai, added strength, and the Marines brought their own rations with them. Nevertheless, even on Corregidor rationing was in effect almost from the first day of war, and two meals a day was the routine.

And so the slow death started with no hope of succor, near or far.

Corregidor, a rugged rocky island, with three high hill masses—the highest rising to 550 feet—and a low, flat, tadpole-shaped tail to the east, is almost four miles long and one and a half miles wide at its extremities. It was covered at the beginning of the siege with tropic verdure, and it stood out green and glowing against the lovely background of Manila Bay. "The Rock," at the outbreak of war, was famous as a fortress, but it was built in the days when the plane was not a menace, and, like Singapore, its designers had anticipated that the main assault would come from the sea, not from the nearby shores of Bataan. Its coast-defense guns were rather well sited to repel an attack by naval vessels, but were of little use against land targets.

Corregidor's defenses were formidable on paper—and in some respects formidable in fact. Its batteries of World War I design, mounted a total of 56 coast-defense guns and mortars, plus some 24 3-inch antiaircraft guns and 48 .50-caliber machine guns. These were mounted behind concrete barbettes, in open pits or in sandbagged positions vulnerable to

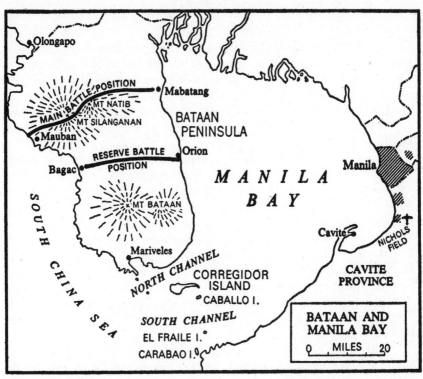

Olongapo

MAIN BATTLE POSITION
MT NATIB
MT SILANGANAN
Mauban
Mabatang

BATAAN PENINSULA

RESERVE BATTLE POSITION
Bagac
Orion

MANILA BAY

Manila

MT BATAAN

SOUTH CHINA SEA

Mariveles

NORTH CHANNEL

CORREGIDOR ISLAND
CABALLO I.

Cavite

CAVITE PROVINCE

NICHOLS FIELD

SOUTH CHANNEL
EL FRAILE I.
CARABAO I.

BATAAN AND MANILA BAY

0   MILES   20

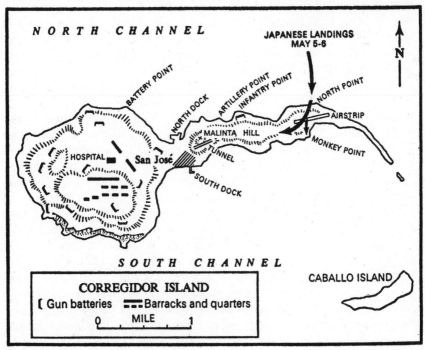

NORTH CHANNEL

JAPANESE LANDINGS MAY 5-6

N

BATTERY POINT

NORTH DOCK
ARTILLERY POINT
INFANTRY POINT
NORTH POINT
AIRSTRIP
MALINTA HILL
MONKEY POINT
HOSPITAL
San José
TUNNEL
SOUTH DOCK

SOUTH CHANNEL

CABALLO ISLAND

CORREGIDOR ISLAND
{ Gun batteries   ▄▄▄ Barracks and quarters
0   MILE   1

air attack. There were eight 12-inch guns and ten 12-inch mortars, plus many of smaller caliber. But there were few star shells for illumination at night, little high explosive or shells useful against land targets, and the mechanical fuses for the 3-inch AA high-explosive shells were critically short. The AA guns, with an obsolescent fire control system, were too few, too small and too old to be very effective against modern high-flying bombers.

Corregidor's famous tunnel system provided underground bomb-proof and shellproof protection for stores, ammunition, communications, headquarters and medical spaces. Malinta Tunnel, 1,400 feet long and 30 feet wide, gouged by a far-seeing general through the 400-foot mass of Malinta Hill, gave a protected route of access from the eastern to the western portions of Corregidor. A small electric railroad ran through it. Laterals opened off the main tunnel, and a separate network of connecting tunnels, which took their names from the activities housed in them, provided hospital space, quartermaster storage area, headquarters, gasoline storage, the "Navy Tunnel" and so on. The weakness was the air supply; in the humid, hot Philippines the tunnels, crowded with men, could become stifling.

One of the island's greatest deficiencies was the water supply. There were some 21 wells on the island, but the supply was insufficient for the wartime population; much of it had to come, in the initial stages of the war, by barge from Sisiman Cove on Bataan.[12] An even greater weakness was the island's exposed power plant, which provided electricity to pump water from the wells, ventilate the tunnels, run the railroad, preserve perishable foods and train and elevate the seacoast batteries. The power plant was sited on what was called "Bottomside," a narrow, low-lying area only slightly above sea level; it had no protection against bombing. It was too small for the demands made upon it, and power and communication wires were strung on the surface, or so close to the surface that, during the siege, they were severed repeatedly by enemy shells and bombs.

The outlying, or satellite, islands around Corregidor were in some ways even more powerful than "The Rock," though each was so small that it could not hope, without Corregidor's support, to withstand a long siege. Fort Hughes on Caballo Island boasted 11 coast defense guns, including two 14-inch and four 12-inch mortars, and a battery of four 3-inch antiaircraft guns. Fort Frank on Carabao, a small island, with precipitous 100-foot cliffs, about a quarter of a mile from Cavite Province, mounted two 14-inch and eight 12-inch mortars in addition to smaller batteries. Fort Drum on El Fraile Island was called the "concrete battleship" and was the most heavily protected of all the Manila Bay fortifications. The top of the tiny island had been shaved off and four 14-inch guns in armored turrets, buried in heavy concrete, covered the seaward approaches. Smaller coast-defense guns were also heavily protected by walls of concrete and steel varying from 20 to almost 40 feet thick. With overhead protection for most of the gunners, and even a latticework steel mast (like an old battleship's) for observation, Fort Drum was considered "impregnable."

Indeed, the defenses of Manila Bay had once been properly called "the Gibraltar of the East." But, like Singapore's guns, Corregidor's batteries and those of the outlying forts were sited against attack from the sea, not from the land or indeed from the air. The fortifications were built for another, and now vanished, era of warfare, before the plane had brought new peril to fixed emplacements. And a stroke of a pen in 1922, when the Washington Naval (Disarmament, or Limitations) Treaty was signed, condemned the "Gibraltar of the East" to increasing obsolescence. For the United States agreed in the treaty that it would not construct additional fortifications or naval bases in the Western Pacific or modernize those already built in Guam, Wake, Midway and the Philippines.

Little did the hopeful disarmament advocates and pacifists of that day realize that their action had condemned thousands of Americans in a future war to death and imprisonment.

The defense of Bataan, closely coordinated with the defense of the fortified islands, was exercised by General MacArthur from his headquarters on Corregidor, through an advanced echelon on Bataan.

A 20-mile "main battle" line stretched across the peninsula from Mabatang—separated by the wild mountain massifs of Mount Natib and Mount Silanganan—to Mauban on the South China Sea. Major General Jonathan Wainwright commanded the I Philippine Corps on the west; Major General George M. Parker, Jr., the II Philippine Corps on the east. Wainwright's command, numbering about 22,500 men, included three Philippine Army divisions, part of another division, the 26th Cavalry (Philippine Scouts) which had lost heavily in covering the withdrawal into Bataan, and miscellaneous troops and light artillery. Parker's II Corps included four Philippine Army Divisions, some artillery and a regiment of the Philippine Scouts—in all about 25,000 men.

Filipinos, half-trained and poorly equipped, comprised by far the greater portion of the defense strength. The Philippine division, a unit of the regular U.S. Army, was the best of General MacArthur's units. It consisted of one regiment—the 31st Infantry—of U.S. officers and enlisted men, two regiments of Philippine Scouts and supporting artillery and other units of Philippine Scouts. The division, which had numbered before the fighting started more than 10,470 officers and men, was officered initially almost entirely by Americans, and included a total of about 2,056 U.S. enlisted men; the rest were Filipinos. These troops, plus the few small U.S. Army units that had reached the Philippines before hostilities started, were the real backbone of the defense.

But it was a weak backbone. For the combat strength of the U.S. infantry on Bataan—one regiment—numbered only about 2,000 men, bolstered by about 4,300 Filipinos of the 45th and 57th Philippine Scout regiments, by some 300 men of the understrength 43rd Infantry, Philippine Scouts, and by the 26th Cavalry, Philippine Scouts, which originally had numbered more than 842 officers and men, but had incurred sizable losses in covering the withdrawal into Bataan. General MacArthur could count therefore upon less than 6,000 reliable and well-trained infantrymen. These were backed up, however, by a U.S. MP company, and two tank battalions—the 192nd and 194th—composed chiefly of U.S. personnel.

Eight miles behind the main battle position from near Orion to Bagac stretched a "rear battle position"—originally envisaged as the peninsula's main defensive line. But this position had not been completed, and reserve troops were assigned to work on it, while the forward position was held. Around the extreme tip of the peninsula was the service command, supplics, hospitals, support and maintenance units and so on.

This was a heterogeneous army. U.S. troops backed up, stiffened and supported the Filipinos; the beaches and coastal flanks were held by mixed units of Marines, sailors without ships, airmen without planes, and supply, quartermaster and maintenance troops converted into provisional infantry. Even civilians participated in the defense.

Corregidor and its satellite islets had mixed and motley garrisons. The prewar strength of the fortified islands had not exceeded 6,000 men, mostly coast artillerymen and support and maintenance personnel. These included originally about 5,200 men of the Harbor Defenses, all of them, except 1,500 Philippine Scouts, Americans. But this cadre had been swollen by headquarters and supply units and refugees: the 4th Marine Regiment, sailors, nurses, Filipinos, a military police company, ordnance companies, engineer companies, a service detachment and many "bits and pieces." The total approximated 9,000 to 10,000 men.

The first attacks on Corregidor occurred even before the headquarters had "shaken down" in their new surroundings. A heavy Japanese bombing raid on December 29, the first of more than 300 air attacks on Corregidor, blasted the Middleside Barracks, where the 4th Marines, bolstered by attached Marine detachments from abandoned Olongapo and Cavite, were quartered, and killed one man and wounded one. The Marines moved out to beach defenses all over "The Rock," and from then until the end lived in scattered groups near their guns—in foxholes, shelters, tunnels.

The troops on "The Rock" turned to in the sweltering heat while guns boomed on Bataan. More than 20 miles of barbed wire were strung in the eastern sector; the miscellaneous collection of light artillery available as antiboat or beach-defense guns were adapted, sited and dug in. Foxholes and tank traps were constructed, concrete trenches poured, cable barriers and mines laid off the little harbors of the island, bombs and other homemade land mines fused and emplaced.

Some of the defense positions had to be hacked with bolo knives out of the thick jungle vegetation, for Corregidor at the beginning of the siege was densely overgrown. Monkeys, who pilfered soap and flashlights, chattered and swung from the long lianas, and there were even a few small deer on the island. But they died quickly beneath the shells and bombs, and the deer provided a welcome addition to a meager diet.

From December 29 through January 6 "The Rock" was bombed almost daily, and Battery Smith (12-inch guns, barbette carriage) and Battery Way (12-inch mortars) were damaged, supplies were burned or destroyed, the island's little railroad was wrecked. Many of the buildings were destroyed. Telephone and communication wires, which should have been buried deep beneath the surface, were continually riddled by fragments; the damage done by one bombing was no sooner cleared up than another attack compounded it. It was dig and work and toil, and lie flat on the belly and claw the earth when the whoosh of the bombs gave warning of death.

There was a marked falling off in the rain of death from the skies between January 7 and 11. Then there were for a long time only sporadic and intermittent attacks, usually by a few planes, but with alarms several times a day. The bombing continued, impassive, deliberate, unhurried, demoniac.

There was not much to be done about it; the Japanese often flew above the range of the 3-inch "sky" guns, and at best there were only a few seconds when the guns could reach them. But the gunners fired anyway, to keep up morale, and occasionally a Japanese bomber plummeted into the bay or disappeared above the hills of the mainland, trailing smoke.[13]

On "The Rock" the Marines and their Army "buddies" worked and sweated. They gradually grew lean and bronze and tense, with fine lines about the eyes, and the faint facial shadows of sleepless nights and hours of strain. They came to look a bit like the island about them. The fulsome loveliness of Corregidor was dying; great trees were splintered and burned; the good earth showed the raw pockmarks of the bombs; at any position on the island there was a bomb crater within 25 yards.

As early as January 5 all personnel on Bataan were placed on half-rations—2,000 calories per day, a starvation diet for men working and fighting in rugged terrain and climate.

There were no great battles on Bataan—except in the newspapers back home. In the communiqués—many of them with the rolling phrases

which were to be characteristic of MacArthur's pronouncements throughout the war—we often "defeated" the enemy, and the size of the Japanese
forces and the scale of their attacks were exaggerated.

On January 10, just as the first Japanese assaults against Bataan
were starting, MacArthur paid his first—and perhaps his *only*—visit to
Bataan.[14] The Commander in Chief inspected I and II Corps positions
and then returned to his tunnel headquarters on Corregidor.

General Homma commenced his first assault against the II Corps on
January 9 with an inferior force. His best division, the 48th, had been
ordered south along with the 5th Air Group after the capture of Manila,
to invade Java. The 16th Japanese Division, the 65th Brigade and the
7th Tank Regiment—none of them first-rate units—totaling collectively
about 25,000 men, attacked a Filipino-American Army almost twice its
strength. Japanese intelligence estimates were, however, grossly overoptimistic. Nevertheless, within one week the Japanese had driven a wedge,
in the rugged mountain area, between the I and II Corps and had turned
the II Corps inland flank.

So serious was the situation that an historic and controversial order
was issued:

FORT MILLS, P.I.

JAN. 15, 1942

SUBJECT: MESSAGE FROM GENERAL MACARTHUR

TO: ALL UNIT COMMANDERS

THE FOLLOWING MESSAGE FROM GENERAL MACARTHUR WILL BE READ AND EX-
PLAINED TO ALL TROOPS. EVERY COMPANY COMMANDER IS CHARGED WITH PERSONAL
RESPONSIBILITY FOR THE DELIVERY OF THIS MESSAGE. EACH HEADQUARTERS WILL
FOLLOW UP TO INSURE RECEPTION BY EVERY COMPANY OR SIMILAR UNIT:

"HELP IS ON THE WAY FROM THE UNITED STATES. THOUSANDS OF TROOPS AND
HUNDREDS OF PLANES ARE BEING DISPATCHED. THE EXACT TIME OF ARRIVAL OF RE-
INFORCEMENTS IS UNKNOWN AS THEY WILL HAVE TO FIGHT THEIR WAY THROUGH
JAPANESE ATTEMPTS AGAINST THEM. IT IS IMPERATIVE THAT OUR TROOPS HOLD UNTIL
THESE REINFORCEMENTS ARRIVE.

NO FURTHER RETREAT IS POSSIBLE. WE HAVE MORE TROOPS IN BATAAN THAN THE
JAPANESE HAVE THROWN AGAINST US; OUR SUPPLIES ARE AMPLE; A DETERMINED
DEFENSE WILL DEFEAT THE ENEMY'S ATTACK.

IT IS A QUESTION NOW OF COURAGE AND DETERMINATION. MEN WHO RUN WILL
MERELY BE DESTROYED BUT MEN WHO FIGHT WILL SAVE THEMSELVES AND THEIR
COUNTRY.

I CALL UPON EVERY SOLDIER IN BATAAN TO FIGHT IN HIS ASSIGNED POSITION, RE-
SISTING EVERY ATTACK. THIS IS THE ONLY ROAD TO SALVATION. IF WE FIGHT WE WILL
WIN; IF WE RETREAT WE WILL BE DESTROYED.

MACARTHUR

BY COMMAND OF GENERAL MACARTHUR

This order briefly raised the hopes of some but was an ultimate
depressant, since its promise of aid could never be kept, and MacArthur

must have known this. For the "thousands of troops and hundreds of planes" (in itself a generalized exaggeration) were being sent to Australia and the Malay barrier, not through the iron ring of the Japanese blockade to the Philippines. Captain John W. Clark wrote that "by the middle of January it had become apparent that ours was a holding scrap out here, with no hope of reenforcement or aid."

And soon others saw this was so; even Corregidor felt an ominous sense of foreboding.

On "The Rock" they scanned the skies and the tropic seas to westward, but the only planes they saw bore the "fried egg" insignia of Japan upon their wings, and the only reinforcements they received were the casuals and the stragglers, the broken units of Bataan, and the bloody wounded, crowding now into the tunnel laterals of Malinta.

By January 23–24 both I and II Corps, their lines infiltrated and penetrated, were in full retreat to the Bagac-Orion position. Against the Japanese combat aggressiveness, their will to die and their infiltration tactics, the Filipinos and Americans had little to offer. The Japanese losses were heavy—1,472 combat casualties in the 65th Brigade, of an original strength of 6,651—but I Corps lost most of its field artillery; one regiment, the 51st (Philippine Army), disintegrated in rout and panic, and MacArthur estimated his losses at 35 percent, with some divisions depleted by as much as 60 percent. Before the end of January the defenders of Bataan were occupying their final, no-retreat, last-stand positions.

In early February shells began falling on Corregidor and the other islands in the bay from the Cavite shore. The enemy emplaced at first 105's, later 150's and 240's, on the high ground south of Manila Bay and began a systematic attempt to silence the island's batteries.

The shellings usually occurred between 0830 and 1130; the morning haze and the rising sun made it impossible for American gunners to spot the enemy's gun flashes.

Corregidor's garrison quickly accustomed itself to artillery fire and carried on, but the furrows and the gouges and the shadows across the face of the island and the faces of its defenders grew and lengthened. Slowly damage and casualties mounted, and Signal Corps linemen, ordnance repairmen and the medicos were busy day and night.

The men of the 4th Marines, the island's only infantry, shaved when they could, and bathed by crawling through the barbed wire on the beaches and swimming at night in the warm waters of the bay. They found themselves stumbling over things in the darkness; the lack of Vitamin A in their monotonous ration gave them night blindness.

On Bataan the surging, clashing lines came wearily to rest from Bagac to Orion, and the campaign settled into bloody piecemeal struggles divided and dispersed by the green compartmentation of the jungle.

The Philippines were isolated; the tide of conquest had spread far to the south, and its backwash eddied, ever rising, about Bataan and Corregidor.

Time worked for Japan. There was not food enough for both the civilians and the fighting men on Bataan. The newly inducted, badly trained and poorly disciplined Philippine Army privates and corporals handled many of the QM supplies, and food had a habit of disappearing between the QM depots and the front. Some of the Filipino civilians on Bataan lived well off pilfered Army rations and some of the men in the rear areas ate slimly but passably, but the men at the front had virtually nothing but rice from January on, pieced out occasionally with mule steak, carabao and the horses of the famous 26th Cavalry.

On Bataan, as the weeks dragged on, the field hospitals were full; many of the patients mumbled in the grip of the shivering ague and the hot delirium of malaria. Dengue and dysentery were spreading; sleeplessness and hopelessness and hunger made potential victims of all the Army of Bataan. Sleeplessness was part of the Japanese strategy; all night long the tropic dark flickered with the lightning of the guns, and the detonation of the enemy's heavy mortar shells murdered rest.

There was little reflection of this situation in the papers in the States. The official communiqués spoke vaguely of "heavy Jap losses." The headquarters of General MacArthur on Corregidor on March 8, in an announcement broadcast throughout the world, pictured Lieutenant General Masaharu Homma, then the Japanese commander of the forces besieging Luzon, as dying under a hara-kiri knife, "disgraced by his defeats."

The communiqué from Bataan on March 8, 1942, said:

FROM VARIOUS SOURCES HITHERTO REGARDED AS RELIABLE GENERAL MACARTHUR HAS RECEIVED PERSISTENT REPORTS THAT LIEUT. GEN. MASAHARU HOMMA, COMMANDER IN CHIEF OF THE JAPANESE FORCES IN THE PHILIPPINES, COMMITTED HARA-KIRI. . . .

THE FUNERAL RITES OF THE LATE JAPANESE COMMANDER, THE REPORTS STATE, WERE HELD ON FEB. 26 IN MANILA. . . .

AN INTERESTING AND IRONIC DETAIL OF THE STORY IS THAT THE SUICIDE AND FUNERAL RITES OCCURRED IN THE SUITE AT THE MANILA HOTEL OCCUPIED BY GENERAL MACARTHUR PRIOR TO THE EVACUATION OF MANILA. GENERAL MACARTHUR ADVISES THAT HE IS CONTINUING HIS EFFORTS TO SECURE FURTHER EVIDENCE OF THE TRUTH OR FALSITY OF THE REPORTS.

The communiqué next day, March 9, 1942, said:

THE NEW COMMANDER IN CHIEF OF THE JAPANESE FORCES IN THE PHILIPPINES IS GEN. TOMOYUKI YAMASHITA. . . . GENERAL YAMASHITA SUCCEEDS GENERAL HOMMA, WHO IS REPORTED TO HAVE COMMITTED SUICIDE.

The communiqué, like so many others, was fiction. General Homma conquered Bataan and "The Rock" and survived the war, only to be executed four years later for "The Death March" of the Bataan prisoners and for other alleged war crimes.

There was, as the weeks went on, no mention in the communiqués and press releases of the Marines who participated in the defense, and when at last a radio from Corregidor casually named them, the Navy Department had to assure the people of the United States that the 4th had been in the Philippines all along, and that this belated mention of Marines did not mean that the fleet had broken through the Jap blockade and landed reinforcements.

So widespread was the American illusion that Bataan and Corregidor were doing pretty well, with the Japs on the receiving end, that broadcasts from the States, cast in a cheerful mood of utter unreality, depressed the morale of the beleaguered men of the Philippines who heard them. The Marines on Corregidor usually listened in about 6 P.M. each evening to Station KGEI, broadcasting from the West Coast of "God's Country." This station had a particularly brash commentator, who flexed his muscles for the benefit of the Japanese, 10,000 miles away, and one night incautiously defied the enemy: "I dare you to bomb Corregidor!"

The Marines' epithets were unprintable; perhaps one old China hand put it best: "I wish I had that s.o.b. in my foxhole."

Several inter-island steamers from Cebu and Panay ran the blockade in February with a little food and supplies.

The Navy, with submarines and seaplanes, maintained an intermittent and precarious communication with Corregidor. *Seawolf* delivered 37 tons of ammunition to "The Rock" on January 27–28. On February 3 submarine *Trout* brought in 3,500 rounds of 3-inch AA ammunition, and took out 20 tons of gold and silver—still paradoxically precious in the eyes of government even when men were dying and wasting away. On February 20 *Swordfish* felt her way into the mouth of the bay, lay on the bottom during the daylight hours, and at dusk surfaced and took aboard President Manuel Quezon of the Philippine Commonwealth, his family and Philippine officials. Four days later, she repeated her exploit and took out High Commissioner Sayre and his party.[15]

On March 11 General MacArthur, his wife, infant son, Chinese amah, and an official party, including staff officers and Rear Admiral F. W. Rockwell, Commandant of the Sixteenth (Philippine) Naval District, left, by Washington order, for Australia. They slipped through the ever-tightening noose in Navy PT boats to Mindanao, and then flew to Australia. MacArthur designated General Wainwright as his successor, but only for the troops on Luzon. MacArthur personally retained command of the over-all Philippine defense from 4,000 miles away in Australia, and he left behind him on Corregidor a deputy chief of staff to represent MacArthur's headquarters—the top echelon of a pyramided and complicated command: United States Army Forces in the Far East (USAFFE). On March 20, a few days after MacArthur reached Australia, the War Department, unaware of MacArthur's arrangements, promoted Wainwright to lieutenant general and appointed him to command of all United States forces in the Philippines. He was authorized to communicate directly with Washington but was under the general over-all command of MacArthur, who was designated Supreme Commander, Southwest Pacific Area. But MacArthur, until the end, sent advice and instructions to "The Rock" from Australia and even tried to influence tactics.

The departure of General MacArthur definitely eased some friction on Corregidor. A clash of personalities between General MacArthur and Admiral Thomas C. Hart, then commander of the Asiatic Fleet, a clash as bitter as it was pronounced (and which predated the war), had marred early Army-Navy cooperation in the Philippines. It had even been reflected in the 4th Regiment by early fears—perhaps entirely unsubstantiated—that the Army wanted to break the regiment up and use it for training and guard duties. Intelligence cooperation between the Army and Navy had not been good, and the aggressive, egoistic personality of General MacArthur's chief of staff, Major General Richard K. Sutherland, did nothing to pour oil on troubled waters. The situation almost reached the crisis stage about March 9, two days before MacArthur's departure, when, in a message to the War Department, the General recommended all units on Bataan and Corregidor, with the exception of the Marines and the Navy, for unit citations. Indignant Marine and Navy questioners were told by staff officers that this was no oversight. Sutherland let it be known that the Marines had gotten their share of glory in World War I, and they weren't going to get any in this one. This error was one of the sources of the bitterness that too often marred Army-Navy relationships in the Pacific later in the war.

General Wainwright rectified this misjudgment almost immediately after he took over, and Marines and Navy both got to like this unpretentious commander, who inspected the beach defenses and the front lines frequently and dived for foxholes like the rest of them.

Wainwright declared flatly, "If the Japanese can take 'The Rock,' they will find me here, no matter what orders I receive."

The remark got around; to fighting men with no hope of escape it represented "loyalty down" by their commander.

There was little change, as March wore on and spring approached back home in the States, in the life on Corregidor. The bombs and shells still fell; the work went on; the attrition of time and hunger and disease and bombardment took its slow toll.

Corregidor, like Bataan, was full of Filipinos, many of them non-combatants, the servants of officers or refugees from Manila. There were probably spies on "The Rock"; sometimes strange lights flickered at night, and once or twice rockets split the sky and were seemingly answered by Japanese rockets from Cavite. Nor was all the garrison staunch and brave. There were many "tunnel rats," who, despite the heat and dust of Malinta, never left its safety, and who gradually came to assume the pallor and the morale of men who dwell forever underground. "Tunnelitis" became an occupational disease. There were shirkers and slackers, as there have been in all armies since the beginning of time. There were those, of all services, who cracked under strain, mentally and physically; and there were some who "performed unbelievable tasks with ease." But until close to the end some officers of the tunnels used their *lavanderos* and house boys to keep them supplied with freshly washed and pressed uniforms. The troops in the field scrubbed their khaki—when it was scrubbed—in buckets.

It must have been about this time, before the gathering of the last Japanese attack against our lines on Bataan, that the men began to hum that lugubrious ditty attributed to Frank Hewlett, the war correspondent. It typified a growing sense of forsaken helplessness, for the Army of Bataan was a gaunt and scarecrow army—the men bearded, dirty; the frayed khaki trousers cut off at the knee to make ragged shorts; the Filipinos mostly shoeless; the eyes of all deep and sunken and hopeless.

> *We're the battling bastards of Bataan;*
> *No momma, no poppa, no Uncle Sam,*
> *No aunts, no uncles, no nephews, no nieces,*
> *No rifles, no guns or artillery pieces,*
> *And nobody gives a damn. . . .*

Toward the end of March "all hell broke loose." The bombings and bombardments of the fortified islands were intensified, and on Bataan the enemy was plainly massing for a big attack. The weary, desperate defenders had no chance—and knew it. At such a time, MacArthur radioed Wainwright that "you should attack" and "advance rapidly" and drive through to Subic Bay to seize Japanese supplies! But these men, who had been moving backward, ever backward, since the war's start, would never attack again; the I and II Corps were skeletons and scarecrows, and some of the men scarcely had strength to hold their rifles.

Many on Corregidor knew that the end was near on Bataan, but tails were still over the dashboard, despite the unrelenting, remorseless bombardment, despite a growing hunger. The 4th Marines and most of the units on Corregidor were on two meals a day, as they had been since the war's beginning: a couple of slices of bread a meal, the inevitable rice, some dried fruit salvaged from wrecked barges stranded on Corregidor's beaches, occasionally other items—a monotonous and debilitating diet, which neither filled the stomach nor nourished the body. For some few, especially those bivouacked in Government Ravine, this diet was occasionally pieced out by mule meat. The Army's QM mules were picketed near one Marine bivouac, and the Japanese shells sometimes provided meat for dinner. But by the end of March the Bataan forces were virtually starving; even on Corregidor the garrison had lost perhaps 20 pounds a man.

The Japanese on Bataan, as well as the Americans, were in a bad way. Disease, semistarvation—23 ounces of rice a day instead of the normal 62, a reflection of the breakdown of Japanese logistic planning—and heavy battle casualties had reduced Homma's effectives to about 3,000 men on Bataan at the end of February. Like the Americans, most of the Japanese had malaria.[16] But in March replacements filled the ranks of the depleted 16th Division and 65th Brigade, and the 4th Division of about 11,000 men, plus a reinforced regiment of the 21st Division, were added to Homma's order of battle. The Japanese artillery was heavily strengthened with 240 mm. howitzers, 300 mm. mortars and other guns; 70 to 80 more aircraft were assigned to the bombardment of Bataan and Corregidor; more special troops were added to Homma's force; and two additional divisions fresh from victories in the south were assigned the conquest of the outlying islands of the archipelago. Japanese general headquarters were irked at U.S. tenacity; the Japanese Fourteenth Army was in disgrace.

As April opened, the remorseless cacophony of the Japanese barrage sounded the knell of hope; the enemy attack was intensified on Bataan, and the II Corps line had buckled. The unequivocal orders of MacArthur left no room for local judgment: "When the supply situation becomes impossible there must be no thought of surrender. You must attack."

Magnificent phraseology but impossible tactics; Bataan was doomed; three-quarters of the troops had malaria; the men were slowly starving on 1,000 calories a day.

Lieutenant (j.g.) Murray Glusman, a young Navy doctor, who had served with the Army on Bataan, was evacuated by orders to Corregidor in the last hours, and was subsequently attached to the 4th (Reserve) Battalion of the 4th Marines. He described Bataan's end in a report preserved with other records by Commander Thomas H. Hayes, senior "medico" of the 4th:

Four tunnels were blown (near Mariveles, on Bataan's tip) by extremely heavy charges of dynamite, destroying the whole mountainside. The air was filled with smoke, dust and flying debris. The din was terrific and terrifying. When [Dr. Glusman] had reached mid-channel . . . en route to Corregidor, number four tunnel was blown. There was gasoline storage in this tunnel which added to the explosions and intensified the blast which hurled large rocks, boulders and . . . human fragments all over the area and into the sea, sinking small boats in the harbor, injuring occupants of small boats. . . . Days later an unidentified human head was found where it had landed in a small boat after having been hurled at an almost unbelievable distance through the air.

The end came in a hideous spectacle which those who saw it will long remember. "Dry heat had turned the earth to dust" on Bataan, and "here and there the woods were ablaze from the last great Japanese bombardment. From these huge pyres, great clouds of smoke and heat arose."[17] There were the last and desperate orders from the tunnel HQ on Corregidor to Bataan, then silence, and the uneasy men in foxholes on "The Rock" watched the trickling stream of stragglers from Mariveles, watched the end of organized resistance on the mainland of Luzon.

The night was split asunder by the crashing jar of great explosions; the retreating Americans blew up caches of gasoline, ammunition and supplies near Mariveles; and from "The Rock" the defenders saw a whole mountainside dissolve into dust and debris. And nature, too, seemed to mourn. About midnight of the eighth an earthquake caused Malinta Tunnel to "weave like a snake." Smoke palls wreathed the dying army, and the noise of explosions, the dull voice of artillery and the desultory crackle of small arms were the Valkyrian accompaniment to the fall of Bataan on the ninth of April, 1942.

Major General Edward P. King, Jr., quiet, modest, strong and able, the commander of the Luzon force (all the troops on Bataan), sent a flag of truce to the Japanese commander early in the morning. It was time; his battered units were completely broken; "in [the last] two days an army evaporated into thin air."[18] There was only a half-ration of food in the QM stores. "We have no further means of organized resistance," King said.[19] King, like the strong man he was, took the responsibility for the decision without informing Wainwright on Corregidor. He felt, he said, when he went to seek the Japanese conquerors in his last clean uniform, like Lee at Appomattox. With him, in piecemeal units and in scattered groups, surrendered some 76,000 exhausted men—most of them Filipinos —the greatest defeat for American arms in history. At the time of the surrender Homma had about 81,000 men on Luzon.[20]

The fall of Bataan had been foreseen, and, beginning on April 3, empty powder cans had been filled with water and distributed to beach defense positions on Corregidor and all possible reservoirs stocked. New wells had been dug at the entrance to Malinta Tunnel and there was an excellent well in San José barrio, but the water was brackish and all of it had to be boiled. Fort Frank on little Carabao Island near Cavite

Province on the south side of the bay was supplied with water by an underwater pipeline leading to a reservoir at the head of a ravine on the mainland. The Japanese cut the pipeline in the daytime, and the Philippine Scouts paddled ashore at night and patched it up.

The terrible aftermath of Bataan—the wrecked, the wounded, the starving—straggled to "The Rock" for many hours after the surrender. When the day came, the Marines watched the frantic attempts of fleeing survivors to cross the North Channel in several small launches. Jap artillery ranged on them; the men on "The Rock," helpless, saw two boats holed and sunk, and one grounded on Artillery Point. Some of the gaunt survivors swam through the oil-streaked waters to doubtful security; most of them died in the sea.

It was a grim prelude to the last terrible act.

The morale of "The Rock" was lowered by the deplorable condition of the 2,000-odd men who escaped from Bataan. The survivors of Bataan were "defeated, demoralized and demilitarized"—without arms or equipment, some of them almost naked, nearly all of them half-starved and ill of malaria, jaundice, fever.

Wainwright felt the inevitable sag in his men's morale and he issued an order: Corregidor could and would be held. And on April 12 one Flying Fortress—"the first and only outside help we ever saw"—bombed Japanese-held Nichols Field, and it "cheered our hearts tremendously," Lieutenant Commander T. C. Parker reported.

The Japanese wasted no time. As the coast artillerymen and the Marines stood to their guns, the enemy established forward "OP's" in the Bataan cliffs and commenced to plaster "The Rock" with the greatest artillery bombardment the Orient had ever known.

The scarecrows from the mainland were incorporated—those who could stand on their feet—in the beach-defense battalions of the 4th Marines, now plumped out by accretions and increments of rag, tag and bobtail formations to almost 4,000 men.

The refugees from Bataan increased the garrison of Corregidor and the three other smaller fortified islands in the bay to 11,600 men, most of them herded together in the less than three square miles of Corregidor, and the greater number of them noncombat troops—headquarters personnel, casuals, wounded, and the men of all ranks and services who go to make up the top echelons of a great command.

The 4th Marines with their incorporated elements were the only guardians of Corregidor's beaches, and on April 9 and 10 they slept by their guns, ready for a quick Japanese attempt to overrun "The Rock."[21]

No combat estimate could brighten Corregidor's situation. The water supply was particularly serious. Some types of ammunition were low.

Rations, if halved, might last until July or August. There were more than 1,000 wounded, and hundreds of others were sick; the tunnel laterals were filling up, and some patients were out in the open.

Two days after Bataan's fall friendly Filipinos from Manila smuggled in at night some $650 worth of quinine and medicines they had collected from the city's drugstores. But it was a drop in the bucket. Fifty percent of the 4th Marines' 1st Battalion already had undergone an epidemic of acute gastroenteritis, and 114 of the cases had been severe. Most of the attached personnel from Bataan had malaria and a good many of the Marines, too; there had been a mild outbreak of tonsilitis; all hands had been vaccinated for cholera; and there had been many cases of jaundice.

Communications, never good, were severed time after time, and the "CP's" in Malinta Tunnel were out of touch, hour after hour, with whole sections of the beach defenses. Many of the Navy's mine sweepers, local defense and naval district craft and small boats had been sunk; others clustered closely to "The Rock," looking vainly for protection from the enemy's murderous fire.

The beach defenses, isolated from the command and from each other, cached water supplies, rations and ammunition.

So, facing the end, Corregidor girded for defeat.

From April 10 on, when enemy batteries at Cabcaben, Bataan, commenced firing on Corregidor, living on "The Rock" was "like living in the center of a bull's-eye." The heights of Bataan, now in enemy hands, and the ridges of Cavite towered over "The Rock" and its island subposts. The fortified islands were under cross fire from both shores and almost continuous bombing from the skies.

By April 14 only five days after Bataan's surrender, all the seacoast batteries—155's and 3-inch—on Corregidor's north shore were destroyed or out of action; confidently the Japanese put up two observation balloons on Bataan, emplaced more guns and proceeded methodically to range on Corregidor's big guns and south shore batteries.

Throughout April the bombardment was progressively stepped up.

Japanese bombers, in groups of three to nine, flew over "The Rock" every couple of hours from 8 A.M. to sunset. At first, they flew at 20,000 feet, but when the AA's opened up, Jap "OP's" spotted their positions and enemy guns on Bataan smothered them in gunfire. Gradually the AA fire slackened; soon the enemy planes were swooping leisurely over Corregidor and dive bombers were hurtling to within a few hundred feet of Malinta's crest. The enemy did not escape unscathed; a few planes were shot down, but much fewer than the number claimed in the communiqués.

But the enemy artillery fire was far more damaging than the bombing. Colonel Stephen M. Mellnik later reported in the *Coast Artillery Journal* that the "effect of massed artillery fire . . . was tremendous. . . . Whole areas were blasted out. One day's shelling did more damage than all the bombing put together. James Ravine, which was heavily wooded before the war, looked completely bare after the shelling."[22]

Batteries Rock Point (two 155's), Sunset (four 155's), James (four 3-inch) and Hamilton (two 155's) were out. Fifteen AA guns were salvaged and moved to new locations. The 155's used for counterbattery work were shifted after each 20 rounds of fire to new positions. All mobile guns were moved into one-gun defiladed positions.

But these measures merely postponed the inevitable.

The enemy ringed "The Rock" with from 80 to 150 batteries, up to 240 mm. in size, and the unending barrage destroyed the defenses faster than they could be rebuilt and gradually chipped away the taut nerves of the defenders.

Gun emplacements were wrecked, land mines exploded, the little vessels of the Navy's inshore patrol sunk one by one, wire destroyed, beach defenses—painfully built up in weeks of toil—razed in one crushing barrage.

Corregidor's counterbattery fire was brave but intermittent; "The Rock's" batteries fired "blind," and even in the first half of April the ratio was at best one shell against four.

And ammunition was running low; ordnance technicians, working steadily, modified the fuses of armor-piercing shells to explode on impact, but their best efforts added only 25 rounds a day to the magazines.

The artillerymen and the 4th Marines, crouching, eating, sleeping, waiting in foxholes or in shallow tunnels dug into the sides of the hills, bore with dull stoicism this unending bombardment. Meals now were haphazard; kitchens were hit; cooking had to be done in the dark. Some units were on one meal a day; all had breakfast before dawn, dinner after dark. The menu was monotonous, sufficient to sustain life but not to satisfy.

On and on through the endless days the shelling continued—unrelenting, impersonal, Wagnerian. Perhaps 200 to 600 guns on Bataan and others on Cavite provided the orchestra of doom, day after day, night after night.

Malinta rocked and shuddered to the crash of explosions; the reeking tunnels stank of powder fumes and stale sweat; the feverish wounded moaned. One by one, Corregidor's guns and batteries were wrecked; food and ammunition dumps were buried, cliff faces blasted into the sea, trenches and barbed wire leveled, the whole topography of the island changed. Casualties mounted; the Marines suffered more killed and wounded in April than in the previous four months of war.

Ammunition dumps went up in sputtering fireworks; toward sunset parts of "The Rock" were sometimes veiled in dust and smoke, a haze so thick that the shores of Bataan and the evening skies were obscured.

One night a group from Malinta came to the sandbagged entrance to get a breath of the fresh night air. The night was momentarily quiet; a soft breeze from the China Sea cooled the battered island. Back home in the States it was spring, and the breeze spoke of home. . . . Without warning a Jap 240 mm. landed in the midst of the group. Hours later, after the bloody work with the scalpel and bandages had been done in the hospital laterals, a soldier found a young Army nurse, weeping bitterly. . . .

Probably never before in the Orient had there been such a bombardment. The island's north shore road was blown into the bay. Battery Way and Battery Geary—with 12-inch mortars, the most effective guns Corregidor had—were located and smothered by enemy artillery; at Geary the 240 mm. shells smashed into the magazines; the ten-ton mortars were hurled a hundred yards away; a six-ton concrete slab was thrown 1,000 yards to cut down a tree almost four feet in diameter. Major Francis Williams, United States Marine Corps, whose name shines out in all these final days of disaster and tragedy as "a man without fear," led a rescue party as he had done when Battery Crocket was hit.

Toward the end of April many men began to crack; morale sagged and shell shock increased. During all this period the 4th Marines, Navy personnel, and the splendid cadre of Regular Army men who had held together our whole makeshift military structure in the Orient were "the individuals who inspired the weaker ones to carry on."

On the twenty-ninth, the Emperor's birthday, "The Rock" shuddered and trembled to a day-long bombardment as more than 10,000 shells smashed into gun positions, tore its beach defenses to shreds and clawed and raked at the trapped garrison. When the "All Clear" sounded, Corregidor was "on fire all over—ammunition dumps, magazines, grass, brush and anything else that would burn."

And that night two Navy PBY flying boats (twin-engined patrol planes) from Australia landed in the darkness with medicines and AA fuses—a last despairing gesture. They flew out, barely staggering off the water, with 50 nurses and key officers of MacArthur's staff.

Up to May 2, the 4th Marines had about 10 percent casualties— killed, wounded, died or missing, plus a small number cut off and captured on Bataan. Those who remained were glassy-eyed from lack of sleep and from shell shock; many of them were ill of dysentery, malaria and malnutrition.

But they were still the mainspring of the Corregidor defense, and detachments of the regiment bolstered the strength of the subposts—Fort

Hughes and Fort Drum on Caballo and El Fraile islands. On "The Rock," from Monkey Point to Battery Sunset, the Marines crouched in their foxholes and waited.

As the gun batteries were destroyed, coast artillerymen became part of the beach-defense organization, and as the Navy's mine sweepers and small craft were sunk, sailors came ashore to join the defense. At the last the 4th Marines were the stiffening of a composite force the like of which had never yet been seen in war: Coast Guard, Navy, Naval Reserve, Insular Force, U.S. Army, Philippine Army, Philippine Scouts and Philippine Constabulary, the whole trained, led and inspired by the tradition and *esprit* of the Marines.

On May 3 submarine *Spearfish* ran the blockade—the last contact with the outside world—and took off 25 passengers, including 13 women. One of the passengers, Lieutenant Commander T. C. Parker, was told by General Wainwright just before the *Spearfish* left, "They [the Japanese] will have to come take us. . . . They will never get this place any other way."

By May 5 Corregidor was broken and blasted; the lovely green-capped hills now lay bare and naked, the earth scourged and flayed and ulcered. All structures and buildings in the open were destroyed; in some areas "not a stick, not a leaf" was left; trees "once so dense . . . that they shut out the sun were reduced to charred stumps"; shell cases from burned-out ammunition dumps pocked the landscape. Two more tunnel laterals had been cleared for hospital use, and yet the sick and wounded overflowed. . . .

The railroad and most of the roads were destroyed, some portions of them literally blasted into the bay; communications except by runner and radio were nonexistent. Most of the beach defenses—the barbed wire, the foxholes—were wiped out. Forty-six of 48 beach-defense guns were destroyed, and all "The Rock's" great batteries were silenced: the mortars, the 12-inch rifles, the 8- and 10-inch disappearing guns, the 155's. The star shells were burned, the searchlights—except for one or two—were wrecked; of the AA guns a few remained, but the fire control instruments were destroyed, and Japanese planes swept leisurely a few hundred feet above "The Rock" to strafe and bomb. The great 14-inch guns on the outer fortified islands were still firing, but except for those on Fort Drum, the "concrete battleship," only intermittently. A thousand shells struck the deck of Fort Drum in one day; some 15 feet of its concrete was chipped away by shellfire during the siege, but its turrets still spoke. On Corregidor 16,000 shells in 24 hours on May 4 were the culminating blow; there was little left on "The Rock" save the rock itself and men with heart and courage. And on May 5 there were only three or four days' supply of water remaining. . . .

Corregidor was all but silenced; it was time for the *coup de grâce*.

The 4th Regiment had absorbed into its ranks—after a fashion—895 officers and men of the Navy, 397 men of the United States Army (including a few from the 31st Infantry, which had fought magnificently on Bataan), 929 from the Philippine Army and 246 artillerymen of the Philippine Scouts. There were even Filipino mess boys of the Naval Reserve, ground crews from the Philippine Army Air Force, one officer and 18 men from the Philippine constabulary, and at least one civilian—who fought stoutly.

These additions were welcome, but they added doubtful strength; the resulting force was heterogeneous in character; none of the Navy men and few of the others had had more than cursory training as infantry, and, as Colonel Howard later reported, "With the exception of three Philippine Scouts, all personnel that joined at this time (after the fall of Bataan) had to be re-equipped and at least partially clothed.

"Due to sickness from malaria and dysentery and malnutrition," the report continued, "the physical condition of these officers and men was generally deplorable and they were unfit for combat duty."

Nevertheless the increments were assigned to bring up the strength of the 1st and 3rd Battalions to about 1,100 men each; the 2nd Battalion's strength was increased to about 900; and the rest were assigned to the General Reserve, and to creation of a 4th Tactical Battalion (sometimes called the "Naval Battalion" because of its preponderance of naval personnel).

James Ravine and the eastern end of the island were battered all day on the fifth, and that night about 10:40 a terrific barrage was put down all over the island, but particularly on the eastern end. "They polished it off with phosphorus shells." A sound of barges was heard off the north and south shores, and at long last, after four months of siege, suffering and bombardment, the defenders of Corregidor were face to face with their foes.

The enemy landed first a few minutes after eleven, before the moon rose, near North Point on the low eastern tail of the island, and immediately extended his landings to the west.

Corregidor's topography favored a landing on the north shore, which faces Bataan, two miles away. There are good landing beaches around North Point and the shore line curves to the southeast. The south shore's rocky cliffs rise almost straight up from narrow, rocky beaches, and they are enfiladed by the high western end of the island.

"On the high ground between the [north and south] shores," Lieutenant Robert F. Jenkins later wrote, "there was a small landing field (Kindley Field) and on the ridge or hogs-back, extending westward from the airfield there were several 3-inch AA batteries," among them Battery Denver.[23]

Their guns were depressed and the gunners were ordered to hold the center of the Marine 1st Battalion line.

The 1st Battalion was responsible for everything east of Malinta, to the tail of the island, a shoreline of at least 10,000 yards. The 3rd Battalion held the middle sector of "The Rock," and the 2nd Battalion the western end of the island.

In reserve were the headquarters and service company of the regiment and the 4th Battalion of attached supernumeraries—who never before had fought as infantrymen and who never would do so again.

The Japanese landings, on the heels of their shattering barrage, were made in the 1st Battalion area, near A Company's beachhead. Some landing boats veered off from the defensive fire and lay to, but the enemy filtered through a weak point to the east and drove in over his dead. Some of the barges were sunk and at least one of the landing attempts was turned back. The remaining guns on the outlying islands, answering the call for help from Corregidor, blasted Japanese troops and boat concentrations at Cabcaben on Bataan. Tracers flickered over North Point, Infantry Point, Artillery Point and all the low tail of the island, and shell splashes rose white and shining from the dark waters of the North Channel.

But the enemy came on.

Platoon Sergeant "Tex" Haynes, a two-gun man, met the enemy head on. Haynes emptied his two pistols, grabbed up the rifle of a dead buddy, and then, as more and more Japanese flooded toward him, he cradled a .30-caliber machine gun in his arms and fired it from the hip. Despite the red-hot barrel, he sprayed two belts of ammo into the enemy's midst until the tide of men engulfed him and a grenade left him, half-blinded and hideously wounded, there at his post.

A Company of the 1st Battalion got the brunt of the attack; the company commander and his second-in-command had been killed just 24 hours before by artillery fire, and B Company was commanded by a gunnery sergeant. The Marines lobbed hand grenades onto the beaches and died in their positions, but the Japanese came on.

Back at Marine Regimental Headquarters in Malinta Tunnel, communications were bad; the wires to battalions were in and out; field radio, runners and patrols were the sources of information. Colonel Howard and his staff, and General Moore, commander of the fortified islands, knew only that the Japanese were ashore—perhaps 500 or 600 of them in the eastern end of the island. About midnight they got a clearer picture: the hogs-back in the center extending from Kindley Field toward Malinta was the key. At all costs, the Japanese must be kept clear of Malinta Hill.

They did not know it then, but Battery Denver had pulled back and A and B Companies' flanks were wide open. The first sergeant of the battery (Philippine Scouts) had been killed by artillery fire and his men, without a leader, had gone to pieces. The Japanese had gotten through the hole on the hogs-back and were in behind the 1st Battalion's beach-defense positions. Colonel Howard ordered in the reserves. They were a composite lot: a headquarters outfit of all ranks and services, and the 4th Tactical Battalion under Major Williams composed of bluejackets under Marine, Army and Navy officers and noncoms, and coast artillerymen whose batteries had been destroyed. They were all that Corregidor had.

The 2nd and 3rd Battalions were pinned down to their beach-defense positions by the threat of another Japanese landing, and the platoons of the 1st Battalion that were not engaged in the counterattack were repelling landings or enduring intensive Japanese artillery. Some platoons had taken heavy casualties. Reserve squads furnished replace-ments, but before the night was old there were more casualties than there were replacements. One squad leader reported that he had two men left in his squad.

As the last reserves—forlorn hope—moved to attack, the men were loaded down with hand grenades and ammunition, but they walked silently in two single-file columns on either side of the South Shore Road from their bivouac area down through Middleside—which was under desultory enemy shellfire—and then across the low ground of "Bottom-side." The battalion was held up by an artillery barrage for about 15 minutes just before reaching "Bottomside." The silent men passed through a "scene of utter desolation—thousands of shellholes, wrecked buildings, upturned automobiles," and entered the west entrance to Malinta Tunnel.

"Inside it was hot, terribly hot," and the ventilation was so bad men labored for breath.

At 0400 General Wainwright had received a final message from President Roosevelt in Washington, ending in sad exaltation:

"You and your devoted followers have become the living symbols of our war aims and the guarantee of victory."

Battalion HQ was set up in the eastern end of Malinta Tunnel, and after a company officer conference, the battalion filed out of the tunnel at 4:30 A.M. to the attack.

It moved out upon a confused and confusing battlefield.

The Japanese landing and penetration through the 1st Battalion position had split up elements of A and B Companies, and some were isolated behind the enemy lines in the Kindley Field area and to the east. A few Japanese had penetrated in the darkness up toward Malinta. American units were behind the Jap lines; Japanese units were behind ours. It was a fire and grenade fight with the main lines only 30 yards apart. So closely interwoven were the combatants in the darkness that when the Japanese called for an artillery barrage, it bracketed both sides; the enemy sent up a rocket to silence their guns.

While the scrapping was going on for the hogs-back, the Jap barges, stuttering away in the North Channel, were coming in toward other beaches. Five or six of them came in toward the outflanked and isolated men at Cavalry Point. The Marines had only one .30- and one .50-caliber to meet them; they had lost six .30-caliber machine guns to Japanese shells, and the emplacement of their single .37 mm. had been damaged. But the Marines were exultant. For four months they had been on the receiving end; now they had a chance to dish it out. They dropped hand grenades down on the beaches; they let the barges have it with point-blank fire.

There were other brushes along the north shore. One of the 75's that was still functioning (sited far beyond the main action) took some Japanese landing craft under fire and sank a number of them. At dawn the enemy approached the North Dock area, where a cable barrier and a string of twenty-one 500-pound TNT sea mines were awaiting them, but Corregidor's remaining artillery opened up and drove them off.

But the Japanese still clung to the hogs-back reaching westward toward Malinta from Kindley Field, and they had inched forward in the dark hours, leaving behind them isolated units of still fighting Marines.

So Major Williams and his composite battalion smashed out in counterattack in the last effort.

They moved out from Malinta—this last vain hope—in platoon columns.

Dawn broke upon the wreckage of a fort. On Corregidor not a stick was standing; the beaten earth was pulverized, and grim-faced, bearded men, bleeding from their wounds, crept from crater to crater.

Exactly what happened that night and early morning on the shell-shattered eastern slopes of Corregidor will never be known in full detail, for most of the men who could tell are dead. And even those who lived saw only segments of action; the fighting was inchoate, wild, vicious.

The counterattack made initial progress, but it was slow and painful. Two guns, one in the ruins of a powder magazine and the other to the right of a road leading to the North Point OP, held up the advance, but by 6 A.M. they had been knocked out. The line moved on, rooting out determined enemy resistance. But not for long. Heavy machine-gun fire came from a nest near a water tower near Mays Point. Two of the "Old Breed"[24]—apparently Sergeant Major Thomas F. Sweeney and Quartermaster Sergeant John H. Haskins—Marines from their tough jaws to their big feet, climbed the stone water tower under fire. They lobbed grenades into the Japanese lines and climbed up and down the tower several times to replenish their supply. They knocked out the machine-gun nest, but one of them died at the bottom of the tower, and long afterward American prisoners of war, working on Corregidor, found the body of a sergeant on top of the tower—"one of the great unsung heroes of the war."

There were many others who rose above and beyond the call of duty. A sergeant, assigned to a safe paper work job in Malinta Tunnel, got permission to leave his job for an hour, organized a voluntary patrol of clerks, typists and telephone men, got one machine gun and two snipers, and then reported his return: "I'm sorry I'm late, sir; it took me longer than I expected."

The line moved on; it moved in blood and anguish, but now its progress slowed. The price was too high.

In the early morning of May 6, the U.S. lines were "enfiladed by a terrific artillery barrage from Bataan and bombed and strafed by high-level and dive bombers."

The Jap shells were walking back and forth; the bombers, now the day had risen over the smoking wreckage, were leisurely pinpointing their objectives. Machine guns, mortars and light artillery had been landed; the enemy came in the thousands. For dead Americans there were no replacements; behind the Japanese were thousands more on Bataan. The hospital laterals of Malinta were filled with the wounded, and they lay now in the open beneath the shells.

The 4th Battalion and Major Max W. Schaeffer's outfit had been riddled. The officers were virtually wiped out. Lieutenant Bethel V. Otter and Ensign William R. Lloyd of the Navy were dead; Lieutenant Charles B. Brook with a terrible leg wound lay on the amputation table in Malinta; Captain Calvin Chunn of the Army, S-2 of the battalion, was wounded in the stomach; Lieutenant Edward N. Little, USN, CO of S Company had a chest wound, and Ensign Andrew W. Long, USNR, was wounded in the arm. At least 90 bluejackets were dead, others wounded. And still the enemy came on.

The exact number of Americans killed in that last battle may never be known, but at least 40 lay dead in the shambles of "The Rock," many times that number were wounded, and the hospital tunnels were double-banked with bleeding, unconscious men.

The Japanese made another landing attempt in the North Dock area, but the cable barrier and fierce defensive fire drove them off. Then, some time around 1030, Japanese tanks came into action; the antitank barriers had been blasted to bits, and there were no AT guns to stop them.

The Marines commenced to withdraw to the final defensive line in front of Malinta. But the concrete trenches were unrecognizable; they had been chewed to bits by artillery fire.

The last messages started to go out from Corregidor:

From the Navy—Captain K. M. Hoeffel:

ONE HUNDRED AND SEVENTY-THREE OFFICERS AND TWENTY-THREE HUNDRED AND SEVENTEEN MEN OF THE NAVY REAFFIRM THEIR LOYALTY AND DEVOTION TO COUNTRY, FAMILIES AND FRIENDS. . . .

The Marines were silent, save with their guns.

From the Army—Private Irving Strobing tapping with his key in the depths of Malinta Tunnel, while America hung on his words:

THEY ARE NOT NEAR YET. WE ARE WAITING FOR GOD ONLY KNOWS WHAT. HOW ABOUT A CHOCOLATE SODA? . . . WE MAY HAVE TO GIVE UP BY NOON, WE DON'T KNOW YET. THEY ARE THROWING MEN AND SHELLS AT US AND WE MAY NOT BE ABLE TO STAND IT. THEY HAVE BEEN SHELLING US FASTER THAN YOU CAN COUNT. . . .

On the torn and blasted battlefield of Corregidor, the shells still fell and the Marines still fought, but an order went out: "Execute Pontiac; execute Pontiac."

It was the code name for that last bitter order which in their hearts they long had known would someday come. It was surrender, by Wainwright's orders as of 12 noon, May 6, 1942, a date that will always live in sorrow and in pride.

(At his headquarters on Bataan, General Homma, the Japanese commander, was "moaning" as he listened to reports of the fighting: "My God! I have failed in the assault.")

Surrender was Wainwright's decision, but Colonel "Sam" Howard of the Marines agreed with it, and so did Colonel "Don" Curtis, his able "exec," who was a tower of strength until the end. "All general reserves [had been] committed; the enemy was making additional landings . . . ammunition in the east sector was practically exhausted"; Japanese tanks were within a few hundred yards of Malinta Tunnel, where the blood-soaked wounded lay; water was low. Wainwright thought of his hostages to fortune—more than 1,000 wounded and 150 nurses. MacArthur had said to hold until he returned, but his return was still 90,000 lives and three years away. Corregidor was finished.

Around the scorched earth and in the shambles that had been called the "Gibraltar of the East," the Marines were crying—openly, unashamed. At the Regimental HQ, in the Navy Tunnel, Colonel Curtis ordered Captain R. B. Moore, adjutant of the 4th Marines, to burn the regimental and national colors. Captain Moore came back with a tear-streaked face.[25]

In the middle and western parts of the island, where there had been no land fighting—the Marine beach-defense battalions had stood their ground against the threat of new landings—the officers called their men together and made little talks.

The psychological and emotional tragedy of surrender, especially to a corps with the pride of the Marines, is racking.[26] Particularly to the 2nd and 3rd Battalions defending the beaches of the central and western parts of the island, surrender was bitter anticlimax. For months these men with the stoicism born of discipline had been "taking" it, had seen some of their comrades blown to bits, had watched the gradual destruction of the fortress of Corregidor. At last, when the Japs landed, these men who had been "taking" it would have a chance to "dish it out".

But it was not to be. The Japs landed in the 1st Battalion area, but the threats of new landings were sufficient to immobilize and pin down to their beach-defense positions the men of the 2nd and 3rd Battalions. They scarcely fired a shot. Keyed up to great effort, the sudden ending of months of hardship left them dull with fatigue, blank with depression, weighed down by that awful leaden feeling of the mind and the heart and the stomach which the word "surrender" means.

Captain William F. Prickett said, "I've lived pretty close with you men for the past five months and I've grown pretty fond of you all—and proud of you too, mighty proud. . . ."

Prickett broke down.

They hurled their rifle bolts into the bay, and then, while the shells whistled overhead and the smoke from Corregidor curled upward, they washed, scraped the beard from their strained faces, donned the cleanest uniforms they had and prepared to show the Japanese the pride of the Marines.

Strobing tapped on:

WE'VE GOT ABOUT FIFTY-FIVE MINUTES AND I FEEL SICK AT MY STOMACH. I AM REALLY LOW DOWN. THEY ARE AROUND NOW SMASHING RIFLES. THEY BRING IN THE WOUNDED EVERY MINUTE. WE WILL BE WAITING FOR YOU GUYS TO HELP. THIS IS THE ONLY THING I GUESS THAT CAN BE DONE. GENERAL WAINWRIGHT IS A RIGHT GUY AND WE'RE WILLING TO GO ON FOR HIM, BUT SHELLS WERE DROPPING ALL NIGHT, FASTER THAN HELL. DAMAGE TERRIFIC. TOO MUCH FOR GUYS TO TAKE . . . THE JIG IS UP. EVERYONE IS BAWLING LIKE A BABY. . . . THEY ARE PILING DEAD AND WOUNDED IN OUR TUNNEL. . . . I KNOW NOW HOW A MOUSE FEELS. CAUGHT IN A TRAP WAITING FOR GUYS TO COME ALONG AND FINISH IT UP. . . .

On Corregidor the white flags of surrender were flying; it was noon. The key tapped on:

MY NAME IS IRVING STROBING. GET THIS TO MY MOTHER. MRS. MINNE STROBING, 605 BARBEY STREET, BROOKLYN, N.Y. THEY ARE TO GET ALONG O.K. GET IN TOUCH WITH THEM SOON AS POSSIBLE. MESSAGE. MY LOVE TO PA, JOE, SUE, MAC, GARRY, JOY AND PAUL. ALSO TO MY FAMILY AND FRIENDS. GOD BLESS 'EM ALL, HOPE THEY BE THERE WHEN I COME HOME. TELL JOE, WHEREVER HE IS, TO GIVE 'EM HELL FOR US. MY LOVE TO YOU ALL. GOD BLESS YOU AND KEEP YOU. LOVE. SIGN MY NAME AND TELL MOTHER HOW YOU HEARD FROM ME. STAND BY. . . .

The shells still fell. The 14-inch turrets of Fort Drum—the tiny "concrete battleship," a subpost of Corregidor—were firing to within five minutes of the end. This was the one battery in all the fortified islands that was never out of action. Drum, on El Fraile Island, a pinpoint at the entrance to Manila Bay, was hammered by at least 1,000 shells on the last day, but its guns still fired.

But it did no good.

The earth still shook on Corregidor; the tunnel lights in Malinta glowed and flickered fitfully to the crash of explosion. And, in parts of the island, Marines and soldiers, because they were tough troops and the orders to surrender had not gotten through, holed up in foxholes and dugouts and fought through the long and blistering afternoon to their deaths.

The messages broke off. . . .

Corregidor was silent.

The epilogue was suffering.

When "The Rock" surrendered, the battle casualty list was not excessive, considering the months of bombardment. Some units of the Marine beach-defense forces suffered heavily in the last brief battle. The improvised 4th Battalion lost approximately 90 enlisted men of the Navy and two naval officers killed in action in its abortive counterattack on May 5–6, and many others were wounded. The reinforced headquarters company, part of the 4th Regiment's reserve, was decimated, and the 1st Battalion, which took the brunt of the Japanese attack, incurred severe losses. Some 31 enlisted Marines were killed in action prior to May 5 (a tribute to the deep foxholes, caves and dispersion of the 4th Regiment) and about 43 in the final vicious fighting May 5–6. Scores of others were wounded, hundreds were out of action due to illness or near-starvation. In all there had been at least 600 to 800 Army troops, Navy sailors, Marines and Filipinos killed and more than 1,000 wounded during the siege. Among the dead were some 70 Filipinos entombed alive when cliffsides collapsed and sealed their caves and dugouts during a heavy bombardment.

Japanese losses have never been accurately compiled.

Commander Thomas H. Hayes, Medical Corps, USN, the Regimental Surgeon who died in prison camp, kept some very complete medical records which he hid from the Japanese, copied and cached in various places on Luzon. Copies have been recovered, and his estimate was that the enemy had lost some 4,000 men in the final assault. Colonel Stephen M. Mellnik, in the *Coast Artillery Journal,* puts the number at 5,000 killed or drowned, 3,000 wounded in the landing operation. This, however, seems excessive, since it is improbable that the Japanese landed more than a regiment on Corregidor prior to the surrender. Though some landing craft were sunk, probably not enough were destroyed to account for 4,000 or 5,000 dead. On February 2, 1946, at the trial of

Lieutenant General Masaharu Homma for war crimes, Major General Shusuke Horiguchi, chief medical officer of the Japanese Fourteenth Army at the time of Corregidor, testified that in the Corregidor campaign (from April 10 to May 7, 1942, *only*) the Japanese casualties were 400 dead, 460 wounded, and 50,000 sick with malaria, dysentery and beriberi. These figures, however, are not to be trusted—particularly the latter one—since Horiguchi was testifying in Homma's defense, and was attempting to extenuate the mistreatment of American prisoners by claims that the Japanese Fourteenth Army did not have enough drugs or medicines for its own soldiers, much less for its prisoners.

The figures of Japanese losses probably will always be conflicting, but it is safe to say "The Rock's" defenders in the final battle inflicted five to twenty times as many casualties as they received and the total Japanese casualties were numbered in four figures.

It is idle to speculate what might have been on Corregidor on May 5–6 had Battery Denver on the hogs-back held its position, or if General Moore and Colonel Howard could have scraped together another 400 or 500 men to throw in against the Japanese. There is no doubt that one of the principal Japanese landings—at the North Dock area—was beaten off, that a good many landing craft were sunk, that the enemy had been mauled severely at the time of surrender and that General Homma's anxiety reflected these reverses. But it seems unlikely that even another counterattack could have cleared Corregidor, and even so, the game was up. Another landing attempt was almost certain to succeed; indeed, Corregidor was beaten by artillery bombardment before the landing was actually made.

The brutal treatment of American prisoners by the Japanese is not a part of this story. This treatment can be summarized in statistics. Between 5,000 and 10,000 Filipinos and a maximum of about 650 Americans died in the "Death March" from Bataan to prison camps soon after the surrender.[27] Thousands of others died more slowly in captivity from illness, malnutrition, brutality and despair. Only about one-third of the officer personnel of the 4th Marine Regiment (and attached Navy) returned to the United States, and the enlisted survivors represented an even smaller fraction. Most of them died as "POW's." Army prisoners fared as badly.

It must be recorded, however, from the Hayes medical records—in the words of Lieutenant Edward Francis Ritter, Jr. of the Navy Medical Corps—that the worst as well as the best in men came out in captivity. Lieutenant Ritter was speaking of American prisoners generally, not specifically of the Marines, when he recorded that in prison camp discipline among the Americans broke down; "selfishness and greed" manifested themselves everywhere, and many of the men would do little work for themselves.

But throughout, men like Major Francis W. Williams of the 4th Battalion, who died as a POW a few months before our final victory, demonstrated the same steadfastness and courage and serenity of spirit that so distinguished them in combat.

Around Corregidor and Bataan have clustered the myths of history.

Through the long months of bloodshed in World War II, the very names became for the American people symbols of fortitude and endurance, combat skill and brilliant generalship. MacArthur's daring escape to Australia by motor torpedo boat and plane, and his promise—"I shall return" (redeemed three and a half years later)—stirred the imagination of millions and gave the nation a symbolic hero in the darkest days of the war.

We gilded the lily. It was not until after the fighting was over that the "SNAFU's" (Situation Normal—All "Fouled" Up), the mistakes, the inadequacy of planning commenced to leak out, but even with most of the facts available a score of years afterward, the reality has not caught up with the myth.

Colonel E. B. Miller, who commanded the 194th Tank Battalion, a National Guard outfit that had been mobilized and sent to the Philippines before war started, tried to dispel some of the myths in a little-noticed book he published after the war. Colonel Miller, describing what he called "our fiasco in the Philippines," was bitterly critical of General MacArthur, the Army and the country.

"Maj. Gen. George Grunert," he wrote, "was commander of the Philippine Department before MacArthur was recalled to active duty. . . . Why was General Grunert sent home . . .? It was because he differed sharply with MacArthur in the defense plans of the Philippines. . . . Grunert was realistically sure of what was needed. MacArthur was steeped in the theoretical."

Colonel Miller in his book stressed particularly the failure to move available supplies into Bataan Peninsula, and he asked a series of rhetorical embarrassing questions:

"Why was not the Orange Plan (WPO-3) put into effect until Dec. 3, 1941?

"What happened to the plans to evacuate the Port Area in Manila of pertinent supplies? . . . Why was no rice moved from . . . Cabanatuan . . .? Why was Bataan put on half-rations immediately after the troops withdrew into the peninsula . . .?"[28]

Colonel Miller's book posed questions which rubbed some of the gilt off the myths, but it did not provide very specific or detailed answers.

Yet history has clearly provided the answers.

Corregidor and Bataan were doomed before war began by:

1. Planning vacillation in Washington and the Philippines.

The shift in emphasis by MacArthur, with Washington's approval, from the Orange Plan—the defense of Manila Bay—to defense of all the Philippines complicated fatally supply and logistic preparations.

Three discordant plans—Orange, Rainbow 5, and the Philippine Commonwealth plans—for the defense of the islands existed, and "no single one [of them] was followed in its entirety when war came."[29] Overdependence upon the Philippine Army, which existed chiefly on paper, and a gross overestimation by the Army High Command of the capabilities of air power contributed to debacle.

MacArthur put a ridiculously high value on the Philippine motor torpedo boat "navy," with which he hoped to repel Japanese landing attempts. There were only about two Philippine MTB's available when war started, and they played a negative role. MacArthur's prewar assessment of the combat value of the Philippine Army, composed largely of five-and-a-half-month drafted men, was far higher than was warranted, and his mobilization and training schedule apparently was predicated on a belief that hostilities probably would not start until April 1, 1942. Time did not favor MacArthur, but even so the Philippine Army's overall combat effectiveness would not have been materially improved in another six months.

We first discovered in the Philippines—a lesson to be emphasized again and again later—that air power to be effective against surface power had to be used in massive numbers and with great skill. The Philippines showed that the definition of air power was complex, that a few bombers minus other elements had little combat meaning. The campaign demonstrated, too, that the Army Air Forces' prewar emphasis upon bombers had been overstressed, that fighters in great numbers were required to win air superiority—a lesson not to be wholly learned until later war years.

Secretary of War Henry L. Stimson made this point strongly later:

It was quickly apparent [after the campaign started] that the hopes of the previous autumn could not be realized; there would be no successful defense of the Philippines by air power. The preparations had not been completed; the Japanese were too strong; most important of all, there had been no adequate realization of the degree to which air power is dependent on other things than unsupported airplanes.[30]

2. Planning differences between the Army and Navy.

When the Army shifted to defense of all the Philippines, Admiral Hart enthusiastically requested permission to abandon prior plans to move his fleet southward and, instead, to concentrate his fleet in Manila Bay. The Navy Department—wisely, in the event—rejected this proposal; the rejection demonstrated that the Navy had little faith in the

Army's new-found beliefs that the Philippines could be defended. There was no unified command in the Philippines until January 30; Army and Navy exercised independent commands.

Navy planning, too, was fundamentally deficient in one major respect, as Admiral Frederick C. Sherman has written:

> Our naval high command . . . little realized that control of the sea was dependent on the air power of carriers and not upon the obsolete battleships which were put out of action at Pearl Harbor. . . .
>
> At the opening of the war [the Japanese] had ten carriers . . . we had only three in the Pacific. This disparity was the main factor in forcing us to take the defensive in the early part of the war, and not the loss of our battleships, as popularly believed.[31]

The defense was marred by personality clashes and combat deficiencies.

The grandiloquent communiqués of MacArthur, his assertion that help was on the way to his beleaguered men, the emplacement of his command post in the Malinta Tunnel on Corregidor and his eventual escape to the Philippines—plus the presence in a combat zone (contrary to his own regulations) of his wife, baby son and Chinese nurse—were causes for criticism by his own officers and men, and were an ultimate depressant of morale. The false and misleading phraseology of some of the MacArthur announcements contributed to confusion, adding by words rather than deeds to the making of a myth. Tension and feeling between the Army and Navy—in part the product of clashing personalities (particularly MacArthur and Sutherland and Admiral Hart[32]), in part the product of clashing plans—added, until General Wainwright assumed command, to the problems of the doomed defense.

The ultimate failure of the defense was due not only to the ineffectiveness of the Philippine Army but also to the ineffectiveness of the U.S. Navy and the Army Air Force. In fact, no defense of the Philippines was possible in 1941–42 unless naval and air superiority could be maintained. As later actions in the war were to prove, island positions, deprived of naval and air support, could ultimately be overwhelmed or passed and left to "wither on the vine." Given America's lack of adequate preparedness on December 7, 1941, the fall of the Philippines was inevitable.

But few would have predicted that the Japanese could land in the archipelago more or less at will without suffering *any* really consequential losses from sea or air attack. U.S. air power in the islands was virtually crippled by *surprise* air attack nine hours after news of Pearl Harbor was received. And 29 submarines of the Asiatic Fleet—on paper a very formidable underwater arm—had virtually no effect on the Japanese landings and sank only three minor units of the attacking forces.[33] The surface forces of the Asiatic Fleet, which most Americans had believed would die gloriously in defense of the Philippines, instead retired under order southward, and later were virtually wiped out in futile attempts to defend the Malay barrier and the Indonesian archipelago. And on land a U.S. Philippine force, 140,000 strong, *superior in numbers* to the Japanese, was totally destroyed in the greatest single defeat of American arms in history.

Yet there *was* the true glory.

Bataan and Corregidor remained a rock slowly engulfed by the rising tide of Japanese conquest after the supposedly impregnable fortress of Singapore had fallen (on February 15), and Malaya, Borneo and the Celebes had been overrun. In early February the repulse of the Japanese offensive against the Bagac-Orion line had reduced enemy morale and enemy capabilities to their lowest ebb; as General Homma was later to testify, the Fourteenth Japanese Army was "in very bad shape." The Japanese had expected to complete their Philippine conquest by mid-February, but it was not until June 9—some four months later—that virtually all forces in the outlying islands had surrendered. General Homma, certainly never a great commander, was relegated to the sidelines until war's end; he never again held an active command. And after the war he paid the price of temporary victory in a dubious *ex post facto* war crimes trial. The "Death March of Bataan" and the brutalization of our captives by the Japanese were held by an American military court to be the responsibility of General Homma, and on April 3, 1946, he died before a firing squad in Manila, the city he had so quickly won in 1941.

The true glory of Bataan and Corregidor belongs neither to MacArthur nor to Wainwright—indeed, to no one man. It belongs to those who kept the faith and fought the good fight; in some units these were few, in others many. It belongs not exclusively to Army, Navy or Marines but to the professionals—the hard core of the services who did much with little. They won time; they forced the Japanese to reinforce Homma with more men and planes than had been intended; they held Manila Bay for five long months—as the Orange war plans had long envisaged—and they became, in President Roosevelt's words to General Wainwright prior to surrender, "the living symbols of our war aims and the guarantee of victory."

CHAPTER 5

STALINGRAD—

POINT OF NO RETURN

June 28, 1942–February 2, 1943

The Field Marshal sat waiting in cataleptic stillness, his face waxen, in the dark, deserted basement beneath the ruins of the Univermag department store.

History, he had said, had already judged him. Now he was to disappear from its stage.

The Russians moved into the bunker; mute, the Field Marshal stood up and followed them—into captivity and oblivion.

The scene: Stalingrad, January 31, 1943.

The man: Field Marshal Friedrich Paulus, commanding the German Sixth Army, first to break a long tradition that no German field marshal had ever surrendered to an enemy.

With him went into captivity more than 100,000 prisoners; with his surrender disappeared the myth of Nazi invincibility and the hope of German victory. Stalingrad, an epic four-month battle, marked the high-water mark of German conquest in World War II.

Stalingrad (until 1925 it was named Tsaritsyn) was in 1942 a provincial Soviet town of about 500,000 that hugged the western bank of the Volga, where the great river makes its sweeping loop to the west. For 30 miles along the high bluffs of the west bank, the city stretched, from tractor and tank factory and Red October steel works in the north through apartment houses and public buildings in the south.

Stalingrad in 1942 was an important part of the Russian war arsenal—the third industrial city of the Soviet Union. In that year of the war red banners and slogans in the streets exhorted the workers to maximum effort, and in the factories the party members and the commissars spurred the laggards, threatened the lazy. Yet, in early 1942, the front was about 250 to 300 miles to the west at its closest point; and though there had been air raids, the war seemed far away.

But the "Motherland" was in peril. The year before another conqueror had invaded Russia; unlike Napoleon he had almost but not quite reached Moscow. Blitzkrieg had been succeeded by attrition; the hoped-for three months' victory gradually bogged down in the huge drifts and icy frosts of a winter on the steppes. German units, laagered in "hedgehogs" and *"Kessels"* (pockets), fought and froze and died, but obeyed Adolf Hitler's orders to hold what they had won and to await the spring. And now the spring, with melting snows and muddy bogs, had come and gone; the roadless steppes were firm, and Stalingrad's days of glory and of trial were at hand.

At the end of June, 1942, Russia was beleaguered. Everywhere, from Leningrad, grim city under siege in the north, to the Crimea in the south, German armies stood deep on Soviet soil. A year of war had resulted in what seemed almost mortal blows. In the summer and fall of 1941 perhaps 2,000,000 to 3,000,000 Red Army soldiers had surrendered to the Nazis.[1] Hundreds of thousands had been killed; at the beginning of 1942 the Red Army had reached its lowest strength—2,300,000. Most of Russia's iron and coal areas were occupied.[2] Kerch was captured; the fortress of Sebastopol was falling.

It is true that, like a sponge, the vast spaces of the Soviet states absorbed more and more of the blood and brawn of the Third Reich. "General Winter" alone had cost the German Army about 113,000 frostbite cases.[3] Casualties (killed in action, wounded, missing) of the war on the Eastern Front (since Hitler's invasion on June 22, 1941) totaled, by the end of June, 1942, 1,332,477 officers and men, including more than 277,000 killed.[4]

German divisions on the Russian front were below strength and were particularly short in transportation; 75,000 vehicles had been lost in the winter battles, and 180,000 horses had been killed or "had died from hunger and exposure."[5]

And Germany's strategic position was far different than it had been in the summer of 1941. The United States, with all its immense potential, had entered the war; England's isolation had ended; the Reich had commenced to feel the fury from the skies; the fruits of the North African victory were still unrealized; and Hitler faced the specter that even he dreaded—war on many fronts.

But the Fuehrer had sounded the tocsin of alarm in the capitals of all his allies; 69 satellite divisions—27 Rumanian, 9 Italian, 13 Hungarian, 17 Finnish, 1 Spanish and 2 Slovak—had bolstered the 171 understrength German divisions on the Eastern Front.[6]

Hitler thought it was enough; his plans were grandiose, untrammeled by advice or objections from the General Staff. The recuperative powers of the Russians he dismissed; when a statement was read to him stressing the tremendous numbers of men (2,000,000) the Russians had massed on the Central Front and in the Caucasus, Hitler called it (according to General Franz Halder) "idiotic twaddle" and "flew at the man who was reading with clenched fists and foam in the corners of his mouth."

"Der Russe ist tod," he said.[7]

For the 1942 campaigns, the German and Axis forces on the 2,300-mile Eastern Front were organized in four great army groups. Army Groups North and Center—the Leningrad-Moscow fronts—were to remain on the defensive (except for pressure against Leningrad). Army Groups A and B, formed out of Army Group South, were to march to new Germanic glories.[8]

In 1942 Hitler substituted economic for military goals. Moscow, rail and communications center and political capital of "Mother Russia"—with the bulk of the Red Armies concentrated in its defense—still beckoned, but Hitler's eyes had shifted to the oil fields of the Caucasus. Gasoline shortages in the Third Reich and the vast fuel expenditures on the Eastern Front influenced him; but even more important was the advice, not of his generals but of leading German industrialists, economists and geopoliticians.

The Caucasus, and its oil fields, with its mighty mountain barrier from Batum on the Black Sea to Baku on the Caspian, was the basic objective, but beyond these snowcapped ramparts lay the far horizons of the old German dream, the *"Drang nach Osten"* ("Push to the East"). Hitler, like so many conquerors before him, had envisaged a possible eventual drive to the fabled riches of the East, the portals of India, where the hated British Raj still flew the flag on which the sun never set.[9]

In Directive No. 41, dated April 5, personally dictated by Hitler, the objectives of "Operation Blau" were outlined as the destruction of enemy forces in the Don bend, to be followed by seizure of "the oil resources of the Caucasus" and penetration of the mountain barrier. The Russians, he thought, would have to defend their principal oil fields and would

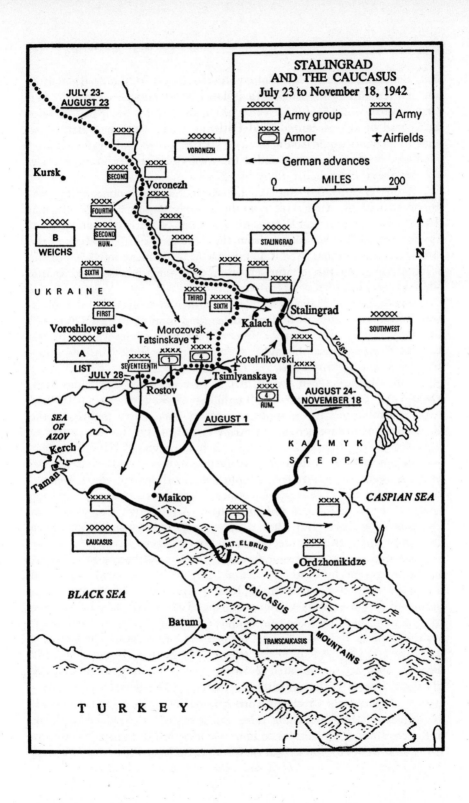

STALINGRAD
AND THE CAUCASUS
July 23 to November 18, 1942

XXXXX ☐ Army group   XXXX ☐ Army

XXXX ⬭ Armor   ✟ Airfields

⟵ German advances

0   MILES   200

JULY 23-
AUGUST 23

Kursk

XXXX
SECOND

Voronezh

XXXXX
VORONEZH

XXXX

XXXX
FOURTH

XXXX
SECOND
HUN.

B
WEICHS

XXXXX

XXXX
SIXTH

UKRAINE

Don

XXXXX
STALINGRAD

XXXX

XXXX

XXXXX
N

XXXX
FIRST

XXXX
THIRD

XXXX
SIXTH

XXXX

Voroshilovgrad

Morozovsk
Tatsinskaye

Kalach

Stalingrad

Volga

XXXXX
SOUTHWEST

XXXXX

A
LIST

JULY 28

XXXX
SEVENTEENTH

XXXX
1

XXXX
4

Rostov

Kotelnikovski

Tsimlyanskaya

XXXX

XXXX

AUGUST 1

XXXX
4
RUM.

AUGUST 24-
NOVEMBER 18

SEA
OF
AZOV

Kerch

Taman

K A L M Y K

S T E P P E

CASPIAN SEA

Maikop

XXXX

XXXX
1

XXXX

XXXX
CAUCASUS

MT. ELBRUS

Ordzhonikidze

XXXX

BLACK SEA

C A U C A S U S

Batum

XXXXX
TRANSCAUCASUS

M O U N T A I N S

T U R K E Y

thus be forced to stand and fight. His objective was "the destruction of the last remaining human defensive strength of the Soviet Union." As a step toward this objective, "every attempt was to be made to seize Stalingrad or at least bring the city within reach of German artillery so that the Soviets would be deprived of its production and transportation facilities."[10] Stalingrad was to be a by-product, a steppingstone; the Caucasus was the goal.

Army Group A—Field Marshal Wilhelm List commanding—was entrusted with the Caucasian operation; Army Group B—Field Marshal Maximilian Freiherr von Weichs commanding—was to clear the banks of the Don of all Russian forces and to hold the long northern flank of the deep Caucasian salient. About 100 of the Axis divisions and 1,500 of the 2,750 German aircraft on the Eastern Front were concentrated in the south to carry out these grandiose designs.[11]

Opposite them Marshal Semyon Timoshenko commanded the southwest, south and Caucasus fronts, with a grand total of at least 120 to 140 divisions. The Soviet strategic reserve had been concentrated in the Central Front between Moscow and Voronezh, where the Russians anticipated the main German blow.

Both General Alfred Jodl, Chief of Armed Forces Operations Staff, OKW, and General Franz Halder, Chief of Staff of the OKH, had expressed some misgivings about Operation Blau, based mainly on the inadequacy of the forces and their shortages. But they do not appear to have raised any strenuous objections; their criticisms of Hitler's strategy —as in the case of so many of the German generals—were retroactive. Hitler's propensity for relieving from command anyone who disagreed with him did not encourage objections. The dictator had, in any case, usurped the functions of the OKH (the Army High Command) on December 19, 1941, and after dismissing Field Marshal Walter von Brauchitsch had assumed direct command of the Army.

German timing was seriously affected, as it had been a year before, by the enemy and by weather. Marshal Semyon K. Timoshenko launched a massive counteroffensive in the Kharkov area on May 9, and made major initial penetrations. Paulus and the Sixth Army played a key role in stemming the Russian onslaught and in turning it into crushing defeat for the U.S.S.R. By the end of May, when the battle ended, the Germans had captured 215,000 Russian prisoners, 1,812 guns, 1,270 tanks and 542 aircraft, and had annihilated 2 Soviet armies totaling more than 22 divisions. But as Walter Görlitz has written, "The Soviet counteroffensive . . . completely wrecked all the original German plans for May."[12]

Then weather—drenching rains and a sea of mud—added to delay, as the Germans struggled against immense logistical difficulties to position men and supplies for the start of their summer offensive.

The start of the offensive appeared to justify Hitler's boundless optimism, despite some ominous indications that the Russians had breached German security. (A few days before the start of the offensive, the operations officer of a German Panzer division was shot down while flying over the front, and the Russians apparently recovered from his body a secret corps order outlining the attack plan.[13])

On June 28 the first of the hammer blows fell. The Fourth Panzer Army broke through the Russian lines in the Kursk area and by July 6 had taken Voronezh on the Don, which was to be the pivot point for the whole operation. The Sixth Army jumped off on June 30. Soon the whole Southern Front was fluid; masses of tanks, men, trucks, horses, guns pushed eastward across the wheat fields and the steppes into the fertile black-dirt area where the Don makes its great sweeping loop to the east.

The initial advances in the Don loop were "so rapid that it appeared to Hitler that Russian resistance was at an end."[14]

The Fourth Panzer Army in Army Group B and the First Panzer Army in Army Group A drew curved arcs of conquest—marked by plumes of dust—and surrounded chopped-up, struggling Russian units in confused fighting.

In the first three weeks of July the fruits of conquest seemed so easily won that Hitler, from his temporary command post at Vinnitsa in the Ukraine, ordered List to start his drive into the Caucasus. But—fatal error—on July 17 he diverted the bulk of the Fourth Panzer Army from Army Group B to Army Group A—from the middle to the lower Don—in order to help List seize the river crossings between Rostov and Kalach. This left the Sixth Army, then meeting little resistance, unsupported in its drive toward Stalingrad; it soon bogged down, west of the Don, in "wild battle."

Halder protested, but was overruled; within six days (he noted in his diary on July 23) as a result of the diversion

it is becoming obvious even to the layman that the Rostov area is crammed with armor which has nothing to do, while the critical outer wing at Tsimlyanskaya is starving for it. . . .

Now that the result is so palpable he [Hitler] explodes in a fit of insane rage and hurls the gravest reproaches against the General Staff.

This chronic tendency to underrate enemy capabilities is gradually assuming grotesque proportions and develops into a positive danger. The situation is getting more and more intolerable. There is no room for any serious work. This "leadership," so-called, is characterized by a pathological reacting to the impressions of the moment and a total lack of any understanding of the command machinery and its possibilities.[15]

Mistake Number One.

And already the German Army was outrunning its logistics; drenching downpours turned the roadless steppes into mud, and ammunition and fuel lagged far behind the armored spearheads. The First Panzer Army, driving toward the Don crossings east and north of Rostov, had only one tank battalion in each division; it had started the offensive at 40 percent war strength; by mid-July it was down to 30 percent.

But still the Panzers rumbled east and south. On July 23 Rostov fell. The Sixth Army, without the diverted Panzers of the Fourth Panzer Army to help it, was stalled in violent fighting near Kalach.

But units of Army Group A poured across the Kerch Strait, fanned out from Rostov, cut the last rail links from central Russia, pushed deep into the Caucasus. Russia's Southern Front was gaping and rent. Hitler's confidence was illimitable, his strategy wavering. He now thought the Caucasus battle won; in late July he started transferring troops away from Army Group A. The Fourth Panzer Army (weakened by the detachment of one Panzer corps to Army Group A and its replacement by a weak Rumanian corps) shifted its *"Schwerpunkt"* or main point of attack northward from the Caucasus toward Stalingrad.

Mistake Number Two.

Stalingrad, originally regarded as a by-product, a steppingstone to Caucasian triumphs, now became a prime objective; belatedly Hitler and Jodl realized (in Halder's words) "that the fate of the Caucasus will be decided at Stalingrad." The shift in objectives, the transfer of troops back and forth from Army Group A to Army Group B, plus the overextended supply systems, had made both commands "too little and too late" in both the Caucasus and in the great bends of the Don and the Volga. The Russians were in deep danger, but they had averted major encirclements and final catastrophe.

Yet August was a black month for Moscow; the German tide of conquest was still lapping to the flood.

The German Panzers rumbled ever eastward. "Like destroyers and cruisers at sea, the tank units maneuvered in the sandy ocean of the steppe, fighting for favorable firing positions, cornering the enemy, clinging to villages for a few hours or days, bursting out again, turning back, and again pursuing the enemy." Like water, the German advance sought the weakest channels; inexorably it swept eastward, ever eastward.

In early August the German XIV and XXIV Panzer Corps, and the XI and LI Infantry Corps, closed a *"Kessel"* near Kalach around the remnants of some nine Soviet divisions and nine brigades.[16]

Sixth Army cleared the Don bend, bridged the river and probed toward the Volga, the heart of "Mother Russia." In the Caucasus the front was fluid; Nazi tanks overran the Maikop oil fields; German mountain troops planted the swastika on 18,481-foot Mount Elbrus on August 21.

At Dieppe, on August 19 the British and Canadians, raiding the coast of France, were slaughtered in an abortive attempt to ease the pressure on Russia.[17] Hitler, confident about Russia, worried about the West, shifted a Panzer division to France.

After a 275-mile advance in two months, on August 23 at 6:35 P.M. tanks and Panzer Grenadiers of the 16th Panzer Division, Sixth Army, reached the Volga in strength in the northern outskirts of Stalingrad, and the trial by fire started.

It was a day of terror. The hot August sun shimmered in merciless heat against the clouds of fine dust stirred up by the tracks of the Panzers. The Luftwaffe heralded the assault on August 23, 24 and 25 with an unending attack against factories, homes, apartments. Buildings collapsed in rubble or burned in unchecked conflagrations; oil tanks by the river blazed in an inferno of leaping flame and towering black smoke; the burning oil spread across the surface of the river "until it seemed that the Volga itself was on fire."[18] The city was chaos. Hundreds of thousands of civilians still lived in Stalingrad when Hitler's legions reached its gates. Thousands died those first few days. Others, the factory workers, downed their tools and took up guns.

Women workers from the factories joined the men behind the barricades, and death levied its indiscriminate claims. Tanks were driven straight out of the tractor works into battle, "some of them still without paint and without gunsights."[19] Thousands of civilians tried on that and other nights to flee across the Volga by ferry and rowboat and anything that would float. Many made it; others drowned in the swift currents of the wide river.[20] Then, on the east bank, with the endless steppes before them, they wandered—women and children, old men and boys—seeking the sanctuary of space. On September 7 Stalin issued an order of the day:

"Not another step backward . . . The Volga has now only one bank."

Field Marshal List of Army Group A was the first of many to feel the Fuehrer's wrath; Hitler blamed others for the mistakes he himself had made. He was displeased because the entire Caucasus had not fallen to the German yoke. List went in early September and Hitler assumed remote command of Army Group A until Field Marshal Ewald von Kleist was assigned in November.

From September until November Hitler wore three hats: Commander in Chief, Army Group A; Commander in Chief of the German Army, and Commander in Chief of the German Armed Forces.

At Hitler's headquarters in early September, Colonel General Alfred Jodl also felt the mania of Hitler's wrath. For a time it appeared several heads might fall and that Paulus, commanding the Sixth Army, might relieve Jodl. But, though Hitler withdrew into himself and "shut himself up in his sunless blockhouse," Jodl had learned his lesson:

"[He] admitted he had been wrong; one should never, he said, try to point out to a dictator where he has gone wrong since this will shake his self-confidence, the main pillar upon which his personality and his actions are based."[21]

But new commanders could not solve the immense problems of an unprecedented front. Kleist's force had been milked away in large numbers for transfer to the north to reinforce the German offensive against Leningrad and, bit by bit, to strengthen the attack on Stalingrad. And behind, his foremost divisions stretched to the bottleneck of Rostov on the Don 370 miles of distance, serviced only by one dilapidated railroad, and from Rostov to Warsaw, another 1,000 railroad miles—a tenuous supply line, severed intermittently by sabotage and guerrilla attacks. For days on end Kleist's spearheads were immobilized by dry gasoline tanks; to save fuel, camel trains were improvised to transport petrol tins to the front.

Nor was the Sixth Army, with the Fourth Panzer Army to its south, in much better shape. Army Group A had been given supply priority and almost half of Army Group B's motor transport had been shifted to the south. Ammunition and gasoline shortages were persistent. Hitler, trying to be strong everywhere, was compounding weakness. The supply lines and facilities were totally inadequate to maintain both the Stalingrad and the Caucasus offensives; as Ziemke has noted, "He could not maintain both and ended up maintaining neither." By mid-September, when Paulus commenced a concentrated assault upon Stalingrad, the area between the Don and the Volga had been cleared of the Russians, and supply dumps and airfields were being completed. But the German divisions, far below strength, were spread thin across an immense and stiffening front, and food, ammunition, spare parts and, above all, fuel were in short supply.

To strengthen the battering ram at Stalingrad, Hitler milked away most of the few German divisions from the vital northern flank. The result: The hinge of the Stalingrad and Caucasian front, the exposed flank upon which the entire offensive depended, was held from Voronezh along the Don to Kletskaya by the Hungarian Second, the Italian Eighth and the Rumanian Third armies—the weakest of the Axis forces in the most important area.

It was Mistake Number Three—a fatal one.

And south of Stalingrad almost to the communications bottleneck at Rostov, there lay an open flank, across the Kalmyk steppes, held only by a single German motorized division which patrolled hundreds of miles of front (reinforced in early November by more weak troops—the Rumanian Fourth Army, transferred from the Crimea and the Caucasus).[22]

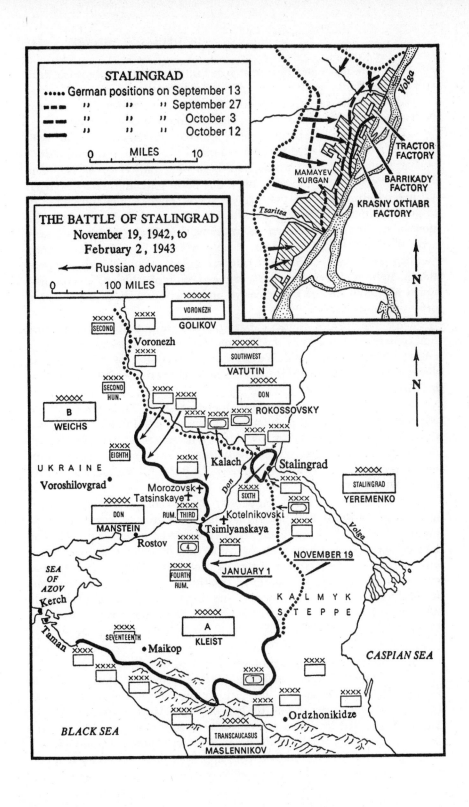

STALINGRAD
•••• German positions on September 13
━ ━ ━ "   "   " September 27
━ ━ ━ "   "   " October 3
━━━━ "   "   " October 12

0   MILES   10

TRACTOR FACTORY

BARRIKADY FACTORY

KRASNY OKTIABR FACTORY

MAMAYEV KURGAN

Tsaritsa

Volga

N

THE BATTLE OF STALINGRAD
November 19, 1942, to
February 2, 1943

← Russian advances

0   100 MILES

XXXXX
VORONEZH
GOLIKOV

XXXX
SECOND

Voronezh

XXXX

XXXXX
SOUTHWEST
VATUTIN

XXXX
SECOND HUN.

XXXXX
DON
ROKOSSOVSKY

XXXXX
B
WEICHS

XXXX

XXXX

XXXX

XXXX
EIGHTH

UKRAINE

Voroshilovgrad•

Kalach

Stalingrad

XXXXX
STALINGRAD
YEREMENKO

Morozovsk ✝
Tatsinskaye ✝

Don

XXXX
SIXTH

XXXX

XXXX
DON
MANSTEIN

XXXXX

Rostov

XXXX
RUM. THIRD

Kotelnikovski

Tsimlyanskaya ✝

XXXX

XXXX

Volga

XXXX
4

XXXX

NOVEMBER 19

SEA OF AZOV

Kerch

Taman

XXXX
FOURTH RUM.

JANUARY 1

K A L M Y K
S T E P P E

XXXX
SEVENTEENTH

XXXXX
A
KLEIST

•Maikop

XXXX

CASPIAN SEA

XXXX

XXXX
1

XXXX

XXXX

XXXX

•Ordzhonikidze

BLACK SEA

XXXX
TRANSCAUCASUS
MASLENNIKOV

N

Army Groups A and B were engaged in divergent attacks, with weak and insecure flanks, separated by 1,500 miles of hostile "Heartland."

Distance, the vast spaces of the Russian earth which had defeated Napoleon, had muffled the German blows. And summer had gone.

It was all too much for Halder, Chief of the Army General Staff. Hitler and Halder had differed for months. Arguments, recriminations and a raging spate of words had been the daily fare at Supreme Headquarters. From mid-September on, both Jodl and Field Marshal Wilhelm Keitl, Chief of the Armed Forces High Command, were in disgrace; Hitler cut his contacts with his military staff; he sought seclusion in his hut, and refused ostentatiously to shake hands with any general of the OKW.[23] Halder, deeply worried by the overextended German positions, the thin and vulnerable flanks, the mounting opposition in Stalingrad and the reports of the massing of Russian reserves, had urged abandonment of the offensive and a withdrawal to less exposed defensive positions.

On September 24 Halder's diary carried the notation: "After situation conference, farewell by the Fuehrer: My nerves are worn out, also his nerves are no longer fresh. We must part. Necessity for educating the General Staff in fanatical faith in the Idea. He is determined to enforce his will also in the Army."

General Kurt Zeitzler, former Chief of Staff of Army Group West, was promoted to general of infantry and succeeded Halder. But Zeitzler could work no miracles. He found the atmosphere at Supreme Headquarters "not only weird but positively incredible. It was compounded of mistrust and anger. Nobody had any faith in his colleagues. Hitler distrusted everyone."[24]

From then on, Hitler's propensity for directing even the detailed movements of divisional and regimental units from a command post hundreds of miles behind the front was accentuated, with all the inevitable delays, mistakes and confusion that overcentralized command always causes. The German Supreme Command was forever behind events; Hitler ignored the shattered condition of the German divisions, the immense difficulties of supply, and issued orders which had little relation to reality. The Great Dictator was like a boy playing with tin soldiers.

But the soldiers at Stalingrad were flesh and blood.

Paulus, ever obedient to Hitler's orders, drove the steel fist of the Sixth Army squarely against the city on the Volga. Just a few weeks before, had the diverted Fourth Panzer Army been available to help Paulus, Stalingrad might have been easily won, for the city, in July and early August, was virtually undefended. Now in September and October, as the days grew shorter and the cold approached, it was a city stripped for siege, grim in resolution, prepared for extinction, ready to fight.

The German attack on the main part of the city started in mid-September; for more than four months Stalingrad was to die slowly.

Paulus and his Sixth Army, with the Fourth Panzer Army on his southern flank (about five corps—20 divisions in all), held the 40-mile isthmus between the Don and the Volga and opposed in Stalingrad Lieutenant General Vasili Chuikov's Sixty-second Army, originally of about five to eight understrength divisions (later considerably reinforced).[25] Moscow created a special Stalingrad front and elements of the Sixty-fourth Army (Lieutenant General M. S. Shumilov commanding) astride the Volga assisted in the city's defense, and with the Fifty-seventh Army faced major elements of the German Fourth Panzer Army in and to the south of the city.

Stalingrad, an elongated "ribbon city," along the high west bank of the Volga, was dominated by three large groups of factories in the north (which had produced more than a quarter of the U.S.S.R.'s tractors, tanks and mechanical vehicles). Just to the west and south of the southern group was Mamayev Kurgan hill (an old Tartar burial ground), the so-called "Iron Heights." Known as Hill 102 on military maps, it rose 331 feet above the Volga. Factory smokestacks and industrial buildings dominated the high western banks and shut off the residential districts—the strange agglomerate of drab apartments and log houses—from direct access to the river. The high plateau on which the city was built was seamed by seven ravines which tended to canalize and restrict urban life and military movement.

The Germans were handicapped by their own tactics of frontal assault upon a city; their mobility was neutralized; there were no open enemy flanks. Modern cities with masonry structures, steel-beamed factories and a maze of streets make natural fortresses, as the war had shown at Warsaw and Leningrad.

The Russians were handicapped by the Volga. They fought with their backs to the river, in an elongated pattern with no depth for maneuver, and across the Volga had to come the ammunition and supplies which are the lifeblood of any army.

General Chuikov maintained his command post during part of the battle in a deep bunker on the west bank dug into the northern bank of a small tributary of the Volga, the Tsaritsa, which bisected the city.[26] On the west bank of the Volga, soldiers and civilians tunneled into the cliffs in a labyrinthine pattern of shelters and dugouts.

When the major German assault started in mid-September, there had been no general planned evacuation of the city's civilian inhabitants; Stalin had forbidden it; the soldiers, he had said, were more likely "to fight for a live town than an empty" one! Some women and children, fleeing by night, had crossed the Volga after the first heavy bombings; others had wandered westward through German lines. As the siege drew on, and the supply lines across the Volga—rafts and boats and ferries—

became strained with military traffic, the civilians either dug underground and were squeezed in little pockets up against the western bank, or they fled westward behind the German lines, across the already devastated land to die by the thousands from exhaustion and starvation. Neither side had plans or facilities to care for the civilians; the civilians lived or died—they mostly died—on their own. Some, including many of the factory staffs, stood by their lathes to the last, then picked up rifles to join the defense; others served the German conquerors as *"Hiwis"* (abbreviation for *"Helfswillige"* or voluntary helpers) as hundreds of thousands of Ukrainians had done before them.

The initial German assault carried by sheer power deep into the jumbled wreckage of the factory district and to the Iron Heights, but at desperate cost. The Sixth Army faced a battle for every house, for each rubble heap. Counterattack drove the Germans from a shell-pocked part of Hill 102. The Nazis brought up more men and tanks and bombers—milking away still more strength from their flanks—and by day and by night, hour without end, the grim assault continued, house by house, street by street, cellar by cellar, man to man.

The streets were "no longer measured by metres but by corpses."[27]

In mid-October the Germans commenced a titanic effort to liquidate the Russian bridgeheads across the Volga. Chuikov, commanding the Sixty-second Army, thought it a "battle unequalled in its cruelty and ferocity throughout the whole of the Stalingrad fighting." The tractor plant was surrounded, fighting continued within its shattered walls; casualties on both sides were enormous. Some 3,500 wounded Russians, casualties in one day's fighting, were transported across the Volga the night of October 14.

The fruit of blood was littered rubble, a few square blocks of conquest. The Germans compressed the Soviet bridgeheads, cut the positions in two, pushed their front lines almost, but not quite, to the Volga.

It was a near thing; the situation was, in Chuikov's words, "desperate."[28]

But "Stalingrad had become a second Verdun,"[29] in part because of "Mother Russia," in part because the muzhik feared the iron discipline of the commissars and the Soviet execution squads.

By the end of October about nine-tenths of the city was in German hands.[30]

Bomb and shell in Wagnerian cacophony reduced the rubble to shard, blasted for week after week the skeletonized houses, the jumble of steel and concrete and masonry that had once been a city. Through the cellars and the sewers, in the blocked and broken streets, from smashed windows and rooftops and rubble heaps, men fought and died in sudden quick assault, in shocked surmise or in prolonged agony. It was, as the somber men who fought it agreed, the *Rattenkrieg* ("War of the Rats").

Yet it was more.

Sometime in these weeks of stench and strain and smoke and flame when the Sixth Army was inching toward the Volga, Stalingrad ceased to be a battle, and the city—what was left of it—no longer was a military objective.

It became, to both sides, a symbol, a test of wills between Stalin and Hitler, between Germany and Russia, between muzhik and Panzer Grenadier. Stalingrad, once envisaged as a means to an end—the conquest of the Caucasus—had now become an end in itself.

"Where the German soldier sets foot, there he remains. You may rest assured," Hitler told the Germans, "that nobody will ever drive us away from" Stalingrad.[31]

The German defeats in North Africa and the threat of Allied air power to Field Marshal Erwin Rommel's supply lines had forced the transfer during 1942 of many aircraft from the Russian to the Mediterranean front at a time when they were vitally needed in the Stalingrad-Caucasus campaign. Now on November 8, with the Battle of El Alamein lost in Egypt, and American and British troops landing in Algeria and Morocco, Adolf Hitler in a ranting beer hall speech in Munich, far from the misery of shattered Stalingrad, screamed that "not one square yard of ground will be given up."[32]

But the Sixth Army, exhausted, cynical, had almost shot its bolt. Already, a few days before the beer hall speech, Paulus had radioed to Hitler's permanent command post, the *"Wulfschanze"* ("Wolf's Lair") near Rastenburg in East Prussia:

"Final occupation of the town with present forces not possible due to high rate of casualties. Army requests assault groups and street-fighting specialists."[33]

Four special engineer battalions, highly trained in house-to-house assault and street fighting—the greatest concentration of these specialists in so small an area during the entire war—were flown to Stalingrad, and on the night of November 9-10 the last German effort began. The objective was the elimination of the final Russian bridgeheads in Stalingrad—*"Der Tennisschläger"* ("the tennis racket"), so named for its shape—a six-square-mile area in the center of the city, and another large bridgehead in the factory district—"a place of huge and awful desolation."[34]

The ruins of the factory buildings were still partly standing with their steel framework and their walls of corrugated iron. Cellars and roofs had been turned by the enemy into pillboxes and strong-points. Piles of rubble, iron girders, parts of guns . . . broken tank transporters and shell craters made the whole terrain impassable . . . death lurked around every corner. There was danger everywhere.[35]

The assault battalions attacked and gained a building here, a block there; they reached the Volga at several points and compressed the Russian bridgeheads into tight perimeters of rubble. But there was no fresh infantry to support them, no follow-up punch; Sixth Army was drained; the last effort petered out by mid-November.

There were ominous indications that the Russians, with remarkable restraint, were feeding in just enough replacements to the ruined city to hold their bridgeheads, while concentrating major forces north and south of Stalingrad opposite the weak and exposed flanks.

And far to the south, where the attempt to conquer the Caucasus had stalled, German patrols had reached the Caspian, but only in brief exhilaration and in probing force.

In addition to the small bridgeheads in the rubble of Stalingrad, the Russians had succeeded, despite persistent German attacks, in holding several bridgeheads north and south of the city: several across the Don, to the west and *behind* the foremost positions of the Sixth Army; another across the Volga in the Fourth Panzer Army area south of the city.

And here danger loomed.

In early November Paulus urged Hitler to "break off the attack and withdraw the troops to a fortified winter line extending from Kharkov to Rostov."[36]

Hitler's answer was adamant; Stalingrad had become an obsession.

For months the Soviet counterblow was in preparation. It was the conception of the Stavka or Soviet High Command and particularly of General Georgi Zhukov, "savior" of Moscow, aided by Generals Alexander M. Vasilevski (Chief of the General Staff) and Nikolai N. Voronov.[37] All during the fall, as the Germans inched ahead in the rubble of Stalingrad, powerful forces had been concentrated in the forests north of the Don bend. Constant attacks were made on the Voronezh "hinge" to pin down the German Second Army, and fords across the Don were seized.

Three army "fronts" were created west of the Volga and north of Stalingrad: the Voronezh (Lieutenant General Filipp I. Golikov), the Southwest (Lieutenant General Nikolai F. Vatutin), and the Don (Lieutenant General Konstantin Rokossovsky). The Stalingrad front (Lieutenant General Andrei Yeremenko) included the city and, south of it, the Ergeni Hills and the northern part of the Kalmyk steppe.[38] A mass of more than half a million Soviet troops and some 900 to 1,500 tanks and 13,500 artillery pieces and mortars had been concentrated on the flanks of the Don and Volga bends until the ground froze and the mud of fall congealed. (The first snow fell on November 16; the bitter wind blew off the steppes, and the ground was hard as iron.)

The objectives were ambitious—to trap the Sixth Army in Stalingrad. Later (it was hoped but not planned) Rostov might be recaptured and parts of Army Group A isolated in the Caucasus. A holding offensive on the Central Front, opposite Moscow, was intended to pin down German divisions and prevent their transfer to the threatened southern areas.

The Germans apparently saw the thunderbolt poised, but Hitler's strategic inflexibility prevented a logical reaction.

On November 19, when the Communists struck, the Nazis were still inching forward in Stalingrad; they had seized Ordzhonikidze in the Caucasus, and their thinly held front was within 75 miles of the Caspian Sea. It was the high-water mark of German conquest; from November 19, 1942, onward for two and a half bitter years it was an ebbing tide for Nazi hopes.

The Russians concentrated their assault against fronts held by Germany's hapless allies—first the Rumanians, later the Italians and the Hungarians.

Rokossovsky and Vatutin struck first—southward toward Kalach—against the Third Rumanian Army, which was thinly holding about a 100-mile sector with battalion frontages averaging one to two miles. Yeremenko (with the Fifty-first and Fifty-seventh Soviet Armies) on November 20 broke through the Fourth Rumanian Army to the south of Stalingrad and drove northward toward Kalach.

From the beginning, it was Russian weather. It began to snow in the early dark of the nineteenth, the temperature was 21 above zero Fahrenheit and visibility was "nil."

For seven and a half hours the Russian massed artillery thundered; then, across terrain which looked as though "cast from molten earth—the surface . . . twisted into weird shapes,"[39] thousands of Russian tanks debouched across the ridge lines, with the Twenty-first Soviet Army and Fifth Soviet Tank Army—about 21 divisions in all—in the van.

It was immediate rout. The Soviet troops tore a gap 50 miles wide in the north, 30 miles across in the south. Rumanian divisions disintegrated, fled, fought, died, surrendered. . . . A weak German Panzer division (part of an understrength so-called German corps), ordered only a few days earlier to back up the Rumanian front, arrived piecemeal too little and too late and was engulfed bit by bit.[40] By November 23 Vatutin and Yeremenko had closed their pincers at Sovetskiy near Kalach on the Don bend. A series of green flares heralded the closing of the pincers; the converging Russian units understood their triumph; soldiers hugged and kissed each other.[41] The encirclement cut the railroad to Stalingrad and cut off more than 200,000 soldiers of the Sixth Army, most of the German elements of the Fourth Panzer Army, parts of two Rumanian divisions, Luftwaffe units, a Croat regiment and some 70,000 noncombatants ("*Hiwis*," prisoners of war and others). Soon the vast Don bend was littered with the flotsam of military disaster—fleeing men, wounded dragging across the snow, blazing tanks, abandoned arms and dumps, a scraggle of isolated battles as small units stood and died—and tried, in vain, to stem the Russian tide.

Back at Rastenburg in East Prussia, where Hitler had returned from his barn-storming political speeches in Bavaria, General Zeitzler, the new Army Chief of Staff, tried to persuade the dictator to order an immediate breakout attempt by the Sixth Army.

Hitler, in a fury, "crashed his fist down on the table, shouting, 'I won't leave the Volga. I won't go back from the Volga.' "[42]

Late on November 22 Paulus knew he was surrounded and so reported to Hitler. Hitler's orders: move army headquarters into the city of Stalingrad; form a hedgehog (all-around defense) and hold fast. Thus, in a pocket of open steppe and little village and shattered city, originally about one-third the size of Connecticut, then reduced to an area about 37 miles wide from east to west, and 23 miles deep from north to south, the Sixth Army stood at bay.

Hitler proudly dubbed them "the troops of Fortress Stalingrad."

It was an ill-prepared "fortress"—its defenders decimated, disorganized, wearied by months of fighting, inadequately supplied and equipped, a "fortress" whose new front lines (to the west) had to be prepared in raging blizzard and icy cold on open steppe.

And its supply lines were severed.

But, ironically, so, too, were the supply lines of the Russian defenders. For Soviet troops in Stalingrad itself, the very moment of triumph—when Paulus was encircled—was the period of maximum danger and greatest toil. From late October to December 17 (when the river froze), the water in the Volga rose; great fields of heavy shifting ice formed, pontoon bridges were swept away, and the river crossing—by ferry, icebreaker, tug, rowboat—became at times impossible, always arduous, five to ten hours per crossing, instead of 40 to 50 minutes.[43] It was a period of superhuman toil when the Russian bridgeheads in Stalingrad were held by sweat and muscle as much as by blood, when the enemy was nature as much as the Germans.

Sixth Army required a minimum of 500 tons of supplies per day to keep fighting—or even living.[44]

In East Prussia Reich Marshal Hermann Göring, the corpulent drug-taker, assured Hitler that the Luftwaffe could supply the Sixth Army's minimum needs by air. He was challenged by Zeitzler, but Hitler believed what he wanted to believe: Sixth Army was to stand fast; the Luftwaffe would deliver its needs; help would come from without.

The airlift started, unpropitiously, about November 25, and on the twenty-seventh Field Marshal Fritz Erich von Manstein, shifted from the Northern Front, hurriedly took command of a newly created Army

Group Don, composed of the shattered remnants of the Third and Fourth Rumanian armies, the Fourth Panzer Army and the encircled Sixth Army, plus such few reinforcements as could be spared from the Caucasus and the Northern Front.

The 6th Panzer Division was ordered from faraway Brittany to provide a spearhead of fresh troops. The 80 trains that moved it were delayed by blown bridges, ripped-up rails and guerrilla attacks; it reached the cold steppes and the forlorn prospects somewhat late but with 160 tanks and 40 assault guns. Manstein's task: to break through the Russian encirclement and relieve "Fortress Stalingrad." It was a formidable mission; by the end of November the Russian ring of steel had thickened to some 30 to 60 kilometers.

Manstein, possibly the ablest German commander of World War II, moved with vigor; in an offensive code-named "Winter Storm" he attacked Yeremenko along the Kotelinkovski-Stalingrad railway on December 12, and made major initial gains. The LVII Panzer Corps— initially composed of the 23rd and 6th Panzer divisions, later reinforced by the 17th Panzer Division—spearheaded the attempt to break the ring. By December 21 Manstein's Panzers were some 30 miles from the Sixth Army's outposts; the Germans saw "on the horizon the reflection of the gunfire" at Stalingrad.[45]

But it was already too late. For the Russian offensive broadened; Vatutin and Golikov had crashed through the Italian Eighth Army on the Don ("the entire front fell apart" in complete rout[46]) between the sixteenth and the nineteenth, and Manstein's flank was threatened. On December 19 Manstein radioed Paulus to drive south to meet him. But Paulus was never a commander with a "blind eye"; his obedience to orders was literal. He told Manstein he had only 20 miles of fuel for his tanks (Paulus had at this time only 60 operational tanks), yet it was not primarily lack of fuel but Hitler's orders which chained him to impassivity. The attempt at relief had failed; the German debacle was broadening. On Christmas Day the Fourth Army was in full retreat; Paulus was doomed.[47]

Within Stalingrad and on its surrounding steppes, the rapid deterioration—body, soul and mind—of the surrounded legions had well started.

An army was dying.

The pocket was short of all things—save misery. The airlift had failed. Instead of 500 tons daily—60,000 gallons of fuel; 40 tons of bread; 100 tons of other supplies, including food; 40 tons of ammunition and weapons—the average amount flown in had been less than one-fifth of the bare minimum needed. It was no fault of the pilots or air crews; the vainglorious Göring had promised the impossible. Stalingrad lay in a weather "pocket" at the edge of a "meteorological frontier" which severely restricted flying. There were not enough planes—180 Ju-52's, some Junkers 86's, and less than 100 Heinkel 111's; there were not enough airfields—two main ones at Pitomnik and Gumrak within the pocket (with two alternatives). Two key air resupply fields outside the pocket (Tatsinskaye and Morozovsk) were engulfed in Vatutin's December and January offensives. The planes ran the gantlet of Soviet antiaircraft and fighter opposition; in the whole operation, 500 to 600 transport aircraft were lost,[48] and by the end of December—due in part to transfers to the Mediterranean—there were only 375 single-engined fighters with the swastika on their wings on the entire Eastern Front.

It was a grim Christmas in Stalingrad. There was little cheer—for many only "German tea," or melted snow. On Hill 135, a little pine tree, decorated with paper ornaments and a few candles, stood glimmering for an hour before mortar fire destroyed it. Beneath a wrecked tank in the ruins of a factory the graves of four German soldiers were marked by the wavering light of a single candle. In the cellars and the dugouts, a few soldiers sang *"Stille Nacht, heilige Nacht"* and *"O du Fröhliche."*

And over the radios, where Christmas carols and messages of hope came from faraway Germany, there intervened, with rasp of static at frequent intervals, the voice of Radio Moscow:

"Every seven seconds a German soldier dies in Russia. Stalingrad—mass grave. One . . . two . . . three . . . four . . . five . . . six . . . seven . . . Every seven seconds a German soldier dies."

Sixth Army was starving.

The stiff carcasses of frozen horses were hacked to bits for meat; rats, cats and dogs and bits of food scrounged from the wreckage of Stalingrad went into empty bellies.[49] The prisoners suffered, too—even the "tried and trusted" Russian auxiliaries, who collaborated with the Germans. At Voroponov POW Transit Camp No. 204 Russians died by the hundreds. Fifty scrawny horses were sent to the camp, but it was not enough.

Sixth Army was freezing.

Many of the German troops were inadequately clothed. Whole trainloads of winter clothing and equipment had been shipped to the Eastern Front, but much of it arrived too late; the trains were stalled far from Stalingrad.[50]

The implacable winter held the Germans in its iron grip. Those in the ruins of Stalingrad were lucky; they had some shelter and huddled over fires fueled by rubble. The temperature fell to 20 to 30 below zero. Those on the open steppes froze and died in the awful wind, the impersonal, searching, cruel cold. And the snow soon hid their deaths.

Sixth Army was ill and exhausted.

Dysentery, typhus, spotted fever, frostbite, ravaged the ranks; dirty, bearded specters stood sentinel and died, too weak to fire a shot.

Sixth Army was wounded.

There were not enough drugs, dressings, doctors, plasma, anesthetic; not enough planes to take the wounded out. Thirty thousand wounded were ready for evacuation long before the end; most of them died. Each wounded man was tagged for air evacuation; "Hans" called these tags "reprieve tickets." The walking wounded staggered or crawled to the airstrips; the stretcher cases were parked in tents and in the snow by the strips. Each time a plane came in there was a staggering, winding trail of blood to its parking place; as the end came on, "the whole organization broke down."

"The numbers of the wounded increased by the thousands, and they often stormed the aircraft . . . many being killed in their struggles to get aboard."[51]

But Sixth Army was still fighting as the New Year dawned—endlessly, ceaselessly, bitterly, hopelessly, by day and by night, until whole units ceased to exist, as the encirclement tightened, as the cold deepened, as hunger knotted the bowels, as the wounded screamed in delirium or unassuaged agony, as the Russians waited. . . . There was never an end to fighting, to shellfire, to mortars, to the staccato of machine guns and the sharp crack of rifles, to the stab in the dark. The Volga was solid now; the Soviet supply problem within the city was eased. The German problem was hopeless.

On New Year's Day, 1943, Hitler radioed to the starving troops in Stalingrad:

"The men of the Sixth Army have my word that everything is being done to extricate them."[52]

About December 28 General Hans V. Hube, a corps commander (XIV Corps) under Paulus, was flown out of the pocket to report to Hitler and to be decorated with a high Nazi medal—the Swords to the Oak Leaves of the Knight's Cross to the Iron Cross. When Hube flew back to Stalingrad on January 8, he brought with him Hitler's message to hold until the spring. Hitler, with his monomania, was still playing toy soldiers.

But spring was far away; life was ebbing from the Panzer Grenadiers in Stalingrad and Sixth Army was already in dissolution.

And now a greater disaster threatened. For all these weeks, while Sixth Army was fighting for its life, two armies of Kleist's Army Group A in the Caucasus had held their vulnerable and far-flung positions, while the Don flank, on which their safety depended, collapsed behind them. Grudgingly, toward the end of December, Hitler permitted Zeitzler to order their withdrawal. It was the last moment. Manstein, repulsed in his attempt to relieve Stalingrad, was now fighting desperately to hold open the gateway to safety at Rostov, against the onpouring Russian legions of Vatutin, which had smashed the Italian Eighth Army. And thus, while Sixth Army died, Kleist conducted a brilliant though precipitate retreat from the Caucasian high-water mark of German conquest, as Manstein held open the Rostov gateway.

But what was going on outside the pocket, few in Sixth Army knew—or cared.

At the beginning of January Sixth Army held a shattered area about 20 miles long by 30 miles deep. It was under constant attack from Rokossovsky's Don Army front, reinforced now to seven armies.[53] On January 8 three Russian officers, under a flag of truce, brought a demand for immediate surrender to Paulus. Sixth Army transmitted the Soviet ultimatum to Hitler and requested freedom of action. Hitler refused. There was to be no surrender. It was to be to the death.

At 0804 on the tenth of January a general assault on the pocket, with the main effort from the west—or across the open steppes—started, supported by 7,000 guns and mortars. The Russians expected to finish off the Sixth Army in three to seven days. But the Germans fought on. It was a grim, relentless battle. Slowly, the ring compressed; the German lines in the open steppes to the west of Stalingrad were driven inward. The snowy wastes were littered with frozen dead, their limbs and features petrified by the cold into contorted immobility. Those who crossed that eerie landscape forever remembered it; the track was marked by "the frozen legs of horses which had been hacked off the dead animals [and] had been stuck into snow, hooves upward."[54] By the fourteenth the main airfield at Pitomnik had been taken; within a few days the western defense perimeter had been breached; the Germans began to collapse.

Paulus again reported to Hitler that his army was dying, that his survivors were enduring the unendurable.

The scenes in the cellars and dugouts of Stalingrad made the drawings of Goya or the inferno of Dante seem pale. The wounded lay untended, bleeding, their anguish uneased by morphia, the dead beside the dying, the living yearning for the end. The sweet, sick stench of human excrement, of putrefying bodies, of decay and filth and dissolution pervaded nearly every dugout. And the lice crawled. . . .

The masonry cellars, with the piled rubble of Stalingrad above them, were secure from shell and bomb (though never from cold or disease or death or misery, from gangrene or diphtheria or despair). *Rattenkrieg*—the war of the human rats—went on, drawing now to its inevitable conclusion.

"In the cellar under Simonvich's warehouse," Heinz Schröter reported, "800 men lay pressed against the walls and all over the damp and dirty floor. . . . A man lay on the steps dying of diphtheria, and beside him lay three others who had been dead for days, but no one had moved them because it was dark and they had not been noticed."[55]

By mid-January the Stalingrad pocket was compressed to an area about 15 miles long by 9 miles deep, with Russian salients and re-entries —bridgeheads across the Volga—thrust into the German citadel. The airlift was petering out in snow and squall and disaster as the Russian front lines, pushing both west and east, overran airfield after airfield. On January 17 a second Russian ultimatum was rejected.

In the second half of January as the Soviets, driving hard, were chopping the Stalingrad pocket in two, Kleist's Army Group A retreating from the Caucasus found sanctuary in the Taman peninsula bridgehead or reached the Don and crossed it near Rostov—just in time to escape disaster. For the Russian offensive broadened. Golikov's Voronezh Army front struck between January 13 and 16 against the remaining Italians (and captured 17,000 of them) and then broke through the Hungarian Second Army and the German Second Army near the Voronezh hinge on the Don, and turned victory into rout. Within a few days the entire German Don front was, in euphemistic terms, "fluid"; there was no stable front for 200 miles between Manstein at Voroshilovgrad and Voronezh. And all the while the long and bitter frozen miles between the entrapped and dying army at Stalingrad and its nearest allies outside the pocket lengthened. Sixth Army was battered on all sides by elements of seven Soviet armies.

In Stalingrad trapped men under stress bent and broke or died; each in his own way endured the unendurable. There was to be no surrender; Hitler had made this clear again and again. Paulus, with the queer dignity of quiet stubbornness, had reiterated Hitler's orders since the days when he had been urged to disobey and to break out of the pocket to meet Manstein in the south.

"For me," he had said, "the first duty of a soldier is to obey."

And so the orders had gone out: no surrender—fight to the last, death in battle or suicide. Some followed them literally; some defied them; others ignored them; some commanders surrendered themselves and their entire units; but for the most part Sixth Army just melted away, like flesh sloughing off a burned body. As each day passed casualties wiped from the rolls another unit.

On January 22 the Gumrak airstrip fell. On the next day the last physical link with the outside world—the Stalingradski field—was lost; 150 to 200 miles of frozen, ravaged land now lay between the Stalingrad pocket and the main front. But the loss was anticlimactic; the airlift had averaged only 80 to 90 tons of supplies a day instead of the minimum 500 tons needed and promised.

Again on January 24 a stark message was flashed to Hitler:

TROOPS WITHOUT AMMUNITION OR FOOD. CONTACT MAINTAINED WITH ELEMENTS OF ONLY SIX DIVISIONS. EVIDENCE OF DISINTEGRATION ON SOUTHERN, NORTHERN AND WESTERN FRONTS. EFFECTIVE COMMAND NO LONGER POSSIBLE. LITTLE CHANGE ON EASTERN FRONT: 18,000 WOUNDED WITHOUT ANY SUPPLIES OR DRESSINGS OR DRUGS: 44TH, 76TH, 100TH, 305TH AND 384TH INFANTRY DIVISIONS DESTROYED. FRONT TORN OPEN AS A RESULT OF STRONG BREAK-THROUGHS ON THREE SIDES. STRONG-POINTS AND SHELTER ONLY AVAILABLE IN THE TOWN ITSELF, FURTHER DEFENSE SENSELESS. COL-LAPSE INEVITABLE. ARMY REQUESTS IMMEDIATE PERMISSION TO SURRENDER IN ORDER TO SAVE LIVES OF REMAINING TROOPS.   SIGNED: PAULUS.[56]

The answer was terse:

CAPITULATION IS IMPOSSIBLE. THE SIXTH ARMY WILL DO ITS HISTORIC DUTY AT STALINGRAD UNTIL THE LAST MAN, IN ORDER TO MAKE POSSIBLE THE RECONSTRUCTION OF THE EASTERN FRONT.[57]

". . . until the last man . . ."

By January 24, with the pocket split in two, a concerted defense was impossible. German gunners were firing their last artillery and mortar shells and destroying their guns; some of the remaining trucks, out of gasoline, were burned or crippled. A Rumanian unit deserted en masse, with weapons and equipment, to the Russians. Hundreds tried to filter through the Russian encirclement and started the long and hopeless trek across the frozen, devastated steppe toward German lines 200 miles away. One sergeant reached sanctuary weeks later, only to die in a front-line dressing station.

There was no longer, as January ended, a controlled battle—only a series of individual fire fights: the yammer of the submachine guns, the thrown grenade, the ferocious struggle for a shattered building, the fight of the doomed. . . .

"The struggle petered out, now here, now there, as a candle gutters and dies."[58]

As Sixth Army sent its final hopeless situation report—the defense split into three pockets: "Army calculates its resistance must finally collapse not later than February 1st"—the world watched the Wagnerian end, and Germany awoke, with horror, to the slow death of an army. The High Command communiqués toward the end of January for the first time hinted of complete disaster, and the vacuous Göring in a speech on January 30 compared the Stalingrad soldiers to the defenders of Ther-mopylae.

Yet even to the end the Germans fought, without hope, with little strength, but with the same instinctive skill and drive that has made the armies of Germany the scourge of modern Europe. On January 30, as the long battle died, the 295th Infantry Division counterattacked and recaptured a block of shattered buildings just lost to the Russians.[59]

On January 31 Paulus, who believed the first duty of a soldier was to obey, sat in a state of shock, with blank face and staring eyes, on his cot. He was in his last command post, deep beneath the ruins of the Univermag department store in a dead city gutted by four months of combat. He had been promoted to field marshal; upon Paulus and his surviving officers and men had been showered in the final hours radio accolades from Hitler far away, promotions, decorations. . . .

They were bitter apostrophes to dissolution and disaster, yet the sense of form, not the reality of tragedy, dominated most of Sixth Army's official reactions until the end.

"The Sixth Army," the Field Marshal had wirelessed, "true to their oath and conscious of the lofty importance of their mission, have held their position to the last man and the last round for Fuehrer and Fatherland unto the end."

At the last, Paulus funked his own "no surrender" orders and left surrender details to his chief of staff.[60]

On January 31, 1943, Sixth Army headquarters sent its last message: "The Russians stand at the door of our bunker. We are destroying our equipment."

And the operator added: "CL"—"This station will no longer transmit."

It took a few days longer to mop up. The northern pocket, held by the XI Corps, was overrun on February 2, and that day a German reconnaisance pilot reported: "No sign of any fighting at Stalingrad."

The German Reich was stunned, numbed with apprehension; the despised *Untermensch* had defeated the Nazi "Supermen." For the first time, in those early days of February, the full dimensions of catastrophe became apparent to the German people. Deliberately, Goebbels emphasized the "glories" of defeat, and the German radio played, over and over again the Siegfried Funeral March and *"Ich hatt' ein' Kamaraden."*[61] The shock was traumatic, but effective. In place of the arrogant confidence of the past, the Nazis fought in the future with desperation.

With Paulus into captivity went 23 generals, 2,000 to 2,500 officers and almost 90,000 German enlisted men—all that was left of the Sixth Army—some Rumanians and an unknown number (perhaps 30,000 to 40,000) of German noncombatants, and Russian "auxiliaries" and civilians. (An additional 17,000 prisoners had been captured by the Russians between January 10 and 29.)

The statistics of Armageddon will be forever incomplete, but no matter how estimated they are appalling. In mid-October the ration strength of the Sixth Army had been something like 334,000 men. A segment was separated from the main part of the Army, and retreated westward to rejoin the main German forces during the Soviet break-through in mid-November. On November 23 Paulus estimated Sixth Army strength in the Stalingrad pocket at 220,000. Between 40,000 and 50,000 wounded and specialists were evacuated from the Stalingrad area by ground and air before and during the siege. Another 60,000 to 100,000 were killed, or died of illness or starvation or cold in and around Stalingrad, or were among the thousands of unfortunates who were suffering in the so-called medical bunkers in Stalingrad when the end came. For many of these wounded survival was not for long; some were entombed alive as bunkers and cellars were sealed by explosives as the victorious Russians mopped up. Others met their ends as grenades or flame throwers sought out the crevices in the ruins.

Those Germans who died in Stalingrad were, perhaps, more fortunate than those who lived. At Beketovka POW camp on the Volga, just south of Stalingrad, thousands of German prisoners—some estimates say 40,000 to 50,000—died of starvation, cold and hardship in the first weeks of captivity. Thousands of others died in the subsequent years. Life was cheap on the Eastern Front. About 5,000 to 6,000 lived throughout the long night of captivity to return to Germany years after the war.[62]

Paulus, castigated by Hitler for his failure to choose death among the ruins rather than life in captivity, lived to testify at Nuremberg. He emerged a shrunken figure, faintly ignoble, ambivalent, with his value judgments shaken, his mind seemingly confused.

Friedrich Paulus—he who was known when a handsome young officer as "The Lord" or "The Major with the Sex Appeal"—was the centerpiece of the Battle of Stalingrad. Upon him and his decisions depended the fate of an army. Walter Görlitz' oversympathetic portrait reveals the man as a painstaking master of minutiae, reserved almost to the point of introversion, with no flair, an experienced and dependable staff officer but with little prior command experience, methodical, slow in decision but stubborn, "a cog in the highly functionalized system of command, completely centralized and controlled by Hitler." Paulus was "the painstaking traditional soldier, who weighed every aspect thrice before reaching a decision."

History will sympathize with Friedrich Paulus; he faced the crucial conflict of any soldier—the conflict of when to disobey. He chose obedience—largely, he later said, because he did not, and could not, know the "big picture." But he won disaster, and in part because he lacked the boldness and the moral courage which are the fundamental requirements of a great commander. He who could have saved an army lives in history as an example of the blind obedience to authoritarianism which has so often been the cause of Germany's downfall.[63]

For Germany, after Stalingrad, the long road of retreat began—in Russia, in North Africa, eventually in Western Europe. By early February, 1943, Kleist still held a Kuban bridgehead across the Kerch Strait in the Caucasus, but the rest of the German Southern Front—all idea of the *"Drang nach Osten"* abandoned—had reeled back through bloody snow to where the great Caucasus offensive had started in the full flesh of summer hopes.

It was the "end of the beginning" for the German Army, which knew now that Russia would never surrender. And it was the beginning of the end for the offensive power of the German Air Force; in Göring's later words, at Stalingrad and in the Mediterranean during those months of crisis in 1942–43 "there died the core of the German bomber fleet." Many of the bombers were downed in flaming destruction, not as eagles striking their prey but pressed into service as cargo carriers in a vain attempt to save the Sixth Army from the destruction which would not be denied.

Stalingrad "was a turning point in the air battle on the eastern front," Richard C. Lukas has written.

As the scale of Soviet operations unfolded during the battle of Stalingrad, it became increasingly apparent that the Luftwaffe was unable to match the strength of the Soviet Air Force. . . . From that point until the end of the war, the Soviet Air Force had virtually unchallenged air superiority on the eastern front.[64]

For Russia Stalingrad was a tremendous, though costly, victory. Exact Soviet casualties will probably never be known; the Germans could estimate them, but their records were lost with the Sixth Army. Moscow did not compile reliable casualty statistics; then as now, there were no Russian graves registration details; if men did not come home, they were presumed dead or missing. One "guesstimate" of Soviet casualties is 400,000 to 600,000 in the entire Stalingrad campaign (exclusive of the Caucasus), as compared to an Axis over-all loss of perhaps 600,000 (exclusive of the Caucasus).

The consequences of Stalingrad were unending.

As Fuller expresses it, "Stalingrad was a second Poltava in which Hitler was as much the architect of his own ruin as was Charles XII in 1709. Into the minds of a hundred million Muscovites flashed the myth of Soviet invincibility, and it forged them into the Turks of the North."[65]

The tremendous strengthening of Russian morale was accompanied by an immediate drop in German spirit. The specter of defeat and the threat of Red Bolshevism for the first time stalked the German mind.

"The German soldier was highly reluctant to go to the Eastern Front."[66]

But Stalingrad was the "signal of Hitler's ruin . . . not its cause."[67]

The Nazi legions had been greeted in large parts of Russia (particularly in the Ukraine, yearning for freedom) the year before Stalingrad as liberators with cheers and flowers. But Hitler's contempt for any non-German, and particularly for the "subhumans" of Russia, dictated a policy of conquest rather than of liberation, and the invaded areas were turned over, despite Army protest, not to Army rule but to the cruel barbarities of the Gauleiters. In March, 1941, the "Commissar Order," issued by Hitler, directed the shooting of all captured Soviet commissars. This was followed in May by a decree which explicitly excluded Russian civilians in the occupied areas from any appeal to a military court; it also stated that offenses against civilians by members of the Wehrmacht would not necessarily lead to court-martial. Such edicts, even though enforced more in theory than in fact by some German commanders, were superimposed upon Hitler's reluctance to utilize effectively, either in combat or for propaganda, the vast numbers of captured Soviet soldiers, and his failure to capitalize politically upon Ukrainian separatist ambitions. Partisan warfare behind the German lines, inconsequential in 1941, became worrisome in 1942 and ominous in 1943. Whole provinces that had welcomed the conquerors soon turned into areas dominated by a great hatred for all things German. The Nazi policies had inevitably consolidated Soviet opposition, and the Communists skillfully dramatized the peasants' love for "Mother Russia."

But Allied policies—specifically the "unconditional surrender" demand issued at Casablanca on January 23, 1943, and the failure to differentiate between Hitler and the German people—provided a stiffening of determination to Germany at the very time the nation was shaken with the specter of Bolshevism triumphant. The situation was made to order for Goebbels. The Propaganda Minister pictured the Nazis as knights-errant, standing between the civilization of Western Europe and the dark abyss of the godless hordes. The Franklin D. Roosevelt–Winston Churchill ultimatum cut the props from beneath several factions in Germany who were plotting to replace or subordinate Hitler. After Stalingrad, many of the high officers in the German Army were in at least subconscious rebellion, but the Casablanca declaration, with its strong implication of a prostrate Germany ravaged by Communist hordes from the East, quenched even the inner fires of revolt. Given so stark an alternative as "unconditional surrender," there seemed to be to most Germans no choice but to fight on.[68]

Because, primarily, of its political and psychological effects Fuller saw Stalingrad—with the exception of the Normandy landing—as "the most decisive of all the battles of the war."[69]

Von Senger und Etterlin, who participated as a division commander in the abortive attempt by the Fourth Panzer Army to relieve Stalingrad, saw the battle as "one of the few decisive battles of the Second World War, not merely because it marked the loss of an army . . . but because it represented a culminating point, after which the Axis powers were forced on to the defensive. The war potential of the Allies had clearly proved itself superior."[70]

Stalingrad was a battle whose tortured architecture was carved from many mistakes, where little went according to plan.

The strategy of both sides was faulty. The Germans, under Hitler's command, had, from the beginning, a confused picture of their objective; they violated military principles by shifting from one objective to another in the midst of a campaign. Forces were dispersed instead of concentrated. The Caucasus offensive should never have been started until the exposed flank along the Don and Volga from Voronezh through Stalingrad to Rostov had been completely consolidated and was firmly held. And properly speaking, it should never have been launched at all; the correct German objective was the destruction of the Soviet Army, not the conquest of terrain or economic goals.

Actually—and ironically—Stalingrad itself was not an essential element of the German strategy, but a secure flank along the Don was.

Once the Sixth Army was committed fully to Stalingrad's capture, the Germans should have employed to the full their superior power of maneuver instead of becoming entrapped and pinned down in endless bloody street fighting. Later—at the latest by early November, when Paulus suggested breaking off the battle and withdrawal—the Sixth Army should have been pulled back at least beyond the Don. When the Russian breakthrough of November 19 closed a ring around the Sixth Army, a quick breakout could have saved most of the Army and might have restored the front. Even until December 21, when Manstein's relief drive stalled, breakout was probably possible, certainly it should have been attempted. Even the Russians admitted subsequently that such an effort might have succeeded; their military historians, writing a few months later not for public history but for military eyes, stated that "the failure of the encircled enemy to make any determined effort to break out of encirclement saved our troops from a situation which might have been serious."[71]

For most of this Hitler and his rigid centralized system of command were to blame—Hitler and some of the moral cowards of the German

Army, who possessed little of the instinct for greatness, and whose obedience was almost subservient.

Hitler was, in fact, a poor loser. His mad genius included an intuitive instinct for timing when he held the initiative, but his obsessive rigidity doomed his armies when they were forced to the defensive. He insisted upon holding whatever he won; he based his defense on an obsolescent linear concept, thus depriving the German armies of their greatest asset: mobility and the highly trained professional initiative of the German officer and noncom. These became but robots answering, like puppets, to the ruler's will. The dead hand of Hitler's command dominated the Stalingrad campaign.

At the last from Christmas on, when the Sixth Army was dying in its final convulsive agonies, Hitler was correct in forbidding its surrender and Paulus was right in his acquiescence. Hitler was right for the wrong reasons; his own megalomania had sent the First Panzer Army and the Seventeenth Army deep into the Caucasus; their safety hung on what happened at Stalingrad. Had Paulus surrendered in early January, Army Group A—or large parts of it—would probably have been doomed in a disaster greater than Stalingrad, for the Rostov gateway and the Kerch Strait were its lifelines to the west. As it was, it was a near thing.

Elements of Army Group A did not cross the lower Don—where Manstein was fighting desperately to hold the gate—until after January 18, and Kleist's headquarters and much of the Seventeenth Army were not pulled back to a more or less secure bridgehead covering the Kuban and the Taman peninsula until the end of the month. Rostov was finally captured after a desperate defense on February 14. Had the Russian forces around Stalingrad been freed for other operations early in January, Kleist would probably have been doomed.[72]

So, at the end, in the last horrible weeks of dissolution and agony, Sixth Army did not die in vain; Hitler was at length right when he exhorted Paulus to final effort with the phrase that "every day Sixth Army holds out helps the entire front."[73]

But the German mistakes were not Hitler's alone. In retrospect German commentators have placed nearly all the blame for the entrapment of Sixth Army and for the success of the initial Russian blow of November 19 upon Hitler and his "no-retreat" orders. But German intelligence, perhaps influenced by Hitlerian policy which kept insisting the Russians were defeated, appears to have been only partially successful in estimating Soviet capabilities and in identifying the areas of maximum Russian build-up.

"Evaluation and interpretation was often colored by wishful thinking."[74]

It is true that radio silence, troop movements by night, deception and other security measures made it difficult to predict either the time or the exact place of any attempted Soviet counterblow. The Germans did believe something was coming (and Hitler's "intuition" about the point of attack was correct). Uneasiness steadily increased from October on, and in the Sixth Army area signs of enemy concentrations on the flanks were noted and recorded, and intelligence estimates noted new Soviet bridge-heads across the Don in the area of the Third Rumanian Army. Some even predicted the places and times with approximate accuracy. Nevertheless, what intelligence experts call "the indicators" were not (a) assessed too seriously or (b) adequate in number or importance. The Germans lost track of the Russian Fifth Tank Army altogether before the Soviet blow, and as late as November 6 a high-level German intelligence estimate stated:

"The main effort is expected in the area of Army Group Center [far to the north of Stalingrad]. It is uncertain whether the Russians, in addition, are planning a larger operation across the Don."[75]

A fundamental factor in the German defeat was that the Nazis attempted far too much with far too little, and their entire campaign was based on a supply and logistics structure completely incapable of dealing with the vast distances, sparse communications and climatic extremes encountered. A single railway bridge across the Dnieper at Dniepropetrovsk was the tiny funnel through which all supplies for Army Group A and most of Army Group B had to pass. No officer in prewar times who had dared suggest such a logistical solution in the paper wars at the German Kriegsakademie would ever have passed.

The Russians, too, made major mistakes, tactically and strategically.

They early misjudged the German intentions and believed the drive toward Stalingrad portended an attempt to outflank and isolate Moscow from the south. Too many of their troops were massed on the Central Front, far too few in the south.

When Sixth Army was safely trapped in Stalingrad, the last drive to annihilate it required 23 days for completion instead of six. No such offensive was necessary; in fact, it probably prevented a greater Russian triumph. Sixth Army should have been contained and left to wither on the vine; the bulk of the Russian troops, had they been thrown against Manstein holding the Rostov gate, might have slammed it in Kleist's face and accomplished a double victory.

As von Senger und Etterlin notes, "Only weak forces should have contained the besieged German Army . . . while correspondingly strong forces should have been set free for the pursuit and its many alluring strategical prospects."[76]

The Russians were sluggish in exploitation and too inflexible in adapting to opportunity; there was little brilliancy in their strategy, they simply exploited, sluggishly and ponderously, the German mistakes.[77]

Their own view of their own shortcomings, expressed in detail in *Combat Experiences,* reveals many tactical weaknesses.

In the early Stalingrad battles of September and October the Communists fought with mass, not skill.

The troops were committed to battle unit by unit. . . . The troops went into battle not knowing the system of defense of the enemy. . . . Reconnaissance was conducted in a superficial manner. . . .

The main body of the infantry was inactive on the battlefield. . . .

There was no cooperation between infantry, tanks, artillery and aviation. Each branch of the service operated for itself.

[There were] weaknesses in command of troops and their combat training.[78]

Later, as victory bestows its laurel wreaths, the comments in *Combat Experiences* become more laudatory; it is probably fair to agree that Stalingrad "marked the beginning of a new chapter in Soviet military art," from the massed armed hordes of the past to a better articulated, better trained, more integrated and more skillfully commanded army. Yet the Russian victory was essentially one of mass. Psychologically, the Soviets stimulated their troops by the carrot of Russian nationalism and patriotism and the stick of harsh Communist discipline—literally, death rather than surrender.

On either side two leaders stand out—Marshal Zhukov, the Russian, who was a principal architect of the victorious plan, and Field Marshal Manstein, the German, who almost foiled the plan.[79]

The aftermath of Stalingrad was, for the German Army and its leaders, loyal (on the battlefield) unto death, bitterly ironic. General Walter von Seydlitz-Kurzbach, the commander of the destroyed LI Corps who had repeatedly urged breakout, headed a Soviet-sponsored group of captive German officers (Federation of German Officers) in an attempt to do what the Allies had scorned—separate the German leaders from the German led. Paulus, but particularly Seydlitz and his *Bund Deutscher Offiziers,* part of the "National Committee of Free Germany," bitterly attacked Hitler and his conduct of the war in radio broadcasts to their homeland (after the abortive anti-Hitler plot in the summer of 1944). Paulus lived to testify at Nuremberg against the fellow generals he had once admired, but his honors had tarnished and only in Communist East Germany were Paulus, Seydlitz and their few followers welcome after the war.

The German defeat at Stalingrad was fundamentally the responsibility of a crazed genius with a lust for global power. He made the mistake that most of those who wield great power make sooner or later:

he attempted to achieve unlimited aims with limited means, and he became obsessed with his own infallibility.

And so men perished by the thousands at Stalingrad and lie today in rubbled cellars or unmarked graves beneath the Mamayev Kurgan and in the bluffs beside "Mother Volga."

"What millions died that Caesar might be great!"[80]

At Stalingrad, as Winston Churchill wrote, "The hinge of fate had turned."[81]

CHAPTER 6

THE SICILIAN CAMPAIGN—

STRATEGIC COMPROMISE

July 10–August 17, 1943

The Sicilian campaign, the largest amphibious assault of World War II, represented the "end of the beginning" in the long Allied road to victory in World War II.

It was the first step in Winston Churchill's planned assault against the "soft underbelly" of *Festung Europa*. The Allied conquest of Sicily secured British maritime communications through the Mediterranean and led directly to the overthrow of Mussolini and the collapse of Italy.

Yet the 38-day conquest of a rugged, arid island that had been the cockpit of battle since the dawn of recorded history opened a military chapter that had no logical ending. Sicily was a strategic compromise conceived in dissension, born of uneasy alliance—a child of conflicting concepts and unclear in purpose. The campaign was fought because "something had to be done."

To the British, the Mediterranean-Suez sea route had long been the lifeline of empire. The oil of the Middle East, the tough little Gurkhas and the fighting men of India—the stuff of war and the goods of peace—moved in the tankers, and the P. and O. liners and tramps with the "Red Duster" at their gaffs over the shortest route from Britain to the East. The British keystone position in Egypt and the campaign in North Africa had to be nourished by the sea, through the Mediterranean and the Suez Canal. Prior to World War II, enemy control of the Mediterranean would have been viewed as catastrophic, well-nigh unbearable. Britain might be sustained, the blood of empire moved, via the far longer route around the Cape of Good Hope, but only at tremendous, perhaps impossible, cost, in ship tonnage and in time.

The early years of World War II demonstrated the importance of the Mediterranean route but, at the same time, showed that Britain, under stress, could live—though barely—without it. Thanks to Malta and its stout defense, thanks to Malta and its naval dockyard, thanks to Malta and its airfields, specialized and heavily protected British convoys were able to transit the Mediterranean—though only intermittently and sporadically and usually at high cost in blood and tonnage. And thanks to Malta, the Italian, and later the German, sea communications to North Africa were harried, hampered and hurt. Nevertheless, though Mussolini's proud boast that the Mediterranean was an Italian *"Mare Nostrum"* was never realized, the sea became too dangerous for any but the most important convoys where speed of maritime transit was the overriding priority. For most shipping, and all tankers and troop ships, the long route round the Cape was mandatory. Britain was able to exist, but barely.

Nowhere was the British lifeline more threatened than in the Sicilian Strait, where the Mediterranean narrows to a 90-mile-wide passage between Cape Bon in Tunisia and the island of Sicily, pocked with good harbors and airfields. From the southern tip of Italian Sardinia to the west on past the Italian fortress islands of Pantelleria, Linosa and Lampedusa in the strait, to Malta on the east, British shipping had to run the gantlet of more than 300 miles of dangerous sea.

It was natural then that even early in the war Sicily should play a part in British planning, long before means were available to achieve British ends.

As early as October 16, 1941—before the Battle of Moscow had been fought and prior to Pearl Harbor—Prime Minister Winston Churchill seized upon one of many contingency plans under study by the Imperial General Staff, christened it "Whipcord," ordered it developed in some detail, and caused the British Army planning staff to "curse it heartily for ten days and nights." The Prime Minister, according to Major

General Sir John Kennedy, Director of Military Operations of the Imperial General Staff, "regarded Sicily as virtually taken already."[1]

Although Mr. Churchill's expectations were premature—his plans had to wait for almost two years—the conquest of Sicily was always prominent in British planning, and particularly in Churchill's concept of strategy.

From the beginning Churchill had envisaged the ultimate defeat of Germany in terms of the Napoleonic era. The utilization of superior British sea power would permit peripheral operations around the sea rims of Europe at selected points where German strength would be restricted and canalized by terrain and where limited British land power could be used to best advantage. The blood bath of the Western Front in World War I and the near-success of the ill-fated Gallipoli campaign—magnificent in concept, botched in execution—influenced the Churchillian concept.

The British expedition to Greece, the battle for Crete and the German attack upon Russia had emphasized, in Churchill's mind, the importance of the Mediterranean and an attack upon German-dominated Europe from the south. The wish—an ephemeral one—that Turkey might be induced to enter the war on the Allied side and that a supply route to Russia might be opened through the Dardanelles almost became father to the thought. The eastern Mediterranean—Rhodes, the Aegean islands, the Balkans, Italy, Sicily—provided the strategic magnets that again and again attracted and held Churchill's attention, and indeed, perforce, the attention of British planners.[2]

As the conflict broadened, and the specter of British defeat faded after the Battle of Moscow and the entry of the United States into the war, the political objectives of the Churchillian peripheral strategy became more and more important. Churchill and his ministers were clearly looking to the postwar future; uneasiness about Russian Communist aims, about the postwar British position in the Mediterranean and in Eastern Europe, increased. Assault from the south, from the Mediterranean, might well save Allied lives, would strike at the flank of the German attack upon Russia and could put the West in position in the Balkans to counter Soviet Russia's ambitions.

Churchill did not intend, as he once said, to preside over the liquidation of the British Empire; neither did he intend to allow the substitution of one form of totalitarian tyranny over Europe for another.

But it was his tragedy, and the world's, that his country, bled white by World War I, reduced in all save the outward panoply of power and the inner spirit of steadfastness, lacked the means to match the ends.

British Mediterranean strategy, therefore, was one of retreat and defeat—almost entirely defensive, except for the seesaw battles in Libya, which in balance were to the German advantage—until the fall of 1942, almost a year after Pearl Harbor.

Then on November 8, 1942, U.S. troops, raw to war, struggled ashore through the creaming surf of Northwest Africa:

. . . the first of more than 1,000,000 Americans to see service in the Mediterranean area during World War II—men of the II Army Corps in Tunisia, the Seventh Army in Sicily, the Fifth Army in Italy from Salerno to the Alps, and an elaborate theatre organization . . . The stream of American military strength which was to pour into that part of the world during the next two and one half years would include the Twelfth, Ninth and Fifteenth Air Forces; the U.S. Naval Forces, Northwest African Waters; the Eighth Fleet; and a considerable American contribution to Allied Force Headquarters.[3]

To Major General Kennedy and many other British planners, North Africa, rather than Sicily, had always appeared to be the logical first step in any Mediterranean strategy.

By the time of the Anglo-American Arcadia Conference in Washington shortly after Pearl Harbor, the first of many high-level U.S.-British conferences that were to chart the course of World War II, Churchill had temporarily postponed his Sicilian dream in favor of the "liberation" of French North Africa—Morocco, Algeria and Tunisia—an idea in which President Franklin Delano Roosevelt showed "marked interest."

Events and Allied differences combined, as the months of blood and sweat and tears dragged on, to emphasize North Africa in Allied strategic planning.

To U.S. planners—particularly to General George Catlett Marshall, Army Chief of Staff—the guidelines to victory were clear: Germany first, Japan second; and the best, surest and quickest way to defeat Germany was the shortest and straightest—a blow to the heart from the British Isles across the Channel and the Strait of Dover to the French coast and the Low Countries. Most U.S. planners had little use for, or little understanding of, peripheral strategy. The U.S. Army dominated the planning for the defeat of Germany; the U.S. Navy looked toward the Pacific, and most Army leaders of those years knew little of the strategic uses of sea power. To many, the Navy was essentially a transport service. Moreover, Russia, imperiled by the German invasion, had to be kept fighting; if Moscow left the war, victory over Germany might become close to impossible.

These, at least, were the concepts that then dominated American strategic planning in Europe. Consequently, U.S. planners insisted that major U.S. efforts during 1942 be devoted to the build-up of U.S. and British ground and air power in the British Isles in preparation for a cross-Channel invasion in 1943, with a preliminary attack—"Operation

Sledgehammer"—to seize a beachhead and to relieve pressure on the Russians, envisaged in 1942.

But the British, never enthusiastic about a direct assault across the Channel, least of all in 1942 or 1943, did their best to dampen U.S. enthusiasm.

The result was a kind of military stalemate; except for bombing and blockade and build-up the Allies would do little in Europe in 1942. But Churchill and Roosevelt insisted upon action—the first still focusing on peripheral strategy, the second insistent for domestic political and psychological reasons upon the use of U.S. ground troops in "action against the enemy in 1942."[4]

Thus "Operation Torch," the invasion of North Africa, was adopted in the summer of 1942, and the events of the summer and the early fall only served to underscore its importance. For Rommel and his Afrika Korps advanced to the gateway of Egypt; at Stalingrad and in the Caucasus the Russians appeared to have reached the edge of defeat; Germany had to be diverted.

Thus the first step toward Churchill's strategy of attrition, of encirclement, was, as the Army official history puts it,

hesitant, and somewhat reluctant; like the first step of a child it was more a response to an urge for action than a decision to reach some specific destination.

The responsibility for this beginning rested more with the civilian than with the professional military leaders of the two countries . . . the critical factors . . . were largely political rather than military.[5]

But there was no end in view; no decision was reached as to what should be done once North Africa was conquered.

It was not until January, 1943, in a setting of bright skies, "palm trees, bougainvillaea and orange groves,"[6] at the Casablanca Conference that Sicily became the avowed goal, for want of any other agreed objective, of the Allied forces. It was an objective, strangely enough, that no one, except Churchill, particularly wanted.[7]

The American planners, especially General Marshall, favored concentration upon "Operation Bolero-Roundup"—the invasion of Western Europe in 1943—and upon continued pressure against Japan in the Pacific. But they had no real meeting of the minds among themselves or with Roosevelt, who favored an opportunistic and compromise strategy: a build-up in both North Africa and the British Isles. The British, on the other hand, showed that unanimity of view which always characterizes official British positions in discussions with other nationalities. They were all in favor of expanding the Mediterranean commitment and against any attempt to cross the English Channel in 1943.

Churchill described North Africa as a strategic "springboard" and not a "sofa." Field Marshal Alan Brooke, Chief of the Imperial General Staff, was from the beginning consistent and insistent about what he felt was the proper strategy for victory:

the conquest of North Africa, so as to re-open the Mediterranean, restore a million tons of shipping by avoiding Cape route; then eliminate Italy, bring in Turkey, threaten southern Europe, and then liberate France. This plan, of course, depended on Russia holding on. . . . Russia (by the end of 1942) had . . . withstood the attacks against Moscow, Leningrad and Stalingrad; was getting stronger and better equipped every day. It seemed a safe bet that she would last out.[8]

The key to the British position was provided, years afterward in a pregnant sentence by Arthur Bryant: "Brooke's strategy, like that of all Britain's greatest commanders, depended on salt water."[9]

The combined front of the British, the divided counsels of the Americans and the agreement of Churchill and Roosevelt weighted the scales in favor of the Mediterranean. There was some discussion of alternatives to Sicily—Sardinia and Corsica, both lightly held and far north on the flank of the Italian peninsula, but Admiral Ernest J. King, the tough-minded U.S. Chief of Naval Operations and Commander in Chief of the U.S. Fleet, characterized this project as "merely doing something just for the sake of doing something."[10] The view of General Dwight D. Eisenhower, then the Allied commander in North Africa, also favored Sicily.[11]

And so the decision was made to undertake "Operation Husky"—the invasion of Sicily, in July, 1943.[12] The objectives were: "(1) to make the Mediterranean line of communications more secure; (2) to divert German pressure from the Soviet front; and (3) to intensify the pressure on Italy."[13]

Thus the Sicilian operation was initiated because, in Morison's words, "something had to be done in the European theatre in 1943," and it was "entered upon as an end in itself; not as a springboard for Italy or anywhere else."[14]

Nobody knew what came next; there was no agreement at Casablanca about subsequent strategy or subsequent objectives.

Nor was there any agreement, and then only a vague one, until the Tunisian campaign was ending and the German-Italian forces in North Africa were collapsing in May, 1943. Then, at the Trident Conference in Washington, the British at last conceded that a cross-Channel operation should be mounted in 1944—not in 1943—and the Americans agreed to additional, limited operations in the Mediterranean (after Sicily) "with the object of eliminating Italy from the war. . . . No precise method of eliminating Italy was adopted. . . . General Eisenhower was to plan such operations, but the final decision was to be reserved to the CCS [Combined, or Anglo-American, Chiefs of Staff]."[15]

The Americans were still asking in May of 1943, "Where do we go from here?"[16] and the British were still irritated by the query.

Thus the Allied Mediterranean campaigns had difficult birth pangs; until almost the last moment no one, indeed, even knew whether the baby would be born, or, if born, whether it would ever grow into strategic maturity.

It was therefore not surprising that discord and differences complicated and delayed the actual operational plan for the invasion of the island.

The initial plan for Operation Husky was developed in February and March by Task Force 141 (so described from the number of the room in the Allied headquarters at the Hotel St. George in Algiers, where the planning group first convened). It was developed while the Tunisian campaign was still in full spate, and while the principal commanders assigned to the Sicilian invasion were still commanding the Allied forces in North Africa. It contemplated full utilization of the Allied superiority at sea and envisaged widely separated and staggered British and American landings in Sicily extending over a period of four to five days. Ports and airfields were the initial objectives from which later operations to clear the island could be supported. The British were to land in the southeastern and eastern part of Sicily from Catania around to Gela, the Americans in the western portion and around Palermo.

The initial plan, Morison comments caustically, was flown back and forth for months between London, Algiers and Cairo (headquarters of Vice Admiral Sir Bertram H. Ramsay, commanding the British Eastern Naval Task Force, which was to be mounted chiefly from Egypt). There were comments, objections and criticisms; ultimately too many cooks spoiled the broth. The original plan conceded that the key point of Messina, just across the strait from the toe of Italy, would have to be captured from land; that two good harbors in Sicily would be needed to sustain the island's conquest; that these harbors, too, would have to be captured from land to avoid unnecessary casualties and that hence the initial landings would have to be made over beaches; and that airfields must be seized quickly in the southeastern portion of the island to help provide air superiority.

General Sir Bernard L. Montgomery, commanding the British Eighth Army, which was then helping to administer the *coup de grâce* to the German Afrika Korps in Tunisia, found time to condemn the plan in no uncertain terms on April 23. He felt the projected assault was too dispersed, spread too thin over too large an area, and that it had made no adequate provision for the early capture of two important airfields.

Despite the opposition of U.S. commanders and of Admiral of the Fleet Sir Andrew B. Cunningham, British Naval Commander in Chief, Mediterranean, who believed the initial plan was sound, "Monty" was able to substitute what was basically his own concept of how the invasion should be mounted.

On May 2 "Monty," in Algiers, "sold" his revision of the original Sicily invasion plan to General Walter Bedell Smith in a lavatory in the St. George Hotel, where Smith was "run to ground" by the persistent Englishman. "Ike" also tentatively accepted the revised plan. At a staff conference "Monty" explained his reasoning in detail: his belief in a concentrated rather than a dispersed assault, the need for two more divisions and for quick capture of airfields in the southeast and a port, and his fear of a "disaster" if the dispersed assault were mounted.

I know well [he said] that I am regarded by many people as being a tiresome person. I think this is very probably true. I try hard not to be tiresome; but I have seen so many mistakes made in this war, and so many disasters happen, that I am desperately anxious to try and see that we have no more; and this often means being very tiresome. If we have a disaster in Sicily it would be dreadful.[17]

It was not until May 13, just about two months before the scheduled D-Day, that the revised "Husky" plan was finally approved. . . . Two months before the largest amphibious and airborne assaults ever attempted; two months before the Allies' first attempt to storm the ramparts of the citadel of Europe . . .

General Dwight D. Eisenhower, a gregarious, outgoing and friendly officer, who was Allied Supreme Commander in North Africa, continued in over-all command for "Husky." Under him, Admiral Cunningham, wise, tough, beloved sea dog, was the top naval commander, with Admiral Ramsay in command of the Eastern (British) Task Force, and Vice Admiral H. Kent Hewitt in command of the Western (U.S.) Task Force. Air Chief Marshal Arthur W. Tedder commanded all Allied air forces in the Mediterranean theater under "Ike," and General Sir Harold R. Alexander, who had performed the same role in the Tunisian campaign as Eisenhower's deputy, commanded the 15th Army Group, composed of the British Eighth Army (General Montgomery commanding), and the U.S. Seventh Army (Lieutenant General George S. Patton, Jr. commanding). The U.S. Seventh Army was to "mount out" from Bizerte and other North African ports to the west, the British Eighth from Malta and ports in the eastern Mediterranean as far west as Alexandria and Port Said.

The two armies were to concentrate their assault in contiguous areas of southeastern Sicily from north of Syracuse to west of Licata—more than 100 miles of coast—with the immediate objectives a group of important airfields; the capture of ports was to come later. The amphibious landings constituted the equivalent of almost an eight-division front—an unprecedented operation over open beaches. It was to be supplemented by the largest airborne operation yet mounted: a simultaneous drop of one U.S. airborne regiment and the glider landing of one British regiment during the night preceding the amphibious landings, and additional paratroop drops later.

Each army was to consist of the equivalent of two corps—the II Corps of the U.S. Seventh Army was commanded by General Omar Bradley, a quiet, folksy kind of an officer. The U.S. forces included the 1st, 3rd, 9th and 45th Infantry divisions and the 2nd Armored and 82nd Airborne divisions, three Ranger battalions and other units.

Token representation for the Free French—of considerable psychological but little military importance—was provided by including some 900 of the famous "goums," the 4th Moroccan Tabor (battalion), to operate with the Americans. About 900 Berber *goumiers*, with a liking for cold steel and a bloodthirsty reputation for toughness, night fighting and throat-slitting, fought in Sicily under French officers and noncoms, with 117 horses and 126 mules as their supply train.

The British forces included the 1st Canadian Division, in action for the first time,[18] and the 5th, 50th, 51st and 78th Infantry divisions, plus a regiment of paratroopers, a glider-borne brigade and other units. The total included close to half a million men—160,000 in the initial assault —14,000 vehicles, 600 tanks, 1,800 guns, transported, supported and protected by 2,600 ships.

The Sicilian assault was to be—though none could know it then— "at once the largest and most dispersed amphibious assault of World War II."[19]

Sicily, its 10,000 square miles—an area as large as the state of Vermont—rugged, seamed with mountains and ravines, a tortured, punishing terrain, was defended by the Sixth Italian Army, commanded by 66-year-old General Alfredo Guzzoni, who had led the glory-seeking Italian invasion of Albania at war's beginning. General Guzzoni's headquarters were at Enna, in the center of the island. Under Guzzoni were two corps headquarters—the XII (west) commanded by General Mario Arisio, and the XVI (east), commanded by General Carlo Rossi.

The first, and weakest, part of the Axis defense—the defense of the 485-mile-long Sicilian coastline, including the beaches and principal ports—was entrusted to six Italian coastal divisions (one of which existed only in cadre strength) and specially organized "maritime strong points." The coastal divisions were composed chiefly of Sicilian reservists, understrength, undertrained, overage, with little modern equipment, virtually no mobility, few guns and those of light caliber, and depressed morale. They represented no threat to Allied plans; indeed, since the shadow of strength was often mistaken for substance by Mussolini, they represented more of a problem to the defense than to the attack. The "maritime

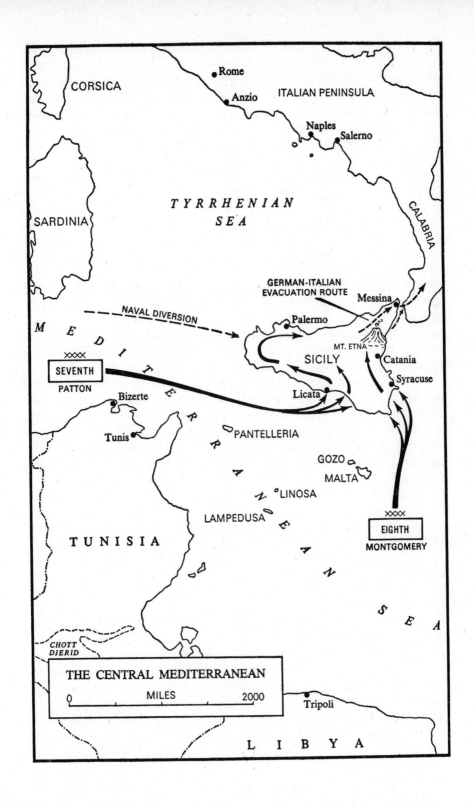

CORSICA

Rome
Anzio

ITALIAN PENINSULA

Naples
Salerno

CALABRIA

TYRRHENIAN SEA

SARDINIA

GERMAN-ITALIAN
EVACUATION ROUTE

Messina

NAVAL DIVERSION

Palermo

MT. ETNA

SICILY

Catania

Syracuse

SEVENTH
PATTON

Bizerte

Licata

Tunis

PANTELLERIA

GOZO
MALTA

LINOSA

LAMPEDUSA

EIGHTH
MONTGOMERY

TUNISIA

CHOTT
DJERID

THE CENTRAL MEDITERRANEAN

0   MILES   2000

Tripoli

L I B Y A

strong points," each organized under naval command, consisted of larger-caliber coast-defense guns and antiaircraft batteries. Their men apparently were of somewhat better quality than the coastal division's homesick reservists, but they were limited to a static defense of specific ports. The kernel of the Axis strength consisted of four Italian field divisions and two German divisions.

The Assietta (26th) and Aosta (28th) Infantry divisions, assigned to the XII Corps, each numbered about 11,000 men with weak artillery support, mostly horse-drawn. They were supported, in their stations in the western part of the island—roughly from Sciacca to Palermo—by an independent regiment of Bersaglieri, the picturesque, "plumed-hat" soldiers, and by a major part of the German 15th Panzer Grenadier Division.

In the east, under the XVI Corps the Livorno (4th) Light Division—about two-thirds motorized and with some light tanks—the Napoli (54th) Infantry Division, the rest of the 15th Panzer Grenadiers, a German brigade combat group called Task Group Schmalz, and the Hermann Göring Panzer Division with about 100 tanks were deployed from Caltanissetta through the southeastern corner of the island to Catania.

These approximately 30,000 German troops were to be reinforced during July and August—during the battle—with whole or major elements of two more divisions (29th Panzer Grenadier Division, and 1st Parachute Division), which about doubled the original German commitment. (Probably as many as 70,000 to 75,000 German troops participated at one time or another in the Sicilian fighting, but the total at any one time apparently never exceeded 60,000.)

The total—250,000 to 300,000 men, about one-third of them mobile (after a fashion), one-eighth of them German—looked formidable on paper, but the Italians were riddled with the dry rot of defeat and dislike for a war that most of them never wanted.[20]

On the sea and in the air, the Allies held a tremendous superiority in both quality and quantity.[21]

The German Air Force was spread thin—along the vast Russian front, in the West where Allied bombers were striking at the heart of Germany, and all along the coastlines and island positions of the underbelly of Europe.

There were an estimated 1,000 to 1,600 Axis planes, spread from southern France and Corsica and Sardinia through Italy and Sicily, as compared to about 3,700 to 4,000 available Allied aircraft organized in the North African strategic and tactical air forces. In Sicily itself there were at least a dozen main fields and seven satellite ones. On July 10—D-day—there was a total of 220 Italian aircraft of all types in Sicily, of which only 79 were "on the line" or operational. Bombers and attack planes had been withdrawn to the mainland in June; only fighters were left on Sicilian fields.[22]

The Allied naval forces were superior to available Axis sea power, though the Italian Navy still represented, despite defeat and decimation, a "fleet in being." Sicily itself harbored no naval vessels except patrol and harbor craft and a very few motor torpedo boats. The Italian heavy ships based at Italian mainland ports and in Sardinia were still a formidable force—on paper. They included 6 battleships, 2 of them new, 7 cruisers, 48 submarines and about 75 supporting destroyers, torpedo boats and escort vessels. But they were "doomed to defeat," as Morison puts it, by "lack of radar, a continual shortage of fuel oil (which penned the heavy ships in port most of the time), and want of a fleet air arm."[23] The Italian Air Force provided little or no air cover when the fleet put to sea, and the war had shown long before that modern sea power also meant seagoing air power. To make its plight even worse, the Italian ships by July, 1943, had no secure base; they were harried, bombed and damaged, even in port, by Allied bombers.

And the Allied invasion armada was being supported and protected, near and far, by 6 British battleships, 2 aircraft carriers, 10 British cruisers, 4 antiaircraft ships and 3 monitors, as well as by 5 U.S. cruisers, 71 British destroyers, 48 U.S. destroyers, and Dutch, Greek, Polish, Belgian and Norwegian light craft, escort vessels and auxiliaries.

So the odds were loaded, as the Allied convoys put to sea; Eisenhower himself estimated the Sicilian campaign might require about two weeks.

But the two weeks were stretched into 38 days. And for this, the altered Allied plan, Allied differences and American inexperience, the cautious Montgomery and superb German delaying actions were to blame.

SHADOW OF THE PAST

What had gone before in north Africa shaped to some degree what was to come in Sicily.

North Africa, despite the victory, had been to the Allies a campaign of disillusionment in a land foreign to past experience. In this strangely melancholy and beautiful setting—a depressed and arid land, a cold country with a hot sun—from the milky-white salt marshes of the Chott Djerid, across the rolling dunes of the desert, through the stark djebels and in the deeply bitten water courses, amid the remnants of ancient and long-gone glories—the American Army had its first great trial by fire in

World War II, and the British and French rebounded from defeat and depression to a costly and, in some ways, sterile victory—a victory on a continent not their own, a victory that was not, even yet, the end of the beginning.[24]

For the Allies the long road back still lay ahead, but North Africa had shaped its course.

To the British, North Africa—and especially the victory at El Alamein which sent Field Marshal Rommel and his Afrika Korps into final retreat—was a moral tonic of tremendous significance. No matter that it was not, in strategic context, a decisive battle; no matter that, with Rommel's sea-borne supply lines all but severed by Allied air and sea power, and with U.S. and British forces landing in Morocco and Algeria in his rear, it was a battle that the British could not ultimately lose. For Rommel, regardless of what happened at El Alamein, would have had to retreat. Nevertheless, the Eighth Army's victory at El Alamein stimulated a victory-hungry nation and restored confidence to an army, and created, in "Monty," a general and a legend. Rommel had had the Eighth Army jinxed; until "Monty" and El Alamein, it was in a defeatist mood. North Africa created in this hard core of British strength around Montgomery an experienced, tough and now confident army, prepared for the trials that were to come.

Nevertheless, for the Allies North Africa had been somewhat of a disappointment. Many had hoped that the Torch Operation—the invasion of Morocco and Algeria—would lead to a quick seizure of Tunisia and a sudden collapse of the entire German position in North Africa. It had not happened that way. Instead, Rommel conducted a masterly retreat from Egypt; the Germans with great tactical and technical ingenuity rapidly reinforced their forces in Tunisia;[25] and the western prong of the Allied offensive bogged down through the winter of 1942–43. Each of the Allies blamed the others for delay and defeat: the Americans said their British allies on the northern flank in Tunisia (the British First Army, Lieutenant General Sir Kenneth A. N. Anderson commanding) stopped too often for tea; the British said the Americans were inexperienced and not well led.

Both observations were true. General Anderson was not a thrusting commander; his First Army had none of the drive and *élan* that Montgomery had developed in the Eighth Army. And the Americans *were* inexperienced; save for a few units, under top-notch professionals, their early performance against the Germans in Tunisia left something to be desired.

General Alexander, who became Eisenhower's deputy in North Africa and who was to command the Fifteenth Army Group in the Sicilian operation, put his finger on one of the causes when he said, "I say; your chaps don't wear the old school tie."[26]

He meant by this that many of the hastily trained reserve officers and other officers commissioned from civilian life had not been imbued with the sense of obligation to their men and to their unit—the sense of *noblesse oblige*—which characterized most of the West Point graduates and the British Sandhurst officers.

Many of the Americans, too, in this early stage of the war had not developed a concept of what they were fighting for. Too many were fighting for "blueberry pie"—a kind of home-and-mother concept, a negative rather than a positive aspiration.

And some of the early U.S. leaders were badly picked; they were round pegs in square holes, perhaps good staff men but poor battlefield commanders.

There were amazing deficiencies, too, in many of the fundamentals of the battlefield, such as map-reading, and there was rigidity about American tactical actions and reactions, which pleased the Germans and disturbed those who had always thought of the U.S. soldier as possessing a high degree of flexibility and initiative.

In short, except for the small hard core of professionals who provided the amalgam for the whole mass, the Americans entered North Africa as an army of amateurs; they grew to professionalism and maturity the hard way on the field of battle. North Africa was a school for the soldier, but not without strain and stress. The Americans were rudely shocked when the Germans, operating from interior positions, were able to exercise, despite smaller forces, definite air superiority until toward the end of the campaign.[27] It was the first and last time in the European phase of the war in which U.S. ground forces had to operate without air superiority. At Kasserine the Americans took a nasty knock; their cocky self-confidence was deflated. But even at the battle of the Mareth Line—Rommel's last stand before his retreat into Tunisia—"Monty's" Eighth Army received a rude surprise and barely snatched victory from defeat; indeed, during the battle some of the British officers thought and said: "The flap's on again" ("Retreat has started").[28]

Thus North Africa revealed once again—and to the surprise of Americans who had believed their own propaganda that the Germans were battlefield robots—the tough, fighting qualities of the German soldier, even in adversity, and his capability for exercising great combat initiative.

And it had demonstrated some of the weaknesses—different national characteristics, aspirations and jealousies and the personality conflicts—of the Allied team.

These had been reflected up to the top; even such an easy personality as that of General Eisenhower had been irritated by the showmanship and arrogance of Montgomery. "Ike," under strict instructions to develop an Allied team, had had to relieve several officers who had been critical of their British allies. Even Eisenhower, under fire from his superiors because of delay and defeat and the dealing with the French Pétainist, Admiral Jean François Darlan (which had been much criticized in America) reportedly had told his chiefs that "I'm the best damned Lieutenant Colonel [his then permanent rank] in the U.S. Army!"—thus implying that he was prepared to be relieved if Washington disapproved of his leadership.

That the Allies surmounted these difficulties and did develop ultimately a smooth-working team was due in large part to Eisenhower, a "general-manager" type of leader with charm and intelligence, and to General Alexander, his deputy, a handsome, florid British type with good judgment and quiet and easy manners.[29]

But the Allied leadership was riding a team of wild horses as it prepared for Operation Husky, for some of the principal American and British generals, developed and proven in North Africa, mixed, in personality, like oil and water.

"Monty," commanding the British Eighth Army, personalized his command; it was "My" army, "My" soldiers, "My" plans. He deliberately dramatized himself as a cocky, confident soldier of Puritan breed, who neither smoked nor drank. He was arrogant, egoistic, often rude, slightly condescending to Americans, nearly always difficult, and actually— despite his image—a cautious, careful, able planner, who did much with much but not much with little, master, as "Ike" called him, of the "set-piece battle." Montgomery was the type of Englishman most Americans— and many Englishmen—found insufferable and infuriating.

General George S. Patton, commanding the U.S. Seventh Army, was a hell-for-leather cavalryman, who had now gotten his spurs into tanks— a driving, even reckless, thruster, who lived for battle. A complex, emotional man, a student of warfare, a fine "tanker" and a master of mobility, he too was histrionic in dress, appearance and manner, but far more flamboyant and emotional than "Monty."

He was given to outbursts, talked of "mealy-mouthed limeys," sometimes roared and ranted with profanities and obscenities, was patriotic and nationalistic to the core, and could not understand Eisenhower's statement that "I have reached a place where I do not look upon myself as an American but an ally."[30]

Many people, including some of Patton's own "GI's," hated their commander, but by others he was beloved and admired, and he was a leader of whom all who served under him would say in later years with pride, "I served with Patton."

Even some of the lesser commanders for "Husky" did not easily meld into a team; Omar Bradley, who commanded the II Corps of the Seventh Army, was not only revolted by Patton's form of leadership but developed a steady and growing dislike for "Monty's" snide and superior manner.[31]

Down the line both British and Americans had developed some excellent division commanders, like Major General Lucian K. Truscott, who commanded the U.S. 3rd Infantry Division in "Husky," an outfit trained to steel-edged hardness by the "Truscott Trot"—a high-speed marching pace of up to five miles an hour.[32] But even on lower levels there were problems, as in the "Fighting First" Division, commanded by two courageous, battling extroverts: Major General Terry de la Mar Allen, and Brigadier General Theodore Roosevelt, Jr., his assistant—two of a kind, men who loved the smell of powder, who rallied, exhorted and led their men, by whom they were beloved, but whose "glory-hunting" personalities grated and who tended to leave discipline and the running of the division to the chief of staff.[33]

The command problem was still further complicated by the separation, both physically and psychologically, of the Allied air forces from the ground forces. The air forces of both countries believed in the centralized control of all air resources under a theater commander, not in control at lower levels; the Marine-Navy closely integrated system of air support that existed in the Pacific and the intimate collaboration of the tactical air forces with the ground troops that was to come later in France had not yet developed.

Even a key, but minor, operation, preliminary to "Husky" developed before the event such acerb differences that Eisenhower was eventually forced to ask for the relief of a senior British staff officer and to describe (later) the planning for the conquest of Pantelleria as one of the few major strategic differences with the British he had experienced during the war.[34]

Pantelleria, an Italian island, some 60 miles from the western coast of Sicily, commanded the Sicilian strait, and was needed by the Allies as an additional base for fighter planes for support of Operation Husky. It was a rocky island, about as large as the Bronx, seamed with tunnels and heavily armed with coastal and antiaircraft batteries, "popularly known as 'the Gibraltar of the Central Mediterranean' and . . . assumed by many as unassailable. . . . Many of our experienced commanders and staff officers strongly advised against attempting this operation," Eisenhower later noted.[35] They feared an assault upon the tiny harbor—the only means of landing on the island—would be repulsed with disastrous effects upon troop morale and upon "Husky" itself.

But "Ike," with Admiral Cunningham's support and the enthusiastic efforts of the Allied air forces who foresaw an opportunity to "prove" the capabilities of air power for independent conquest, overrode his opposition.

The result was anticlimax. The fortress proved no stronger than the hearts of its defenders. Twenty days and nights of air bombardment (which did relatively little damage to the coast-defense batteries) plus heavy naval bombardment preceded planned amphibious assault. But on June 11, 1944, just as the Allied troops were embarking in their assault boats for the attack so many dreaded, the garrison of 11,199—all except 78 of them Italians—surrendered without a fight.[36] There was one Allied casualty: a British "Tommy" was bitten by a mule.

The capture of two other little islands in the strait—Linosa and Lampedusa—soon followed, and Pantelleria was quickly developed for use by the short-legged American P-40 fighters.

U.S. Army aviation engineers astonished the British by building a new airstrip on Gozo, a little island near Malta in some 17 to 20 days, and more Spitfires were established close to Sicily's southeast coast.[37]

By the selected D-day for "Husky"—the night of July 9–10, during the second quarter of the moon, with sufficient light in early darkness for paratroop operations, and with darkness after midnight for naval approach—the Allied forces were ready, despite the past history of dissension and the African heritage of frustration, for their first great assault against the "underbelly" of a continent.

Sicily, despite the lack of heart of its Italian defenders, was no soft and flabby gateway. The "stormily beautiful and harshly patterned"[38] island was, in July, 1943, as it had been for thousands of years, a rugged, ridged, sun-baked land, as inhospitable in terrain and climate and primitive communications to the Allied invaders as it had been to Greeks, Carthaginians and Romans.

It was a perpendicular land—little of it flat, most of it mountainous, with precipitous ravines, one after the other, few winding roads on most of which two vehicles could not pass abreast, a land in which defense was easy and tactics canalized by nature. It was thickly settled; the stone walls of the little towns provided natural defenses. Olive and almond trees and some terraced vineyards were tended carefully in the same primitive way the peasants of the poor land had used for hundreds of years. Donkeys and burros hauling brightly painted carts and trudging swarthy farmers —there were few motorcars—used the roads and tracks.

Sicily is a hot land in summer; in July the temperatures reach 100 degrees. Parts of it were malarial; both attackers and defenders suffered from fevers, some of them brought from other areas, other campaigns.

Messina, across the strait where in ancient legend Scylla and Charybdis ruled, was the key strategic city, bottleneck for supplies and reinforcements, opposite the toe of the Italian boot.

The land approaches to Messina from the southeast coastal plain, where the British Eighth Army was to land, are canalized and guarded by the 10,741-foot bulk of Mount Etna, which almost shoulders into the sea the railroad and road from Syracuse to Messina. From the U.S. invasion beaches on the southern coast, the land rises sharply to north and west in a succession of peaks and ridges, tortured and tumbling terrain with peaks more than 5,000 feet high. All roads from the southern beaches lead either northward to the transisland central road and railroad which cross Sicily from Catania to Palermo, or, eventually, to the coastal road and railroad on the north coast from Palermo to Messina, which, like the east coast routes, are pushed against the sea by a succession of peaks and ridges, and which bridge many defiles.

Sicily—then, today and yesterday—offers ideal terrain, sculptured by nature for delay, to determined defenders. And the Germans, though few in numbers, were both determined and skilled.

The invasion of Sicily was no real strategic surprise to anyone but Hitler. Even before the marshaling of the invasion fleets, the OKW operations staff had prepared an appreciation which indicated that "the Balkans were the most likely target for Western strategy in the Mediterranean," but that the initial enemy objectives were likely to be the "large Italian islands" and then, perhaps, Italy itself.[39]

Hitler agreed with this appreciation initially, but later thought that the first landings would be made in Sardinia, not Sicily, and in the Peloponnesos and the Dodecanese. He was aided in coming to this conclusion—one which the British hoped he would reach—by an elaborate British deception: the "planting" of a body with documents, arranged to appear to be that of a British courier lost in a plane just off the Spanish coast. The "secret" documents spoke of Greece and Sardinia as the real objectives, and Hitler took the bait. Both areas were reinforced.[40]

The German Army High Command thought on May 21 that defensive measures for Sardinia and Greece should take priority; the German Navy, on the eve of invasion, pointed to "Sardinia and Corsica" as "first targets," with an assault on Greece probable.[41]

Yet neither the Italian High Command nor the responsible German and Italian commanders in the area were fooled. Even Mussolini had feared Allied attack upon Sicily, but he had refused Hitler's offer of German reinforcements, apparently in fear that increased German numbers would lead to German command. Field Marshal Albert Kesselring, who originally had been German Air Force Commander in Italy, had become in fact as well as in title OB South (Oberbefehlshaber Sud), commander of all German forces in the Mediterranean and senior German liaison officer with the Comando Supremo, the Italian High Command, in January of 1943. Perhaps, in part because of German influence on the Italian staff, both the Italians and Kesselring believed that Sicily would be the most likely Allied target. Indeed, on June 20

Kesselring started the Hermann Göring Panzer Division—a recently reconstituted and reorganized outfit—across the Strait of Messina; it was in position, along with another German division previously sent to Sicily, by the time of the invasion.

And just before the invasion, German and Italian reconnaissance planes sighted Allied convoys;[42] scouts were observed coming ashore near Gela, and there were contact reports from various points along the southeastern coast. By 0100 July 10, before the amphibious landings had started, General Guzzoni, the Italian commander of all German and Italian forces in Sicily, who had anticipated a landing where it actually occurred, had ordered a state of emergency in the southeastern part of the island.[43]

THE ASSAULT

Off the beaches and in the vineyards of Sicily Allied troops had relatively little to fear from the vaunted might of the Luftwaffe. For almost two months before D-day Allied air forces had been ranging all over the central Mediterranean, hammering Sicilian, Italian and Sardinian targets. The attack was intensified in the last few days, and round the clock the crump of bombs echoed on or near Catania, Gerbini, Palermo, Chinisia (Borizzo) and other fields. By July 1 the number of airstrips usable in Sicily by the Italian Regia Aeronautica and the Luftwaffe had been reduced to about a baker's dozen.

So far, so good; air superiority, though not air domination, had been won. But there was some promiscuous and unnecessary "strategic" bombing; the cities as well as the airfields of Catania and Palermo were hit; civilians were killed; ancient buildings were destroyed, narrow streets were clogged with rubble. And the beach defenses were left untouched; the mobile divisions in the interior of the island were never bombed.[44]

And weather promised a bad beginning. While the assault convoys were at sea, approaching and passing Malta[45] and Gozo, an old Mediterranean scourge—the mistral, or stiff northerly wind—kicked up a "nasty, steep sea,"[46] and the small craft, crammed with seasick soldiers—the LCI's (Landing Craft, Infantry), LCT's (Landing Craft, Tanks)—and the patrol craft took green water aboard, wallowed and pitched in the seaway and made slow work of it. But for once the weatherman was right; the mistral eased soon after midnight of the ninth of July.

But not in time to help the "devils in baggy pants"—a reinforced regimental combat team of the 82nd Airborne Division, scheduled to drop a half-hour before midnight on July 9 near the Ponte Olivo airport, just six miles behind one of the important American landing beaches at

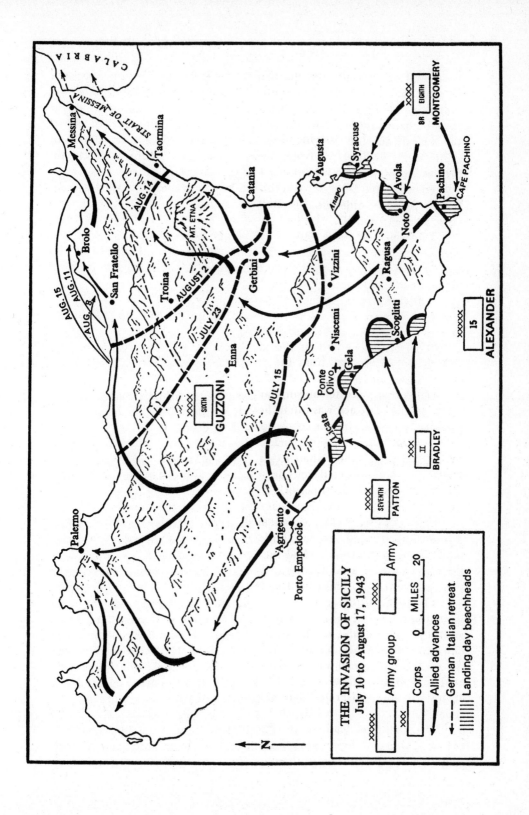

THE INVASION OF SICILY
July 10 to August 17, 1943

Army group
Corps
Allied advances
German Italian retreat.
Landing day beachheads

XXXXX Army group
XXX Corps
XXXX Army
MILES 0 20

MESSINA
CALABRIA
STRAIT OF MESSINA
Taormina
Messina
AUG. 14
Brolo
San Fratello
AUG. 15
AUG. 11
AUG. 8
Troina
AUGUST 2
JULY 23
MT. ETNA
Catania
Gerbini
JULY 15
Augusta
Syracuse
Avola
Anapo
Noto
Pachino
CAPE PACHINO
Vizzini
Ragusa
Enna
Niscemi
Scoglitti
SIXTH GUZZONI
Gela
Ponte Olivo
Licata
XXXX 15 ALEXANDER
Agrigento
Porto Empedocle
Palermo
XXX II BRADLEY
XXXX SEVENTH PATTON
XXX BR EIGHTH MONTGOMERY
N

Gela—and one regiment of the British 1st Airborne Division, supposed to glide to earth near Syracuse. The stiff 40-mile mistral blew the lumbering C-47's and other transports off their approach courses, and as their human cargoes, in answer to the green jump lights, spewed out of the aircraft to "hit the silk," they were "strewn over a large part of southeastern Sicily—from Ponte Olivo to Niscemi, Vizzini, and Ragusa, even as far east as Noto in the British Eighth Army sector."[47]

For the paratroopers, tense for the leap into the dim, moonlit void, the jump was the moment of truth.

"Stand up and hook up!"

Fourteen men—one "stick" of jumpers—stood up, each in two chutes and battle equipment, and hooked the snap fasteners of the anchor lines leading from the primary chutes to the static line running along the overhead of the fuselage.

"Check your equipment!"

Each jumper checked the chute and equipment and rip cord of the man in front of him, and sounded off:

"Fourteen, okay!"

"Thirteen, okay!"

"Twelve, okay . . ."

"Okay," the leader and jumpmaster yelled as he crouched in the open doorway, looking down toward the hidden face of danger. "We jump when the green light comes on. Make it good!"

We stood waiting, our knees buckling beneath the tremendous loads, hearts thudding against our ribs, nerves steeled for the dive into darkness, minds sealed against . . . nerve-wrecking thoughts.[48]

More than 3,000 men of the 505th RCT, 82nd Airborne Division—young Colonel "Jim" Gavin commanding—scattered along some 50 to 60 miles of coast. But part of one battalion dropped near its objective—a blocking position at a key road juncture; another group organized a strong point in a stone-walled house near Niscemi.

The 1,600 British paratroopers were also widely dispersed; 47 gliders landed in the sea; most others were far from their objectives. But a small group glided to a safe landing near one of two bridges—their key objectives—which crossed high above Syracuse Harbor and over the Anapo River. Some 73 officers and men took Ponte Grande bridge and held it against Italian counterattack until, with 19 men left and the bridge still unblown, they were relieved by British infantrymen late on D-day.[49]

The airborne troops were down, so widely scattered in village, roadside, vineyard, field and mountain that it would be days before they could assemble and form a formidable fighting force. But the very dispersion of the drop created consternation and confusion among Sicily's defenders. The Italians, in wild confusion, estimated that 20,000 to 30,000 paratroopers had dropped; to the defenders, the enemy was everywhere!

The moon had set; the false dawn was still only a promise in the sky when the first troops hit the beaches about 0245, July 10. The initial landfalls were generally good, in part due to fine navigation by a British beacon submarine, HMS *Safari*, which buoyed her position off Licata and served as a flank guide to one of the American assault forces.

The U.S. Seventh Army landed on and around the wide, shelving beaches of the 37-mile Gulf of Gela—the 3rd Division and part of the 2nd Armored to the west around Licata; the 1st Division in the center near Gela, just south of the paratroop objective at Ponte Olivo; and the 45th Division on the eastern flank near Scoglitti.

Off Gela, about 0200 on July 10, as the landing craft were approaching the beaches, four Italian searchlights "flared and swept seaward in a wide arc" and impaled the *Biscayne*, flagship of Rear Admiral R. L. Conolly, and CP of General Truscott, commanding the 3rd Division.

"There we stood," Truscott recalled, "silhouetted in the searchlight beams, so bright on deck that one could read a book. . . . But no shots came."[50]

In the British sector, in Sicily's extreme southeastern coast, the British Eighth Army landed on a four-division front: the 1st Canadian Division on the extreme southern and western flank southwest of Pachino (nearest the Americans); the 51st at Cape Passero; the 50th near Avola; and the 5th, with the British airborne troops, south of Syracuse.

The dawn of July 10 broke to reveal to astounded Sicilian eyes thousands of ships—the greatest amphibious armada until then assembled.

The initial landings in most instances brushed aside light opposition and produced only mild initial enemy reaction. In many areas tactical, or local, surprise was achieved by the invaders, even though the Axis higher commanders had anticipated the invasion.

General Guzzoni and other Axis generals had estimated that the principal Allied landings would probably be made in the southeastern part of the island around Cape Passero (as, in fact, they were), but Field Marshal Kesselring thought a subsidiary landing to outflank Axis forces in the southeast might be made on the western coast near Palermo or Trapani, and he had persuaded Guzzoni to move a major part of the 15th Panzer Grenadier Division to the western part of the island a few days before the assault.[51]

In part two naval diversions—one a demonstration by British naval forces in the Ionian Sea which appeared to threaten the coast of Greece, the other an apparent diversionary attack against western Sicily—confused the enemy. The western feint appeared to be fully successful, for on the morning of July 10 a major part of the German 15th Panzer Grenadier Division and two Italian mobile divisions, in position in extreme western Sicily between Palermo and Mazara, did not commence to move to the east against the Allied beachheads until the landings were many hours old.

In part, the mistral had helped: Italian weather experts and naval officers had told their commanders the weather was too bad to permit beach landings; in part, it was the old problem of crying "Wolf, Wolf!" once too often. German radar crews and Italian coastal divisions had been keyed to the alert for so long that they found it difficult to credit first indications of a landing.

At Beach Yellow, near Licata, where the Americans overran an abandoned Italian beach command post, an American correspondent—Michael Chinigo, of International News Service—picked up a ringing telephone and asked in his perfect Italian, *"Chi e?"* ("Who's there?")

An Italian general officer, a sector commander, queried about a reported American landing which he couldn't believe was possible on such a bad night. Chinigo assured him "all was quiet on the Licata beaches; and both parties, well satisfied, hung up."[52]

The invasion started in low key.

Beach defenses were weak, and few of the troops of the Italian coastal divisions in the direct path of the landings had any stomach for a fight; many faded away back into the stark hills, others raised their hands in surrender, some fled in panic. The Germans were disgusted.

But no matter how complete the surprise, how overwhelming the attack, how easy the landings, invasion always means to some the end of all things—death and extinction. That July 10 of 1943 was no exception—to attackers as well as to defenders.

Red Beach on the western flank near the Torre de Gaffi, to the west of Licata and outside the gulf, was heavily pounded by white creaming surf and swept by Italian gunfire. The landing craft, floundering and broaching in the seaway, had a tough time; some GI's, swept into deep water, drowned, and several Italian batteries found targets; blood spilled in the landing craft, and the Navy and the 3rd Division paid the first price of victory.

Near Scoglitti, on the eastern flank of the American beaches exposed to the wind, an Italian air raid, under the light of fat yellow flares, heralded, with the tympany of the bombs, a rugged H-hour. The heavy surf, green boat crews, bad landfalls and the rocky coast taxed the invaders more than did the enemy. Many landing craft were lost, and at least 38 GI's drowned, dragged down by their heavy gear, as their boats collided and sank or broached on rocky headlands in the darkness.

The British landings encountered less surf and little initial resistance. The Canadians got ashore on the Pachino peninsula handily; each beach flashed "Success" by 0530 of D-day.[53]

White flags appeared on some of the beaches; an Italian crew of a beach-defense gun was captured asleep; the 51st Division went ashore with bagpipes playing. The "maritime strong point" of Syracuse collapsed, and by 2100 (9 P.M.) on D-day, July 10, the 5th Division had marched, virtually unopposed, over the Ponte Grande bridge into Syracuse by the main road. The Allies had captured their first major port.

But it was, despite the preinvasion air bombardment, first blood for the Luftwaffe. A Stuka dive bomber found U.S. destroyer *Maddox* on antisubmarine patrol at 0458, 16 miles off the coast, and the little ship died in one great rending explosion.

"A great blob of light bleached and reddened the sky, tearing the night into shreds. It was followed by a blast . . . sullen and deafening."[54]

It was sudden death for 7 officers and 203 Navy men, and to others death was soon to come.

Just 12 minutes later—at 0510—still too dark to see the falcons diving from the skies, mine sweeper *Sentinel* was holed by a bomb; in quick succession she suffered four more air attacks. Soon after dawn, with the forward engine room awash and the ship sinking slowly in a heavy sea, what was left of her ship's company was taken off by rescue craft. The toll was 10 dead, 51 wounded; 40 survived unhurt.

Here and there as the assault troops waded ashore and encountered sporadic enemy resistance, naval gunfire sparkled like fireflies along the whole reach of coast from Licata to Syracuse. Sometimes it was needed; often a few rounds served to convince the Italians—a crescendo of noise and flame against minor resistance.

Near Gela there was brief crisis, quickly passed. The Hermann Göring Panzer Division moved into action early in the day. Two task forces—one including some of the new German Mark VI Tiger tanks (not yet very effective technically), the other with Mark III's and IV's, and both with supporting artillery and some infantry—were sent in a two-pronged attack toward the U.S. beaches east of Gela. At the same time an Italian mobile group, with some obsolescent light French tanks, started south in several sections from Niscemi. The attacks were uncoordinated, piecemeal.

Most of the Italians were quickly stopped. The paratroopers, few in number but determined in spirit, had a go at them first, and the column was observed by cruiser *Boise*'s observation plane, which had spent the morning dodging Messerschmitts. The *Boise*'s 6-inch guns dropped shells among the Renault and Fiat light tanks at 10,000 yards.

But 13 (unlucky number!) Italian light tanks, supported by a small infantry force, took their losses, pushed through destroyer gunfire, leaving some of their vehicles flaming torches, and into the streets of the little beachhead village of Gela, held by Lieutenant Colonel William O. Darby's 1st Ranger Battalion and elements of the 1st Division. In the town Americans and Italians "began a deadly game of hide and seek," as the "GI's" dodged "in and out of buildings, throwing hand grenades and firing rocket launchers." In 20 minutes the Italians had had enough; they pulled back—what was left of them—bearing the scars of combat. No sweat!

But now, in the afternoon, the Hermann Göring Panzers finally got rolling, five hours late, after General Conrath, the division commander, had finally whipped his inexperienced forces into some kind of shape.[55] But again, the tenacious "doughfeet" and the Navy's guns—plus the piecemeal nature of the attack and the failure of the German infantry to coordinate their tactics well with the armor—halted the enemy. "The tankers could not go on because they had nothing to cope with the five- and six-inch naval shells that came whistling in from the sea."[56]

One German thrust, led by the Tigers, temporarily had better luck, mauled an American battalion and captured its commander. But another battalion filled in the gap, and suddenly the Germans, in inexplicable battlefield panic, "ran in wild disorder."[57]

So far, so good. July 10 was a proud day for the Allies; everywhere their landings on the coasts of Sicily had been made good; GI's thronging the drab coastal towns had already liberated bottles of Sicilian wine, and happy Italian captives were asking their captors about relatives in Brooklyn.

The overage, underspirited men of the Italian coastal divisions "stampeded to the safety of [the Allied] prisoner-of-war cages . . . in such terrific disorder that [Allied] troops faced greater danger from being trampled upon than from bullets."[58]

As dusk came down on the smoke-rimmed shores, some of the beaches were piled high with a "monstrous and ever-growing heap . . . of material . . . an endless, confused mass of men, of tiny jeeps, huge, high-sided DUKW's [amphibious trucks, tried for the first time in Sicily] . . . heavily loaded trucks, stuck and straining in the thick sand."[59]

It was requiem, just at sunset of D-day, for LST-313, helping to rig a pontoon causeway (also used for the first time in Sicily) on Green Beach No. 2, near Monte Sole. One bomb turned No. 313—an unlucky number—into a charnel house; land mines, ammunition, guns, trucks, jeeps and half-tracks with tanks full of gasoline went up in infernal explosion, "and filled the air with singeing death."[60]

Worse was to come. The eastern beaches in the American sector were cluttered and congested by the night of D-day; shore parties and beach parties, exhausted, had bogged down; the Luftwaffe appeared to be roaming the air at will.[61]

That night, July 10–11, antiaircraft gunners in the hundreds of ships of the invading fleet eyed the night skies tensely; they were "bomb-happy" and trigger fingers were "itchy." The Luftwaffe knew now exactly where the fleet was, how it was committed 'twixt land and water, anchored to the beachheads until the great armies and their supplies were all ashore. The night was bright with alarms; "the moon mocked us by its beauty"; parachute flares dropped by the German raiders exposed the gaunt steel decks as if they were "naked at noon"; task force guns "roared . . . into action . . . sending tracer bullets arching from all sides above us, until they formed the nave of a Gothic cathedral made of neon"; bombs burst on land and sea.[62]

Off Syracuse the night of the invasion, the British lost the white-hulled, brightly lighted hospital ship *Talama,* which was struck by a bomb and sunk while embarking wounded.[63]

Crisis came on D-plus 1—July 11. General Conrath and the Hermann Göring Panzers tried again.

Soon after dawn, tanks—Mark III's and IV's and Tigers—of the Hermann Göring Panzer Division, supported by elements of the Livorno Division and some Italian infantry, in answer to Guzzoni's orders of the day before, drove from the highlands and from the west toward Gela and the 1st Division beachhead on the coastal plain. At a regimental command post of the 26th Regiment, near the road to Ponte Olivo airfield, and to Niscemi, not far from Gela, Brigadier General "Teddy" Roosevelt telephoned General Allen at the division CP.

"Terry—look! The situation is not very comfortable out here. . . . No antitank protection . . . Is there any possibility of hurrying those medium tanks?"

It became "less comfortable" rapidly. The German attack was determined; the 1st Division had lost some of its AT guns in the landing; few were ashore; artillery was still scarce; and only a few U.S. tanks had waddled up onto the beaches.

It was quick crisis. Destroyer guns opened up; everything that could shoot was firing on the German monsters.

But by about 0930, July 11, the enemy spearhead had debouched from the hills and was still coming hard across the plain within four miles of Gela.

General Patton, on a visit to a Ranger CP in a building on Gela, saw them plainly, and expressed his disgust and anxiety in sulphurous terms.

In answer to a hail from Patton, a Navy ensign of a shore fire-control party, equipped with a walkie-talkie radio, asked politely, "Can I help you sir?"

"Sure," Patton yelled, "if you can connect with your goddam Navy tell 'em for God's sake to drop some shellfire on the road."[64]

The "goddam Navy" obliged in the person of the cruiser *Boise;* 38

6-inch shells fell on the road and slowed but did not halt the Panzer charge. (Later, 500 rounds of 6-inch from the *Savannah* chopped an Italian infantry column to ribbons.)

By 1100 the German tanks had pushed to within 500 yards of the beach; the "Fighting First" was fighting for its life. With tank shells falling on the beachhead, the divisional artillery—what there was ashore —was lined up atop the dunes, firing point-blank at the lumbering monsters. The Navy, offshore, for the first time in World War II was dueling with tanks.

It was a near thing; the division had clung to its positions "by tooth and toenail."[65]

But it was an action that was less dangerous than it seemed. The tank assault came in piecemeal, with little infantry support until late afternoon; the Germans had sacrificed speed for coordinated attack, hoping to catch the invaders off-balance.[66] Almost—at Gela—they succeeded, but they failed and Conrath withdrew, about a third of his tank strength shattered.

But that morning of July 11, when a Navy ensign with a walkie-talkie perhaps turned the tide of war, was the high-water mark for Nazi counterattack.

It was not over.

The two combat teams of the 15th Panzer Grenadier Division, stationed in western Sicily, came hard toward 1st Division beaches, as the Hermann Göring Division and the battered Italians retired to the east to take up the defense of the Catania Plain against the British. The Germans, with some Italian infantry, tangled again with the "Fighting First" on the morning of the twelfth. The 1st beat them to the punch. Two regiments of the 1st Division and some tanks of the 2nd Armored attacked inland, stood off the German assault, knocked out 43 German and Italian tanks, seized the Ponte Olivo airfield and took 4,206 prisoners —most of them happy Italians. There were other challenges, but to all intents and purposes the beachheads were secure.

But not the ships at sea. "Bogies" and "bandits"—Messerschmitts and Stuka dive bombers—roared over the invasion fleet time after time. In broad afternoon on the eleventh a bomb hit Liberty Ship *Robert Rowan,* loaded with ammo; she exploded in flaming but largely harmless pyrotechnics shortly before dusk, and her beached and burning hulk belched clouds of smoke over the beaches for long hours.

The guns claimed victims, plucked German and Italian aircraft from the skies, but their exploding shells downed with catholic impartiality friend and foe alike. On the evening of July 11 just after a German raid had ended, some U.S. C-47 transports, carrying the 504th Parachute Battalion to Sicily to join their brothers on the ground, blundered above the beachheads and the fleet at low altitude. About one-half of the 144 aircraft were damaged by "trigger-happy" Allied gunners; 23 were shot down. The stricken transports flared, flaming, into the sea; paratroopers leaped, some with their chutes afire, from falling planes. Some 97 Americans died, not by enemy steel but cut down, impersonally, by U.S. fire.[67]

On the night of July 13, despite the tragedies of the prior air drops, another airborne operation was laid on (in conjunction with a Commando landing) by the British—the objective the Primosole bridge over the Simeto River, gateway to the Catania Plain. Once again Allied as well as Axis batteries plucked the low-flying troop carriers from the skies. Some 50 of the 124 aircraft were damaged, 11 shot down, and 27 returned to base "with partial or full loads."[68]

The British fleet, only 40 to 100 miles from Axis airfields in Italy, took the brunt of Luftwaffe fury, particularly after July 13; at least six cargo and auxiliary vessels were hit, two were lost.

But the air raids were mostly sound and fury, signifying little in the scales of battle. This was no Crete; the rules were reversed in Sicily. The Allies had an overwhelming air preponderance; the Axis was hopelessly outnumbered. By July 15 the Allies held a continuous front, which included all southeastern Sicily from just east of Porto Empedocle to north of Augusta, including numerous important airfields safely beyond German artillery fire.

DELAY

To Italian defections and Allied victories, the Germans reacted with speed and decision. Two regiments of the German 1st Parachute Division commenced to land in Sicily a few days after the invasion; one element, which had just dropped from the skies, riddled a flight of British gliders coming in for a landing, and turned them into flaming coffins for their passengers and crews.

Advance elements of the German 29th Panzer Grenadier Division moved to Calabria across the Strait of Messina and commenced to move into Sicily to reinforce the greatly outnumbered German troops about July 19. As early as July 12, the XIV Panzer Corps, under General Hans Valentin Hube, was ordered to Sicily to assume command of all German troops, and, in effect, to supersede the Italian, General Guzzoni, in command of the island.[69]

By July 15 the operations staff of the OKW had faced reality: Sicily could not be held, but German troops were to exact delay—to sell space for time—and, at the last, to insure the evacuation of the German divisions across the Strait of Messina.

It was a large task. Within less than a week, the nine to ten Italian divisions in Sicily ("divisions" in name only) had virtually ceased to exist. Thousands of Italians were resting happily in Allied POW cages; other thousands had simply taken off their uniforms and vanished into the hills. There had been heavy casualties in the abortive counterattacks of the first week. Thousands of stragglers behind the German lines were corralled and diverted into the northeastern part of the island. A few small units were more or less incorporated into German divisions, but the Italian infantry fought for the most part with ill-will and scant enthusiasm; most of these had melted away before the end came. The Italian artillery was somewhat better; some light mobile batteries that escaped the early debacle later fought hub to hub with the German guns, and won some grudging encomiums from their allies.

The German strength in Sicily never exceeded about 60,000 men; before the end, as the Allied build-up continued, the Germans were outnumbered between six and ten to one. Given such odds, and with Allied superiority in the air and at sea, there was no possibility but delay; the entire western portion of the island would have to be abandoned, and a defensive line established, based on the Mount Etna massif.

The broad Catania Plain, flat and with "no place to hide," and the "vast slope of Etna and the hot blue sea"[70] which dominated the main road and the shortest route to Messina were the key strategic features in Sicily and the pivot of the first of many German delaying positions.

This had been recognized before the invasion, but "no specific plans to develop the land campaign" after the initial beachheads were secured had been made by the Allies. Alexander, who as an army group commander appeared to be more of a conciliator than a firm leader, had expected the British Eighth Army to drive quickly through Catania, past Etna up the coastal road to Messina. Alexander had little confidence, as a result of his North African experiences, in American combat effectiveness, and his concept of the campaign was the use of the Seventh Army as flank protection for the British: "Patton's Army would be the shield in Alexander's left hand; Montgomery's Army the sword in his right."[71] The secondary role assigned the Americans caused considerable resentment. But soon after the beachheads were secured, Patton saw his chance and took it.

Guns well sited on the high ground on the southern slopes of the Etna massif to command the Catania Plain met the British Eighth Army as they tried to push to the north, and immediately the "Tommies," bloodied and hurt, had slow and heavy going.

But not the U.S. Seventh Army. To Patton's great glee, resistance melted away in front of the Americans.

Major General Geoffrey Keyes, Deputy Commander of the Seventh

Army, and General Truscott, 3rd Division commander, had mounted a successful "reconnaissance in force" toward Agrigento, and Patton soon wangled Alexander's approval of a rampage into western Sicily. A Provisional Corps under General Keyes was formed to take over the Seventh Army's left flank. The 3rd Infantry Division, the 82nd Airborne and some units from the 9th Division formed the corps, with elements of the 2nd Armored Division joining later. The 45th Division, under General Troy Middleton, assigned to General Bradley's II Corps, had been forced out of its position on the right flank of the Seventh Army, next to the British, by General Montgomery's unilateral decision— approved after the event by Alexander—on July 12 to mount a "left-hook" drive by his XXX Corps against Enna and around the western flank of the Etna position.

A road, essential to this operation, had been assigned to the U.S. Seventh Army in the invasion plans, and the Army boundaries clearly put this road network in the U.S. sector. But "Monty" was riding a high horse; he started his plan and commenced moving his XXX Corps squarely across the right front of the Americans even before Alexander rubber-stamped it. The 45th Division was thus squeezed out as the Army boundaries were shifted to the west, and the 45th moved around to the left (western flank) of the 1st Division, and participated in the drive into western Sicily.

Moving at high speed, the Seventh Army went high-balling into western Sicily. Within eight days it had taken Trapani and Palermo, against slight resistance from a few disheartened Italians who retreated rapidly to the east and north, and despite delay caused by German roadblocks and demolitions.

The 82nd Airborne, with the help of a battery of 155 mm. guns, borrowed from the 9th Division, captured Trapani. An Italian admiral surrendered the city and its port with 5,000 hapless Italians to General Matthew B. Ridgway, the division commander, who "also took [the admiral's] sword and field glasses, a fine pair which [Ridgway] later gave to [General] Mark Clark."

"I returned the Admiral's sword later, a gesture which he seemed to appreciate," Ridgway wrote afterward.[72]

The 82nd had "moved 150 miles in six days in its drive to the west, capturing 15,000 prisoners."[73]

The skillful demolitions, the "terrific heat," the mountainous terrain and the serpentine roads were the principal enemy. "And the dust! A compound of cattle dung and pulverized chalky rock, it penetrated the throat and made men desperately thirsty. Old desert hands swore it was worse than the dust of Africa."[74]

Beautiful Palermo—beautiful no longer, its harbor cluttered with the wrecks of more than 50 sunken craft, some of its ancient palaces and irreplaceable mosaics in bomb-shattered ruins,[75]—was captured late on July 22, and Patton established Seventh Army headquarters in the palace of the Norman kings, after a triumphal entry into the city to the sound of cheering Sicilians shouting, "Down with Mussolini! Long live America!"

"The boldness of maneuver and the unflagging speed with which the Seventh Army had moved" captured the imagination of the public in both England and the United States, and Patton's swift progress was compared with Montgomery's slow, inching gains. No matter that the conquest of western Sicily encountered little opposition more formidable than terrain; it was, nevertheless, an achievement in mobility. One U.S. battalion marched 54 miles, some of it cross-country, in 36 hours, and one regiment marched 30 miles in one day, after an all-night motor movement.[76]

Major General Kennedy, Assistant Chief of the Imperial General Staff, recorded that

the success in Sicily inflamed Churchill, and he immediately began to press for bold action to follow it up and bring about the fall of Italy.

He sent a note to the Chiefs of Staff in which he gave his view that we should not "crawl up the leg of Italy like a harvest bug, but strike boldly at the knee," the knee being Rome. . . .

In the middle of July (after the success of the amphibious assault on Sicily was assured) Churchill was reported to have said, "It is true, I suppose, that the Americans consider we have led them up the garden path in the Mediterranean—but what a beautiful path it has proved to be. They have picked peaches here, nectarines there. How grateful they should be."[77]

And Sir Alan Brooke wrote in his diary in July, 1943, that "we had now arrived in the orchard and our next step should be to shake the fruit trees and gather the apples."[78]

But Palermo, psychological prize, moral tonic, was virtually undefended; on the eastern flank of the island where "Monty" had hoped to race up the coastal road into Messina, the XIII Corps of the British Eighth Army had butted its head against a stone wall. The 5th and 50th Divisions had suffered heavy casualties in frontal attack across the flat Catania Plain and had gotten nowhere. About the time Palermo was captured, "Monty" was stopped at dead center.

Nevertheless, for the British "Tommy Atkins"—patient, irrepressible, good-humored—the island campaign was not too bad.

The British Eighth Army "enjoyed Sicily after the desert." It was—behind the front—almost literally wine and roses; as Montgomery describes it, it was "high summer; oranges and lemons were on the trees, wine was plentiful; the Sicilian girls were disposed to be friendly."

Nor was "Monty" too much of a stickler about uniform regulations and spit and polish—"so long as the soldiers fought well and we won our battles." Later he recorded that in Sicily he issued the only order about "dress in the Eighth Army" he ever issued. He had encountered a lorry on the road; the driver (stripped to the waist) appeared to be naked, and he was wearing a "silk top hat. As the lorry passed me, the driver leant out from his cab and took off his hat to me with a sweeping and gallant gesture. I just roared with laughter."

But back at his headquarters the uniform order he issued was simple: "Top hats will not be worn in the Eighth Army."[79]

By July 23, the date by which Eisenhower had thought Sicily would be secured, the battle line was shaping up square across the island. To the east, the German Hermann Göring Division (reinforced) held the Etna massif and dominated the coastal road and the Catania Plain; to its northwest, guarding the hilly approaches to the Etna position, were other German units and two regiments of the 1st Parachute Division; then on Etna's northwest flank, the 15th Panzer Grenadiers, and gradually filling in the front as its units transited the Strait of Messina was the 29th Panzer Grenadier Division, holding the western coastal road from Palermo to Messina, and stretching over the spiny ridges inland. Sandwiched in between and among the German units were the hodgepodge remnants of Italian units, a few fighting strongly, most decimated and defeated.

The Allied order of battle numbered eight divisions—five in the British Eighth Army, three in the U.S. Seventh. The 50th and 5th were on the southeast; the 51st on their flank; the 78th, brought over from Army reserve in Africa, to the west; and the 1st Canadian Division (described as "magnificent" by Montgomery) linking up with the Americans until pinched out as the front narrowed. The 1st, elements of the 9th Division (which had been Patton's reserve) and the 3rd (which had relieved the 45th) on the coastal road held the Seventh Army front; the others were squeezed out for mopping up and support in the rear, as the island narrowed to the northeast.

The toughest fighting for Sicily still lay ahead.

But for the Italy of Benito Mussolini, the Italy that entered the war hungry for spoils as France was dying, the war was about over.

On July 19, as Sicily was falling, Hitler and Mussolini were meeting near Feltre in northern Italy. Mussolini, belatedly, asked Hitler for more armor and 2,000 more planes to defend Sicily. Hitler launched into a harangue.[80]

As they talked, Rome—the Imperial City—was bombed for the first time by Allied planes. The moral and psychological shock, added to the impending loss of Sicily, was far greater than the physical destruction.[81]

The Italian war effort and the glittering pattern of Fascism had long been coming apart at the seams. Instead of a march to glory, instead of an empire greater than ancient Rome's, Mussolini, "tired and senile," had led his country to defeat after defeat.[82] And now it was the end.

On July 20 King Victor Emmanuel III called Mussolini to the palace and told him, "We cannot go on much longer."

On the late afternoon of July 24, as heavy fighting continued across the middle of Sicily, the Fascist Grand Council, each of its members dressed in his black uniform, met at the Palazzo Venezia in Rome to discuss Italy's desperate situation. A coup had been carefully prepared, led by Dino Grandi, former Foreign Minister and former Ambassador to Britain, as figurehead, but with Marshal Vittorio Ambrosio, Chief of the Italian General Staff, and Marshal Pietro Badoglio as the "King's men," wielding the actual power. Mussolini's personal bodyguard had been relieved of their duties as the Council met; the dictator was taken completely by surprise.

Grandi led the attack; like vultures Mussolini's old Black Shirt comrades turned upon him. Even Ciano, who owed him all, even Ciano, Mussolini's Foreign Minister and his son-in-law, voted against the dictator. After a session that lasted most of the night the Grand Council voted overwhelmingly early on July 25, 1943, in favor of a motion presented by Grandi: a resolution calling upon the King to assume more power. It seemed innocuous, but there was no doubt about its meaning: the vote was to end 21 years of Mussolini's rule.

The same day, the *de jure* proceedings became a *de facto fait accompli* when Mussolini called upon the King, who

frowned, fluttered his shriveled little hands impatiently.

"*Il giuoco e finito,* the game is over, Mussolini," he said. . . . "You'll have to go. . . ."

Finally, the ex-Duce, whose thunderings from the Balcony had frightened a whole world, mumbled, "Sire, this—this is the end of Fascism."[83]

And it was.[84] Mussolini was placed in "protective custody"; Badoglio took over the Italian Government and commenced to try to find a way to take Italy out of the war.

The news of Mussolini's downfall came like a thunderclap to the Third Reich. "It is simply shocking," Goebbels wrote in his diary, "to think that . . . a revolutionary movement that has been in power for twenty-one years could be liquidated."[85]

It was a grim period for the Axis. About the time of Mussolini's fall Hamburg, proud, rich *grande dame* of German cities, was reduced to ashes by incendiary bombs dropped by the Royal Air Force. The resultant fire storm, with swirling winds of up to 150 miles an hour, resulted in one of the greatest holocausts of World War II. . . .

"Monty," stopped on the coastal route to Messina, shifted the weight of his attack to the west and north—inland—in a "left hook," to outflank the strong Etna–Catania Plain position to the west.

The three-pronged attack—the British and Canadians curling around the inland flank of Etna; the American 1st Division and elements of the 9th Division pushing east and north over hill and mountain and defile in the center of the island; the 3rd Division on the coastal road from Palermo to Messina—met tough going. Tanks were of limited use in such terrain; it was work for the infantryman, and the 100-degree temperatures dehydrated and exhausted the toiling foot-sloggers.[86]

And work they would never forget. In front of Troina, a mountain town and "natural strong point" on a key road leading past Etna to the north, the "Fighting First" Division met the "Heartbreak Ridge" of World War II.

From August 3, when the attack jumped off, what the communiqués were to describe as "stubborn enemy resistance" developed. The words cloaked tragedy. The Axis forces had slowed the Allied advance from the first day of the invasion by masterly delaying tactics—blown bridges, cratered roads, skillfully planted mine fields. And now, in the defense of Troina, the enemy had lost none of his skill.

Most of the water courses were dried gullies, parched in the searing heat; the few springs and trickles were mined and booby-trapped by the retreating Germans. It was a land where a few could and did hold the gate against many.

Hour after hour and day after day, the 1st Division, wearied, dispirited, bloody, tried to take Troina. The attack on August 3 got nowhere.

General Patton, tense, eager to keep his army moving, visited the 1st Division front that day; his emotions—always sensitive to men and environment (he was "like a high-tension wire that quivers and hums when it is overloaded"[87])—were deeply stirred by the hard battle. On the way back to his CP, the general visited the 15th Evacuation Hospital. He was moved by the newly wounded men, some without arms or legs.

In the hospital, there also was a man trying to look as if he had been wounded. I asked him what was the matter, and he said he just couldn't take it. I gave him the devil, slapped his face with my gloves and kicked him out of the hospital.[88]

It was the first of two "slapping incidents" that were to affect the career of General Patton and of history.

On August 4 the 1st Division tried again. A heavy bombing and concentrated artillery fire preceding an infantry assault near dusk failed to budge the Germans. All day on the fifth the 1st tried again, but made inching gains. The German defenders of Troina were successfully covering the withdrawal of Axis forces around the western and northern flank of Etna.

The 39th Regiment of Major-General Manton Eddy's 9th Division, temporarily attached to the "Fighting First," had its try against Troina, led by an Army "character"—one of the finest fighting regimental commanders of World War II, Colonel "Paddy" Flint (Harry A. Flint of St. Johnsbury, Vermont). Flint took a regiment that had no soul, no confidence and made them "fighting fools." At Troina he walked up and down in front of his men, where the bullets sang, a rifle in his hand, stripped to the waist, his helmet on and a black silk scarf around his neck.[89]

The 9th Division, brought into Palermo by sea on August 1, had been scheduled to relieve the battered 1st when Troina was captured. Outflanking operations of some of its units north of Troina may have helped slightly to lead to the hill town's fall—but at a time of German choosing. It was not until about dawn on August 6 that a patrol of the 1st Division penetrated Troina and reported the Germans had withdrawn. It had been a tenacious and, to the Allies, a costly defense—"one of the most fiercely fought smaller actions of the war." The Germans had launched no less than 24 separate counterattacks.[90]

The 1st Division lost 267 dead, 1,184 wounded and 337 missing in the Sicilian campaign; it captured in 37 days of combat some 18 towns and 5,935 prisoners.[91]

After Troina and the prior three weeks of fighting, sergeants were commanding platoons in the tired and battered "Fighting First."

On August 10, with Troina captured but Truscott's 3rd Division still making slow progress on the coastal road, Patton visited the 93rd Evacuation Hospital. Again his tense emotions burst all bounds. A

patient was sitting huddled up and shivering.

When asked what his trouble was, the man replied, "It's my nerves," and began to sob. The General then screamed at him, "What did you say?" He replied, "It's my nerves. I can't stand the shelling any more." He was still sobbing.

The General then yelled at him, "Your nerves Hell, you are just a Goddamn coward, you yellow son of a bitch." He then slapped the man and said, "Shut up that Goddamned crying. I won't have these brave men here who have been shot seeing a yellow bastard sitting here crying."[92]

The war went on. But many who had witnessed the incidents were outraged; official reports started up the chain of command; soon the Seventh Army was abuzz with wild rumors. The day of reckoning was delayed, but the fat was in the fire.

On the coastal road—a tourists' paradise "bordered by pink and white oleanders and lemon orchards,"[93] but a military nightmare—the 3rd Division had by-passed, with the help of the Navy, some of the enemy strong points and the delaying positions. General Truscott mounted two small battalion-size amphibious end runs—the first on August 8—behind a strong enemy position on 2,400-foot Monte Fratello, which had held up the 3rd Division for five days. The first operation landed a battalion nine miles behind the Monte Fratello position in the dark hours before dawn.

"It's the chance that few outfits get, so let's cut the rug and knock them all the way back to Messina," the battalion commander told his troops.

But the Germans were already withdrawing;[94] the landing did not "knock them back," though it killed and captured several hundred Germans and destroyed tanks and vehicles.

The second end run, on August 11, put an infantry battalion ashore at Brolo, behind a German position. But they stuck their noses into a hornet's nest; the Germans reacted fiercely, and seven U.S. Army planes, trying to help, bombed the American battalion CP and also destroyed the battalion's supporting artillery. The battalion lost 99 dead, 78 wounded; it exacted a tribute of blood from the enemy, but at the most helped to force, but did not block, a German retirement a few hours earlier than planned.

Patton tried a third small landing at the last, but it was "dated" by the time it got ashore; the front had passed it by.

Similarly, on the east coast a small Commando landing, south of Scaletta, on the night of August 15–16—the only British attempt in the campaign to by-pass by sea Sicily's natural defenses—was mounted too late for meaningful tactical result. It produced skirmishes but little else.

British Commandos landing in the night encountered sudden death —brief, flaring fire fights—as they crept stealthily toward their objective. An officer, Douglas Grant, walked slowly toward the enemy trenches in the darkness.

They were all empty except for one into which a rag doll had been carelessly thrown . . . it was an undersized boy. He lay dead on his back. . . . His unbuttoned tunic was ripped and torn. . . .

A light wind blew up and a heavy drift of perfume, sweet and pervasive, filled the air and mixed with the dry scent of the baked dust. . . .

A scream suddenly rang out with a violence that showed it had been long suppressed, and a voice, exasperated by pain and fear, cried "Mama! Mama!" It called again and again from the seaward side of the cliff in . . . high pitch and slowly dwindled to a monotonous tearful moan of "Mama! Mama!" . . . It was horrible to lie in the darkness and listen to the eerie repetitive cry.[95]

On the southern and eastern flank, the British took the abandoned German positions in the town of Catania on August 6, and inland, the 78th Division, which had pinched out the 1st Canadian Division as the front shortened, fought alongside the right flank of the U.S. 9th Division toward Adrano and Randazzo, along the road winding through lava beds beneath the cone of Etna.

The Etna position had been won; the German XIV Corps and thousands of disorganized Italians were now penned at last in the small northeastern peninsula of Sicily, with Messina and its fabled strait at their backs.

But for the Germans it was "no sweat." They still compelled delay. Hube—not Patton, not Montgomery—commanded the situation; Alexander and Eisenhower might propose, but Hube and Kesselring disposed.

Hube's job was to get the cadre of his German forces safely out of Sicily to the mainland, and this he did, despite tremendous Allied air superiority and Allied command of the sea.

The staff work and organizing genius for which the German military are justly famous was never better exemplified than in the evacuation of Sicily.

A heavy concentration of flak guns lined the strait to keep Allied planes at bay; E-boats (motor gunboats) and light craft patrolled its waters; coast-defense guns dominated its entrances. Ferries, barges and many other kind of craft were used, most of them heavily armed with AA guns.

On the night of August 10–11, as the German troops fell back to the first of a number of preselected delaying lines, the first German soldiers crossed the strait without serious interference. By early morning August 17, General Hube, among the last to leave in "conformity with approved German tradition"[96] evacuated Sicily with the last of his men.

The Germans crossed the strait in good order, with weapons and light equipment, tactical organizations intact, some heavy equipment and no serious interference by the Allies. Thousands of Italians, barred from Messina by German order to prevent interference with the German evacuation, nevertheless made their own way across the strait from points as far south as Taormina in train ferries, small steamboats and motor rafts organized by General Guzzoni.[97]

On that last night of the campaign a full moon shone upon thousands of men, and hundreds of vehicles, hurrying across a wrecked and burning landscape to their prize. The roads were littered with ruined transport, camions still smoking and abandoned, burnt-out cars. A vanguard of bulldozers ploughed through heaps of rubble. Shells from the German batteries now mounted in the Italian toe fell among the ruins and the advancing troops.[98]

Patton won the race to Messina, and preened himself on his success, but the first GI patrol cautiously entered the city August 16 only after nearly all the Germans had left. Other troops, and General Patton himself, entered Messina on the morning of the seventeenth. A couple of hours later "a column of Eighth Army tanks rumbled in from the south amid shouts from GI's of 'Where you tourists been?' To which the Tommies replied with a grin, 'Hello, you bloody bastards!' "[99]

The Sicilian campaign was over, but its dissonance lingered on.

THE RESULTS

Sicily was an Allied physical victory, a German moral victory.

From the Allied point of view it had accomplished its purpose, though that purpose was somewhat vague.

Allied conquest of the island made possible more or less continuous use of the Mediterranean maritime routes, though it could not insure them against loss.

The Sicilian campaign revealed in full starkness the war weariness of Italy and led directly to the internal coup in Rome which resulted in Mussolini's downfall and—ultimately—to the establishment of the Badoglio government, the armistice, the surrender of the Italian Fleet and the virtually complete collapse of the Italian war effort.

It opened a new front against the Axis underbelly of Europe.

The campaign cost the Axis some 160,000 to 164,000 casualties— killed, wounded, prisoners and missing—but less than 12,000 of them were German dead or captured (more than 5,000 dead, the rest captured); the great majority were willing Italian prisoners.[100] The Allies captured 3,500 motor vehicles,[101] several hundred German guns, 70 tanks, mountains of Italian supplies.[102] The Seventh Army lost about 1,425 dead, almost 5,200 wounded, 791 missing; the total Eighth Army casualties were 11,843. The U.S. Navy lost 546 men killed and missing, 484 wounded; the Royal Navy, 314 killed, 411 wounded, 4 prisoners.[103]

The grand total of about 20,000 Allied combat casualties showed that the Germans had sold space for time at a high price in Allied blood.

Sicily spelled the end of the Regia Aeronautica, and it helped to break the back of the Luftwaffe in the central Mediterranean; total Axis air losses—in addition to fields and facilities overrun, destroyed and captured—probably amounted to 200 to 1,500 planes.[104] The Allies lost about 375 planes.

Admiral Cunningham estimated that

during the actual operations, and the period covering the transportation of men and material to Sicily from Great Britain and the United States through the U-boat zone in the North Atlantic, the total of Allied merchant shipping lost amounted to 85,000 tons. . . . British naval losses were two submarines, three motor torpedo boats, one motor gunboat and a few landing craft.

The naval losses of the Sicilian campaign were not onerous. Ultimately, of course, Sicily led to the surrender or neutralization of the entire Italian Fleet. But the fighting itself cost the Axis only 3 German and 9 Italian submarines sunk or captured, and these 12 "boats" had sunk 4 British cruisers. Air attacks "caused far more trouble and dislocation." The British lost, to the end of July, 3 landing craft and 6 merchantmen or auxiliaries (41,509 tons of shipping); the carrier *Indomitable,* the monitor *Erebus,* 2 destroyers, 4 landing craft and 3 merchantmen were damaged. The U.S. lost 1 destroyer, 1 mine sweeper, 2 LST's and 1 merchantman, and several transports, mine sweepers and LST's damaged.[105]

And the Allies "inherited" Sicily, a devastated, impoverished island, its marginal economy wrecked, its peoples a burden, not an asset, to the Allied war effort.

Sicily made and marred reputations of men and units; it left psychic scars on both sides. The German-Italian combat relationships, always under strain except for a brief time in North Africa, were forever shattered by Sicily; the fury and contempt the Germans showed for the Italian ineffectiveness would have henceforth doomed any real combat cooperation even had Italy continued to fight.

Once again, even more than in North Africa, the German soldier had demonstrated his thorough professionalism, and General Hube had proved a master of his trade.

On the Allied side, the two leaders—Montgomery of the Eighth and Patton of the Seventh—emerged with reputations somewhat tarnished. Both were ambitious, avid for fame. "Monty," a Puritan ascetic, cautious and deliberate, showed little flair in Sicily; once more, as after El Alamein, the Germans eluded his slow pursuit. No matter that the British Eighth Army faced the pivot position in Sicily—the Etna massif; no matter that against the Eighth was concentrated, after the initial days, the bulk of German strength. The public imagination had been captured by Patton's sweeping thrusts through western Sicily and his prior capture of Messina. "Monty" seemed overshadowed.

Patton, a swashbuckling cavalier, emotional, complex and aggressive, had won the spotlight of fame, but the slapping incidents (which were publicized in a garbled account by Drew Pearson, the columnist, three months afterwards)[106] cost him heavily in public esteem; and for the drive from Normandy against the German heart, Bradley, Patton's subordinate corps commander in Sicily—Bradley, quiet, dependable, "safe"—became Patton's boss.

And for the glory hunters—Terry Allen and Teddy Roosevelt—and their beloved 1st Division, Sicily was an end of an era. The two men, brave to the point of recklessness, human and humane, warm and eccentric, were too much alike; for their good and the division's, they had to be parted. Somehow, by Troina, the division was wearied, dull, sorry for itself; it had lost its drive; somehow, it had become a kind of a tactical prima donna, which felt itself apart; somehow, many of its men believed that after North Africa they were finished with war, they were to go home; somehow, Sicily seemed to them unfair.

Even so the 1st Division fought well in Sicily, superbly in the beachhead days, but it was a division going downhill with war weariness and a vague malaise when Bradley, with Patton's approval, relieved its two beloved generals on August 7 after the division had fought its last Mediterranean battle at Troina.

It was not the end of the road for either the division or its generals; under a tough, strong, fair and square soldier named Huebner, the "Fighting First" was to achieve its greatest glory at Omaha Beach in Normandy and in the drive into Germany's heart. Teddy Roosevelt, shifted to the 4th Division as Assistant Division Commander, was to die of a heart attack—rather than, as he would have wished, from an enemy bullet—after leading his troops ashore at Utah Beach in Normandy with a walking stick; and Terry Allen, sent back to France by General George Catlett Marshall in command of a new division, the 104th, demonstrated his great capacity for leadership.[107]

But Sicily was a campaign that marred reputations as much as it made them; in Washington and London there was a vague disquiet about its results.

For to the Germans went the moral triumph. Their few divisions had surmounted their Italian's ally's defections and rout; some 60,000 to 75,000 German troops had stood off an Allied force of close to 500,000 men,[108] had protracted a campaign expected to require two weeks to 38 days, and, despite overwhelming Allied air and sea superiority, had safely retired to the mainland in what Morison calls "an outstanding maritime retreat . . . in a class with Dunkirk."[109] The land worked for them, it is true, but the Germans had been able, figuratively, to thumb their noses at the Allies. As Morison says, "The German concept of the Sicilian campaign, a delaying action followed by the salvage of 'valuable human material,' was carried out to the letter despite Allied superiority in land, naval and air forces."[110]

Sicily was a clear-cut Allied victory—wars are not won by evacuations—but it was scarcely a glorious one that went "according to plan."

Plainly, Germany was far from finished; Sicily might be the end of the beginning, but a long, hard road still lay ahead. And plainly the Allies still had much to learn.

CRITIQUE

Sicily was a campaign without an objective, an end in itself, and the troops who fought it and the Allies themselves suffered from this strategic aimlessness.

Napoleon is said to have remarked, "Give me allies to fight against." Sicily illustrated the kernel of this aphorism. Allied cross-purposes had led to Sicily in the first place, because "something had to be done," but what was to be done—except to win a victory in the island—and where it was to lead was never enunciated. Churchill knew where he wanted to go—into the Balkans;[111] his purpose was strategic in the largest sense of the word in that it had a postwar purpose: the establishment of a strong western position in Eastern Europe. But he could not persuade his ally, the United States, and as junior partner Britain did not call the tune.

As it was, what followed Sicily was as aimless as its beginnings. Salerno and the invasion of Italy itself did not lead to the formal Italian surrender; Sicily had done that, and in the event, Marshal Badoglio signed a formal armistice on September 3, the day Montgomery's Eighth Army began crossing the Messina Strait—six days before the landing at Salerno. The principal objective—knocking Italy out of the war—had therefore been accomplished, but to it was added the somewhat vague goal of securing southern Italian airfields around Foggia as bases for Allied bombers in the air war against Germany.[112] This objective, never a very important one, and of relatively minor significance, as events showed, in the strategic bombing offensive, was also paralleled by a kind of vague aspiration, a hope: the capture of Rome.

This was to become an *idée fixe*. All roads led to Rome, but Rome led nowhere strategically.

That in a nutshell was the tragedy as well as the costly glory of the Italian campaign, of the Sicilian campaign and of the entire Allied effort in the central Mediterranean. Allied dissension led to Allied infirmity of purpose; the United States and Britain defied a principle of war and had no clear-cut strategic objective.

Thus the Allies moved one piecemeal step by another: into Sicily, across to the boot, to Salerno, to the airfields and Naples, to Anzio and Rome, and up the stony spine of the Apennines the length of the peninsula to the Po and war's end. But never along the only road that this Via Dolorosa could justify strategically—across the Adriatic into the Austrian plain and the heart of the Balkans.

Italy, it has been said, justified itself because of the strain it placed upon the German armed forces. It diverted men, planes, divisions from the Russian front and from Western Europe where the Normandy invasion was still to come.[113] Perhaps this contention is sound, but it is, indeed, difficult to determine who diverted whom. The American commitment of 227,000 troops in the Tunisian campaign (at the end of December, 1942) had grown by the end of 1943 to 597,000 in the entire Mediterranean theater, and to a peak of 742,000 (in August, 1944) in the Mediterranean. The British, the French, a dozen other nations and races contributed hundreds of thousands more. Italy and the Mediterranean adventures, no matter how viewed, represented an expensive diversion, to the Allies even more than to the Germans.

And it was a diversion that was far more costly to the Allies than it should have been. For the Allied strategy in Sicily and Italy was not only aimless in the largest sense; it was unimaginative and overcautious and failed to use to the optimum the priceless Allied asset of command of the sea.

The original plan for the invasion of Sicily, discarded by Montgomery's insistence, utilized the flexibility of sea power to a far greater degree than did the formal frontal assault in the southeastern part of the island. It contemplated successive, widely separated landings in eastern and western Sicily from Avola to Palermo. It utilized naval mobility to put troops ashore on the flank and in the rear of Axis defenses in the southern and southwestern part of the island and would have forced a major dispersion of Axis defensive strength. The initial plan, based in part upon the early capture of a port (Palermo) and not, as in the plan actually used, upon the supply of the Seventh Army over open beaches (a task of this magnitude had never before been attempted), was heavily backed by the U.S. and British navies, by Admiral Cunningham and by General Patton. But "Monty," with Alexander supporting him, had sufficient influence to force a change; the ultimate landings were a compromise heavily slanted toward "Monty's" views—sound enough in view of the new amphibious techniques and equipment available, but certainly neither daring nor enterprising.

Eisenhower, in his book *Crusade in Europe*, defends the discarding of the original plan as follows:

Some professionals . . . have since vigorously asserted to me that if we had correctly evaluated the low combat value of the huge Italian garrison we would have stuck to the "encircling" plan and so overrun the island in 10 to 15 days rather than in the 38 eventually required. Moreover, it is alleged, we would have captured the German core of the defending forces instead of merely driving it back into Italy. It is possible that with Syracuse, Gela and Palermo quickly in our hands we might have been able to capture Messina, the key point, before the Germans could have concentrated sufficiently to defeat any of our attacks. But not even by hindsight can it be said with certainty that the whole Italian garrison would quit—I still believe that we were wise to concentrate as much as possible, and to proceed methodically to the conquest of an island in which the defending strength was approximately 350,000.[114]

But, as Morison notes, "Admiral Cunningham still believes the initial plan was the better and so do many others."[115]

And all the postwar German comments are shot through with references to Allied "caution," to Allied "frontal attack," and with amazement that the Allies did not land near Messina or Catania, or in the northern part of Sicily to cut off and destroy the Axis garrisons in the south.[116]

Even the U.S. Army official history describes the invasion, "based (falsely) on anticipation of strenuous Italian resistance," as "cautious and conservative," essentially "Montgomery's plan."

"No one, except Montgomery was particularly happy with it. The strategic conception inherent in the plan was both disadvantageous to and disparaging of the American force."[117]

Once they were ashore, conservatism influenced Allied strategy in execution just as it had in planning. The two small amphibious end runs mounted by the Seventh Army to outflank obstacles on the Palermo-Messina road were helpful, though mounted too late and in too small force to really influence the campaign.[118] Montgomery sent a Commando group ashore in a small operation (mounted much too late and after the Germans had retired) that had no effect; the Eighth Army lost heavily in frontal attacks against the Etna massif.

Cunningham, in his book *A Sailor's Odyssey*, wrote later that "I thought at the time we might have lessened our difficulties and hastened the advance if we had taken a leaf out of the American book and used our sea power to land troops behind the enemy lines."[119]

The pattern of cautious frontal attack by toiling foot-sloggers against the natural ramparts of rugged terrain established in Sicily was to continue in Italy. Anzio, ill-fated through no fault of Allied sea power, was the sole attempt to utilize naval dominance and the broad reaches of the seas to outflank the strong German positions in the punishing mountains of the peninsula.

The step-by-step involvement of the Allies in Italy, without ultimate strategic aim, was, indeed, to cost heavily.

As Eisenhower comments, "The doctrine of opportunism, so often applicable in tactics, is a dangerous one to pursue in strategy."[120]

An official study, *Operations in Sicily and Italy*, prepared for use at West Point, comments:

Looking back over the broad picture, it is perhaps justifiable to conclude that the Allied high command took a conservative course in deciding to invade Sicily. The bolder and more decisive course would have been an operation against Sardinia and Corsica, followed by an invasion of the Italian mainland. Napoleon is credited with a statement to the effect that the proper way to invade Italy is from the top of the boot and not from the toe. An Allied attack launched from Sardinia would have followed more closely the sound tenet enunciated.[121]

Eisenhower himself wrote later:

Sicily was the proper objective if our primary purpose remained the clearing of the Mediterranean for use by Allied shipping. . . . On the other hand, if the real purpose of the Allies was to invade Italy for major operations to defeat that country completely, then I thought our proper initial objectives were Sardinia and Corsica. . . . Since Sardinia and Corsica lie on the flank of the long Italian boot, the seizure of those islands would force a very much greater dispersion of enemy strength in Italy than would the mere occupations of Sicily, which lies just off the mountainous toe of the peninsula.[122]

The dual nature of the tragedy of the central Mediterranean campaign is clear: (1) the Allies had no clear-cut, agreed-upon ultimate strategic objective; (2) the Allies did not lead to German weakness, at sea and in the air, but to German strength on land; failure to use to the optimum naval and air superiority permitted the defense to enlist as ally the heart-breaking, back-breaking terrain of the island of Sicily and of the peninsula of Italy.

In Sicily both sides made mistakes, both sides learned new lessons.

The escape of almost 40,000 Germans (with 9,600 vehicles, 47 tanks, 94 guns and about 17,000 tons of supplies[123] across the three-mile wide Messina Strait despite Allied air domination, an evacuation which never experienced serious interruption, cast a shadow on the navies of Nelson and Farragut and demonstrated the need for tremendously improved Allied air capability. Admiral Cunningham states, "There was no effective way of stopping [the Germans at Messina] either by sea or air."

The German defenses of the strait were strong: searchlights, barrage balloons, more than 150 German and Italian guns, ranging from 280 mm. coast-defense batteries to light antiaircraft, and E-boats and other craft.[124] Allied motor torpedo boats made nightly sallies into the strait but accomplished nothing.

But there was, really, little serious attempt to interfere with the German evacuation. Within 17 days of the end of the evacuation of Sicily, Montgomery's Eighth Army landed in the toe of Italy. There was nothing to prevent such a landing before the evacuation was completed. The Allied air forces proved singularly ineffective in dealing with the shipping traffic across the strait. It is true that the Germans evacuated many of their troops at night—the original plan contemplated movements across the strait only at night, but the Germans found Allied interference so ineffective they also moved by day. There was virtually no

Allied night capability for attack upon shipping; high-level pattern bombing of the strait area was a "hit-or-miss" proposition, inaccurate and ineffective. In daytime the heavy concentration of flak kept the Allied attack planes at bay; yet the Allied air fleets demonstrated a lack of training, a lack of accuracy and a lack of aggressiveness in attacks against the Messina crossings, and Allied air power was never fully concentrated against the strait.[125]

Nor did the Allied navies show the dash and vigor that one might have expected. Large parts of both the British and U.S. fleets were tied down, it is true, in providing gunfire support and convoy protection for the ground operations in Sicily. Nevertheless, it is impossible to avoid the conclusion that determined large-scale naval attacks and naval bombardment upon the strait, carefully coordinated with air attack and air protection, would have seriously interfered with the German evacuation. No such attacks were made.

The key perhaps to many of the Allied shortcomings in Sicily was the lack of intimate, closely integrated air-surface cooperation. The centralized command of the Allied air forces, though useful for so-called strategic bombing and for air superiority missions, led to inordinate delays in the provision of close air support, to failure to provide adequate air protection to the invading fleets in the first days of the invasion, and to other errors of omission and commission. It was difficult, at best, in Sicily, to "lay on," without great delay, the kind of closely coordinated air-surface missions that were taken for granted in the Navy–Marine Corps operations in the Pacific, and that later in France became the hallmark of the tactical air forces that supported the drive into Germany.[126] Nevertheless, the Allied air superiority, overwhelming in Sicily, constantly impressed and hampered the German defenders, and contributed mightily to the ultimate victory.

The United States and Britain learned much about both the flexibility and the fragility and difficulties of airborne operations. The tragic destruction by Allied guns of Allied paratroop transports emphasized more sharply than any other single event the necessity of the closest kind of low-level, intimate collaboration in any operation of combined forces.

The airborne operations in Sicily required many post-mortems. Colonel Gavin called them, in a take-off on the old military description "snafu," a "safu"—a self-adjusting foul-up. It was the first time that paratroopers had been dropped by night, and it was obvious that much more work, training and study were needed before airborne operations could become really effective against a first-rate enemy. As Colonel Gavin later wrote, the Sicilian operation demonstrated that the troop carrier wings needed far more training in navigation and night operations, that rapid assembly of the paratroopers on the ground must be improved, and that the paratroopers had to carry with them more weapons and ammunition.[127]

The German evaluation of the Allied airborne operations in Sicily was that, despite the dispersed nature of the landings, the airborne troops "operating as nuisance teams . . . considerably impeded the advance of the Hermann Göring Panzer Division and helped to prevent it from attacking . . . promptly after the landings at Gela and elsewhere."[128]

New amphibious techniques tested for the first time in Sicily—notably the Navy's pontoon causeways and the Army's amphibious truck, the "duck," which could swim from transport to shore and then roll up on the beach—paved the way to even more advanced concepts in later operations. The need for effective shore and beach parties to make order out of chaos was emphasized.

The actual invasion plan utilized depended for its success upon supply of the assault forces

over the beaches to an extent that had never before been deemed acceptable.

The dilemma, which at one time appeared virtually insoluble, was in fact solved by the arrival from America of the new amphibious vehicles called DUKWS (colloquially "Ducks," or amphibious trucks—D—year of origin; U—utility—K—front-wheel drive—W—six-wheeled) whose remarkable performance in carrying men and stores direct from the assault ships and up the landing beaches reduced the need for the very early capture of a major port.[129]

This judgment, however, represents a somewhat oversimplified reason for the supply success achieved in "Husky." The "ducks" used for the first time *were* highly successful, but other new types of landing craft and vehicles—LST's (Landing Ships, Tanks), LCT's, LCI's, etc.—in their first extensive use, and pontoon causeways were also responsible. In addition, the light initial enemy resistance permitted the quick capture of a number of small and intermediate and, finally, large ports.

From the Allied point of view, two of the most heartening developments of the Sicilian operation were the effectiveness of naval gunfire support for ground troops in the initial stages of an amphibious operation (the U.S. Army, with few exceptions, had never been "sold" on this concept until Sicily) and the tremendous logistical and engineering achievements of U.S. forces.

The Sicilian campaign was, for the Allies, the final training ground for the Battle of Europe. In its battles U.S. troops proved themselves, despite the misgivings of both Montgomery and Alexander, and "GI" and "Tommy" learned a mutual respect. Sicily did not end Anglo-American rivalry; at high levels it stimulated it, but the fighting man of each nation learned that he could depend upon the other.

For the Axis, Sicily was the end of an uneasy alliance, a marriage of convenience that had never been really consummated. Hitler had long put tremendous confidence in Mussolini; he was greatly shaken by the Duce's downfall, and he was not prepared—though Rommel and others had long predicted it—for the lackadaisical performance and the whole-sale defections of Italian troops.

For the Italians, Sicily was certainly not a glorious chapter. The Germans were bitterly contemptuous of their allies; postwar German accounts imply—with overstatement—that the Italians did virtually no fighting. Yet, in truth, they did little—just how much history possibly will never ascertain. Morison gives them considerable credit for the defense, even though ineffective, of Sicily—more credit than they deserve.

The Germans tended to dismiss their Italian allies too lightly. Nevertheless, one German comment seems eminently fair:

Even though a few commanders still wanted to fight, and even though some units (the Italian artillery, for example) still gave a fair account of themselves, nothing was left of coordinated leadership and combat effectiveness. The Italian soldier was tired, aimless, and undisciplined. Consequently, Italian units only rarely constituted an asset in combat, and for the most part only proved to be a liability.[130]

Operations in Sicily and Italy speaks of "the general defection of Italian troops who deserted and surrendered at the first opportunity. Within ten days the Italian Sixth Army ceased to have combat value."[131]

Yet some Italian units fought, and many bewildered Italian peasants in uniform, knowing little of what the war was about or why they fought, died to no good end.

General Guzzoni, a weak leader, nevertheless appears to have been more correct than Kesselring in his preinvasion appraisal of Allied intentions. It was on Kesselring's insistence that the bulk of the 15th Panzer Grenadier Division, which had been in eastern Sicily, was transferred to western Sicily just before invasion. Kesselring believed one Allied amphibious assault would be made in the west; Guzzoni pinpointed where the actual invasion occurred. Kesselring was wrong, and his error was in part responsible for "an initial dispersion of Axis forces that materially decreased the chances of a successful defense."[132]

Even so, in retrospect it is clear that a successful defense of Sicily by the forces the Axis then had available would have been impossible; the Germans were overwhelmed by sheer power.

During the fighting the Germans time and again stressed the difficulties of their communications; their inadequacy unquestionably played a part in the lateness and piecemeal nature of the Axis counter-attacks against the initial Allied beachheads. The transmission of orders to individual units was uncertain, delayed, intermittent. There were no land lines, and radio communications were erratic and subject to interruption and interference—due in part to the mountainous nature of the country, in part to local phenomena, in part to the inadequacy in quality and quantity of the German signal equipment, satisfactory for combat in flat terrain but totally inadequate for the mountains. Time and time again the Germans had to resort to couriers and liaison officers, who were often delayed by broken bridges and air attacks; orders sometimes reached lower units long after they were pertinent. In Sicily the German ground units were controlled much as Napoleon controlled the Grand Army more than a century before.

The tenuous nature of the German command and control system emphasized even more sharply the high degree of training and initiative and tactical "savvy" of the German officers and noncoms. German lower units knew, in general, General Hube's plan for delay and evacuation; in the absence of orders they conformed to the plan and in detail played it by ear, withdrawing on their own initiative when the situation indicated.

But Sicily, which proved once again the strength of the German Army and its thorough training and high degree of professionalism, was to be one of the last battlefields on which military initiative, unhampered by political control, was to be possible.[133] More and more as World War II continued, Hitler's "no retreat" orders, his attempt to hold everything, led to the loss of all his conquests. In Sicily the German Army won a moral victory—and conducted a highly successful delaying action and evacuation—largely because General Hube, the commander, exercised initiative without restraint.

Sicily was no glory road for either side. An Allied force that reached a total ground strength of 467,000 at its peak was baffled and held in check by German units which probably never totaled, at any one time, more than 60,000 men.

In the years ahead in World War II, the dead hand of Hitler and the tremendous and overpowering weight of the products of the "arsenal of democracy," the United States, doomed the Third Reich. Sheer weight of men and metal overpowered the Germans in Sicily and sealed their fate in the campaigns to come.

CHAPTER 7

TARAWA—A STUDY IN COURAGE

November 20–23, 1943

On November 20, 1943, the tropic surf round a Pacific island of which few Americans had ever heard was frothed with blood. "Operation Galvanic," one of the famous battles of World War II, emblazoned a new name—Tarawa, epic of reef and sand—in the history books, and added a new episode of glory to the Iliad of the United States Marines.

The long road back from Pearl Harbor had been but barely started in November, 1943. The rising sun flag of Japan still flew above Wake, the Philippines, the lovely islands of the Malay barrier and of the Southern Seas. From the legendary fortress of Truk in the heart of Pacific Micronesia the spiderweb of the Carolines, the Marianas, the Marshalls and the Gilberts—with their airstrips, seaplane ramps and gun emplacements—dominated the Central Pacific, barred the direct route to the gateways of Nippon.

Guadalcanal had been fought for and won; most of the Solomons were ours; and MacArthur's green troops, racked by malaria and battling jungle leeches, tropical ulcers and Japs fighting to the death behind ramparts of the dead, had won the initial campaigns in New Guinea. At

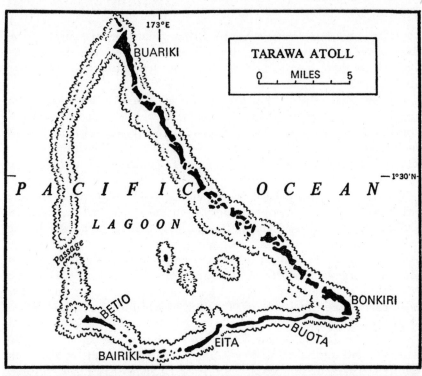

TARAWA ATOLL

0   MILES   5

BUARIKI

173°E

PACIFIC OCEAN

— 1°30'N

LAGOON

Passage

BETIO

BONKIRI

EITA

BUOTA

BAIRIKI

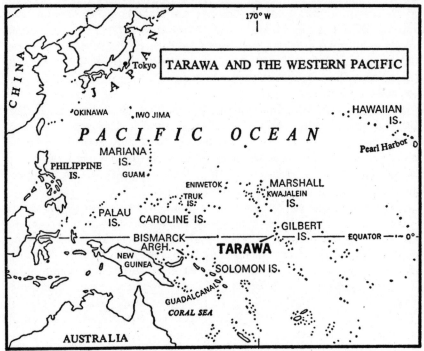

TARAWA AND THE WESTERN PACIFIC

170° W

CHINA

JAPAN

Tokyo

PACIFIC OCEAN

OKINAWA

IWO JIMA

HAWAIIAN IS.

MARIANA IS.

Pearl Harbor

PHILIPPINE IS.

GUAM

ENIWETOK

MARSHALL IS.

KWAJALEIN

TRUK IS.

PALAU IS.

CAROLINE IS.

BISMARCK ARCH.

GILBERT IS.

EQUATOR

0°

NEW GUINEA

TARAWA

SOLOMON IS.

GUADALCANAL

CORAL SEA

AUSTRALIA

long last, as Allied armies struggled in the mountains of Italy, and the armed hordes of Soviet Russia moved inexorably westward, the growing fleets of the largest navy the world had ever seen gathered for the long road back.

Operation Galvanic was to be no hit-and-run raid, but a campaign to seize and conquer, for the first time in modern history, heavily fortified coral atolls, some of the outer defenses of the Japanese island citadels which controlled the Central Pacific. For the first time since the debacle of Pearl Harbor almost two years before, the United States was to utilize its stong right arm in the Pacific and to open a new approach to Japan.

Until the Gilbert Islands campaign (of which Tarawa was the principal battle), the American offensive in the Pacific had been limited to Guadalcanal and to General Douglas MacArthur's Southwest Pacific attack, based on Australia, and moving up the long ladder of the Bismarcks and New Guinea toward the Philippines. Each steppingstone along the large land masses near Australia was to be carefully calculated; MacArthur's drive never outpaced its land-based air power and, when possible, by-passed Japanese garrisons and left them in the ruck of war to "wither on the vine."

But MacArthur's route was the long way home, and supply routes to Australia and the Bismarck–New Guinea–Philippine offensive were constantly menaced by the flanking threat of Japanese sea-air power, based on the island bases of Micronesia. At the Casablanca Conference the opening of a Central Pacific offensive was provisionally agreed upon (though with qualifications), to protect the flank of MacArthur's advance and to open a more direct route to the Philippines, the China coast and Japan. And the "Quadrant" conferences at Quebec on August 24 proposed the Gilberts as the first step.

The Joint Staff planners of the Joint Chiefs of Staff reasoned that "strategically speaking the Central Pacific route is decisive . . . success here is most certain to sever the [Japanese] homeland from the overseas empire to the south." The decision to embark upon what derisive but uninformed critics were later to call "island hopping" was based upon the firm faith of the Navy in the aircraft carrier.

"The old maxim," the Joint Staff planners wrote before the event, "that carriers and carrier aircraft are at a disadvantage when exposed to shore-based air is subject to revision when large carrier forces become available. . . . There are strong reasons to believe that carrier aircraft, although untested, are equal to the task of supporting amphibious operations against island fortresses in the absence of land-based air-[craft] . . ."

"Galvanic" was directed against the Gilbert Islands, tiny coral outcroppings crowned by palm trees, and spread across languorous watery latitudes, astride the Equator, as large as Texas. The Gilberts represented the southeastern-most extension of the Micronesian spiderweb; they flanked our Pacific supply routes and were steppingstones to the important Marshall Islands to the north. The Japanese in the early months of 1943 had started to exploit the strategic possibilities of the Gilberts. An airfield was in use on Betio Island, Tarawa; a seaplane base was operational at Makin; and the phosphates of nearby Nauru and Ocean islands were being worked as Jap planes thundered from the coral strips.

"Galvanic's" specific objectives were Makin Island; Tarawa, dubbed in the war plans with the code name of "Helen"; and the lightly held islet of Apamama—"Land of Moonshine"—once described by Robert Louis Stevenson as a "treasure trove of South Sea Island beauty."

The newly formed Fifth Fleet, under Vice Admiral Raymond A. Spruance, was to conduct the largest amphibious operation yet mounted in the Pacific against objectives more than 700 miles from the nearest U.S. land air base. Two hundred ships, with 35,000 troops, 6,000 vehicles and 117,000 tons of cargo, converged on the smiling equatorial seas near the Gilberts from ports all over the Pacific. They were protected by the largest carrier task force yet assembled: 19 flattops, with 5 new battleships, 7 old ones and a whole covey of lesser men-of-war—"the most powerful naval force ever assembled under one flag" up to that time.

The entire Gilbert Islands operation was under over-all command of Admiral Chester W. Nimitz, Commander in Chief of the Pacific Fleet, with headquarters at Pearl Harbor. In command afloat was Admiral Spruance, flying his flag in the cruiser *Indianapolis*. Rear Admiral Richmond K. Turner in battleship *Pennsylvania* commanded the assault force for both the Tarawa and Makin attacks, and also wore another hat as commander of Task Force 52—the Northern Attack Force. With him in *Pennsylvania* was Major General Holland M. ("Howlin' Mad") Smith, USMC, Commander of the V Amphibious Corps. Under "Kelly" Turner and under Admiral Spruance was Rear Admiral Harry W. Hill, with flag in battleship *Maryland*. Hill commanded Task Force 53, the Southern Attack Force which was to seize Tarawa.

Admiral Hill and his Marine Commander, Major General Julian C. Smith, were subordinate to both "Kelly" Turner and Admiral Spruance, and Julian Smith was also under "Howlin' Mad" Smith. But Turner and Spruance chose what they thought was the post of greater danger—off Makin Island several hundred miles from Tarawa.[1] Makin was much closer to Japanese air bases than Tarawa, and it was thought the Northern Task Force would be far more exposed to Japanese retaliation than Hill's force. In practice, therefore, Hill was the senior commander in the Tarawa area, and the slowness and unreliability of radio communications were to mean that, in most cases, crises had been resolved at Tarawa or decisions taken before the higher command had time to intervene.

The 2nd Marine Division, victors of Guadalcanal, rested and re-

organized in New Zealand, had the primary task in the Gilberts operations: assault upon the stronghold of Betio, key to the atoll of Tarawa
and to the nexus of the Gilberts. They sang as they left port:

> Good-bye, Momma,
> We're off to Yokohama. . . .

Operation Galvanic was prefaced by wide-ranging carrier strikes and
land-based air raids upon Tarawa and supporting Jap bases scattered
across hundreds of leagues of watery distance. The Solomons campaign
and the open sore of Rabaul, constantly bombed and neutralized by
American planes, had sapped Japanese strength more than the Navy
knew. On D-day—November 20, 1943—the Japanese did not have a
single operational aircraft carrier in their Micronesian bases, and only 46
planes in the entire Gilbert-Marshalls archipelago.

But U.S. intelligence estimates anticipated strong Japanese reaction
and believed that heavy enemy air and submarine assaults could be made
on the Fifth Fleet within three days of the landing. Speed of conquest
was, therefore, considered to be of the essence; "it was agreed that the
Gilberts had to be taken in a hurry," lest enemy submarines and planes
ravage the vulnerable transports like wolves among the fold. There
would be no time for slow attrition or the prior seizure of other, less
strongly defended islands in the Tarawa atoll. Betio, the stronghold,
must be speedily overrun, its airstrips utilized by American planes, and
the thin-skinned transports and supply ships withdrawn from the zone of
danger.

The preliminary intelligence reports from air reconnaissance, the
wide-ranging preparatory air strikes and the heavy bombardment laid
down upon Betio prior to D-day—plus the sheer superlatives of the Fifth
Fleet, the largest yet mobilized in the Pacific—led to optimism. Rear
Admiral Howard F. Kingman, commanding the naval fire support group,
promised the 2nd Marine Division's officers in a preparatory briefing,
"We will not neutralize; we will not destroy; we will obliterate the
defenses on Betio!"

And another speaker: "We're going to steam-roller that place until
hell wouldn't have it."

But the wise were not deluded. One commander warned his Marines, "There's always some damn jackass that doesn't get the word and
will still be shooting."

Major General Julian C. Smith, commander of the 2nd Marine
Division, said in a prebattle briefing, "Gentlemen, remember one thing.
When the Marines land and meet the enemy at bayonet point, the only
armor a Marine will have is his khaki shirt!"

And Rear Admiral Keiji Shibasaki—soon to die—atoll commander of Tarawa, had boasted that the Americans could not take Tarawa with a million men in a hundred years.

Kichi Yoshuyo, a lieutenant in the Imperial Japanese Navy, was the first to move from the wings onto the stage of history in the early dark of November 19, 1943. The young lieutenant, his fist nervous with the impact of the message he sent, hunched in the seat of the patrol bomber (homeward-bound to Tarawa after a 600-mile predawn patrol) and broadcast ominous news:

"Enemy contact report . . . fleet sighted . . . several carriers and other types too numerous to mention."

Soon, to Jap-held Kwajalein, to Truk, heart of the spiderweb, to Tokyo, the news went forth: enemy fleet approaching the Gilberts! And on Tarawa, where the picked men of the Sasebo 7th Special Naval Landing Force, the 3rd Special Base Force and other units more than 4,800 strong[2] waited, the orders were to "defend to the last man . . . and destroy the enemy at the water's edge."

The tropic moon was on the wane, with a "faint golden ring surrounding it and one lone star," when the TBS (talk-between-ships radio) squawk box aboard battleship *Maryland,* flagship of Rear Admiral Harry W. Hill, commanding the Southern (Tarawa) attack force, came alive:

"CTF 53 [Commander Task Force 53] from *Ringgold* [destroyer]. We now have Tarawa atoll in sight."

Reveille that morning of destiny—the last bugle call that many who heard it were ever to hear—was in the middle of the night. Soon after, as the ships closed the dull, dark loom of the land, the clangor of General Quarters and the "thin pipings" of boatswains' whistles—"All boats away!"—echoed through the armada.

A score of transports, cargo vessels and amphibious craft were in position by 0355 (3:55 A.M.), and the Marines started clambering down the cargo nets, each "with three units of K rations, two canteens of water and shaving kit, toothbrush and spoon."

They appeared, to Marine Captain Earl J. Wilson, Public Relations Officer of the 2nd MarDiv (Marine Division) like men "dressed for a ballet," with "camouflaged helmet covers that looked like toadstools."

Lieutenant Paul Hospide of the machine-gun platoon, wore his life jacket tossed back over his combat pack, "like a hussar." He carried a cigar box, the contents of which he later distributed to his platoon—those who survived—on the beach.

One chaplain passed the word as the men manned the boats: "In a few minutes you will be over there. . . . This will be a great page in the history of the Marine Corps. . . . Wherever you men are, stop and give a prayer. . . . God bless you all."

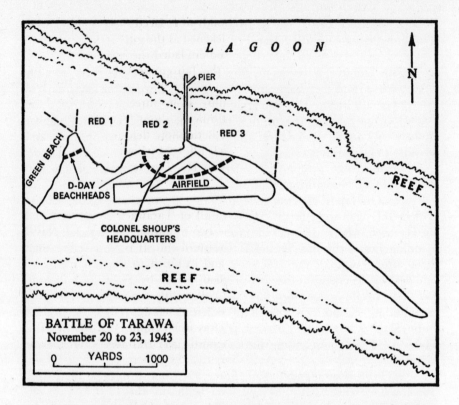

LAGOON

PIER

N

RED 1   RED 2   RED 3

GREEN BEACH

D-DAY
BEACHHEADS

×   AIRFIELD

REEF

COLONEL SHOUP'S
HEADQUARTERS

REEF

BATTLE OF TARAWA
November 20 to 23, 1943

0   YARDS   1000

It was not until almost 5 A.M. of D-day—Saturday, November 20—
that Betio showed a sign of life. A Jap signalman challenged with blinker
light, and then the enemy opened the ball. A red star cluster rose from
the south shore of Betio and two 8-inch guns opened on the *Maryland*.
Shell splashes commenced to erupt in the sea near battleships and
transports, and—suddenly, surprised—the Marines and sailors about the
decks started to "try to dig foxholes in the steel." The big ships and the
little, the medium and the small thundered back; soon bright flashes
illuminated the dark pall of the land, and smoke, with leaping flames at
the base, trailed across the calm sea. The sun rose like thunder in
ominous, flaming red, with "only one planet—and it was Mars—bright
and significant." The sky was a "painter's dream."

But the transports, straddled by Japanese shell splashes, were in the
wrong position; they were too close to the enemy batteries. The transport
group got under way and steamed a mile offshore. Some of the Marines
debarked in landing craft and amtracs trailed alongside their mother
ships. It was a bad beginning.[3]

The 16-inchers of *Maryland* silenced one Japanese battery; counterbattery fire continued, then lifted, in the day's early beginnings, for a
tardy seven-minute air strike from carriers *Essex, Bunker Hill, Independence.* Then, again, the ships' guns laid down upon the tortured land a

crazy quilt of shell bursts; the palm fronds were laced and shredded, fires burned upon Betio; the smoke pall thickened as the gunfire support ships moved to Betio's northwestern flank and enfiladed the beaches where the Marines were soon to land. And yet the Jap gunners spoke in flaming answer.

"Two and a half hours of gunfire from three battleships, four cruisers and a number of destroyers, throwing about 3,000 tons of naval projectiles, were expected to knock out Betio shore defenses and leave the defenders dazed and groggy," Samuel Eliot Morison observes in his history of naval operations in World War II. "This was a gross miscalculation."[4]

The island of Betio, part of the atoll of Tarawa, is nowhere more than ten feet above the sea. It is some two miles long, 500 to 600 yards wide, tapering to a point on the southeastern end. It is framed by white surf boiling over fringing coral reefs, and its northern shore fronts upon the placid green-blue waters of the lagoon formed by Tarawa atoll. Here in this constricted battlefield, scarcely half a square mile in area, where death lurked in each square foot of sand, 5,500 men were to die.

The "small boys" lead the parade—as usual; mine sweepers *Pursuit* and *Requisite,* with sweep wires and acoustic gear trailing, puff valiantly through the channel into the lagoon, their 3-inchers popping, smoke-screening them from Jap gunners.

In their wake, with a bone in their teeth and the white bow waves curling high, steam destroyers *Ringgold* and *Dashiell* in support, coral heads close to their keels, Jap guns aiming at point-blank range, against the "tinclads" side. At 0711 *Ringgold* is hit in the after engine room with a 5-incher, but the shell's a dud. It's *Ringgold's* lucky day; a moment later another dud strikes a forward torpedo mount and ricochets off to chew its way through the thin steel of sick bay and radio room. *Ringgold* fires back. . . .

Behind the van the assault waves move into the lagoon, the amphibious tractors crawling like water beetles across the brightening sea.[5]

The rasping static of radio chatter streams from the squawk boxes, ships calling boats, boats calling ships:

"Thirst calling Grocer; Thirst calling Grocer . . . Can you hear me, Grocer?"

Lieutenant William D. Hawkins, "The Hawk" of the Scout-Sniper Platoon (Posthumous Medal of Honor), who was to win from brave men the accolade of "*the* bravest man," leads his 34 men to a 750-yard wooden pier jutting into the lagoon astride the landing area on the northern shore of Betio. Flame throwers, demolition charges, rifle fire and grenades clean out Jap machine-gun nests, as the pier burns.

The amtracs of the assault wave, scrambling across the coral reef, churning through shoal water, chug to Beaches Red 1, 2 and 3, with the lagoon geysered by shell splashes, bullets pinging off the amtracs' steel flanks, the shoal water furrowed with Japanese fire. No "steam roller" this, no "obliteration"; the Jap garrison is full of fight. The first three waves of amtracs of 2nd Battalion, 8th Marines, led by a "prodigious red-head who had risen from the ranks," Major H. P. Crowe, swarm ashore to the east of the pier with moderate casualties, but on Red Beaches 1 and 2 to the west, where the shoreline curves into a dangerous re-entrant, the Marines are caught like sitting ducks in a searing cross fire. Amtracs take direct shell hits—"The concussion felt like a big fist—Joe Louis maybe—had smacked me right in the face." The assault waves are late; the ships' gunfire support has lifted too soon; now it is the United States Marine, armored only by his khaki shirt, against invisible men in log bunkers and concrete pillboxes.

It is about 0922 A.M. on that November day that is to make history. Back home the football crowds are gathering; chickens and turkeys dressed and ready for Thanksgiving crowd the markets, and on Broadway *Life with Father* is in its fifth year and *Oklahoma!* takes the mind off war.

Marines are dying on Red Beaches 1 and 2, caught in the cross fire, amtracs bellied down in shell holes or stalled on the beach barricade. Many men are killed as they try to tumble out of the clanking steel monsters. Lieutenant Colonel Herbert R. Amey, Jr., commanding 2nd Battalion, 2nd Regiment, dies as a leader should.

"Come on men," he says. "We're going to take the beach; those bastards can't stop us."

His words are true, but not for him; he falls, shot through the head, as he leaves his amtrac.

To the west of the pier on Red 1 and 2, the assault waves hold only a toehold; many Marines lie in the water; most crouch clustered beneath the two-to-four-foot shelter of the beach barricade; above the rim of the coconut logs a hail of fire scythes and mows.

Before 1000 A.M. the ominous messages come in to Admiral Hill and General Smith aboard flagship *Maryland:*

From Red Beach 3: "Heavy opposition."

From Red Beach 2: "Meeting heavy resistance."

From Red Beach 1: "Boats held up on reef, right flank, Red 1. Troops receiving heavy fire in water." And later: "We have nothing left to land."

Corporal Dan Swarts is in an amtrac straddling the coral reef near the pier when a Jap mortar shell ignites the gas tanks—kills or burns most of the crew. The driver is wounded; Swarts drags him across the shallow reef into hip-deep water near the smoldering pier where they shelter crouched beside the coconut logs of a machine-gun nest. Swarts touches a Marine standing still, spraddle-legged, facing the beach; the Marine falls silently into the water. Swarts notices a clean, neat bullet hole through his head. And the lapping waves are "foaming red over yellow coral."

Chance, arbiter of so many battles, deals the cards at Tarawa. The sandy shores of Betio are armored with a fringing coral reef, which extends to seaward and into the lagoon from 300 to more than 700 yards from shore. The tides of Betio are unpredictable; in fact, no accurate tables exist, and Fifth Fleet's calculations are based on gleanings from the experience of New Zealand and British officers who had known Tarawa in better and more peaceful days. All except one of them predict five feet of water over the reef on the morning of November 20, enough to permit the boats which are to follow the amphibious tractors to reach the beach. One officer disagrees; he forecasts "dodging" or irregular and unpredictable tides for November 20, with possibly three feet of water or less over the reef—too little to float the boats. And some of the boats must get in, for "an amphibious assault must pack a sustained wallop"; the assault waves must be quickly supported by follow-up troops. The Marines have anticipated trouble at the reef; they plan to shuttle from boats to amtracs to shore.

Second MarDiv had combed the Pacific for amphibious tractors—those alligator-like machines of World War II (adapted from commercial vehicles used in the Everglades)—and there were just enough for the assault units. The Marines use about 100 amtracs for the first waves; 25 are kept in division reserve; there are no more. The follow-up waves essential to victory must come ashore in landing craft—LCVP's (Landing Craft, Vehicle, Personnel)—and boats and by shuttling from the reef in amtracs. But chance deals out death; the "dodging tide" stays low; the reef is barely covered. The boats are stranded or balked; and many of the amtracs are knocked out. The following waves must wade instead of shuttling; the attack loses momentum.

Fourth wave, boated in LCVP's with 37 mm. guns, embarked, are stuck on the edge of the reef; they retract and wait for higher tides. Fifth wave is tanks, badly needed ashore; they splash from LCM's (Landing Craft, Medium) into three feet of water and wade beachward. Some bog down in shell holes or drop deep into coral pockets; some are hit; few long survive. The battalion commander, Lieutenant Colonel Alexander B. Swenceski, is badly hit in shoal water; he pulls himself bleeding onto a heap of the slain "to avoid drowning" and is found there, unconscious and all but dead, hours later.

Before 1100 A.M. Colonel David M. Shoup ("Dave" Shoup, Medal of Honor, described by his first sergeant in rare encomium as "the bravest, nerviest, best soldiering Marine I have ever met") reaches the fire-swept pier. Shoup, commanding the 2nd Marines and the assault force, wades through waist-deep water to the beach with a sergeant with a radio strapped to his back as his "communications." By this hour two landing craft and perhaps a score of amtracs are stranded on the reef or wrecked in the shoals between deep water and white sand. They are full of dead and wounded, and bodies bob gently in the seaway. As the LCVP's ground on the reef and lower their ramps, a Jap gun, still firing accurately, drops shells squarely in the midst of the floundering Marines; pools of blood brighten the waters.

Shoup calls for "all possible fire support." The great guns boom, Betio is wreathed in smoke and flame, but still the enemy's hail of fire decimates the few reinforcements.

Long before noon Shoup's regimental reserve has been ordered into Red Beach 2, and General Smith, aboard *Maryland*, releases half of his divisional reserve to Shoup, who directs it to Red Beach 3. (The other half, bobbing in its boats, is soon ordered in but doesn't get the word for many hours.) The "dodging tide" still helps the defense; the landing craft strand on the reef, and the reserves wade 700 yards through waist-deep waters to a thin and bloody strip of sand. Many of them die in the water; some step into holes and, festooned with heavy equipment, drown; others are hit but drag themselves to shoal water. The reserves reach the beach—if at all—drenched, disorganized, sometimes weaponless, exhausted and cut to pieces.

Overhead, a Kingfisher float plane from the *Maryland*—Lieutenant Commander Robert A. McPherson, pilot—soars and circles above the smoke and carnage, reporting the details of inferno to Admiral Hill and General Smith.

"The water never seemed clear," McPherson says, "of tiny men, their rifles held over their heads, slowly wading beachwards. I wanted to cry."

At noon, as the tropic sun beats down in merciless intensity on the slaying and the slain, the word is chaos. Here is no well-ordered panoply of battle; nothing is going according to plan. Landing craft and boats, filled since predawn darkness with Marines and supplies, are circling madly off the transports, milling about in the lagoon, lying to at sea, frustrated by the low tide. Flagship *Maryland*'s communications, racked by the blast of her big guns, are often broken; Hill and Smith get much of their information from the Kingfisher observation planes circling over Betio.

The beachhead—if it can be called that—is held by an eyelash; some 1,500 living Marines, many wounded, are pinned down under the coconut-log and coral-block beach barricade. Officers are dead, organizations destroyed or inextricably mixed; what remains of the dead Amey's command—2nd Battalion, 2nd Regiment—is commanded by an "absolute stranger," an observer from another Marine division—Colonel Walter I. Jordan, who has helped to lead one company 100 yards inland, only to report to Shoup: "We need help. Situation bad."

Five battalions, all but one decimated by heavy casualties, have been committed by early afternoon of the twentieth. Two M-4 medium tanks have finally waddled ashore; four others have been drowned out in potholes. The tanks help the Marines push to within 30 yards of the south shore of the island from Red Beach 1, but their combat life is short; one tank is quickly disabled, the other damaged.

At 1330 of D-day, about four hours after the initial landing, General Julian C. Smith aboard *Maryland* radios General Holland M. ("Howlin' Mad") Smith, the V Amphibious Corps commander, aboard battleship *Pennsylvania,* off Makin Island far to the north, requesting release of the corps reserve. The message concludes: "Issue in doubt."

Through the afternoon of D-day, the slugging match goes on—man against man, Marine against pillbox and dugout. Satchel charges, hand grenades, flame throwers, dynamite, covered by rifle fire, machine guns and the 5-inchers of destroyers *Ringgold* and *Dashiell,* dashing about in the lagoon, make for inching progress, measured in blood. Betio is a network of more than 200 strong points defended by about 200 guns: near the beach edge a coconut-log barricade, housing machine-gun emplacements; then field guns sited in sand-covered log pillboxes, with armored or concrete tops; dug-in tanks and six-foot-thick compartmented bombproof shelters and pillboxes, constructed of coconut logs, sand, corrugated iron and concrete, with an interconnecting system of trenches. The Japs have burrowed like rats; each strong point presents a separate problem in assault; snipers are everywhere, lashed to the riddled palms, behind a hummock of sand, under the pier.

Throughout the long hot daylight hours, Marines straggle ashore in groups and by twos and threes, wading through the reddened water, units cut up, officers missing. All over the littered beach sprawl the quick and the dead; the plasma bottles hang from rifles jabbed into the sand; the Navy medics ferry the wounded to the reef in rubber rafts. . . .

At sunset a line of straggling foxholes astride the pier extends some 700 yards along Red Beaches 2 and 3. A few bold spirits have pushed inland 100 to 300 yards. Well to the west at the end of Red Beach 1, and on the western extremity of Betio, called Green Beach, another isolated beachhead buttons up for the night. After dark 75 mm. pack howitzers are carried in pieces on the backs of the cannoneers; reinforcements use the log pier to reach the island.

By midnight there are some 5,000 Marines ashore—1,500 of them dead or wounded. At sundown on D-day the "situation of the Marines . . . was precarious."[6]

D-plus 1—November 21—starts in horror as the last of the division reserve, which had spent 20 hours in the boats and only now gets the word to land, is raked and slaughtered as it fights its way to shore. During the night the Japs have infiltrated back to the cribwork of the pier, to wrecked amtracs and boats, to an old hulk, sunk nearby, which had been cleared of the enemy the day before. Planes and mortars attack the hulk; a mortar destroys a privy used as a machine-gun nest; but in five hours the last of the division reserve loses about as many men as the D-day assault battalions.

Colonel Shoup's command post, now in the lee of a Japanese bunker, is a hole in the sand; there are still a score of live Japs in the bunker, and Marine riflemen are posted at the vents and entrances to keep them down.

Captain John B. McGovern, naval boat control officer, sets up a command post aboard *Pursuit,* rounds up some 18 amtracs, bellows through a bull horn and brings some order out of the milling boats, most of them loaded to the gunwales with men and equipment they can't get ashore.

And still the island of Betio, a bit of bloody sand in a vast immensity of sea, is clothed in smoke "with great licking flames about the base of the clouds."

The Marines are swimming in sweat; there is a "kind of skin-cracking heat that was as sharp as a physical blow on the head . . . lips break and crust and break again . . . noses blister and peal and blacken."

Aboard the transports and the support ships sailors and Marines waiting to debark suddenly and sharply comprehend the price of war. The wounded come back, with the gray mask of shock, the bright blood staining, the labored breath, the rasp of pain.

"The ship's doctor, dressed in a pair of sneakers, and a bloodstained pair of pants," tends them with gentle hands.

And the chaplains bury the dead:

"Oh, death, where is thy sting? Oh, grave, where is thy victory?"

Around the flag-draped, canvas-shrouded bodies the fighting men stand, "bare to the waist, unshaven in their crumpled dirty jungle suits, with matted, uncombed hair and solemn faces. . . .

"The concussions were shaking our ships; corpses were floating by," and the sea is littered with debris—"books, V-mail forms, chunks of coconut palms, artillery boxes, papers."

As the bodies slide over the side, the "sound of canvas rasping on wood sent a shiver over me that I will never forget," Captain Earl J. Wilson recalls.

And still men die in murderous battle on that half square mile of sand called Betio. . . .

For the first day and a half the Battle of Tarawa is fought by makeshift, patchwork teams; during this period no Marine unit "reached the beaches intact."

In the heat of the long morning the battle is still fluid, the situation still in doubt; Colonel Shoup, a "squat, red-faced man with a bull neck"[7] who "carries the biggest burden on Tarawa," radios repeatedly in the morning of D-plus 1:

"Imperative you land ammunition, water, rations and medical supplies . . . on Beach Red Two. . . ."

"Imperative you get all types ammunition to all landing parties immediately. . . ."

"Situation doesn't look good ashore. . . ."

But Shoup, "the tough Marine officer in the best tradition," and his kind of man—the kind that always storms in the van of battle and wins all wars when the chips are down—tip the scales at Tarawa.

Lieutenant Hawkins, shot twice through the shoulder and chest, bloodstained, bearded but fighting, rides an amtrac like a wild Valkyrie in the van of the fight. Then, with his men, he crawls forward, storming pillbox after pillbox to die with many of those he led.

"It's not often you can credit a first lieutenant with winning a battle," Shoup later says, "but Hawkins came as near to it as any man could. He was truly an inspiration."[8]

There is redheaded Crowe on Red Beach 3, and a quiet, scholarly-looking, little man, blond and wearing glasses, an ex-professor of economics, Major William C. Chamberlin, an unlikely-looking fighting man but a true Marine.

He grabs a boy who, terror-stricken, has dropped his gun and started to run and says, "What kind of a Marine are you? Get back in there."

And leads the way himself, his jacket bloodstained. . . .

There are others, the natural sons of battle, who rise to their highest moments; and there are many, "even well-trained men with battle experience on Guadalcanal," who are appalled by the hail of fire, the mounting bodies of the slain and the terror of the Japanese interlocking defenses. They cower behind the beach barricades and dig foxholes with their fingernails; officers and noncoms find it hard to move them forward.

Robert Sherrod, war correspondent, recalls a young major complaining to Shoup: "Colonel, there are a thousand goddamn Marines out there on that beach, and not one will follow me across to the airstrip!"

Shoup says, wearily, "You've got to say, 'Who'll follow me?' And if only ten follow you, that's the best you can do, but it's better than nothing."

It is often darkest before the dawn. . . .

Between noon and dusk that day the tide of battle turns.

Marines, pinned down astride the long pier, fight their way across the airfield to Betio's south shore. Elements of the V Amphibious Corps reserve, the 6th Marine Regiment, land on Beach Green on the western end of the island after three 80 mm. coast-defense guns have been knocked out. Divisional artillery is established on nearby Bairiki, the islet next to Betio, and their guns add to the cacophony of called fire from destroyers and strikes from the air.

And the fickle goddess turns her smile upon the Marines; a normal neap tide, more than 36 hours late, puts deeper water over the reef; some boats can make the shore; other Marines land in rubber rafts.

By 1600 on D-plus 1 Colonel Shoup, weary, bearded but indomitable, feels the pulse of change, says to Sherrod, "Well, I think we are winning, but the bastards have got a lot of bullets left."

His 1600 situation report to division headquarters ends:

". . . Casualties many; percentage dead not known; combat efficiency: we are winning. Shoup."

He is right; the island is cut in two; the beachheads are expanded; reinforcements are moving in in ordered boat waves; casualties are evacuated.

By early morning of D-plus 2, November 22, the enemy knows it is the end; the Japanese radio on Tarawa broadcasts its final message:

"Our weapons have been destroyed and from now on everyone is attempting a final charge. . . . May Japan exist for ten thousand years."

But the Japs die hard and take many Marines with them. During all of D-plus 2, under the terrific blazing heat of the tropic sun, there is still the slow advance and inexorable death. More tanks are ashore; pillbox after pillbox, position after position is assaulted under covering fire from tanks and riflemen and artillery; TNT blocks are hurled into apertures, grenades follow and flame throwers sear the screaming enemy. The Marines reach at dusk the eastern end of the airstrip.

The island is a scene of infinite and indescribable carnage, yet incongruously "red little Jap chickens, a pig, a dog and a gray kitten" run across the sand. A Marine stops beside a burned-out Jap tank and gives the kitten some precious water from his canteen.

And "Sergeant Siwash," the duck mascot of a pack howitzer unit, won at a raffle in New Zealand, waddles, quacking in alarm, past the riflemen and the flame throwers.

At dark November 22, General Julian Smith is "far from hopeful of a rapid cleanup." Some Jap strong points are still intact despite incessant naval gunfire and bombing; officer casualties are heavy and mounting.

But that night the animal cries of men who are about to die echo over Betio. That night—two nights too late—the Japs counterattack, with "terrible screaming," in straggling determined groups, with grenades and swords and bayonets, leaping upon the Marines in their foxholes, shouting, "Banzai!"

"Marine, you die."

"Japanese drink Marines' blood."

Company B, 1st Battalion, 6th Marines, takes the brunt of the attacks, stiffened by a mortar platoon and part of another rifle company. Artillery fire, mortars, destroyers' 5-inchers, machine-gun and rifle fire slaughter the enemy as they advance, but some reach the Marine line to stab and be stabbed in the dark. . . . Rifle butts and bayonets, knives and the kick to the groin, the thud of bodies, the yelling curse and the dying scream . . . More than 300 Japs are slain in their fanatical delirium. Their contorted bodies in the morning light, as a "rooster crows somewhere amidst the ruins," form a horrid carpet leading from the eastern tail of Betio to the Marine line.

At 1312 on D-plus 3, November 23, Betio is declared "secured." The 3rd Battalion, 6th Regiment, sweeps down the tail of Betio; and the last big bombproof, that no shell has been able to pierce, back of Red Beach 1 is assaulted. At noon a carrier plane lands on the airstrip, already repaired by Seabees under fire.

There is still more killing, and a few nests to wipe out. A Marine patrol almost shoots by mistake a Seabee rummaging in a dugout. He emerges, his hands high to pointed rifles, a Jap captain's cap on his head and his tongue thick: "Shay, I found some *sake* in there."

For days to come the rifles will still fire and the demolition charges echo over the island as snipers are flushed out and the remnants of a once mighty garrison are harried and hunted down in the shambles of Betio and on nearby islets of the atoll.

But on D-plus 3, after 75 hours and 42 minutes of "the bitterest fighting in the history of the Marine Corps," Betio and Tarawa are "secured."

"Secured" at the cost of brave men dead: 1,115 Marines, 25 Navy men, killed in action missing or dead of wounds; 2,309 wounded. Of the 125 amtracs ferried to Tarawa—those amphibious machines which had climbed the reef and tipped the scales of battle—90 were sunk or wrecked, and 323 of the 500 men who manned them were killed, wounded or missing.

"Secured" at the cost of an islet, "littered, devastated, desolated and ripped to shreds," the "overpowering stench" of torn and shattered death a reeling assault upon the senses of those still alive. Betio's sands and waters were strewn with "masses of twisted, bloated and burned Japanese corpses" in the ruins of their blockhouses, under the coconut logs that failed to save them—almost 4,700 enemy dead; only 1 officer, 16 enlisted men and 129 Korean laborers, prisoners.

So the fighting waned, leaving a landscape "like a living drawing from Dante's Inferno"—fires still raging, ammunition exploding, the debris of battle strewn across the sands, "grenades, bullets, bandoliers, weapons, papers, shells, shoes, kimonos, books" and everywhere "bodies." . . .

They lined up on "the dusty ruined beach they had fought so hard to win," the survivors of Tarawa, "wild men," with matted beards and the numbed, gray pallor of shock and fatigue, their uniforms torn, reeking with sweat and blood.

And there, as they waited to embark, beside them on the beaches and on the sands still lay the bodies of their "buddies" facing the foe. One dead Marine lay against the beach barricade, one limp clenched hand stretched up above the coconut logs full in the field of fire. At his fingertips, where it had fallen as he was hit, lay the beach marker flag which it had been his job to emplace. And in the waters of the lagoon, gently drifting now to seaward with the tide, still afloat, face down, the dead who tried to land across the fatal reef. . . .

"I always expected them to lift their heads for air, but they never did," one eyewitness said.

Tarawa came as a considerable shock to the American people, partly because of the vividness of the reporting, partly because of incomplete and unbalanced initial accounts, partly because the nation had not fully learned that there is no easy road in war and that the price of victory is always blood. There followed recriminations and regrets, praise and blame, tears from the bereaved and long suffering for the wounded.

Gradually, with time and background the battle came into clearer perspective; the Marine casualties for some units were probably as high as any in the Pacific War, but the total dead of the 2nd Marine Division at Tarawa scarcely exceeded the Navy men who were lost when the light carrier *Liscome Bay* was torpedoed and sunk by a Japanese submarine off Makin Island to the north.

For the preinvasion forebodings about Japanese submarine and air attacks were not entirely mistaken. The sinking of the escort carrier *Liscome Bay* by the Japanese submarine I-175 cost the Navy 53 officers and 591 men lost, scores of others terribly wounded. The 165th Regimental Combat Team and other units of the Army's 27th Division, which seized Makin, against light enemy resistance—290 Japanese combat personnel, 271 laborers—had easy going (only 64 American soldiers were killed and 150 wounded), but the blowing up of the *Liscome Bay* and some small losses in air battles cost the Navy far more heavily. Samuel Eliot Morison correctly observes that "the United States paid relatively dearer for Makin considering the size of the opposing forces involved than for Tarawa."[9]

However, the losses might have been far greater if the Japanese High Command had anticipated U.S. intentions accurately. But Admiral Mineichi Koga, Commander in Chief of the Japanese Combined Fleet, missed by about three weeks. From radio intelligence and other sources he thought, in September and again in October, that the Americans were going to invade the Marshall Islands, and he disposed his planes and ships accordingly. But when nothing had happened in late October, Koga sailed back to the Japanese base at Truk, canceled the alert in the Marshalls and, to comply with orders from Tokyo, sent 173 aircraft from three carriers to stiffen the defenses of Rabaul.[10] When the invasion was actually mounted, Koga and his ships and planes were hopelessly out of position—an achievement that may have been due in part to inadequate interpretation by the Japanese of the intelligence available and in part to U.S. communications deception techniques.

But though the enemy dispositions eased the task of the invading fleet, fanatic Japanese resistance, the small size of the island and U.S. inexperience and mistakes were responsible for the heavy Marine casualties.

The invasion of Tarawa had had to be hastily prepared; there were many loose ends, but, as Admiral Spruance later noted, "War is a tough business and often we gain more than we lose by pushing forward against the enemy before we are entirely ready.

"This," he said, "was certainly true against the Japanese in the Central Pacific."

General Holland M. Smith disagreed; he wrote in 1949, in his book *Coral and Brass*, that "Tarawa was a mistake," that Betio was too small an island to be frontally assaulted, that far more gunfire support and bombing were needed, that "better cooperation between all units" was essential. But "Howlin' Mad," always a dour maverick, was one of the few professionals who took such an iconoclastic point of view, and even he admitted that "the Marine doctrine of amphibious assault stood the test."[11]

Years later historians of the Marine Corps Historical Section were to write:

"There had to be a Tarawa. This was the inevitable point at which untried doctrine was at length tried in the crucible of battle."

The heavy Marine casualties were "a high price to pay for a few hundred acres of coral," military historians were to write later. "Yet in the minds of most American military planners and strategists the cost of the capture of the Gilberts was justified both in the terms of the strategic gains realized and the tactical lessons learned."[12]

Tarawa taught many lessons, above all the need for more amtracs, which the factories of America subsequently produced in tremendous quantities. Tarawa also led to the improved gathering of intelligence. A makeshift UDT (Underwater Demolition Team) was assigned to the "Galvanic" operations but played no preinvasion operational role. From Tarawa the "frogmen" were really born, and underwater demolition teams, trained to remove beach obstacles and to reconnoiter beaches and landing areas, later became a familiar part of the amphibious technique.

Supply procedures were improved.

Radio sets, many of which were inoperable at Tarawa because of immersion in salt water, were waterproofed.

Ship-to-ship and ship-to-boat communications were improved. Amphibious command ships with adequate communications specifically designed for the mission replaced battleships in the specialized job of directing a sea-to-shore assault. The Navy's boat procedures and logistic support were strengthened. Fire support ships restudied their plans to determine why the Betio defenses had not been "obliterated," and in subsequent operations the Navy's prelanding bombardment and gunfire support were far more effective. Tarawa, in short, "revolutionized the concept of naval gunfire." Armor-piercing shells and other means of destroying highly fortified positions were utilized to a greater extent in later operations. Greater volume, more accuracy and close-in fire support were stressed.

Night air defense from carriers, first tested in the Gilberts operations, became a part of fleet doctrine and was specialized and improved. The protection of a large surface fleet and many thin-skinned transports, against enemy air and submarine attack, by carrier aircraft and screening destroyers proved not only feasible but extremely efficient—despite the loss of *Liscome Bay* and a torpedo hit in carrier *Independence.* And timing, the essence of amphibious operations, became in the Marianas and at Okinawa a split-second miracle of coordination.[13]

So Hawkins and his fellows did not die in vain.

American planes were soon thundering off Hawkins Field at Tarawa; Makin and Apamama (which had been easily seized against light enemy resistance) were also converted into U.S. bases, and the Marshall Islands were next.

"Tactically Betio became the textbook for future amphibious landings and assaults," Jeter A. Isely and Philip A. Crowl noted after the war:

Thirty-three hundred casualties (including those incurred in the seizure of Makin and Apamama) are low when compared with the total for any other Central Pacific offensive, with the exception of the seizure of Kwajalein and Eniwetok in the Marshall Islands. Assaults against the Marianas, the Palaus, and Iwo Jima were not only more expensive in terms of lives lost—it may confidently be said that these later victories were possible at all only because of the lessons learned at Tarawa.[14]

But the greatest lesson learned was the oldest lesson of war. Tarawa was won by stout hearts beneath the khaki shirts, by men willing to die. For the red badge of courage, war and life itself know no substitute.

To the 2nd Marine Division, "dauntlessly advancing in spite of rapidly mounting losses," locked in "the toughest fight in Marine Corps history," to Dave Shoup and Hawkins and redheaded Crowe, and to their comrades beneath the crosses in the sand, the Commander in Chief, Fifth Fleet, paid the ultimate homage:

The part that will be longest remembered in American history was the magnificent courage and tenacity of the [Marines] in carrying on their assault . . . after suffering staggering losses. Nothing in the record of the Marine Corps can exceed the heroism displayed at Tarawa by the officers and men of the Second Marine Division and by the naval units that accompanied them in their landing.[15]

CHAPTER 8

NORMANDY—

THE BEGINNING OF THE END

June 6, 1944

The yellow gorse was blooming in the hedgerows and the green hills of England were never lovelier than on that spring evening of crisis, fulfillment and culmination in June of 1944.

At Waterloo station a RAF corporal stood silently, his arm around a girl, her head upon his chest, their faces inexpressibly sad.

In all the southern towns of England the pubs were strangely quiet, the streets were empty; the troops were on the move. In England and the Western world time seemed to have stopped; there was a bated stillness, a waiting tension. For many millions on the eve of battle the nations prayed.

For this was the Day and this the Hour; the ancient ports were crammed, the Channel lop was furrowed white with history's greatest armada, its course set for the Far Shore, for the bloody beaches of

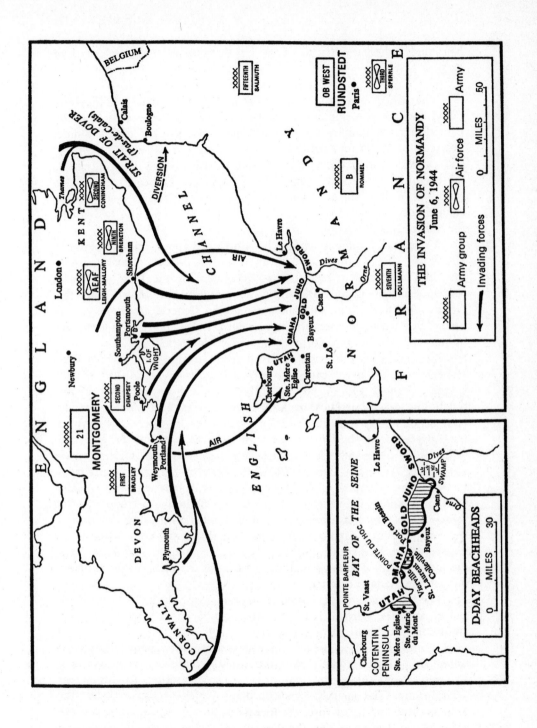

THE INVASION OF NORMANDY
June 6, 1944

Army group — Air force — Army

Invading forces

D-DAY BEACHHEADS

Normandy, where the destiny of empires hung upon an Homeric clash of arms.

The Allied invasion of France on June 6, 1944, was both the emotional and the strategic climax of World War II. For Britain and the United States it came as the end and the beginning—the end of almost five years of defeat and struggle, of frustration and hardship, of peripheral victories costly won, of strategic debate, discussion and compromise; the beginning of decision, the dawn of hope. For France it promised a return of freedom; to most Germans it was do-or-die, hurl back the foe from France or take the low road to *Götterdammerung*, the twilight of the Nazi gods and inevitable catastrophe.

The cross-Channel attack had been dreamed about, studied, planned almost since the beginning of the war. It was the product of many minds, the child of none. It represented the climax of the basic American strategic concept: Europe first and a direct and massive blow toward the German heartland. The supreme commander, General Eisenhower, had been appointed just six months before. For this day and for this hour, the toiling staffs had labored, the sweating soldiers trained.

The concept of the invasion was immense, imaginative, massive. The invaders were to move from many of the ports of Britain across the choppy Channel with 5,300 ships and craft—the largest fleet of any time![1] The greatest aerial armadas in history, some 12,000 planes, were to land major elements of three airborne divisions in Normandy, protect the surface forces, batter the German defenses, cut the bridges and railroads to Normandy, isolate the beach defenses. Six infantry divisions—three American, two British, one Canadian—were to assault from the sea a 60-mile stretch of the German West Wall between Caen and the Cherbourg peninsula. One hundred and seven thousand troops, 14,000 vehicles, 14,500 tons of supplies were to be landed on the open beaches in the first 48 hours. Artificial ports, sunken ships and bombardons and improvised docks, flexible undersea pipelines, amphibious tanks and the thundering guns of scores of mighty men-of-war were part of the supporting paraphernalia of conflict.

The Germans knew crisis was imminent; on June 3 German intelligence estimates warned that "invasion could be considered possible within the next fortnight."

Admiral Wilhelm Canaris, chief of German intelligence, had penetrated the Allied-French underground net. He had warned German communications intelligence monitors to listen carefully for broadcasts from Britain. The operative code message, which would first alert the underground and then with the broadcast of the second line prepare them for a landing within 48 hours, was taken from the *"Chanson d'Automne"* ("Song of Autumn") by Paul Verlaine:

Les sanglots longs des violons de l'automne
Blessent mon coeur d'une langueur monotone. . . .
(The long sobs of the violins of autumn
Wound my heart with a monotonous languor. . . .)[2]

A German monitoring service at Fifteenth Army headquarters near the Belgian border intercepted the first line on June 1, and interpreted it correctly. The second line was intercepted and correctly interpreted about 9:15 P.M. June 5. The Fifteenth Army along the Pas-de-Calais was alerted, but not the Seventh in Normandy.

Yet for many months, spurred by the energy of Erwin Rommel, who had gained lasting fame as the commander of the Afrika Korps, soldiers and laborers had strengthened the Atlantic Wall, pouring concrete, installing guns, mining beach exits, setting up in open fields *Rommelspargel* ("Rommel's asparagus"—tall mined poles to prevent glider or parachute landings), peppering the shelving beaches with underwater obstacles of all kinds—Teller mines, hedgehogs and tetrahedra, "Belgian gates," or "Element C" and stakes.

But there was dichotomy in the German command. Field Marshal Karl Gerd von Rundstedt, supreme German commander in France and the Low Countries, retained his mobile reserves grouped far to the rear of the coast in the belief that he could mass them rapidly after the main Allied landing had been developed. Under Rundstedt were two army groups. Army Group B, with Rommel in command, consisted of the LXXXVIII Corps in Holland; the strong Fifteenth Army, massed along the Strait of Dover from Antwerp to the Orne; and the Seventh Army scattered from the Orne to the Loire and defending the Normandy, Cotentin and Brittany beaches. Rommel, with his long experience of Allied air superiority in North Africa, knew that the Germans must win on the beaches or not at all; under the shadow of Allied planes, mobile reserves from the rear would reach the battle too little or too late.

By June 6 there were 547 naval coastal guns along the French and Belgian coasts—47 of them in Normandy—about half under concrete, additional hundreds of lighter Army guns and five to six million mines laid in or near the beaches. But Rommel had planned a deep barrier of 50 million mines and the girdle of steel was thin; Rommel had had no chance to deepen it.

The German Navy, save for submarines and a few E-boats, was spent; the German Air Force was weak and attenuated; the Germany Army faced Allied sea, air and land power alone.

But it was not the German Army of the years of blitzkrieg and triumph. In 1943 alone, the Germans had suffered about 2,086,000 casualties in the vast and bloody battles on the Eastern Front and additional scores of thousands in North Africa and Italy. Like the South in 1865, replacements for the youthful dead were almost exhausted; the Reichswehr, which had conquered a continent, had become in some of its units a polyglot army, with Croatians, Hungarians, Poles, Russians, French, Negroes, Arabs, Turkomans, Kazaks and even Indians in its ranks. Many of the static coastal divisions manning the Atlantic Wall were composed of the old and the very young, and of foreign "volunteers"—Russian "Ost Battalions" of doubtful reliability. But they were backed up by numerous first-class units, with a hard core of veterans from the Russian front.

Manning the beach defenses and garrisoned a few miles inland were eight German divisions along the 60-mile stretch of coast from east of Caen to Cherbourg; there were more than 60 in France and the Low Countries. But, unknown to Allied intelligence, strong elements of one division, the 352nd, had moved into the defense belt along a beach that will be forever known as "Omaha."

"Operation Overlord" is ready—the troops embarked, the convoys moving, from Portland, Weymouth, Poole and Plymouth, debouching from the Irish Sea and the Strait of Dover, sortieing from the little ports of Cornwall and of Devon. . . .

The weather is marginal; already D-day has been postponed one day, but now at last the great decision has been made and the Supreme Commander, Allied Expeditionary Force, is carrying out his directive: to "enter the continent of Europe and in conjunction with the other United Nations, undertake operations aimed at the heart of Germany."

In the pocket of Eisenhower's battle jacket, that June evening is a handwritten communiqué, undated, never to be used, a concession to the gods of war and to blind chance that sets the fate of men.

"Ike" himself has penned it sometime on June 5, after he had set the whole vast machinery in motion with the simple words "Okay. We'll go."

The communiqué reads:

OUR LANDINGS IN THE CHERBOURG-HAVRE AREA HAVE FAILED TO GAIN A SATISFACTORY FOOTHOLD AND I HAVE WITHDRAWN THE TROOPS. MY DECISION TO ATTACK AT THIS TIME AND PLACE WAS BASED UPON THE BEST INFORMATION AVAILABLE. THE TROOPS, THE AIR, AND THE NAVY, DID ALL THAT BRAVERY AND DEVOTION TO DUTY COULD DO. IF ANY BLAME OR FAULT ATTACHES TO THE ATTEMPT IT IS MINE ALONE.[3]

The same sense of impending fate, or courage screwed to the sticking point, but tinctured, too, with dread, permeates soldiers and civilians. The immensity of the task has staggered many minds; *"Festung Europa"* has been built up by Allied warnings and Goebbels' propaganda alike; predictions of heavy casualties have been discussed widely.

In Germany and in France the refrain of a new song, *"Die Wacht auf Kanal"* ("The Watch on the Channel") echoes in the barracks and restaurants:

> *We stand in the West; we are fully prepared;*
> *Let the enemy come today.*
> *We are on guard, our fists are hard,*
> *We shall stand in the West at bay. . . .*

The Fifth Army captures Rome, the Eternal City, this fourth of June; glad headlines speak the news, but men's hearts are tuned to Normandy and the Channel tide where slowly the great armada wallows, rolls and pitches toward the coast of France. . . .

JUNE 5

6:30 p.m.

First touchdown on the sandy beaches is just 12 hours away; the paratroopers are to start to drop soon after midnight.

This is the calm before the storm, but it is first blood for the enemy. USS *Osprey* of Mine Squadron 10, sweeping in mid-Channel, strikes a mine; the sea rushes into her forward engine room; she flames and sinks with six American sailors, the first of many dead.

But behind the little sweepers and converging now at "Piccadilly Circus," a great area of wind-swept sea southeast of the Isle of Wight, steam inexorably the big ships and the small to alter course southward into five swept lanes across the Channel. For mile on endless mile fading into the westering light, the seascape is crowded; watchers on the headlands of the south coast see in the dying day armed trawlers and battleships, tugs and landing craft, cruisers and destroyers, many of them towing barrage balloons. The wind drops, the waters calm, but the small ships still roll and flounder. . . .

In shoal water in the Bay of the Seine, off the landing beaches two X-craft—British midget submarines—are lying on the bottom, awaiting the full dark, their mission to surface and mark, with shadowed lights to seaward, the limits of the British assault area.

Far to the north off Calais and in the strait feints are made at

Boulogne; dummy landing craft clog the Thames, and at Dover Lieutenant General George ("Blood and Guts") Patton occupies a phantom headquarters, with smoke still rising from cooking fires and trucks moving in deserted camps.

Back in England, an ascetic general, who has quoted to his troops:

> *He either fears his fate too much,*
> *Or his deserts are small*
> *Who dare not put it to the touch*
> *To win or lose it all,*

goes "up to Hindhead that evening" to make "final arrangements" about his motherless son, David, and to put his "plain clothes" away "in a wardrobe." His name is Bernard L. Montgomery, commander of all the ground forces in the invasion.

"While the Allied invasion force stream[s] across the Channel, the Germans in France, so long schooled for this moment, [have] no direct knowledge that it [is] at hand. The enemy [is] all but blind. There had been no air reconnaissance during the first five days of June. Naval patrols scheduled for the night of 5–6 June, along with the minelaying operations for that date, [are] cancelled because of bad weather."

Field Marshal Rommel, en route to see Hitler, stays this night at Herringen (Germany), with his family.[4]

In England the airborne troops prepare. Each American paratrooper has about ten dollars' worth of newly minted French money in his pocket; a small U.S. flag is sewn to his right sleeve; he has a brass compass and "dime store" metal crickets for identification purposes: one squeeze (click-clack) to be answered by two (click-clack, click-clack). Strips of brown and green burlap are woven into helmet nettings for camouflage; some men shave their heads and leave only a Mohawk scalp lock; others daub their faces with "fierce Indian camouflage"; still others smear coal black beneath their eyes. General Maxwell D. Taylor, commanding the "Screaming Eagles"—the 101st Airborne—asks his men to shout "Bill Lee" as they jump into the French dark, in tribute to the "father of American paratroopers," Major General William C. Lee of Dunn, North Carolina, just hospitalized with a heart attack.

The men eat a "hurried meal of stew" and march off to the nearby airfields. "Nobody sang, nobody cheered. It was like a death march."[5]

The summer days are long in England. In June the sun doesn't go down until nine o'clock. You can sit for hours and watch the big soft hills change color and wonder what it's like back in the States now. Trapped in your harness and your solitude, you look south to the winding valley to the sea. And what are the Germans thinking now? Of home, perhaps, and better days? When will it get dark? Why do I go on doing this? What chance does a paratrooper have? Stay light, stay on forever, and we'll never get to Normandy.[6]

10:15 p.m.

All southeastern England hears it now—in London and Portland and Kent—the throb of engines, the steady roar of the largest aerial fleets of all time passing overhead for hour after hour, southbound, toward the Far Shore.

"This is it." People kneel to pray.

At the airfields the C-47's, crammed with paratroopers, take off into the cloud-racked sky.

The darkened sea armada moves on in blackout toward its rendezvous with history. The day has ended in a burst of sunshine, but the queasy Channel still heaves as moonlight filters through the ragged clouds, and *Texas* and *Tuscaloosa, Chickadee* and *Nuthatch, Black Prince* and *Montcalm* and *Georges Leygues* and their thousand kin move quietly to the south. The landing craft and "small boys" take it wet and green; the troops are tired, seasick, tense; a young lad quotes Shakespeare *sotto voce:*

> *Your son, my lord, has paid a soldier's debt;*
> *He only liv'd but till he was a man;*
> *The which no sooner had his prowess confirm'd*
> *In the unshrinking station where he fought,*
> *But like a man he died. . . .*

In England, near Newbury, the Supreme Commander, Allied Expeditionary Force, wanders through groups of "hundreds of paratroopers with blackened and grotesque faces," "chinning with this and that one," cheering his men with a phrase. One GI offers "Ike" a postwar job in Texas, "rassling" cattle.[7] The men emplane—13,000 Americans, 5,300 British; the engines roar, the gliders lift in tow; the destiny of men and nations is committed to the skies.

In France, the light at Pointe Barfleur burns brightly; the Germans sleep. Admiral Theodor Krancke, the German naval commander thinks the tides and weather "not right" for an invasion. But the British Broadcasting Corporation broadcasts a code message: "The arrow pierces steel."

And in shadowy lanes and tiny villages of the bocage country men gather; the French underground blows a bridge, rips a rail; the time has come.

The Germans have broken the code; Fifteenth German Army, which guards the coast from the Orne to Antwerp, stands to full alert. Army Group B takes no action: "On the basis of past experience, Rommel's staff consider[s] it unlikely that the intercepts warn of an imminent invasion."

And "Rundstedt's intelligence officer . . . reject[s] the warning on grounds that it would be absurd for the Allies to announce their invasion in advance over BBC."[8]

11 p.m., June 5, to Midnight

In New York it is drawing on toward curtain time for *Life with Father,* still playing to capacity audiences in its fifth year.

In the Bay of the Seine the first ships are moving now toward the hidden loom of the land; behind them, stretching far away to the headlands of England, the immense procession steams past the lighted dan buoys which mark the swept channels.

Over the lighthouse on Portland Bill as midnight approaches, hundreds of troop carriers, with identification stripes on wings and fuselages, roar southward at 500 feet, carrying for the Western world "Caesar and his fortunes."

Aboard USS *Augusta,* cruiser flagship of Rear Admiral Alan G. Kirk, commanding Western Naval Task Force, Lieutenant General Omar N. Bradley, who looks like a Kansas farmer and speaks with a nasal twang, lies in a bunk with his boots on. Bradley, who commands all American ground forces in the invasion—the U.S. First Army—listens to the muted tumult of a ship under way, thinking of the wedding of his daughter, which he has missed, musing until sleep comes on the responsibilities he bears. . . .

Over the Channel in Horsa gliders towed by Halifax bombers, three platoons of the "Ox and Bucks" (Oxford and Buckinghamshire Light Infantry) are wisecracking with Cockney accents and singing "Abie, My Boy" as they approach their objective, the Orne River bridges, near Caen.

Fifty miles to the west flying toward the Cotentin Peninsula, the pathfinder teams of the American paratroopers check their equipment, "let out a yell as they [see] the French coast," and shout "Hell, Yes!" when the jumpmaster bellows down the fuselage of the C-47, "Is everybody happy?"[9]

In the farms and villages of the Cotentin Peninsula, the German 709th Infantry Division—average age 36—fleshed out with Russian and Polish prisoner-volunteers, guards some 30 miles of Channel coast. At midnight: "Achtung!"—an air raid alert. But this is normal—no need for alarm.

D-DAY, JUNE 6

12:15 a.m.

The fireworks are starting. Aboard *Augusta* an observer notes: "From midnight on occasional gun or bomb flashes on horizon far away. But nothing else. So far nothing else. Have we surprised the enemy?"

RAF night bombers—1,333 of them—are plastering the enemy coastal batteries from the Seine to Cherbourg with more than 5,000 tons of bombs.

The pathfinders of the "Screaming Eagles," the men who are to mark and light the drop zones to guide the main body in, fly near the Channel Islands, greeted by haphazard flak; make landfall on the French coast on the west side of the Cherbourg Peninsula and start to hit the silk, shouting "Bill Lee" as they step from the doors. The C-47 "goonie birds"—work horses of the war—cross the coast at 1,500 feet, slant down to 700-feet jumping altitude, slow to 110 miles an hour, as the multi-colored flak rises to greet them in beautiful pyrotechnics of the night.

But the men are scattered, much of the equipment lost; only one DZ (drop zone) is properly marked. . . .

12:20 a.m.

Far to the east, the pathfinders of the British 6th Airborne Division are leaping into the night, and Horsa gliders cast off their tow lines and crash-land with breaking wings and splintering fuselages near the Orne River bridges and the Caen Canal.

"The concussion is shattering. The glider [tears] into the earth at ninety miles an hour, and careen[s] across the tiny field with a noise like thunder as timber crack[s] and split[s]. . . ."

An astounded German soldier named Helmut Römer, one of the sentries on the Orne River bridge, leaps into a trench as men with blackened faces and Cockney voices run yelling toward him.[10]

1:30 a.m.

The midget submarines have surfaced, their shielded lights blinking to seaward. The ships are closing into the transport area, about seven miles off the British beaches; 11 miles off the American, the gunfire support ships take stations; the sweepers steam slowly on their appointed rounds; the sleepless armada approaches, prays, prepares. . . .

Over Normandy the airborne assault, "by far the largest and most hazardous ever undertaken," starts in full strength. One thousand and eighty-seven transport aircraft fly back and forth from Portland Bill to Normandy in all the hours of darkness through carefully charted channels in the night sky.

The first serials over the Cherbourg Peninsula run through a cascade of antiaircraft; the planes "bounce and bob like a ball on a waterspout."

The jumpmasters crouch in the doorways; the equipment bundles are ready.

"Stand up!"

"Hook on!"

"Check equipment!"

The planes throb; the green lights come on; the men leap into the unknown night. One chutist forgets to count while waiting for the opening shock and yells instead, "Open, you bastard!"

Some of the planes, flying in formation of V of V's, cruise into thick cloud near the jump point; Brigadier General James M. Gavin, in the lead plane of a formation transporting three para regiments of the 82nd Airborne Division, leaps as the fog begins to dissipate and the "flak and small-arms fire thicken[s]."

Major General Matthew B. Ridgway, division commander, lands in a "nice, soft grassy field," rolls, spills the air from his chute, unbuckles, loses his .45 in the grass, hears "something moving," recognizes "in the dim moonlight the bulky outline of a cow."

"I could have kissed her."

But the pilots, confused by flak and cloud, and with most DZ's unmarked, scatter the paratroopers over wide areas: one "stick" lands in the sea; others drop in swamps or flooded areas; their chutes, still inflated by the wind, pull the men through black water and mud; some drown before they can unbuckle; others, gasping, reach hard ground. The 82nd and 101st Divisions are scattered far and near; some troopers land 25 miles from their objectives.

But the sheer dispersion confuses the enemy. The war diary of German Seventh Army, which holds the Cotentin Peninsula, notes reports of Allied paratroop landings near Caen, at Montebourg, on both sides of the Vire River and all along the east coast of the peninsula. Lieutenant Colonel Hoffman, battalion commander of the 709th Division, hears aircraft approaching and within a few minutes his battalion staff and security guards are heavily engaged in a fire fight. From Cherbourg to Saint-Lô to Caen, the alarums sound; the Germans stand to arms.

1:40 a.m. to 3 a.m.

The sea armada debouching from the swept lanes scatters in ordered confusion to assigned stations along 60 miles of beach; the Bay of the Seine is alive with ships. The transports anchor—"Anchor holding, sir"; the LST's and amphibious craft close up; the control boats to guide the boat waves move slowly toward the beaches.

The crews and troops eat breakfast, the last meal many will ever have; two Ranger battalions slated to assault the sheer cliffs of Pointe du Hoc with raw will and scaling ladders gulp hotcakes, coffee and seasick pills.

In the distance above the dark, low-lying coast, stricken planes flame briefly and die; bombs erupt with flash of flame; flak bursts against the clouds; tracers and small-arms fire arc into the night.

In the Cotentin Peninsula and again along the Orne, the black-faced men are fighting desperately by twos and threes in little groups, joining up with other groups as crickets chirp "click-clack"—"click-clack, click-clack." This is a cat and dog fight in the dark—no front, no rear, no flanks—as parachutes billow in unending waves against the night sky, as desperate men crawl through the ditches and search frantically for weapons and equipment.

At 3 A.M. the German Seventh Army Chief of Staff correctly estimates Allied intentions. The big show is on, he reports, with the main efforts near Carentan and Caen. But his superiors, including Hans Speidel, Rommel's chief of staff, still are cautious; this may well be a diversion in Normandy; keep tight the gate of the Pas-de-Calais. The Dover deception and Patton's phantom army have done their work; for days the Germans wait, holding much of Fifteenth Army in reserve to guard the strait— until it is too late.

3 a.m. to Dawn

At 0309, an hour or more after the first ships had reached the transport areas, German radar picks up some of the invasion fleet; Admiral Krancke "promptly issues[s] orders to repel . . . invasion."

The night is muggy, with heavy overcast and the moonlight occasionally gleaming through; an eighteen-to-twenty-knot wind roils up the Bay of the Seine; the PT boats and spitkits make rough weather of it.

General quarters sounds aboard the men-of-war spread for mile on sea mile around the vast and silent fleet. From *Augusta,* an observer sees gunfire in the distance; then ten charioteer flares light up the sea and silhouette the ships hard on the starboard bow.

At 4:50 A.M. out of the cacophony above the land, a flaming flare breaks away heading seaward in a gigantic, curving arc above the invasion fleet. It is an American B-25, its engines still running, outlined in flame. It arches over gracefully to splash into the sea. There are no chutes.

At 4:58 the air blitz is on—the bombing preparatory to landing. Another plane is hit; it flames and dies on land in a tremendous cascading flash of fire.

"Away all boats!" Slowly the light breaks in the east, as troops, heavily laden, clamber down cargo nets into the heaving craft.

P-38 Lightnings fly toward the Far Shore; aboard the men-of-war huge battle flags are streaming from the gaffs.

But the seas are high; the small boats bob and duck, and many of the assault troops are seasick, cold and wet as the boats move shoreward on the last long miles.

Ashore the battle waxes in the hedgerows, the ditches, the cow-pocked fields, the swamps and towns; nettles sting the knees and wrists of crawling men. The sound of battle stupefies: the crash of explosions, the rattle of machine-gun fire, the thrown grenade, a "prolonged screaming out of the night which dies in crescendo as if a man had been bay-oneted," the chirp of a cricket, the hasty password: "Flash"—"Thunder" —"the most joyful noise of a lifetime."

Colonel Robert F. Sink, CO of the 506th Parachute Infantry (101st Division) bangs on the door of a French house in Sainte-Marie-du-Mont to confirm his position. A Frenchman looks out a second-story window.

"The invasion has begun!" Colonel Sink announces in his best French.

"Très bien," the Frenchman replies, and only after prolonged knock-ing can he be persuaded to come downstairs, "shivering from fright."

The dead lie now, scattered and forlorn in Norman fields, American and German and British; the dead and those soon to die, moaning in agony of wounds, dragging through ditches. Beside them lie the cattle, the dead Norman cows, bellies swelling already in the dissolution of death. And just before sunrise on that day of destiny there are many more to die. The gliders come arching in—the Wacos and the Horsas—to crash-land in meadows, roads and swamp. Nearly all are damaged by hedgerows, tree trunks, obstacles; some are literally ripped apart and shredded, their passengers decapitated, crushed. So to die is Brigadier General Don F. Pratt, Assistant Division Commander of the 101st. . . .

The Germans open the ball. At 5:05 A.M. a shore battery, one of 28 defending Utah Beach, fires on destroyers Fitch and Corry three miles off the sands. Then the big guns of Saint-Vaast join the chorus against the little sweepers close to the land, and at about 5:30 HMS Black Prince gives tongue of thunder. Soon the duel is general: battleship *Nevada,* monitor *Erebus, Soemba, Quincy* and *Tuscaloosa,* and His Majesty's Ships *Hawkins* and *Enterprise,* together with two divisions of "small boys," rip and ravage the land.

Again the Germans taste first blood; just before sunup PC 1261 guiding LCT's toward the beaches hits a mine and sinks.

Dawn to H-Hour

The sun rises above the coast of France at 5:58; for 60 miles the milling landing craft are moving toward the land; for league on league the guns are thundering in the greatest duel of sea against shore in this or any war. The stealth of the approach has yielded now to an "almost continuous wall of sound." The clouded skies echo the roar of bomber engines; gardens of flame blossom behind the invasion beaches.

Just as dawn is breaking three German torpedo boats—T-28, Jaguar *and* Möwe—*out of Le Havre, steaming at 28 knots, penetrate a smoke screen shielding the Eastern Task Force off the British beaches and fire a spread of 18 torpedoes. Two barely miss British battleships* Warspite *and* Ramillies; *one gives the death blow to Norwegian destroyer* Svenner. *But this is a flea biting an elephant, and it is the only blow the German Navy, raddled and wrecked by years of attrition, delivers that day.*

Admiral Krancke, the German naval commander, writes in his diary: "It was only to be expected that no effective blow could be struck at such a superior enemy force."

Heavy and medium bombers pass overhead in an unending sky procession, their targets the beach defenses and landing areas. The mediums, flying beneath the overcast, have some luck; about one-third of the 4,404 bombs they drop crater sections of Utah Beach between high and low water. But the heavies, flying above the clouds, move back the bomb line to insure the safety of the assault troops. Some 13,000 bombs from 329 Liberators fall from a few hundred yards to three miles inland. Omaha Beach is unscarred by air attack.

The dawning day is gray and ominous; the wind is making up and the white-crested seas in the Bay of the Seine surge into four-foot waves. Off Utah Beach to the west, the small boats come under the lee of the peninsula as they near the shore, but further east off Omaha and at the British beaches the landing craft toss and pitch and ship green water, and the hapless troops use again and again an item of issue equipment which the British War Office frankly dubs "Bags, Vomit." Already craft are foundering; men are drowning in the seaway.

Small craft and rocket ships steam close to the shore, and the fiery trails of rockets arch above the landing craft.

H-Hour: 6:30 a.m. to Noon

Touchdown that day on Utah Beach to the west is at 0630; 600 GI's in the first assault waves of the 4th Division leap from the landing craft ramps into waist-deep water, "yell like Indians," and wade ashore waving their rifles: "Goddamn; we're on French soil!"

There is light initial opposition; the paratroopers inland have done their work; German attention is distracted. By a fortunate turn of chance such as the gods of war arrange with blind impartiality, the troops land on the wrong, but a more lightly defended, beach. Brigadier General Theodore Roosevelt, Jr., leading the assault waves with a walking stick and his father's famous grin, makes a personal reconnaissance of the causeway beach exits over the flooded areas and redirects the attack.

Captain Robert C. Cresson, CO of Charlie Company, 8th Infantry (Colonel James C. Van Fleet commanding), 4th Division, is stumped. One of his men in great excitement runs to him near the beach and says, "I have two women over here!"

"Where?"

"In a ditch . . ."

"What the hell are you doing with two women in a ditch?"

"I don't want them to get shot."

A sergeant nearby chimes in, "How old are they?"

Captain Cresson moves the women to safety, and the war goes on.

U.S. destroyer *Corry*, in action with several German batteries, steams at high speed, her guns erupting flame. Mines—the most effective German sea weapon that day—are her undoing; one erupts beneath her keel and she is almost cut in two, with both fire rooms and foreward engine room flooded. Before 7 A.M. the bridge passes the word: "All hands, abandon ship!"

Hobson and *Fitch* fish the survivors out of the sea—13 dead, 33 wounded.

Back in England at SHAEF's advanced CP near Portsmouth, Air Marshal Sir Trafford Leigh-Mallory "rings up" the Supreme Commander at 0640 A.M. Leigh-Mallory, air commander of the invasion, has bitterly opposed the paratroop and glider operations and has predicted catastrophe. Now he eats crow; he tells Eisenhower's aide that only 21 of 850 American C-47's are missing; 8 out of 400 British.

About 7:30 A.M. on the British beaches—Gold and Juno and Sword —between Port-en-Bessin and the Orne River, Second British Army, Lieutenant General M. C. Dempsey commanding, sends its assault troops from three divisions storming toward the land. DD tanks are in the van, "swimming" through rough seas with the aid of accordion-pleated canvas "bloomers" as flotation gear. Allied fighters swarm overhead and dive and dip toward the beach as the first waves of the 3rd Canadian Division and the 3rd and 50th British touch down on the fire-swept beaches.

With the British in No. 4 Commando are 171 French marines, first to regain their native soil.

On Gold and Sword, the beach obstacles damage landing craft, but the "Tommies" drive ahead against pockets of resistance; the defenders have been stunned by the two-hour bombardment, and the 716th German Division, one-fourth Poles and Ukrainians, appears to have little stomach for a fight.

The fortified stronghold of Le Hamel, garrisoned by a battalion of the veteran German 352nd Division, is virtually untouched by bombs or shells. It delivers "accurate and intense" fire against the right flank of the British 50th Division, and its stout resistance makes the western end of Gold Beach almost impassable until the Hampshires after hours of fighting finally kill or capture the last of its defenders.

On Juno the Canucks swarm ashore behind time at a little after eight. Strong points still fight along the British beaches and an 88 "brews up" several British tanks. But the British paratroopers have dispersed the German effort, and British flail tanks thrash their way through the mine fields.

At 0930 above Juno, Sword and Omaha beaches the once invincible Nazi Luftwaffe makes its only attack during daylight hours on D-day. Two FW-190's make one pass over the crowded beaches, bomb ineffectively and turn tail for home. Lo, how the mighty have fallen![11]

The assault troops overrun the enemy's forward observation posts on the beaches.

German soldiers at battery positions in the rear hear their battery commander make his last alarming call: "They're coming right in the post," he crie[s] with a frantic note in his voice. "Lebt wohl, Kameraden!"

The vaunted Atlantic Wall is crumbling; save for stubborn resistance at a few strong points it presents no problem here.

By now the Germans are alerted all over France; reserves are moving up; back in Paris, von Rundstedt fears a ruse; he thinks another landing is to come in the Pas-de-Calais.

On Omaha the battle reaches climax. . . .

The Bay of the Seine is littered with the flotsam and jetsam, the debris of war. Life jackets, mattresses, wreckage, bodies drift with the tide; the amphibious "ducks," heavily laden and sandbagged against mines, make heavy weather of it. Some of them, their bilge pumps clogged by sand, sink with their cargoes; artillery to buttress the assault never reaches the beaches.

The gage of battle is now fully joined. From Cherbourg to Le Havre, the invasion coast is swathed in smoke and early morning mist through which the flash of explosions bursts like gigantic stars. The red sun, climbing in the east, looks down upon an awesome scene: the churning waters, frothed with white and pocked with the scum of battle; the sands, where summer bathers once played, violated now by bomb and shell; the embattled casemates and pillboxes; and, over all, the inhuman noise of human conflict, the whining roar of shells, the crump of bombs, the rattle of small arms and the screams of men.

At Omaha nothing goes right . . .

The Rangers take Pointe du Hoc, but the German batteries which are their objective have been withdrawn; the Rangers flounder in a landscape cratered like the surface of the moon by Allied bombs and shells.

The "Fighting First" Division, with one regiment of the 29th attached and the others hard on its heels, leads the assault.

But the seas are up—three to four feet of surf—and a strong current with the rising tide sets easterly along the beach. "A majority of landing craft during the first hour" beach well to the east—sometimes as much as 1,000 yards—of their assigned sectors; units are mixed in disordered confusion.

The LCA's (British Landing Craft, Assault) and LCVP's moving toward the beach pass men in life jackets, men on rafts floating in the water—survivors of the ill-fated DD tanks swamped by the seas. Of one unit of 32 tanks two swim to the beach, three others are landed by amphibious craft; the rest lie on the bottom of the Bay of the Seine. Even the small craft have trouble from the sloshing seas; soldiers bail with their helmets.

A heavy, well-aimed fire greets the assault waves; elements of the 352nd German Division—no static, listless unit this, but an "offensive division of good quality with a core of veterans" from the Russian front—man many of the defenses.

Bullets patter like hail against the steel landing ramps, even before touchdown. One boatload of troops is wiped out to a man. As the ramps are lowered, men leap into waist-deep water, slip and fall and drown; are hit and sag; wade through neck-deep runnels toward the terrible sands; shrink and cower, diving to escape the undiscriminating fire.

"Within seven to ten minutes after the ramps [drop] Able Company, 116th Infantry [is] inert, leaderless and almost incapable of action." Most of its officers are dead or wounded. Lieutenant Edward Tidrick is shot through the throat as he leaps from the ramp into the water, and hit again in the body as he flops on the sand. Private Leo J. Nash hears him gasp his last command as he sprawls beneath the enemy fire 15 feet away: "Advance with the wire cutters!"

But the wire cutters lie on the bottom of the Bay of the Seine.

In a few minutes Omaha Beach is an appalling panorama. Little groups of clustered men hug the sands; some, shrinking from the withering fire, seek shelter behind the German beach obstacles, to be driven slowly toward the shore as the tide rises—or to drown.

The beach and the lapping waters are strewn with the dead, the dying and those soon to die, but the boats still come in to disgorge their fear-raddled cargoes. . . .

In the midst of chaos and under the thunder of the guns, 16 underwater demolition teams—seven sailors and five Army engineers each—commanded by a stocky, spirited Reserve officer, Lieutenant Commander Joseph H. Gibbons, try to blast boat channels through the beach obstacles in a race with death and the rising tide. Theirs is a suicide job; almost one-third die; more than half are casualties. One crew has its primacord all set to blow on a big obstacle. A direct hit detonates the charge prematurely; all men but one are dead. A whole team is wiped out by an enemy salvo as it touches down. "A naval officer, about to pull the . . . igniters to explode his charge, [is] hit by a piece of shrapnel that cut[s] off his finger and the two fuses."

But out on the wet sands, as the inexorable tide creeps up a foot every eight minutes, sailors stand on sailors' shoulders to defuse Teller mines on beach obstacles while enemy fire whips about them. Soldiers sheltering behind some of the obstacles, paralyzed with fear, are deaf to the entreaties of the demolition teams; only the spluttering of the detonating fuses forces them up the beach.

The statistics of Armageddon are sickening. Easy Company, 116th, loses its captain and 104 of other rank.

To the east, the 16th Regimental Combat Team, 1st Division, is in the toughest fight of its distinguished life; its men are pinned down "like a human carpet."

Captain John G. W. Finke, commanding F Company, 16th Infantry, hobbles ashore, his ankle sprained, on a stick. Soon he is lashing at his men with his stick trying to force them from behind the beach obstacles up the sandy strip of death to the esplanade. A degree of ruthlessness must be part of the equipment of any good battlefield commander; Finke, watching with horror, has to order the wounded to be abandoned to the rising tide. Each time two men try to aid one, the casualties mount to three.

The landing sites on Omaha Beach offer scant protection against the merciless fire. The strip of sand rising from the surf is 50 to 300 yards wide; it ends in steeply rising rocky shingle, bordered by sandy dunes or a sea wall 2 to 12 feet high and in places by a promenade, the whole interspersed with mines and barbed wire, and dominated by high bluffs from which the German guns "fire down our throats." There are only five beach exits to the high ground, all mined and heavily defended.

"All along Omaha there [is] a disunited, confused and partly leaderless body of infantry, without cohesion, with no artillery support, huddled under the seawall" or pinned to the beach. "There [are] two long stretches of beach where nobody [lands]. Only two companies out of eight are on the beaches where they are supposed to be. German gunners concentrate on each tank as it comes ashore and disable or explode many of them before they can fire."[12]

Here, on Omaha, the gigantic gamble hangs now in balance; the invasion meets its fate. Here is no overwhelming "assault of matériel, operated by man"; the bombing and bombardment have left the beach defenses largely unscarred. Here there is no static, listless enemy but a crack German division. Here the ultimate arbiter of all battles and all wars—the raw will of man—holds the key to history.

At H-plus 80 minutes—ten minutes of eight—Captain Robert Ellis, Assistant Division Engineer of the 29th Division, sees the United States Coast Guard LCI No. 91 attempt to beach near the Vierville exit. A German shell scores a direct hit on the crowded deck, striking an enlisted man with a flame thrower strapped to his back.

"His body stiffen[s] with such convulsive reaction he is catapulted clear of the deck, completely clearing the starboard bulkhead and plunging into the water. The burning fuel from the flame thrower covers the foredecks and superstructure; most of the troops and the ship's crew plunge into the sea." LCI No. 91, beached and burning, dies in flaming crescendo for 18 hours, spraying the beaches with lead as the ammunition for her Oerlikon guns explodes.

Nebelwerfer and mortar fire and "screaming meemies" rake the sands and search out men crouched behind the sea wall. Chunks of shrapnel as "large as the blade of a shovel" practically "cut bodies in two"; medics strive futilely with gaping head and belly wounds. Colonel Charles D. W. Canham, commanding the 116th Regiment, is shot through the wrist, refuses evacuation, establishes his first CP at 8:30 at the foot of the bluffs.

A private takes over command of a tank, as his sergeant skulks, white with fear, in a foxhole.

Another tank—its painted name "Always in My Heart" incongruous in the midst of carnage—fires furiously at a pillbox and a fortified house near a beach exit.

A man from Love Company of the 116th, shot through the head, "spins round like a chicken."

A captain, shrapnel through both cheeks, blood spouting as he talks, leads the attack.

Men paralyzed with fear crawl across the sands. Easy Company, 16th Infantry, takes an hour to move its survivors across 300 yards of sand to the foot of the bluffs; George Company loses 63 men between boat ramps and shingle. Most of the regimental radios are "destroyed or useless"; units are scattered and leaderless.

In time of trial a few men always rise to their greatest hour. So it is this day on Omaha, as the world waits.

Brigadier General Norman D. Cota, Assistant Division Commander of the 29th Division, leads the assault on one section of the beach. He is an imperturbable general, who "waves a .45 around," cajoles, exhorts and leads. He has a gap blown by a bangalore torpedo in the barbed-wire, double-apron fence near the edge of the bluff. The first soldier through is hit by "a heavy burst of machine gun fire."

"Medico, medico," he screams. "I'm hit; help me." He "moans and cries for a few minutes and finally dies after sobbing 'Mama' several times."

The troops are stalled; none dares to brave the gap. Cota leads the way, pushes through the marsh grass up toward the dominating bluffs. As they near the crest, they see below them on the promenade a lone American rifleman herding five German prisoners. A burst of machine-gun fire mows down two Germans; the rifleman and one prisoner dive to safety. The two remaining sink to their knees. "They seem to be pleading with the operator of the machine gun on the bluffs to the east not to shoot them. The next burst catches one kneeling German full in the chest."

In the 16th RCT sector Colonel George A. Taylor lands about 8:15 and finds his men "still hugging the embankment, disorganized, suffering casualties from mortar and artillery fire."

"Two kinds of people are staying on this beach," he yells, "the dead and those who are going to die—now let's get the hell out of here."[13]

He herds his men through gaps in the wire, across the flat and up the bluffs.

Cota gains the bluffs about 9 A.M.

In New York, where the night still lingers, deserted Broadway suddenly echoes with the dead voice of yesterday. A recording of the Bow bells of London's famous Bow Church, destroyed in the blitz of 1940, rings out via amplifier from St. Luke's Lutheran Church on Forty-sixth Street, just off Times Square.

But on Omaha no bells peal.

A dying officer calls with his last breath, "Senior noncom, take charge and get the men off the beach!"

Off the beach, off the deadly beach swept by fire—but the men shrink and cling to the sea wall; officers and noncoms rage and rant and swear, lead and drive, threaten and cajole:

"Get your ass on up there!"

"Come on, come on!"

"This is what separates the men from the boys."

"Let's see what you're made of."

Slowly as the morning wears on, some of the beach exits are conquered, the mine fields overcome, the barbed wire cut; here and there small companies of brave men have gained the heights.

But Omaha is in bloody chaos, the enemy fire still strong and many beach obstacles still unblown; the follow-up waves mill about off the beach; burning and wrecked landing craft litter the shoals; the sea is black with the awful debris of battle.

The beaches are becoming clogged; the beachmaster halts all landings of vehicles until some of the bluffs are won.

The 111th Field Artillery Battalion suffers "complete disaster." Lieutenant Colonel Thornton L. Mullins, its CO, lands in chaos, quickly takes charge: "To hell with our artillery mission. We've got to be infantrymen now."

Twice wounded he organizes little groups of infantrymen for the assault, leads a tank forward, is killed by a sniper. Behind him in the seas his battalion is drowning; every gun but one sinks to the bottom of the Bay of the Seine as the amphibious "ducks" are swamped with green water.

By 11:30 A.M. the face of General Bradley, aboard flagship *Augusta*, is grim. The sea is rough and choppy, a brisk wind blows from the west-nor' west, and Bradley says to war correspondents, "Well, do you know all about what's going on? I don't."

The fog of war, as always in the first hours of battle, has cut off command from forward elements; the reports are few; only the aura of the horror of the beaches has filtered back. . . .

At high noon Winston Churchill stands up in the House of Commons. With maddening deliberation, in which he takes a puckish glee, he talks for ten minutes about the fall of Rome on June 4 and then to a tense House, he says:

"I have also to announce . . . that during the night and early hours of this morning the first of a series of landings in force upon the European Continent has taken place. . . . So far the commanders who are engaged report that everything is proceeding according to plan. And what a plan! . . ."

"According to plan . . ."

But not upon the beach at Omaha. At noon Major Stanley Bach, liaison officer of the 1st Infantry Division attached to the 29th, makes a scratched note: "Beach high tide. Bodies floating—many dead Americans . . . at HWM [high water mark]."

Noon to 6:30 p.m.

The stores are closed in New York; in Britain the waiting women sob over their factory lathes. Churches are crowded; many men to whom prayer is strange pray this day.

On Omaha the assault, slowly, inchingly, leaving the bloody wake of its passage behind it, gains ground.

By 12:30 P.M. F Company, 16th Infantry, has 95 men left out of the 200 who had stormed ashore those brief hours before. Finke, the company CO, is the last of seven officers still in action; he gets his on the bluffs about 1,000 yards inland when a mortar shell breaks his elbow, rips his leg.

Destroyers and small-fire support ships creep close to the land, almost put their keels in sand, blast German casemates and guns at point-blank range. The "big boys" further out send 12- and 14-inch shells screeching into the German defenses.

"Cor'," a British Tommy says. "What next? They're firing jeeps."

Through' the long, blood-drenched afternoon the attack builds up; men die in windrows, but others move in from the sea. An LCT hits three mines, disintegrates; two "Navy men go flying through the air into the water. They never come up."

At 1:20 Major Bach's notes record a direct hit on a beached LCM: "Flames everywhere; men burning alive." At 3:30 another holocaust: "Direct hit on 2½ ton truck gasoline load; another catches fire; then entire load goes up; area 100 yards square—men's clothes on fire— attempt to roll in sand to put out flames . . . some successful, others die."

But the outflung flanks of the huge attack are solid now; the paratroopers and the 4th Division hold some of the causeways from Utah Beach across the marshes and the inundated areas to the Cotentin Peninsula; the flag flies above Sainte-Mère-Église; the British are firmly ashore astride the Orne and pushing inland near Bayeux. And on Omaha at 3:40 P.M. Major Bach notes: "Infantry moving by us on path over crest. . . . We get to open field—follow path—see one man that had stepped on mine; no body from waist down."

The Germans do not quit; at 4:30 the major notes again: "Barbed wire, mines, mortars, machine gun, rifle and 88 fire everywhere it seems. Prayed several times—why do these things have to be forced upon men?"

By 4:50 Major Bach reaches the town of Saint-Laurent, three-quarters of a mile from the sea; Colleville is ours and Vierville-sur-Mer. German artillery still ranges along the beaches; the Omaha foothold is shallow and tenuous, but flesh and blood and guts and courage have broken the Atlantic Wall. . . .

Far away, near Salzburg, Hitler learns of the invasion just before attending a reception for the new Hungarian prime minister. He has a "radiant face" at the reception. "It's begun at last," he says, confident that the beachheads will be eliminated by counterattack.

But the Allies are in Normandy to stay, and the Nazi Reich that was to last a thousand years faces catastrophe.

As the westering sun draws down toward the smoke-clouded Channel after that long, long day, the build-up starts; the bridge of ships and planes to England has no ending; by D-plus 26, less than one month after

June 6, 929,000 men, 177,000 vehicles, 586,000 tons of supplies will be upon French soil; the German counterattacks are destined to be stalled and broken by naval gunfire, air attack and stout land resistance. This is the beginning of the end.

In New York at Madison Square by the Eternal Light 50,000 people bow in prayer in the late afternoon of that day as a priest, a minister and a rabbi ask "God's grace for the Allied invaders."

And from the throne of England that June evening King George VI in slow and halting voice calls the empire to prayer. "The Lord," he quotes from Psalm 29, verse 11, "will give strength unto his people; the Lord will bless his people with peace."

THE SUMMING UP

D-day in Normandy, described by Winston Churchill as "the most difficult and complicated operation that has ever taken place," was a *coup de main* to Germany.

It was for the Third Reich the beginning of the end; once the landing was made good, Berlin had no strategic choice, as many of the German generals realized, but to bring the war to an end as quickly as possible at the best terms possible. But Adolf Hitler was still the implacable dictator of Germany's destinies.

From the Allied point of view the invasion was the quickest way to the German heart, though also the hardest and bloodiest.[14] Normandy meant the end of the "eccentric" operations around the periphery of German-held Europe, which Winston Churchill favored. It doomed, in time, his dream of the trans-Adriatic operation, through the Ljubljana Gap into the Austrian plain. Churchill's strategic concepts, too often decried both in America and in England, were, nevertheless, the proper blend of reality and imagination, of political and military factors. He wanted no blood bath for English youth similar to that of World War I, when whole generations went to France to "chew on barbed wire in Flanders." He foresaw the danger of Russian Communist imperialism in Eastern Europe, and he hoped to forestall it in the Balkans by right of conquest in the Danube area. He wished to wear down Germany by a series of operations on her more lightly defended flanks, while pounding the heartland from the air.

This strategy, had it been implemented, might have delayed the Normandy invasion and probably would have prolonged the war, though the ultimate cost in human lives to the United States and Britain might have been less. Whether or not it would have delayed the Soviet conquest of eastern Germany seems considerably more doubtful, though it almost certainly would have limited the postwar Soviet sphere of influence in Central Europe and the Balkans.

The invasion of southern France by U.S. and French troops—code name "Anvil"—was originally timed to coincide with the Normandy assault. This "Anvil" and hammer concept originally was sound (though, as events showed, unnecessary), particularly since logistic experts estimated that Marseilles and southern French ports would be required to support our armies. But when shortage of landing craft forced the postponement of "Anvil" (then renamed "Dragoon") until August 15 (after the breakout in Normandy), "not even the code name of the operation made sense," as Field Marshal Earl Alexander of Tunis, then commanding in Italy, notes bitterly in his memoirs.[15] It was an "unwise dispersion of force."

The diversion of troops from the Italian campaign and from Churchill's hoped-for trans-Adriatic operation committed the Allied armies in Italy to a bloody inching campaign up the backbone of the Apennines. It doomed British hopes of occupying the Balkans and the Danube plain before the Communist hammer and sickle could fly over the area. As General Mark Clark, Commander of the U.S. Fifth Army in Italy, noted:

"Save for a high-level blunder that turned us away from the Balkan States and permitted them to fall under Red Army control, the Mediterranean campaign might have been the most decisive of all in post-war history."

The Normandy invasion was, in perspective, a sound *military* conception, but American planners gave far too little weight to postwar *political* factors. The Churchill strategy—a drive into the Danube plain —might have been substituted for the invasion of southern France (which lost its major strategic purpose of diversion when it had to be postponed until more than two months after the Normandy D-day). The two months' delay meant that the forced dispersion of the German armies, and the possibility of trapping the Nazi forces in southern France between the hammer of Normandy and the anvil of the southern attack, had been eliminated. Indeed, the German withdrawal from France started *before* the southern France landings, and many of the enemy combat units in the south completed a successful withdrawal to Germany. Nor were the supply ports of the Mediterranean coast vital to victory.

General Clark repeatedly stresses in his book *Calculated Risk* that the

weakening of the campaign in Italy in order to invade Southern France instead of pushing on into the Balkans was one of the outstanding political mistakes of the war. . . .

Had we been there [in the Balkans] before the Red Army, not only would the collapse of Germany have come sooner, but the influence of Soviet Russia would have been drastically reduced.[16]

Even if one discounts the testimony of General Clark and many other of the great and near-great leaders of World War II, the historical record is clear:

The invasion of southern France two months after the Normandy attack had little military and no political significance; our main effort in the Mediterranean should have been transferred from France and Italy across the Adriatic. Churchill was right and Roosevelt was wrong. We forgot that all wars have objectives and all victories conditions; we forgot that winning the peace is equally as important as winning the war; we forgot that "politico-military" is a compound word.

Normandy did not lead therefore to the *political* triumph this great military victory deserved. Normandy meant the beginning of the end for Germany; it was sound, if not imaginative, *military* strategy.

It was a battle that from the Allied point of view was on the whole sound in both planning and execution. General Montgomery's insistence, emphatically endorsed by both General Eisenhower and his chief of staff, Lieutenant General Walter Bedell Smith, in early 1944 that the invasion frontage be extended from about 25 to almost 60 miles, from three assaulting divisions (over the beaches) to six, quite probably insured the success of the invasion. Montgomery, despite his prickly personality, was a thorough though cautious planner; he always required assurance that he had enough before he would move.

On the other hand, the German defense was split between two antipathetic concepts and personalities: Rundstedt and his counterattack plan and Rommel and his "lick-'em-on-the-beaches" plan. The effect was an unhappy compromise.

Nevertheless, other factors led to Germany's undoing. She had been bled white by more than four years of war, and her air power—key to modern victory—was spent. Without control of the air or the sea the Reich's hold on Europe was doomed; the Allies could land where they willed, and when.

The Allied foreboding which had preceded the attack—the expectation of tremendous casualties and perhaps, like the Dieppe Raid, a costly repulse—was not justified by the actual events. The airborne troops and the assault waves on Omaha Beach lost heavily, but the Utah casualties were light. The entire U.S. First Army, including all U.S. ground troops engaged (but excluding smaller naval and Army Air Force casualties), reported 6,603 casualties for June 6: 1,465 killed, 3,184 wounded, 1,928 missing, 26 captured. The Second British Army kept no such comparable figures, but Chester Wilmot in *The Struggle for Europe* estimates their total D-day casualties "can hardly have exceeded 4,000." The German casualties for D-day—estimates only—ranged from 4,000 to 9,000.[17]

The assault on June 6 breached the Atlantic Wall, but it failed to penetrate inland nearly as rapidly as the planners had hoped. Caen, a

D-day objective, was not captured until July 9, and the Allied armies, handicapped by a fierce storm in the Bay of the Seine (June 19–21), which interrupted supply and destroyed some of the artificial ports, were contained in bloody hedgerow fighting in Normandy until the breakout at Saint-Lô on July 25.

"The slow advance southward," G. A. Harrison comments in *Cross Channel Attack*, "and especially the failure to push out into open country south and southeast of Caen . . . meant a reduction in the planned progress of airfield construction," which, however, was "much less serious than planners had anticipated."[18]

Nevertheless, despite desperate German resistance in the difficult *bocage*, bad weather and a costly fire in a large ammunition dump, the Allies, aided by their air power, won the battle of the "build-up."

"In the first seven weeks," Chester Wilmot writes, "one and a half million men were transported across the Channel with all their arms, equipment and supplies, an unparalleled achievement." (The Allied forces landed on the Far Shore by July 29 included 903,061 Americans, 176,620 U.S. vehicles and 858,436 tons of U.S. stores; 663,295 British troops, 156,025 British vehicles and 744,540 tons of British supplies.) "While the Germans were reinforcing Normandy with 20 divisions, the Allies landed thirty-six plus a vast number of supporting troops, air squadrons and service units."[19]

The cross-Channel attack did not go "according to plan"; war never does.

George Patton's Third Army, once scheduled to land in Brittany and overrun the Breton ports, came ashore instead over the Normandy beaches and built up its strength quietly in the orchards of the Cotentin until it formed a sweeping right flank in the drive toward Paris.

The inaccuracies and limitations of air bombardment against beach defenses and fortified positions were clearly revealed. But the preinvasion air bombardment contributed, anachronistically, both to tactical surprise and to the success of the Allied deception measures. German radar and radio stations from Boulogne to Cherbourg were "heavily and accurately attacked by the R.A.F." in the week before D-day, and in the night before H-hour many of the remaining radar stations were jammed, but "sufficient sets were left operating north of the Seine to enable the Germans to pick up the faked convoys" headed for the Pas-de-Calais area. As Air Marshal Leigh-Mallory put it: "In the vital period between 0100 and 0400 hours when the assault was nearing the beaches only nine enemy radar installations were in operation, and during the whole night, the number of stations active in the [invasion] area was only eighteen out of a normal ninety-two."[20]

Air bombardment also provided, as *Cross Channel Attack* puts it, "perhaps the biggest and most important surprise" of the invasion; with ancillary aid from French saboteurs it crippled the enemy's transportation system. "It would be difficult to overestimate the handicaps imposed on the enemy by his lack of mobility. It was the primary reason why the big counterattack that figured in all Allied estimates never materialized."[21]

Rommel, who was the best and most energetic German commander in the West, had been right: the Allies had to be contained and repulsed on the beaches or not at all. His energy and imagination had greatly strengthened the Atlantic Wall during his short period of command of Army Group B; Omaha, in particular, reflected the growing strength of the German defenses. Had Rommel had a few additional months, the entire assault might have resulted in as bloody an epic as Omaha. Yet during the assault the German command was confused and misled—a by-product, in part, of Allied air superiority. And even prior to the assault German intelligence had vastly overestimated the Allied amphibious capability and divisional strength—a tribute to the Allied preinvasion cover and deception techniques.

Naval gunfire failed to produce the anticipated results in the short *preinvasion* bombardment; only on the British beaches, where the bombardment was longer (due in part to the later hour of the landings, a circumstance dictated by the tide), did it even approximate hopes. These hopes were, of course, unrealistic; all the experience of the Pacific had shown that a long period of heavy and smothering preparatory fire was essential against fortified positions. But in the Pacific island campaigns, where the Japanese were isolated and there was no possibility of reinforcing the defenders, long preparatory fire was possible. In an assault upon the continent of Europe, it had been believed that the importance of surprise—which was partially achieved, to the astonishment of everyone—outweighed the value of a long period of preparatory bombardment, which would tip our hand and might permit the Germans to concentrate reserves at the point of threatened landings.

Gunfire support *after* touchdown—and particularly during the desperate battle on Omaha—was, however, a keystone of victory. Point-blank bombardment of German gun positions and casemates helped the doughboys to breach the Atlantic Wall and heavy-caliber fire ranged far inland against enemy artillery positions and broke up incipient counterattacks. Its morale importance, debilitating to the enemy, encouraging to our own troops, was also major. Colonel S. B. Mason, Chief of Staff of the 1st Infantry Division, wrote to Rear Admiral John L. Hall (who commanded Task Force 124—Assault Force "O" for Omaha Beach) that "I am now firmly convinced that our supporting naval fire got us in; that without that gunfire we positively could not have crossed the beaches."

The utilization of airborne troops—despite the inaccurate navigation of many of the troop carrier aircraft, the failure of the pathfinders to mark the proper drop zones, the tragedies of the gliders, the wide dispersion of the paratroopers—was a key factor in the relatively easy landings at Utah and on the British beaches. The airborne troops had heavy casualties; their divisional organization was virtually nonexistent in the first day after the drop (radios were lost, the men widely scattered), and by the end of D-day only 2,500 men of the 6,600 men of the 101st Division dropped that morning were "working together" in "mixed units of varying size." Nevertheless, surprise and the very dispersion of the attack "had in fact achieved such complete tactical success" behind Utah Beach that "the sea-borne infantry had had little to do but walk ashore."

Similarly, the smaller British airborne effort—despite the loss of a number of gliders in the Channel when tow ropes broke, wide dispersion and the drowning of many paratroopers in the Dives swamps—helped to distract the Germans and to weaken their defenses against assault from the sea.

On Omaha a variety of factors contributed to carnage: the poor navigation of landing craft and control boats which landed units in confused masses at the wrong beaches; the sinking of overloaded "ducks" with supporting artillery in the rough sea; and the lack of a sufficient number of armored vehicles in the assault waves. British historians have been critical of American planning for Omaha; some small part of the criticism is justified, though few of their histories have emphasized, as *Cross Channel Attack* does, that "the First Division had gone in against the one sector of the Normandy coast that had anything like the kind of cordon defense which Field Marshal Rommel counted on to hold and smash the Allies on the beaches." The undetected presence of the German 352nd Division in the Omaha sector cost us dearly.[22]

The use of flail tanks to break through the beach mine fields, as on the British beaches, would have eased the doughboys' job. But the failure of the British-developed DD tank—an awkward, vulnerable device to provide precarious flotation while the tank swam ashore—was basically due to its unseaworthiness, although poor judgment in launching and handling also contributed to the sinking of most of these vehicles. The longer distances to the American beaches and the more exposed anchorages off Omaha also contributed to the high toll of the much vaunted DD tanks.

More important at Omaha—and in the invasion generally—was the failure of SHAEF and its subordinate echelons to assimilate and properly weigh the many technical lessons learned in the hard-fought amphibious assaults in the Pacific. At the time of Normandy amtracs, armored and unarmored, had been in use in the Pacific for many months to transport troops ashore and to provide close gunfire support during the actual assault. The bloody epic of Tarawa had shown the necessity for a vehicle which could swim from ship to sand, crawl out of the sea and maneuver on land like a tank. Amtracs were far superior to landing craft for the assault; they could land their troops dry-shod, and they were far superior to the British DD tanks in their seaworthiness.

Major General Charles H. Corlett, who commanded the U.S. XIX Corps—a follow-up corps, which became operational in Normandy on June 13—had had Pacific experience, and when he was transferred to England to prepare for the invasion he urged the use of amtracs in the assault wave. His suggestions were not heeded. Shortage of these vehicles or lack of time to procure them may have played a role in this rejection. But two other factors were important. One was a dichotomy between the European and the Pacific theaters of war—a feeling on the part of the Army commanders in the European theater that they knew the answers; that Europe, the major theater, had nothing to learn from the Pacific. Another factor was that British planning, even in small details, greatly influenced assault concepts; the DD tanks were British developments and were therefore the front runners—particularly in a race with a vehicle which few in Europe had ever seen. (This British influence was marked throughout the invasion phase; the arrangements for press dispatches and public relations were a result of British planning and British control, and they suited the age of Nelson rather than that of Eisenhower.)

Thus there were mistakes in detail in planning and in execution on Omaha and elsewhere in the battle for the Atlantic Wall.

But they were rectified by the courage of Man.

The pride and power and fighting heart of the divisions that broke the Atlantic Wall is best epitomized by the report of the 82nd Airborne Division, after its survivors had been withdrawn from France following more than a month in action.

The words of this report speak for all the brave men, living and dead, who dropped from the skies into Norman fields or stormed the beaches from the Orne to Utah:

Thirty-three days of action without relief, without replacements. Every mission accomplished. No ground gained ever relinquished . . .

Combat Efficiency: Excellent; short 60 per cent infantry; 90 per cent artillery . . .

CHAPTER 9

THE GREATEST SEA FIGHT—

LEYTE GULF

October 23–26, 1944

In October, 1944, the greatest sea fight in history—perhaps the world's last great fleet action—broke the naval power of Japan and spelled the beginning of the end of the war in the Pacific. The Battle for Leyte Gulf, fought off the Philippine Archipelago, sprawled across an area of almost 500,000 square miles, about twice the size of Texas. Unlike most of the actions of World War II, it included every element of naval power from submarines to planes. It was as decisive as Salamis. It dwarfed the Battle of Jutland in distances, tonnages, casualties. But, unlike Jutland, there was no dispute about the outcome. After Leyte Gulf, the Japanese Fleet was finished. Yet it was a battle of controversy. . . .

The empire was dying, and there were some who faced the fact. The long retreat was over, the great spaces of the Pacific had been bridged by the countless ships of the American "barbarians," and the enemy was knocking upon the inner strongholds of the Samurai. For Japan it was now the desperate gamble, the all-out stroke: to conquer or to die.

And so, the *Shō* ("To Conquer") plans were drawn: if the inner citadel—the Philippines, Formosa, the Ryukyus, the main islands—were penetrated by the U.S. Fleet, all the remaining Japanese naval power that could steam or fly would be mobilized for a desperate assault.

Four separate *Shō* plans were drawn up to deal with different contingencies, but, as Morison notes, Japanese intelligence was "betting on the Philippines."

"The Japanese high command obtained very little advance intelligence from reconnaissance, but a good deal from other sources and by inference. One important bit came from Moscow on 6 October."

The Soviet Foreign Office informed the Ambassador from Japan, representative of their "ally's enemy," that through diplomatic sources they had learned that the U.S. Fourteenth and Twentieth Army Air Forces, then China-based, had been ordered to make attacks intended to isolate the Philippines. The U.S. assault on Leyte came sooner than the Japanese had expected but about where they expected it.

U.S. intelligence was far less perspicacious; indeed, it was grossly overoptimistic, as many of our estimates of Japanese island garrisons were throughout the Pacific War. Lieutenant General G. C. Kenney, Commander, Allied Air Forces Southwest Pacific, described the objective (Leyte) as "relatively undefended," and predicted the Japanese would not offer strong resistance and that a fleet action was unlikely.*

Famous last words!

In October, 1944, when U.S. troops in Europe were smashing into German Aachen street by street and the opposing armies faced a bitter winter of grudging gains, the time for *Shō* I—the defense of the Philippines—had almost come. Tarawa, with its bloody reef, was proud history; so, too, were the Gilberts, the Marshalls, the Marianas, New Guinea, Biak, Palau and Morotai. B-29's were converging on the new fields in Guam, Saipan and Tinian to bomb Japan; U.S. submarines were preying upon the enemy's commerce; the U.S. flag flew above palm-fringed islands once remote strongholds of the Emperor's power.

From August 31 to September 24 the fast carriers, supported by the battleships, of Admiral William F. Halsey's Third Fleet had raked over Japanese bases from Mindanao to Luzon, and on the twenty-first, while Radio Manila was playing "Music for your Morning Moods," naval pilots combed Manila Bay. The bag throughout the islands was large, the enemy opposition was surprisingly feeble, and Admiral Halsey reported to Admiral Chester W. Nimitz, Commander in Chief, Pacific: "No damage to our surface forces and nothing on the screen but Hedy Lamarr."

---

* Samuel Eliot Morison, *Leyte, June 1944–January 1945* (*History of United States Naval Operations in World War II*, Vol. XII), Boston, Little Brown, 1958, pp. 71–72.

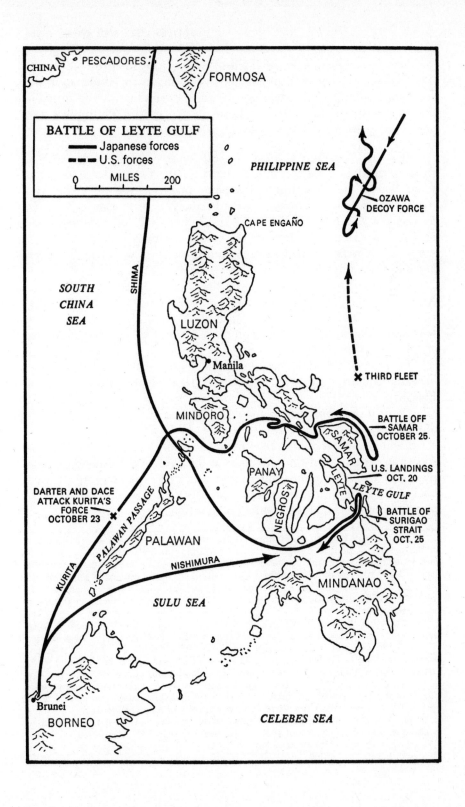

CHINA

PESCADORES

FORMOSA

BATTLE OF LEYTE GULF
—— Japanese forces
- - - - U.S. forces

0   MILES   200

PHILIPPINE SEA

OZAWA
DECOY FORCE

CAPE ENGAÑO

SOUTH
CHINA
SEA

SHIMA

LUZON

Manila

THIRD FLEET

MINDORO

BATTLE OFF
SAMAR
OCTOBER 25.

SAMAR

PANAY

LEYTE

U.S. LANDINGS
OCT. 20

LEYTE GULF

DARTER AND DACE
ATTACK KURITA'S
FORCE
OCTOBER 23

PALAWAN PASSAGE

NEGROS

BATTLE OF
SURIGAO
STRAIT
OCT. 25

KURITA

PALAWAN

NISHIMURA

MINDANAO

SULU SEA

Brunei

BORNEO

CELEBES SEA

The weak Japanese reaction led to a change in American strategy.*ᵃ The planned capture of Yap and step-by-step moves to Mindanao in the southern Philippines and then northward were eliminated; the amphibious assault upon the island of Leyte in the central Philippines was advanced by two months to October 20, 1944.

It started according to plan. A great armada of more than 700 U.S. ships steamed into Leyte Gulf at dawn on the twentieth; a lone Jap plane braved the skies. Initial Japanese opposition was weak; the vast American armada—the greatest of the Pacific War, with some 151 LST's, 58 transports, 221 LCT's, 79 LCI's and hundreds of other vessels—may have overawed the defenders. By the end of A-plus 2—October 21—thousands of American troops had been landed on Leyte with few casualties, and only three warships had been damaged.

Four hours after the first landing on Leyte, General Douglas MacArthur waded ashore; later Colonel Carlos Romulo, the little Filipino, who was with him, was to quip, "There was the tall MacArthur, with the waters reaching up to his knees, and behind him there was little Romulo, trying to keep his head above water."

In front of a Signal Corps microphone on the beach just won and beneath rain-dripping skies MacArthur recalled the bloody epic of Bataan:

"This is the Voice of Freedom, General MacArthur speaking. People of the Philippines: I have returned. . . ."*

Light cruiser *Honolulu*, the "Blue Goose" of the Pacific, was the first American casualty. On the afternoon of the landing a Japanese torpedo plane put a "fish" into the cruiser's port side. The explosion tore a jagged hole in *Honolulu*'s side, gave her a heavy list in a few minutes, killed 60 men and put the first of many ships out of action.

---

* Notes to this chapter are of three kinds. Author's notes, marked by asterisks, are at the bottom of pertinent pages. Notes with Arabic numerals refer to special comments by Admiral Kinkaid. Alphabetical references relate to comments by Admiral Halsey. Some corrections and additions to the narrative have been made since this account was first published, but the comments of the two admirals are unchanged. Admiral Robert B. Carney has also furnished a brief critique, which appears in the notes at the rear of the text.

* A nostalgic dispatch to the *New York Times* of October 6, 1964, by Seth S. King noted that twenty years after the Leyte landings, which led to the fateful naval battle:

". . . the Red and White beaches where the 24th. Division and the 1st. Cavalry waded ashore and two beaches at Dulag, 11 miles to the south where the 96th. and 97th. Divisions landed hold few reminders of those great amphibious operations.

"All that remains at the Red Beach are hulks of four amphibious tractors half-buried in the sand, rusted and splotched with barnacles. One tractor is overturned, its shattered tracks grinning at the sky like the gaping teeth of a beached whale.

"The White Beach is clear and inviting, occupied today only by Filipino children running among outrigger canoes and rushing into the cool surf. A hundred yards behind them a cluster of fishermen's huts has risen over the rotting stumps of palms shattered that day by gunfire."

At 0809, October 17, just nine minutes after the USS *Denver* fired the opening gun in the liberation of the Philippine Islands, Japanese forces had been alerted to carry out the *Shō* I plan.* Admiral Soemu Toyoda, Commander in Chief of the Japanese Combined Fleet and leader of what he knew was a forlorn hope, had his last chance to "destroy the enemy who enjoys the luxury of material resources." From his headquarters at the Naval War College just outside Tokyo, he sent the word "To Conquer" to his widely scattered units.

The *Shō* plan was daring and desperate, fitted to the last months of an empire strained beyond its capabilities. The Japanese Fleet had not recovered from its cumulative losses, particularly from the heavy blow it had suffered four months earlier in the Battle of the Philippine Sea, when Admiral Raymond W. Spruance, covering our Marianas landings, had destroyed more than 400 Japanese planes, sunk three Japanese carriers, and helped to break the back of Japanese naval aviation.[b] In mid-October, when Halsey—in a preliminary to the Leyte Gulf landing —struck heavily at Formosa, Toyoda had utilized his land-based planes and had also thrown his hastily trained carrier replacement pilots into the fight. The gamble failed. But the "pathology of fear" and the curious propensity of the Japanese for transforming defeats into victories in their official reports magnified the normally highly inflated claims of enemy aviators; Tokyo declared the Third Fleet had "ceased to be an organized striking force."

An enemy plane dropped leaflets over recently captured Peleliu:

FOR RECKLESS YANKEE DOODLE:
DO YOU KNOW ABOUT THE NAVAL BATTLE DONE BY THE AMERICAN 58TH [*sic*] FLEET AT THE SEA NEAR TAIWAN [FORMOSA] AND PHILIPPINE? JAPANESE POWERFUL AIR FORCE HAD SUNK THEIR 19 AEROPLANE CARRIERS, 4 BATTLESHIPS, 10 SEVERAL CRUISERS AND DESTROYERS, ALONG WITH SENDING 1,261 SHIP AEROPLANES INTO THE SEA. . . .

Actually only two cruisers—*Canberra* and *Houston*—were damaged, less than 100 U.S. planes lost; the Japanese were to have a rude awakening as the great invasion armada neared Leyte Gulf.[1]

But for Toyoda, the Battle of the Philippine Sea and his futile gamble in defense of Formosa had left the Japanese Fleet naked to air attack. Toyoda had carriers, but with few planes and half-trained pilots.[c] *Shō* I, therefore, must be dependent upon stealth and cunning, night operations and what air cover could be provided, chiefly by land-based planes operating from Philippine bases and working in close conjunction with the fleet.

---

* The Japanese were alerted locally about 0650 after sighting the U.S. attack force. The first soldiers to land were Rangers, who seized a small island in the mouth of Leyte Gulf.

Toyoda also confronted another handicap—a fleet widely separated by distance. He exercised command, from his land headquarters, over a theoretically "Combined Fleet," but Vice Admiral Jisaburo Ozawa, who flew his flag from carrier *Zuikaku,* and who commanded the crippled carriers and some cruisers and destroyers, was still based in the Inland Sea in Japanese home waters. The bulk of the fleet's heavy units—Vice Admiral Takeo Kurita's 1st Diversion Attack Force, of 7 battleships, 13 cruisers and 19 destroyers—was based on Lingga Anchorage near Singapore, close to its fuel sources. The Japanese Fleet was divided in the face of a superior naval force; it could not be concentrated prior to battle.

These deficiencies, plus the geography of the Philippines, dictated the enemy plan, which was hastily modified at the last minute, partially because of the Japanese weaknesses in carrier aviation. Two principal straits—San Bernardino, north of the island of Samar; and Surigao, between Mindanao and Dinagat and Leyte and Panaon—lead from the South China Sea to Leyte Gulf, where the great armada of MacArthur was committed to the invasion. The Japanese ships based near Singapore —the so-called 1st Diversion Attack Force—were to steam north toward Leyte, with a stop at Brunei Bay, Borneo, to refuel. There the force would split: the Central Group, Vice Admiral Takeo Kurita, flying his flag in the heavy cruiser *Atago,* with a total of 5 battleships, 10 heavy cruisers, 2 light cruisers and 15 destroyers, would transit San Bernardino Strait at night; the Southern Group, Vice Admiral Shoji Nishimura,[2] with two battleships, one heavy cruiser and four destroyers, was to be augmented at Surigao Strait by an ancillary force of three more cruisers and four destroyers under Vice Admiral Kiyohide Shima, which was to steam through Formosa Strait, with a stop in the Pescadores, all the way from its bases in the home islands. All these forces were to strike the great American armada in Leyte Gulf almost simultaneously at dawn of the twenty-fifth of October and wreak havoc among the thin-skinned amphibious ships like a hawk among chickens.

But the key to the operation was the emasculated Japanese carriers, operating under Vice Admiral Jisaburo Ozawa from their bases in Japan's Inland Sea. These ships—one heavy carrier and three light carriers, with about 116 planes aboard, "all that remained of the enemy's once-great carrier forces"—were to steam south toward Luzon and to act as deliberate decoys or sacrificial "lures" for Admiral Halsey's great Third Fleet, which was "covering" the amphibious invasion of Leyte. The northern decoy force was to be accompanied by two hermaphrodites—battleship-carriers, the *Ise* and *Hyuga,* with the after-turrets replaced by short flight decks, but with no planes—and by three cruisers and nine destroyers. Ozawa was to lure Halsey's Third Fleet to the north, away from Leyte, and open the way for Kurita and Nishimura to break into Leyte Gulf.

At the same time all three forces were to be aided, not with direct air cover but by intensive attacks by Japanese land-based planes upon American carriers and shipping. As a last-minute "spur-of-the-moment" decision, the Japanese "Special Attack Groups" were activated, and the kamikaze (Divine Wind) fliers commenced their suicidal attacks upon U.S. ships. As early as October 15, Rear Admiral Masabumi Arima, a subordinate naval air commander, flying from a Philippine field, had made a suicide dive and had "lit the fuse of the ardent wishes of his men."[d] When Vice Admiral Takijiro Ohnishi took command of the First Air Fleet on October 17, there were only about 100 operational Japanese planes available in the entire Philippine Archipelago. (They were subsequently reinforced.) There were at least—and Admiral Ohnishi knew this—20 to 30 U.S. aircraft carriers nearby. To solve this equation the kamikaze was born. Admiral Ohnishi made the mission clear in an address to Japanese air group commanders in the Philippines on October 19.

The fate of the empire depends on this operation. . . . Our surface forces are already in motion. . . . The mission of our First Air Fleet is to provide land-based air cover for Admiral Kurita's advance. . . . To do this, we must hit the enemy's carriers and keep them neutralized for at least one week.

In my opinion, there is only one way of assuring that our meager strength will be effective to a maximum degree, and that is for our bomb-laden fighter planes to crash-dive into the decks of enemy carriers.*

All these far-flung forces were under the common command of Admiral Toyoda far away in Toyko.

Such was the desperate Shō I—perhaps the greatest gamble, the most daring and unorthodox plan, in the history of naval war.

It committed to action virtually all that was left of the operational forces, afloat and in the air, of Japan's Navy: 4 carriers, 2 battleship-carriers, 7 battleships, 19 cruisers, 33 destroyers, and perhaps 500 to 700 Japanese aircraft—mostly land-based.

But the opposing American forces were far more powerful. Like the Japanese forces, which had no common commander closer than Tokyo, the U.S. Fleet operated under divided command. General MacArthur, as theater commander of the Southwest Pacific area, was in over-all charge of the Leyte invasion, and through Admiral Thomas C. Kinkaid he commanded the Seventh Fleet, which was in direct charge of the am-

---

* From the unpublished manuscript of a speech, "Contradictory Pacific War," by Roger Pineau, delivered at Colorado College, January, 1964. Mr. Pineau points out that the pilots volunteered as kamikazes and that 40 or 50 of them died, but succeeded in sinking only one baby flattop. However, it was to be a different story off Okinawa later in the war. The manuscript was later published in Shipmate, U.S. Naval Academy Alumni publication, February, 1965.

phibious operation. But Admiral Halsey's powerful covering force of the Third Fleet—the strongest fleet in the world—was not under MacArthur's command; it was a part of Admiral Chester W. Nimitz' Pacific Command forces, and Nimitz had his headquarters in Hawaii. And above Nimitz and MacArthur the only unified command was in Washington.

The gun power of Kinkaid's Seventh Fleet was provided by 6 old battleships, 5 of them raised from the mud of Pearl Harbor, but he had 16 escort carriers[3]—small, slow-speed vessels, converted from merchant hulls—8 cruisers and scores of destroyers and destroyer escorts, frigates, motor torpedo boats and other types. Kinkaid's job was to provide shore bombardment and close air support for the Army and antisubmarine and air defense for the amphibious forces.

Halsey, with 8 large attack carriers, 8 light carriers, 6 fast new battleships, 15 cruisers and 58 destroyers, was ordered to "cover and support forces of the Southwest Pacific [MacArthur's command] in order to assist in the seizure and occupation of objectives in the Central Philippines."[e] He was to destroy enemy naval and air forces threatening the invasion. And: "in case opportunity for destruction of major portion of the enemy fleet is offered or can be created, such destruction becomes the primary task." He was to remain responsible to Admiral Nimitz, but "necessary measures for detailed coordination of operations between the [Third Fleet] . . . and . . . the [Seventh Fleet] will be arranged by their . . . commanders."[f]

The combined Third and Seventh Fleets could muster 1,000 to 1,400 ship-based aircraft—32 carriers, 12 battleships, 23 cruisers, more than 100 destroyers and destroyer escorts and numerous smaller types and hundreds of auxiliaries. The Seventh Fleet also had a few tender-based PBY patrol planes (flying boats).[g] But not all of these forces participated in the far-flung air attacks and the three widely separated major engagements which later came to be called the Battle for Leyte Gulf.

Such was the stage, these the actors, and this the plot in the most dramatic and far-flung naval battle in history.

It opens with first blood for the submarines. At dawn on October 23 the U.S. submarines *Darter* and *Dace,* patrolling Palawan Passage, intercept Admiral Kurita. The *Darter* puts five torpedoes into Kurita's flagship, the heavy cruiser *Atago,* at less than 1,000 yards range, and damages the cruiser *Takao. Dace* hits the cruiser *Maya* with four torpedoes. The *Atago* sinks in about 20 minutes as Kurita shifts his flag to the destroyer *Kishinani* and later to the battleship *Yamato.*[4] The *Maya* blows up and sinks in four minutes; *Takao,* burning and low in the water, is sent back to Brunei, escorted by two destroyers. Kurita steams on, shaken but implacable, toward San Bernardino Strait.

OCTOBER 24

Aboard battleship *New Jersey*, flying "Bull" Halsey's flag, the plans are ready for this day as the sun quickly burns away the morning haze. In the carriers, bowing to the swell, the bull horns sound on the flight decks: "Pilots, man your planes."

At 0600 the Third Fleet launches search planes to sweep a wide arc of sea covering the approaches to San Bernardino and Surigao straits. Submarine reports from *Darter*, *Dace* and *Guitarro* have alerted the Americans, but not in time to halt the detachment of Third Fleet's largest task group—Task Group 38.1 commanded by Vice Admiral John S. ("Slew") McCain—with orders to retire to Ulithi for rest and supplies. The fleet's three other task groups are spread out over 300 miles of ocean to the east of the Philippines from central Luzon to southern Samar; one of them, to the north, has been tracked doggedly all night by enemy "snoopers." As the planes take off to search the reef-studded waters of the Sibuyan and Sulu seas and the approaches to San Bernardino and Surigao, Kinkaid's old battleships and little carriers off Leyte are supporting the GI's ashore.

At 0746, Lieutenant (j.g.) Max Adams, flying a Helldiver above the magnificent volcanic crags, the palm-grown islands and startling blue sea of the archipelago, reports a radar contact, and a few minutes later Admiral Kurita's 1st Diversion Attack Force lies spread out like toy ships upon a painted sea—the pagoda masts unmistakable in the sunlight.

The tension of action grips flag plot in the *New Jersey* as the contact report comes in; the radio crackles "Urgent" and "Top Secret" messages —to Washington, to Nimitz, to Kinkaid, to all task group commanders. McCain, 600 miles to the eastward, en route to Ulithi and rest, is recalled and Third Fleet is ordered to concentrate off Bernardino to launch strikes against the enemy.

But at 0820, far to the south, the southern arm of the Japanese pincer is sighted for the first time; Vice Admiral Nishimura—with battleships *Fuso* and *Yamashiro*, heavy cruiser *Mogami* and four destroyers—steaming toward Surigao. *Enterprise* search planes attack through heavy AA fire; *Fuso*'s catapult is hit, her planes are destroyed, and a fire rages; a gun mount in destroyer *Shigure* is knocked out, but Nishimura steams on to the east, his speed undiminished.[5] And Halsey continues the concentration of his fleet near San Bernardino to strike the Japanese Central Force.

There has been no morning search to the north and northeast, and

Ozawa's decoy carriers, steaming southward toward Luzon, are still undiscovered.

The *Shō* plan now moves toward its dramatic denouement. Japanese planes flying from Ozawa's carriers and Philippine bases commence the most furious assault since the landing upon the Seventh and Third Fleets. To the north off Luzon, carriers *Langley, Princeton, Essex* and *Lexington* face the brunt of the winged fury. Seven Hellcats from the *Essex*, led by Commander David McCampbell, intercept 60 Japanese planes—half of them fighters—and after a melee of an hour and 35 minutes of combat the Americans knock down 24 Japs with no losses. *Princeton* claims 34 enemy from another large raid; the *Lexington*'s and *Langley*'s "fly-boys" are also busy; over the air comes the exultant "Tally-hos" and "Splash one Betty—Splash two Zekes" of the pilots.

But the Japs draw blood. At about 0938, as Third Fleet starts converging toward San Bernardino and the carriers prepare to launch deckloads to strike the enemy's center force, a Jap Judy (dive bomber or fighter-bomber) dives unseen and unrecorded on the radar screen out of a low cloud. She drops a 550-pound bomb square on *Princeton*'s flight deck; the bomb penetrates to the hangar deck, ignites gasoline in six torpedo planes, starts raging fires. The fight to save her starts, but at 1002 a series of terrific explosions splits open the flight deck like the rind of a dropped melon, throws the after plane elevator high into the air, and by 1020 *Princeton*'s fire mains have failed and she is dead in the water, with a 1,000-foot pall of smoke above her and hundreds of her crew in the water. The task group steams on southward to the San Bernardino rendezvous, while cruisers *Birmingham* and *Reno* and destroyers *Gatling, Irwin* and *Cassin Young* hover about the wounded *Princeton* in a day-long fight to save her.

But as *Princeton* flames and staggers, Kurita's Central Force of five battleships, accompanied by cruisers and destroyers, is running the gantlet. Carrier strikes start coming in against Japan's 1st Diversion Attack Force about 10:25 A.M., and the exultant U.S. pilots concentrate against targets none of them had ever seen before—the largest battleships in the world. *Yamato* and *Musashi*, long the mysterious focus of intelligence reports, lie beneath the wings of naval air power—their 69,500-ton bulks, 18.1-inch guns, 27.5-knot speeds dwarfing their sisters. *Musashi* is wounded early; oil smears trail on the blue water from her lacerated flank as a torpedo strikes home. But she is strong; her speed is undiminished. Not so *Myoko*'s. This heavy cruiser is badly hurt in the first attack; she drops to 15 knots and is left astern to limp alone into port; Kurita has lost four out of the ten heavy cruisers that sortied so gallantly from Brunei.

But he has no respite. At three minutes past noon another strike comes out of the sun. The Jap AA fire blossoms in pink and purple bursts; even the battleships' main batteries are firing. Several American planes are hit; one goes down flaming, but *Musashi* takes two bombs and two torpedoes; she loses speed and drops back slowly out of formation.

An hour and a half later *Yamato* takes two hits forward of her No. 1 turret, which start a fire, but her thick hide minimizes damages; the fire is extinguished. But *Musashi* is now sore wounded; she takes four bomb hits in this attack and three more torpedoes; her upper works are a shambles, her bow almost under water, her speed down first to 16 and then to 12 knots.

Kurita's slow agony drags on during this long and sunlit day. He hopes in vain for air cover. *Yamato* is hit again in the fourth attack and the older battleship *Nagato* damaged.

At six bells in the afternoon watch (3 P.M.) Kurita orders the limping *Musashi* to withdraw from the fight. But not in time. The final and largest attack of the day seeks her out as she turns heavily to find sanctuary. In 15 minutes *Musashi* receives the *coup de grâce*—ten more bombs, four more torpedoes; she's down to six knots now, her bow is under water, and she lists steeply to port, a dying gladiator.

Kurita is shaken. He has had no air cover; he has been subjected to intense attack; his original strength of 5 battleships, 12 cruisers and 15 destroyers has been reduced to 4 battleships, 8 cruisers and 11 destroyers; all his remaining battleships have been damaged; fleet speed is limited to 22 knots. There is no sign that Ozawa's northern decoy force is succeeding in luring the Third Fleet away from San Bernardino. At 1530 (3:30 P.M.) Kurita reverses course and steams away toward the west. And American pilots report the "retreat" to Admiral Halsey aboard *New Jersey*. . . .

To Admiral Halsey there is "one piece missing in the puzzle—the [Japanese] carriers."

The northern task group of Third Fleet has been under attack by enemy carrier-type planes, which might have been land-based, but none of the sightings has reported enemy carriers. Where are they?

At 1405 (2:05 P.M.), as Kurita's Central Force is pounded in the Sibuyan Sea, *Lexington*'s planes take off to find out.[6] They are under orders to search to the north and northeast in the open seas untouched by the morning search.

The search planes fly through a cloud-speckled sky and intermittent rain squalls, leaving behind them a task group harassed by fierce, though intermittent, Jap air attacks.

The flaming *Princeton*, billowing clouds of fire and smoke, is still afloat, with her covey of rescue ships around her. Despite intermittent explosions and singeing heat, cruisers *Birmingham* and *Reno* and destroyers *Morrison*, *Irwin* and *Cassin Young* have clustered alongside, pouring water from their pumps on the blazing carrier. Submarine contacts and enemy air attacks interrupt the fire fighting; the rescue ships pull off. At 1523 (3:23 P.M.), about the time Kurita, 300 miles away, reverses course and heads to the westward in the Sibuyan Sea, cruiser *Birmingham* comes alongside *Princeton*'s blazing port side again. The cruiser's open decks are thick with men—fire fighters, line handlers, antiaircraft gunners, medical personnel, fire and rescue squads, watchstanders. There are 50 feet of open water between blazing *Princeton* and her salvor, *Birmingham;* a spring line is out forward between carrier and cruiser.

Suddenly a "tremendous blast" rips off *Princeton*'s stern and after section of the flight deck; steel plates as big "as a house" fly through the air; jagged bits of steel, broken gun barrels, shrapnel, helmets, debris rake *Birmingham*'s bridge, upper works and crowded decks like grapeshot; in a fraction of a second the cruiser is a charnel house, her decks literally flowing blood—229 dead, 420 mangled and wounded—the ship's superstructure sieved.

Aboard *Princeton* all the skeleton fire-fighting crew are wounded. Captain John M. Hoskins, who had been scheduled to take command of *Princeton* shortly and had remained aboard with the skipper he was relieving, puts a rope tourniquet around his leg, as his right foot hangs by a shred of flesh and tendon. The surviving medical officer cuts off the foot with a sheath knife, dusts the wound with sulfa powder, injects morphine. . . . Hoskins lives to become the Navy's first "peg-leg" admiral of modern times.

But still *Princeton* floats on even keel, flaming like a volcano, manned by a crew of bloody specters. . . .

At 1640 (4:40 P.M.) the search to the north pays off. U.S planes sight Ozawa's decoy force of carriers. The contact reports electrify Third Fleet, but mislead it, too; Ozawa's Northern Group of ships, which were sighted about 130 miles east of the northern tip of Luzon, includes two hermaphrodite battleships, but our fliers mistakenly report four.[7] Nor do our fliers know Ozawa's carriers are virtually without planes.

The contact reports decide *Princeton*'s fate; her weary crew of fire fighters are removed, the day-long struggle is ended, and at 1649 (4:49 P.M.) *Reno* puts two torpedoes into the flaming hulk and the carrier blows up, breaks in two and sinks. Mangled *Birmingham*, which has lost far more men than the ship she was trying to save, steams with her dead and dying to Ulithi—out of the fight. . . .

Two hours later, near Sibuyan Island, the giant *Musashi*, pride of Kurita's Central Force, loses her long fight. Fatally wounded, she settles slowly deeper and deeper in the calm sea, and as the evening closes down, the greatest battleship in the world capsizes and takes with her to the depths half of her crew. But no American sees her passing. . . . And no American has seen Kurita, earlier in the afternoon, alter his course once more and at 1714 (5:14 P.M.) head once again with his battered but still powerful Central Force back toward San Bernardino Strait. . . .

At 1950 (7:50 P.M.), with the tropic dusk, "Bull" Halsey makes his decision and informs Kinkaid, commanding Seventh Fleet:

"Central Force heavily damaged according to strike reports. Am proceeding north with three groups to attack carrier force at dawn."[8]

Third Fleet concentrates and steams hard to the north in what irreverent historians of the future are to call "Bull's Run." Night snoopers from *Independence* shadow the Jap Northern Force, and orders go to the carriers to launch planes at sunrise.[h] San Bernardino Strait is left uncovered—not even a submarine patrols its waters;[i] Kinkaid and Seventh Fleet, protecting the Leyte invasion, believe it is barred by Halsey; Halsey, banking too heavily on exaggerated claims from his pilots,[j] thinks Kurita's Central Force has been stopped by the day's air attacks and the battered Jap survivors can be left safely to Kinkaid. On such misunderstandings rest the course of history and the fate of nations.[k]

Surigao Strait is dark under the loom of the land. Since the morning there have been no sightings of the Japanese Southern Force; even its exact composition is not known. But Kinkaid and the Seventh Fleet have no doubts; the Japs will try to break through this night. Kinkaid and Rear Admiral Jesse B. Oldendorf, his "OTC" (officer in tactical command), have made dispositions for a night surface battle. They have provided a suitable reception committee, including PT boats deep in the strait and covering its southern approaches, three destroyer squadrons near the center, and at the mouth, where the strait debouches into Leyte Gulf, six old battleships and eight cruisers.[9]

Into this trap the Japanese Southern Force blunders in two divisions, each independent of the other. Nishimura, with battleships *Fuso* and *Yamashiro*, cruiser *Mogami* and four destroyers, leads the way. Cruising 20 miles behind Nishimura is Vice Admiral Shima with three cruisers and four destroyers from Jap home bases. The two Jap forces attack piecemeal and uncoordinated; neither knows much of the other's plans. Shima and Nishimura were classmates at the Japanese Naval Academy; their careers have bred rivalry; Nishimura, formerly the senior, has been passed in the processes of promotion by Shima, who commands the smaller force but is now six months senior in rank to Nishimura. But Nishimura, a seagoing admiral, has seen more war. Neither seems anxious to serve with the other; there is no common command.

Radars on the PT boats pick up the enemy about 2300 (11 P.M.) as "sheet lightning dims the hazy blur of the setting moon and thunder echoes from the islands' hills."

Thirty-nine PT boats, motors muffled, head for Nishimura and attack in successive "waves" as the enemy advances. But the Japs score first. Enemy destroyers illuminate the little boats with their searchlights long before the PT's reach good torpedo range; a hit starts a fire in PT 152; a near-miss with its spout of water extinguishes it; PT 130 and PT 132 are also hit.[10] But Nishimura is identified; course, speed and formation are radioed to Kinkaid's fleet and the harassing PT attacks continue.*

Aboard destroyer *Remey*, flag of Destroyer Squadron 54, Commander R. P. Fiala turns on the loudspeaker to talk to the crew:

"This is the captain speaking. Tonight our ship has been designated to make the first torpedo run on the Jap task force that is on its way to stop our landings in Leyte Gulf. It is our job to stop the Japs. May God be with us tonight."

The destroyers attack along both flanks of the narrow strait; their silhouettes merge with the land; the Japs, in the middle, can scarcely distinguish dark shape of ship from dark loom of land; the radar fuzzes and the luminescent pips on the screen are lost in a vague blur.

It is deep in the mid-watch—0301 of the twenty-fifth—when the first destroyer-launched torpedoes streak across the strait. In less than half an hour Nishimura is crippled. His slow and lumbering flagship, the battleship *Yamashiro*, is hit; destroyer *Yamagumo* is sunk; two other destroyers are out of control. Nishimura issues his last command:

"We have received a torpedo attack. You are to proceed and attack all ships."

Battleship *Fuso*, cruiser *Mogami*, destroyer *Shigure* steam on toward Leyte Gulf.

But before 0400 a tremendous eruption of flames and pyrotechnics marks *Yamashiro*'s passing; another American torpedo has found her magazine, and the battleship breaks in two and sinks, with Nishimura's flag still flying.

Fuso does not long outlive her sister. Up from the mud of Pearl Harbor, the avengers wait—six old battleships patrol back and forth across the mouth of the strait. This is an admiral's dream. Like Togo at Tsushima and Jellicoe at Jutland, Kinkaid and Oldendorf have capped the T; the remaining Jap ships are blundering head on in single column against a column of American ships at right angles to the Jap course. The concentrated broadsides of six battleships can be focused against the leading Jap, and only his forward turrets can bear against the Americans.

---

* Reports of the enemy's movements were the most important part of the motor torpedo boats' accomplishments. Morison (*op. cit.*, pp. 210, 211) says that 30 of the 39 boats got into "some sort of a fight" during the entire night's action. Some 34 torpedoes were launched; only one hit a target—the *Abukuma*. The boats "neither stopped nor confused the enemy and were chased away by his gunfire," but they "performed an indispensable service through their contact reports." Of the 30 boats, which came under fire, 10 were hit, but only 1 was lost, and total casualties were 3 killed, 20 wounded.

BATTLE OF SURIGAO STRAIT

A. PT boats **B.** 3 destroyer squads
C. 6 battleships, 8 cruisers
1. PT boats attack Nishimura
2. Battleship Yamashiro sunk, two destroyers hit
3. Battleship Fuso crippled, Mogami crippled
4. Shima arrives, Abukuma hit and left behind
5. Shima meets retreating Shigure
6. Nachi collides with burning Mogami. Shima retreats

SAMAR

BEACH HEAD

LEYTE GULF

LEYTE

DINAGAT

BOHOL

Surigao Strait

SIARGAO

MILES 0   50

NISHIMURA

SHIMA

MINDANAO SEA

MINDANAO

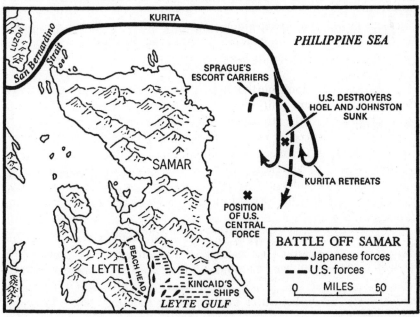

KURITA

PHILIPPINE SEA

LUZON

San Bernardino Strait

SPRAGUE'S ESCORT CARRIERS

U.S. DESTROYERS HOEL AND JOHNSTON SUNK

SAMAR

KURITA RETREATS

POSITION OF U.S. CENTRAL FORCE

BEACH HEAD

LEYTE

KINCAID'S SHIPS

LEYTE GULF

BATTLE OFF SAMAR
—— Japanese forces
- - - U.S. forces
MILES 0   50

Climax of battle. As the last and heaviest destroyer attack goes home in answer to the command, "Get the big boys," the battle line and the cruisers open up; the night is streaked with flare of crimson.

Fuso and *Mogami* flame and shudder as the "rain of shells" strikes home; *Fuso* soon drifts helplessly, racked by great explosions, wreathed in a fiery pall. She dies before the dawn, and *Mogami*, on fire, is finished later with the other cripples. Only destroyer *Shigure* escapes at 30 knots.

Into this mad melee, with the dying remnants of his classmate's fleet around him, steams Vice Admiral Shima—"fat, dumb, and happy." He knows nothing of what has gone before; he has no cogent plan of battle. *Abukuma*, Shima's only light cruiser, is struck by a PT torpedo[11] even before he is deep in the strait; she is left behind, speed dwindling, as the two heavy cruisers and four destroyers steam onward toward the gun flashes on the horizon. About 0400 Shima encounters destroyer *Shigure*, sole survivor of Nishimura's fleet, retiring down the strait.

Shigure tells Shima nothing of the debacle; she simply signals: "I am the *Shigure*; I have rudder difficulties."

The rest is almost comic anticlimax. Shima pushes deeper into the strait, sees a group of dark shadows, fires torpedoes and manages an amazing collision between his flagship, the *Nachi*, and the burning stricken *Mogami*, which looms up flaming out of the dark waters of the strait like the Empire State Building. And that is all for futile Shima; discretion is the better part of valor; dying for the Emperor is forgotten, and Shima reverses course and heads back into the Mindanao Sea and the obscurity of history.

The Battle of Surigao Strait ends with the dawn—debacle for the Japanese. One PT boat destroyed, one destroyer damaged for the Americans. The southern pincer toward Leyte Gulf is broken.[1]

OCTOBER 25

By this day, more than 114,000 troops and almost 200,000 tons of supplies have been put ashore on Leyte, and most of the great amphibious fleet has cleared Leyte Gulf. But as the day of battle opens, there are still more than 50 thin-skinned Libertys, LST's and amphibious ships anchored in Leyte Gulf.

Dawn of the twenty-fifth of October finds Admiral Ozawa with his decoy force[m] eastward of Cape Engaño (fortuitous name: "Engaño" is Spanish for "lure" or "hoax"), prepared to die for the Emperor. At 0712, when the first American planes appear from the southeast, Ozawa knows he has at last succeeded in his luring mission. The day before he has at times despaired; more than 100 of his carrier planes—all he has, save for a small combat air patrol—have joined Japanese land-based planes in attacks upon Halsey's northern task group. But his planes have not come back; many have been lost, others have flown on to Philippine bases. This day less than 30 aircraft—token remnants of Japan's once great flying fleets—are all that Ozawa commands. A few are in the air, to die quickly beneath American guns, as the first heavy attacks from Halsey's carriers come in.

The American carrier pilots have a field day; the air is full of the jabberwock of the fliers.

"Pick one out, boys, and let 'em have it."

The Jap formation throws up a beautiful carpet of antiaircraft fire; the colored bursts and tracers frame the sky-sea battle. The Japanese ships twist and turn, maneuver violently in eccentric patterns to avoid the bombs and torpedoes, but their time has come. Before 0830, with the day still young, some 150 U.S. carrier planes have wrought havoc. Carrier *Chiyoda* is hit; carrier *Chitose,* billowing clouds of smoke and fatally hurt, is stopped and listing heavily; the light cruiser *Tama,* torpedoed, is limping astern; destroyer *Akitsuki* has blown up; light carrier *Zuiho* is hit; and Ozawa's flagship, the *Zuikaku,* has taken a torpedo aft, which has wrecked the steering engine; she is steered by hand.

A second strike at 1000 cripples *Chiyoda,* which dies a slow death, to be finished off later by U.S. surface ships. In early afternoon a third strike sinks carrier *Zuikaku,* the last survivor of the Japanese attack upon Pearl Harbor. She rolls over slowly and sinks, "flying a battle flag of tremendous size." At 1527 (3:27 P.M.) carrier *Zuiho* "follows her down." The hermaphrodite battleships, with flight decks aft—*Hyuga* and *Ise,* "fattest of the remaining targets"—are bombed repeatedly, their bilges perforated, their decks inundated with tons of water from near-misses. *Ise*'s port catapult is hit, but they bear charmed lives. Admiral Ozawa, his flag transferred to cruiser *Oyodo,* his work of "luring" done, straggles northward with his cripples from the battle off Cape Engaño. Throughout the day he is subject to incessant air attack, and in late afternoon and in the dark of the night of the twenty-fifth U.S. cruisers and destroyers, detached from the Third Fleet, finish off the cripples.

The price of success for Admiral Ozawa's decoy force is high: all four carriers, one of his three cruisers and two of his eight destroyers are gone. But he has accomplished his mission: Halsey has been lured, San Bernardino Strait is unguarded, and the hawk Kurita is down among the chickens.

Off Samar that morning of the twenty-fifth, the sea is calm at sunup, the wind gentle, the sky overcast with spotted cumulus; occasional rain squalls dapple the surface. Aboard the 16 escort carriers of Seventh Fleet and their escorting "small boys" (destroyers and destroyer escorts) the dawn alert has ended. The early missions have taken off (though not the search planes for the northern sectors). Many of the carriers' planes are already over Leyte, supporting the ground troops, the combat air patrol and ASW (Anti-Submarine Warfare) patrols are launched, and on the bridge of carrier *Fanshaw Bay* Rear Admiral C. A. F. Sprague is having a second cup of coffee.

The coming day will be busy; the little escort carriers have support missions to fly for the troops ashore on Leyte, air defense and antisub-marine patrols, and a large strike scheduled to mop up the cripples and fleeing remnants of the Japanese force defeated in the night surface battle of Surigao Strait. The escort-carrier groups are spread out off the east coast of the Philippines from Mindanao to Samar; Sprague's north-ern group of six escort carriers, three destroyers and four destroyer escorts is steaming northward at 14 knots 50 miles off Samar and halfway up the island's coast.

The escort carriers, designated CVE's in naval abbreviation, are tinclads, unarmored, converted from merchant ships or tanker hulls, slow, carrying 18 to 36 planes. They are known by many uncompli-mentary descriptives—"baby flattops," "tomato cans," "jeep carriers"— and new recruits "coming aboard for the first time were told by the old hands that CVE stood for Combustible, Vulnerable, Expendable!" Their maximum of 18 knots speed (made all-out) is too slow to give them safety in flight; their thin skins and "popguns"—5-inchers and under—do not fit them for surface slugging; they are ships of limited utility, intended for air support of ground operations ashore, antisubmarine and air defense missions, never for fleet action.

Yet they are to fight this morning a battle of jeeps against giants.

Admiral Sprague has scarcely finished his coffee when a contact report comes over the squawk box. An ASW pilot reports enemy battle-ships, cruisers and destroyers 20 miles away and closing fast.

"Check that identification," the Admiral says, thinking some green pilot has mistaken Halsey's fast battleships for the enemy.

The answer is sharp and brief, the tension obvious. "Identification confirmed," the pilot's voice comes strained through the static. "Ships have pagoda masts."

Almost simultaneously radiomen hear Japanese chatter over the air; the northern CVE group sees antiaircraft bursts blossoming in the air to the northwest; blips of unidentified ships appear on the radar screens; and before 0700 a signalman with a long glass has picked up the many-storied superstructures and the typical pagoda masts of Japanese ships.

Disbelief, amazement and consternation are felt; the escort carriers, Admiral Kinkaid himself, in fact most of the Seventh Fleet, had been convinced the Japanese Central Force was still west of the Philippines[12] and that, in any case, Halsey's fast battleships—now far away to the north with the carriers in the battle for Cape Engaño—were guarding San Bernardino Strait. But Kurita has arrived. And about all that stands between him and the transports, supply ships and amphibious craft in Leyte Gulf and Army headquarters and supply dumps on the beach are the "baby flattops" and their accompanying "small boys."

There's no time for planning; within five minutes of visual sighting, Japanese heavy stuff—18.1-inch shells from *Yamato,* sister ship of the foundered *Musashi*—is whistling overhead. Sprague, giving his orders over the voice radio, turns his ships to the east into the wind, steps up speed to maximum, orders all planes scrambled. By 0705 escort carrier *White Plains,* launching aircraft as fast as she can get them off, is straddled several times, with red, yellow, green and blue spouts of water from the dye-marked shells foaming across her bridge, shaking the ship violently, damaging the starboard engine room, opening electrical circuit breakers, and throwing a fighter plane out of its chocks on the flight deck.

White Plains makes smoke and the Japs shift fire to the *St. Lô,* which takes near-misses and casualties from fragments. The "small boys" make smoke, and the carriers, their boiler casings panting from maximum effort, pour out viscous clouds of oily black smoke from their stacks, which veils the sea. There is a moment of surcease; the planes are launched, most of them armed with small-size or antipersonnel or general-purpose bombs or depth charges—no good against armored ships. But there has been no time to rearm. . . .

The air waves sound alarm. Sprague broadcasts danger in plain language at 0701; at 0707 Admiral Kinkaid, aboard his flagship *Wasatch* in Leyte Gulf, hears the worst has happened: the Jap fleet is three hours' steaming from the beachhead; the little escort carriers may be wiped out. Just five minutes before, Kinkaid has learned that his assumption that a Third Fleet cork was in the bottle of San Bernardino Strait was incorrect; in answer to a radioed query sent at 0412, Halsey informs him that Task Force 34—modern, fast battleships—is with Third Fleet's carriers off Cape Engaño far to the north.

Kinkaid in "urgent and priority" messages asks for the fast battleships, for carrier strikes, for immediate action.

Even Admiral Nimitz, in far-off Hawaii, sends a message to Halsey: "Where is Task Force 34—the world wonders?"[13n]

But in Leyte Gulf and Surigao Strait the tocsin of alarm sounded via the radio waves puts Seventh Fleet, red-eyed from days of shore bombardment and nights of battle,[o] into frenetic action. Some of the old battleships and cruisers are recalled from Surigao Strait, formed into a task unit, and they prepare feverishly to ammunition and refuel. Seventh Fleet's heavy ships are in none too good shape for surface action; their ammunition is somewhat low from five days of shore bombardment, some of their armor-piercing projectiles having been used in the night battle; destroyers are low on torpedoes, many ships short of fuel.[p]

And in the battle off Samar, Sprague is fighting for his life.

Within 20 minutes, as the baby carriers steam to the east, launching planes, the range to the enemy has been decreased to 25,000 yards—easy shooting for the big guns of the Japanese, far beyond the effective reach of the American 5-inchers. . . .

Destroyer *Johnston,* Commander Ernest E. Evans commanding, sees her duty and does it. Anticipating orders (which were issued by Admiral Sprague at 0716), she dashes in at almost 30 knots to launch a spread of ten torpedoes against an enemy heavy cruiser *Kumano* working up along a flank of the pounding carriers. She spouts smoke and fire as she charges, her 5-inchers firing continuously as she closes the range. She escapes damage until she turns to retire; then a salvo of three 14-inchers, followed by three 6-inch shells, hole her, wound her captain, wreck the steering engine, the after fire room and engine room, knock out her after guns and gyro compass, maim many of her crew, and leave her limping at 16 knots.

Sprague and his carriers, veiled in part by smoke, find brief sanctuary in a heavy rain squall; the curtain of water saves temporarily the wounded *Johnston.* But well before 0800 Kurita has sent some of his faster ships seaward to head off and flank the escort carriers; gradually Sprague turns southward, the enemy coming hard on both his flanks and astern.

"Small boys, launch torpedo attack," Sprague orders over the TBS circuit.

Destroyers *Heermann* and *Hoel* and wounded *Johnston,* her torpedoes already expended but her guns speaking in support, answer the command—3 destroyers in a daylight attack against the heaviest ships of the Japanese fleet, 3 tinclads against 4 battleships, 8 cruisers and 11 destroyers.[14]

"Buck," Commander Amos T. Hathaway, skipper of the *Heermann,* remarks coolly to his officer of the deck, "Buck, what we need is a bugler to sound the charge."

Hoel and *Heermann,* followed by limping *Johnston,* sally forth to their naval immortality.

In and out of rain squalls, wreathed in the black and oily smoke from the stacks and the white chemical smoke from the smoke generators on the fantails, the destroyers charge, backing violently to avoid collisions, closing the range. They hear that "express-train" roar of the 14-inchers going over; they fire spreads at a heavy cruiser, rake the superstructure of a battleship with their 5-inchers, launch their last torpedoes at 4,400 yards range. Then Hathaway of the *Heermann* walks calmly into his pilothouse, calls Admiral Sprague on the TBS, and reports: "Exercise completed."

But the destroyers are finished. *Hoel* has lost her port engine; she is steered manually; her decks are a holocaust of blood and wreckage; fire control and power are off; No. 3 gun is wreathed in white-hot steam venting from the burst steam pipes and in flames from No. 3 handling room; No. 5 is frozen in train by a near-miss; half the barrel of No. 4 is blown off; but Nos. 1 and 2 guns continue to fire.

By 0830 power is lost on the starboard engine; all engineering spaces are flooding; the ship slows to dead in the water and, burning furiously, is raked by enemy guns. At 0840, with a 20-degree list, the order is given to "abandon ship." Fifteen minutes later she rolls on her port side and sinks stern first, holed repeatedly by scores of major-caliber shells.

In *Heermann* the crimson dye from enemy shell splashes mixes with the blood of men to daub bridge and superstructure reddish hues. A shell strikes a bean locker and spreads a brown paste across the decks. *Heermann* takes hits but, fishtailing and chasing salvos, she manages to live.

Not so, wounded *Johnston*. Spitting fire to the end, and virtually surrounded by the entire Jap fleet, she is overwhelmed under an avalanche of shells, to sink about an hour after *Hoel*.

The four smaller and slower destroyer escorts make the second torpedo attack. *Raymond* and *John C. Butler* live to tell about it; *Dennis* has her guns knocked out; but *Samuel B. Roberts,* deep in the smoke and framed by shell splashes, comes to her end in a mad melee. She is hit by many heavy-caliber projectiles, her speed is reduced, and by 0900 a salvo of 14-inch shells rips open her port side like a can opener, wrecks an engine room, starts raging fires. The *Roberts,* abaft her stack, looks like "an inert mass of battered metal"; she has no power, she is dead in the water.

But the crew of No. 2 gun load, ram, aim and fire by hand. They know the chance they take; without compressed air to clear the bore of the burning bits of fragments from the previous charge, the silken powder bags may "cook off" and explode before the breach can be closed. But they fire six rounds, despite the risk. The seventh "cooks off" and kills instantly most of the gun crew; the breach is blown into a twisted inoperable mass of steel. But Gunner's Mate 3/c Paul Henry Carr, the gun captain, his body ripped open from neck to groin, still cradles the last 54-pound shell in his arms, and his last gasping words before he dies are pleas for aid to load the gun.

But smoke screens, rain squalls and torpedo attacks have not saved the slow and lumbering baby flattops. Kurita has sent his cruisers curving seaward; slowly the fight swerves round from south to southwest; Sprague's carriers, strung out over miles of ocean, steam wounded toward Leyte Gulf, with the enemy destroyers coming hard on their landward flank, battleships astern and Jap cruisers to seaward.

The flattops dodge in and out of the 150-foot waterspouts from the major-caliber Japanese shells; they chase salvos and fire their 5-inchers defiantly. *Fanshaw Bay* takes five hits and one near-miss from 8-inch shells, which wreck the catapult, knock holes in the hull, start fires. *Kalinin Bay* takes 15 hits; *White Plains* is racked from stem to stern by straddles. But their thin skins save them; most of the huge armor-piercing projectiles pass clean through the unarmored carriers without exploding. *Gambier Bay*, trailing and on an exposed windward flank where the smoke screens do not shield her, takes a hit on the flight deck, a near-miss close alongside, loses an engine, drops to 11 knots, then loses all power— and is doomed. For an hour, far behind the chase, she dies in agony, hit about once a minute by enemy fire. She sinks about 0900, flaming brightly, gasoline exploding, a Jap cruiser still riddling her from only 2,000 yards away.

Well before 0930 the chase, which is drawing closer and closer to crowded Leyte Gulf, where frantic preparations are in progress, has enveloped the Northern Group of escort carriers; the Central Group is now under fire, and the 16 jeep flattops have lost 105 planes.

Observers thought it would be "only a matter of time" until the two groups were destroyed or crippled.

Two destroyers, a destroyer escort and a carrier are sunk or sinking; two carriers, a destroyer and a destroyer escort are badly hurt.

Aboard *Kitkun Bay* an officer quips, "It won't be long now, boys; we're sucking 'em into 40 mm. range."

Suddenly at 0911, Vice Admiral Kurita, with victory in his grasp, breaks off the action, turns his ships to the north and ends the surface phase of the battle off Samar.

"Damn it," a sailor says. "They got away."

Kurita's action, inexplicable at the time, has some, though incomplete, justification. The charge of the American "small boys"—one of the most stirring episodes in the long history of naval war—and the desperate gallantry of the uncoordinated and improvised air strikes by the pilots of the escort carriers have had their effect. During the early action off Samar, U.S. carrier pilots, from the little CVE's, have harassed Kurita constantly, have shot down more than 100 enemy land-based planes, dropped 191 tons of bombs and 83 torpedoes. The enemy ships have turned and maneuvered violently to avoid torpedoes. Effective smoke screens have confused the Japanese. The air attacks have been mounting in intensity and effectiveness as planes have been launched from the center and southern groups of escort carriers and have been diverted from ground-support missions on Leyte to the new emergency. Pilots have strafed the Japanese ships recklessly, have dropped depth charges and antipersonnel bombs, have zoomed above Japanese mastheads with no ammunition and no weapons to win time and to divert and to distract.

The torpedo attacks by surface ship and aircraft have damaged enemy ships, and Kurita's fleet, composed of units now capable of widely differing speeds, is strung out over miles of ocean. Cruiser *Kumano*, torpedoed, is down to 16 knots; cruisers *Chikuma* and *Chokai* are crippled; superstructures, charthouses and communication equipment in other ships are damaged by 5-inch shellfire and aircraft strafing. The Japs are shaken. Kurita, who has lost close tactical control of his command,[15] does not comprehend his closeness to victory; he thinks he has engaged some of the big, fast carriers of Third Fleet instead of merely the escort carriers of Seventh Fleet. Intercepted U.S. radio traffic convinces him—erroneously—that Leyte airstrips are operational.[q] He believes the rest of Halsey's powerful forces are nearby; he knows that Nishimura's southern pincer has been defeated in Surigao Strait; he has never received messages from Ozawa, far to the north, reporting the success of his decoy mission. So Kurita recalls his ships and assembles his scattered forces—and his chance has gone.

Admiral Sprague notes (in his after-action report) his thankful bewilderment: "The failure of the enemy . . . to completely wipe out all vessels of this Task Unit can be attributed to our successful smoke screen, our torpedo counterattack—and the definite partiality of Almighty God."

AFTERMATH

The rest was anticlimax.

Kurita's irresolution was reinforced by mounting American attacks. Only two hours from the soft-skinned amphibious shipping in Leyte Gulf—his original goal—Kurita wasted time assembling his scattered forces and aiding cripples, and his fleet milled around in much the same waters, steering varying courses. Cruiser *Suzuya* was fatally damaged by air attack, and at 1030, two to three hours' flying time to the eastward, Admiral "Slew" McCain's Task Group 38.1 (which had been sent to Ulithi for rest and replenishment, hastily recalled, and was steaming hard to the rescue) launched a heavy strike.* The bell had tolled for Kurita, and Japan's sun had passed the zenith. And far to the north, "Bull" Halsey, striking at Ozawa's decoy force, was at last alarmed by Kinkaid's frantic appeals for help, and particularly by the query from Nimitz. A major part of his fleet reversed course when within 40 miles of decisive surface action, and Halsey detached some of his fast battleships to steam southward at high speed, but too late to intervene.[16]

The rest of that day, the twenty-fifth, and all the next, the twenty-

---

* Admiral McCain, who had intercepted some of the battle messages, actually broke off replenishment prior to receipt of Halsey's orders and steamed hard toward the west. He launched the heaviest naval air attack "in the history of that time."

sixth, was mop-up and fierce stab, as the Japanese survivors fled and Jap land-based aircraft struck hard in angry futility. Japanese kamikaze planes, attacking after the crescendo of battle, hit the escort carriers, damaged three and broke the back of *St. Lô*, which had survived the 18.1-inch guns of *Yamato*. But Kurita, who reached so closely to the verge of fame, paid heavily for the luxury of indecision. Air attacks struck him again and again during the afternoon of the twenty-fifth. Three of his damaged cruisers, crippled and on fire, had to be sunk. *Tone*, one of his two remaining heavy cruisers, was hit aft and damaged, and during the night of the twenty-fifth, as Kurita took his battered survivors back through San Bernardino Strait, U.S. surface forces caught and sank destroyer *Nowaki*. At midnight of the twenty-fifth only one of Kurita's ships, a destroyer, was wholly undamaged.

On the twenty-sixth there was more slow dying as Halsey's and Kinkaid's fliers, augmented by some Army Air Force land-based bombers, chivvied and attacked the retreating Japs; and the 1st Diversion Attack Force, "which had already undergone more air attacks than any other force in naval history, once again braced itself for the final ordeal." Destroyer *Noshiro* was sunk; *Yamato*, with its gigantic but futile 18.1-inchers, was hit twice and its superstructure sieved with splinters; and other cripples of the battle off Samar and the Battle of Surigao Strait, including cruiser *Abukuma* and destroyer *Hayashimo*, were finished off. And there still remained the gantlet of U.S. submarines.

At 2130 (9:30 P.M.), October 28, "what remained of the Japanese Battle Fleet re-entered Brunei Bay."

The *Shō* plan—the great gamble—had failed completely. In the sprawling naval Battle for Leyte Gulf, Japan had lost 1 large and 3 light aircraft carriers, 3 battleships, including one of the 2 largest warships in the world, 2 heavy cruisers, 4 light cruisers and 12 destroyers; most of the rest of her engaged ships were damaged severely or lightly; hundreds of planes had been shot down, and between 7,475 and 10,000 Japanese seamen died. The Japanese Navy as a fighting fleet had ceased to exist; Leyte Gulf was a blow from which the enemy never recovered.

But for the United States it was, nevertheless, incomplete victory when we might have swept the boards. The penalty of divided command, of failure to "fix definite areas of responsibility," and unwarranted assumptions by both Kinkaid and Halsey[17r] led to the surprise of our jeep carriers and to the escape of Kurita with his battered survivors, including 4 battleships, and of Ozawa with 10 of his original 17 vessels.*

---

* It should be stressed that this critique, and what follows, was written with the benefit of hindsight, and that there is considerable disagreement in naval circles with

Admiral Halsey ran to the north, leaving behind a force (the Seventh Fleet) inadequate in strength and speed to insure Kurita's destruction, and then just at the time when he was about to destroy all of Ozawa's force, he turned about and ran to the south in answer to Kinkaid's urgent calls for help.[8] The Japanese "lure" worked, but the Shō plan, which depended fundamentally upon good communications, split-second coordination and bold leadership, foundered in complete and fatal failure.

To the United States the cost of overwhelming victory was 2,803 lives, several hundred aircraft, one light carrier, two escort carriers, and the "small boys" who had helped turn the tide of battle—destroyers *Johnston* and *Hoel* and destroyer escort *Samuel B. Roberts*—fought by "well-trained crews in an inspired manner in accordance with the highest traditions of the Navy."*

THE JUDGMENT

The Battle for Leyte Gulf will be, forever, a source of some controversy, comparable to, though in no way as bitter as, the Sampson-Schley controversy after the Spanish-American War or the Jellicoe-Beatty differences after Jutland.[18] Admiral Halsey and Admiral Kinkaid believed their judgments were justified; each felt the other could, and should, have covered San Bernardino Strait.†

Leyte Gulf is a case history of the importance of communications to victory. Grossly inadequate communications made the coordination essential to Japanese success impossible; Kurita, for instance, never received Ozawa's messages.[19] But in the U.S. forces too many messages— and some messages improperly phrased[20]—led to the assumptions which made possible Kurita's surprise of Sprague's jeep carriers.

---

some of these judgments. Rear Admiral E. M. Eller, USN (Ret.), Director of Naval History, quite cogently asks:

"How do you know that united command would have swept the boards any better than divided command? Nearly every commander sees his own immediate problems in especially strong light and he will not take what he assumes to be risks by removing forces for distant operations. Had MacArthur and Kinkaid controlled the whole fleet, they might possibly have concentrated at Leyte Gulf, hence we might not have struck the northern force."

Many of the facts here presented were not known to the commanders at the time, and in any case there always have been, and always will be, human errors in war.

* Both combatants suffered additional ship, plane and personnel losses before and after the naval battle, incident to the landings on, and conquest of, Leyte Island and, later, other Philippine islands. *The History of the Medical Department of the United States Navy in World War II—The Statistics of Diseases and Injuries,* prepared by the Division of Medical Statistics of the Bureau of Medicine and Surgery of the Navy Department (Navmed P-1318, Vol. 3, Washington, U.S. Government Printing Office, 1950) gives total Navy and Marine casualties in the "Return to the Philippines" as 11,201, of which 4,158 were killed in action.

On October 24, while Third Fleet was launching its air attacks against Kurita, who was then in the Sibuyan Sea, Halsey sent out "a preparatory dispatch"[u] to his principal Third Fleet commanders designating four of his six fast battleships, with supporting units, as Task Force 34.[8] This task group was to be detached from the main fleet and used as a surface battle line against the Japanese surface ships if developments warranted. Halsey did not actually form this task force; he merely informed his own commanders that this was a "battle plan" to be executed when directed. However, Kinkaid, Nimitz and Vice Admiral Marc A. Mitscher intercepted this message, though it was not directed to any of them, and later in the battle—and partly because of subsequent messages—all misconstrued it.

When Halsey made his decision late in the evening of the twenty-fourth to steam north with all his available fleet and attack Ozawa, he informed Kinkaid that he was "proceeding north with three groups." Kinkaid, having intercepted the earlier message about Task Force 34, thought Halsey was taking his three carrier groups to the north and leaving four of his six fast battleships to guard San Bernardino Strait. But Kinkaid, busy with preparations for the night action of Surigao Strait, did not specifically ask Halsey whether or not Task Force 34 was guarding San Bernardino Strait until 0412, October 25, and he did not get a negative reply from Halsey until just about the time Kurita burst out of the morning mists upon the surprised Sprague.

If Kinkaid had tried to clarify the situation earlier, if he had *not* intercepted the Task Force 34 message, or if Halsey had reported to him that he was "proceeding north with all my available forces" instead of "proceeding north with three groups," the surprise would not have occurred.[v]

There was one other factor that contributed to surprise. Kinkaid *did* send one or two aircraft to scout southward of San Bernardino Strait along the coast of Samar on the night of the twenty-fourth–twenty-fifth and the morning of the twenty-fifth. There was no report from the night search plane, a lumbering PBY "Black Cat," and the dawn search did not start until about the time Kurita's top hamper appeared over the horizon.[21] Halsey's fleet also sent out night "snoopers," and one report was received by Third Fleet on the night of the twenty-fourth indicating Kurita had turned east again toward San Bernardino.

The fact remains, however, that there had been no clear understanding, prior to the event, between Seventh and Third Fleets about San Bernardino Strait; the "coordination" required by Admiral Halsey's orders was defective, and he himself has written (in the *U.S. Naval Institute Proceedings*[22]) that Leyte Gulf "illustrates the necessity for a single naval command in a combat area, responsible for, and in full control of, all combat units involved."[w]

"Division of operational control in a combat area leads at the least to confusion, lack of coordination, and overloaded communications (a fault which was pronounced during the battle on the American side), and could result in disaster."

In Third Fleet's after-action report of January 25, 1945, Admiral Halsey's reasoning which led him to take all his available forces to the north in answer to Ozawa's "lure" is phrased as follows:

Admiral Kinkaid appeared to have every advantage of position and power with which to cope with the Southern (Japanese) Force. The Center Force might plod on through San Bernardino Strait toward Leyte, but good damage assessment reports, carefully evaluated, convinced Commander Third Fleet, that even if Center Force did sortie from San Bernardino Strait, its fighting efficiency had been too greatly impaired to be able to win a decision against the Leyte forces [Seventh Fleet]. The Northern Force [Ozawa] was powerful, dangerous, undamaged, and as yet unhampered. Commander Third Fleet decided to (a) strike the Northern Force suddenly and in full force; (b) keep all his forces concentrated; and (c) trust to his judgment as to the fatally weakened condition of the Center Force—judgment which happily was vindicated by the Japs' inability to deal with the CVE's and small fry which stood toe-to-toe with them and stopped them in their tracks.[23]

Admiral Kinkaid's position, as stated in *Battle Report*, obviously does not agree with these conclusions:

"One must keep in mind the *missions* of the forces," Admiral Kinkaid is quoted.

The key to the Battle for Leyte Gulf lies in the missions of the two fleets.

The mission must be clearly understood. The mission of the Seventh Fleet was to land and support the invasion force. My title was Commander of the Central Philippines Attack Force. Our job was to land troops and keep them ashore. The ships were armed accordingly with a very low percentage of armor-piercing projectiles.[x] The CVE's carried anti-personnel bombs instead of torpedoes and heavy bombs. We were not prepared to fight a naval action. . . .

The only thing I can think of that I would have done differently if I had known Kurita was definitely coming through San Bernardino unopposed is that I would have moved the northern CVE group more to the south and I would have had a striking group from the escort carriers up looking for him at dawn.

What mistakes were made during the battle were *not* due to lack of plans. Any errors made were errors of judgment, not errors of organization. The two areas coming together—the Central Pacific and the Southwest Pacific—posed a difficult problem of command, but one head would not have altered things.[24y]

In retrospect, it seems clear that : (1) San Bernardino Strait should have been carefully patrolled by either the Seventh Fleet, by Halsey's forces or by both; (2) that Halsey was "lured" to the north and left the strait open to Kurita; (3) that Kurita's timidity and ineffectiveness and the brave delaying actions of the escort carriers and destroyers prevented the Japanese Central Force from reaching Leyte Gulf; (4) that delay rather than disaster would have resulted had Kurita succeeded in bombarding the Leyte beachhead and the shipping in Leyte Gulf. Admiral Halsey is dead, and judgments are easily made from the vantage point of hindsight and with the aid of information not available then. But it seems likely that three major considerations led to his decision to take his entire fleet to the north when he learned that Ozawa's carriers had been sighted.

Concentration of force is an ancient principle of war; every commander has been taught from youth that it is dangerous to divide one's force in the face of the enemy. Halsey must have known that at this stage of the Pacific War the United States Third Fleet alone (even without Kinkaid's forces) had an overwhelming superiority to the Japanese Center and Northern Forces and could easily afford to divide its power to meet dispersed Japanese threats. But principles, once taught, are hard to violate.

Second, Halsey was an air admiral and one of the most successful of World War II. He, more emphatically than most, believed that the Japanese carriers were the proper objective of his fleet, the most feared and dangerous ships. He knew Kurita's Central Force had no carriers; judging from his own words he did not realize that Ozawa's carriers had so few planes.

Third, Halsey's orders—which he probably had a hand in formulating—stressed the destruction of a major portion of the Japanese Fleet as his primary task, if such opportunity offered. This phrase, as Morison points out, contrasts with orders for other major amphibious invasions in the Pacific. Much the same situation as the one that confronted Halsey had occurred during the invasion of the Marianas Islands when Admiral Raymond A. Spruance was attacked by strikes launched from Japanese aircraft carriers. The Japanese planes were then overwhelmingly defeated in what came to be known as the "Marianas Turkey Shoot," but Spruance, who interpreted his primary mission as coverage of the amphibious invasion, resisted the temptation to pull his fleet away from the islands in pursuit of the Japanese Fleet.

Halsey, of different temperament and, unlike Spruance, an air admiral, could not resist the opportunity, particularly when his orders required it. Halsey was aggressive, with a touch of the Nelsonian tradition and with a great flair for leadership; his South Pacific campaign was touched with greatness. But Halsey did not possess the calculating coolness and thoroughness of Spruance. Spruance, on the other hand, did not have the dynamic, colorful leadership qualities of Halsey and was not as well known to either the Navy or the public. But, judged by performances, he was a great fighting admiral. As Admiral Robert B.

Carney has written, "Each was a remarkable man in his own way and style."

If Kurita had reached Leyte Gulf, it is highly unlikely, in view of the earlier Surigao Strait defeat, that he could have achieved decisive success. Most of the amphibious shipping had been unloaded. He would have faced six U.S. battleships, each with 13 to 24 rounds of armor-piercing ammunition per gun, and, without much supporting air power of his own, he would have been harried continuously by U.S. planes. Naval losses on both sides would probably have been heavier; Kurita, for instance, would have found San Bernardino Strait guarded by Halsey's detached battleships had he delayed his turnabout another two hours. But he could not have wiped out the beachhead or cut its sea-borne umbilical supply cord. As Halsey pointed out in his notes to this chapter, Japanese raiding forces—some of them virtually unopposed—repeatedly bombarded the U.S. beachhead in Guadalcanal and occasionally our supply shipping, yet we hung on there, despite the then Japanese naval, and at times air, superiority. There was very little chance, so great were the odds against them at the time of Leyte Gulf, that the Japanese Shō plan could have been successful. After the Surigao Strait defeat, the best Kurita could hope for was to sink many American ships and to delay the conquest of Leyte; he could not prevent it.

Despite errors of omission and commission and initially exaggerated reports of damage by our fliers, Leyte Gulf was indubitably a major American victory. But the Japanese, who had a gambling chance, never of all-out victory but at the best of causing the United States sufficient losses to extend the war, contributed to their own decisive defeat—by their communications failure,[z] their lack of air cover, the uncoordinated nature of their air and surface operations, amazing deficiencies in timing, poor judgment and the irresolution or blundering ineptitude of three of their four principal commanders. Only Admiral Ozawa, the "bait," really carried out his mission.

The Japanese tried to carry out one of the most complicated plans in the history of naval warfare, a plan requiring for success perfect timing, excellent communications and sacrificial courage. The plan was far too complex but was boldly conceived, deplorably executed.

Luck, as well as judgment, obviously played a major part in the battle. But luck lay, in the final analysis, with the larger fleet and the more skilled commanders. The Japanese took their "eye off the ball," abandoned their fundamental objective—the thin-skinned amphibious shipping in Leyte Gulf—in the midst of battle, and thereby violated a cardinal military principle.

And the Americans—Third and Seventh Fleets—as Admiral Halsey radioed to Hawaii and Washington, broke "the back" of the Japanese Fleet "in the course of protecting our Leyte landings."

Leyte was a magnificent valedictory for the battleship—probably the world's last naval battle in which the big-gunned ship was to play a major role.

It sealed the doom of Japan and opened the final chapter of the war in the Pacific.

CHAPTER 10

THE BATTLE OF THE BULGE—

A CASE HISTORY IN INTELLIGENCE

December, 1944–January, 1945

SUPREME HEADQUARTERS, ALLIED EXPEDITIONARY FORCE, DEC. 17, 1944—COM-
MUNIQUÉ 253:

ALLIED FORCES YESTERDAY REPULSED A NUMBER OF LOCAL COUNTER-
ATTACKS. . . .

Thus the Battle of the Bulge opened for the American public—quietly, inconspicuously, distorted by censorship and obscured by security. But the "local counterattacks" were in reality a major breakthrough, and in the dripping Ardennes Forest and along the narrow, muddy roads of Belgium, American troops were in precipitate retreat and amazed confusion.

From Monschau to Luxembourg, where the lovely hills of the Schnee Eifel lift against the weeping sky, the staggering colossus had gathered his strength in final effort and on 70 miles of front the armies were grappling. Here was no "ordered confusion of battle," here no planned retirement, here no thrust and riposte of textbook tactics—but here the bludgeon of desperate effort and the dazed reaction of broken units. . . .

Between Eupen and Malmédy, a First Army patrol was stopping officers and men at gunpoint and asking such curious questions as:

"Who is Mickey Mouse's gal friend?"

"Who are 'Dem Bums'?"

The road to Saint-Vith was choked, verge to verge, with streaming men and vehicles, many of them wearing the shoulder patch of a new division—a rampant lion's head. They did not stop for shouted command or personal threat; they blocked the road and moved in endless columns westward, ever westward, out of the path of juggernaut, out of the way of Armageddon. . . . A screaming major, defying rank and custom and frightened colonels rushing to the rear, cursed and bullied them and used his tanks as battering rams to smash a way toward the front through the snarled traffic.

There were many such, men of stout heart and spirit, in all that area, but from Saint-Vith to Bastogne the roads were clogged with snaking columns of army vehicles, mixed without rhyme or reason in inextricable confusion. And the woods were creeping with smashed and shattered units, men with dazed faces and the gray look of exhaustion and of shock, men without rifles, without guns, broken men and broken units. Behind the retreating American Army, flowing back upon itself in disordered chaos around the hairpin curves and through the postcard towns, behind the broken units, came the Panzers and the guns of the Nazis, taking the old route of conquest, the old high road to victory, smashing through the Ardennes in final gigantic effort for Fuehrer and Fatherland. . . .

Thus began in death and retreat the Battle of the Schnee Eifel, variously called the Battle of the Ardennes or the Battle of the Bulge— that controversial campaign which saw American troops in defeat and panic and in splendid victory, that campaign which changed the face of war. The Battle of the Bulge was perhaps the greatest single battle in which American troops have ever fought, and in it "GI Joe" showed all the abject weaknesses of man and rose to unprecedented heights. It was a battle which cost the United States dearly in blood and time, but from defeat the pendulum swung to victory. . . .

The great Nazi attack in the Ardennes was a shattering surprise; Germany, it had been thought, was almost finished, and the Allied armies were gripped with an attack psychology; the enemy's offensive strength was discounted.

The thundering surge across France had broken, in blood and fire, against the borders of Germany some months before; now the waves of conquest no longer marched in rapid phalanx across the land. Allied hopes of victory in 1944 had faded, but the rising tide of Allied might was lapping slowly but inexorably through a rift here, a weak spot there, into the ramparts of the Reich.

Arnhem was a fresh memory, and Antwerp, crouched beneath the V-bombs, had become a great supply port.

From the snow-covered Vosges Mountains to the sea along a front about 500 miles long, three great army groups—almost seventy divisions—were hammering at the gateways to Germany. General Jacob L. Devers' Sixth Army Group (including some French troops) held the southeastern flank; General Omar N. Bradley's Twelfth Army Group (the Ninth, First and Third American Armies, the largest group of armies the United States had ever put in the field) fought from the Saar to the Roer; and "Monty's" Englishmen and Canadian Twenty-first Army Group, buttressed by American units, drove toward the Rhine in the north.

For the first time since the "phony war" of the winter of 1939–40, the war was on German soil in the West, and on the Eastern Front the Russian hordes were halfway across Poland, poised on the Vistula, reorganizing for another great offensive. *"Festung Germania"* was under direct assault, and in early December the Allies were perfecting plans for a great winter drive to the Rhine.

The U.S. First Army, Lieutenant General Courtney H. Hodges commanding, held about 120 miles of front from Aachen to Luxembourg with Lieutenant General George S. Patton's Third Army on its southern flank and Lieutenant General William H. Simpson's Ninth Army to the north. Three corps were in line under Hodges in December, 1944: the VII Corps in the north, pushing toward the Roer; the V in the center, driving toward the dams that controlled the level of the Roer; and the VIII in the south. The VIII Corps was spread thin—deliberately. Less than four divisions held about 85 miles of front in the quiet Ardennes sector. The bulk of U.S. strength had been concentrated to the north and south of the Ardennes to support the main efforts then planned, and the Ardennes sector, with its difficult terrain and limited road network, was considered a "quiet rest" area and was held by new outfits and by divisions blooded and weary from the slugging match of the "bloodiest battle" beneath the shattered pines in Hürtgen Forest. It was a weakly held front, "the nursery and the old folks' home of the American Command."[1] But the enemy couldn't attack; he was licked—all it would take was time.

The Germans were hurt, there could be no doubt of it; their casualties in November along the long front from Holland to Switzerland approximated the equivalent of four divisions. "Stomach" battalions, prison outfits, the aged and unfit, and the new Volksgrenadier divisions were manning the line. Some of the American propaganda was having effect; captured German documents depicted men under stress. In late November one German colonel in the 18th Volksgrenadier Division went into a ranting fury about the desertion and surrender of six of his men:

Traitors from our ranks have deserted to the enemy. . . . These bastards have given away important military secrets. . . . Deceitful Jewish mud slingers taunt you with their pamphlets and try to entice you into becoming bastards also. Let them spew their poison! We stand watch over Germany's frontier. Death and destruction to all enemies who tread on German soil. As for the contemptible traitors who have forgotten their honor, rest assured the division will see to it that they never see home and loved ones again. Their families will have to atone for their treason. The destiny of a people has never depended on traitors and bastards. The true German soldier was and is the best in the world. Unwavering behind him is the Fatherland.
And at the end is our Victory.
Long live Germany! *Heil* the Fuehrer![2]

There was a clear note of frenetic desperation, of a nation at bay, in such pronouncements. True, the enemy had rallied, recuperated and by herculean effort had held, a few short months before, in what the Germans called the "West Wall Miracle," and they were fighting tenaciously now, as German soldiers had nearly always fought.

But Christmas was near and the Allies were attacking. In the American First Army "the whole air was one of slightly angry bafflement" at continued German resistance, of weary frustration; few "seemed seriously to consider that the Germans had a Sunday punch left."

But war seldom goes according to plan, and to those of the Allied armies who had read Clausewitz, the warning was there:

When the disproportion of power is so great that no limitation of our own object can ensure us safety from a catastrophe, or where the probable duration of the danger is such that the greatest economy of forces can no longer bring us to our object, then the tension of forces will, or should, be concentrated in one desperate blow. . . . He who is hard pressed . . . will regard the greatest daring as the greatest wisdom—at most, perhaps, employing the assistance of subtle stratagem.

Clausewitz' advice to the despairing blended well with Hitler's Wagnerian concepts, and the first act of the Battle of the Bulge opened months before the great attack. Even before September, when the beaten armies of the Reich were streaming back across France, the German Supreme Command had decided to group all the newly activated Panzer and infantry divisions into a fresh assault army. This process was halted to "plug the gaps" in the West Wall, but the Sixth Panzer Army, new to war, slowly grew in strength and numbers during the fall.

At the end of October, an officer of the Operations Section, Supreme Command, appeared at the headquarters of the German Seventh Army and carefully inspected the terrain of the Schnee Eifel. The decision was made; the blow of "greatest daring" and "subtle stratagem" was to be launched from the western Rhineland province where the fir and birch and evergreen forests and the rugged hills of the Hohe Venn, the Schnee Eifel and the Ardennes stand like sentinels along the borders of Germany and Belgium.

And on November 6 the Chiefs of Staff of the Seventh Army, the Sixth Panzer Army and the Fifth Panzer Army were summoned to the headquarters of Army Group B (Field Marshal Walther Model commanding) and given a message in code, which read as follows:

The German war potential enables us by summoning all our powers of organization and by straining every nerve to form an offensive force by rehabilitating and completely reconstituting the twelve Panzer and Panzer Grenadier divisions at present employed on the West Front as well as some twenty Volksgrenadier divisions and two airborne divisions. With the aid of these forces, the last that Germany is able to collect, the Fuehrer intends to mount a decisive offensive. Since such an operation would offer no prospect of a decisive success on the vast Eastern Front, and since a similar operation on the Italian Front could not be of decisive strategic significance he has resolved to unleash his attack from the West Wall. The success of this operation will depend fundamentally upon the degree of surprise achieved; therefore the time and place for this offensive will be such as to completely deceive the enemy. Considering the situation, the time and the weather, the enemy will be least likely to expect such an attack shortly before Christmas, from the Eifel, and against a front only thinly held by him. The objective of the offensive will be Antwerp in order to rob the Allies . . . of this very important supply point and to drive a wedge between the British and American forces. After achieving the objective we will annihilate the British and American forces thus surrounded in the area of Aachen-Liege, north of Brussels. In the air the operation will be supported by several thousand of the best and most modern German fighters, which will secure, at least temporarily, supremacy in the air. The most important factor will be first—SURPRISE, and next—SPEED. . . .[3]

It was a great gamble and the Germans knew it. Here, in the Ardennes, was the route to the great conquests of 1940; southward lay the Sedan Gap and the road to Paris and the Channel ports; north and westward were the Meuse and its key bridges, the great supply dumps and communication centers at Liége, the city of Brussels and, on the misty coast, the port of Antwerp.[4] The forested, hilly terrain, which limited cross-country mobility, and weather—the mists and freezing rains and snow and cold of winter—should aid surprise. There were only three main north-south lateral road systems: Eupen–Malmédy–Saint-Vith–Arlon;   Liége–Aywaille–Houffalize;   and   Aywaille–Hotton–Marche–Jemelle. Interruption of those would handicap the Americans' lateral movement, while a series of good east-west roads should facilitate the Germans' lightning debouchment.

The preparations were masked by some of the greatest security measures known to the history of war. Until the last moment only a few high officers were briefed in the great secret, and each of these took several oaths to guard secrecy and to accept the death penalty for any breach of security. Any and all civilians of doubtful heritage were evacuated from the front line areas; troops of Alsatian or other doubtful lineage were weeded out of forward combat units. Armies and corps changed the code names for their headquarters (the Seventh German Army, prophetically, to "Winter Storm"); all troop movements into assembly areas were made at night to muffle noise; German motor movements were prohibited within five kilometers of the Ardennes front; most of the Nazi troops were not shifted into attack positions until the final hours, and an elaborate program of deception was readied. By mid-November the concentration of units was well under way, but the date first set for the offensive—the last of November—had to be postponed since the Fifth Panzer Army, which was to side-slip southward and turn over the Aachen sector to the Fifteenth Army, had been pinned down in heavy fighting at Aachen, and neither men nor equipment were ready.

By the end of November the whole area between the West Wall and the Rhine and the Moselle was jammed with Nazi troops—hiding in the pine forests, keeping off the roads, pinpointing the artillery positions of the Americans in the Ardennes, ready for the battle that was to win the war.

X-day or "O-Tag" was first set for December 12 but was postponed because the desired period of bad weather was not predicted. On December 11–12 the men who were to command Germany's final effort—army, corps and division commanders—were summoned to Ziegenberg, near Bad Nauheim, the HQ of "High Command, West," Field Marshal Karl Gerd von Rundstedt. But it was not von Rundstedt who was to harangue them, but the Fuehrer himself. He rambled and he ranted, but his was the cold fury of calculation, and he left with them the sense of final, maddened, desperate effort—Wagnerian effort.

As the commanders filed out, General Erich Brandenberger, gray-haired, slightly bald, pot-bellied and "with shell-rimmed eyeglasses which interrupted the roundness of his face," got a brief word with Colonel General Alfred Jodl, Chief of the Operations Section of the Ober-kommando der Wehrmacht. Brandenberger explained his fears about the success of the offensive unless his Seventh Army was given the supplies it had so long requested—engineer equipment, bridging material, more ammunition.

"Jodl promised further assistance as Army Group B had done," Brandenberger explained to U.S. intelligence officers after the war, "But actually on the day the attack began the catastrophic nature of Seventh Army's engineer situation had not been remedied one iota."

The German security measures were excellent, but there were not lacking some signs of the approaching storm.

The VIII Corps, Major General Troy Middleton commanding, held the long line of the Ardennes front. The Germans had used the Eifel-Ardennes area to "blood" and train new Volksgrenadier divisions. The Americans knew that the three enemy divisions normally opposite VIII Corps had been increased to six, and Middleton wanted more troops. General Omar Bradley, commanding the Twelfth Army Group, had discussed the possibility of a German offensive in the Ardennes with Middleton, with Brigadier General Edwin L. Sibert, Twelfth Army Group G-2, and with General Eisenhower, and all G-2's along the front had kept their eyes fixed on the newly organized German Sixth Panzer Army, the existence of which was known and the whereabouts of which were last reported near Cologne.

Photo-reconnaissance missions also picked up enemy activity of various kinds, some of it back of the VIII Corps front—including gun emplacements, troop concentrations, rail and road movements, and some aircraft concentrations.

Two divisions noted increased German vehicular activity behind the front.

But in early December planning was being completed for a great offensive by the Twelfth Army Group to the Rhine, and the Ardennes sector had been stripped of all possible troops to "beef up" our blows elsewhere. And the Ardennes was not the only weakly held area; more fear was felt about the possibility of a German drive through Alsace toward Metz than a German offensive in the Ardennes.

So Bradley and Eisenhower deliberately accepted the famous "calculated risk." But it was not rated as much of a risk; the American front, though frustrated and weary, was "offensive-minded"; the "mental approach from the lowliest man in the front line to the highest brass on the staffs was one of attack."

Those who saw vaguely the shape of things to come had little influence. For the intelligence estimates of different echelons of command were at sixes and sevens, and clashing personalities hampered coordinated staff work in the First Army and between First Army and Twelfth Army Group.

DECEMBER 16

The day which was to change the face of the war opened in somber drabness after intermittent "drizzling, bone-chilling rain combined with snow and mist."

The United States First Army with three corps in line—the VII in the north, the V in the center and the thinly spread VIII on the south flank—held about 120 miles of front. The 2nd and 99th Infantry Divisions of V Corps, the latter division still relatively green to war, held the southern flank nearest VIII Corps, and the 14th Cavalry Group, (Mechanized) under VIII Corps control plugged the gap between the two corps.

In the VIII Corps sector, where the front was kept by troops riddled by the holocaust of Hürtgen Forest and sick to death of war, or by green units yet to be blooded in battle, the night of December 15–16 passed quietly. On the northern flank of the VIII Corps front east of Saint-Vith, the 106th Division, which had landed at Le Havre on December 6 and had relieved the 2nd Division just five days before, was worried about its artillery; only one battery was in position with covered routes of withdrawal—a cardinal artillery principle. But the division was green to combat; it had taken over positions held for two months by the veteran 2nd; some of its equipment was still mired in the mud between the front and Le Havre. It was getting "everything in good shape for the expected advance," and it had not "gotten around" to shifting positions. There were few, if any, mines or roadblocks and little wire.

To the south, the 28th Division, used up and battered from Hürtgen Forest, was "resting" in a "quiet sector," its three regiments stretched thin for 27 miles in front of Bastogne. The 9th Armored Division, relatively new to war, had a combat team in the line north of Echternach, and on the extreme southern flank of the VIII Corps front, where the Third Army flank joined the First Army near Luxembourg, the 4th Division, which had suffered 4,053 combat casualties[5] in the pine woods of Hürtgen, was licking its wounds, trying to absorb replacements and to forget the hell of dreadful memories in which its survivors lived. The "general attitude" on the VIII Corps front was "that of an uneasy armed truce—a 'Don't bother me, and I won't bother you' outlook." And the battle-weary troops were fiercely grateful for this brief respite.

At 0530 in the morning of December 16, "all hell broke loose." Heavy artillery concentrations fell in the rear areas of the 106th and 28th Divisions; V Corps reported heavy shelling and enemy "counterattacks"; and the battle had opened.

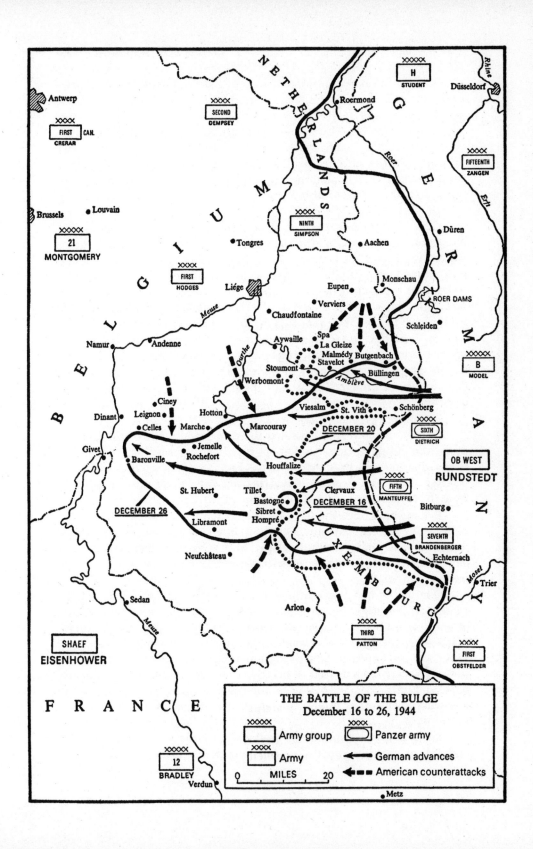

THE BATTLE OF THE BULGE
December 16 to 26, 1944

The alarm came over miles of wire to a sleepy-eyed G-2 watch officer in the Hotel Britannique at Spa, where the First Army headquarters was established in the spacious, ornate, rococo building in which Kaiser Wilhelm II and von Hindenburg had directed from Imperial German Headquarters the campaigns of 1918. Before 0800 scores of reports flooding over the wires from all sections of the VIII Corps and V Corps fronts showed "that something big was happening, and as the morning wore on, and as more reports came in, there was no doubt that this was it."

General Courtney Hodges, First Army commander—quiet, courteous, soft-spoken—put a line through to SHAEF at Versailles sometime on the Sixteenth and got General Omar Bradley on the telephone. Hodges told "Brad" the situation, said he had no reserves, and asked for assignment to his army of the 82nd and 101st Airborne Divisions. "Brad" said (thinking simultaneously in the same terms) that he agreed but would have to ask "Ike" about them, since they were in SHAEF reserve.

At Versailles, where General Bradley had arrived from his Luxembourg headquarters for a conference about replacements and to iron out details of the forthcoming American offensive, early reports of the German attack brought "Ike" and "Brad" and their staffs into a quick huddle.

Eisenhower's reaction was rapid.

As soon as the reports revealed the power and scope of the German drive, the Supreme Commander approved the transfer of the two airborne divisions to Bradley's control. Eisenhower also authorized the transfer of the 10th Armored Division from Patton and the 7th Armored from the Ninth Army to the flanks of the salient.

But in the Schnee Eifel, where the snow blanketed the green sprigs of the pine forests, the thin American line was broken, and shattered units—some streaming in full retreat, and grim men standing to their guns—knew only that the German gray-green legions were roaring in full freshet to the west.

One of the first breakthroughs came on the northern flank of the 106th Division, where the mechanized 14th Cavalry Group held a section of the front. One squadron was relieving another when the Germans struck; the enemy quickly flooded through the lightly held line; the sector was in confusion, and the commanding officer of the 14th, acting without orders, commenced a hasty withdrawal. He was subsequently relieved, but the damage had been done; the northern flank of the 106th was wide open and a raging tide of men and machines flowed to the west.

Another major penetration was made southeast of Saint-Vith; by nightfall of the sixteenth two regimental combat teams, the 422nd and

423rd of the 106th Division, were almost encircled. Major General Alan W. Jones, the division commander, "thinking out loud," tried to decide whether to withdraw the regiments closer to Saint-Vith. His boy was a platoon commander in the 423rd, an island now in the rising tide of German aggression, but war has no place for fathers. The General's responsibility was to 15,000 other men of his division—and to the whole staggering, sprawling army. General Jones deferred withdrawal orders.

The entire front was shrouded in the fog of war; communications with forward units had been cut by the rapid German advances; division and regimental CP's were in turmoil; the whole great army was groping blindly. In the G-3 operations room of the 28th Division CP at Wiltz, Major General Norman D. Cota, the division commander, rushed in, talked briefly with the air officer, looked at the situation map and said, "Looks like those bastards are trying to come through at Wallendorf—trying to establish a bridgehead." Cota asked for a bombing mission, but the air officer said it was too late in the day to get planes off the ground and on a target. Cota stalked from the room agitated and disturbed.

At Clervaux that night, the CO of the rest center, "tired and worried," was already trying to form a provisional defense group composed of men on leave who had been cut off from their outfits. The Germans were coming fast and hard, and within a few hours the 110th Regiment's command post in the village was under direct assault. Belgian women were "crying, screaming, moaning. . . . The firing had grown . . . intense and the night sounded as though it would come apart."

The Nazis attacked with 3 armies—some 19 divisions, and at least 5 in reserve.

One corps of the Seventh Army on the south attacked toward Luxembourg to protect the southern flank; and in the north the hoarded and fanatical Sixth SS Panzer Army, Sepp Dietrich commanding, drove toward Malmédy, Spa, Verviers, Liége and Antwerp, while the Fifth Panzer Army smashed in the center toward Saint-Vith, Bastogne, Namur, Brussels and Antwerp.[6]

By nightfall of the Sixteenth of December the VIII Corps front was broken, a deep penetration had been made between V and VIII Corps, the 99th Division in V Corps was hard-pressed, and the 2nd Division was fighting off attacks on its flanks and rear.

The Germans had achieved completely the first of their requirements for victory: "surprise." The surprise was absolute, tactically and strategically. As the veteran of another war, General Peyton C. March, was to put it later, the enemy had moved a force equivalent to the population of Richmond, Virginia, a score of miles without our knowing it.

DECEMBER 17

The dawn broke on new perils: the Rhineland provinces, Belgium and the roads of France shook with the heaving struggle of tremendous battle; for miles on endless miles behind both fronts the armies stirred in frenzied movement. The broken surf of retreating men and vehicles was followed hard by the roaring wave of the German armies. Hitler was again upon the march, and from Monschau to Luxembourg the inhabitants of the little towns and hamlets watched with despairing, hopeless eyes the retreating Americans, hauled down the Star-Spangled Banners, and either wept and moaned or openly rejoiced.

But here and there, at Saint-Vith and other road junctions, the strong-flowing tide of retreat met American reserves rushing toward the front. The opposing streams of traffic—one piling pell-mell toward the east, the other driving resolutely toward the west—raised riffles of boiling confusion; traffic snarled and jammed and overflowed the road shoulders.

Overhead through rain patches and gray sky and mist the robots roared; the V-1's rode the skyways toward Verviers, Brussels, Liége and Antwerp. The unmistakable pulsation of their engines dominated the heavens; unseen above the overcast the Germans' "bad-weather air force" operated in stepped-up tempo against the flanks and rear of the army. The men below, behind them the sound of bursting shells and the staccato rapid bursts of the "burp guns," waited for the cut-offs and counted the sinking seconds; the end of sound in the sky above meant death for someone on the earth beneath.

Men fled but did not trust their neighbors. Several hundred German parachutists of *"Kampfgruppe* [Battle Group] *von der Heydte"* had landed in the night in the Eupen-Malmédy area, their mission to cut the Eupen-Malmédy road. Other scattered groups had dropped elsewhere; occasionally "burp guns" fired from thick woods far behind the shifting front, and GI's slumped dead at the wheels of jeeps.[7]

The sheer bruising power of the German drive, the identification of numerous enemy divisions, the parachute drop and captured Nazi orders destroyed all doubts; this was *it*—this battle was the pay-off.

Von Rundstedt proclaimed it. "We gamble everything now; we cannot fail," he told his men in an order of the day.

Field Marshal Model, Commander of Army Group B, verified it: "We will not disappoint the Fuehrer and the Fatherland, who created the sword of retribution. Forward in the spirit of Leuthen [the victory of Frederick the Great over the Austrians in Silesia in 1757]. . . ."

And Panzer General Hasso von Manteuffel, commanding the Fifth Panzer Army: "We will march day and night, if necessary, fight all the time. . . . 'On toward the enemy and go through him.' "

The answer was the greatest and most rapid concentration in the U.S. history of war. The 82nd and 101st Airborne Divisions were released from SHAEF reserve, and through all the ganglions and nerve cells of the huge machine the impulses started that were to set in motion the entire Western Front. American attacks halted all along the front from the flooded lowlands of Holland to the snow-covered mountains of the Vosges. Patton prepared to face about toward the north; divisions side-slipped and moved to new locations; combat engineers built roadblocks and laid belts of antipersonnel and antitank mines. Troops in France and England started to move from strategic reserve toward the battle front, and in England the "repple-depples" (replacement depots) were alerted for quick action, and the 17th Airborne and 11th Armored Divisions were ordered to France. Even some of the service troops of the Communications Zone, who (the "doughfeet" used to say) had never heard a shot fired in anger, were ordered to the principal crossings of the Meuse to protect the bridges against sabotage and the fast-coming enemy.

The front was formless and so was the rear.

General Bradley left SHAEF early on the seventeenth for "Eagle Tac"—the Twelfth Army Group advance headquarters in Luxembourg. He left behind him at Versailles the wreckage of the winter's plans, but neither desperation nor fear. War was a chessboard; "Ike" and "Brad" hoped that here was an opportunity to turn enemy daring into enemy defeat.

But to the men who fought from foxholes or who plodded through the trampled snow in sullen retreat these things were not known; for them there was still the nightmare of confusion.

Near Büllingen enemy tanks and parachutists had driven deep into the 99th Division area; Butgenbach was under shellfire and a large ammunition dump nearby was in danger of capture. At Wirtzfeld the 2nd Division had to shift abruptly from attack to defense; staff sections in the division CP, which were almost surrounded, burnt their documents, as clerks and headquarters personnel formed a perimeter defense. The antiaircraft gun positions in this northern area, which formed part of the belt of AA defenses against the V-1's, were overrun by the enemy. Some guns and equipment were abandoned by their crews; some braver men depressed the gun barrels and used them as antitank and antipersonnel weapons; and still other batteries retreated with a vast miscellany of other units.

"The jam of men and vehicles around Hünningen-Büllingen . . . added to the confusion . . . and hampered . . . speedy counter measures."

The 99th Division, relatively new to war, was "rapidly forced back in confusion," but rallied, and the veteran 2nd Division, outnumbered, beleaguered, its units inextricably mixed with those of the 99th, "fought one of the brilliant divisional actions of the war" and doggedly retreated or stood and died.[8]

Near Malmédy, *Kampfgruppe Peiper*, an element of the 1st SS Panzer Division overran a convoy of some 200 men of Battery "B" of the 285th Field Artillery Observation Battalion. The Americans—First Lieutenant Virgil P. Lary, Jr., among them—were herded into a field near the road, their pockets looted and their weapons taken from them. The sky was murky and overcast; above the prisoners the buzz bombs roared on their way to Liége.

Lary and a handful of other wounded survivors later recalled that a German private in a "command car stood up and fired two shots into" the group of unarmed American prisoners. "Machine guns opened fire at point-blank range, first killing those who did not fall to the ground quickly enough, then began raking back and forth over the prostrate forms. . . . Gradually the groans and moans ceased."

But the Germans were thorough. Several Nazi noncoms, members of a panel platoon of an engineer battalion attached to the 1st SS Panzer Division, walked about among the bodies, "shooting in the head those who still showed signs of life. When doubtful they kicked a man in the face to see if he winced."[9]

The "Supermen" were on the march, and they could not be bothered with prisoners. . . .

The enemy advance caught up supply installations, hospitals and all the assorted paraphernalia of the army in the vortex of the retreat and muddled them with the shattered remnants of combat units. The hospitals were full; the doctors worked endlessly over bloody wounded. Long lines of stretcher cases waited their turns.

The battle reached crisis near Saint-Vith. Here was the 106th Division CP, here the focus, the traffic choke point for all the men and vehicles pulling back from what had been the front. To the north the 14th Cavalry Group, withdrawing by orders of its commander, was almost nonoperational, its units shattered and dispersed, but by precipitate retreat not by the enemy. Eighty-seven of the group's 99 officers and warrant officers "were not battle casualties at any time."

Seven or eight miles to the east of Saint-Vith, the 422nd and 423rd combat teams of the 106th Division—two-thirds of the division's fighting strength, 8,000 to 9,000 Americans—were outflanked and virtually surrounded near Schönberg; radio communication with them was intermittent. To the south, part of the 9th Armored Division was counterattacking the advancing enemy; still further south, the 424th Regiment of the 106th was fighting its way to the rear; still further south, the situation was "hazy." The flanks of nearly all these units were "open." The front was what generals and commentators often called "fluid"; rumors of "Tiger tanks were prevalent; there was an air of impending disaster."

"CC-B" (Combat Command "B") of the 7th Armored Division, Brigadier General Bruce C. Clarke commanding, was driving hard toward Saint-Vith from the north and west—to plug the breach, to hold the town, to counterattack toward Schönberg and relieve the beleaguered and cut-off regiments of the 106th. The command was pushing hard; time meant lives; if the surrounded regiments were to be saved, the counter-attack would have to be mounted no later than the afternoon of the seventeenth.

But the roads were clogged with the retreat. The road from Viesalm to Saint-Vith was double-banked with traffic.

Here would come an empty 2½ [ton truck], then another 2½ but this time with two or three men in it (most of them bare-headed and in various stages of undress) in the rear, next perhaps an engineer crane truck or an armored car, then several artillery prime mover tractors—perhaps one of them towing a gun, command cars with officers (up to and including several full Colonels) in them, quarter-tons—anything which would get the driver and the few others he might have with him away from the front. It wasn't orderly; it wasn't military; it wasn't a pretty sight—we were seeing American soldiers running away.[10]

The tanks and half-tracks of "CC-B" moving toward Saint-Vith were caught in the jam, slowed and finally stalled.

A major, fighting mad, used his 30-ton tanks to clear a way for the advancing reserves, but it was almost a futile gesture: "The fear-crazed occupants of the vehicles fleeing to the rear had lost all reason." The major ordered a company commander to "force his way on the road even if he had to wreck or run over fleeing vehicles and their drivers, and to pay no attention to the rank of anyone who might be fleeing and attempt to prevent him."[11]

But one company moved only three miles in two and a half hours. The jammed roads doomed the two isolated regiments of the 106th.

There was one of the biggest tragedies of St. Vith; that American soldiers fled, and by fleeing they crowded the roads over which reenforcements were coming and prevented those reenforcements from arriving in time to launch a counter-attack to save the 422nd and 423rd Infantry Regiments.[12]

But it was not all disaster; in many areas brave men stood to their posts and died. Outside Saint-Vith a first sergeant from an artillery outfit retreating to the west saw the advancing tanks of "CC-B," jumped out of his jeep, climbed on the turret of a tank and yelled, "I'm going with those damned tanks. They know how to fight, and goddam it, I joined the Army to fight—not to run!"[13]

And there were others—many, many others—who joined the Army "to fight and not to run." A small group of fighting engineers, men of the 291st Engineer Combat Battalion, held tenaciously to their roadblocks near Malmédy. The 2nd Division, aided by reinforcements, tightened its hold on the shoulder of the penetration. The German parachutists who had dropped between Eupen and Malmédy were scattered over a wide area by high winds, lost most of their equipment in the brush, failed conspicuously to hold the vital road, and were quickly killed or captured. Clear weather along portions of the front aided our artillery OP's and our air force.

More important, the Germans were already behind schedule;[14] they had achieved one element—*surprise*—in their formula for success, but the second vital factor was *speed*. Delays here and there, the delays imposed by men of will and courage, could throw awry the entire Nazi plan.

And there were delays—at Monschau, at Malmédy, at Butgenbach, at Saint-Vith. Even the parachutists had vainly expected elements of the II SS Panzer Corps to break through to a junction with them by 1700 (5 P.M.) of the seventeenth. And the Seventh German Army in the south, which was to exploit and hold the southern shoulder of the salient, was already reporting spotty but considerable American resistance at various strong points (especially in the 4th Division sector, whose troops made a "formidable impression" on the enemy) and delays due to inadequate bridging equipment—"Valuable time, the precious moment of surprise, had been lost."

And by midnight of this day 60,000 men, 11,000 vehicles, of the Third Army were moving to support the U.S. First Army.

DECEMBER 18

An American jeep, operated by English-speaking Germans, was captured well behind the front of an alert First Army unit. This coup, plus captured German documents, revealed the full extent of "Operation Greif" ("Grab") a part of the German offensive, which involved the use of English-speaking German soldiers, dressed in American uniforms with American insignia and forged credentials.

A special enemy task force, using captured American vehicles, weapons and insignia, was organized as the 150th Panzer Brigade, which was to operate when breakthrough was made as the spearhead of the Sixth SS Panzer Army. The captured documents verified the earlier estimates of Colonel "Monk" Dickson (G-2, First Army) that these units were part of a novel and audacious attempt to add to the surprise and speed of the enemy assault.

But the stout American defense from Monschau to Malmédy and at Saint-Vith averted breakthrough in this vital northern sector, and the G-4 and Quartermaster of First Army, working frantically, performed a miracle of supply—moving truck heads, dumps and depots west of the Meuse. QM companies sometimes pulled out with the last loads only a few hundred yards ahead of the advancing German Panzers, and some depots were overrun.

"*Einheit Stielau*," a part of 150th Panzer Brigade, operated 30 to 50 American jeeps behind U.S. lines, cutting wires, spreading rumors, misdirecting American traffic, reconnoitering for the Panzer spearheads. One or two of these patrols reached the Meuse and pushed into the outskirts of Liége. The credentials of "*Einheit Stielau*" were impeccable, the insignia and uniforms perfect. Unorthodox defenses against unorthodox attack were improvised. Some jittery MP's at gas dumps and truck heads took action first and asked questions afterward; a phosphorus bomb in the gas tank of a suspected vehicle was a sure deterrent to further mobility. But most kept their heads and improvised passwords, demanding the name of last summer's world's champions or the capital of Rhode Island.

The contagion of fear and the exhilaration of danger, which all men feel in moments of supreme stress, spread to Paris and commenced to sweep across the world. Otto Skorzeny, "spy, saboteur, assassin," the notorious abductor of Mussolini and Horthy, had planned—and now commanded—Operation Greif. His saber-scarred likeness was soon placarded in a hundred Belgian towns and villages, and in Paris, where rumors of an enemy plot to assassinate Eisenhower were circulating, MP's were reinforced and trigger-conscious. . . .

At Supreme Headquarters in Versailles a French delegation, infected with the virus of fear, expressed puzzled wonderment that SHAEF was "not packing."

This day was a day of crisis; the Nazis drove hard.

But the mobilization continued, the British halted concentration for their Rhineland offensive, some divisions were switched west of the Meuse, a British corps was held south of Brussels. Eisenhower ordered Devers to extend the frontage held by his army group and to revert to the defensive. Patton took over command of VIII Corps troops south of the Bulge, prepared his army to wheel to the north. Corps and divisions were shifting to new areas, supply lines crossing supply lines. More than 11,000 vehicles of the Third Army roared endlessly toward Belgium; 57 tons of maps of the Ardennes sector were printed and distributed to 13 divisions. And like young Lochinvar out of the west, the van of the 82nd and 101st

Airborne Divisions, coming hard after forced night marches from their rest camps 100 miles away, reached, respectively, Werbomont and Bastogne.

In the south where Luxembourg shuddered to the sound of the guns, the city was saved by the 4th Division's firm stand and the 10th Armored's reinforcements; the southern "shoulder" was firm.

Along the northern shoulder of the Bulge, the 2nd and 99th Divisions fought off persistent enemy attacks; the 30th moved into blocking position in the Malmédy-Stavelot area; an assorted and conglomerate group of task forces filled in the gaps.

At Spa, the "palace guards" at First Army headquarters took to the field, as enemy Panzers roaring up the valley of the Amblève, battered at the First Army's door. Censors, clerks, MP's, cooks, bakers and headquarters personnel, armed with tommy guns, carbines, bazookas and grenades, marched out for a last-ditch stand. Some of them died, some were wounded, but by one of those lucky breaks which so often tip the scales of war, the air artillery officer of First Army, flying a cub liaison plane low over the congested roads, spotted a German armored column moving out of La Gleize. Above him, flying almost "on the deck" in the low overcast that cut visibility to a few hundred feet, roared a flight of P-47's. The major in his cub "put" the fighter-bombers on the target; the planes swooped down out of the low clouds. The Nazi column, hurt, confused, some vehicles burning wrecks, turned at the threshold of Spa and detoured toward Stoumont. But at Stoumont a tank battalion hastily equipped with a miscellany of vehicles hit them again. And the planes came out of the sky at Stoumont and Stavelot, and the winding roads in the valley of the Amblève were littered, as the dark came down upon the land, with the burned-out carcasses of Nazi trucks and tanks and with the twisted bodies of men violently slain.

It was a check, but a check was not enough. In the Amblève, at Spa and Saint-Vith and a score of towns, the night was broken with the roar of demolitions, and the skies were red with the furious flames of burning gasoline and the fireworks of exploding shells, as supply dumps were burned by retreating troops.

And at First Army headquarters the gloom was as perceptible as fog. In the morning of that day of crisis, most of the headquarters had moved—out of the path of the Panzers, out of the sweep of juggernaut— to Chaudfontaine on the Meuse, not far from Liége. The Belgians wept as the Americans retreated; the pictures of Roosevelt in the shop windows disappeared. This night, they held the death watch, those of First Army that remained, waiting for word from Chaudfontaine that the displacement was complete. General Hodges waited at Spa looking old and worn and serious, with Major General William B. Kean, his chief of staff, tired but hard and cool. The roar of the buzz bombs on the way to

Liége, the motors of German planes—low in the dark—fluttered the great blackout curtains across the windows of the Britannique, and the dull thump of the field guns, the sharper burst of machine-gun fire echoed from the fighting lines—on the threshold, now, of Spa.

In the G-2 office, where Colonel Dickson, back from leave in Paris, sat and waited, the field phone rang. It was (Lieutenant Colonel) "Bob" Evans, the G-2 of the "Fighting First" Division, reporting in from the positions near the "hot corner" at Butgenbach, which the division had occupied after a forced march.

"The general wants you to know that we are in place," Evans said cheerily, "that our artillery is right where we want it, that we are dug in, and that if you send us within the next four or five hours, so that we have them by early morning, fifty copies of the 1:50,000 sheet [map] of the area, we will start tomorrow morning to teach those SS bastards the lesson of their lives."

It was a small thing, this message, but it bucked up the HQ: the "Fighting First" was in position; the northern shoulder of the bulge was congealing. The hastily built dam, constructed of American bodies and American machines, was forcing the German tide away from the north and the northwest, away from vital Liége and Antwerp and into a canalized channel to the west. So Hodges and Kean and Dickson and the forward echelons of First Army HQ cut the telephone wires, went out into the dark night of the buzz bombs and the weeping Belgians and took the road of retreat to Chaudfontaine, their grim thoughts a little lightened. . . .

But it was sparse comfort.

The front was shapeless; checked here and there, the Nazi tide by-passed obstacles and roared on to the west.

In Bastogne Major General Troy Middleton, commanding the VIII Corps, was telling Brigadier General "Tony" McAuliffe, interim commander of the 101st Airborne, that "there has been a major penetration . . . certain of my units, especially the 106th and 28th Divisions, are broken."

. . . Broken men and broken units . . .

Around Saint-Vith the 7th Armored Division with elements of the 9th were dug in, but it was a hodgepodge outfit that faced the Germans. Some of the 7th's artillery was still tied up in the traffic jam near Viesalm; other elements were mixed in with many shattered outfits; in one small command a colonel had men from 14 different units. The hard fighting started, but there was no thought now of counterattack; the Yanks were holding vital Saint-Vith, commanding crossroads town, by their eyelashes. The strategy was expedient and primitive; it was plug a gap here and then plug one there, hold and die. For lesser men and lesser outfits no such strategy, built squarely on the will to fight, could have succeeded. But General Clarke of "CC-B" knew his men; they were tough "tankers" of a tough outfit and they and 100,000 other GI's were soon fired to fury by news of the Malmédy massacre.

But it was defense, not attack, and out there somewhere in the Schnee Eifel, two of the three regiments of the 106th Division, cut off, surrounded, were dying a slow death.

In the early morning of the eighteenth the two regiments—the 422nd and 423rd—received orders by radio from 106th Division HQ to attack "and destroy" enemy forces behind them at Schönberg and to retire westward along the Schönberg–Saint-Vith road. The order was brave, but tardy and unrealistic. On the sixteenth or even early on the seventeenth it might have been possible, but now it was too late. The 106th Division had been struck in the past two days by the 18th Volksgrenadier Division, the 62nd Volksgrenadier Division, and elements of the 116th Panzer Division and other units. The 106th now was scattered and shaken, and the encirclement of the 422nd and 423rd Regiments was virtually complete. They had been under heavy but intermittent artillery fire and ground attacks, but they had held their ground and even mounted local counterattacks; on the night of the seventeenth the 2nd Battalion of the 422nd had been faced to the north to meet a flank threat. The men were cold and wet and sleepless, short of ammunition and short of food, and the groaning wounded lay on the ground about them.

Transport planes had been poised for two days to bring them supplies by air, but the weather seemingly had prohibited. (Strange "alibi," though, to the men cut off, for over Schönberg and the beleaguered regiments the weather was moderately clear on the seventeenth, eighteenth and nineteenth and both German and American fighters were in the skies.[15])

The two doomed regiments started their cross-country march on the morning of the eighteenth, eluding the advancing Germans in the woods and broken terrain of the Eifel. But things went wrong from the start. The 106th Division CP, miles away and in intermittent communication with the isolated regiments only by radio, apparently attempted to retain remote control of the withdrawal. Moreover,

neither Cavender [Colonel Charles C. Cavender, commanding the 423rd Regiment] nor Descheneaux [Colonel George L. Descheneaux, Jr., commanding the 422nd Regiment] was given command in the field.

Cavender was reluctant to take command without an order and Descheneaux was apparently unwilling to submit to Cavender's authority voluntarily with the result that the march on the morning of the 18th was not coordinated. Both commanders had only sketchy knowledge of the other's plans, and liaison between the two columns went from inadequate to nonexistent as the day progressed.[16]

Some of the regimental units became intermingled and strayed off from the main body, and the bivouac, made at dark that night in the woods, was confused and confined to too small an area. And the 423rd already had run into heavy opposition, and its 3rd Battalion, off on an unreconnoitered route, lost contact and communication with the regimental CP. The attack on Schönberg and the withdrawal to Saint-Vith was twice doomed before it started.

And the front moved west before the retiring men, for the Germans still were on the march; and still the hour of crisis cast a pall across the world.

DECEMBER 19 AND 20

The crisis continued; the impetus of the Nazi offensive was not spent.

On the nineteenth at "Eagle Main" (Twelfth Army Group HQ) at Verdun, there was a solemn meeting of the "Brass." "Ike" and "Brad" were there, and Air Chief Marshal Sir Arthur William Tedder, Deputy Supreme Commander, as well as Devers and Patton and their principal staff officers. Patton was the man of the moment, and he knew it. He and his staff arrived outside the HQ building in three jeeps; he made an impressive entry, saluted slowly, took off his coat with calm deliberation to show his resplendent uniform and sat down at one end of a long table. Others clustered about him, then gazed with consternation at the situation map. General Bradley asked a G-2 officer, "What the hell is this?"

He pointed to a red arrow marked "20 German tanks" pinned on the map at a point about 10 to 12 miles east of Namur, much further west than any previous reports of the Nazi penetration.

The G-2's didn't know the answer; for a time, as the report was traced, the tension in the conference room was terrific; then, as a G-2 officer removed the red arrow from the map and announced a mistake, General Bradley took a deep breath, turned to one of his officers, smiled quizzically and said simply, "Whew!"

General "Ike" looked at the glum men in front of him and opened the conference by declaring, "I want only cheerful faces."

Eisenhower then described his plan: Devers was to extend his front to the west to take over part of the Third Army's Saar frontage; Third Army was to wheel two corps to the north and drive into the south flank of the German salient; later the salient would be attacked from the north by First Army; elsewhere along the front the Allies were to assume the defensive.

"How long will it take you, George, to turn those divisions to the north and to attack?" Ike asked, indicating that the twenty-third would be a satisfactory date for the start of the counterblow.

Patton, who already had prepared some plans and moved many troops, preened himself with his answer: "I can do it by the twenty-second, Ike."

"That'll be perfect timing; I don't want any piecemeal attack, though. And, Brad, I want that right flank secure."

The Verdun meeting confirmed and expedited the most rapid shift in major plans, and consequently in troop movements, in the American experience of war. These few words set in motion a million men, moved mountains of supplies, performed prodigies of logistics. . . .

And that night, back at SHAEF, General Eisenhower telephoned 21st Army Group HQ in Belgium. He got Field Marshal Montgomery out of bed and said, "Monty, I want you to take command of everything up there."

"You want me to take command of everything here?"

"Yes, everything north of Givet."

"Very well, very well; I'll hop to it."

Eisenhower told Montgomery of the plans for the Third Army attack and said the shift in command would be effective, and confirmed in writing, the next day.

Later, "Ike" called Bradley and told him of his decision to put all the First Army north of the German penetration and the Ninth (American) Army under Montgomery. Bradley did not like it, but Eisenhower pointed out that Bradley's Twelfth Army Group tactical headquarters were not in a central location but were in Luxembourg, near one shoulder of the German bulge; that Bradley had decided for good political and psychological reasons not to retire them to the west but to retain them there; that telephone communications between Luxembourg and First Army HQ at Chaudfontaine in Belgium had been severed by the German penetration; and that physical communication between Luxembourg and the north was roundabout and difficult because of the German bulge. "Ike" assured "Brad" that this was a temporary and emergency measure, forced primarily by problems of communication.

Not until the next morning, the twentieth, did Prime Minister Churchill get Eisenhower on the phone from London to ask, "What's this all about—this change in command?"

The P.M. was worried and alarmed, not so much by what he knew of the situation but by the change in command, which he seemed to regard as an index of the seriousness of the battle. Eisenhower reassured him, and the conversation ended with Churchill endorsing the shift.

At 1 P.M. on the twentieth "Monty," wrapped in a bearskin and carrying his own lunchbox and thermos jug, appeared in his green Rolls Royce at First Army HQ at Chaudfontaine. The "great man" had already ordered the XXX British Corps west of the Meuse to hold a general line from Liége to Louvain, with patrols commanding the river crossings, and he had sent out the night before half a dozen of his young staff officers to gather for him the exact situation on the disorganized front. General Hodges had had luncheon prepared for "Monty," but he refused it and (as Iris Carpenter recalls in *No Woman's World*) he munched his sandwiches and drank his tea as the First Army staff stood around in discomfort. Then "Monty" pulled out a small-scale map of the area and, ignoring the well-marked large-scale American wall maps, plotted his moves.

"Monty's" first inclination was to "tidy up" the battlefield, and he suggested a withdrawal from the "hot spot" at Butgenbach and a retirement of the northern shoulder to straighten out the lines between Monschau and Malmédy. The faces of the First Army's staff turned grim, and Hodges politely demurred. Such a retirement would broaden the base of the German bulge and negate the sacrifices of the 1st, 2nd and 99th Divisions which had held this area. Moreover, there was only one road through the swamps north toward Eupen, and a retirement under such conditions might be disastrous. "Monty" did not press the point that day, but he returned to it later, even suggesting (but again futilely) that the V Corps front ought to be swung back as far as Verviers.

The American Ninth Army to the north was ordered to extend its flank to take over some of the First Army's front, as Devers had done with the Third Army in the south, and "Fighting Joe" Collins' VII Corps was freed for a possible counteroffensive, toward the tip of the bulge.

The 101st Airborne Division was dug in around Bastogne, and fighting well; the XVIII Airborne Corps, "Matt" Ridgway commanding, was moving in troops to block south of the Amblève River, and the 82nd Airborne was in action around Werbomont. Saint-Vith was held by the fighting fools of the 7th Armored Division, supported by a conglomeration of units, mixed together in a fashion rarely known to war.

The great mobilization was well under way, and the north and south shoulders of the salient were firmly anchored in the Monschau-Butgenbach area and at Echternach. The German drive had been canalized to the west—toward the Meuse but away from Liége and Antwerp.

But from Saint-Vith to Bastogne the front was still "fluid"; Saint-Vith lay at the bottom of a pocket, Bastogne was virtually surrounded, and the roads still were filled with weary, dazed stragglers, retreating from broken units.

And out there in the Eifel where the bodies lay stiffly in the woods, the two lost regiments of the 106th fought their last fight. An attempt on the nineteenth to drive the enemy out of Schönberg and to break through to U.S. lines via the Schönberg–Saint-Vith road had failed. The attack was uncoordinated; elements of the two regiments fired on each other. Some of the companies in the 422nd held out for a time outside Schönberg, but the riflemen were down to a few rounds apiece, most of the machine guns were silenced and there was no artillery support.

[We] could go neither forward nor backward.
The Krauts were closing in slowly and there was heavy machine gunning to our front and left—some shelling from our right. We had nothing but .30 caliber—no food, medicines, or blankets. The latter items were the worst because there was a steady stream of wounded from the gully to our west and without dressings or blankets there was nothing that we could do except let them lie there in their gore and shiver—with the most goddam pitiful look in their eyes. I put my coat over one—when it was all over I felt like a heel going back for it—but he didn't need it any more. The situation was hopeless.[17]

Colonel Descheneaux surrendered most of the 422nd on the nineteenth; the bulk of the 423rd was captured the same day; some held out until night of the following day, a few a day longer. But there in the Eifel two regiments were destroyed; many dead, some never to be found.[18] The Germans claimed thousands of prisoners and destruction of the 106th, and a German lieutenant near Saint-Vith noted exultantly in his diary:

Endless columns of prisoners pass; at first, about a hundred; half of them negroes, later another thousand. Our car gets stuck on the road. I get out and walk. Generalfeldmarshal Model himself directs traffic. (He's a little undistinguished looking man with a monocle.) Now the thing is going. The roads are littered with destroyed American vehicles, cars and tanks. Another column of prisoners passes. I count over a thousand men.

And Lieutenant Martin Opitz, 1st Company of 295 Volksgrenadier Regiment, noted:

All the advancing units are picking up American vehicles to become motorized. It is like a gigantic flood forward which gives proof of German power and German organization. Who would have expected a German attack like this one, right before Christmas? Everybody is enthusiastic, especially the *landsers* [the German "GI Joe"].[19]

DECEMBER 21

Day and night, night and day, the bitter battle continued.
Supply dumps were moved in endless convoys to the rear; the Meuse bridges were prepared for demolition; the VII Corps was pulled out of

the Roer River line and started moving toward the tip of the Bulge, with General Collins, corps commander, ordered to be prepared to "attack south, southeast, east or northeast."

The Nazis gradually were being fenced in, but the front still was "fluid" to the west, the drive still had momentum, German tanks were rambling toward the Meuse, and the enemy smashed furiously against the northern shoulder.

The 1st Division beat back heavy and sustained attacks near Butgen-bach by the 12th SS Panzer Division; the vital "shoulder" still was firm.

The 84th Division, a fine fighting outfit, first of the units that was to bottle up the neck of the Bulge, moved into a "vacuum" near the Ourthe River, with its flanks wide open, but ordered to hold the Marche-Hotton line—a 12-mile front with foxholes "150 yards apart"—at "all costs."

On the southern shoulder of the Bulge, the German Seventh Army had inflicted 2,000 casualties in the first five days, but the U.S. resistance had been in most cases dogged and determined. The Americans had defended the towns and denied the Germans use of the road network.

"Strength sufficient to achieve a quick, limited penetration the German divisions possessed, so long as assault forces did not stop to clean out the village centers of resistance," Cole comments. "Strength to exploit these points of penetration failed when the village centers of resistance were bypassed."[20]

Patton's attack was in gestation; the III Corps of Third Army, after a sharp wheel to the north, had already set up its CP near Arlon. The battered units of VIII Corps were now under Patton's command; six new supply points with 235,000 rations and 300,000 gallons of gasoline had been established near Longwy; the roads around the southern shoulder from Luxembourg to Arlon and for scores of miles back to the supply ports in France were crawling with thousands of vehicles. "Stonewall" Jackson's lightning movements and miracles of supply had been trans-lated now into the gasoline age.

"Old Blood-and-Guts" was supremely confident. "I'm gonna shove the Third Army up the First Army," he declared, and news of his impending assault cheered the tired defenders of Saint-Vith. One first sergeant said, "Hell, we've got it made if Georgie is coming!"[21]

But others jeered, "Yeah, *his* guts and *our* blood!"

General Hodges issued a confident letter of instructions to all the corps in the First Army, stating optimistically that

the enemy's attack had been blunted and slowed down. . . .

The enemy has paid a heavy price for the local gains he has made over the past few days, and he has been frustrated in the main direction of his attacks. . . . He has failed completely to capture any sizeable amount of supplies to sustain his drive. By his "all or nothing" gamble, he has presented us the opportunity of destroying him and ending the war in the shortest possible time.

But optimism sounded premature to the hard-pressed GI's along the front.

Saint-Vith and Bastogne were all but islands, ringed round by the rising enemy tide.

At Bastogne the last road to Neufchâteau had been cut by Nazi Panzers, and "Tony" McAuliffe and his men of the 101st Airborne, and a combat command of the 10th Armored Division, with a jumbled mixture of stragglers, were ready for their moment in history. On this day they received the order from VIII Corps to "hold the Bastogne line at all costs."

At Saint-Vith a narrow corridor to the rear was still propped open, held ajar by the bodies and the guts of more paratroopers—young "Jim" Gavin's 82nd Airborne. But the fighting was of unprecedented ferocity; at Cheneux on the gentle Amblève—its waters white with snow and red with blood—the paratroopers in hand-to-hand fighting leaped aboard the German half-tracks and knifed the Nazis at their posts.

It was not good at Saint-Vith. Here the 7th Armored, with elements of the 106th, the 9th Armored and other units, had stood, like a rock, since December 17, but supply routes had been interrupted, ammunition was dwindling, casualties mounted.

Troop "B," 87th Cavalry Reconnaissance Squadron, was cut off to the east of Saint-Vith in the night, as the Germans drove hard to take this vital crossroads town; First Sergeant L. H. Ladd brought back about 50 men from a troop that "entered the line on 17 December with six officers and 136 men."

This was the day for Saint-Vith:

This was von Rundstedt's "grand slam" play to seize St. Vith before which he had been stalled for more than four days; this was his "all out" assault to smash the forces which had prevented his Panzer spearheads (already at Stavelot and almost to the Salm River in the north, and well beyond Houffalize in the south) from linking up on a broad front.[22]

Von Rundstedt gave the 7th Armored "the works," and the 38th Armored Infantry Battalion took the brunt of it, hour after hour this day of Saint-Vith's crucifixion:

The Krauts kept boring in, no matter how fast we decimated their assault squads.

All machine guns were employing swinging traverse and taking a deadly toll. But again and again there was a flare of flame and smoke (the explosion could not be heard because of the general din), as some "Kraut" got in close enough to heave a grenade into a machine gun crew or to launch a dread Panzerfaust [German antitank rocket]. One caliber .50 squad which hitherto had been dishing out a deadly hail of fire all along the front, was hit by a Panzerfaust which struck the barrel halfway between the breech and the muzzle. The gunner fell forward on the gun with half his face torn off; the loader had his left arm torn off at the shoulder and was practically decapitated while the gun commander was tossed about fifteen feet away from the gun to lie there quite still.

The men were magnificent, their fire never ceased . . . [but] always there were more Germans, and more Germans, and then more Germans![23]

Tiger tanks broke through at last, and by midnight of the twenty-first the 38th Armored Infantry Battalion had found its Valhalla. "Of an estimated 670 men who had manned the line to the right of the Schönberg road in the morning, there were only approximately 185 men [left] at 2300 [11 P.M.]. The rest were dead or severely wounded."[24]

Saint-Vith was evacuated, but the thin American line reformed west of the town and Yank guns still commanded its crossroads; Hitler's legions still broke in blood and death against the bastion of American courage.

It was so in many sectors along the front. Out of the rubble and the rabble of defeat and disaster had somehow coalesced a rampart of fortitude.

Stragglers still moved to the rear, dazed and wandering, gray-faced and twitching, but here and there, in a dozen, a score, of places, men of many different units had formed themselves, spontaneously or under some paladin in khaki, into grim battle groups and task forces, which fought with whatever weapons came to hand.

The history of all these units will never be written; some of these leaders will remain forever unsung, for the canvas is too vast to detail each bloody encounter, and some there were, perhaps many, who, overwhelmed beneath the flood of Nazi might, fought unhonored, unreported and unknown until the end.

Of such stuff was born "Team Snafu," formed of 600 stragglers from the 9th Armored and the 28th Divisions, which fought at Bastogne.

And of such heroic clay was molded "Task Force Jones," and its smaller counterpart which it absorbed, "Team Stone."

Lieutenant Colonel Stone was "located at Gouvy with an assortment of about 250 stragglers, including ordnance, quartermaster, engineer, and signal personnel whom he had collected. He had established a defensive position and said, 'By God, the others may run, but I'm staying here and will hold at all costs!' "

"Task Force Jones" of the 7th Armored—so named for its commanding colonel—absorbed the dauntless Colonel Stone, and grew in a few days into an amazing and conglomerate assortment of units, which guarded with skill and success—not common in *ad hoc* forces—the southern flank of the 7th Armored.[25]

Of such men, stalwart in resolution, grim in humor—men who could hum, "This is the Army, Mr. Jones; no private rooms or telephones"—out of such men was molded in this and succeeding days the spirit of victory.

And it spread and permeated the Army. . . .

DECEMBER 22

The real struggle from this day on was to the west; the battle was a constant extension of the front toward the Meuse, as the enemy—held in his attempts to break out of the Bulge toward the northwest, toward Verviers, Spa, and Liége—tried to outflank the First Army to the west.

Von Rundstedt had hurled in these past few days the better part of four German divisions against the Monschau-Butgenbach area and the Elsenborn Ridge and had seen them recoil in bloody confusion, leaving behind to mark the high tide of their attacks the broken bodies of their dead. The German General shifted now from insensate assault upon the "shoulder" to stratagem and wile; he moved the II SS Panzer Corps, heretofore in reserve, to the west to "beef up" the German drive between the valleys of the Ourthe and the Amblève.

But Saint-Vith, far behind the flood tide of the German advance, was still under the fire of American guns; it stood like a rock against the swift-flowing German assault. The defending troops were forced back under the increased German pressure and formed a tighter perimeter defense, broken only by one secondary road for withdrawal to the west.

To their north German elements were trapped in a pocket at La Gleize; to the west the VII Corps was quickly assembling near Marche to counterattack and put the cork in the bottle.

And on this day a forlorn and bedraggled German hero of other years, hobbling on frostbitten feet, was captured south of Eupen, and Colonel von der Heydte, veteran of Crete, onetime holder of a Carnegie fellowship and commander of the Nazi parachutists dropped December 17, admitted the complete failure of his mission.

This day, the ground fog lifted somewhat, and our planes commenced to range the airways. Despite the new Nazi jets, the hunting was good over the crowded roads of the Eifel and the Ardennes.

On the ground the tanks used "grousers" and yet slithered and skidded on the icy roads. The GI's, lacking snow camouflage suits, reversed the usual order of things and donned their white underclothes last. Shoes and galoshes seeped up the snow; cases of trench foot mounted into the thousands; the American Army was ill-prepared for a winter war.

But on this day the air of victory spread; "Georgie" had mounted his attack from the south, and the III Corps stuck a knife into the belly of the German Bulge. And around the flanks of the German penetration artillery had been massed; concentrated fire smashed some of the Nazi attacks; the proximity fuse, new to land war, detonated the shells just above the foxholes of the enemy with uncanny accuracy; "Jerry" was confounded.[26]

And down at Bastogne a handful of men ordered to hold the town "at all costs" fought to the death.

It was on this day, at 1130, that four Germans carrying a white flag came into the outposts of the 326th Glider Infantry. A German captain said, "We are *parlementaires*."

The rumor quickly spread among the feckless, reckless paratroopers, cocky with their past successes, that the "Heinies had had enough and wanted to surrender"—to an entrapped and surrounded garrison!

But the reality was different; the Germans came to demand surrender from the Americans:

DEC. 22ND, 1944

TO THE U.S.A. COMMANDER OF THE ENCIRCLED TOWN OF BASTOGNE:

THE FORTUNE OF WAR IS CHANGING. THIS TIME, THE USA FORCE IN AND NEAR BASTOGNE HAVE BEEN ENCIRCLED BY STRONG GERMAN ARMORED UNITS. MORE GERMAN ARMORED UNITS HAVE CROSSED THE RIVER OURTHE NEAR OURTHEVILLE, HAVE TAKEN MARCHE, AND REACHED ST. HUBERT BY-PASSING THROUGH HOMPRÉ-SIBRET. TILLET-LIBRAMONT IS IN GERMAN HANDS.

THERE IS ONLY ONE POSSIBILITY OF SAVING THE ENCIRCLED U.S.A. TROOPS FROM TOTAL ANNIHILATION: THE HONORABLE SURRENDER OF THE ENCIRCLED TOWN. IN ORDER TO THINK IT OVER, A TERM OF TWO HOURS WILL BE GRANTED BEGINNING WITH THE PRESENTATION OF THIS NOTE. . . . THE ORDER FOR FIRING WILL BE GIVEN IMMEDIATELY AFTER THIS TWO HOURS' TERM.

ALL THE SERIOUS CIVILIAN LOSSES CAUSED BY THIS ARTILLERY FIRE WOULD NOT CORRESPOND WITH THE WELL-KNOWN AMERICAN HUMANITY.

THE GERMAN COMMANDER

The written German demand for capitulation was taken to General McAuliffe's CP in Bastogne. Told what the paper contained, "Tony" McAuliffe laughed in contemptuous unbelief and said, "Ah, nuts!"

That was the answer the Germans got: "Nuts."

The Nazi *parlementaires* did not understand.

An American officer translated. *"Quatsch!"* he said scornfully. "Go to hell!"

"And I will tell you something else," the American officer volunteered. "If you continue to attack, we will kill every goddamn German that tries to break into this city."

DECEMBER 23

This day it was bitter cold and deep snow mantled the bodies of the slain.

On the northern shoulder the German lines lay dormant; the bloody attempt to storm Elsenborn Ridge and clear a path to Liége had ceased, and the Fifth and Sixth Panzer Armies were driving toward the west.

Saint-Vith, "focal point of five main highways and three rail lines," still lay beneath Allied guns—but not for long. The gallant defense of the area already had delayed the Nazi schedule for many days; 21,000 men, decimated now and disorganized, had held 87,000 Germans at bay, first in the town and then on its western heights.[27] But the end was now; German tanks had broken through the perimeter defense. "Daisy chains" of high explosives placed beneath the treads of the tanks by men who braved certain death, grenades dropped down their turrets, bazookas fired at point-blank range had exacted high casualties from the enemy's Panzer forces but had not stopped them.

A message from Field Marshal Montgomery to Major General R. W. Hasbrouck, commanding the 7th Armored Division and its attached conglomeration of units, ordered withdrawal:

"You have accomplished your mission—a mission well done. It is time to withdraw."[28]

Time and high time; the decision was completely sound. The battered defenders of Saint-Vith, short of food and ammunition, mauled for six days of bloody fighting by elements of eight German divisions, were out on the end of a limb—at the bottom of a deep pocket east of the Salm River, with only one exit route.

But again they accomplished the impossible—probably the most difficult maneuver in military operations—a daylight withdrawal in the face of a hard-pressing and vastly superior enemy, a withdrawal restricted to one road.

Division headquarters was plastered with German 88's and the gunners of the 440th Field Artillery Battalion had to fight hand-to-hand for their guns, but ubiquitous "Task Force Jones" covered the withdrawal, and by midnight of this day the defenders of Saint-Vith were in safety.

The 7th Armored Division retreated in sullen glory, its laurels greater far for the blood it had shed and the stand it had made, and in its ears ringing a dramatic telegram of congratulations from the VIII British Corps *"Á bas les Boches; á bas les Boches!"*

At another key crossroads town miles to the south, the defenders of

Bastogne passed the crisis of defense. Low on ammunition, "Tony" McAuliffe had ordered his batteries not to fire "until you see the whites of their eyes," but it "was still a neat question whether relief would come before the ammunition ran out."

And it was this day that the 3rd Battalion of the 327th Glider Infantry—part of the 101st—hard beset by the enemy, made its final retreat. "This is our last withdrawal," the colonel said. "Live or die—this is it."

But the supplies arrived—by air through the long day; 144 tons were dropped by parachute to the hard-pressed defenders.

And far to the south Patton was on the march; that was the glad word that spread from Echternach to Monschau. The Belgian villagers, forlorn and frightened by retreat, took heart and brightened as the American tanks skidded and slithered over the icy roads toward the front.

"Pat-ton?" they asked in broken English. "T'ree Arm-ee?"

Third Army had performed a logistical miracle: six divisions had faced to the north and were roweling the German flank. From December 17 until this day, 133,178 motor vehicles, shuffling and shifting corps and divisions, facing a whole army about, had passed through Third Army traffic control points; the trucks had rumbled half a million miles, moved 20,000 tons of supplies.

And the weather was looking up; on parts of the front the twenty-third was fair and clear and our planes rose to harry the Germans. Nazi fighters also roved the skyways as they had done in the gray overcasts of the early days. But Patton, the lust of battle in his eyes, was not satisfied; he called in his chaplain and ordered him to distribute to all his Army the following prayer:

Almighty and most merciful Father, we humbly beseech Thee, of Thy great goodness, to restrain these immoderate rains with which we have had to contend. Grant us fair weather for Battle. Graciously hearken to us as soldiers who call upon Thee, that armed with Thy power, we may advance from victory to victory and crush the oppression and wickedness of our enemies and establish Thy justice among men and nations.

Amen.[29]

Back in Paris, all Allied officers and men were ordered off the streets by 2000 (8 P.M.). Skorzeny's saboteurs were still at large; the MP's kept their guns ready; these Germans were in American uniforms and supposedly armed with little vials of acid to blind the unwary.

And Eisenhower, at Versailles, a "prisoner of our security police" who feared attempt at assassination, paced restlessly in the snow, watching the course of battle ebb and flow, imprinted forever upon his mind the map of the Ardennes. He was harassed, not by the battle but by other things. Back home, the nation was alarmed by the German blow. "Monty" had called for payment on an old five-pound bet: "Ike" had wagered that the war would be over by Christmas. "Monty" had suggested that a high-ranking American general might have to be removed from command (he subsequently reversed this). "Monty" had criticized emphatically SHAEF strategy; the British press, which had gotten wind of the shift in command, had embarked upon a campaign to supersede Bradley, have "Monty" appointed "supreme ground commander." The trials and tribulations of a war of allies![30]

But "Monty's" troops were covering the crossings of the Meuse, and the battlefield was being "tidied up."

DECEMBER 24

Patton's prayer was answered; Christmas Eve dawned fair and clear; the snow-laden forests glistened in the sun; the roads were frozen hard, and the toiling GI's flapped their arms and shivered in the cold.

The clear blue sky was laced with vapor trails; the greatest air force in the world was out in strength, and the Germans "took" it from 5,000 planes. Their airfields miles behind the front were bombed in a concerted attack, but major havoc came to the enemy supply lines, where for mile on endless mile throughout the Bulge German vehicles, motor-driven and horse-drawn, were piled up in endless convoys on the few roads. The fighter bombers had a field day, and the smoking wreckage of tanks and trucks, the mangled bodies that were men, were ominous forecasts of the end.

But it was a grim day in Bastogne, and that night the town was bombed twice. Twenty wounded and a Belgian nurse were killed in a battalion hospital, and a forlorn Christmas tree set up in a message center was knocked down. But the irrepressible GI's put the tree up again, and "in an elaborate ceremony one of the sergeants pinned the Purple Heart on a mangled doll."

It was bad, too, elsewhere along the front, for the Nazi tide was still swift-flowing to the west. The 82nd Airborne, under orders, pulled back from the salient it had so stoutly defended. "Jim" Gavin worried only about one thing:

"I was greatly concerned with the attitude of the troops toward the withdrawal, the Division having never made a withdrawal in its combat history."

The Nazi advance had roared so rapidly to the west that "Fighting Joe" Collins' VII Corps, on the right (southern) flank of First Army, intended for counterattack, found many of its units quickly embroiled in fierce defensive action.

The strong 3rd Armored Division, full of fighting "tankers"—which had been having a long series of ding-dong, hell-for-leather actions all the way from La Gleize to Houffalize, were helping to screen the corps concentration, but were heavily engaged at Hotton, Manhay and elsewhere—and "Task Force Hogan," with all its tanks, were cut off at Marcouray, and "attempts to supply by air were unsuccessful."

And the 2nd Armored Division, "Gravel-Voice" Harmon in command, already had had to commit one combat command to clear up the Ciney-Leignon road and clean up elements of the German 2nd Panzer Division which had filtered through a corps screen and around the "open" flank of VII Corps. This day 2nd Armored had good hunting, and in a moonlight ambush had knocked out "several hundred" enemy vehicles. Concentrated corps artillery fire had eased the "almost unbearable pressure" of the twenty-third on the 84th Division positions.

But the Germans still were driving hard—up toward Aywaille at the junction of VII and XVIII Corps, and around the open western flank of VII Corps.

The Nazis surrounded Rochefort, reached Marche and Celles, and drove a bulge 60 miles deep and 45 miles wide at the base into U.S. lines. Their van stood four miles from the Meuse.

And the First Army headquarters had withdrawn again—this time to Tongres, across the Meuse.

But it was westward that danger lay; the VII Corps right flank was still "up in the air"; there was no junction with the Third Army on the southern flank of the Bulge; the cork was not yet in the bottle. To the west, German patrols meandered around the outskirts of Givet; and British tanks of the 29th Armored Brigade, the only British troops east of the Meuse (in the Bulge sector), engaged and checked an enemy force near Dinant.

The situation was still "fluid" in the mouth of the Bulge: VII Corps was now meeting the brunt of the enemy assault; enemy tanks were licking northward around the corps's western flank.

It was the last crisis. . . .

"Monty" came to Tongres, to the "dreary much-bombed barracks," now the HQ of First Army. He looked at the situation map, discussed the "fluid" right flank of First Army gravely, and immediately put the 51st Highland Division at Hodges' disposal. Hodges asked that it be "assembled south of Liége."

Field Marshal Montgomery, carelessly dapper, cocky, self-assured, "prescribes, if forced, a refusal [in military parlance, a swinging back]" of First Army's right flank to a line from Andenne on the Meuse to Hotton, "which line, he stated, had to be held at all costs."

"Monty" left, and Hodges, gray and grave, studied his maps, undisturbed by the throbbing roar of the buzz bombs on their way to Antwerp. He discussed the situation with Major General William B. Kean, his chief of staff, and with his operations officer. After long deliberation, an officer courier—Colonel R. F. ("Red") Akers, Jr.—was sent to General Collins to give him, "in view of Marshal Montgomery's desires, the full picture."

It was Christmas Eve, and Akers, stiff with the cold of his long ride to the VII Corps CP near Marche, was given a drink of hot rum. He described the "full picture" to "Lightnin' Joe" Collins; long telephone conversations in carefully guarded double-talk preceded and followed his visit. In one of them VII Corps was told: "Now get this. . . . Roll with the punch."

Collins "got it"; "Monty" obviously favored a swing-back to the Andenne-Hotton line, and First Army had passed this along, releasing all troops in VII Corps—some of them held heretofore for offensive purposes by First Army—for Collins' use. Collins was "authorized," not ordered, to retreat to the Andenne-Hotton line, and though there was little suggestion in the various directives that he might attack, he was not forbidden to do so. In other words, the decision was up to Collins.

It was a key decision; to retire the corps's right flank to the suggested line meant to uncover the whole west bank of the Meuse and its crossings from Givet to Namur and Andenne.

But Collins did not have his nickname for nothing; all his instincts were scrappy, aggressive.

He got Major General Ernest Harmon, commanding the 2nd Armored Division, out on the exposed right flank of the corps, on the phone, and in guarded double-talk he told Harmon to give Combat Command "B" their head.

"Ernie . . ." he said.

The result was history—history of attack, not of withdrawal, attack to keep linked up with the British at Dinant, attack to knock the Panzer out of 2nd Panzer Division.

Old "Gravel-Voice" Harmon roared delightedly at the other end of the phone, "The bastards are in the bag!"

And they were. This Christmas Eve decision marked the final crisis in the defensive phase of the Battle of the Bulge; next morning on Christmas Day, "Ernie" Harmon, supported by the Ninth Air Force's fighter-bombers, racked and ruined the 2nd Panzer Division at Celles. Many of the German self-propelled guns were out of gas, their crews gaunt with hard going; ammunition was low, and by sunset of Christmas Day the high tide of the vain German effort had recoiled upon itself, leaving behind at Celles burned-out tanks and sprawling bodies as monuments to futility. The right flank of VII Corps and First Army was secured; the cork was in the bottle; the Germans were stopped short of the Meuse.

And Christmas was fair, the break in the weather continued; throughout the length and breadth of the Bulge the enemy cringed beneath a terrible pounding from the air.

The next day, December 26, Bastogne was relieved, the Seventh German Army recorded that it was now painfully clear that the offensive had failed, and von Rundstedt reported to Hitler that the great gamble was lost.

On December 28 Hitler, in an address to his generals, admitted failure. But he grasped a straw of hope: his plans for a new offensive by eight divisions in northern Alsace (which was to open on January 1, to gain a few brief and inconclusive miles and to peter out in agony). To Hitler and to his Third Reich there was now little left but "fanaticism."

"I have never in my life," the Fuehrer said, "learned the meaning of the word capitulation."[31]

It was to be a Wagnerian end—and it was.

FINALE

The Germans never quit. The cause was lost, but the Bulge had yet to be reduced. On New Year's Day, long after the German effort had reached its high-water mark and had begun to recede in blood and wreckage, the Luftwaffe dealt a savage blow with 700 planes against Allied airfields in the Netherlands and Belgium, a raid which cost the Allies 156 aircraft.[32]

On January 3 Hitler officially "abandoned the objectives of the Ardennes offensive," and on the eighth he permitted the Sixth SS Panzer to be withdrawn to constitute a reserve.[33]

The Nazis retired doggedly, aided by snow and cold. Many died but few surrendered. When the skies cleared, Allied air power cluttered the road with debris. But it was not until January 23, 1945, that Saint-Vith was recaptured, and the U.S. First and Third Armies, pushing from north and south, eliminated the final vestiges of the Bulge.

But the entire Western Front had been thrown awry. The German offensive, even though it failed, had averted simultaneous attacks upon the Nazi citadel from east and west; when the Russians jumped off from the Vistula on January 12, the Americans were still painfully whittling away at the salient thrust into their lines. The Ardennes drive completely altered Allied plans, quite possibly lengthened the war by some weeks,[34] and probably had a postwar political impact. Concentration of German strength in the West and the setback to the Western Allies facilitated the

Russian advance, bolstered subsequent Communist boasts that Russian armies had saved the West and aided the Soviet capture of Berlin.

In retrospect, the Battle of the Bulge was for the United States and its Western allies both defeat and victory. A reeling enemy suddenly regained his strength and dealt a blow to Allied morale and Allied war plans that history can never minimize.

Some American troops ran away in panic and American losses were severe: two divisions broken, others severely mauled. The Third Army lost 20,000 battle casualties, and 13,778 noncombatant casualties (including thousands of cases of trench foot) in the last two weeks of December alone. The First Army had 22,000 battle casualties and thousands of sick. One U.S. infantry division—the 106th—was virtually destroyed, two badly hurt and one armored combat command almost wiped out. The final toll of the Bulge was about 76,000 U.S. casualties (8,607 dead, 47,139 wounded, 21,144 missing and prisoners). The enemy captured 1,284 machine guns, 542 mortars, 1,344 trucks and 237 tanks, and some supply dumps were destroyed to prevent capture. (The U.S. First and Third Armies lost a total of 471 medium tanks in the last two weeks of December.)

But at terrible cost. The Germans sustained by the middle of January, 1945, 100,000 to 120,000 casualties in the Bulge campaign and lost matériel impossible to replace. They did not even reach their minimum objective—Liége and the line of the Meuse. Their bitter defense of their borders—and their desperate gamble in the Ardennes— weakened their subsquent defense of the line of the Rhine.

The German offensive through the Ardennes, as *Command Decisions* states,

inflicted on the U.S. Twelfth Army Group the first and only serious reverse it suffered in its sweep from Normandy to the Rhine. . . .

For the Germans, the Ardennes did not officially end until January 28, when Field Marshal Model's armies had been forced back to their original jump-off positions. They could claim to have inflicted on them [heavy] casualties. The offensive had achieved a temporary respite though Hitler now referred to it as a "tremendous easing of the situation." The Allies had been forced to abandon their attacks on the Roer dams and the Saar and to delay their final offensive toward the Rhine for two months. But even Hitler had to admit that it had not gained "the decisive success that might have been expected." For this modest achievement compared to the ambitious aim, Hitler had paid an exorbitant price. . . . German casualties were in the neighborhood of 100,000 men (about one-third of the attacking force); at least 800 tanks (out of over 2,000 employed); and about 1,000 planes (about half of the total fighter force assembled . . .).

These losses were irreplaceable.[35]

The enemy failed primarily and fundamentally because of inadequate power—in men, divisions, equipment, planes and guns. He accomplished his first objective, *"surprise,"* but failed to maintain the necessary *"speed"* of his planned advance. The very secretiveness of the preparations, which forbade any extensive briefing of junior officers and men, handicapped to some extent the tactical development of the offensive, and the difficult topography of the Ardennes, though a "victory road" in summer, proved to be a trail to defeat in the snow and mud and ice of winter. Bad weather, which aided surprise, handicapped movement, and, when good weather firmed the roads with ice, superior Allied air forces throttled the German supply system and blunted the armored spearheads. The enemy's failure to capture sizable supplies of gasoline was another, though minor, factor in his defeat; many of our supply dumps were west of the Meuse, but 3,500,000 gallons of gasoline and many tons of ammunition were transferred from Spa and other points out of his reach.

The failure of the German Sixth Panzer Army to widen the base of the salient by capturing the Monschau–Elsenborn Ridge area canalized the German advance, and the Fifth Panzer Army became, in effect, the spearhead. The stout and successful defense of the northern shoulder restricted the Sixth Panzer's advance to two main roads instead of four, and one of them was under U.S. artillery fire. Likewise the underpinning of the southern shoulder of the Bulge confined and trammeled the enemy's movements to the west.

At its extreme width the base of the salient driven into the American front was never longer than 47 airline miles, whereas the depth of the German penetration reached a maximum of 60 miles. An old military rule of thumb—a guide rather than a principle—holds that the base of any salient must be twice as long as the depth of penetration. The danger to the Germans in the salient was obvious. In their counterattack against the salient the Americans took the small solution: they did not attack from the shoulders, thus pinching off the whole salient, but about midway down its length. The availability of road networks had a good bit to do with this decision, but in the event, the Germans, fighting tenaciously, succeeded in withdrawing many of their forces, though at a great cost in casualties.

Air power shared the victory, as well as the defeat. The days of greatness of the Luftwaffe were over by the time of the Bulge; the Germans mounted a maximum of 849 sorties on December 18; on December 24 Allied air forces flew 1,138 tactical sorties and 2,442 bomber sorties. U.S. air superiority helped, but "GI Joe" on the ground eventually won the Battle of the Bulge.

The American dependence upon a linear defense—our lack of a defense system in depth—which cost us heavily in the early phases of the Bulge, was eventually more than compensated by superior American mobility and by prodigies of supply.

The fundamental reason for the German failure was a lack of

military power to match Hitler's imaginative but extraordinary aims. And, as so often happens in totalitarian societies, the Germans underestimated the staying power of their enemies.

After the first shock of surprise had been dissipated, U.S. troops, especially the blooded veteran divisions, rallied, fought and died.

As Alan Moorehead has written in *Eclipse,* many "American units in the midst of the German flood—without orders or information—simply took things into their own hands and fought back."

This is probably the major imponderable of warfare—to know just when men will suddenly, and often of their own free will, commit an act of unthinking, desperate bravery. "They held on long after the time when normally all hope would have been lost."

THE LESSONS

The Battle of the Bulge is a case history in the "Do's" and "Don'ts" of intelligence. It provides, in the annals of war, a remarkable example of deception and surprise, and the results that can be achieved, even against a more powerful enemy, by masking intentions.

"The American Army," an Australian critic has written, "tends to concentrate upon the development of its own strength and, unlike the British Army, does not normally seek victory by playing upon its opponent's weaknesses."[36]

"A shocking deficiency that impeded all constructive planning existed in the field of intelligence [at the war's start]," Dwight D. Eisenhower wrote after the war. "The stepchild position of G-2 in our General Staff system was emphasized in many ways."[37]

The Battle of the Bulge portrayed these weaknesses in bold relief.

The German armies, with their extreme secrecy and their carefully prepared security and deception plans, indeed made the task of the combat G-2 (intelligence officer) difficult.

The organization of the Fifth Panzer Army was masked by keeping many of its divisions engaged in active operations at the front until mid-November. Corps and army boundaries were shifted gradually and imperceptibly. Units brought from the east or elsewhere, or newly organized, were concealed under new names. Radio deception for some units was practiced extensively, and the Sixth Panzer Army, the key unit upon which the success of the offensive depended, observed complete radio silence for at least three weeks prior to the start of the operation.

Small elements of divisions were left in line to permit continued identification by the Allies, long after the bulk of the divisions had been removed (2nd Panzer Division and 12th SS Panzer Division were among the units that used this deception). Infantry divisions earmarked for the assault did not move into assembly areas until a few days before the attack; during the moves to the assembly area—all at night—unit emblems and vehicular markings were covered and light bulbs in vehicles were removed. Along much of the U.S. First Army front, including the quiet VIII Corps sector, extensive use was made of deception sound trucks. The sound of tracked vehicles was simulated by loudspeaker each night for a month prior to the offensive, so that when the actual concentrations started a few nights prior to jump-off, the actual noise of tanks and half-tracks was like the boy's cry of "Wolf, wolf."

Despite all these precautions, there were signs. The Germans could not possibly keep secret, for instance, the existence of the Sixth Panzer Army, which they had started to form early in the fall. The Allies had long known of its existence, and intelligence reports for weeks before the offensive had emphasized it and had discussed its potential. The risk in the Ardennes was known, faced and discussed, but as Lieutenant Colonel Wilbur E. Showalter has demonstrated in *Military Review*, it was not calculated as carefully as it might have been.[38] The Germans, like the Americans, had used the Ardennes front to "break in" new divisions and to rest weary ones. The Allies knew that the enemy strength in the sector had been "beefed up" from three to more than six divisions prior to the offensive.

"The Ardennes was considered a danger spot by General Eisenhower and General Bradley, but not the only one, inasmuch as the Alsace sector was also critical," wrote Colonel James O. Curtis, Jr., who in December, 1944, was Deputy to the Chief of the Operational Intelligence Subdivision at SHAEF and intelligence member of the SHAEF planning staff, in a letter to this writer of June 28, 1946.

In fact from our point of view, the Alsace sector was a much more dangerous one, everything considered, than the Ardennes, for you can imagine what would have been the effect of a German slice through and seizure of Metz upon the French and our own Sixth Army Group. The fact that the Germans, in desperation, might employ their last remaining strategic reserves in a gamble to achieve some tactical or strategic advantage was also, I believe, fully appreciated by Gen. Eisenhower and by Gen. Bradley in a conference at SHAEF which took place long before December 16th [the start of the German offensive].

Brigadier General Edwin L. Sibert, then G-2 of the Twelfth Army Group, recalls (letter of January, 2, 1947) that

perhaps two and one-half weeks prior to December 16, I called General Bradley's attention to the German capability of an attack in the Ardennes. After my return from a visit to the 6th Army Group, I noted for General Bradley, in connection with the above capability, that two German assault corps had been withdrawn from the line. However, I want to emphasize that I only noted the German capability of an attack through the lightly held Ardennes and at no time did I specifically state that this capability would be—to use our own peculiar intelligence language—"implemented."

"It is also significant," Colonel Curtis notes, "that Gen. Patton had appreciated the danger of a German counteroffensive in the Ardennes, as well as one through Alsace, and had made tentative plans for the U.S. Third Army in the event of such a contingency."

"We always considered a German attack here [in the Ardennes] a capability," writes (May 29, 1946) Lieutenant General W. H. Simpson, then commander of the U.S. Ninth Army.

This was raised in priority by us on December 5th when, on my return from a conference with General Bradley at Luxembourg, I stopped off to have a short visit with General Troy Middleton [VIII Corps commander] at Bastogne. He told me then of his great concern about the German forces on his front. It was his feeling, and I might say that he felt very strongly on the matter, that whereas previously the Germans had been unloading troops in the rear area, bringing some up to the front line and then moving them to other sectors, he felt that now they were trying to keep the same picture as far as we were concerned, but were actually building up a large force in the rear areas. He further stated he had made known his concern to First Army headquarters.

Although this well-nigh universal perspicacity, as quoted, was recorded after the event, the diaries and intelligence documents and independent recollections of numerous participants agree that the existence of the Sixth Panzer Army and the weakness of the Ardennes sector were factors that were *mentioned* at many staff presentations in the days and weeks prior to the German drive.

There were, despite the German secrecy, far more specific signs, which became particularly noticeable after December 1.

On November 20, a German general was captured by the French. He again confirmed, when interrogated, the existence of the uncommitted Sixth Panzer Army, commanded by SS General Sepp Dietrich, and declared that this Army was to be "used for a single large-scale counterattack on the Western Front scheduled for the end of December."

In early December a copy of a letter signed by "Wissman, Chief of Staff" of the German LXXXVI Corps, was captured, which declared that "the Fuehrer has ordered the formation of a special unit of a strength of about two battalions for employment on reconnaissance and special tasks on the Western Front." The battalions, the letter stated, were to be drawn from volunteers who knew English and the "American dialect," and "captured U.S. clothing, equipment, weapons and vehicles" were to be collected and utilized by this special unit. Otto Skorzeny was known to have established a special school at Friedenthal near Berlin for these men.

Prisoners of war commenced to speak of shifts of army boundaries south and east (specifically, shifts of the Fifteenth Army and Fifth Panzer Army southward were reported), and two Panzer divisions, the 2nd and 116th, disappeared from the line. The 2nd was subsequently reported (among other places) near Wittlich, behind the Ardennes front.

Troop and train movements into areas opposite the U.S. VIII Corps front were noted: "A conservative estimate [12 December Daily Periodic Report, U.S. First Army, G-2] would place at least two Volksgrenadier and one Panzer Grenadier divisions in the enemy's rear area opposite VIII U.S. Corps."

On December 13 various POW's spoke of three divisional shifts, and on December 14 and December 15 (the German offensive started on December 16) VIII Corps reported statements of a German woman, "believed reliable," who had seen considerable movement of equipment including pontoons and bridging material "behind the German lines" (near Bitburg, opposite VIII Corps front) and noted "an abrupt change of routine of enemy personnel opposite U.S. 9th Armored Division," which "suggests that new troops may have arrived in that area."

Visual air reconnaissance, although periodically hampered by weather, flew a total of 48 missions along the U.S. Army front in the first 15 days of December. Five daily missions were planned for each corps front, but along the VIII Corps front, in the Ardennes, a total of only eight missions were flown during the period December 1–15 (both inclusive). Both road and rail movements were intermittently detected (when weather permitted) all along the front, most of it to the north in V and VII Corps areas.

"Considerable" activity was noted in the Trier area northwest of Luxembourg, opposite the VIII Corps front on December 14.

In a study of enemy armored reserves, by the "Target Subsection" of G-2, U.S. First Army, (dated December 8) Bitburg and other towns, railheads and rail junctions behind the VIII Corps front, as well as numerous towns behind V and VII Corps fronts were listed as profitable targets—troop concentration areas or railheads.

And about December 11 a warning was sent out by teletype from the headquarters of the U.S. Ninth Air Force to the Ninth Tactical Air Force and lower units that the German Air Force had built up sufficient strength opposite the U.S. First Army front to make air penetrations of about 60 miles above our front lines, and that these penetrations were likely to be attempted during the next two weeks.

Perhaps most important of the straws in the wind was the interception and decoding of a German message (by U.S. Twelfth Army Group G-2) about two weeks before the attack which ordered certain GAF units to reconnoiter the Meuse River bridges.

And in England agents in German POW camps reported that December 16 had been set as the date for a mass break.[39]

Despite all these signs the intelligence reports of the period failed to evaluate the gathering storm in proper perspective.

British Major General Kenneth Strong, Eisenhower's intelligence deputy at SHAEF, stated on November 26, in his weekly intelligence summary, that "the intentions of the enemy in the Aachen sector (north of the Ardennes) become quite clear. He is fighting the main battle with his infantry formations and army panzer divisions and with these, he hopes to blunt our offensive." Like most other G-2's, Strong thought the Sixth Panzer Army would be used in this sector defensively, or in counterattack when we attempted to cross the Roer River. On December 3 Strong recorded that the "longest term problem [of the enemy] is to find enough men and equipment to stand up to the present rate of attrition." He felt that to date attrition losses had been met "to a large extent by feeding the fat from the Ardennes and from Holland to the battle sectors."

SHAEF's "Weekly Intelligence Summary No. 38" of December 10, the last before the German offensive started, opened with the sentence: "On the Western Front an unstable equilibrium is still maintained." The withdrawal of infantry divisions from "quiet sectors for use in the battle areas" was noted, and similar withdrawal of armor "for refit" was reported. "The number of nominal enemy divisions in the west is increased by one to 71. . . . Continuing troop movements toward the Eifel [Ardennes] sector . . . suggest that the procession is NOT [caps are Strong's] yet ended. Other considerable road movement . . . in the direction of Holland and in direction of First Army sector." Under "enemy capabilities," the SHAEF report noted heavy German losses; defined the Cologne-Düsseldorf area as the "vital sector" for the enemy; noted that German morale showed "no signs of cracking"; said that so far the battle "must have gone better for him [the enemy] than he had anticipated," and so "we cannot expect anything else but continued reenforcement [in the Cologne-Düsseldorf sector, north of the Ardennes], hard and bloody fighting, every sort of defense. . . . It will be a bitter and hard struggle to reach the Rhine."

There was no reference to a possible German offensive and only a slight note of apprehension: until the Sixth Panzer Army is committed, "we cannot really feel satisfied," Strong declared.

Field Marshal Montgomery's Oxford don, Brigadier "Bill" Williams, G-2 for the British Twenty-first Army Group, also produced in early

December a glowingly optimistic estimate of German weaknesses, which "Monty" liked so well that he incorporated the main elements in a Top Secret order—which he signed himself—of December 16 dealing with future Allied operations. Paragraph 3 of this order read:

The enemy is at present fighting a defensive campaign on all fronts; his situation is such that he *cannot stage major offensive operations* [italics mine]. Furthermore, at all costs he has to prevent the war from entering on a mobile phase; he has not the transport or the petrol that would be necessary for mobile operations, nor could his tanks compete with ours in the mobile battle.

Paragraph 4 started: "The enemy is in a bad way. . . ."

The U.S. Twelfth Army Group's report of December 12, "Weekly Intelligence Summary No. 18" (for the week ending December 9), was almost equally definite. Brigadier General Sibert, the G-2, had used the writing skill of a well-known author, Ralph Ingersoll, then in uniform and assigned to Twelfth Army Group staff, to produce this report from the facts provided him. It was unfortunate that this estimate, which reached the front-line divisions just before the Germans struck, was unequivocal in the opening sentence:

It is now certain that attrition is steadily sapping the strength of German forces on the Western Front and that the crust of defenses is thinner, more brittle and more vulnerable than it appears on our G-2 maps or to the troops in the line.

The report went on to state that

the deathly weakness of the individual infantry division in the line, plus the inevitability of the enemy falling still further in replacement arrears make it certain that before long he will not only fail in his current attempt to withdraw and rest his tactical reserve but he will be forced to commit at least part of his Panzer Army to the line.

The enemy's primary capabilities continue to relate to the employment of the Sixth SS Panzer Army but it may not be possible for the enemy to have complete freedom of choice as to the time and place of its employment. The situation is becoming similar to that which existed at Caen and St. Lô. . . . If the situation deteriorates seriously in the South, he will be forced to transfer some of the armor quickly to that area. At the same time, he must keep a strong reserve in the North to deal with a potential break-through in that area.

The U.S. Third Army G-2, Colonel Oscar Koch, came closer to the mark. He reported that enemy rail movements in the early part of December "indicated a definite buildup of enemy troops and supplies directly opposite the north flank of Third [U.S.] Army, and southern flank of First Army." On December 9 he thought there were some six and a half enemy divisions in the Eifel (Ardennes) area, and on December 10 Colonel Koch specified that the enemy was able to "maintain a cohesive front" without committing the bulk of his infantry and armored reserves. He declared that the "massive armored force" the enemy was building up in reserve gave him "the definite capability of launching a spoiling offensive."

Colonel B. A. ("Monk") Dickson, the First Army G-2, was even more explicit. He was optimistic in his report No. 36 of November 20, 1944, and thought "the enemy's capability of a spoiling attack is now lost." His "strategic plan appears to be based on counter-attack rather than a planned offensive opened on his own initiative."

On December 2 in his periodic report Dickson noted the formation of a special German unit of two battalions to be composed of German soldiers speaking English with an American dialect, and to be clothed and equipped in American uniforms. These units, he recorded, had been ordered to report to "Hq Skorzeny" at Friedenthal near Oranienburg. On December 4 Dickson's estimate reported the "very probable" instead of "just possible" movement of the German Fifteenth Army southward from Holland to the Aachen area, where it relieved Fifth Panzer Army. On December 7 he noted enemy troop movements toward the VIII Corps front.

By December 8 Dickson had discovered what he felt were strong enough concentrations of the enemy in the Eifel to warrant bombing. General Hodges requested concentrated air attacks and Major General Elwood R. Quesada endorsed the proposal, but higher Air Force echelons thought the targets "unremunerative."[40]

In the famous "Estimate No. 37," dated December 10, Dickson changed his tone sharply. The signs he had noted in late November and early December convinced him that

it is plain that his [the enemy's] strategy in defense of the Reich is based on the exhaustion of our offensive to be followed by an all-out counter-attack with armor, between the Roer and the Erft, supported by every weapon he can bring to bear. . . .

It is notable that morale among PWs freshly captured, both in the Army cage and at Communications Zone cage, recently achieved a new high. . . . It is apparent that Von Rundstedt, who obviously is conducting military operations without the benefit of intuition, has skillfully defended and husbanded his forces and is preparing for his part in the all-out application of every weapon at the focal point and the correct time to achieve defense of the Reich west of the Rhine by inflicting as great a defeat on the Allies as possible. Indications to date point to the location of this focal point as being between Roermond and Schleiden [in the Aachen area, north of the VIII Corps front, where the German attack was actually made].

Under "Enemy Capabilities," Dickson listed:

(1) The enemy is capable of continuing his defense of the line of the Roer north of Düren, his present front line west of the Roer covering the dams, and thence south along the West Wall.

(2) The enemy is capable of a concentrated counter-attack with air, armor, infantry and secret weapons at a selected focal point at a time of his own choosing.

(3) The enemy is capable of defending on the line of the Erft and subsequently retiring behind the Rhine.

(4) The enemy is capable of collapse or surrender.

Dickson thought that Capability No. 1 was "current," and that the exercise of No. 2 "is to be expected when our major ground forces have crossed the Roer River, and if the dams are not controlled by us, maximum use will be made by the enemy of flooding of the Roer in conjunction with his counter-attack."

But Dickson concluded the famous "Estimate No. 37" with a prophetic statement: "The continual building up of forces to the west of the Rhine points consistently to his staking all on the counter-offensive as stated in capability 2."

This estimate, widely distributed, alarmed some; in England Lieutenant General Matthew B. Ridgway, commanding the XVIII Corps, read it and used it as a warning against overconfidence in a Christmas message he was preparing for his troops; in Belgium the 9th Armored Division—one of the divisions in the Ardennes sector—was alarmed, but was subsequently somewhat reassured by the Twelfth Army Group estimate which arrived later.

In his last report before the storm struck, a "periodic" dated December 16, Dickson reported recent information compiled before that date, and stated:

Reenforcements for the West Wall between Düren and Trier (VIII Corps front) continue to arrive. . . . Although the enemy is resorting to his attack propaganda to bolster morale of the troops, it is possible that a limited scale offensive will be launched for the purpose of achieving a Christmas morale "Victory" for civilian consumption.

Many PW's now speak of the coming attack between the 17th and 25th of December, while others relate promises of the "recapture of Aachen as a Christmas present for the Fuehrer."

But by the time this warning had been distributed the enemy had struck.

What happened is history. The Germans achieved almost complete tactical surprise. The strength, drive and ferocity of their offensive came, especially, as a stunning blow; and the time and place of their assault also surprised the U.S. forces. Surprise was, in fact, the decisive factor in the enemy's early successes.

The enemy had committed to battle in the Ardennes on December 16 some 19 divisions, with about 10 more divisions in reserve which were subsequently committed before January 4. A total of some 240,000 to 300,000 men had been moved into position to strike, against the weakest link in the long Allied line from Switzerland to the sea, and our maximum preattack estimate of enemy strength in the Ardennes area had been six and a half divisions! Scores of thousands of men had been shifted into the area without our knowing it. Moreover, hundreds of fighters moved from bases in central Germany to fields in western Germany to support the ground offensive, again with little warning of the shift.[41]

Field Marshal Wilhelm Keitel, OKW Chief of Staff, and Colonel General Jodl later said with absolute correctness that the Battle of the Bulge was "fundamentally one of surprise, and to this extent we believe it was a complete success."[42]

Any appraisal of what went wrong with our intelligence prior to the Battle of the Bulge has to start with a state of mind. The American Army was and is attack-minded. That was at once its strength and its weakness. We paid lip service prior to World War II to the defensive at our military schools, but our thinking was geared to the attack, and, as the Germans learned, an offensive psychology overdone can pave the way to G-2 mistakes.

Captain William J. Fox, who was with the V Corps at the time of the Bulge Battle has depicted in correspondence with the author this state of mind:

The whole air of the First Army zone was one of slightly angry bafflement, for we had been trying since early November to crack through to the Cologne Plain and reach the Rhine. The psychology still was one of attack, however, and no one seemed seriously to consider that the Germans had a Sunday punch left. The mental approach from the lowliest man in the front line to the highest brass on the staffs was one of attack. . . . None of us found any evidence among our troops or commanders of awareness that a possible large-scale German counter-attack might be in the wind.

Coupled with this attack psychology were frustration and resignation, and, as always, an attempt, wherever conditions permitted, to make the best of any small luxuries the field allowed. This was true on the VIII Corps front, where the badly battered 28th Division and the 4th, both veterans of Hürtgen, were trying to catch their breath, and where the 106th, new to war, was shakily fitting into line.

It was true, too, of First Army headquarters at Spa, Belgium. A staff officer of that time, who prefers anonymity, writes:

Until then, we had been in the field in tents. I mention this because there is no doubt that once we moved into buildings we began to feel more civilized, and on the whole I don't think the headquarters was on its toes as much as it had been when the men were out in the swamps or fields. Spa, an almost untouched city, is one of the great European resorts, and the buildings into which we moved offered many luxuries. The brains of the headquarters—the Commanding General, the Chief of Staff, and the G-2 and G-3 sections, as well as a few others were stationed in the Hotel Britannique, five minutes off the main square at Spa . . . [a hotel which] had served in 1918 as the Imperial German headquarters.

These psychological influences could not help but affect intelligence officers, British as well as American.

"We were completely, utterly fooled," Robert E. Merriam writes in *Dark December*. General overconfidence and intelligence officers who competed with each other in destroying the German Army "with words" were major factors in the success of the German surprise.[43]

The "attack psychology" and the doctrine of the offensive also had another effect in the American Army: it resulted, almost universally, in the downgrading of G-2. In theory, but rarely in fact, though sometimes in rank, were the G-2's and G-3's coequal and supplementary partners.

There was then, and there still is today, a tendency on the part of most commanding generals to lean more heavily on G-3 than on G-2; the perfect staff blend was rarely found.

General Bradley used to say, "My -2 [Intelligence] tells me what I should do; my -4 [Supply] tells me what I can do, and I tell my -3 [Operations] what I want done." The then Twelfth Army Group commander made his decisions after a careful briefing from his G-2 and a subsequent long study of a terrain map. But this was not universal practice; too often the dash and aggressiveness of American commanders could be reflected in the Farragut phrase: "Damn the torpedoes; full speed ahead."

This is admirable courage, but if it is to result in victory it must be based, as it was in Farragut's case, on knowledge of the enemy. A proper appreciation of the enemy is the key to success in war; the German and Japanese armies possessed the aggressive spirit to as high a degree as any armed services on earth, yet their lack of understanding of the enemy who defeated them often verged on the contemptuous.

In the First Army headquarters at the time of the Battle of the Bulge, that happy melding between G-2 and G-3 which is the key to success in battle did not exist. Colonel Dickson, the G-2, was outranked by the G-3, who was promoted during the earlier part of the continental fighting. At the time of the Bulge, Dickson was very much opposed to the

Hürtgen Forest battle, and the dichotomy that existed between him and G-3 was more marked than normal because of the existence at the Spa headquarters of two separate staff messes, with Dickson as a colonel assigned to one, and with the chief of staff, G-3 and G-4 and other general officers in charge of staff sections in another.

This downgrading of intelligence, about which General Eisenhower and so many other American officers have commented, was compounded at the time of the Battle of the Bulge by personality differences. Nearly all official histories of war—our own included—treat these human conflicts lightly, if indeed at all, but men, not machines, make war and the interplay of personalities, inescapable in all human endeavors, has often changed the course of campaigns.

"Within the First Army headquarters," a staff officer then assigned writes, "personalities played a big role."

The differences between G-2 and G-3 in this headquarters, and to a lesser extent between G-2 and the chief of staff, were in part due to personality clashes; the three men were utterly different in methods, temperament and outlook. At the daily conferences it seemed to some of Dickson's officers that his intelligence estimates, sometimes livened by the peculiar slang of the trade (Dickson called prisoners "customers"), were not always taken too seriously.

There was also what might be described as a "coolness" between G-2, First Army—Colonel Dickson—and G-2, Twelfth Army Group—Brigadier General Sibert. Again, rank intruded; Dickson, the veteran of First Army action, who had served in North Africa and Sicily, and had landed in Normandy, was still a colonel, and was still G-2 of First Army, though his chief, General Bradley, had "fleeted up" to command Twelfth Army Group. Dickson and Sibert both came from old Army families; their fathers had known each other in Panama years before. Dickson, a West Pointer, had left the Army but returned to service in World War II; Sibert, a year ahead of Dickson at the Point, had stayed in.

The difference in rank and position, plus the entirely different personalities of the two men, had an effect upon their relationships, which were always correct and never hostile, but certainly not cordial. One—Sibert—who had had no World War II combat service prior to his Twelfth Army Group assignment, felt the diffidence a man green to battle always feels for a veteran; the other—Dickson—felt the diffidence of inferior rank and position. Dickson was tall, lean and histrionic; Sibert, shorter, heavier, more stolid. Dickson was brilliant, volatile, unconventional and with a quick mind. He was not always easy to get along with and he required careful handling. Sibert was thorough, a staff man, and tended to go by the book. The two contrasting characters did not mix.

This feeling was never expressed openly by either man; in correspondence and interviews with this author both have discounted it, but their staffs felt and expressed it. The OSS operatives, for instance, who worked out of Twelfth Army Group headquarters had a picture of Hitler at their CP, and under it was the totally unfair legend:

"He fools some of the people some of the time but he fools Dickson all of the time."

This almost sophomoric display did not stem, however, entirely from the First Army–Twelfth Army Group frictions, but in the case of the OSS it resulted in part because Dickson, with General Bradley's support, had strictly limited OSS operations in the First Army area.

The friction seems to have been worsened somewhat by the lack of a sense of humor of an OSS officer at the Twelfth Army Group. Someone at First Army wrote a humorous parody of a PW report, alleging to represent the results of an interrogation with Hitler's latrine orderly. The one OSS officer then permitted to head a section (counterespionage and antisubversion) in the First Army took this parody to his superior at Twelfth Army Group "for a laugh." Unfortunately, the paper was taken seriously; and when the explanation that it was all in fun was made, there seems to have been considerable embarrassment among the Twelfth Army Group OSS personnel.[44]

There were also lesser frictions—due in part to personalities, in part to individual interpretations of national interests—at SHAEF itself. And General Strong, the British G-2 at SHAEF, and one of his deputies found themselves at odds on occasions with the British Oxford don, Brigadier Williams, who was Field Marshal Montgomery's able intelligence officer.

These personality frictions were complicated by differing American and British intelligence concepts. General Strong, for instance, seemed to feel, in accordance with British practice, that he occupied a sort of command position in relation to the G-2's of the army groups and field armies; and he actually undertook to take both Brigadier Williams, a Britisher who understood this concept, and Colonel Dickson, an American who was not accustomed to such a concept, to task for what he, Strong, felt were mistakes in their order of battle estimates.

Among American G-2's there was relatively little coordination, no real "meeting of the minds" and only intermittent attempts to reconcile differing estimates. There was no such "command concept" as that which motivated General Strong.

There was a strong feeling that G-2 estimates should be made readable and "lively"; many of them were embellished with quotations and historical analogies, but some paid too much attention to this literary surface dressing and not enough to the solid subsoil of fact.[45]

The lack of direction and coordination was further complicated by the old problem of "capabilities" or "intentions." The British often undertook to establish the enemy's intentions with all the risks inherent in such prophecy; the U.S. listed every possible capability under the sun, some of them differing so markedly—from all-out offensive to "collapse and surrender"—that as guides to what the enemy might do they were largely worthless.

Another and more basic failure was the inadequacy of collection; the Allies simply did not get all the facts that were available. There were a variety of reasons for this.

In General Sibert's words:

We may have put too much reliance on certain technical types of intelligence, such as signal intelligence . . . and . . . we had too little faith in the benefits of aggressive and unremitting patrolling by combat troops. We had no substitute, either, for aerial reconnaissance when the weather was bad; and when we came up to the Siegfried Line, our agents had great difficulty in getting through, particularly in the winter.[46]

Dependence upon "Magic," or decoded signal intercepts, was major —particularly at higher echelons; when the Germans maintained radio silence, our sources of information were about halved.

Our own failures were not only passive and negative; they were also positive. U.S. security measures were lax, and our communications procedures and methodical and routinized habits at the front greatly helped the German intelligence officers to estimate (with extreme accuracy) U.S. strengths.

The most outstanding failure was in aggressive patrolling, the textbook weakness that is constantly emphasized in every maneuver and in every recent war in which Americans have engaged. This failure to probe deep into the enemy's lines in order to bring back many prisoners and force him, by reaction, to reveal his intentions was particularly pronounced on the VIII Corps front, where the natural letdown of exhausted troops who had been shifted from bloody carnage to a "quiet sector" was a factor. And at higher headquarters too little attention was paid to the few ground patrol reports available.

The reduced reports of agents behind the enemy's lines due to tighter German security measures also reflected, however, a lack of adequate coordination between the Office of Strategic Services, an outfit for which too many of the combat units had little use, and the Army. There was also a misuse of the intelligence sources available to a field army.

The limited success of air reconnaissance was in part due to the atrocious weather, but the night air effort was also handicapped by major shortage of adequate aircraft. Moreover, the value of visual reconnaissance, as distinct from aerial photography, could not be measured by the numbers of missions flown or the reports made (many of which were erroneous), for the pilots and observers were largely untrained in identification of ground targets.

Martin M. Philipsborn, then a major and S-2 of Combat Command "B" of the 5th Armored Division, in a "Summary of Intelligence Operations from July '44 to May '45" (May 27, 1945), commented on "the absolute and complete failure of aerial reconnaissance." Increased "tank and vehicular recognition courses for the air force" were indicated.

The ground-air organizational liaison also left something to be desired. The official history comments that:

the air force was responsible for the initial screening of the results of its own reconnaissance.

Perhaps the chief fault was one of organization, for there seems to have been a twilight zone between air and ground headquarters in which the responsibility had not been sufficiently pinned down.[47]

There was, finally, a failure in evaluation. For no one predicted accurately the German offensive. Colonel Dickson, G-2 of the army most involved, was closest; his estimates just prior to the attack warned clearly of the danger of a heavy German blow, quite possibly before Christmas. But he was wrong as to place; the German security measures were successful in that they made us believe the attack, when it came, would be toward the Aachen area, north of the Bulge. And he was somewhat inexact as to time; Dickson expected the "counterattack" or "counteroffensive" (as he variously called it) when we had crossed the Roer or controlled its dams. Neither Dickson nor anyone else correctly assessed the power of the enemy drive. Moreover, Dickson's definite note of warning was diffused, as were the estimates of all other G-2's, by inclusion of numerous "capabilities." We hedged against all bets.

Correct evaluation might have rectified weaknesses in organization, differences in concept, personality frictions and inadequate collection. But it did not do so. As Colonel Showalter demonstrates:

Aggressive patrolling increased [on the part of the Germans], high-caliber units were reported in the front line, river-crossing equipment was located in the forward areas, troops were recalled from the rear, and a large build-up, including armored divisions, was reported in what previously had been a quiet sector. In spite of these telltale signs, intelligence estimates were *not* materially revised. [Colonel Dickson's particularly and to a certain extent the reports of Colonel Koch were exceptions] . . . intelligence did not measure up to the trust of its commanders.[48]

The failures in evaluation were, in one sense, a composite of all the weaknesses previously noticed, plus other factors.

There was far too much of a "scratch-my-back-I'll-scratch-yours" attitude among various G-2's. Each echelon was eager to pad out and expand its factual output. Bits of information, often reported speculatively, or evaluated as possibilities, not certainties, by lower echelons, would be picked up by higher G-2's, and would appear and reappear in higher-echelon estimates, often with the qualifying factors omitted, until they came to be accepted as facts instead of possibilities.

Higher-echelon G-2's, privy to a flow of information from "Magic," British Intelligence, OSS, etc., often incorporated so much in their reports that front-line combat units received a plethora of data, much of it of little use to them. The lower-level G-2 had great difficulty in separating the chaff from the wheat.

The deficiencies of much of this "high-level stuff"—which gave, for instance, the strategic situation on the Russian front, and described the psychology of the Rhinelanders—is best illustrated in the official words of Major Philipsborn:

"While it is perhaps an exaggeration, nevertheless there is a certain amount of truth in the statement that while we knew to a nicety where bridges, fords and brothels were located in towns all around us, we rarely—if ever" knew where the enemy's antitank gun was sited.[49]

Cole sums up the intelligence failure as "general," as one which "cannot be attributed to any person or group of persons." It was "a gross failure by Allied ground and air intelligence."

One of the greatest skills in the practice of the military art is the avoidance of the natural tendency to overrate or underestimate the enemy. . . . The enemy capability for reacting other than to direct Allied pressure had been sadly underestimated. Americans and British had looked in a mirror for the enemy and seen there only the reflection of their own intentions.[50]

Such, then, was the case history of intelligence in the Battle of the Bulge.

History, many say, is simply "Monday morning quarterbacking." But the intelligence lessons of the Battle of the Bulge are still pertinent today, in an era when accurate intelligence may mean the difference between national life or death.

The lessons of the Bulge are clear: (1) Maintenance at all levels of an objective frame of mind; the "attack psychology," overdone, can lead to disaster. (2) Maintenance of G-2 officers at all levels as heads of staff sections coequal with all other staff sections. A proper mating of G-2 and G-3 is a key to victory; the sections must work as one; there can be no downgrading of intelligence. (3) Elimination of staff and personality frictions at all levels is the responsibility of command. (4) Improved coordination between differing-echelon G-2's; reports sent to lower commands must be carefully sifted to eliminate unnecessary detail. (5)

Modification of U.S. estimates to something perhaps halfway between the British emphasis upon enemy "intentions" and our own tendency to list enemy "capabilities" as a means of hedging all bets. (6) *Aggressive patrolling at all times and at all parts of the front.* (7) Better training of air-reconnaissance units and improvement of night "recon" techniques. (8) Full utilization of *all* available collection sources. (9) Careful selection of intelligence officers for their (a) analytical ability and aptitude in the collation of facts and their synthesis, (b) knowledge of the enemy and (c) judgment and ability to work in harness. (10) Establishment of career intelligence officers and the training of specialists, particularly in the field of evaluation.

The aggressive spirit is a priceless heritage of the American armed services. Without it there can be no triumph in war. But its overemphasis—and consequent neglect of the defensive and of a knowledge of your enemy—can lead to disaster, particularly in the age in which we live, where we face an enemy more nearly comparable in strength to ourselves than any in our history.

Today, inscribed in the brain of every commander there should be one slogan:

"Know your enemy—or die."

CHAPTER 11

THE GREATEST SEA-AIR BATTLE

IN HISTORY—OKINAWA

April 1–June 22, 1945

This is the story of "the last battle" of World War II, the gigantic struggle at Okinawa, in the East China Sea, between the "fleet that came to stay" and the Japanese "kamikazes"—a battle which Winston Churchill correctly described as one of "the most intense and famous of military history."

Easter Sunday, April 1, 1945, a time of prayer and hope in a world at war, is a shining day in the East China Sea. The ocean is calm, the weather cool, the visibility good, the sun strong; the escarpments of Okinawa, a dim and distant island soon to become part of American tradition, are shadowy on the horizon.

The greatest naval armada in history—more than 40 carriers, 18 battleships, 200 destroyers, hundreds of transports, cruisers, supply ships, net layers, submarines, mine sweepers, gunboats, landing craft, patrol vessels, salvage ships and repair vessels, more than 1,500 ships transporting 182,000 assault troops—is steaming deep into Japanese waters.[1] The objective is "Operation Iceberg"—the seizure of Okinawa.

After the months of intensive preparation and weeks of hair-trigger

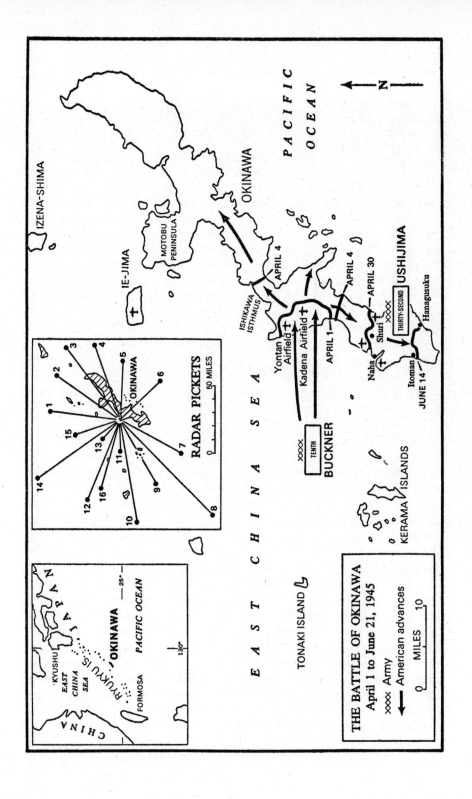

THE BATTLE OF OKINAWA
April 1 to June 21, 1945

xxxx Army
American advances

0   MILES   10

N

PACIFIC OCEAN

OKINAWA

IZENA-SHIMA

IE-JIMA

MOTOBU PENINSULA

ISHIKAWA ISTHMUS

APRIL 4

APRIL 4

APRIL 30

USHIJIMA

Yontan Airfield

Kadena Airfield

APRIL 1

Shuri

THIRTY-SECOND

Hanagusuku

Naha

Itoman

JUNE 14

BUCKNER

TENTH

EAST CHINA SEA

TONAKI ISLAND

KERAMA ISLANDS

RADAR PICKETS

0   50 MILES

OKINAWA

1 2 3 4 5 6 7 8 9 10 11 12 13 14 15 16

JAPAN

KYUSHU

EAST CHINA SEA

OKINAWA

RYUKYU IS.

FORMOSA

PACIFIC OCEAN

CHINA

25°

130°

tension that always precede battle, the start of the operation seems anticlimactic.

Well offshore cruises famed Task Force 58 under Vice Admiral Marc A. "Pete" Mitscher, the admiral with a gnomelike face framed in a peaked baseball cap. Southward, where the swells of the East China Sea break against the rocky pediments of Sakishima Gunto and Formosa, a British carrier task force, first to operate in the Pacific, rakes Japanese airfields. Off Blue Beach and Purple Beach, the transports and landing ships and cargo vessels are disembarking their Marine and Army assault units with almost incredible ease. The bright waters are laced with the wakes of small boats and landing craft. In the distance the guns of battleships flame and thunder, but they are American guns. In the skies the planes dip and wheel and bomb, but they are American planes.

The enemy is strangely silent. An infantryman of the 7th Division, the tightness gone from his chest, wipes his brow after climbing one of Okinawa's knoblike hills and says, "I've already lived longer than I thought I would."

Yontan and Kadena airfields, deserted by the Japanese, are captured before noon on the first day of the invasion—objectives which it had been expected might require a week to secure.

But the ease of the landing is to be succeeded by some of the most bloody, vicious fighting in the history of warfare. The Japanese have prepared a "showdown" battle.

Okinawa, largest of the Ryukyu island chain stretching southward from Japanese Kyushu, is a lizard-shaped land mass fringed with coral reefs, about 60 miles long and from 2 to 18 miles wide. Its two-mile waist divides the northern two-thirds of the island—rugged, mountainous and heavily forested—from the rolling, hilly land of the south. It is in the southern sector, seamed by escarpments and ravines, dotted with ancient Okinawan tombs and limestone caves, and with every foot of arable ground planted in sugar cane, sweet potatoes, rice and soybeans, that the Japanese have erected their main defense lines.

The assault upon Okinawa is a logical development of the Pacific strategy of the United States. The island is within medium-bomber range of Japan, and it is estimated that 780 bombers can be based there to intensify the assault being conducted by the B-29's from the Marianas. From Okinawa and its satellite isles planes and ships could sever virtually all Japanese shipping routes. Okinawa also is wanted as a supporting position for "Operation Olympic"—the invasion of the Japanese island of Kyushu, 350 miles away, which is scheduled for the ensuing November 1, 1945.

In retrospect it may be argued that the assault upon Okinawa was not essential to final victory; less than two months after its capture the enemy was ready for peace. But at the time the predominant military opinion was that Japan would fight on indefinitely. The Japanese defeat at Okinawa was, moreover, a major contributory cause to the enemy's quick surrender. The final desperate hope of the militarists—to force a negotiated peace—died at Okinawa.

The war in Europe was drawing to its end when the assault upon Okinawa was mounted. Most strategists thought the Japanese, though beleaguered and in a hopeless position since the Battle for Leyte Gulf, would fight to the last gasp, and many feared the bloody task of invading the home islands and mopping up Japanese forces on the mainland of Asia would require at least another year of war. The atomic bomb had not even been tested at Alamagordo, and Japan's desperate straits at home had not been reflected in any lessening of the Japanese soldier's will to fight.

Okinawa and the Ryukyus were the last bastion to Japan itself. The sheer task of projecting American power across thousands of miles of sea into an area surrounded by enemy bases was unprecedented in warfare. The invading fleet was assembled, literally, from all over the world; logistic planning for the giant invasion began in the summer of 1944. "A vital factor in the success of Operation Iceberg was the Navy shipping control system, which after much trial and error nearly reached perfection in 1945."[2] The technique of refueling and replenishment at sea had been routinized and refined. Naval ammunition expenditures alone surpassed all prior operations: 247,000 rounds (through May 20) of 5-inch 38-caliber antiaircraft, a total of more than 27,000 tons of AA and bombardment ammunition, plus almost 35,000 5-inch rockets and about 44,000 bombs.[3] The brains, the brawn, the might and the majesty of a nation were exemplified at Okinawa.

The invasion, it is hoped, will be a "quick" operation, lasting a month or less. Intelligence estimates that the enemy has about 55,000 to 65,000 troops on the island and 198 artillery pieces of major calibers. But intelligence is to be rudely surprised and hopes of a quick victory are soon to bog down. More than 110,000 of the enemy are to die and 7,400 to surrender; about 75,000 Americans will be killed, wounded, missing or ill before the "Last Battle" ends.[4]

For the Japanese High Command is determined to hold Okinawa and to employ the major portion of the empire's remaining air and sea strength to destroy the American armada that is making the invasion possible. The destruction of the U.S. Fleet is the major enemy objective. To accomplish this, the enemy is counting chiefly on bomb-laden planes guided to their targets by suicide pilots, members of the Japanese Navy's Special Attack Corps and by volunteer Army pilots, better known as the suicidal Kamikaze (Divine Wind) Corps.

A shadow of the terror impending at Okinawa has touched the

invasion fleet even before the first landings. *Indianapolis,* the flagship of the armada under Admiral Spruance, commanding the Fifth Fleet, has been hit on the port quarter by a bomb-carrying kamikaze suicide plane on March 31; the *Adams* also has taken a suicide hit; the *Murray* has been disabled by an aerial torpedo; the *Skylark*—strange, lilting name for a plodding sweeper—has been blown up by a mine. By April 3 the sheltered anchorages at Kerama-Retto already are beginning to clot with limping and crippled ships.

April 6, 1945, is clear, with wind riffling the East China Sea. Ashore, around a hill called "The Pinnacle," where Matthew Perry had raised the American flag almost a century before, a desperate battle rages—the first in a bruising, terrible struggle to break the enemy's fortified Shuri Line. The enemy stands and fights.

Afloat, the great armada is spread wide around the island.

Task Force 58 has already raked the Kyushu airfields and Japanese naval ports in a series of wide-ranging preinvasion strikes during March, and Army Air Force B-29's, flying from the Marianas bases, have plastered the enemy air bases. As the invading fleet bombards enemy positions on Okinawa, the fast carriers are launching aircraft in the open seas from a position about 70 to 100 miles northeast of the island. Today—and for many days unending—Task Force 58 flies combat air patrol over the invading fleet, and its planes range far and wide to Kyushu, alert to intercept kamikazes or surface sorties from the Inland Sea.

To the southeast are 17 United States "jeep" carriers, their planes furnishing air support for the ground troops ashore and flying CAP (Combat Air Patrol) for the surface ships. Cruisers and battleships steam back and forth within easy range of Okinawa's high escarpments, shelling the Japanese positions. Huddled off the beaches are the landing ships, transports and cargo vessels which keep the stream of men and supplies moving over the coral reefs and through the surf to the fighting men ashore. And ringing the whole island and the amphibious force, in a great circle some 100 miles out from the beaches, are the "tin cans," the "spitkits," the "small boys," officially designated the "5th Amphibious Force Area Screen" but universally called the radar picket line.

The "small boys," clustered in 15 main picket stations, detect the enemy first; the kamikazes show up as dots of light on the radar screens long before the diapason of their engines can be heard.

The mid-watch notes enemy snoopers on April 6, and, before daylight, "heavy air attacks." Nine enemy planes are "splashed" in the transport area by AA fire. The day clouds up; by afternoon the sky is heavily overcast, and from all directions the "bandits" roar in. The radiotelephone TBS (talk-between-ships) circuits chatter as the Japanese attack, and the CIC's (Combat Information Centers) aboard the destroyers are a babel of radioed reports: "Pedantic, this is Riverside; I see bogy one eight zero. Do you concur? Over."

"This is Pedantic. Affirmative. That makes three raids . . . out."

Between 1 and 6 P.M. of this gray and somber day 182 enemy planes in some 22 different attacks reach the Okinawa area. Many drop bombs or torpedoes, but more than a score crash into American ships in suicide dives. The victims are mostly the lowly sweepers, destroyers, escorts and landing craft in the far-flung radar picket line.

One of the victims is USS *Rodman*, who meets her fate. At about seven bells in the afternoon watch, the sea is smooth and *Rodman's* white wake scarcely roils the surface as she loafs along at eight knots, screening —with her sister destroyer-sweeper, the *Emmons*—a group of sweepers. The crew is at General Quarters, but there are no pips on the radar screen. Suddenly three planes break out of the thick cloud rack close aboard and commence a coordinated attack. One crashes into the port side of the main deck and a great sheet of flame burgeons over the superstructure, to be followed seconds later by a blinding spray of water from a near-miss close aboard to starboard.

The whole bow of *Rodman* is opened to sea and sky. The struggle for life commences; steering control is lost as *Rodman* backs into the wind to keep the fire forward and the bridge clear of flame and smoke. The ship settles deep; the main deck is awash. Overboard go the topside weights. Jettison the anchor, pump clear the ballast. Working near the licking flames, seamen manhandle the ammunition out of the fire's path and dump it overboard. Lighten the ship, lighten the ship! Fight fires! Plug leaks!

By eight bells the fire is under control, but the Japanese come again. They come from all directions, the young men of Japan who would die for their Emperor, and their wishes are fulfilled as their blazing planes flame, like meteors, across the skies. Many of the Japanese, shot down by the CAP, crash close aboard the *Rodman*. One kamikaze nearly cuts her in two with a bull's-eye on the port side water line; the rupture extends almost to the keel. Four 5-inch powder charges detonate; most of the others in the forward magazine are tumbled and torn, but—miraculously —the magazine does not "blow." Another suicider smacks into the captain's cabin; the flames gut the superstructure and force "conn" to shift from the bridge aft.

Some of the crew are blown overboard, some jump. Fifty-eight remain aboard as salvage crew; the rest—those who still live—shift to rescue vessels. As dusk begins to settle down, the fires are out, the rudder is cleared, the ship has worked up to a speed of six knots, and at 0325 the next morning, April 7, the torn ship limps into Kerama-Retto, the bodies of her dead, singed and battered, still aboard. *Rodman* has survived. She is of "the fleet that came to stay."

But *Emmons* is not so lucky. She is among those who died that day. The score card is ominous: besides foundered *Emmons*, two destroyers are sunk; LST-447 is burned "end to end"; the *Logan Victory*, an ammunition ship, dies in an awesome pyrotechnical display after being crashed by two suicide Zekes; another ammunition ship is sunk and nine escort types are heavily damaged, one by depth charges attached to floating planks pushed by swimmers.

But the blanks in the radar picket line are filled in; the unloading continues, and the Japanese losses are huge—almost 400 planes on April 6 and the early morning of the seventh. Of these, 300 are stopped at the picket line at the cost of only two United States planes. And on this day—the seventh—there dies in a sudden convulsive shudder and a pyramid of spiraling smoke the largest battleship in the world, the last pride of the Japanese Navy; the 18.1-inch-gunned *Yamato*. *Yamato*'s sortie from the Inland Sea, in a desperate but forlorn attempt to attack the U.S. invasion fleet off Okinawa, is planned as a sacrificial accompaniment to the kamikaze attacks. *Yamato* has only enough fuel for a one-way trip; she is accompanied by one light cruiser—the *Yahagi*—and eight destroyers. Her officers and crew are prepared to die for the Emperor. But—fatal omission—she has no air cover.

The Japanese "Surface Special Attack Force" is sighted early by U.S. submarines, and Admiral Mitscher and Task Force 58 prepare a warm reception. An *Essex* plane sights the *Yamato* and her escorts at 0823 April 7, west of the southernmost point of Kyushu, far from Okinawa. The first large strike from the fast carriers comes in on the Japanese task force about 1232, and from then until *Yamato* sinks at 1423 (2:23 P.M.) it is the final agony. She dies hard and takes five bombs and ten torpedoes before, a shambles, she up-ends and slides under, taking with her most of her crew. (Some 23 officers and 246 men, of a crew of 2,767, survived.) With her go *Yahagi* and four of the eight destroyers—all a futile sacrifice which contributes nothing to the defense of Okinawa.[5]

The "Sons of Heaven" came again in great numbers out of the clouds on the eleventh and twelfth. The Okinawa area is only harried on the eleventh; the Japanese concentrate on Task Force 58, 100 miles to the east. *Enterprise*—"the Big E"—one of the "fightingest" carriers of the Pacific War, takes "considerable damage" from two suicide near-misses; *Essex* is damaged; destroyers and DE's are hit.

Ashore, the Marines are cleaning up the northern part of the island against limited resistance, but the doughboys, driving south, meet the enemy's "iron defense" of the Shuri Line.

The Japanese strategy is now painfully clear. The Japanese Army ashore is to fight to the death, protracting the battle to the utmost, to pin the U.S. Fleet to close support of the land forces. Intensive conventional air attacks, kamikaze assaults, suicide boat raids, naval surface and submarine sorties and all the desperation measures which can be envisaged by a militaristic nation facing certain defeat are invoked against the U.S. support ships, transports and men-of-war.

The U.S. defense is offense—smashing raids against the Japanese air and naval bases by Task Force 58 and the Army's B-29's. The defense is a combat air patrol, sizable and continuous, flown from the fast carriers of Task Force 58, from the jeep carriers closer to Okinawa, and from captured Yontan and Kadena airfields on Okinawa. (Thirteen to 16 fast carriers in TF 58 were constantly deployed to the east of Okinawa from March 23 to April 27, a somewhat fewer number thereafter, and in addition there were 14 to 18 escort carriers, and British Task Force 57, with four large and six converted carriers. The combat air patrol numbered at least 50 to 120 U.S. aircraft in daylight hours.[6]) The defense is the radar picket line, flung wide around the island—destroyers and destroyer-type vessels initially, but beefed up, as the kamikazes take their dreadful toll, with the fire power of gunboats. The defense is guns—AA guns afloat and ashore, from the tiny 20 mm. to the thundering 5-inchers.

It is a formidable cordon, and the Japanese pay heavily. But still they come.

The twelfth—the day of President Roosevelt's death—is a day of great attack. At home a nation mourns; at Okinawa the news spreads suddenly from foxhole to foxhole, from flight deck to gun turret, but there is no time to mourn, scarce time to pray. That day many another American dies. In the clear bright afternoon perhaps 175 enemy planes in 17 separate raids reach the Okinawa area. They are met by a strong CAP and the guns of the most powerful fleet in history, but they exact a grim toll. The picket line takes the brunt of it.

At 1358 (1:58 P.M.) *Cassin Young* splashes four "Vals," but takes a suicider in the forward engine room: 1 killed, 54 wounded. At 1402 (2:02 P.M.) *Jeffers,* in picket station No. 12, is lashed by fire from a near-miss. Less than an hour later the new destroyer *Mannert L. Abele* is struck by a bomb-laden Zeke, which breaks her back and stops her shafts. Dead in the water, she is the target a few moments later for a "human guided missile," what Morison describes as a "little horror." It is a so-called *baka* bomb—the first used in the Pacific War—a tiny glider, with rocket boosters and a 2,645-pound warhead, launched from a bomber, and piloted to its target at some 500 knots speed by a suicide pilot. The *baka* strikes *Abele;* the dying ship disintegrates: 6 killed, 34 wounded, 74 missing. The battleship *Tennessee* is hit; blisters on the *Idaho* are flooded; the *New Mexico* is holed by a shell from a shore battery.

Meanwhile, in the foxholes in front of the still unbreached Shuri Line, the Japanese propaganda leaflets already are proclaiming:

We must express our deep regret over the death of President Roosevelt. The "American Tragedy" is now raised here at Okinawa with his death. You must have seen 70 per cent of your CV's [Carriers] and 73 per cent of your B's [BB's—battleships] sink or be damaged causing 150,000 casualties. . . . A grand "U.S. Sea Bottom Fleet" numbering 500 has been brought into existence around this little island.

Once you have seen a "lizard" twitching about with its tail cut off, we suppose this state of lizard is likened to you. Even a drop of blood can be never expected from its own heart. . . .

April 15–17 is another bad period.[7] On the sixteenth, during the third major *kikusui* ("floating chrysanthemum") attack, the destroyer *Laffey,* in picket station No 1, survives 80 minutes of unparalleled horror. Some 50 planes show simultaneously on her radarscope; some are shot down by the CAP, but *Laffey* fights off 22 separate attacks from all quarters. She is crashed by six kamikazes and takes four bombs, but she shoots down nine aircraft, and lives to tell about it, chiefly due to her skipper's superb ship handling. She limps into anchorage in tow, with 31 dead, 72 wounded and only 4 20 mm. guns still in operation but with both engines and all boilers still operational. The carrier *Intrepid* is hit, a destroyer sunk, many of the "small boys" damaged. The "hot corners" of the radar picket line—stations 1, 2, 3 and 14—are given a standing CAP of two planes each, and each station is "double-banked with two destroyers to provide greater anti-aircraft fire power." But Spruance reports to CINCPAC (Nimitz):

"The skill and effectiveness of enemy suicide air attacks and the rate of loss and damage to ships are such that all available means should be employed to prevent further attacks. Recommend all available attacks with all available planes, including Twentieth Air Force, on Kyushu and Formosa fields."

The attacks are made; the Japanese fields are raked and pounded relentlessly by bombs and rockets, but the Emperor's Special Attack Corps is well dispersed and carefully camouflaged; the suicide raids continue. The damaged ships clog the anchorage at Kerama-Retto; there is a trail of limping cripples all the way across the Pacific; the fire-gutted carrier *Franklin,* hurt in Task Force 58's preliminary strike against Japan, even transits the Panama Canal for repairs at New York.

But the traffic across the Pacific is two-way. The cripples steam home; replacements of flesh and steel move steadily westward; destroyer divisions from the Central Pacific, the North Pacific, the Atlantic are ordered to Okinawa to take up their stations in the battered picket line.

Gone now—afloat and ashore—are the hopes of a quick victory. The Shuri Line is still intact. The "bong, bong, bong" of General Quarters sounds by day and by night. The fleet settles down for a long trial by blood and fire. By the end of the month 20 United States ships have been sunk—14 by suiciders—and 157 damaged—90 by kamikazes.

But the fleet stays, on the doorstep of Japan. The battleships, cruisers, destroyers, jeep carriers of imperturbable and determined Rear Admirals M. L. Deyo and W. H. P. Blandy stand off the rocky escarpments of Okinawa and carry out their major objective—support of the ground forces. Day and night, night and day, the guns thunder, and the close air support missions drop bombs or napalm on the enemy lines. Smoke often veils the transport and supply area, where the vulnerable thin-skinned ships unload without cessation; Admiral Turner uses all the tricks of defense to meet the enemy's imaginative but desperate assaults.

Ashore, after the Marine amphibious corps has cleaned up the lightly defended northern part of the island, Buckner shifts them southward to help the weary doughboys smash, in blood and mud, against the caves and pillboxes and fortified hills of the unbreached Shuri Line. The Marines suggest—indeed argue—for an amphibious assault behind the enemy line or on his flank; they are overruled by the Army, and the bloody frontal slugging match goes on.

With the end of April the *kikusui* (Special Attack) operations do not falter; the terrible battle is to drag on for almost two more months.

Many a "small boy" is still to be hurt. Light mine layer *Aaron Ward*, a brave ship, is attacked on May 3 by 25 Japanese planes; several are shot down, but she takes hit after hit from bombs and kamikazes, flaming gasoline sprays her decks, ammunition explodes in fiery pyrotechnics, she loses power and lists to port, "with fires raging uncontrolled." But she limps into harbor, flag still flying.

But never again, after April, are the ship losses and damages to be so threatening. During May and June Okinawa becomes less and less a struggle of bombs against steel and more and more a sheer test of human will and endurance.

There are alerts unending. For more than 40 consecutive days, until foul weather brings a brief but blessed break, there are air raids every night and every day. Sleep becomes a thing yearned for, dreamed about. Heads droop over gun sights; nerves frazzle, tempers snap; skippers are red-eyed and haggard. "Magic"—the Navy's system of breaking the enemy's codes and divining his intentions—has enabled the fleet to forecast the days of big attacks. Loudspeakers sometimes warn the crews the night before to be prepared. But this practice has to be stopped. The strain of waiting, the anticipated terror, made vivid from past experience, sends some men into hysteria, insanity, breakdown. Only that saving American trait, a sense of humor, keeps most from the brink of horror. On one picket station a tiny gunboat, its crew fed up with close brushes with death, rigs up a huge sign with a pointing arrow: "To Jap Pilot— This Way to Task Force 58."

Ashore, the bloody slogging progress inches into the Shuri Line, but the Japanese defenses are still intact, and on May 22 the commanding general of the III Amphibious Corps reports that the Marines are encountering the most effective artillery fire yet met in the Pacific. The "plum rains" deluge Okinawa in late May; fields become swamps, tanks are mired. Mud is king, and ammunition and fuel are moved to the front in amphibious vehicles.

Back in the rear areas, the "gyrenes," huddled in the dripping tents, raise their cans of beer and let forth with the famous MacArthur parodies:

> *Now the greatest of generals is Douglas, the proud,*
> *Writer of fine flowing prose.*
> *He paces the floor as his orders ring out*
> *Down through his aquiline nose. . . .*

Afloat, as ashore, the "no-quarter" fight goes on. Enemy submarines, midget submarines and suicide boats join the kamikaze planes in harassment of the fleet. Many submarine contacts are reported, but some of them are false; the sonar gear detects a school of fish or a "knuckle" in the current; the sailors dub the contact the "underwater ghost of the Ryukyus." In one suicide boat attack the Japanese use everything "from a thirty-foot raised-deck cruiser to an open dugout canoe with paddlers."[8]

Then they try a new twist. They bomb the American airstrips ashore at Yontan and Kadena, and follow up with an airborne landing. Five bombers try to make it; four are shot down in the air; the fifth makes a wheels-up belly landing on a Yontan runway, and 10 or 11 Japanese jump out and begin to shoot up the neighborhood. Before their riddled bodies line the airstrip they have destroyed 7 American planes, damaged 26 others, ignited 70,000 gallons of gasoline and in general raised "pluperfect hell."

The suiciders come again in swarms and coveys on the twenty-seventh, and 115 enemy planes are "splashed" that day, and they return in lesser force on the twenty-eighth. The destroyer *Drexler* joins the company of her peers fathoms deep on May 28, and a long list of ships with lyrical names—*Gayety, Anthony* and *Braine, Sandoval* and *Forrest, Gilligan* and *Loy,* the *Mary Livermore* and the *Brown Victory*—are hurt.

At midnight of the twenty-seventh Admirals Spruance and Mitscher, who have commanded the greatest land, sea and air battle Americans have ever fought, turn over command to "Wild Bull" Halsey, he of the rakish air, and John Sidney McCain, the tobacco-chewing admiral.

By the end of May the flower of the Japanese Thirty-second Army, 50,000 men, lies dead in the rubble and shell-pocked debris of their fortifications, and Lieutenant General Mitsuru Ushijima withdraws his remaining troops for a last "back-to-the-sea" stand in the south.

The flag now flies above the site of Shuri Castle, the strong point of the Japanese line. Built by an ancient, long-forgotten king, the castle has walls 20 feet thick. They are now reduced to rubble out of which the Marines dig two antique bells, scarred and dented by shellfire, and inscribed in Chinese: "And how will the bell sound? It will echo far and wide like a peal of thunder, but with utmost purity. And evil men, hearing the bell, will be saved."

Round about in the craters where men have lived hangs the unforgettable stench of rotting human flesh.

But the end is not yet. The war diary of the Third Fleet soon is noting "alarming losses of ships on the radar picket stations."

On Okinawa the weary, destitute survivors of the Thirty-second Imperial Army stand along a rocky line of hills and bluffs from Itoman to Hanagusuku. On June 3 the kamikazes come again in 18 raids by 75 planes, and on June 4 nature joins the malevolent forces of the enemy. A typhoon, with gigantic waves, tosses the invasion fleet like chips upon rapids, shears off the bow of the cruiser *Pittsburgh* and damages the carrier *Hornet* and many other ships. On June 5 the *Mississippi* and *Louisville* are struck by suiciders; on June 6 there are heavy raids from the north. The enemy is dying hard.

Still victory is in sight. But there are many now who never will savor the triumph. Ashore the principal commanders on both sides are among the dead. Simon Bolivar Buckner, Lieutenant General, United States Army—he of the rolling name, the rugged frame and distinguished heritage, who commands the American Tenth Army—dies on June 18 when a Japanese shell bursts above a Marine observation post, and a fragment of coral, broken off by the explosion, strikes him in the chest.

Early on June 22 General Ushijima, commander of His Imperial Majesty's Thirty-second Army, and his chief of staff, Lieutenant General Isamu Cho, die the ceremonial death of hara-kiri just outside a cave in a cliff Americans hereafter will know as Hill 89. A captured Japanese diary later describes the event:

Their [the generals'] *cook prepared an especially large meal to be served shortly before midnight. When the meal was finished, the two generals and their staff drank numerous farewell toasts with the remaining bottles of Scotch whiskey which had been carried from Shuri. . . .*

Alas! The Stars of the Generals have fallen with the setting of the waning moon over Mabuni.[9]

That same night the world is told that organized resistance has ceased on Okinawa. The next morning, as the band plays "The Star-Spangled Banner," the color guard raises the American flag over the blood-drenched island. "A sudden breeze swept the flag out full against a blue and quiet sky."

In retrospect, the battle for Okinawa can be described only in the grim superlatives of war. In size, scope and ferocity it dwarfed the Battle of Britain. Never before had there been, probably never again will there be, such a vicious, sprawling struggle of planes against planes, of ships against planes. Never before, in so short a space, had the Navy lost so many ships; never before in land fighting had so much American blood been shed in so short a time in so small an area; probably never before in any three months of the war had the enemy suffered so hugely, and the "final toll of American casualties was the highest experienced in any campaign against the Japanese."[10] There have been larger land battles, more protracted air campaigns, but Okinawa was the largest combined operation, a "no-quarter" struggle fought on, under and over the sea and the land.

The statistics of combat prove "the last battle" expensive. Besides their 110,000 dead, the Japanese lost 16 combat ships, including the *Yamato;* tens of thousands of tons of commercial shipping sunk by patrol planes operating from Kerama-Retto; and 287 guns. Of the 12,000 American dead, more than 4,000 were Navy men.[11]

The Navy ship casualties were 34 small ships lost and more than 300 damaged (including damage due to storm, collision and grounding), and of this number 26 were sunk and 164 damaged by kamikazes. Two were sunk and 61 damaged by conventional air attack.[12]

But 7,830 Japanese planes were destroyed in three months, about 3,047 shot down by Navy and Marine planes and 409 others by guns of the fleet. Another 2,655 were lost in operational accidents; hundreds were destroyed on the ground; 558 were credited to the Army's B-29's and hundreds were deliberately wrecked in the suicide crashes.

Our losses, including those of the big Air Force bombers which smashed at Japanese fields, were 768 planes, and only 458 of these were lost to enemy antiaircraft or in aerial combats. The rest were operational losses. Nothing larger than a destroyer was sunk by the enemy; of the larger ships damaged, all except one—an escort carrier—ultimately were repaired, most of them quickly. The Japanese failed to sink a single American carrier, battleship, cruiser or transport.

The "fleet that came to stay" and made Okinawa's conquest possible gave far more than it received. The simple accolade applied to the brave men of the little ships, "They stuck it out with demonstrated valor," is equally applicable to all those of Okinawa, dead and living, who stood, fought and endured in the greatest battle of U.S. arms. But to the "small boys," the "spitkits," the "tin cans"—the little ships of the radar

*picket line—belongs a special glory. They bore the overwhelming share
of death and destruction; they were the thin and bloodstained line that
stood between the Sons of Heaven and the dominion of the East China
Sea.*

Okinawa was an epic of human endurance and courage. The Japanese forms of attack represented ingenious desperation; the U.S. defense
against them and the successful seizure of Okinawa were a masterpiece of
logistics, operational planning and determined implementation.

Many lessons were learned. The armored flight decks of the British
aircraft carriers proved worth their weight; the damage done by kamikazes to British ships was limited by the armor; U.S. carriers, like the
Franklin, suffered horribly when bombs penetrated the flight decks, and
caused roaring fires below decks. Light guns were not adequate to deflect
a determined kamikaze attack. Radar, it was discovered, had its limitations; many attacks were not discovered, or the screens were saturated.
The importance of damage control and seamanship was emphasized, and
ship repair in improvised forward bases became a fine art.

The kamikaze attacks on the fleet at Okinawa could be described as
the preface to the missile age. The kamikazes, and particularly the *baka*
bomb, were in a sense guided missiles, with human guidance mechanisms.
They clearly foreshadowed the new menace to the surface man-of-war
which has now, two decades later, come to fruition with the development
of the homing missile.

The threat, even in World War II, was clearly understood by the
Navy. After Okinawa, with the invasion of the main islands of Japan
planned, the prospects appeared grim indeed. Vice Admiral Willis A. Lee
was detached from his battleship command and ordered to establish an
operational research unit to find means of meeting the kamikazes.
Admiral Lee died before the war ended, and the atomic bomb and the
unexpected Japanese surrender in August, 1945, relieved the pressure of
time. But a new 3-inch automatic rapid-fire gun, the development of
which was initiated as the result of the kamikaze attacks, replaced the
light 20 mm. and to a large extent the 40 mm. in the postwar Navy. The
lighter shells did not have the explosive power to stop a determined
suicide pilot.

What would have happened had the war continued and the invasion
of Japan been mounted is one of the "if's" of history. But it seems
clear:

1. That heavy losses probably would have been suffered by the radar
picket line and the smaller ships, as well as by some of the transports and
supply ships. These ships, unlike the carriers and larger vessels, would
have been restricted to relatively small offshore areas, in order to support

and protect the beachheads and amphibious landings, and hence their mobility—the greatest attribute of sea power—would have been to a large degree lost.

2. That some new methods, new arms and perhaps new types of ships would have been developed, to provide a shield against the suicide attacks. The 3-inch gun probably could not have been ready in time, but a more powerful combat air patrol would undoubtedly have been maintained.

3. That the factor of human will in war is still in this mechanistic age a—and perhaps the—fundamental intangible which makes the difference between victory and defeat. The Japanese possessed the will to fight to a high degree, but it was built on a negative philosophy—a fatalistic will to die. At Okinawa the will to die and the will to live met in head-on conflict; in this instance the will to live—aided by far superior material—won. Yet it is well to remember that the will to live must, in war, have more than a selfish context, or men who are willing to die for a cause will defeat those who put life ahead of their cause. In the case of the Japanese the kamikaze represented more than a technique; it might be called a self-destructive urge, a death wish. And in the long roll of history the sole reason for man's persistence has been that the will to live has triumphed through the ages over the will to die.

Okinawa, the island so dearly won, helped to break the back of enemy resistance, though the long-planned invasion of the Japanese main islands became unnecessary. As an Allied air base, Okinawa was only in the initial stages of development when the Japanese surrendered. Nevertheless, it was an important base in the closing months of the war in tightening the blockade around Japan, and Army Air Corps planes, based on Okinawa, flew 6,435 sorties against Kyushu. And so the last battle was not in vain.

NOTES, BIBLIOGRAPHIES
AND ACKNOWLEDGMENTS

GENERAL ACKNOWLEDGMENTS

Some of the chapters in this book originally appeared in much shorter and in quite different form in the *New York Times Sunday Magazine.*

The *Marine Corps Gazette* published in installments parts of the chapter on Corregidor.

The chapters on Leyte Gulf and Okinawa appeared in my book *Sea Fights and Shipwrecks* (Garden City, Hanover House, 1955). They have been revised for this book.

My gratitude for general help, criticism and detailed information is due, particularly, to the Office of the Chief of Military History, Department of the Army, (Brigadier General Hal C. Pattison, Chief of Military History, and Dr. Stetson Conn, Chief Historian) for basic data and many courtesies. The thick green volumes of the Army's official histories represent collectively a model of historical research and provide the historians of today and tomorrow with the basic framework of any military narrative of World War II.

Rear Admiral E. M. Eller, Director of Naval History, has also been most helpful in research and judicious in appraisal.

I have also drawn heavily, as noted in individual chapter acknowledgments, upon the British, and particularly the New Zealand, official histories.

Mrs. Freeda Franklin of the *New York Times* Library has, as always, been diligent in helpfulness.

Notes

1. William L. Shirer, *The Rise and Fall of the Third Reich*, pp. 509, 532. Also Nuremberg Document 1014 PS Washington, 1956, Exhibit USA-30, and *Documents on German Foreign Policy.* Count Galeazzo Ciano, *The Ciano Diaries, 1939–1943*, pp. 118–119. John A. Lukacs, *The Great Powers and Eastern Europe*, p. 248.

2. Various accounts of the Gleiwitz incident have been published. Until recently most authorities believed that the Naujocks raiding party wore Polish uniforms and that the body of the man left behind was an unknown inmate of a concentration camp, sacrificed brutally to achieve persuasive "authenticity." It is possible that this version is correct, but the weight of evidence is against it. I am indebted to Kurt Rosenbaum of the Department of History of West Virginia University for calling my attention to a comprehensive article on the Gleiwitz incident by Jürgen Runzheimer in the October, 1962, *Vierteljahrshefte für Zeitgeschichte,* entitled "Der Uberfall auf den Sender Gleiwitz." Mr. Runzheimer concludes after painstaking examination of the evidence that the raid was planned and carried out by the *Sicherheitsdienst* of the SS. Five men participated, led by Naujocks. All were attired in civilian clothing. One of the men was shot, apparently accidentally, by an SD man who passed by after the fake transmission had gone out over the air. The various versions of the Gleiwitz incident and the confusion surrounding it are due to several factors, including the obscurity of some of the Nuremberg documents dealing with the affair. A reference by General Halder in a diary entry of August 17 to a request from Himmler to the Wehrmacht for Polish uniforms, the objective, "a simulated raid . . . against Gleiwitz," and other references in various publications to plans to furnish concentration camp inmates to serve as "bodies" of Polish raiders combined to distort somewhat what actually happened at Gleiwitz. It seems probable that the raid was actually planned to include the accouterments of verisimilitude—Polish uniforms and the body of a concentration camp inmate left behind—but it apparently did not happen that way. The Runzheimer article and evaluations of it by Mr. Rosenbaum, Major R. M. Kennedy and Mr. Herbert H. Schellenberger of Albany, New York, former German artillery officer and document translator at Nuremberg, are convincing evidence to the contrary. However, other Polish border "incidents"—little known to fame—were staged by the Nazis with all the props mentioned in numerous publications, including, apparently, bodies of concentration camp inmates.

3. The leaders of World War II offer a fascinating study in psychology. The two great protagonists were Adolf Hitler, malevolent genius, and Winston Churchill, a towering, inspirational leader.

The various characters of 1939 could only have been produced by the capricious dice of genetics; the dramatist who conceived them would have been labeled ludicrous:

Adolf Hitler—Master of the Third Reich, a World War I corporal come to high estate. A vegetarian, a hater of Jews, who apotheosized himself and Germany in his image. A man, like many before him, with a sense of mission and destiny but ruthless, determined, with a great gift for mob-stirring oratory, a sense of political timing, an intuitive generalship, a natural mimic, an untidy administrator, a megalomaniac ambition, shouting passion and (in Sir Nevile Henderson's words) "sheer vindictiveness." He was a man who "believed neither in God nor in conscience ('a Jewish invention, a blemish like circumcision') . . . a Siegfried come to reawaken Germany to greatness, for whom morality, suffering and the 'litany of private virtues' were irrelevant." And, withal, a perverted genius who, in Bullock's phrase, "like[d] cream cakes and sweets . . . flowers in his rooms, and dogs . . . the company of pretty—but not clever—women."

Herman Göring—The No. 2 man of the National Socialist hierarchy—a World War I air ace, grown fat and dissolute, corrupted by power, a taker of drugs, a collector of art, antlers and decorations, a lover of fine foods and wines, a seeming Falstaff, vain and petty, but behind the bulky joviality a keen and cunning mind and strong will, a political infighter.

Benito Mussolini—Dictator of Italy, exemplar of Fascism, the "sawdust Caesar" who made the trains run on time.

General Maurice Gamelin—Chief of the French General Staff, who depended upon the Maginot Line, and whose fatuous remark, "My soul is at peace," epitomized the misjudgments of the time.

Pierre Laval and many opportunistic French politicians who feared the left wing more than the Nazis.

Neville Chamberlain—Prime Minister of Great Britain, who had returned from the Munich conference a year before, brandishing an umbrella and predicting "peace in our time."

The British Establishment—who thought they could do business with Hitler, and who agreed with Chamberlain (in his broadcast of September 27, 1938) that British blood should not be shed "because of a quarrel in a faraway country [Czechoslovakia] between people of whom we know nothing."

And *Winston Churchill*—almost a lone voice—gadfly, oppositionist, a Cassandra warning of Nazi aims.

Joseph Stalin—whose paternal face belied a ruthless will. Dictator of Russia, master of terror and repression, leader of the Communist conspiracy. He knew no friends, tolerated no enemies. To Stalin the ends justified any means. He matched Hitler in cynicism but restrained his megalomania with a shrewd peasant cunning.

Ignacy Mościcki—President of Poland; *Józef Beck*—Foreign Minister; *Marshal Edward Rydz-Smigly*—Inspector General of the Armed Forces—inheritors of Paderewski's and of Pilsudski's mantles, authoritarian rulers of a feudalistic state, beset by ethnic minorities, squeezed between Moscow and Berlin.

And, across the sea, "F.D.R."—*Franklin Delano Roosevelt*—President of a United States still emerging from a great depression, a leader loved and hated, master politician, paralytic, ambitious, idealistic, dreamer of dreams and schemer of schemes, an aristocrat with the common touch, who, in his "Fireside Chats," made the phrase "My friends" a household term and a subject for satire.

4. Mr. S. Nilson of Oslo, Norway, points out that the name of "Quisling" and what it stands for "should not be eliminated from history," but he urges that Quisling's role in Norway should not be "misunderstood." He points out that "the mere existence of a number of sympathizers within the borders of another country has never proved to be of decisive advantage to any nation." Though "never" is too strong a word, it is true that Quisling had relatively few followers in Norway. They became important—in a minor way—solely because the might of the German war machine overwhelmed the Norwegian defenders. But in the German occupation Quisling and his followers were never able to "pacify" Norway or to command the political loyalty for which Hitler had hoped.

5. History's condemnation of Chamberlain, and indeed of the British and French surrender at Munich, has another side. Chamberlain was told unanimously by the British Chiefs of Staff prior to Munich that Britain was in no military condition to go to war. This estimate was written and extensive; confronted with it, Chamberlain had virtually no other choice than to get the best terms he could without war. The Allies, moreover, probably did gain by the year of uneasy peace that Munich gave them. The British radar detection system was virtually completed; British aircraft factories increased their production, and the RAF got the new Hurricane and Spitfire fighters in some quantity. Moreover, Hitler's continued aggrandizement united the British people. The attack on Poland was such a clear-cut case of aggression (as compared to the Czechoslovakian crisis complicated by the cloudy but plausible claims of the Sudeten Germans) that it provided a bugle call to battle, hitherto lacking. (See Lukacs, *op. cit.*, pp. 169–172, and Lieutenant Commander P. K. Kemp, *Key to Victory*, pp. 26–28.) Kemp says that the "categorical" report of the Chiefs of Staff stated "that the country was not ready for war." He adds that it placed Chamberlain in a "position from which there was no escape; national prestige, national honor, the obloquy of future generations, none of these could weigh against his overriding duty to his country, to gain time."

6. A. L. Rowse's bitter and biased little polemic, *Appeasement: A Study in Political Decline 1933–1939*, gives some of the precrisis atmosphere in England's "Establishment" before the blinders were removed. John W. Wheeler-Bennett's *Munich: Prologue to Tragedy* is "must" reading.

7. Shirer, *op. cit.*, p. 454.

8. T. L. Jarman, *The Rise and Fall of Nazi Germany*, p. 251, quoted from Hans B. Gisevius, *To the Bitter End*.

9. Shirer, *op. cit.*, p. 468; Major Robert M. Kennedy, *The German Campaign in Poland (1939)*, p. 39; Walter Görlitz, *History of the German General Staff*, p. 348.

10. An elaborate "cover scheme" to camouflage the mobilization was arranged. The annual fall maneuvers were to be held near the Polish frontier, and a celebration of the twenty-fifth anniversary of the Battle of Tannenberg

(August 27–29, 1914) was scheduled for East Prussia. The operations plan for the invasion was perfected in midsummer by a "General Staff tactical ride" (an actual terrain reconnaissance near the frontier, supplemented by maps, etc.), led by General Franz Halder himself. (See MSC No. C-065c, *Greiner Series, Poland, 1939,* Washington: Office of the Chief of Military History, Department of the Army. Helmut Greiner was Keeper of the War Diary in Hitler's Headquarters from August, 1939, to April, 1943.)

11. Kennedy, *op. cit.,* p. 36.
12. Ciano, *op. cit.,* pp. 119 and 121.
13. General Franz Halder, *The Halder Diaries,* Vol. I, *Polish Campaign.*
14. *Ibid.,* Collenberg commentary. See also Kennedy, *op. cit.,* pp. 42–43.
15. *Ibid.,* p. 43.
16. Shirer, *op. cit.,* p. 532.
17. Lukacs, *op. cit.* (quoted, p. 245). Three versions of this famous Obersalzberg monologue, reconstructed from notes made by participants, were presented to the Nuremberg war crimes trials and a fourth was referred to but not offered in evidence. Each differs slightly in wording but not in substance. Greiner (*op. cit.,* pp. 7 ff.) offers a toned-down and secondhand version of the conference, which took place on August 22, *before* the signing of the Soviet-German pact.
18. The genesis of the Russo-German pact lies deep in the ambivalence of both Soviet and German politics. One school in Germany had always looked toward the East and had urged virtual alliance with Russia at the expense of the West. But Hitler's immediate interest apparently stemmed, according to Greiner (*op. cit.,* pp. 6 and 7), from a meeting between Soviet Embassy and German representatives in the "Berlin Weinrestaurant, Ewest," in April, 1939, during economic negotiations between the Nazis and the Communists.
19. Halder, *op. cit.,* August 24.
20. *Ibid.,* August 28.
21. Sir Nevile Henderson, *Failure of a Mission; Berlin 1937–1939,* pp. 278, 280.
22. *Ibid.,* pp. 284–285.
23. General Walter Warlimont, *Inside Hitler's Headquarters 1939–1945,* p. 31.
24. Shirer, *op. cit.,* p. 588.
25. Ciano, *op. cit.,* p. 134.
26. Shirer, *op. cit.,* p. 591.
27. Warlimont, *op. cit.,* pp. 3–5.
28. Henderson, *op. cit.,* pp. 289–290.
29. Shirer, *op. cit.,* p. 592.
30. *Ibid.,* pp. 588–589; Henderson, *op. cit.,* pp. 290–291; Alan Bullock, *Hitler: A Study in Tyranny,* p. 501; and Jarman, *op. cit.,* p. 263.
31. Ciano, *op. cit.,* p. 134.
32. Bullock, *op. cit.,* p. 500, as quoted from Paul Schmidt, *Statist auf diplomatischer Bühne,* 1923–1945.
33. Bullock, *ibid.,* pp. 502, 505.
34. Henderson, *op. cit.,* p. 294.
35. Shirer, *op. cit.,* p. 608.
36. *Ibid.,* p. 613.

37. Frederick L. Schuman, *Europe on the Eve,* notes (p. 496) that "in its ultimate ramifications the panic which the Russian Revolution inspired among
the wealthy and well-born of Western Europe is the clue to the politics of
the epoch of dread." The Western world found itself between the devil and
the deep blue sea—between Communism and Fascism.

38. Some sources estimate the active peacetime strength of the Polish Army of
1939 at 350,000 (see *Die Gebirgstruppe,* October, 1964, pp. 25 ff.). But this
estimate appears high; except in times of emergency or for special maneuvers, the strength varied between 280,000 and 300,000.

39. Greiner (*op. cit.*) estimates the over-all strength of the Polish field forces as
45 infantry divisions, 12 cavalry brigades and 2 motorized brigades. The
April, 1964, number of the German military magazine *Die Gebirgstruppe*
(Munich, Plankensteinstrasse, 7) gives the peacetime strength of the Polish
Army in 1939 at about 300,000, organized in 28 infantry divisions and 2
mountain divisions, plus some 11 cavalry brigades and 1 motorized brigade.
Its strength at the beginning of the war was estimated by *Die Gebirgstruppe*
at 3,600,000, organized in 39 infantry divisions, 1 mountain division, 3 mountain brigades, 11 cavalry brigades and 1 motorized brigade. However, as
noted, most of the reserve units were never fully mobilized, and hundreds
of thousands of reservists never reached their mobilization centers. These
estimates in any case appear to be high; Lieutenant General Norwid-
Neugebauer (*The Defense of Poland,* p. 33) estimates total strength with
partial call-up of reservists at about 2,200,000.

40. See Flight Lieutenant Poruczynik (pseudonym), *Polish Wings Over Europe.*

41. F. B. Czarnomski, ed., *They Fight for Poland,* p. 33.

42. Lukacs, *op. cit.,* p. 241.

43. One of the SS regiments that fought in Poland, according to Major Kennedy,
was drawn from Hitler's bodyguard—the *Leibstandarte Adolf Hitler*—which
then operated as a motorized regiment, but was later raised after the end of
the Polish campaign to divisional status. The LAH, as the unit was called,
was probably committed to combat in Poland "for prestige purposes," since
the Army was critical and uneasy about the growing strength of the SS and
the priority it was receiving in personnel and equipment. The SS was, in
effect, a political army, which was not under Wehrmacht command except
when in action at the front.

44. "Der Feldzug in Polen, 1939," *Die Gebirgstruppe,* Munich, October, 1964.

45. F. S. Kurcz, *The Black Brigade,* pp. 4 ff.

46. General Heinz Guderian, *Panzer Leader,* pp. 70–71.

47. Lieutenant General W. Anders, *An Army in Exile,* pp. 2–3.

48. Clare Hollingworth, *The Three Weeks' War in Poland,* pp. 25, 26, 29. This
description applied to Cracow as of September 3–4.

49. Czarnomski, *op. cit.,* p. 79 ff. "My First Three Days" by Lieutenant J. S. of
the Bydgoszcz District Office, as told to Jerzy Pomian.

50. Kurcz, *op. cit.,* p. 55.

51. Herbert, *op. cit.,* pp. 33 ff. Descriptions of the Polish aircraft and a rambling
chronicle of the air campaign as seen by one Polish flier are given in this
book.

52. Kennedy, *op. cit.*, pp. 89–90. This work, the best in English dealing with the Polish campaign, is the definitive and most objective treatment of the subject. I have drawn upon it heavily. Other works consulted for this section include Görlitz, *op. cit.*, pp. 357–358; Bullock, *op. cit.*, pp. 505 ff.; and my own account of the Polish campaign in *The New International Year Book*, 1939, pp. 234 ff. For personal experiences, see also Wilhelm Prüller, *Diary of a German Soldier*, edited by H. C. Robbins Landon and Sebastian Leitner, with an introduction by Robert Leckie.

53. Alexander Polonius, *I Saw the Siege of Warsaw*, p. 109.

54. Czarnomski, *op. cit.*, pp. 90–91.

55. But the OKH kept a tight rein on the scope of the envelopments. It was worried about the lightly held Western Front and attempted to limit the depth of the German drive into eastern Poland in order to facilitate the rapid transfer of German troops to the Western Front.

Guderian's armored corps carried out the northern part of this sweeping encirclement, which Liddell Hart describes (*The Other Side of the Hill*, p. 70) as a "deep drive . . . down to Brest-Litovsk, southward across the rear of the Polish armies—a deadly stroke, brilliantly executed."

56. Prüller, *op. cit.*, pp. 22, 25.

57. Kennedy, *op. cit.*, p. 102.

58. Czarnomski, *op. cit.*, pp. 33 ff.

59. Polonius, *op. cit.*, pp. 126–135.

60. Czarnomski, *op. cit.*, pp. 92 ff.

61. Hollingworth, *op. cit.*, p. 40.

62. Schörner, of infamous memory, was "also known to the troops as '*Schreck*'," or "Fright," Major Kennedy states in a letter to the author. His comment follows:

He was accustomed to collecting officers and enlisted men at canteens and troop shows and sending them off to the front, and woe betide any individual on authorized pass in the rear areas when Schörner made one of his forays. On one occasion he overtook General Edward Dietl (who later commanded German forces in Northern Russia) on the road and was addressed for his trouble as "Du Bauerngendarme" or "Yokel Policeman." Dietl, an unprepossessing and popular officer, was not accustomed to traveling with the usual fanfare of senior generals and apparently Shörner had mistaken his car for that of some junior officer off on some purpose of his own with a government vehicle.

63. Shirer, *op. cit.*, pp. 626 ff. The rapid German advance was a disagreeable surprise in Moscow, and the Russians hastily advanced the date for the "stab-in-the-back." The Germans did not know until the seventeenth that the Soviet Army would cross the border at 6 A.M. that day.

64. Some Polish officials remained in Kuty, near the Rumanian frontier until late in September. For many of the Poles who escaped across neutral frontiers, the flight meant not only the end of a way of life but permanent exile. Some returned to Poland after the war, but a great number, implacable foes of Communism and earmarked for prison or liquidation if they returned to their homeland, became citizens of other countries, or kept up the forms of a government in exile. As late as 1963, the Associated Press reported

from London that "nine elderly exiles, dreaming of a thousand miles away and a quarter century ago, reign in London as the Polish Provisional Government in Exile.

"Unrecognized by world rulers, they cling to grand titles and eke out the pennies."

65. Czarnomski, *op. cit.* A graphic description of the siege of Warsaw is provided in this book in the chapter entitled "In Beleaguered Warsaw—The War Diary of Colonel L, Warsaw Defense Command," pp. 89 ff.

66. Polonius, *op. cit.*, p. 177.

67. Field Marshal Gerd von Rundstedt, Manuscript No. B-847, Office of the Chief of Military History, Department of the Army, "Notes on the 1939 Polish Campaign," English translation. The gasoline-filled bottles have now become the hallmark of street fighting, guerrilla warfare and even Harlem riots. They have been dubbed "Molotov cocktails," after V. M. Molotov, the wartime Soviet Foreign Minister. The origin of the phrase is obscure, but the "cocktails" were apparently first used extensively in the Spanish Civil War.

68. Polonius, *op. cit.*, p. 199.

69. Czarnomski, *op. cit.*, chapter entitled "In a Warsaw Hospital," as told by Madame Jadwiga Sosnkonska.

70. Kennedy, *op. cit.*, p. 113.

71. Czarnomski, *op. cit.*, pp. 95 ff.

72. *Ibid.*, p. 119.

73. The Fifth Column activities, though widely noted by the Poles, were of minor importance in the quick victory achieved by the Germans; the major factor was Germany's overwhelming military preponderance. Some of the Fifth Columnists, though technically Polish citizens, were ethnic Germans and had been German citizens before the Versailles Treaty made them Poles. Apparently, relatively few ethnic Poles aided the enemy.

74. Norwid-Neugebauer, *op. cit.*, p. 225.

75. The figures differ widely; accurate Polish losses—particularly killed and wounded—may never be known. "Der Feldzug in Polen, 1939," *Die Gebirgstruppe*, October, 1964, estimates 217,000 Poles fell into Russian hands, and about 100,000 escaped across the border to Hungary and Rumania. It puts the number of prisoners in German hands at 694,000.

76. Lieutenant General Norwid-Neugebauer (*op. cit.*) claimed in his book published in 1942 (p. 199) that "confidential reports of the German war office" indicated far higher German casualties: 91,278 killed, 63,417 seriously wounded and 34,938 slightly wounded, plus 198 tanks and 415 planes destroyed. It was widely believed at the time that the German official figures were too low. Like all casualty statistics, the truth probably depends upon the period for which the casualties were reported. The officially reported German figures may not have included all casualties of the mop-up phase, but the total of about 49,000 appears to be substantially correct, and I know of no sources which substantiate General Norwid-Neugebauer's claims.

77. Winston S. Churchill, *The Gathering Storm*, p. 447. Actually few parachutists—except intelligence agents—were used in Poland, and although the

Germans did not hesitate to bomb towns, their targets were selected primarily because of their military importance as communications junctions, mobilization points, etc. Warsaw was a major exception; as the political and psychological capital of Poland it was bombed and shelled ruthlessly.

78. Liddell Hart, *op. cit.*, p. 50.
79. Warlimont, *op. cit.*, p. 93. See also pp. 5, 30 ff., for a fascinating discussion of the German command arrangements.
80. Görlitz, *op. cit.* (p. 348), quotes General Walter Warlimont, Deputy Chief of Armed Forces Operations Staff (OKW), as having said "on a later occasion that no German Army had gone to war so ill prepared." This is a gross exaggeration or at least conveys a completely erroneous impression. For preparedness is relative, and the German Army of 1939, despite its weaknesses, was better prepared than any other army in the world (the Japanese approached it) for a short war—and probably as well prepared as any, in September, 1939, for a long war.

A curious oversight in the Polish campaign cited by Kennedy (*op. cit.*, pp. 133–134) was the "supply of horseshoes [for the German Army], made to a size common to military horses but far too small for the splayed hooves of many farm horses requisitioned at the time of mobilization."

Rundstedt also reported later (Rundstedt, *op. cit.*) that

our field artillery and infantry vehicles were much too heavy for the poor roads, especially in the large forests. Unfortunately this failed to become apparent prior to the Russian campaign in 1941 because of the speedy operations and the continued good weather experienced in Poland. The heavy vehicles required strong draft horses. Such horses need more fodder, water, and rest. In 1914–17, and also in 1941 we preferred the little hardy *panje*-horses to be obtained locally. Our losses in horses during the Russian campaign were enormous.

The Field Marshal also reported that the combat power of the light motorized divisions was "extremely limited"; as a result of the Polish campaign they were converted to Panzer divisions.

Some of the German weaknesses, revealed to the skilled eye in the Polish campaign, were never remedied—largely because Hitler's ambitions exceeded German capabilities. The problem of supply became insurmountable in the vast Russian spaces. Colonel John C. Kulp comments in "Mobility Is an Endless Belt," *Army Magazine,* March, 1965, that the German planners neglected "their total mobility requirements."

The movement capabilities of individual pieces of equipment were confused with mobility . . . an army is a complete entity whose total mobility capabilities are gauged by the total movement of the entire mass rather than by the speed of its component parts.

In the Russian campaign the immobility of its support system destroyed the German Army. . . . The Soviet advance was eased by short-sighted planners who had riveted their attention on tactical mobility to the neglect of balanced mobility in the support system.

There is an element of importance in these comments, though they are considerably overstated. The Germans based most of their strategic mobility on the railroad, largely because much of their army was horse-drawn. It probably could not have been completely motorized and at the same time supplied by motor vehicles because of the limited supplies of fuel available to the Germans. There were deficiencies—an inadequate number of trucks, a lack of armored personnel carriers to enable infantry to keep pace with the Panzers and so on—but on the whole the Germans accomplished prodigies of supply, often with improvisation.

As Robert Leckie writes in his introduction to Wilhelm Prüller's *Diary of a German Soldier* (*op. cit.*, p. 9), "Military professionalism, when yoked to romantic purpose, however evil, is a most formidable force . . . we might discover how what is best in man can be brought to excellence in the service of what is worst."

81. Rundstedt (*op. cit.*) objects that the Polish campaign, despite the propaganda to the contrary, was not an eighteen-day war. He reported that Army Group South "suffered more casualties after the first eighteen days than before." Nevertheless, the campaign was clearly won within two weeks. The Poles fought proudly but not well. As Rundstedt remarks, after words of high praise for the Polish cavalry, ". . . in general, the bravery and heroism of the Polish Army merits great respect. But the higher command was not equal to the demands of the situation."

Mr. Kurt Rosenbaum of the Department of History of West Virginia University notes that "contemporary Germans" describe the Polish campaign as *Blumenkrieg* to convey the idea that the fighting was a "pushover," or exercise.

82. Major Kennedy makes a point about the use of the phrase *"Deutschland über alles"*—from the German national anthem—which deserves stress. The original intention of the song, as he points out, was to emphasize the unity and supremacy of Germany within its own borders, to "counteract the strong particularism of the Bavarians, Swabians, Prussians and others" who formed a German state united only since 1871. The song itself was not originally associated with aggression, but the quoted phrase was undoubtedly twisted by the Allies in both World Wars for propaganda purposes.

However, during the Hitler regime, there is no doubt that the Nazis meant the phrase literally in the sense of a race of German supermen astride Europe, of world conquest.

83. See Appendix for casualty details.

84. Few of the principal actors of 1939 survived the holocaust; Hitler killed himself in a bunker in Berlin in a Wagnerian finale in 1945. Neville Chamberlain died, broken in heart and body, on November 9, 1940; he had survived long enough to see the fall of France and Hitler's bid for conquest across the Channel turned back in the Battle of Britain. Chamberlain's arch-antagonist and critic, Winston Churchill, rallied the forces of freedom as Prime Minister of Britain, but even he lived to see the words he uttered then (in his Mansion House speech in London in November, 1942) belied: "I have not become the King's First Minister in order to preside over the liquidation of the British Empire."

For World War II confirmed and ended the process World War I started—the decline and fall of the empire upon which the sun had once never set.

Germany and her satellites were completely defeated; Japan was crushed. The Allies achieved Total Victory, but again for the second time in a quarter of a century peace and stability eluded them. The United States and Soviet Russia emerged from World War II as "super-states"; Communism extended its hegemony over Eastern Europe and even to Berlin. Instead of "peace in our time," there emerged from World War II breakups of empires, anticolonialism, racial friction, the downfall of the past order, continents in turmoil and, with the conquest of China by Marxism, a global menace more dangerous than Hitler ever was.

Man, once again, as in the Great War of 1914–1918, was both cause and effect, victor and vanquished, victim of his own worst nature.

World War I, and its imperfect peace, had led inevitably to World War II. The real injustices and, more important, the geographic and ethnic absurdities of the Versailles Treaty, the economic depression and the bitter struggle of right and left helped to lead to Hitler's rise. The appeasers and the shortsighted pacifists and well-intentioned "do-gooders" encouraged aggrandizement by passivity and negation, and the Right Wing in France and England, mesmerized by the dangers of Communism, overlooked, minimized or palliated the dangers of Fascism and Nazism. And Communist Russia contributed mightily to world disaster by international subversion and conspiracy and by the cynical power politics of Joseph Stalin.

It was to lead—this second period of Total War—to the atomic age, with its incipient horrors, and to divided Germany, divided Korea, divided Vietnam, and to the "time of troubles" unending in which we live.

Its consequences linger on unto a third and fourth generation. . . .

Who was to blame?

If one agrees with the Tolstoy theory of history, even great national leaders are but chips on the tidal waves of great events. World War II in this context was part of an epoch of catastrophe and revolution, an inevitable outgrowth of World War I.

Yet if any one man bears primary and major responsibility for World War II, that man is Adolf Hitler, corporal in World War I, nemesis in World War II.

He it was who wanted war—not the war he got, but a war of conquest and triumph, of revenge and aggression; he it was who led a nation to battle and subjected a continent to devastation.

World War II, Hitler's War, dragged on for almost six long years. At its end the Nazi Reich that was to last a thousand years was dust and ashes, a jumbled mass of wreckage where cities once had been, peopled by men and women with shocked, lackluster eyes—a "Master Race" led to destruction by the Master Pied Piper of history.

A Note on the German Command System

The German command system was unified under Hitler as Commander in Chief or Supreme Commander. His principal staff assistants in the OKW

(Oberkommando der Wehrmacht) or High Command of the Armed Forces were at the start and for the duration of the war Field Marshal Wilhelm Keitel as Chief of Staff and General Alfred Jodl as Chief of the Operations Staff (in American parlance, J-3 or Operations Section of the Joint Staff). Under the OKW were the OKH (Oberkommando des Heeres) or Army High Command, with Field Marshal Walther von Brauchitsch as Commander in Chief and General Franz Halder as Chief of Staff; the Oberkommando der Luftwaffe (OKL) or Air Force High Command, with Reich Marshal Hermann Göring as Commander in Chief and General Hans Jeschonnek as Chief of Staff; and the OKM (Oberkommando des Kriegsmarine) or Navy High Command, with Grand Admiral Erich Raeder as Commander in Chief and Admiral Otto Schniewind as Chief of Staff.

Hitler assumed personal command of the Army (in addition to his Supreme Commander's role) after the invasion of Russia, and Army Chiefs of Staff were frequently relieved. There were changes in the high commands of the other services during the war (although Göring continued until the end as head of the Luftwaffe), but the Navy and Air Force enjoyed more stability—largely because Hitler knew less about them, took less interest in them and had more confidence in them politically.

When the war started in September, 1939, the defensive front on Germany's western frontiers was held by three armies—the Fifth, First and Seventh under Army Group West (General Wilhelm Ritter von Leeb). Army Group A was organized, but only as a skeleton force, to cover the Belgian and Dutch borders in September. (See Greiner, *op. cit.*)

Acknowledgments

I am particularly indebted to Major Robert M. Kennedy, USA (Ret.), one-time Army historian, now (1965) professor at Siena College, New York, for his extraordinary kindness, courtesy and patience. Mr. Kennedy supplied some of the material for this chapter, made many suggestions and read the manuscript, though its faults substantively and stylistically are the author's.

I am also indebted to Professor Kurt Rosenbaum of the Department of History of West Virginia University for suggestions, sources and corrections.

Bibliography

Books

ANDERS, LIEUTENANT GENERAL W., *An Army in Exile*. London: Macmillan, 1949
BALDWIN, HANSON W., *The Caissons Roll*. New York: Knopf, 1938
BLOCH, LEON BRYCE, and ANGOFF, CHARLES, eds., *The World Over: 1939*. New York: Living Age Press, 1940
BUCHANAN, RUSSELL A., *The U.S. and World War II*, Vol. I. New York: Harper, 1964
BULLOCK, ALAN, *Hitler: A Study in Tyranny*. London: Odhams Press, 1952
CHURCHILL, WINSTON S., *The Second World War*, Vol. 1, *The Gathering Storm*. Boston: Houghton Mifflin, 1948

CIANO, COUNT GALEAZZO, *The Ciano Diaries, 1939–1943.* New York: Doubleday, 1946

CZARNOMSKI, F. B., ed., *They Fight for Poland.* London: Allen & Unwin, 1941

ESPOSITO, VINCENT J., ed., *The West Point Atlas of American Wars,* Vol. II, 1900–1953. New York: Praeger, 1959

FALLS, CYRIL, *The Second World War.* London: Methuen, 1949

GISEVIUS, HANS B., *To the Bitter End.* New York: Houghton Mifflin, 1947

GÖRLITZ, WALTER, *History of the German General Staff.* New York: Praeger, 1953

GREINER, HELMUT, *Greiner Series, Poland, 1939,* Manuscript No. C-065c (English translation). Washington: Office of the Chief of Military History, Department of the Army

GUDERIAN, GENERAL HEINZ, *Panzer Leader.* London: Michael Joseph, 1952

HALDER, GENERAL FRANZ, *The Halder Diaries,* personal wartime journal of the chief of the German Army General Staff, with commentary by General A. D. Ludwig Freiherr Rüdt von Collenberg. English translation in manuscript form; entries by dates. Washington: Office of the Chief of Military History, Department of the Army, Vol. I, *Polish Campaign.*

HART, B. H. LIDDELL, *The Other Side of the Hill.* London: Cassell, 1951

HENDERSON, SIR NEVILE, *Failure of a Mission; Berlin 1937–1939.* New York: Putnam, 1940

HERBERT, FLIGHT LIEUTENANT PORUCZYNIK (pseudonym), *Polish Wings Over Europe.* Middlesex (England): Atlantis Publishing Co.

HOLLINGWORTH, CLARE, *The Three Weeks' War in Poland.* London: Duckworth, 1940

JARMAN, T. L., *The Rise and Fall of Nazi Germany.* New York: New York University Press, 1956

JONG, LOUIS DE, *The German Fifth Column in the Second World War.* Chicago: University of Chicago Press, 1956

KEESING'S *Contemporary Archives,* 1937–1940

KEMP, LIEUTENANT COMMANDER P. K., *Key to Victory.* Boston: Little Brown, 1958

KENNEDY, MAJOR ROBERT M., *The German Campaign in Poland (1939).* Washington: Department of the Army Pamphlet No. 20–255, 1956

KURCZ, F. S., *The Black Brigade.* Middlesex (England): Atlantis Publishing Co., 1943

LUKACS, JOHN A., *The Great Powers and Eastern Europe.* New York: American Book, 1953

NORWID-NEUGEBAUER, LIEUTENANT GENERAL MIECZYSLAW, *The Defense of Poland.* London: Kolin, 1942

Order of Battle of the German Army. Washington: Military Intelligence Division, War Department (March, 1945)

PAPEN, FRANZ VON, *Memoirs.* New York: Dutton, 1953

POLONIUS, ALEXANDER, *I Saw the Siege of Warsaw.* London: William Hodge, 1941

PRÜLLER, WILHELM, *Diary of a German Soldier,* ed. by H. C. Robbins Landon and Sebastian Leitner, with an introduction by Robert Leckie. New York: Coward-McCann, 1963

ROWE, VIVIAN, *The Great Wall of France.* New York: Putnam, 1961

ROWSE, A. L., *Appeasement: A Study in Political Decline 1933–1939*. New York: Norton, 1961

SCHUMAN, FREDERICK L., *Europe on the Eve*. New York: Knopf, 1938

SHIRER, WILLIAM L., *Berlin Diary*. New York: Knopf, 1941

SHIRER, WILLIAM L., *The Rise and Fall of the Third Reich*. New York: Simon & Schuster, 1960

TAYLOR, TELFORD, *Sword and Swastika*. New York: Simon & Schuster, 1952

WARLIMONT, GENERAL WALTER, *Inside Hitler's Headquarters, 1939–45*. New York: Praeger, 1964

WHEELER-BENNETT, JOHN W., *Munich: Prologue to Tragedy*. New York: Duell, Sloan & Pearce, 1948

General References

The British War Blue Book. Misc. No. 9. New York: Farrar & Rinehart, 1939

The New International Year Book. New York and London: Funk & Wagnalls, 1939

Periodicals

"Der Feldzug in Polen, 1939," *Die Gebirgstruppe*, Munich, October, 1964

GEOFFREY BOCCA, "The Mystery Man Who Triggered World War II," *True* magazine, August, 1963

COLONEL JOHN C. KULP, "Mobility Is an Endless Belt." Washington: *Army* magazine, March, 1964

JÜRGEN RUNZHEIMER, "Der Uberfall auf den Sender Gleiwitz," *Vierteljahrshefte für Zeitgeschichte*, October, 1962

Documents

Documents *Concerning German-Polish Relations and the Outbreak of Hostilities between Great Britain and Germany on Sept. 3, 1939*. London: His Majesty's Stationery Office, 1939

Documents *Concerning the Last Phase of the German-Polish Crisis*. Berlin: Reichsdruckerei, 1939

Documents *Polish-Soviet Relations 1918–1943*. Washington: Polish Embassy

Documents *On the Events Preceding the Outbreak of the War*. New York: German Library of Information, 1940

Henderson, Sir Nevile, *Final Report on the Circumstances Leading to the Termination of His Mission to Berlin*. London: His Majesty's Stationery Office, 1939

Nuremberg Document 1014 PS, Washington, 1956, Exhibit USA-30; and *Documents on German Foreign Policy*

Rundstedt, Field Marshal Gerd von, "Notes on the 1939 Polish Campaign," Manuscript No. B-847 (English translation). Washington: Office of the Chief of Military History, Department of the Army

CHAPTER 2.   THE BATTLE OF BRITAIN

Notes

1. "One of the few men who realized from the start that in any future war technology would play the vital part was General Wever who unfortunately lost his life in a tragic crash in the Summer of 1936 when he was the first Luftwaffe Chief of Staff." Dornier and Junkers had built prototypes of long-range, four-engined bombers during Wever's regime to support his conviction, patterned after Douhet (the Italian apostle of strategic air power), that bombing of enemy industrial cities, ports and communications would play a major role in future warfare. But these developments were abandoned after Wever's death, and Germany entered World War II with only one four-engined aircraft—the Focke Wulf 200 C Condor, a civilian transport which was utilized with modifications, for long-range, antishipping patrols and reconnaissance. It was an improvisation, albeit a highly successful one. (Werner Baumbach, *Broken Swastika*, pp. 21, 22.)

   See also *The Narrow Margin* by Derek Wood and Derek Dempster, pp. 44, 45; *Famous Bombers of the Second World War* by William Green, Vol. II, p. 72.

   Major Raymond H. Fredette believes that "Udet was apparently much more responsible for the 'Stuka madness' than a single-engined fighter design." He points out that Adolf Galland, German fighter ace, wrote in an article, "Defeat of the Luftwaffe: Fundamental Causes" (Air University *Quarterly Review;* 6:18, Spring 1953):

   The strength ratio between bombers and fighters in the autumn of 1939 was about as follows: 30 Bomber *Gruppen* (Groups, about 27 to 31 aircraft each) and 9 *Stuka* (dive-bomber) *Gruppen*, as compared with only 13 Fighter *Gruppen* (40 aircraft each). Thus from the very beginning the fighter arm stood on too slight a development basis. . . .
   Grave concern over the raw material resources of Germany in case of a long war was responsible for the fact that the *Stuka* concept, stimulated by impressions received in the United States, appeared to the German air strategists as the "egg of Columbus." Udet and other observers sent to the States were thoroughly "sold" on this concept. Instead of the commitment of major forces and area operations, small forces with pinpoint accuracy of fire became the slogan. With typical German thoroughness this concept was followed to the hilt; from now on, for instance, full diving capabilities were required of all medium and heavy bombers. . . . The consequences were neglect of pattern bombing, elimination of four-engine bombers from the development and construction programs, and retardation of the remaining types of bombers. . . .
   The German Me-109 fighter plane was not the product of any requirement nor the result of official specifications which might have given impetus to such a design, but rather was originated and submitted by the Messerschmitt Aircraft Works. The Luftwaffe had so many faults to find with it—most of which were in reality long out of date, that its superior technical capabilities won its acceptance and adoption by only a narrow margin.

Curiously, both the Germans and the Japanese were influenced considerably by the U.S. Navy's development of the dive bomber as an instrument to assist in controlling the sea. The dive bomber was a potent weapon against ships, as the Pacific War, Crete and other campaigns were to prove, but it was no weapon for so-called "strategic" or area bombing; its bomb load was too limited, its range too short, its defensive capabilities too weak.

2. Major Fredette points out in a letter to the author that:

The British "bomber obsession" was a blend of: (1) Trenchard's dictum that the airplane was an offensive, not a defensive weapon; (2) the trauma of the World War I raids and the sense of insecurity it generated; (3) the conviction, at least until 1936 or so, that "the bomber will always get through." Hence, the counter-offensive, or the threat of reprisal in kind was the only protection.

General P. R. C. Groves, Director of Flying Operations in the British Air Ministry in 1918, estimated (in 1922) that as the air threat increased, "millions of men, thousands of guns, and hundreds of squadrons" would be required for defense. "The only alternative to such an absurdity is the policy of the aerial-offensive-defensive, for which the weapon is the long-distance striking force consisting of bombing machines."

Douhet undoubtedly received a closer reading from the Germans. Göring was intrigued with the Douhet concept for psychological reasons, but he failed to grasp the technical requirements such warfare would entail. Wever, who did, was killed. Udet had his own obsession—the dive-bomber. The traditionally minded General Staff was only interested in an air force which could support the Army. The result was a politico-tactical hybrid of an Air Force which was ill-suited to fight the Battle of Britain.

Marshal of the Royal Air Force, the Viscount Hugh Montague Trenchard was the so-called "father" of the independent Royal Air Force and one of the first—and in Britain perhaps the most influential—theorists of air power.

3. Robert Watson-Watt was by no means the only, "inventor" of radar (abbreviation for RAdio Direction And Range). Dr. A. Hoyt Taylor and Leo C. Young of the U.S. Naval Research Laboratory started experimentation as early as 1922, and by 1937 the U.S. Navy had an experimental radar installation aboard the destroyer Leary. Other independent developments took place in the United States, France and Germany. German Freya radars were operational in small numbers during the Battle of Britain, but they gave no altitude information and they were not keyed to a comprehensive ground-fighter control system. Britain had the first combat-useful radar warning system around her shores, and it was integrated with an effective fighter control system. (James Phinney Baxter, III, Scientists Against Time.)

4. Lieutenant Commander P. K. Kemp, RN (Ret.), Key to Victory, p. 26.

5. R. J. Minney, ed., The Private Papers of Hore-Belisha, p. 146.

6. H. R. Trevor-Roper, Blitzkrieg to Defeat, pp. 33–37.

7. The grand total evacuated from all of France and Norway numbered 558,032, of which 368,491 were British, 25,000 Poles, 5,000 Czechs and the rest French. Of this number a total of 366,162 were evacuated from the Dunkirk area—338,226 during the nine days of "Operation Dynamo," the last stand and final evacuation. It was a "naval affair"; contrary to common belief, it

was the Royal Navy rather than civilian yachtsmen or RAF pilots who made the successful evacuation possible.

8. The total RAF loss in the Battle of France (including losses of Fighter Command) was 1,526 killed, wounded, prisoners and missing, and 931 aircraft destroyed.

9. Winston Churchill, speech to the House of Commons, broadcast June 18, 1940. Quoted from *Victory; War Speeches by the Right Hon. Winston S. Churchill,* compiled by Charles Eade, Boston, Little Brown, 1946, Vol. I, pp. 206–207.

10. The majority of these—some 30 squadrons—were Hurricanes; there were about 19 squadrons of Spitfires.

11. British production of fighter aircraft increased from 157 in January, 1940, to 496 in July.

12. The British official history describes the thirteenth as "Eagle Day," but the attacks of the fifteenth were far larger, and "for the first time the planned scheme of coordinated attacks in daylight by the three Luftflotten deployed from Norway to Britain was put into effect." (Basil Collier, *History of the Second World War—The Defense of the United Kingdom,* p. 191.)

13. Wood and Dempster, *op. cit.,* p. 333.

14. Dennis Richards, *Royal Air Force 1939–1945,* Vol. I, p. 181.

15. Sir. Charles Webster and Noble Frankland, *The Strategic Air Offensive Against Germany—1939–1945,* Vol. 1, p. 140.

   Earlier raids had been directed against German naval shipping at its bases, but, as in the German Scapa Flow raid, some bombs had inevitably fallen on nearby land.

16. There had been a considerable number of relatively minor raids by RAF bombers on German objectives prior to the summer. The first fairly large raid of about 93 aircraft was undertaken against Ruhr marshaling yards in May at the time of the German attack on Belgium, the Netherlands and France.

   Dennis Richards (*op. cit.,* Vol. I, p. 122) comments that

the destruction of Rotterdam (May 14) settled not only the question of further resistance in Holland, but also the question of how far the German Air Force was respecting civilian life and property. When on 15 May the War Cabinet once more considered the propriety of attacking the Ruhr, its remaining doubts had vanished, and the Air Staff was at last given the signal to go ahead. Of the many benefits that this decision was expected to bring, the greatest would be the anticipated effect on the German Air Force. . . . If the Royal Air Force raided the Ruhr, destroying oil plants with its more accurately placed bombs and urban property with those that went astray, the outcry for retaliation against Britain might prove too strong for the German generals to resist. Indeed, Hitler himself would probably head the clamour. The attack on the Ruhr, in other words, was an informal invitation to the Luftwaffe to bomb London.

However, the bulk of the bomber effort had to be diverted during the land campaigns in the west to attempts to support the hard-pressed Allied ground forces by bombing roads, defiles, bridges, railroads and communication junctions. Since January 31, 1940, Bomber Command had had an Air Ministry plan (WAB) for night attack upon Germany "to produce an immediate dislocation of German war industry." But this attack, due to the small British forces available and the diversion of many of the bombers to communications, ports, shipping and other objectives, did not really commence, and then only in small force, until midsummer, with German aircraft factories as the primary objective. The night raids reached a peak, in terms of sorties, (for 1940) in September, with 3,141 sorties.

17. From August 28 to 31 the GAF dropped 114 tons of high-explosive and 257 incendiary canisters on Liverpool and Birkenhead in night raids.

The British raids were allegedly in retaliation for the attacks on these cities and on London, but may have been a master stroke of Churchill to divert the German bombers from British airfields to London.

During August the main objectives of the German bombers were the airfields of Fighter Command. . . . These attacks by the whole weight of the German bomber force against some 20 vital airfields did a great deal of damage to the ground organization of Fighter Command . . . it was estimated toward the end of August that three more weeks of such operations would have exhausted the British reserves of fighter aircraft.

In these circumstances the Prime Minister decided to play a bold card. On the night of August 24 a number of German bombs were dropped on London—the first since 1918—and the government ordered a heavy raid on Berlin as a reprisal. On the night of August 25, 81 aircraft of Bomber Command carried out a successful attack on the German capital, although the night was scarcely long enough to allow the aircraft to go and return in darkness. The German attack had been switched to London and other towns and cities. The pressure against Fighter Command's airfields, which was imperiling the British defense system, was relieved. Although this meant that the civilian population had to suffer, it was a turning point in the battle, and greatly improved the British chances of victory.

Air Marshal Sir Robert Saundby, *Air Bombardment,* p. 96.

There had been, nevertheless, considerable support in the German Air Force and the German Navy for the bombardment of London.

18. William L. Shirer, *The Rise and Fall of the Third Reich,* pp. 777 ff.

19. There are various versions of this speech by Hitler, given on September 4. The wording differs somewhat—apparently due in part to translation—but the basic meaning is identical. These quotations are compiled from Richards, *op. cit.,* Vol. I, p. 183, and Shirer, *op. cit.,* pp. 779, 780.

20. Favorable moon and tides made an invasion attempt between the eighth and the tenth possible. Concentration of aircraft near the straits and of barges and shipping in invasion ports were other indices which led the British Chiefs of Staff to conclude (mistakenly) at a late afternoon meeting on September 7 that an invasion attempt might be imminent. That night from GHQ Home Forces the "Cromwell" warning was issued to bring troops in eastern and southern England to immediate readiness. Some Home Guard commanders ordered the ringing of church bells to mobilize their forces and thus created the impression that an invasion had actually started. (See Collier, *op. cit.,* pp. 223–224.)

21. Shirer, *op. cit.*, p. 770.

22. Total British civilian casualty figures due to bombing were 51,509 killed, 61,423 seriously injured throughout the war. The grand total for civilian casualties, including deaths and injuries caused by flying bombs and rockets (V–1 and V–2) and long-range artillery, was 146,777 (including 60,595 dead). Of this total more than 80,000 occurred in the London area. (See Collier, *op. cit.*, p. 528.)

23. Anthony Martienssen, *Hitler and His Admirals*, p. 89. See also Office of Naval Intelligence, *Fuehrer Conferences—On Matters Dealing with the German Navy, 1939–1945.*

24. David M. Figart, a veteran of World War I, contributes to the origins of so-called strategic bombing, in a letter to the author, written on December 16, 1964. He states:

> In the middle of 1918 I landed in the Statistics Branch of the General Staff—already an enthusiast for air bombing of transportation. My boss was Col. Ayres, later famous for his Cleveland Trust bulletin. After getting settled in a bit I asked permission of Col. Ayres and my immediate superior Major Lutz to work on my idea and establish contacts with the Air Missions of Britain, France and Italy.
>
> Two members of the British Mission were of great help. Col. Seagraves, a car racer, had been shot down and lost a leg. Major Raikes was the initiator of a series of bombing experiments on a railway in England which fitted in completely with my own ideas. He had some magnificent photographs of damage done to railways by bombs of various sizes dropped from various heights, and I reproduced these in my report. A captured German document said that a German general had observed the fact that planes flying *under* a certain height were free from shell bursts. To further illustrate the general idea, I had a plane photograph the railway yards in Washington and the lines to Baltimore, with results of English pattern bombing plotted—indicating that while all bombs from an air drop might fall on the Washington yards, there still would be tracks available on which transport could be detoured. But a single bomb hitting the isolated section of track between Washington and Baltimore would tie up traffic until crews and materials could reach the section needing repair.
>
> Because our Statistics Branch dealt with logistics, I had to camouflage the report under the title "A Statistical Analysis of Aerial Bombardments."
>
> I regret to report that nothing startling happened—the report was not ready for release until the day the Armistice was signed. When things began to get bad in Europe before the Second World War I reminded both the U.S. and British War Offices of the existence of this report, but do not know if it ever was dug up at that late date. Anyway, it was some satisfaction to see from the Strategic Bombing Survey that a plan which seemed so obvious was in fact finally put into effect and had such decisive results.

> Mr. Figart's report was found—by Major Fredette, almost a half-century later. It dealt with the statistical results of bombing attacks by British and French aircraft near and behind the Western Front in the first half of 1918.

25. The Rotterdam raid on May 14, 1940, occurred as the surrender of the city was being negotiated. The Germans attempted to halt the bombing, but some 60 aircraft killed 980 persons. The results were initially completely distorted, partly by war propaganda, and early reports alleged some 30,000

people had been killed. See *The Destruction of Dresden* by David Irving, pp. 21–25.

26. This was after the Rotterdam attack and during the German land campaign against the Netherlands, Belgium and France. I am indebted to Major Fredette for calling my attention to the following passages which bear on the British decision to bomb Germany.

Air Vice Marshal E. J. Kingston McCloughry (*The Direction of War,* p. 102) provides this further background information:

> At this time we had ten fighter squadrons in France . . . the French Government, but also our War Office, were pressing for fighter reinforcements [from the U.K.]. As a result Air Chief Marshal Dowding, the C.-in-C. Fighter Command was ordered by Whitehall to send more fighters; he refused, and as the Commander responsible for the air defense of the U.K. demanded to see the War Cabinet. He saw the Cabinet and spent some time putting his case that to send more fighters to France was frittering them away. . . . He argued that now was the time to bomb Germany and the enemy bombers would then retaliate on his pitch where he could really put up effective opposition. That is how it came about that at long last political approval was given to bomb Germany. Operations were ordered for that night, but even then we had to keep this secret from the French authorities.

Sir Edmund Ironside (*Time Unguarded,* p. 309) noted in his diary for May 15:

> . . . the Cabinet decided unanimously to bomb the Ruhr. It starts tonight. . . . We at least have a Cabinet with some courage now. I never saw anything so light up as the faces of the R.A.F. when they heard that they would be allowed to bomb the oil-refineries in the Ruhr. It did one good to see it. They have built their big bombers for this work and they have been keyed up for the work ever since the war began. Now they have got the chance. I am wondering what the result in the way of reprisals is going to be. Shall we get it as soon as to-morrow in return?

27. William R. Emerson, *Operation Pointblank,* The Harmon Memorial Lectures in Military History Number Four, United States Air Force Academy, Colorado, 1962, pp. 40–41.

28. Field Marshal Albert Kesselring, *A Soldier's Record,* p. 71. Fuller (Major General J. F. C. Fuller, *The Decisive Battles of the Western World,* London, Eyre & Spottiswoode, 1956, Vol. 3, p. 471) comments:

> The truth is, with the possible exception of Göring, the Luftwaffe commander, nobody believed in Operation Sea Lion. Certainly the German admirals did not, nor the generals, nor Hitler himself who, according to General [Günther] Blumentritt [later Chief of Staff to Rundstedt], in July told Rundstedt privately that he "did not intend to carry out Sea Lion."

29. Walter Ansel, *Hitler Confronts England,* pp. 316, 317.

30. Ansel holds, however, in his remarkably thorough study (*op. cit.*) that even in September the invasion would have been crushed, primarily by superior British sea power. An earlier invasion would have presupposed elimination

of the weaknesses in planning and execution so noticeable in retrospect. Neither, in fact, occurred. Nevertheless, the moral is to the physical as three to one, and quick onslaught after the defeat of Dunkirk would have been hard for the British to meet, had it been coupled to a comprehensive and sound plan.

But the German planning was halfhearted and incomplete. Low-level attacks (to avoid detection by British radar), for instance, directed against RAF fighter airfields, with the sole objective of establishing a localized air superiority in the planned invasion area, might well have crippled the British. See *Wing Leader* by Group Captain J. E. Johnson, pp. 171–174:

Dowding's airfields were not well protected. . . . Antiaircraft resources were so stretched that captured Stuka machine guns were used to defend Tangmere; and one obsolete brass-bound cannon was the only heavy weapon available to another sector station.

Surprise (by low-level attacks) would certainly have been achieved against the radar and coastal airfields, and had the attacks been well delivered, the eyes of Fighter Command would have been put out after, at the very most, three or four strikes. . . .

Working to such a plan, how long would the Luftwaffe have taken to achieve air domination over southern England? When I put this question to Park [Air Vice Marshal K. R. Park, commanding No. 11 Group] he replied: "This was the only thing I dreaded, because had they come in very low we could not have intercepted from the ground readiness, and I should have had to resort to standing patrols, which were no substitute." . . .

In my view the Luftwaffe could have won air domination over southern England within two weeks and would have then been ready for the next phase of their campaign—the isolation of the battlefield. . . . Then, opposed only by a British Army still handicapped by the loss of much equipment at Dunkirk and by a Royal Navy fighting at a great disadvantage in the narrow confines of a Channel dominated by the Luftwaffe, the German airborne troops might easily have seized a suitable piece of Kent in which to establish and build up an invasion force.

31. Kesselring, *op. cit.,* p. 76.
32. The GAF did use, however, the so-called Knickebein beams (a "code-word roughly translatable as 'googly' " or "bent leg"). These electronic beams were not radar, but medium-frequency radio beacons which were used as navigational aids by the German bombers. When two such beams crossed, the German navigators fixed their positions over their targets even in bad weather. The British succeeded in "bending" some of these beams; some were jammed, others were nullified by the establishment of false beacons. This was the start of a "war" still continuing, a quarter-century later, of electronic measures and countermeasures. (See *The Destruction of Dresden* by David Irving, pp. 29–30.)
33. Wood and Dempster, *op. cit.,* p. 301.
34. Richards, *op. cit.,* p. 190.
35. *National Observer,* September, 1965.
36. Collier (*op. cit.,* p. 250) comments that "the battle had been won but by a margin whose narrowness was apparent only to those who had studied its progress in all its aspects and through all its phases."

A Note on the Principal Aircraft in the Battle of Britain

GERMAN FIGHTER AIRCRAFT

Messerschmitt (Me) 109: Single-engined. Maximum speed 354 at 12,300 feet. (The Bf 109–E–3 was the principal model used in the Battle of Britain.)

Messerschmitt (Me) 110: Twin-engined, two-seat, long-range escort fighter. Also used as fighter-bomber. Maximum speed 350 miles per hour at 20,000 feet. (Me–110 C–4, principal model used.)

GERMAN BOMBER AIRCRAFT

Junkers (Ju) 87 ("Stuka"): The famous two-seat, single-engined dive bomber. Max. speed 245 at 15,000 feet.

Junkers (Ju) 88: Twin-engined medium bomber; also employed as a night and day fighter. Maximum speed (with 4,400 pounds of bombs), 287 at 14,000 feet.

Heinkel 111: Twin-engined bomber; also used for reconnaissance. Maximum speed 240 at 14,000 feet, 255 at 16,000 feet. Bomb load 2,200 pounds (maximum 4,400 pounds).

Dornier 17: Twin-engined bomber; also used for reconnaissance. Maximum speed 265 at 16,400 feet. Bomb load 2,200 pounds.

BRITISH FIGHTER AIRCRAFT

Supermarine Spitfire ("Spit"): Single-seat, eight-gun fighter (later models four or six heavier guns). Maximum speed 356 at 19,000 (Mk II–370).

Hawker Hurricane ("Hurry"): Single-seat, eight-gun fighter. Maximum speed 320 at 22,000 feet.

Acknowledgments

I am particularly indebted to Major Raymond H. Fredette, USAF, author of a definitive and pioneering work to be published in 1966 in the United States and Britain describing the origins of strategic bombing (*The Sky on Fire;* New York: Holt, Rinehart & Winston). His careful reading and numerous pertinent suggestions were of material benefit. I have utilized extensively, particularly in the notes, his wide knowledge of the history of air power.

My thanks go to Lieutenant Colonel Gene Guerny, United States Air Force, Magazine and Book Branch, Directorate for Information Services of the Department of Defense, for reading the manuscript.

Bibliography

Books

ANSEL, REAR ADMIRAL WALTER, USN (RET.), *Hitler Confronts England.* Durham: Duke University Press, 1960

BAUMBACH, WERNER, *Broken Swastika: The Defeat of the Luftwaffe.* London: Robert Hale, 1960

BAXTER, JAMES PHINNEY, III, *Scientists Against Time*. New York: Little, Brown, 1946

BRICKHILL, PAUL, *Reach for the Sky*. New York: Norton, 1954

CHURCHILL, WINSTON S., *The Second World War*, Vol. 2, *Their Finest Hour*. Boston: Houghton Mifflin, 1949

COLLIER, BASIL, *The Defense of the United Kingdom*. London: Her Majesty's Stationery Office, 1957

CRAVEN, W. F., and CATE, J. L., eds., *The Army Air Force in World War II*, Vol. 1, *Plans and Early Operations, January 1939 to August 1942*. Chicago: University of Chicago Press, 1948.

FLEMING, PETER, *Operation Sea Lion*. New York: Simon & Schuster, 1957

GALLAND, ADOLF, *The First and the Last—The Rise and Fall of the German Fighter Forces, 1938–1945*. New York: Holt, 1954

GREEN, WILLIAM, *Famous Bombers of the Second World War*, Vol. II. New York: Doubleday, 1960

HILLARY, RICHARD, *Falling Through Space*. New York: Reynal & Hitchcock, 1942

IRONSIDE, SIR EDMUND, *Time Unguarded*. New York: McKay, 1962

IRVING, DAVID, *The Destruction of Dresden*. New York: Holt, Rinehart & Winston, 1964

JOHNSON, GROUP CAPTAIN J. E., *Wing Leader*. New York: Ballantine Books, 1957

KEMP, LIEUTENANT COMMANDER P. K., RN (Ret.), *Key to Victory*. Boston: Little Brown, 1958

KESSELRING, FIELD MARSHAL ALBERT, *A Soldier's Record*. New York: Morrow, 1954

KIRK, JOHN, and YOUNG, ROBERT, *Great Weapons of World War II*. New York: Walker, 1961

LANGER, WILLIAM L., and GLEASON, S. EVERETT, *The Undeclared War, 1940–1941*. New York: Harper, 1953

LEE, ASHER, *The German Air Force*. New York: Harper, 1946

MARTIENSSEN, ANTHONY, *Hitler and His Admirals*. New York: Dutton, 1949

MCCLOUGHRY, AIR VICE MARSHAL E. J. KINGSTON, *The Direction of War*. London: Jonathan Cape, 1955

MIDDLETON, DREW, *The Sky Suspended—The Story of the Battle of Britain*. New York: Longmans, Green, 1960

MINNEY, R. J., ed., *The Private Papers of Hore-Belisha*. London: Collins, 1960.

Office of Naval Intelligence, *Fuehrer Conferences—On Matters Dealing with the German Navy, 1939–1945*. Washington: Navy Department, 1946–1947

RICHARDS, DENNIS, *Royal Air Force 1939–1945*, Vol. I, II, III. London: Her Majesty's Stationery Office, 1953–1954

SAUNDBY, AIR MARSHAL SIR ROBERT, *Air Bombardment*. New York: Harper, 1951

SHIRER, WILLIAM L., *The Rise and Fall of the Third Reich*. New York: Simon & Schuster, 1960

TREVOR-ROPER, H. R., ed., *Blitzkrieg to Defeat: Hitler's War Directives, 1939–1945*. New York: Holt, Rinehart & Winston, 1965

WEBSTER, SIR CHARLES, and FRANKLAND, NOBLE, *The Strategic Air Offensive Against Germany—1939–1945*. London: Her Majesty's Stationery Office, 1961, Vol. 1–4

WHEATLEY, RONALD, *Operation Sea Lion*. Toronto: Oxford University Press, 1958
WOOD, DEREK, and DEMPSTER, DEREK, *The Narrow Margin*. New York: McGraw-Hill, 1961

CHAPTER 3.   CRETE—THE WINGED INVASION

Notes

1. General Walter Warlimont, *Inside Hitler's Headquarters 1939–1945*, p. 55.
2. *Ibid.*, p. 111.
3. *Ibid.*, p. 150. Also see Alan Clark, *Barbarossa: The Russian-German Conflict, 1941–45*, pp. 24–25 ff.
4. Major General I. S. O. Playfair, with Captain F. C. Flynn, Brigadier C. J. C. Molony, Air Vice Marshal S. E. Toomer, *The Mediterranean and Middle East*, Vol. 2, *The Germans Come to the Help of Their Ally (1941) (History of the Second World War)*, p. 14.
5. Eden, who was accompanied by General Sir John Dill, Chief of the Imperial General Staff, had hoped that he could enlist Turkey, Yugoslavia and Greece on the Allied side and form a Balkan front.
6. Admiral of the Fleet Viscount of Hyndhope, Cunningham. *A Sailor's Odyssey*, p. 357.
7. Christopher Buckley. *Greece and Crete*, 1941, p. 138.
8. *Ibid.*, pp. 136–137. See Playfair, *op. cit.*, pp. 104–105, and Cunningham, *op. cit.*

   The total number of British in Greece, including 4,200 sent prior to March, was about 62,500; about 50,700 were evacuated from the mainland, but this figure included a number of Greeks and Yugoslavs.
9. Winston S. Churchill, *The Second World War*, Vol. 2, *Their Finest Hour*, p. 538.
10. Playfair, *op. cit.*, p. 124. Tobruk in Cyrenaica (Libya) had been invested and besieged by Rommel on April 11; its British garrison was supplied by sea.
11. The *York* had to be beached as it could not be repaired before the invasion of Crete; it was hit by a bomb during the Cretan fighting and became a total loss. The tanker *Pericles* was also damaged in the same attack. The British official history (Playfair, *op. cit.*, p. 61) comments: "This was the first success in a series of attacks of an unconventional kind, requiring great individual skill and daring which the Italians made against British ships in the Mediterranean."

    The explosive motorboat was one of a whole bagful of unconventional naval devices developed and used with great success by the Italians. The official history (Playfair, *op. cit.*, p. 270) describes it as follows:

    The E. M. B.'s [explosive motorboats] were one of several weapons which had been developed by a special arm of the Italian Navy, known by 1941 as the Tenth

Light Flotilla, for the purpose of penetrating defended harbors and causing under-water damage to ships inside. The E. M. B. was so designed that on impact with its target small charges exploded which severed the boat in two. Both parts sank rapidly, but when the fore part, containing the main charges, reached a set depth, which depended on the estimated draught of the ship to be attacked, it exploded as a result of water pressure. It had been demonstrated at Suda Bay that an E. M. B. had a reasonable chance of success if it could come within striking distance of its target undetected. The one-man crew then increased to full speed, and when satisfied that his craft could hardly fail to hit, he locked the rudder. He then pulled a lever to detach his back-rest, which also served as a life-saving raft, and threw himself into the water. He quickly climbed on to the raft in order to be clear of the water when the main charge exploded.

12. Buckley, *op. cit.,* p. 162.
13. Directive 28, issued by Hitler on April 25, described the objective as the use of Crete "as a base for air warfare against Great Britain in the Eastern Mediterranean." The genesis of the Crete operation goes back to the fall of 1940. (See D. M. Davin, *Crete (Official History of New Zealand in the Second World War, 1939–1945),* p. 80, and Trevor-Roper, *Blitzkrieg to Defeat,* p. 68.)
14. Buckley, *op. cit.,* pp. 161–162.
15. Davin, *op. cit.,* Freyberg report, p. 41 n.
16. Theodore Stephanides, *Climax in Crete,* pp. 15 ff.
17. The strength estimates of the defenders, curiously enough, vary widely, in various official or semiofficial accounts, in itself an index of the confusion sur-rounding Crete. In part this is due to the fact that just before, and during, the battle, several thousand British troops arrived on the island from Egypt. Another complicating factor was the order of battle of the Greek forces; by some counts there were only about 10,000 to 11,000 Greek regulars (most of them with only token training) on the island, but if gendarmes, cadets, home guard, and so on were included, the total rose to about 15,000, with an un-known number of guerrillas and irregulars. Compare: Buckley, *op. cit.,* p. 155; Gavin Long, *Greece, Crete and Syria: Australia in the War of 1939–1945,* pp. 213, 214; Davin, *op. cit.,* pp. 40, 46 and Appendix 4; Playfair, *op. cit.,* pp. 146–147. Of these, the New Zealand history (Davin) is the most detailed.
18. Actually, 16 light tanks, 7 "I" or infantry tanks. Buckley, *op. cit.,* p. 155.
19. There were "a number of senior commanders with ill-defined and over-lapping fields of authority." Alan Clark, *The Fall of Crete,* p. 28.
20. Churchill, soon after World War I, had counted 27 "separate scars and gashes" on Freyberg's body. The incident, when both were guests during a weekend at Cliveden, apparently made an indelible impression on Chur-chill, for he wrote of the much-wounded Freyberg (*The Second World War,* Vol. 3, *The Grand Alliance,* pp. 272–273) that "he will fight for King and Country with an unconquerable heart."
21. Playfair, *op. cit.,* p. 129.
22. Buckley, *op. cit.,* p. 163.
23. Manuscript No. B-639, pp. 4, 5.
24. Playfair, *op. cit.,* p. 130.
25. *Ibid.,* p. 129.

26. The caïques were motorized sailing vessels of varying size, about 70 to 200 tons, five to six knots speed. (See Army Pamphlet No. 20–260, p. 124.)

27. Actually, a total of about 25,000 German troops and a few hundred Italians were transported to Crete in May. (See "Combat Effectiveness of Allied and German Troops in the World War II Invasion of Crete," Operations Evaluation Group Interim Research Memorandum No. 35.)

28. Buckley, op. cit., p. 156. In early May General Freyberg urged both General Wavell and his own government either to reinforce Crete promptly or to reconsider the decision to hold it. He specifically pointed out the need for more planes, artillery, ammunition, tools and reserve supplies. To his Prime Minister in New Zealand, he urged "pressure . . . on highest plane in London either to supply us with sufficient means to defend island, or to review decision Crete must be held." (Long, op. cit., p. 209.) But just five days later he wired Churchill: "Cannot understand nervousness; am not in the least anxious about airborne attack; have made my dispositions and feel can cope adequately with the troops at my disposal." (Clark, *The Fall of Crete*, p. 31.)

29. Clark, *The Fall of Crete*, p. 39.

30. Buckley, op. cit., p. 166.

31. *Ibid.*, p. 167. Also see Davin, op. cit., table, p. 81.

32. *Ibid.*, p. 168.

33. *Ibid*, p. 172.

34. British bombers from Egypt were making night attacks on German air bases in Greece and the islands. But the efforts amounted to pin pricks; only 42 Wellington sorties were flown in these strikes from May 13 to 20.

35. The evidence on this point differs. Apparently permission was given on May 19 to crater the strip at Maleme and to install demolitions, but the German invasion came too soon. General Freyberg recorded later (Long, op. cit., p. 220) that his request for permission to destroy all three strips was denied by the British Chiefs of Staff in London, who, with misguided optimism, believed the fields should be kept intact so that aircraft from Egypt could be sent later to use them. This was thinking in a vacuum, for there were not enough aircraft in Egypt and no prospects that there would be enough during the course of the anticipated battle. Nor could the fields have been made secure against German bombing; there were not enough antiaircraft guns, in fact too little of everything.

36. In the preliminary bombing attacks, prior to May 20, many of the lighter British antiaircraft guns and some of the heavies had held their fire, to avoid revealing their positions to German recon aircraft. Actually, until the twentieth most of the British antiaircraft positions had not been primary German targets; no gun had been damaged beyond repair and only six AA crewmen had been killed and 11 wounded. However, the preparatory flack-suppression missions had, as one observer put it, exhausted the British gunners (they were described as "jaded") and had forced many of them to keep their heads down in slit trenches and foxholes during attacks. On May 20, with the efficiency of the gunners reduced and with attacks upon known AA positions heavy and prolonged, losses were heavy.

37. Buckley, *op. cit.*, p. 174.
38. *Ibid.*
39. Long, *op. cit.*, p. 221.
40. Davin, *op. cit.*, p. 89.
41. Clark, *The Fall of Crete*, pp. 57, 58.
42. John Hetherington, *Airborne Invasion: The Story of the Battle of Crete*, pp. 100 ff.; Buckley, *op. cit.*, pp. 175 ff.
43. Von der Heydte later reported that Schmeling "practically collapsed with diarrhoea" in Crete, and had to be hospitalized. He explicitly states that "our champion boxer" was innocent of deception and that the medal he received later and the big build-up given him by Goebbels and the German propagandists for his alleged exploits on Crete were not the result of Schmeling's deception. He was an innocent figurehead; even Göring was deceived by the false accounts.
44. Baron Von der Heydte, *Daedalus Returned: Crete, 1941*, pp. 52, 59.
45. Davin, *op. cit.*, p. 89.
46. Von der Heydte, *op. cit.*, p. 12.
47. The German gliders were built with "so-called '*Sollbruchstellen*' (breaking points), that is, joints of purposely weak construction, which would break first in crash landings or collisions with natural or artificial obstacles." Take-off wheels were dropped off when airborne, and the landing runners or skids were sometimes "wrapped with barbed wire to increase the braking effect," and "at least some gliders designed for special types of operation" were equipped with a "strong barbed hook, similar to an anchor, which bored into the ground during the landing." By these means loaded gliders could sometimes stop within 35 yards. Two types of gliders were used—a small one, the DFS 230, which could carry ten men with light equipment, or a larger glider, the Gotha 242, with double tail assembly which could carry a 75 mm. antitank gun and crew, or 20 to 25 men, or their equivalent in weight. The He-111 or the Ju-87 were used for cable towing. (See pp. 17, 88 and 89, MS No. P–051, "Airborne Operations—A German Appraisal.")
48. Clark, *The Fall of Crete*, p. 59.
49. Davin, *op. cit.*, p. 123, report of Captain Watson.
50. Clark, *The Fall of Crete*, p. 63.
51. Report of Major W. D. Philip, B. Troop battery commander, as quoted in Davin, *op. cit.*, p. 130.
52. Buckley, *op. cit.*, p. 192.
53. Davin, *op. cit.*, p. 173 n. Something like 1,260 Germans were still in action in the Prison Valley area west of Galatas on the night of May 20. There had been 540 casualties. East of Galatas in scattered groups were 310 survivors out of an original 1,068. Near Alikianou 590 survived; 150 had been casualties.
54. Von der Heydte, *op. cit.*, p. 87.
55. For a full account of the royal adventures, see Davin, *op. cit.*, Appendix II, pp. 468 ff.
56. *Ibid.*, p. 159, quoted from Bassett (an eyewitness and soldier participant not further identified).
57. The troop carriers had been delayed in take-off in Greece by the great clouds

of dust and other difficulties at the makeshift airfields. The drops had been rescheduled for two hours later than original plans required, but VIII Air Corps combat aircraft had scheduled its fighters and bombers over the targets in accordance with the original timing. Hence the "paratroopers jumped without the least bit of protection into a hail of enemy fire—fire which was all the more intense because the enemy had been forewarned and counted on more parachute landings that day." (MS No. B–639, p. 9.)

58. Buckley, *op. cit.,* p. 205.
59. *Ibid.,* p. 206.
60. Davin, *op. cit.,* p. 181.
61. Actually, though Andrew's other companies had suffered—one of them heavily—they were still fighting stoutly, though in much reduced strength.
62. Davin, *op. cit.,* p. 110.
63. *Ibid.,* p. 182.
64. The Australian official history calls this landing with typical British understatement a "significant event." (Davin, *op. cit.,* p. 231.)
65. MS No. B–639, "Commitment of Parachute Troops by the 2nd Air Transport Wing (Special Purpose); Crete, 21 May, 1941"), p. 10. The same report states "waves of enemy bomber and fighter formations" raided Maleme and attacked the "heavily loaded" transports while they were stacked in the air. But these attacks by Blenheims came later (on May 23) and were in small strength. No British fighters were able to intervene in the air battle with any success.
66. Davin, *op. cit.,* pp. 188, 189, quoted from report of Captain J. N. Anderson.
67. Dispatch from "Creforce" to New Zealand Division, 7:50 P.M., May 21, quoted in Davin, *op. cit.,* p. 196.
68. Manuscript No. B-524, p. 36-G.
69. Bartimeus, *East of Malta, West of Suez,* p. 118.
70. The fracas continued for about two and one half hours. The convoy had been ordered to reach the coast of Crete on May 21 "regardless of enemy fleet movements." (G. Hermon Gill, *Royal Australian Navy 1939–1942,* pp. 344 ff.)
71. Commander Antonio Bragadin, *The Italian Navy in World War II,* pp. 108, 109; Gill, *op. cit.,* Vol. 1, pp. 344, 345; Captain S. W. Roskill, *The War at Sea, 1939–1935,* p. 441.
72. The claims in this brief sea fight differ widely. Apparently *Sagittario* like *Lupo* did a good job, and because Admiral King turned back in deference to German air attack nearly all of the convoy escaped. In any case, Lieutenant Giuseppe Cigala Fulgosi, CO of the *Sagittario,* was "literally carried in a triumphal procession by the German Alpenjäger troops whom he had been convoying" when he returned to the Piraeus (port of Athens). (*Bragadin, op. cit.,* pp. 109–110; Gill, *op. cit.,* p. 346; Toomer, *op. cit.,* p. 137.
73. In modern terms, as Admiral Cunningham expressed it later in his memoirs (*A Sailor's Odyssey,* p. 370). "The safest place [from enemy bombers] was in amongst the enemy convoy."
74. Cunningham, *op. cit.,* p. 371.
75. *Ibid.*
76. Davin, *op. cit.,* p. 217.

77. *Ibid.*, p. 218.

78. *Ibid.*, p. 220.

79. Long, *op. cit.*, p. 236.

80. Davin, *op. cit.*, p. 225, quoted from German XI Air Corps report.

81. Buckley *op. cit.*, p. 210.

82. *Ibid.*, p. 210.

83. Davin, *op. cit.*, quoted from A. Q. Pope, 4 RMT Company, pp. 234–235.

84. Davin, *op. cit.*, Appendix II; and Buckley, *op. cit.*, pp. 211 ff.

85. "In effect," the Australian history says, "this decision [to withdraw] was an acceptance that Crete had been lost." (Long, *op. cit.*, pp. 237–238.)

86. Davin, *op. cit.*, p. 261.

87. In all, 12 Blenheims attacked German-held Maleme in daylight on the twenty-third, other bombers by night.

88. Stephanides, *op. cit.*, p. 73.

89. It was destroyed on the ground later by Messerschmitts.

90. Kenneth Poolman, *The Kelly*, pp. 197 ff.

91. Bartimeus, *op. cit.*, pp. 125–127. See also Admiral Cunningham, *op. cit.*, p. 373. *Kipling* ran out of oil completely 70 miles off Alexandria the morning of May 24 and had to be towed in.

92. See Admiral Cunningham, *op. cit.*, p. 274, for the countermanding orders from London, and Cunningham's (in turn) countervailing orders and his comment about "unjustifiable interference by those ignorant of the situation." The same day, however, destroyers *Jaguar* and *Defender* successfully transited to Suda Bay and discharged ammunition the night of the 23rd–24th.

93. Long, *op. cit.*, p. 241.

94. *Ibid.*, p. 241.

95. Playfair, *op. cit.*, pp. 138–139. The Commanders in Chief were General Wavell, Admiral Cunningham and Air Marshal A. W. Tedder (who was acting, from May 3 to June 1, in the absence in London of Sir Arthur Longmore, and was then Sir Arthur's successor).

96. The Germans later alleged that the defenders had committed atrocities upon their troops near Kastelli and at other points in Crete. After the fighting was over the reports were thoroughly investigated by a German military commission, which found them to be exaggerated. There is no doubt, however, that some atrocities were committed—none, so far as is known, by the British troops, but by the Cretans. The bodies of some German dead were mutilated.

97. Davin, *op. cit.*, p. 303.

98. *Ibid.*, p. 314, quoted from report by Lieutenant Thomas.

99. *Ibid.*, p. 326.

100. Buckley, *op. cit.*, p. 247.

101. Davin, *op. cit.*, p. 367.

102. Long, *op. cit.*, Freyberg quoted, p. 253.

103. Stephanides, *op. cit.*, p. 113.

104. Von der Heydte, *op. cit.*, pp. 146 ff.

105. Churchill, Winston S. *The Second World War*, Vol. 3, *The Grand Alliance*, p. 299.

106. Quoted in Buckley, *op. cit.*, pp. 272–273.

107. MS No. B-524, p. 36.
108. Army Pamphlet No. 20-260, p. 137.
109. Long, *op. cit.,* p. 291, quoted from Captain P. A. Tomlinson's report.
110. Bartimeus, *op. cit.,* p. 142; Gill, *op. cit.,* p. 356.
111. Playfair, *op. cit.,* p. 143.
112. Buckley, *op. cit.,* p. 276.
113. *Ibid.,* p. 278.
114. Army Pamphlet No. 20-260, p. 137. See also note 96.
115. Long, *op. cit.,* p. 318.
116. From a week before the land fighting began until after the evacuation was completed.
117. Playfair, *op. cit.,* p. 147. See also New Zealand and Australian histories.
118. The Air Corps reported 5,255 Greek prisoners. Davin, *op. cit.,* Appendix V.
119. See "Combat Effectiveness of Allied and German Troops in the World War II Invasion of Crete," *op. cit.*
120. Playfair, *op. cit.,* p. 147.
121. MS No. P-051, "Airborne Operations—A German Appraisal," p. 21.
122. MS No. P-051b, p. 21.
123. Davin, *op. cit.,* pp. 461, 462.
124. MS No. P-051, p. 24.
125. *Ibid.,* p. 23.
126. MS No. P-051b, p. 23.
127. Von der Heydte, *op. cit.,* pp. 180-181. Von der Heydte records (p. 97) that the German parachutists in his battalion had worn in the heat of Crete the same-weight uniforms that had been tested in the Arctic Circle and that they carried "northern" rations, which melted in the heat, and resulted in an "extraordinary pot-pourri of melted chocolate, smoked bacon, spiced sausages and rock-hard rusks." For days after landing, his battalion had to scrounge to live and the men often went hungry, since the resupply of food failed. He notes "roasted donkey" for dinner. The high German losses in Crete he attributed (pp. 180-181) to "inexperience in parachute warfare . . . training of officers none too thorough . . . most important encountered for the first time an enemy who was prepared to fight to the bitter end."
128. A German appraisal of airborne operations written after the war (MS P-051, pp. 4 and 5) noted that

in Holland and in Crete elements of Army units, in part by design and in part because of ignorance of the situation, had landed from transport planes in territory still occupied by the enemy or situated within sight of enemy artillery observers. This was recognized as a mistake resulting in serious losses. The only thing that saved the planes landing on the Maleme airfield in Crete from being completely destroyed by direct enemy fire was the fact that the ground was covered with dust as a result of drought and that the planes actually landed in clouds of dust. . . .

The designation of "parachute troops" (Fallschirmtruppe) and "parachutists" (Fallschirmjaeger) . . . is not quite accurate. Fundamentally a major part of the German airborne force was suited for transport glider commitment only. . . . In practice the percentage of trained parachutists steadily decreased and as a result, as the war continued, these troops were almost exclusively used in ground combat.

The German Wehrmacht, because of the scarcity of manpower, found it impossible to keep these special troops in reserve for their special duties. It is evident that only "the rich man" can afford such forces, and that efforts must be made to withdraw these troops as soon as possible after each airborne commitment. Otherwise their value as special troops will rapidly decrease."

The United States was to learn this hard lesson later in Europe, when, after Normandy, numerous plans for the use of U.S. airborne troops were made only to be discarded. The problem persists today: how many "special" or elite troops, trained at great expense for special missions (i.e., Special Forces; airborne forces; air assault divisions, etc.), can an army afford?

Kesselring, in after-the-war comments, noted (MS P-051b, pp. 25 ff.) that "fundamentally, Hitler was no partisan of the Luftwaffe and therefore no friend of airborne operations. . . . The improvised Crete operation caused Hitler and Göring to draw conclusions which they should not have drawn." He noted that there was no suitable replacement for the Ju-52 transport in later years of the war, that unintelligent use was made of airborne troops, insufficient attention was paid at top military levels to "organization, operational and tactical possibilities" offered by airborne troops, and that "senior parachutist officers . . . strove to preserve the glamor of something secret and extraordinary." Consequently airborne troops were never again used by the Germans in mass operations.

129. Von der Heydte describes Student (p. 140) as "inwardly impelled by the passion of an explorer or inventor." Student had what U.S. Marines would describe as "gung-ho" spirit; he was aggressive, restless, energetic, a fine combat leader, but a better field leader than a planner.

130. MS P-051, p. 5.

131. *Ibid.*, p. 32

132. Davin, *op. cit.*, p. 464.

133. Long, *op. cit.*, p. 205.

134. Churchill, *The Second World War,* Vol 3, *The Grand Alliance,* p. 269.

135. The overcontrol exercised from London during the Cretan battle and at other times in World War II (in part a product of Churchill's dynamic, thrusting personality) has its far more dangerous parallel in modern history. In both the Kennedy and the Johnson administrations during the Cuban, Dominican and Vietnamese crises the flood of detailed orders from Washington to the commanders on the scene sometimes by-passed the normal chain of command, severely restricted military flexibility, sometimes confused the execution of orders, and may have caused (notably in the early air attacks against North Vietnam) unnecessary casualties. If modern communications had existed at the time of the Battle of Waterloo, the British probably would have been defeated.

136. Major General Sir John Kennedy, *The Business of War,* pp. 118–123.

137. MS No. P-051, p. 30.

138. Cunningham (*op. cit.*, p. 391) makes it clear that Crete would have been a tremendous burden to the British. "Looking back I sometimes wonder whether the loss of the island was really such a serious matter [as] it seemed

at the time. . . . The problem of its maintenance and supply would have been extraordinarily difficult. We should undoubtedly have required a large garrison, and . . . the drain on our slender resources of arms, ammunition and equipment available in the Mediterranean would have been heavy."

139. Warlimont, *op. cit.,* p. 131. See also footnotes. Warlimont records that after the decision to attack Crete was made his section was ordered to delete from its war diary any mention of Malta or of differences of opinion with Supreme Headquarters.

140. The rest of the war showed the decision to seize Crete was an erroneous one (see Warlimont, *op. cit.,* p. 253, *passim*). It was a drain upon the Germans later, and tied down in purely static defensive tasks numerous trained troops. It never halted British sea traffic in the eastern Mediterranean. Malta, on the other hand, rose like a phoenix from the ashes of its bombings, and became more and more dangerous to German supply lines to North Africa.

The U.S. Army official history (George F. Howe, *Northwest Africa: Seizing the Initiative in the West,* Washington, Office of the Chief of Military History, Department of the Army, 1957, pp. 8, 9) is emphatic about the importance of Malta.

The fortunes of Rommel's command seemed almost directly proportional to Axis success in neutralizing Malta. . . . Rommel's success and the capture of Malta were interdependent. . . . Rommel believed he could continue to Cairo [in June, 1942]. . . . At that juncture, Hitler was lured into a serious blunder. . . . He . . . proposed to Mussolini that Operation Herkules, the seizure of Malta, be postponed in favor of a continued drive into Egypt. . . . In July, 1942, Rommel's army got as far inside Egypt as the El Alamein position, some sixty miles southwest of Alexandria, before being held up by lack of supplies and the opposition of the British Eighth Army.

See also the chapter in this book on the Sicily campaign.

Admiral Franco Maugeri of the Italian Navy, in his book *From the Ashes of Disgrace* (New York: Reynal & Hitchcock, 1948), stresses repeatedly (as most of the Italian strategists did) the strategic importance of Malta: "The war in Europe was decided in 1942 at three focal points; Malta, North Africa and Stalingrad" (p. 75). "Malta was the keystone of the British Mediterranean defense" (p. 76). "Malta was . . . the key to control of the Mediterranean" (p. 80). "In my opinion, the war's turning point was our abandonment of the invasion of Malta. If we had captured and occupied it . . . we would have been the masters of the Mediterranean" (p. 83).

141. Warlimont, *op. cit.,* p. 143.

142. Anthony Eden (1st Earl of Avon), *The Reckoning: The Eden Memoirs,* p. 230.

143. MS No. B-250.

144. MS No. P-030, pp. 61, 69. The Crete campaign itself added congestion to the Balkan railroads but did not cause a "further delay."

145. Charles von Luttichau, "The Road to Moscow—The Campaign in Russia, 1941," Ch. 25, III 54a. The author points out that

> replacing the divisions sent into the Balkans was far less a problem . . . than might appear. . . . The infantry divisions came from a large reserve force that was not to have been committeed until weeks after the offensive had begun . . . the added strains on the concentration for Barbarossa [were] confined to a re-arrangement of transportation schedules. By attracting attention to the Balkans and diverting it from German-occupied Poland and Rumania, the Germans may indeed have reaped an unexpected benefit of surprise.

John Erickson (*The Soviet High Command,* London: Macmillan, 1962, p. 583) points out that

> along almost the entire length of the vast front, the German Army achieved tactical surprise. Soviet troops were caught in their camps and barracks. . . . Germany Army Group Center intercepted plaintive and desperate Russian wire-less signals: "We are being fired on. What shall we do?" to which their head-quarters replied with asperity and reprimand—"You must be insane. And why is your signal not in code?."

Acknowledgments and Bibliography

I am deeply grateful for the criticism and comments of Charles von Lut-tichau, of the Office of the Chief of Military History, Department of the Army, who read the manuscript of this chapter in draft form.

The documentation on the Battle of Crete is voluminous. By far the most detailed and carefully objective account of the struggle is that given in the New Zealand official history by D. M. Davin. This concentrates, of course, upon ac-tions in which New Zealanders participated, but it also provides an over-all picture comprehensive in its grasp. I am indebted to this book for many of the stirring details of action and for objective comments.

Books

BARTIMEUS (pseudonym of Paymaster Captain Lewis Anselm da Costa Ritchie, RN), *East of Malta, West of Suez; The Official Admiralty Account of the Mediterranean Fleet, 1939–1943.* Boston: Little Brown, 1944

BRAGADIN, COMMANDER (R) ANTONIO, ITALIAN NAVY, *The Italian Navy in World War II.* Annapolis: U.S. Naval Institute, 1957

BUCKLEY, CHRISTOPHER, *Greece and Crete, 1941.* London: Her Majesty's Sta-tionery Office, 1952

CHURCHILL, WINSTON S., *The Second World War,* Vol. 2, *Their Finest Hour.* Boston: Houghton Mifflin, 1949

CHURCHILL, WINSTON S., *The Second World War,* Vol. 3, *The Grand Alliance.* Boston: Houghton Mifflin, 1950

CLARK, ALAN, *Barbarossa: The Russian–German Conflict, 1941–45.* New York: Morrow, 1965

CLARK, ALAN, *The Fall of Crete.* New York: Morrow, 1962

CUNNINGHAM, ADMIRAL OF THE FLEET VISCOUNT OF HYNDHOPE, *A Sailor's Odyssey*. New York: Dutton, 1951

DAVIN, D. M., *Crete (Official History of New Zealand in the Second World War, 1939–1945)*. Wellington, New Zealand: Department of Internal Affairs, War History Branch, 1953

Department of the Army, Pamphlet No. 20–260, *The German Campaigns in the Balkans (Spring, 1941)*. Washington: Office of the Chief of Military History, Department of the Army, 1953

EDEN, ANTHONY (1st Earl of Avon), *The Reckoning: The Eden Memoirs*. London: Cassell, 1965

GILL, G. HERMON, *Royal Australian Navy 1939–1942*. Series 2 Navy, Vol. I. Canberra Australian War Memorial, 1957

HETHERINGTON, JOHN, *Airborne Invasion: The Story of the Battle of Crete*. New York: Duell, Sloan & Pearce, 1943

KENNEDY, MAJOR GENERAL SIR JOHN, *The Business of War*. New York: Morrow, 1958

LONG, GAVIN, *Greece, Crete and Syria: Australia in the War of 1939–1945*. Series 1 Army, Vol. II. Canberra: Australian War Memorial, 1953

LUTTICHAU, CHARLES VON, "The Road to Moscow—The Campaign in Russia, 1941." Washington: Office of the Chief of Military History, Department of the Army. Unpublished manuscript.

PLAYFAIR, MAJOR GENERAL I. S. O., with CAPTAIN F. C. FLYNN, BRIGADIER C. J. C. MOLONY, AIR VICE MARSHAL S. E. TOOMER, *The Mediterranean and Middle East*, Vol. 2, *The Germans Come to the Help of Their Ally (1941) (History of the Second World War)*. London: Her Majesty's Stationery Office, 1956

POOLMAN, KENNETH, *The Kelly*. London: Kimber, 1954

ROSKILL, CAPTAIN S. W., RN, *The War at Sea, 1939–1945*, Vol. 1, *The Defensive (History of the Second World War)*. London: Her Majesty's Stationery Office, 1954

SHIRER, WILLIAM L., *The Rise and Fall of the Third Reich*. New York: Simon & Schuster, 1960

STEPHANIDES, THEODORE, *Climax in Crete*. London: Faber & Faber, 1946

TREVOR-ROPER, H. R., ed., *Blitzkrieg to Defeat: Hitler's War Directives, 1939–1945*. New York: Holt, Rinehart & Winston, 1965

VON DER HEYDTE, BARON, *Daedalus Returned: Crete, 1941*. London: Hutchinson, 1958

WARLIMONT, GENERAL WALTER, *Inside Hitler's Headquarters 1939–45*. New York: Praeger, 1964

Manuscripts

Office of the Chief of Military History, Department of the Army, Washington, D.C.

MS No. P-030: "The German Campaign in the Balkans, 1941"

MS No. B-250: Warlimont, General of Artillery, "Answers to Questions Concerning Greece, Crete and Russia"

MS No. D-064: General Hans-Joachim Rath, "1st Stuka Wing (Feb.–May, 1941)"

MS No. P-051: "Airborne Operations—A German Appraisal"

MS No. B-524: General von Greiffenberg, "Supplements to the Study—The Balkan Campaign (The Invasion of Greece)"

MS No. B-639: Major General Rüdiger von Heyking, "Commitment of Parachute Troops by the 2nd Air Transport Wing (Special Purpose); Crete, 21 May, 1941"

MS No. P-051b: Field Marshal Albert Kesselring, "Practical Experience in Carrying out and Opposing Airborne Landings in World War II'
Study No. 11

Department of the Navy, Office of the Chief of Naval Operations, J. H. Engel, Operations Evaluation Group Interim Research Memorandum No. 35, "Combat Effectiveness of Allied and German Troops in the World War II Invasion of Crete," 1963

CHAPTER 4. "THE ROCK"

Notes

I am greatly indebted to Louis Morton, Professor of History at Dartmouth, and author of the definitive official history on Bataan and Corregidor, *The Fall of the Philippines,* for reviewing this chapter. His comments and criticisms have been extremely helpful.

1. Louis Morton, *The Fall of the Philippines,* pp. 63–64.
2. Kent Roberts Greenfield, gen. ed., *Command Decisions,* p. 33 (Louis Morton, "Germany First").
3. Morton, *ibid.,* pp. 26, 28, 30.
4. The author obtained rough transcripts of the Marshall interview from *Time-Life* and *Newsweek* correspondents who were present. On September 16, 1949, the author wrote to General Marshall, describing the gist of the interview, as outlined in the transcripts and requesting his comment. In a letter of September 21, 1949, which could not be quoted in the General's lifetime, Marshall acknowledged that to the best of his recollection the transcripts were "apparently correct."

   In the light of after-events, I would say that there were three things that largely were responsible for defeating prospects indicated [in the interview].
   One was the fact that the group of planes which was to reenforce heavily the "Flying Fortress" concentration in the Philippines was unexpectedly delayed in its departure from California because of adverse winds. . . . I recall this delay was in the neighborhood of 2½ weeks. . . .
   Another factor . . . was the fact that it became evident that planes would not have the reach that the Air Corps then believed possible. In other words, we were over-optimistic as to that phase of the matter.
   The third factor was the inadequacy of the fields in the Philippines for the dispersal of the planes and of the limited antiaircraft protection which was in process of being established.
   Possibly another factor might well have entered into the matter should the planes and their fighter protection have survived the opening attack, and that was

the difficulty [inaccuracy] that developed in the bombing of moving and evading naval shipping from high altitudes.

In other words, General Marshall and Army Air Corps leaders had absorbed the doctrine of Douhet and Billy Mitchell well but not wisely.

5. Morton, *op. cit.,* pp. 42–50.
6. Samuel Eliot Morison, *History of the Rising Sun in the Pacific, United States Naval Operations in World War II,* Vol. III, p. 151.
7. Louis Morton, "American and Allied Strategy in the Far East," *Military Review,* December, 1949, p. 38.
8. Morton, *The Fall of the Philippines,* p. 57.
9. *Ibid.,* p. 77.
10. Stanley L. Falk, *Bataan—The March of Death,* p. 28. Falk breaks the figures down as follows: "more than 78,000 troops . . . 6,000 civilian employees of the Army . . . 20,000 Filipino refugees."
11. Morton, *The Fall of the Philippines,* p. 259.
12. The island's main supply, drawn from a deep artesian well and stocked in a reservoir, was pumped through a conduit to various outlets on "The Rock." The pumping station and power plant, both inadequate to Corregidor's needs even under good conditions, were damaged and out of action frequently and the conduit was holed again and again. Some wooden water tanks were built on Malinta to serve the hospital tunnel laterals if the main supply went out; in the last weeks one of these tanks was destroyed.
13. The exact number of Japanese planes shot down by the Corregidor gunners is questionable. Some authorities believe the toll was in two figures, but few actually saw more than one or two planes crash. Lieutenant Robert F. Jenkins, Jr., then CO of the 2nd Platoon of A Company, 4th Marines, notes in his report:

> One day a large flight of two-motored Jap bombers raided Corregidor. They had released their bombs on the southern side of the island and were headed north toward Bataan. They were just overhead when the AA shells started bursting in their midst. As we watched, a wing of one plane suddenly disintegrated and the plane plunged toward the earth spinning round and round as it fell. Above the din of battle there rose a tremendous cheer. It came from everywhere and seemed to cover the whole of Corregidor. Men jumped out of their foxholes, waved and cheered until they were hoarse and tears came to their eyes. It was a wonderful feeling to see the Japs taking it after being on the uncontested receiving end for months. It was just one Jap plane that finally buried itself in the waters of the North Channel, but it was the first and only Jap plane that we ever actually saw shot down! It was a sight we never forgot. It buoyed up morale, and strained faces smiled when they talked about it for days to come.

There were five 3-inch AA batteries on Corregidor, but at times there was only one height finder for all the batteries.

14. Morton, *The Fall of the Philippines* (p. 268) describes the January 10 visit of MacArthur to Bataan, but mentions no other visits by the Commander in Chief. In actuality, none was made. Major General Charles A. Willoughby, who was MacArthur's intelligence officer at the time, in a letter to the author (August 31, 1964) states:

It was MacArthur's firm habit to send his trusted senior staff officers repeatedly forward into active combat situation and report back to him. . . . MacArthur made occasional unannounced trips himself for some particular inquiry at the top level. The staff did not consider them noteworthy any more than their own investigations or reconnaisances.

The question of MacArthur's visits to Bataan is not in itself important except in conjunction with the friction then existing between the services and certain command echelons in the Philippines and the recriminations that later marred the great campaigns of the Pacific.

MacArthur's grandiloquent and egoistic personality and his occasional purple prose were shining marks for parody. It was probably in the Philippines that he was first dubbed—unfairly, for his personal courage was beyond cavil—"Dugout Doug." Possibly the Navy or the Marines, troubled by the attitude of Major General Richard K. Sutherland, MacArthur's chief of staff, first started this.

But Colonel E. B. Miller, commander of the 194th Tank Battalion, in his postwar book, *Bataan Uncensored*, states that one version of a "Dugout Doug" parody had been widely circulated on Bataan before MacArthur left Corregidor for Australia. This version, the first of thousands, was to the tune of the "Battle Hymn of the Republic" and, according to Colonel Miller (p. 193), the first verse was:

> *Dugout Doug MacArthur lies a shaking*
> *on the Rock,*
> *Safe from all the bombers and from*
> *any sudden shock.*
> *Dougout Doug is eating of the best*
> *food on Bataan,*
> *And his troops go starving on.*

In any case, the appellation stuck, and it spread from the tunnels of Corregidor to Australia. During the first phase of the Australian–New Guinea operations MacArthur's seeming aloofness and his infrequent visits to combat troops drew some muted criticism. When the General realized his image was being hurt, he made it a point to make frequent visits to the front.

Nevertheless, the derogatory nickname stuck throughout the war, and countless service rhymesters produced verse after verse of "Dugout Doug" doggerel, most of it unprintable.

15. For a complete list of the special submarine missions to the Philippines, see Theodore Roscoe, *United States Submarine Operations in World War II*, pp. 508–509.

16. Morton, *The Fall of the Philippines*, p. 412.

17. Falk, *op. cit.*, p. 132.

18. Morton, *The Fall of the Philippines*, p. 442.

19. Falk, *op. cit.*, p. 18.

20. *Ibid.*, p. 66.

21. The beach defense organization was as follows:

East Sector—From Malinta Hill (inclusive) to the tail of the island:

1st Battalion, 4th Marines, Lieutenant Colonel Curtis T. Beecher, USMC, commanding—20 officers, 367 enlisted.

Middle Sector—From Malinta Hill (exclusive) to a line from Morrison Hill (inclusive) to Government Ravine (inclusive): 3rd Battalion (less detachments), Lieutenant Colonel John P. Adams, CO—20 officers, 490 enlisted.

West Sector—From a line running from Morrison Hill to Government Ravine (both exclusive) to the west end of the island: 2nd Battalion, Lieutenant Colonel Herman R. Anderson, CO—18 officers, 324 enlisted.

General Reserve—Bivouac area, Government Ravine: Headquarters and Service Company (less detachments), Major Max W. Schaeffer, CO—8 officers, 183 enlisted. Later increased in strength to a total of more than 300. To the General Reserve was later added the Provisional 4th Tactical Battalion, consisting chiefly of naval personnel under Major Francis H. Williams, USMC, stiffened by some Marine and Army personnel.

The beach defense artillery was organized as follows:

Beach Defense Artillery—Colonel Delburt Ausmus, CAC, USA Artillery Officer.

East Sector—Captain Jules D. Yates, USA Artillery Officer.

    1 75 mm. gun, Malinta Hill (North)
    1 75 mm. gun, Malinta Hill (South)
    1 75 mm. gun, Malinta Hill (West)
    3 75 mm. guns, North Point
    2 75 mm. guns, Hooker Point
    1 75 mm. gun, Monkey Point
    1 75 mm. gun, Tunnel gun
    ———
    10 75 mm. guns

Middle Sector—Captain Smith, CAC, USA Artillery Officer.

    2 75 mm. guns, Breakwater Point
    1 75 mm. gun, Ramsey Ravine
    1 75 mm. gun, Point Conception
    1 75 mm. gun, Spanish Fort
    1 75 mm. gun, C.R. No. 73
    1 75 mm. gun, Stockade
    1 155 mm. gun, Stockade
    1 Navy 3″ landing gun, 200 yds. S.W. North Dock
    ———
    1 155; 7 75's; 1 3″ landing gun

West Sector—Lieutenant Colonel Harry J. Harper, FA, USA Artillery Officer.

    1 75 mm. gun, Wheeler Point
    1 3″ Navy landing gun, 200 yds. W. of Geary Point
    1 75 mm. gun, Craighill
    1 75 mm. gun on beach, James Ravine
    1 75 mm. gun, James Ravine
    ———
    4 75's; 1 3″ landing gun

Beach Defense Searchlights

    1 36" Light, Hooker Point
    1 36" Light, San José Point
    1 36" Light, Malinta Point
    1 18" Light, Cavalry Point
    1 18" Light, North Point
    1 18" Light, Monkey Point
    1 60" Light, Breakwater Point
    1 36" Light, Skipper Hill
    <u>1 36" Light, Battery Point</u>
    1 60; 5 36's; 3 18's

22. Colonel Stephen M. Mellnik, "How the Japs Took Corregidor," *Coast Artillery Journal*, March–April, 1945.

23. From postwar report of Lieutenant Robert F. Jenkins, Jr., at the time of Corregidor commanding officer of the 2nd Platoon of A Company. The regimental records of the 4th Marines were destroyed when the island surrendered, and this account has been based (as far as the Marines are concerned) primarily upon individual reports and memoirs, written for the most part after the war and on interviews, as noted in the bibliography.

24. The "Old Breed" in Colonel John W. Thomason's famous words referred to "the Leathernecks (World War I name for Marines), the old breed of American Regular, regarding the Service as home and war as an occupation."

25. The devotion of all men who served with the regiment to the 4th Marines is well illustrated by an incident during the captivity of the survivors. The regimental colors used to be blue; just before the war they were changed to red and blue. The new standard regimental colors were burned by Captain Moore, as ordered, but one of the discarded blue ensigns was stored with QM stores in one of the old barracks on Corregidor. Louis Novak, Jr., PhM2c, USN, was employed as a typist in a hospital for the Japanese medics after the surrender. About June 15, 1942, he found the old regimental colors. Major Frank P. Pysick, a fellow prisoner who was acting as an interpreter, told Novak it was the colors of the regiment. Novak hid them between his sheet and mattress. A Japanese officer found the colors, questioned Novak and then beat him with his riding crop until he was felled. About June 30 Novak was notified he was being transferred to Manila. He stole the colors from the Japanese officer's quarters during the officer's absence, wrapped the five-by-six flag around his stomach under his clothing, and carried it with him to Bilibid Prison, Manila, where he kept it for a year, when he was ordered by an officer to transfer the colors to the senior officer or to destroy them. Novak burned them in the galley fire. "I have been in the service for fourteen years," he commented in his report to the Commandant of the Marine Corps. "The time spent with the Fourth will be most memorable in my mind for years to come."

26. Lieutenant Colonel A. C. Shofner described the details of the surrender (as related to him by Captain Clark after the surrender) as follows in his postwar report:

The final hour of Corregidor brought to the Marines the honor or dishonor of surrendering the island. When the inevitable decision of surrender came from General Wainwright it was a Marine Officer, Captain Golland L. Clark, Jr. (died aboard Jap prison ship at Formosa), who was assigned the mission of offering surrender to the Japanese commanding officer, and expressing General Wainwright's desire to confer with Lieutenant General Homma regarding terms. Captain Clark's party consisted of a music [Marines' name for a bugler], a flag bearer, carrying a piece of white sheeting on a pole, and an interpreter; all were Marines except the interpreter.

The party left from Malinta Tunnel and proceeded east, about seven hundred yards to the front lines; numerous times the group was forced to seek cover momentarily due to the heavy Jap artillery and mortar fire, but realizing the importance of the mission rapidly continued forward, Captain Clark in the lead.

As the party passed the last Marine outpost the music sounded off and the flag bearer waved the white standard. The party marched erect across the fire-swept no-man's land and, unusual as it may seem, the Japanese did not intentionally direct fire at the group although many ricochets fell nearby. At this time Captain Clark's thoughts turned back five years to a lecture at the Marine Officers Basic School, the conduct of a *parlementaire* at a surrender. At the time of the lecture he never dreamed that he would be sent on a surrender mission, but now he strained his memory for all the details of procedure in order to assure the safety of his party and the men of General Wainwright's command.

The first Jap soldier located was very amazed at this group of four, and after much parley, the soldier conducted the party to his corporal and eventually, after much searching by the guides, Captain Clark reached the senior Japanese officer alive on the island, a Lieutenant Colonel. The Jap Lieutenant Colonel contacted higher headquarters on Bataan and arrangements were made for General Wainwright to proceed to Bataan at about three o'clock that afternoon—thus ended the story of Corregidor.

27. Falk, *op. cit.*, pp. 194 ff.
28. Miller, *op. cit.*, pp. 5 and 7.
29. Morton, *Military Review,* op. cit., p. 39.

Until his death in 1964 MacArthur insisted that the Rainbow 5 plan anticipated the defense of Manila Bay for four to six months and that (in his own words in his memoirs) "the Pacific Fleet would then move in with massive force escorting relieving ground troops." But Rainbow 5 provided no such thing; it specifically committed the United States to a strategic defensive in the Pacific, and, as Morton points out (*Command Decisions,* p. 33), "the Philippines had virtually been written off as indefensible in a war with Japan." Rainbow 5, which stemmed from talks with the British, is published in full in the Congressional Pearl Harbor Attack hearings (1946), Exhibit 129, pp. 2875 ff. The Joint Army and Navy Basic War Plan—Rainbow No. 5 (pp. 2908 ff.), declares that the concept of the war was as follows:

Since Germany is the predominant member of the Axis powers, the Atlantic and European area is considered to be the decisive theatre. The principal United States military effort will be exerted in that theatre and operations of United States forces in other theatres will be conducted in such a manner to facilitate that effort. . . .

If Japan does enter the war the military strategy in the Far East will be defensive. The United States does not intend to add to its present military strength in the Far East [this intention was modified after the basic concept was written], but will employ the United States Pacific Fleet offensively in the manner best calculated to weaken Japanese economic power, and to support the defense of the Malay barrier by diverting Japanese strength away from Malaysia.

The responsibility of the C-in-C Asiatic Fleet for supporting the defense of the Philippines remains so long as that defense continues.

The Navy's specific Rainbow 5 war plans provided for the following task:

"Raid Axis forces and sea communications in the Pacific and Far East areas."

"Divert" enemy strength away from Malay barrier.

". . . prepare to capture and establish control over the Caroline and Marshall island area and to establish an advanced fleet base in Truk."

The Asiatic Fleet was to "support the defense of the Philippines," and other Allied areas, and raid Japanese sea communications and destroy Axis forces. It was to cooperate with the Army in the defense of the Philippine coastal frontier. The Commander in Chief, Asiatic Fleet, was authorized to shift his base of operations to British or Dutch ports at his discretion.

Rainbow 5 plainly stated that the U.S. strategy in the Far East would be defensive. It fudged the question of Philippine defenses; the Navy's task to *"prepare"* for the advance to the westward through the Caroline and Marshall islands plainly indicated that the Philippines were written off even before Pearl Harbor. The Pearl Harbor losses might be termed a *de jure* confirmation of a *de facto* situation; they meant further delay—and consequently the inevitable loss of the Philippines—before any sizable offensive operations could be undertaken. But Pearl Harbor did not "neutralize" the Pacific Fleet; its aircraft carriers escaped destruction. The superiority of Japanese strength and the geographic power of the Japanese network of bases had already "neutralized" it.

In his memoirs (*Reminiscences,* p. 121) MacArthur wrote that

although Admiral King [Ernest J. King, Commander in Chief, U.S. Fleet, and later also Chief of Naval Operations] felt that the fleet did not have sufficient resources to proceed to Manila, it was my impression that our Navy deprecated its own strength and might well have cut through. . . . The Japanese blockade of the Philippines was to some extent a paper blockade. Mindanao was still accessible and firmly held by us. . . . A serious naval effort might well have saved the Philippines and stopped the Japanese drive to the south and east. One will never know.

But the facts are easily marshaled; one *can* know. History sides with Admiral King. Ten Japanese aircraft carriers in the Pacific to the U.S. three; an overwhelming Japanese superiority in battleship strength and in cruisers and destroyers, and a tremendous Japanese advantage in land-based air power would have doomed to disaster any early attempt to penetrate the web of Japanese bases in the Central Pacific by a major fleet and amphibious move.

An attempt to supply the Philippines, on the massive scale needed to clothe and equip 140,000 fighting men, would have meant a continuing and periodic program of large convoys. These would have had to fight their way through enemy-dominated seas from Hawaii or Australia against superior air and naval opposition. The only eventuality that could have insured the integrity of such a maritime supply line would have been the destruction of the bulk of Japanese naval and air power. Yet any wholesale attempt to push a large convoy through the blockade or to provoke a large-scale naval battle would, at that stage of the war, have resulted in inevitable disaster to the United States. The facts of history are now at hand, and it is clear that the Japanese, as Admiral King then said, were far too strong. Blockade running and small-scale supply efforts by submarines, planes, inter-island steamers and small craft were partially successful, but the results merely prolonged agony. Large-scale supply was out of the question.

The course of the war demonstrated its impossibility. MacArthur and Marshall—and many other senior Army officers of that day (with the exception of General Walter Krueger, a graduate of the Naval War College, and a few others)—had no real understanding or appreciation, when the war started, of the capabilities and limitations of either sea power or air power. Nor did the Navy have a comprehensive understanding of the tremendous and specialized maritime strength required to conduct a campaign across the vast reaches of the Pacific against determined opposition. The full strength of carrier-based air power, of submarine operations, of the Navy's under-way replenishment groups and mobile supply system, of underwater demolition teams and highly trained amphibious forces was still to be developed.

30. Henry L. Stimson and McGeorge Bundy, *On Active Service,* p. 395.

As I noted in *Great Mistakes of the War* (p. 72),

MacArthur's then dual status as Field Marshal in the Philippine Army and General in the American Army, his belief—a mistaken one, as the war showed—that the Philippines could, in large measure, provide their own defense, and the American commitment to Philippine independence, seem to have influenced his (MacArthur's) judgment. Faced with an actual act of war—the Japanese attack upon Pearl Harbor some hours previously—he hesitated, apparently, to undertake offensive action while awaiting either an enemy overt act against the Philippines or formalization of hostilities by actual declaration [of war].

This hesitation may have contributed to some degree to the debacle at Clark Field nine hours after Pearl Harbor. But the primary cause was, as Secretary Stimson pointed out, our lack of understanding of what air power entailed.

Dr. Robert F. Futrell ("Air Hostilities in the Philippines 8 December, 1941," *Air University Review,* Maxwell Air Force Base, Alabama, January-February, 1965) concludes that General Lewis H. Brereton, the Army Air Force Commander, "did request and was denied authority to send a B-17 strike against Formosa early in the morning of 8 December." In my opinion, General Sutherland, MacArthur's chief of staff, was probably the key to the mystery of why permission was denied—or at least deferred—until too late. MacArthur was then "thinking defensively," as Futrell points out, a victim of the confusion of plans which he had helped to create. But even if a U.S. air strike had been launched against Formosa, it seems certain it would not have changed the ultimate outcome in the Philippines; our concept then of what air power was, was far too restricted.

The same dichotomy in MacArthur's actions, which undoubtedly grew out of the peculiar commonwealth political status of the Philippines and MacArthur's own dual role, was evident in MacArthur's designation of Manila as an open city, and his transmission to Washington of Quezon's proposals for neutralization of the Philippines.

MacArthur's role in the defense of the Philippines was by no means— as this account has shown—one of brilliant judgment and unalloyed glory. To quote the author's *Great Mistakes of the War* (p. 75):

> The most amazing and least understandable of MacArthur's Philippine actions was his tacit approval of a proposal by President Quezon on February 8, 1942, that the Philippines "receive immediate and unconditional independence from the United States, and that they be forthwith neutralized by agreement between Japan and the United States; all troops were to be withdrawn and the Philippine Army disbanded." This message from Quezon to President Roosevelt railed against the United States for its failure to reinforce the Philippines "in terms as unfair as they were wholly understandable." (Quezon had been misled by MacArthur's early optimism, and relations between him and President Roosevelt had been strained.) What was not understandable was the tacit approval of MacArthur, demigod in his own image, hero of Bataan in the eyes of the world. MacArthur radioed the President that "so far as the military angle is concerned, the problem presents itself as to whether the plan of President Quezon might offer the best possible solution of what is about to be a disastrous debacle." This, just twenty-four days after promising his men that thousands of reinforcements and hundreds of planes were on the way!

31. Admiral Frederick C. Sherman, *Combat Command,* pp. 41–42.

32. In 1963, years after a brief version of the defense of Corregidor was published in the *New York Times Sunday Magazine,* the author received a letter from Admiral Hart declaring in no uncertain terms that I had charged him with forgetfulness of his training and "Sailor's Faith" and with allowing a "personal feeling" to influence his "performance of vital duties." "You really *knew* nothing about any 'feud,'" Admiral Hart wrote; "for that matter, you still can't *know* anything." The word "feud," used in the original article to describe the relationships between the Navy and the Army in the Philippines, particularly that between Admiral Hart and General Mac-Arthur, is too strong. But the relationships were prickly; indeed, until General MacArthur's and General Sutherland's departure, poor. Clashing personalities, lack of a unified command, plans and concepts which differed markedly, General MacArthur's grandiose egoism, Admiral Hart's stiff-necked sense of duty and, particularly, General Sutherland's attitude toward the Navy and Marines were to blame.

In response to a letter from the author, Admiral Hart on April 4, 1963, recounted the following incident:

> About 1958, I was motoring around Oahu and saw a signboard which said that there was the station of the Fourth Marine Regiment. I had never seen any of them since 1941 so I entered the compound and asked if there were any men in it

who were in the Far East when the war began. Was at once told that there were five—all Sergeants.

I was put in touch with them and the following transpired between their leader and myself:

Hart: "I am wondering how you men feel toward me. I was the one who in particular got you moved to the Philippines, from Shanghai, where you lost an inordinate number of your buddies, and went through many horrible months. But for me, you would have had to surrender to the Japanese in Shanghai. You would nearly all have survived because the Japanese would have given you a sort of diplomatic status and treated you fairly well as was the case with the detachment which had to surrender at Peking. I have over the years rather had the very heavy losses which the Fourth Marines suffered on my conscience. Would you tell me very frankly how *you* feel about it?"

The Sergeant: "You should not feel that way at all, Admiral. You placed us where we could fight the good fight. What we went through gave the Regiment a soul; otherwise we would not now have what we've got."

Needless to say, I liked what I was told.

Pretty good, from some Sergeants, don't you think?

Admiral Hart, a crusty old sea dog, is a man of uncompromising integrity.

33. Many attacks were made, but throughout the war narratives of the early days ran the familiar phrase "torpedoes missed." Some hit and failed to explode. Defective torpedoes explain some, but by no means all, of the early months' poor submarine results. See *United States Submarine Operations in World War II* by Theodore Roscoe, *op. cit.*

The text of the message tapped out by Private Irving Strobing (part of it recorded in Chapter IV) was read on the Army Hour radio program on May 31, and was reported, in part, in the *New York Times* of June 1, 1942.

The official Army history (*The Signal Corps: The Test*, by George Raynor Thompson, Dixie R. Harris, Pauline M. Oakes and Dulany Terrett; Office of the Chief of Military History, Department of the Army, Washington, D.C. 1957) points out (p. 120–122) that on the day Corregidor surrendered prior to "1037 . . . a soldier named Irving Strobing had been filling in the time with poignant if unauthorized farewells to his family." It adds that various official messages to Washington, to General MacArthur and elsewhere were despatched from 1105 on, and that Chief Warrant Officer Robert L. Scearce "sent out Washington No. 3, the last word from Corregidor before it blacked out"—a message which simply reported destruction of cipher strips.

Bibliography

Books

BALDWIN, HANSON W., *Great Mistakes of the War*. New York: Harper, 1950
BRERETON, GENERAL L. H., *The Brereton Diaries*. New York: Morrow, 1946
CRAVEN, W. F., and CATE, J. L., eds., *The Army Air Forces in World War II*, Vol. 1, *Plans and Early Operations, January 1939 to August 1942*. Chicago: University of Chicago Press, 1948

FALK, STANLEY L., *Bataan—The March of Death*. New York: Norton, 1962
GREENFIELD, KENT ROBERTS, *American Strategy in World War II: A Reconsideration*. Baltimore: Johns Hopkins Press, 1963
GREENFIELD, KENT ROBERTS, gen. ed., *Command Decisions*. New York: Harcourt Brace, 1959
MACARTHUR, GENERAL DOUGLAS, *Reminiscences*. New York: McGraw-Hill, 1964
METCALF, COLONEL CLYDE H., ed., *The Marine Corps Reader*. New York: Putnam, 1944
MILLER, COLONEL E. B., *Bataan Uncensored*. Long Prairie, Minn.: Hart Publications, 1949
MORISON, SAMUEL ELIOT, *History of United States Naval Operations in World War II*, Vol. III, *The Rising Sun in the Pacific*. Boston: Little Brown, 1948
MORTON, LOUIS, *The Fall of the Philippines (U.S. Army in World War II)*. Washington: Office of the Chief of Military History, Department of the Army, 1953
NAVAL ANALYSIS DIVISION, *U.S. Strategic Bombing Survey (Pacific), Interrogations of Japanese Officials,* Vols. I and II. Washington: U.S. Government Printing Office, 1946
ROSCOE, THEODORE, *United States Submarine Operations in World War II*. Annapolis: U.S. Naval Institute, 1949
SHERMAN, GENERAL FREDERICK C., USN (RET), *Combat Command*. New York: Dutton, 1950
STIMSON, HENRY L., and BUNDY, MCGEORGE, *On Active Service*. New York: Harper, 1948
WAINWRIGHT, GENERAL JONATHAN, *General Wainwright's Story*. New York: Doubleday, 1946

Magazine Articles

This chapter was based upon an article, "Corregidor: The Full Story" by Hanson W. Baldwin, which first appeared in the September 22, 1946, *New York Times Magazine,* and later was published in greatly expanded form under the title "The Fourth Marines at Corregidor" in four successive issues of the *Marine Corps Gazette,* commencing in November, 1946, and ending in February, 1947.
Other magazine articles quoted or consulted include:
LIEUTENANT COLONEL C. STANTON BABCOCK, USA, "Philippine Campaign," *The Cavalry Journal,* March-April, 1943
LIEUTENANT COLONEL C. STANTON BABCOCK, USA, "Philippine Campaign" (Part II), *The Cavalry Journal,* May-June, 1943
STETSON CONN, "Changing Concepts of National Defense in the United States, 1937–1947," *Military Affairs,* Spring, 1964
DR. ROBERT F. FUTRELL, "Air Hostilities in the Philippines 8 December, 1941," *Air University Review,* January-February, 1965
COLONEL C. L. IRWIN, USA, "Corregidor in Action," *Coast Artillery Journal,* January-February, 1943
COLONEL STEPHEN M. MELLNIK, Coast Artillery Corps, USA, "How the Japs Took Corregidor," *Coast Artillery Journal,* March-April, 1945

LOUIS MORTON, "American and Allied Strategy in the Far East," *Military Review,*
   December, 1949

LIEUTENANT COMMANDER T. C. PARKER, USN, "The Epic of Corregidor-Bataan,"
   U.S. Naval Institute Proceedings, January, 1943

CAPTAIN JOHN WHEELER, USA, "Rearguard in Luzon," *The Cavalry Journal,*
   March-April, 1943

Documents

Official Reports and Personal Narratives:

   COLONEL SAMUEL L. HOWARD, USMC

   LIEUTENANT ROBERT F. JENKINS, JR., USMC

   CAPTAIN F. W. FERGUSON, USMC

   FIRST LIEUTENANT WILLIAM F. HOGABOOM, USMC

   CAPTAIN H. M. FERRELL, USMC

   ACTING SERGEANT MAJOR CARL E. DOWNING, USMC

   QUARTERMASTER SERGEANT ALBERT S. LEMON, USMC

   CAPTAIN CHARLES B. BROOK, USN

   FIRST LIEUTENANT OTIS EDWARD SAALMAN, USA

   FIRST LIEUTENANT WILLIAM F. HARRIS, USMC

   CAPTAIN DENNYS W. KNOLL, USN

   LIEUTENANT COLONEL A. C. SHOFNER, USMC

   PHM2C LOUIS NOVAK, JR., USN

   (Ranks as of 1942)

"Hayes Report on Medical Tactics, Fourth Regiment," compiled by Commander Thomas H. Hayes, Medical Corps, USN, from original papers salvaged from Canacao, Manila, Corregidor and Bilibid Prison. Consists chiefly of accounts by medical officers attached to the 4th Regiment, but also includes some other data.

Personnel and administrative details and casualty figures furnished by Colonel Donald Curtis, USMC.

Interviews:

   COLONEL SAMUEL HOWARD

   COLONEL CURTIS

   LIEUTENANT COLONEL WILLIAM F. PRICKETT

   LIEUTENANT WILLIAM F. HARRIS

   LIEUTENANT ROBERT F. JENKINS, JR.

   PLATOON SERGEANT LAURENCE E. MORVAN

   SERGEANT JOHN PATRICK ZIMBA

   MASTER TECHNICAL SERGEANT JOSEPH ANDREWS

   SERGEANT JOSEPH MICELI

   (Ranks as of 1942)

Miscellaneous:

   War Department communiqués
   New York Times, 1941–42; 1946
   War and Navy Department press releases

I am particularly indebted to the Marine Corps Historical Section and to the Public Information Office, USMC. To Colonel Curtis, late of the 4th Marines, I owe a special debt of gratitude for assembling many of the official reports used in this narrative, for checking miscellaneous facts, and in general for acting as a kindly and capable *deus ex machina*.

CHAPTER 5. STALINGRAD

Notes

The Stalingrad campaign is extremely difficult to record and to interpret, not only because of its tremendous scope but because available figures conflict and no accurate records were kept, or, if kept, were lost or suppressed.

The Germans, normally meticulous record keepers and probably more accurate in casualty estimates than the Americans, lost the battle, and with it many of their records. The Russians kept no accurate statistics of casualties, and their published material, even that intended only for the internal consumption of the Red Army, is heavily overlarded with Communist propaganda and the typical distortions of Communist-written history.

Both sides claimed that the other was greatly superior in numbers on the ground and in the air when the campaign started; at its end, when Sixth Army was tightly encircled, the Russians, in *Combat Experiences* (cited in the notes) —the frankest Russian study this writer has seen—admitted only a 1.5 to 1 superiority in numbers on the Don front, and claimed the Germans had a major superiority in tanks, guns, machine guns and motor vehicles. I find the Russian statistics hard to believe, especially since they admittedly used seven armies to smash the Sixth Army. On the other hand, I would feel that German estimates of Soviet strengths were somewhat exaggerated.

It is quite likely that the Germans initially enjoyed a superiority in numbers in the air when the campaign opened, which was reduced—by attrition, losses on the ground, and transfers to the Mediterranean theater—to a marked inferiority in numbers of aircraft at the end. The ultimate Russian power undoubtedly derived from greatly superior Russian mass and from the overextension of the German armies.

Some of the best works dealing with Stalingrad are: *Paulus and Stalingrad* by Walter Görlitz; *The Battle for Stalingrad* by Marshal V. I. Chuikov; *Stalingrad* by Heinz Schröter; Manstein's *Lost Victories;* and the English translation of the Soviet General Staff's *Combat Experiences;* all supplemented—up to his dismissal—by Halder's trenchant diaries. The Soviet official history, *History of the Great Patriotic War of the Soviet Union,* Vol. III, though tendentious and biased, provides supplementary data. Paul Carell's *Hitler Moves East 1941–1943* and Alan Clark's *Barbarossa* provide differing viewpoints and much detail, with Carell's the more comprehensive.

I am greatly indebted to the Office of the Chief of Military History of the Army for access to available documents and studies dealing with the Stalingrad campaign, and to Dr. Stetson Conn, Chief Historian, for his kindly help.

Mrs. Freeda Franklin, *New York Times* librarian, was, as always, efficient and painstaking.

Earl F. Ziemke, Office of the Chief of Military History, kindly read the manuscript and provided important corrections and criticisms. Major General John Shirley ("P.") Wood, onetime commander of the 4th Armored Division and one of the great tank leaders of World War II, also helped with a critical reading.

1. The exact number is in doubt. Ziemke credits the higher figure ("Stalingrad to Berlin—The German Campaign in Russia, 1942–1945," by Earl F. Ziemke, p. 88).
2. Yu. P. Petrov, ed., *The History of the Great Patriotic War of the Soviet Union 1941–1945*, Vol. III. The Soviet official history states (manuscript translation, Department of the Army, p. 1):

> More than 80 million people had lived in the territories now under temporary occupation. . . . The Motherland had been deprived of its greatest industrial and agricultural districts. These . . . regions had possessed the following proportions of national wealth—71 percent of the iron cast, 58 percent of the steel, 63 percent of the coal mined, 42 percent of the electric power generated, 47 percent of the sown areas.

3. *The Goebbels Diaries, 1942–1943*, pp. 112–113.
4. "The Halder Diary, Vol. 7, Pt. 2," p. 341.
5. *The German Campaign in Russia—Planning and Operations, 1940–42*, p. 137.
6. *Ibid.*, p. 131. Major General J. F. C. Fuller reckons the Allied total at 61 divisions in *The Decisive Battles of the Western World*, Vol. III, p. 520. The Soviet official history states there were 242 Axis divisions in Russia in August, 1942, and 266 in November.
7. General Franz Halder, "Decisions Affecting the Campaign in Russia (1941–1942)." General Halder, who answered questions after the war, said in this manuscript that "Hitler's fixed idea was to seize two political and geographic objectives—Leningrad and Stalingrad." The Army High Command knew that there were very strong enemy concentrations near Saratov and north of Baku. But "Hitler considered this information to be childish nonsense. His opinion was: *'Der Russe ist todt.'* "
8. Army Group South, originally commanded by Field Marshal Fedor von Bock, initiated the southern campaign. His command became Army Group B on July 9, and Bock was replaced by General Weichs on July 13, ostensibly because Hitler was said to be displeased with Bock's direction of the initial blows against Voronezh, but actually because Weichs was considered more pliable to Hitlerian direction. Thus two army groups were established in the south—one, Army Group B, operating against Stalingrad and the Don-Volga loops; the other, Army Group A, operating against the Caucasus. Army Group B included the Sixth Army, Fourth Panzer Army, the Second Army (around Voronezh), the Italian Eighth, the Hungarian Second and the Rumanian Third Armies. Army Group A included the First Panzer Army, the Eleventh Army, the Seventeenth Army and the Rumanian Fourth Army,

plus other units. During the campaign the order of battle changed, as new units were thrown into action or were shifted.

9. As early as February, 1941, *before* the invasion of Russia, Hitler had asked General Jodl to prepare a plan for the invasion of India. His dream—a vague one—was, as Mr. Ziemke has noted, "a gigantic encirclement operation through the Near East to link up with the Italian-German drive through Egypt that would take the Suez Canal and cut the British lifeline." But these hopes were a military mirage. The Germans would never have had the strength, or the logistic support, to invade India, even if they had won the El Alamein battle and had overrun Egypt.

10. *The German Campaign in Russia, op. cit.,* pp. 121 ff. Hitler recognized Stalingrad's importance as a transportation nexus and transshipping center for manganese, wheat, oil and other products.

11. Winston S. Churchill, *The Second World War,* Vol. 4, *The Hinge of Fate,* p. 343.

12. Walter Görlitz, *Paulus and Stalingrad,* p. 152n. Ziemke does not agree with this statement. He points out that the Russians lost as greatly in the Kharkov battle as the Germans did later at Stalingrad. He believes that the necessity for cleaning up the Crimea, in June, was probably more significant than the Kharkov battle insofar as delay in initiating the Stalingrad campaign was concerned. See also Paul Carell, *Hitler Moves East 1941–1943,* p. 463, which gives slightly different figures for Soviet losses.

13. Carell gives a comprehensive account of this incident (*ibid.,* pp. 479 ff.).

14. Fuller, *op. cit.,* Vol. III, p. 524. The Russians suffered heavily in this initial phase of the German drive, but their forces avoided a major encirclement and pulled back rapidly. Hitler and the German Army leaders differed as to what had been accomplished. (See Carell, *op. cit.,* pp. 502 ff.)

15. "The Halder Diary," *op. cit.,* 23 July, 1942.

16. Carell's figures on Soviet losses in this encirclement (*op. cit.,* p. 547) appear to be too high.

17. Western plans to relieve the German pressure against Russia predated Dieppe. U.S. units were earmarked, along with British forces, for an attack against the coast of France late in the spring and early in the summer of 1942. These plans were (fortunately for the Allies) canceled. But the preparations and the abortive raid at Dieppe stoked Hitler's anxiety about his western flank, and in August, when every possible division was needed in Russia, Hitler ordered the transfer of two Panzer divisions from the Southern Front to the West. Only one division, the 1st SS Panzer Division (*Leibstandarte SS Adolf Hitler*), was actually transferred; the other became involved in a Russian counteroffensive.

18. Ronald Seth, *Stalingrad: Point of No Return,* p. 69.

19. Carell, *op. cit.,* p. 552. The Soviet official history claims that some 50,000 Stalingrad residents—"volunteers"—joined the "People's Guard"; 75,000 were assigned to the Sixty-second Army, 3,000 girls served as nurses, telephone operators, etc. (Chuikov stresses the services of Soviet women at Stalingrad), and thousands of young boys were inducted into fighting formations as replacements and fillers. All of these—if the figures are, indeed, correct (and

their accuracy is subject to doubt)—learned war the hard way, and death, for many, was their lot.

20. The Volga at Stalingrad is almost a mile wide at its widest point. Opposite the southern part of the city, it is broken into two channels by Sarpinsky Island.
21. Warlimont, *op. cit.,* p. 257.
22. The 16th Motorized Infantry Division patrolled about 250 miles of steppe-land between Army Groups A and B until the Rumanians, after mid-September, filled in part of the gap.
23. B. H. Liddell Hart, *The Other Side of the Hill,* p. 314.
24. Seymour Freidin and William Richardson, eds., *The Fatal Decisions,* p. 135.
25. By November 1 the Germans estimated there were 16 Russian divisions in Stalingrad (the Russians never admitted to more than 11, a maximum of 40,000 to 45,000 men), 33 more on the Don to Volga front and 8 facing the Fourth Panzer Army in the bridgehead of Stalingrad. The Germans used a maximum of about 11 divisions in the city itself. Carell offers slightly different figures (*op. cit.,* pp. 566, 567).
26. The command post was shifted during the battle to several locations.
27. Clark, *op. cit.,* p. 238.
28. See Chuikov's rambling book, *The Battle for Stalingrad,* and Werth's post-battle account of what Chuikov told him at the time (*The Year of Stalingrad,* p. 463), in which he describes October 14 as "the bloodiest and most ferocious" day in the whole battle.
29. Fuller, *op. cit.,* Vol. 3, p. 531.
30. Carell, *op. cit.,* p. 574.
31. Freidin and Richardson, *op. cit.,* p. 141.
32. Fuller, *op. cit.,* p. 532, and *The Rise and Fall of the Third Reich* by William L. Shirer, pp. 922–23.
33. Heinz Schröter, *Stalingrad—The Battle That Changed the World,* p. 34.
34. *Ibid.,* p. 35.
35. *Ibid.*
36. Department of Military Art and Engineering, *The War in Eastern Europe, June 1941 to May 1945,* p. 78.
37. Stavka—the Russian High Command or *Stavka Verkhovnovo Glavnokom-mandovaniya.* Joseph Stalin, rarely mentioned in modern Soviet accounts of Stalingrad and almost ignored in the Soviet official history, was the *de facto* Commander in Chief of Soviet Armed Forces, as well as People's Commissar of Defense. The Stavka formulated Soviet strategy and directed its implementation. It operated, in a sense, as a committee, but Marshal Georgi Zhukov, perhaps Russia's greatest World War II soldier, the savior of Moscow, and at various times Army Chief of Staff and First Deputy Commissar of Defense, was, after Stalin, its most notable member.

Zhukov was a member throughout the war, and more than any other one man was responsible for the formulation and implementation of Soviet strategy. The Stavka was, in effect, the Soviet GHQ, directly subordinate to Stalin, who headed it, and the State Defense Committee (GKO). The GKO, or GOKO, included Stalin, Molotov (the Foreign Minister), Voroshilov,

Malenkov and Beria. John Erickson (*The Soviet High Command,* London, Macmillan, 1962, p. 598) describes it as the "heart of policy making for the Soviet Union at war, with the Stavka acting as a subordinate but complementary body as a kind of 'military Politburo.' "

The Stavka consisted variously of 12 to 20 senior military officers of all services. Marshal Boris M. Shaposhnikov, Chief of the General Staff, until he retired for illness in November, 1942, was the senior military member of Stavka and was probably, as General Guillaume calls him, the "master of modern Soviet strategy" (see B. H. Liddell Hart, *The Red Army,* New York: Harcourt Brace, 1956). Marshal Vasilevski, who succeeded Shaposhnikov, probably shares with Zhukov, Voronov and Stalin the major credit for planning the Stalingrad counteroffensive. But Nikita Khrushchev, a member of the local (Stalingrad) Front soviet, had little share in either planning or execution, despite postwar attempts to crown him with *ex post facto* laurel wreaths.

The wartime title of Commander in Chief, held by Stalin, lapsed after the war until Khrushchev assumed it in 1961—the first time any Soviet dictator had called himself Commander in Chief in peacetime. His overthrow in 1964 had been preceded, ironically, by some second thoughts about Khrushchev's role at Stalingrad by Marshal Malinovski, Defense Minister, who, in the oblique political methods of Communism, belittled Khrushchev by praising Zhukov.

38. The Soviet official history gives the order of battle on the Russian front in mid-November as follows:

Barents Sea to Gulf of Finland (1,600 kms): German Twentieth Mountain Army and entire Finnish Army—25 divisions. Opposed by Soviet Karelian front, Seventh Independent Army, Twenty-third Army of the Leningrad front.

Leningrad-Kholm (1,100 kms.): German Army Group North—Eighteenth and Sixteenth Armies—45 divisions, supported by First Air Fleet. Opposed by Leningrad, Volkhov and Northwest fronts.

Kholm-to-Orel (1,000 kms.): German Army Group Center—Ninth and Fourth Armies; Third and Second Panzer Armies—83 divisions, supported by Operational Air Group "East." Opposed by Kalinin and Western fronts and right wing of Bryansk front.

Army Group B (1,300 km. front): Half German, half Rumanian, Italian and Hungarian troops—German Second; Hungarian Second; Italian Eighth, Rumanian Third and Fourth, German Sixth and Fourth Panzer Armies—85 divisions. Fourth Air Fleet, reinforced by VIII Air Corps in support. Opposed by Southwest, Don and Stalingrad fronts.

Army Group A (1,000 km. in North Caucasus): German First Panzer and Seventeenth Armies, plus Operation Group Crimea—28 divisions. Opposed by Transcaucasus front.

Army Groups B and A had begun their summer offensive on a frontage of 850 kilometers. After advancing 400 to 650 kilometers, they had broadened their front to 2,300 kilometers.

The names of the fronts (roughly equivalent to Western army groups) were changed and boundaries altered during the campaign.

The detailed Russian order of battle for the Stalingrad area as given by the Soviet official history was as follows:

Southwest Front: First Guards Army, Fifth Tank Army (I and XVI Tank Corps; VIII Cavalry Corps and six rifle divisions) and Twenty-first Army; Seventeenth and Second Air Armies supporting. 250-km. front from Verkhnye Mamon to Kletskaya.

Don Front: Sixty-fifth, Twenty-fourth and Sixty-sixth Armies; Sixteenth Air Army supporting. 150-km. front from Kletskaya to Yerzovka.

Stalingrad Front: Sixty-fourth, Fifty-seventh, Fifty-first, Twenty-eighth and Sixty-second Armies, supported by Eighth Air Army. 250-km. front from Rynok-Sarpa.

The Russians claimed a total of 894 tanks on these three fronts to the Germans 675. Actually, the Germans had far less in this area, the Russians probably had more.

Ziemke (*op. cit.*, pp. I-31 and 32) gives comparative strength estimates, drawn from Eastern Intelligence Branch OKH on September 20 as 3,338,700 for the Axis forces on the Eastern Front (only about 3,158,000 were combat troops), as compared to 4,255,840 in the Russian forces. But the Russians had only about 3,000,000 men on the front; the balance were reserves. According to these calculations, Army Group B, with a ration strength of 1,234,000 men, faced 818,250 Russians on the front and another 561,050 in reserve; Army Group A, with a strength of 434,800 men, faced 266,350 Russians on the front and 252,240 in reserve. The German estimates of Soviet strength appear, in retrospect, conservative and, as events showed, were probably underestimates. The great Soviet advantage in numbers of armies, corps and divisions engaged did not represent, however, a similar numerical superiority, much less the same combat superiority. German divisions at this stage of the war were considerably stronger than Soviet divisions. Carell (*op. cit.*, p. 581) equates a Soviet army as equal to the "fighting strength of a German Corps at full establishment," and a "Soviet division was roughly the strength of a German brigade." This may be an overstatement, but, generally speaking, German divisions could be reckoned, until later in the war, as roughly equivalent in combat power to one and a half to two and a half Soviet divisions.

39. Schröter, *op. cit.*, p. 57.
40. See Carell, *op. cit.*, pp. 578 ff.
41. Alexander Werth records a report from Henry Shapiro, the veteran United Press correspondent in Moscow, who visited the scene of the German encirclement a few days afterward. "I found," he said, "among both soldiers and officers [of the Red Army] a feeling of self-confidence, the like of which I had never seen . . . before. In the Battle of Moscow, there was nothing like it." Werth correctly emphasizes this passage. Stalingrad was a moral victory; for the first time, the Red Army came to feel that the Germans were not invincible. (Werth, *The Year of Stalingrad*, p. 360.)
42. Freidin and Richardson, *op. cit.*, p. 153.

43. For details on the Volga crossings, see Chuikov, *op. cit.*, pp. 326–332. Chuikov says: "From the second half of October until the drifting ice came to a standstill (Dec. 17) more than 28,000 men and more than 3,000 tons of ammunition and other cargoes were carried across the river." These figures were for Chuikov's Sixty-second Army alone. The Soviet official history claims there were nine "crossing areas," with 50 ferry sites and 130 ferries along the Volga from Saratov to Astrakhan. The Volga Military Flotilla (Rear Admiral D. D. Rogachev) operated transports across the river. Hundreds of wounded were evacuated in every kind of craft, including rowboats.

44. The Army originally asked for 750 tons "daily"; later it lowered its minimum needs to 500 tons. Göring promised to deliver this amount.

45. By December 19 the LVII Panzer Corps, in hard fighting, had established a small bridgehead across the Myshkova River, a tributary of the Don. (Erich von Manstein, *Lost Victories*, p. 345.)

46. Yu. P. Petrov, ed., *History of the Great Patriotic War of the Soviet Union, 1941–45*, Vol. III, quoted from *Con L'Armata Italiana in Russia* by Major Giusto Tolloy, Italian Eighth Army, Torino, 1947.

47. Manstein had planned two complementary and alternative operations. One—"Winter Storm" (*"Wintergewitter"*)—envisaged driving a supply corridor to Paulus by LVII Corps; the other—*"Donnerschlag"* (*"Thunderclap"*)—contemplated a breakout by Paulus with the help of LVII Corps and the abandonment of Stalingrad. Hitler approved the first (at least in theory)—the establishment of a supply corridor—but not the second. Paulus and his Sixth Army were of no help to either, largely because even a link-up with Manstein ("Winter Storm") would have required a redeployment concentration of some of his Stalingrad forces and a consequent abandonment of parts of the city so bloodily won. Hitler never approved this, and, in any case, Paulus could not disengage his hard-pressed forces to concentrate the reserves needed to establish a link-up with Manstein. Actually, the Sixth Army was so far gone that *"Wintergewitter"* and *"Donnerschlag"* had to meld into one operation; otherwise neither was possible. But Paulus did not try.

Major General F. W. von Mellenthin in *Panzer Battles* (University of Oklahoma Press, 1956) states that just as the Manstein offensive reached its crisis (December 17–19) the Italian Eighth Army crumpled as the Russians broadened their offensive and Manstein was forced to divert the 6th Panzer Division to meet the onrushing hordes. The struggle at the Aksay River—another tributary of the Don—over the Christmas period, with just 35 tanks left to the LVII Corps (and about the same number to the entire Fourth Panzer Army), was described by Mellenthin (somewhat overemphatically) as "marking a crisis in the fortunes of the Third Reich." The attempt at relief had failed. By the day after Christmas, Mellenthin writes (pp. 193–196), "the Corps was almost non-existent; it had literally died on its feet." Manstein records (*op. cit.*, p. 339) that "it was the fuel . . . which finally decided Sixth Army against attempting to break out and persuaded the Army Group [Manstein] that it could not insist on its order being implemented." But the inadequate fuel—the difference between the 20 miles Paulus estimated he had available and the 30-mile distance from Stalingrad of the LVII Corps—

was less important than the overshadowing Nemesis of Hitler and his stand-fast orders.

See also *Neither Fear nor Hope* (pp. 60 ff.) by General Frido von Senger und Etterlin, who commanded the 17th Panzer Division in the attempt to relieve Stalingrad. By Christmas Eve, von Senger und Etterlin writes, "each regiment of the [17th Panzer] Division had shrunk to some 180 to 200 men carrying rifles, and the temperature had dropped to thirty degrees [Centigrade] below zero."

Ziemke and others doubt Manstein's statement in his book that he ordered Paulus to break out. He does not think either general was "ready to ruin his career" and that Hitler held too tight a rein on the whole operation to have permitted defiance of his orders. He cites as authority a teletype conference of December 23 between Paulus and Manstein, in which Paulus asked whether Manstein was ordering him to break out, and Manstein replied in the negative.

Manstein's numerous teletype conferences with Paulus and his staff do add up to some equivocation, but Manstein did, at one point, "order" (or perhaps "suggested" is a better word) Paulus to commence "Winter Storm"—the link-up operation.

48. Schröter, *op. cit.*, p. 164, also lists 149 bombers and 123 fighters destroyed in the Stalingrad battle.
49. The Soviet official history claims that even before the encirclement the German supply system had broken down, and the average German ration provided only 1,800 calories a day (about 3,500 to 4,000 is generally reckoned as the caloric intake required for a soldier).
50. Werth, *op. cit.*, p. 550.
51. Schröter, *op. cit.*, p. 158.
52. *Ibid.*, p. 149.
53. The seven Soviet armies were the Sixty-sixth (Shadov); Twenty-fourth (Galinin); Sixty-fifth (Batovok); Twenty-first (Chistyakov); Sixty-second (Chuikov); Sixty-fourth (Shumilov); and Fifty-seventh (Tolbukhin)—the latter three formerly assigned to the Stalingrad front, which was deactivated on January 1 and replaced by a Southern Front.
54. Carell, *op. cit.*, p. 618.
55. Louis L. Snyder, ed., *Masterpieces of War Reporting: The Great Moments of World War II*, p. 236.
56. Schröter, *op. cit.*, p. 218.
57. Alan Bullock, *Hitler: A Study in Tyranny*, p. 631, quoted from von Paulus' testimony at Nuremberg.
58. Schröter, *op. cit.*, p. 223.
59. Görlitz, *op. cit.*, p. 268.
60. The details of the Paulus surrender were reported, secondhand, by Alexander Werth (*Russia at War*, pp. 540–541), who records that he learned them in Stalingrad right after the battle, from a Soviet lieutenant who arranged the surrender. The lieutenant is quoted as follows: Paulus "was lying on his iron bed wearing his uniform. He looked unshaved, and you wouldn't say he felt jolly. 'Well, that finished it,' I remarked to him. He gave me a sort of

miserable look and nodded." Earlier, the lieutenant—identified as Fyodor Mikhailovich Yelchenko—quotes Paulus' chief of staff as saying that Paulus "no longer answered for anything since yesterday." Later, Werth saw Paulus in captivity, and records (p. 549) that he "looked pale and sick, and had a nervous twitch in his left cheek," though he had "a more natural dignity" than the other prisoners.

61. *Ibid.*, p. 544.
62. The Bonn government announced in 1958 that about 5,000 survivors of Stalingrad had returned to Germany. Since then several hundred others—perhaps 1,000 more—have returned to Germany.

The exact casualty statistics of Stalingrad will never be known, but the approximation given in the text cannot be far wrong. The Russian official history claims more than 91,000 prisoners (apparently exclusive of the unmentionable *"Hiwis"*), and states: "A total of 147,200 dead German officers and men were collected and buried on the battlefield." The later figure is almost certainly exaggerated.

Ziemke estimates the total number of Germans in the pocket shortly before Christmas was about 211,700, including some 6,000 wounded. In addition, according to a ration strength return on December 18, there were some 13,000 Rumanians and about 19,300 *"Hiwis."* But combat effectives were a very small portion of this total. By mid-October Sixth Army's "front line infantry strength," as Ziemke notes, was only 56,500.

To the German losses in and around Stalingrad itself must be added the high cost of the entire Stalingrad campaign, which properly speaking includes the campaign in the Caucasus. Again no exact figures are possible. But German casualty figures on the entire Eastern Front by months were as follows:

COMBAT CASUALTIES

September, 1942	130,550
October	68,150
November	46,900
December	83,665
January, 1943	81,124
February	268,512
March	121,485

The February figures include delayed returns of Sixth Army combat casualties—dead, wounded seriously enough to be transported outside the army area for treatment, and missing (including prisoners)—which totaled 178,505. The March figures also reflect delayed returns from units other than Sixth Army. In many months—December, for instance—the sick and slightly wounded far outnumbered the combat casualties; the total casualties, including sick, for December, were 200,690 for the entire Eastern Front.

Some idea of the total cost of the Stalingrad campaign to the Germans can be gleaned from a comparison of Germany's total cumulative casualties on the Eastern Front when the campaign opened with the cumulative total in March, 1943. The respective figures are 1,332,477 as of June 30, 1942 (including 326,791 killed); 1,589,082 as of August 31, and 2,389,468 as of April 1, 1943—showing that Germany lost more than 1,000,000 men in the fateful nine months from July 1 to April 1.

Italian, Hungarian and Rumanian casualties must be added to these horrendous totals.

These, again, can only be estimated. According to Italian and Russian accounts, the Italian Eighth Army lost about 125,000—or half—of its personnel in killed, wounded, captured and missing. The Rumanians were virtually wiped out. The Hungarians suffered somewhat less severely, but heavily. The total satellite casualties possibly approximated a quarter of a million to 300,000.

Figures compiled by Mario Fenyö ("The Allied-Axis Armies and Stalingrad") in *Military Affairs* (Washington, American Military Institute, Summer, 1965, Vol. XXIX, No. 2) arrive at a somewhat higher total. Mr. Fenyö says that "of the 220,000 Italians sent to the Russian front over 100,000 did not return," and adds that "the Hungarian army was more completely annihilated than the other allied armies had been.

"It has been estimated that of a total of over 200,000 soldiers of all ranks, 7,000 froze to death, 40,000 were killed, and 70,000 ended in Russian captivity. About 70 to 80 per cent of the heavy weapons were lost."

However, the Italian Institute of Statistics, in a geographical breakdown of Italian war casualties, lists only 11,891 Italians as dead in the U.S.S.R., and 70,275 as missing. See Appendix.

For the satellite armies, even more than for the Germans, the Stalingrad campaign was a modern Cannae.

The Russian figures are even more indeterminate. Yet their losses were unquestionably tremendous; both Chuikov and Deriabin speak of divisions reduced to company strengths. Deriabin's own regiment, which fought in the city from September to February, entered action with 2,800 men; 151 were "left alive." (See Peter Deriabin and Frank Gebney, *The Secret World,* pp. 47–52.)

63. Görlitz, *op. cit.,* pp. 5, 145, 257. Paulus himself later wrote (Görlitz, pp. 284–285):

Deeply though I sympathized with the troops committed to my care, I still believed that the views of higher authority must take precedence. . . . I believed that by prolonging to its utmost our resistance in Stalingrad I was serving the best interests of the German people, for, if the eastern theatre of war collapsed, I saw no possible prospect of a peace by political renegotiation.

In the early stages of the encirclement Paulus probably had little choice; he would have been immediately relieved from duty by Hitler had he disobeyed the Fuehrer's orders. His moment of truth came when Manstein's drive reached its climax. He might then have saved what remained of his army had he possessed the intestinal fortitude to break out regardless of orders or had he taken advantage of Manstein's "suggestions" or "orders" that he commence "Winter Storm," the link-up operation. Paulus' point, nevertheless, is well taken; as an army commander he did not know and could not know the "big picture" along the entire Eastern Front; his dilemma was that if he disobeyed orders and saved his own army he feared he might cost the German Army more than he saved. See Carell's point of view, *op. cit.*, p. 597.

64. Richard C. Lukas, "The Velvet Project: Hope and Frustration." The "unchallenged air superiority" enjoyed by the Russians after Stalingrad to which Mr. Lukas refers was, however, successfully challenged locally and periodically by the Germans, though Moscow retained great over-all superiority in numbers of aircraft across the entire Eastern Front throughout the rest of the war. Mr. Lukas in his article points out that the Soviet Air Force

appears to have maintained its strength at 4,000–5,000 planes during the fall and winter of 1942. After that the strength of the Soviet Air Force increased substantially. In addition to its own resources, the Soviet Air Force could also rely on the deliveries of Lend-Lease aircraft from the United States and Great Britain. For example the Army Air Forces delivered approximately 400 aircraft to the Russians in Iran in the period July-November, 1942, thus matching the number of known withdrawals by the Luftwaffe from the Eastern Front during October-November, 1942.

65. Fuller, *op. cit.,* Vol. 3, p. 538.
66. *Combat Experiences,* General Staff of the Red Army Collection of Materials for the Study of the War Experiences, No. 6.
67. Fuller, *op. cit.,* Vol. 3, p. 538.
68. George F. Kennan, former Ambassador to Russia and scholarly diplomat, notes in his book, *Russia and the West under Lenin and Stalin* (Boston, Little, Brown, 1960, pp. 364–367), that the non-Communist German resistance

was composed of men who were very brave and very lonely, and were so much closer to us in feelings and in ideals than they were to either Hitler or Stalin that the difference between them and us paled, comparatively, into insignificance. These men succeeded, at the cost of great personal and political danger, in establishing contact with the Allies during the war. They received literally no encouragement from the Allied side. . . . The unconditional surrender policy, which implied that Germany would be treated with equal severity whether or not Hitler was overthrown, simply cut the ground out from under any moderate German opposition.

In December, 1964, General Dwight D. Eisenhower, former President of the United States, said in an interview with the Washington *Post* that he believed the "unconditional surrender policy" was a mistake and that it caused the Germans to fight longer. He added that while he had never before condemned the policy publicly, because "nobody ever asked me," he had complained about it privately when he was Supreme Commander in the European theater during the war. General George C. Marshall, Chief of Staff of the Army, "intimated," General Eisenhower said, that he, too, thought the policy was a mistake.

And, undeniably, it was.

See also *Unconditional Surrender* by Anne Armstrong (New Brunswick, Rutgers University Press, 1961).

It is difficult to avoid the conclusion that the unconditional surrender policy and all it implied to the political future of Europe was, from the point of view of the United States and the Western world, one of the great mistakes of the war.

To those who object and who assert that the German opposition was apathetic and would never have rallied to any kind of positive Allied policy or propaganda, the answer of history is clear: "Perhaps." But the black mark stands; we made no attempt.

69. Fuller, *op. cit.,* Vol. 3, p. 542.

Görlitz (*op. cit.,* p. 288) agrees it was the "politico-psychological turning point of the whole war," but that it was "not the military turning point of the eastern campaign—that came with the German defeat at Kursk and Bielgorod in the Summer of 1943." The reasoning of Görlitz, though accepted by many Germans, appears faulty. The military turning point of the Eastern Front—and, indeed, of the war—was the Battle of Moscow (and prior to that the Battle of Britain), and the operations immediately preceding and following the Battle of Moscow. For Germany's attempt to achieve a rapid victory over Russia failed at the gates of Moscow, and a war of blitzkrieg, which Hitler might well have won, turned into a war of attrition, which he could not possibly win. Stalingrad, in this context, was the German high-water mark, and the political and psychological, rather than the *military,* turning point in the East. Kursk and Bielgorod followed almost inevitably as a logical consequence of Germany's overextension and prior defeat at Stalingrad.

70. Von Senger und Etterlin, *op. cit.,* p. 78.

71. *Combat Experiences, op. cit.*

72. Manstein in *Lost Victories* (*op. cit.*) gives the the following chronology: 29 December, Army Group A "at last" ordered to withdraw from the Caucasus; 24 January, "withdrawal of bulk of First Panzer Army through Rostov" had been approved by Hitler, though later, the 50th and 13th Panzer Divisions were ordered west into Kuban bridgehead where "some 400,000 men lay virtually paralysed," penned in and useless, remote from the "crucial battleground," Manstein's appreciation of the situation is given graphically (p. 369): "Through Rostov ran the rear communications, not only of the whole of Army Group A but also of Fourth Rumanian and Fourth Panzer Armies." The strategic nightmare confronting the German Armies in south Russia is also dramatically illustrated by Manstein in a few sentences (p. 369): "The two Dnieper railroad crossings at Zaporzhye and Dnepropetrovsk, upon which the principal logistical support of the entire Southern Front depended, were respectively 440 miles from Stalingrad and 560 miles from the left wing of the Caucasus front, and only 260 miles from the enemy [Russian] front." Ziemke (*op. cit.,* p. III–1) points out "how vulnerable Army Groups Don and A were; they dangled like puppets on strings at the end of the few railroads that reached into the steppe east of the Don and the Donets.

73. Schröter, *op. cit.*, p. 169.

74. *The German Campaign in Russia: Planning and Operations (1940–1942)*, *op. cit.*, p. 178.

75. Translation in files of the Office of the Chief of Military History, Department of the Army, Washington, of *"Teil A—Zusammenstellung,* April, 1942 —Dec., 1944, Bewiteilungen der Feindlage vor deutscher Ostfront im grossen," Brigadier General Gehlen.

76. Von Senger und Etterlin, *op. cit.*, p. 122.

77. See Clark's discussion of Zhukov's limited concept (*op. cit.*, pp. 257, 258): his "corps and even . . . army commanders had neither the flexibility nor the imagination" for a more ambitious strategic plan.

78. *Combat Experiences, op. cit.*

79. Manstein is described as "the most gifted [general] produced by Germany in the Twentieth Century and probably the most skillful field commander to appear on either side in World War II" by Earl F. Ziemke in "Stalingrad to Berlin," p. VII-12.

80. Thomas Campbell, *The Pleasures of Hope,* 1799.

81. Winston Churchill, *The Second World War,* Vol. 4, *The Hinge of Fate,* p. 831.

But the consequences go on and on. The battle of Stalingrad was still in 1963 a *point d'appui* for political maneuvering and the dialectical argument which Communism spawns. In a discussion of the book, *Soviet Military Strategy,* conducted by The Center for Strategic Studies, Georgetown University, Colonel Thomas W. Wolfe, USAF (Ret.), pointed out that on the anniversary of the battle

several articles by prominent military men recalled the victory of Soviet arms but assigned credit for planning and organizing the victory to different agencies. . . . One group of military men, including Marshals Yeremenko, Chuikov, and Biryuzov wrote articles which placed the main credit with the local military and Party authorities at Stalingrad. This meant, in turn, a large share of credit for Khrushchev, who was a "political commissar" or a member of the Stalingrad Front's military council (Soviet) at the time. The second group, which included Marshals Voronov, Rotmistrov, and Malinovskii, singled out officers of the *Stavka,* or high command, in Moscow, as the main architects of the Stalingrad plan for victory. . . . Malinovskii's article in Pravda on February 2 [1963] . . . credited Marshal Zhukov, along with Vasilevskii and Voronov, as the *Stavka* representatives who played a key role in conceiving and planning the Stalingrad operation."

(Robert D. Crane, ed., *Soviet Nuclear Strategy,* p. 16. This Malinovski article, incidentally, was—viewed in retrospect—one of the indicators of Khrushchev's subsequent fall.)

These conflicting viewpoints, typical of the Communist interpretation of history, cannot disguise the facts. Malinovski is right; the Stavka, particularly Zhukov, Vasilevski and Voronov and Stalin himself, were the architects of the Soviet plan which led to the German encirclement at Stalingrad. Khrushchev was a Johnny-come-lately in history; he and his followers did not hesitate to indulge in the same "cult of personality" which they condemned in Stalin. As far as one can tell from Chuikov's friendly book, in which a number of flattering references to Khrushchev are dragged in by the heels, Comrade Khrushchev rarely, if ever, set foot in Stalingrad proper during the battle; he and his fellow commissars remained on the eastern bank of the Volga. The Soviet official history, written when Khrushchev was dictator of the U.S.S.R., also goes out of its way to flatter "Comrade Khrushchev," but it, too, never clearly puts him in the city of Stalingrad.

But with Premier Khrushchev's fall from power another revision in Soviet history took place. In May, 1965, a new history of the battle of Stalingrad, edited by Marshal Konstantin K. Rokossovsky and entitled *The Great Victory of the Volga,* minimizes the Khrushchev role in the battle, mentions him only twice as a member of the military council in the area, and gives chief credit for the victory chiefly to military leaders—among them Marshal Zhukov. This account, which mentions Soviet reverses more frankly than prior "histories," is nevertheless only relatively more dependable. Like all Communist history it suffers from the subordination of facts to ideology, and its prose and eyewitness accounts are couched in carefully edited, highly polished, "heroic" phraseology which conveys neither conviction nor realism.

Heroes and history are the stuff of dreams in a Communist society, written and rewritten, made and unmade with the years.

The scene of Stalin's greatest victory no longer bears his name. The city of Stalingrad was renamed Volgograd after Stalin's death and the excoriation of his "cult of personality." But most heroes have feet of clay in Communist ideology; there are suggestions today, that with Khrushchev's downfall and Stalin's "rehabilitation," the city by the Volga—scene of one of the greatest battles of history—may again resume its World War II name.

The modern Volgograd of 1964 has a population of 600,000 people, fine white beaches on the Volga, and river excursions over waters once flecked with blood. The factories are back; the city rebuilt from its rubble. There are more than 150 factories, 10 motion picture theaters but only 3 restaurants, little to buy in the stores and little luxury by Western standards. There are, however, two stadiums and many sports facilities. Lenin's likenesses and Communist slogans are everywhere, but the pedestals where statues of Stalin once stood are—ironically—empty. (See "Life in Volgograd Centers on River" by Robert Daley, *New York Times,* July 19, 1964.)

Bibliography

BULLOCK, ALAN, *Hitler: A Study in Tyranny.* London: Odhams Press, 1952

CARELL, PAUL, *Hitler Moves East 1941–1943.* Boston: Little, Brown, 1964

CHUIKOV, MARSHAL VASILI IVANOVICH, *The Battle for Stalingrad* (trans). New York: Holt, Rinehart & Winston, 1964

CHURCHILL, WINSTON S., *The Second World War,* Vol. 4, *The Hinge of Fate.* Boston: Houghton Mifflin, 1950

CLARK, ALAN, *Barbarossa: The Russian-German Conflict, 1941–45.* New York: Morrow, 1965

Combat Experiences, General Staff of the Red Army Collection of Materials for the Study of the War Experiences, No. 6, responsible editor, Major General P. P. Vechnii. Moscow: Military Publishing House of the People's Commissariat of Defense, April-May, 1943. Translated Document I.D. 547476, Assistant Chief of Staff, Intelligence, Historical Division, Department of the Army

CRANE, ROBERT D., ed., *Soviet Nuclear Strategy—A Critical Appraisal—A Report of the Study Program on Soviet Strategy.* Georgetown University: The Center for Strategic Studies, 1963

Department of the Army, pamphlet No. 20–261a, *The German Campaign in Russia: Planning and Operations, 1940–1942.* March, 1955

Department of Military Art and Engineering, *Operations on the Russian Front, Part 2, Nov. '42 Dec. '43.* West Point: U.S. Military Academy, 1945

Department of Military Art and Engineering, *The War in Eastern Europe, June 1941 to May 1945.* West Point: U.S. Military Academy, 1949

DERIABIN, PETER, and GEBNEY, FRANK, *The Secret World.* New York: Doubleday, 1959

DUPUY, R. ERNEST, and ELIOT, GEORGE F., *If War Comes.* New York: Macmillan, 1937

FREIDIN, SEYMOUR, and RICHARDSON, WILLIAM, eds., *The Fatal Decisions.* New York: Sloane, 1956

FULLER, MAJOR GENERAL J. F. C., *The Decisive Battles of the Western World.* Vol. 3. London: Eyre & Spottiswoode, 1956

GOEBBELS, JOSEPH PAUL, *The Goebbels Diaries, 1942–1943,* Louis P. Lochner, ed. New York: Doubleday, 1948

GÖRLITZ, WALTER, *Paulus and Stalingrad.* New York: Citadel, 1963

GUDERIAN, GENERAL HEINZ, "The Experiences of the War in Russia." Translated and digested from *Revue Militaire Suisse, Military Review,* September, 1956

"The Halder Diary, Vol. 7, Pt. 2, November 29, 1941–September 24, 1942." *New York Times,* mimeographed translation.

HALDER, GENERAL FRANZ, MS No. C-067b, "Decisions Affecting the Campaign in Russia (1941–1942)." Washington: Office of the Chief of Military History, Department of the Army

HART, B. H. LIDDELL, *The Other Side of the Hill.* London: Cassell, 1951

JACKSON, W. G. F., *Seven Roads to Moscow.* New York: Philosophical Library, 1958

KERN, ERICH, *Dance of Death.* New York: Scribner's, 1951

LUKAS, RICHARD C., "The Velvet Project: Hope and Frustration." Washington: *Military Affairs,* Vol. XXVII, No. 4, Winter, 1964-65

MANSTEIN, FIELD MARSHAL ERICH VON, *Lost Victories.* Chicago: Henry Regnery, 1958

Military Intelligence Division, War Department, *Order of Battle of the German Army.* Washington: March, 1945

Military Review, "The Soviet Encirclement at Stalingrad," December, 1952. Translated and digested from *Revue Militaire d'Information,* France.

ORBANN, ALBERT, *With Banners Flying.* New York: John Day, 1960

PETROV, YU. P., chief of editors and authors, *History of the Great Patriotic War of the Soviet Union, 1941-45,* Vol. III. Moscow: Institute for Marxism-Leninism. Department of the Army translation, 1963

PLIEVIER, THEODOR, *Stalingrad.* New York: Appleton-Century, 1948

ROONEY, ANDREW A., *The Fortunes of War.* Boston: Little, Brown, 1962

SCHNEIDER, FRANZ, and GULLANS, CHARLES, translators, *Last Letters from Stalingrad.* New York: Morrow, 1962

SCHRÖTER, HEINZ, *Stalingrad—The Battle That Changed the World.* New York: Ballantine Books, 1958

SENGER UND ETTERLIN, GENERAL FRIDO VON, *Neither Fear nor Hope.* New York: Dutton, 1964

SETH, RONALD, *Stalingrad: Point of No Return.* New York: Coward-McCann, 1959

SHIRER, WILLIAM L., *The Rise and Fall of the Third Reich.* New York: Simon & Schuster, 1960

SNYDER, LOUIS L., ed., *Masterpieces of War Reporting: The Great Moments of World War II.* New York: Julian Messner, 1962

WERTH, ALEXANDER, *The Year of Stalingrad.* New York: Knopf, 1947

WERTH, ALEXANDER, *Russia at War.* New York: Dutton, 1964

ZIEMKE, EARL F., "Stalingrad to Berlin—The German Campaign in Russia, 1942-1945." Office of the Chief of Military History, Department of the Army. Unpublished manuscript

ZIEMKE, EARL F., *The German Northern Theatre of Operations—1940-1945.* Department of the Army Pamphlet No. 20-271, 1959

CHAPTER 6.   THE SICILIAN CAMPAIGN

Notes

1. Major General Sir John Kennedy, *The Business of War,* pp. 174, 175. This is a delightful as well as an important book, with many anecdotes and much insight into the character and personalities of Churchill and of the great and near-great of World War II. General Kennedy writes with an intensely human touch.

2. Churchill viewed control of the Aegean and invasion of the Balkans as "a business of great consequence to be thrust forward by every means." (Arthur Bryant. *Triumph in the West,* p. 30.)

   "While I was always willing to join with the United States in a direct assault across the Channel on the German sea-front in France, I was not convinced that this was the only way of winning the war, and I knew that it would be a very heavy and hazardous adventure." (Quoted in Bryant, *op. cit.,* p. 34.) Churchill wrote: "The fearful price we had to pay in human life and blood for the great offensives of the First World War was graven in my mind."

3. George F. Howe, *Northwest Africa—Seizing the Initiative in the West,* p. 3.

4. Robert E. Sherwood, *Roosevelt and Hopkins,* p. 603.

5. Howe, *op. cit.,* p. 4.

6. Maurice Matloff and Edwin M. Snell, *Strategic Planning for Coalition Warfare, 1941–42,* p. 19.
7. Eisenhower was to write later (*Crusade in Europe,* p. 160) that

> at Casablanca the Sicily operation was decided upon for two reasons, the first of which was its great immediate advantage in opening up the Mediterranean Sea routes. The second was that because of the relatively small size of the island its occupation after capture would not absorb unforeseen amounts of Allied strength in the event that the enemy should undertake any large-scale counteraction. This reason weighed heavily with General Marshall—moreover this decision . . . avoided a commitment to indefinite strategic offensives in the area.

Kennedy (*op. cit.,* p. 276) records that in December, 1942, after the German defeat at El Alamein and the success of the "Torch" landings in North Africa, Churchill suggested that a "halt should be called in the Mediterranean about June, in order that we might concentrate in England for the invasion of France." But Field Marshal Sir Alan Brooke, Chief of the Imperial General Staff, was "quite determined" to continue operations in the Mediterranean during 1943. As Kennedy later notes, the Churchill position then seemed to be that of devil's advocate; he forced the British planning staffs to produce all kinds of statistics and telling arguments to rebut the American demand for the opening of a second front in France in 1943.

At Casablanca Kennedy found (*op. cit.,* pp. 280–281) that the American officers were "extremely difficult to know."

> When I went to bed, I picked up a copy of Oscar Wilde's *The Canterville Ghost,* and in it I came across his well-known remark, "We have really everything in common with America nowadays except, of course, language." I wished very much that that had been true. Some months later I heard the story of a Polish officer who was sent to the U.S.A. for duty, and who was told that he must learn the language before beginning his military work. After a few days, he came to his Chief in a state of frenzy and said, "I cannot learn this language. My muscles are not right for it. My jaws are made to work up and down, but the Americans work their jaws sideways."

That anecdotes such as this were recorded by a high staff officer not only shows that he had a sense of humor but also illustrates the difficult nature, despite surface correctness, of Anglo-American relationships during (particularly) the North African–Sicilian operations.

8. Arthur Bryant, *The Turn of the Tide,* pp. 423–433.
9. *Ibid.,* p. 16.
10. Samuel Eliot Morison, *Sicily, Salerno, Anzio, January 1943–June, 1944.* Some of the British planners favored the invasion of Sardinia over Sicily even to the last minute, and Lord Mountbatten and others agreed. But Brooke, described by Sir Ian Jacob as a "very obstinate man," had fixed his mind on Sicily. (See Bryant, *op. cit.,* p. 456 and footnote.)
11. Eisenhower, *op. cit.,* p. 159.
12. "No real long-range plans for the defeat of the Axis powers emerged from the [Casablanca] conference," Matloff and Snell declare (*op. cit.,* p. 381).

13. *Ibid.,* pp. 26, 151. Morison (*op. cit.,* p. 10) states that another objective was to create a situation "in which Turkey can be enlisted as an active ally," an old objective of Churchill's. But any operations in support of Turkey were specifically left, by agreement between the President and the Prime Minister, as a unilateral responsibility of Britain's.

14. Morison, *op. cit.,* pp. 9, 10.

15. Matloff and Snell, *op. cit.,* p. 134.

16. Morison, *op. cit.,* p. 5.

17. *Field Marshal Bernard Law Montgomery, The Memoirs,* Cleveland, New York: World, 1958.

18. "Monty" briefed the Canadian division when he was on a visit to England and made clear what their mission was to be in their first combat operation. At the end he said: "Of course I shall work up the soldiers. . . . I will give them as their battle-cry 'Kill the Italians.' Every man must be shouting that as he steps ashore." (Kennedy, *op. cit.,* p. 291.)

19. Lieutenant Colonel Albert N. Garland and Howard McGaw Smith, assisted by Martin Blumenson, *Sicily and the Surrender of Italy,* p. 88. The Normandy operation was, of course, larger in terms of *total* troops and supplies, than Sicily. But it was concentrated against a shorter, though much more strongly defended, strip of coast, and the initial assault was made by six seaborne divisions, as compared to Sicily's seven plus.

20. See Morison, *op. cit.,* pp. 47 ff., and Department of Military Art and Engineering, *Operations in Sicily and Italy (July 1943 to May 1945).*

    Both the 15th Panzer Division and the Hermann Göring Division were somewhat "green" and understrength. The latter had been reconstituted after the North African defeats. Apparently there were about 160 German tanks of all types in Sicily at the time of the invasion, and about 100 Italian light tanks. The German tanks included some 17 of the new German Tiger tanks, which later came to be much feared. The first models, however, had some mechanical deficiencies and other weaknesses, and these handicapped their performance even before they got into action.

    The total Axis strength in Sicily is still a matter of dispute among historians. Eisenhower puts it at 350,000 at the time of the invasion; Alexander's figures were even higher. The official Army history, however, estimates the Italian strength at about 200,000. Morison disagrees, and gives the total Axis strength at 300,000 to 365,000, in itself a wide range. The casualties and evacuation figures do not, however, add up to such totals. The answer to the puzzle is to be found, in part, in the large number of Sicilian reservists in the Italian units. Probably many of these simply took off their uniforms and faded into the civilian population. Nevertheless, it seems likely that the grand total of Axis strength at the time of invasion was no more than 250,000 to 300,000.

21. Churchill (*Closing the Ring,* p. 26) estimated the forces available for the invasion in the following proportions: Army: 8 British divisions, 6 U.S. divisions; Air Forces: 55 percent U.S., 45 percent British; Navy: 80 percent British. In addition, there were some small French units—"goums," or North African colonial troops.

22. Morison, *op. cit.*, pp. 56, 57.

23. *Ibid.*, p. 35.

24. Some of these passages describing North Africa are quoted, or paraphrased, from my introduction to a book by Colonel Edson D. Raff, *We Jumped to Fight.*

25. See Howe, *op. cit.*, pp. 366–368, for the details of the emergency air and sea lift the Germans initiated from Italy to Tunisia in 1942–43. Despite Allied fighter aircraft in North Africa and Malta, transport to Tunisia by air continued from 9 November, 1942, until May, 1943. The Germans used an average of 200 Ju-52 aircraft and 15 six-motored heavy Messerschmitt 323 transports daily, flying at about 150 feet above the water to escape radar and Allied fighters. Italian, German and Vichy French merchant shipping, specially built ferries, heavily armed with flak guns, 14 submarines and other craft were used in the surface transport system. Howe concludes that "despite staggering losses . . . from Nov. 1942 through Jan. 1943 (the Allied counter-measures began to be more effective from Jan. on) 8,122 Germans and 30,735 Italians," plus more than 100,000 tons of supplies were transported to North Africa.

26. This remark was made to the author in North Africa in March, 1943.

27. Eisenhower (*op. cit.*, p. 120) describes the German air superiority in November, 1943, as "hostile domination of the air."

28. Told to this writer shortly after the event.

29. Bryant (*The Turn of the Tide*, p. 452) describes Eisenhower and Alexander as "men with a genial gift for accommodating and reconciling divergent views."

30. Ladislas Farago, *Patton—Ordeal and Triumph*, p. 265.

31. General Omar N. Bradley, *A Soldier's Story*, p. 159.

32. The specifications for the marching pace, known as the "Truscott Trot" were published by the General during the training in North Africa. See Lieutenant General L. K. Truscott, Jr., *Command Missions*, p. 185.

33. The author noted this personality rivalry and the informal manner in which the 1st Division was commanded in an amusing but illustrative incident at Gafsa, in March, 1943. The division CP had just been established in a partially wrecked French gendarmery headquarters. I arrived there after dark, was directed to the generals' room, and was immediately invited to have a drink of cognac. Roosevelt was in his long woolen underwear (North Africa can be bitterly cold in winter) and was sitting on the edge of his cot; Terry Allen was leaning on a mantelpiece above a tiny fire in the grate, when a French colonel commanding a conglomerate collection of colonial troops covering the somewhat nebulous southern (desert) flank of the division arrived. He spoke only French and he had come to report to *"Mon Général."* Roosevelt, who spoke some French, immediately responded with *"Mon Colonel"* and an embracing gesture, and the colonel took him to be the division commander and commenced to make his report to "Teddy." It was amusing, but General "Terry" obviously didn't like it. In North Africa both men were at the front line so often that the division acquired a reputation of being "run" by its chief of staff.

34. In a conversation with the author, during Eisenhower's tenure as President of Columbia University.

35. Eisenhower, *op. cit.*, pp. 164 ff.

36. The conquest of Pantelleria really proved little about the so-called strategic capabilities of air power except that bombing was a useful weapon of intimidation against leaders and troops of low morale. Some 7,500 to 8,500 tons of bombs were dropped on the 45-square-mile island in the last 13 days of the bombardment, and there were at least six surface bombardments by naval vessels. Despite this, at least 31 serviceable guns were found near the town and harbor, and there were no serious shortages except for planes.

Craven and Cate point out that "the enemy had certainly not prepared for all-out resistance" on Pantelleria, and that conditions on the island "had been unusually favorable for the use of air power." The water mains had been ruptured, but there was sufficient water if it could be distributed. "Only a few of the batteries were damaged sufficiently to prevent their being fired by determined crews. Bombing had been less accurate than expected. . . . In the final analysis the morale of the defenders was the determining factor." (W. F. Craven and J. L. Cate, eds., *The Army Air Forces in World War II*, Vol. II, *Europe: Torch to Pointblank*, pp. 431–432.

37. See Morison, *op. cit.*, pp. 55, 56. The engineering and logistics achievements of the Americans, who used machines in prodigal quantities where other nations used manpower, outstripped those of any other combatant.

38. Eric Linklater, *The Campaign in Italy*, p. 23.

39. General Walter Warlimont, *Inside Hitler's Headquarters*, pp. 317, 318.

40. The deception plan has been fully described in Ewan Montagu, *The Man Who Never Was*. General Lord Ismay in his *Memoirs* (p. 292) wrote that the deception planners

> procured the body of a man who had just died of pneumonia, dressed him up as an officer of the Royal Marines, and attached a brief-case containing ingeniously faked documents, which gave the impression that our next objective would be the Peloponnese or Sardinia. The body was floated out of a submarine, opposite Huelva, a hundred miles north of Gilbraltar, was washed ashore in exactly the right place, and was discovered by the Spaniards, who passed it over to the Germans for a preview.

41. Morison, *op. cit.*, p. 46.

42. Brigadier General Max Ulich, writing after the war, about "Reconnaissance in the Battle of Sicily" (MS No. D-089, p. 2) commented that "during the fighting in Sicily the Luftwaffe was able to carry out reconnaissance flights only in exceptional instances, because of the overwhelming superiority of the Allied air forces, and the availability of only a small number of German reconnaissance aircraft."

43. Morison, *op. cit.*, p. 69.

44. *Ibid.*, p. 60.

45. Eisenhower moved his headquarters for the invasion to Malta, where the Royal Navy had a long established war room and communications system.

But first news, as always in every amphibious operation, was sparse and confusing.

"Nothing is so agonizing as to sit and wait." (Captain Harry C. Butcher, USNR, *My Three Years with Eisenhower*, p. 353.) As Butcher and others point out, the command setup for the Sicilian operation was far from ideal. Navy headquarters were at Malta, but the advance CP of the Allied forces headquarters was at Amilcar, Tunisia, with air communications at La Marsa. On July 16, for instance, Butcher records, "Cunningham and Alexander are at Malta; Tedder and Eisenhower in Tunisia"; Alexander was uncertain just where Fifteenth Army Group HQ would be established. The separation led to many problems, particularly in air cooperation, and orders were given and countermanded. Butcher noted (p. 364) that "if the battle weren't going so well, the separation of commanders would be most serious."

46. Morison, *op. cit.*, p. 67.
47. *Operations in Sicily and Italy*, pp. 9, 10.
48. Ross Carter, *Those Devils in Baggy Pants*, pp. 20, 21.
49. Morison, *op. cit.*, pp. 160–161, and *Operations in Sicily and Italy*, p. 11.
50. Truscott, *op. cit.*, p. 212.
51. MS T-2-1, "The Battle of Sicily," p. 13.
52. Morison, *op. cit.*, p. 87.
53. Morison, *op. cit.*, p. 152.
54. John Mason Brown, *To All Hands*, p. 131.
55. Some of the division's men and junior officers were green.
56. Garland, McGaw and Blumenson, *op. cit.*, pp. 152–154.
57. *Ibid.*, p. 155.

Some of the soldiers of the Hermann Göring Division—some of whom had never been in action before—"came running to the rear hysterically crying." General Paul Conrath, commanding the division, issued a stern order, threatening "severest measures . . . cowardice punished on the spot . . . death sentences." (See Society of the First Division, *Danger Forward—The Story of the First Division in World War II*, p. 110.) The Germans steadied and fought thereafter with their usual stubborn stability, but not even threats could stiffen the Italians.

58. Lionel S. Shapiro, *They Left the Back Door Open*, p. 48.
59. Jack Belden, *Still Time to Die*, p. 267.
60. *Danger Forward*, pp. 103, 104.
61. Morison (*op. cit.*, p. 109) comments that "the enemy had almost full control of the air," and that "many officers were wondering whether they could hold on to the beachhead." To this author this appears to give an unduly pessimistic impression. German aircraft could roam the skies at night almost at will, and Allied fighter cover in the day over the invasion fleet was inadequate. But the losses due to German air attack, as compared, for instance, to Crete, were very small, and the Allies were learning that air superiority did not mean air domination—that some enemy planes were almost certain to find targets. However, Morison rightly condemns the inadequacy of fighter cover in the initial stage of the invasion; Army Air Force fighters, based on Pantelleria, experienced early morning mists, which

Morison says was their "excuse" (perhaps a strong word) for failure to take off at dawn. But British Spitfires, flying from Malta, had been providing some air cover from the dawn of D-day.

62. Brown, *op. cit.*, p. 160.

63. Admiral of the Fleet Viscount Cunningham, *A Sailor's Odyssey*, p. 557.

64. Quoted in Morison, *op. cit.*, p. 112; also in Farago, *op. cit.*, pp. 298, 299. The exact Patton quotes differ in various accounts, but all agree the general's answer was characteristically sulphurous.

65. *Danger Forward*, p. 107.

66. Conrath was later severely criticized by Kesselring for his piecemeal attack.

67. See Morison, *op. cit.*, pp. 120 ff.; General Matthew B. Ridgway, *Soldier*, p. 73; Carter, *op. cit.*, pp. 20 ff.; Craven and Cate, *op. cit.*, pp. 453–454.

  The flight profile of the 144 C-47's carrying about 2,000 men of the 504th Regimental Combat Team was routed, unfortunately, over about 35 miles of battle front, where soldiers and seamen alike fingered nervously the triggers of AA guns and where a German air raid had just ended. "Insufficient time had been allowed for warning Allied naval vessels along the route." The result—the tragedy of the night of July 11—was thus inevitable, but might have been avoided by better planning. (See Craven and Cate.)

68. Craven and Cate, *op. cit.*, p. 454. Only 200 paratroopers out of 1,900 dropped reached their objectives.

69. See MS No. T-2, "The Battle of Sicily." Colonel Bogislaw von Bonin, Chief of Staff of XIV Panzer Corps, writes (p. 111) that "after the arrival of General Hube, the Italian commander-in-chief never again made the slightest attempt of issuing *(sic)* any orders to the German forces. He himself was, or at least seemed to be, annoyed and ashamed about the complete collapse" of the Italians. Kesselring told the Italian Comando Supremo of Hube's orders on July 14.

70. Linklater, *op. cit.*, p. 32.

71. Garland and Smyth, *op. cit.*, pp. 89, 91.

72. Ridgway, *op. cit.*, p. 75.

73. *Ibid.*, p. 76.

74. Morison, *op. cit.*, p. 183.

75. *Ibid.*, p. 188. "Moles were blasted, quayside buildings shattered, and most of the repair shops and cranes destroyed. The city was without water, light, power or sewerage." The damage was caused by a combination of Allied bombing, German demolitions and somewhat haphazard Italian demolitions.

76. Linklater, *op. cit.*, p. 36.

  Patton himself wrote (General George S. Patton, Jr., *War As I Knew It*, pp. 54 ff.) that "I believe this operation [to Palermo] will go down in history . . . as a classic example of the proper use of armor, and I also believe that historical research will reveal that General Keyes' [provisional] corps moved faster against heavier resistance and over worse roads than did the Germans during their famous Blitz." In retrospect, this is certainly an exaggerated statement; save for intermittent roadblocks and demolitions and occasional stands by some Italians, the drive into western Sicily encountered no real resistance.

On August 1 Patton hailed the men of the Seventh Army as "magnificent soldiers," and after the campaign was over on August 22, he addressed a general message of congratulations to his army, starting: "Born at sea, baptized in blood, and crowned with victory, in the course of thirty-eight days of incessant battle and unceasing labor, you have added a glorious chapter to the history of war." This order estimated that the Seventh Army had "killed or captured 113,350 enemy troops . . . destroyed 265 of his tanks, 2,324 vehicles and 1,162 large guns."

77. Kennedy, *op. cit.*, pp. 294, 295.
78. Bryant, *op. cit.*, p. 559.

Chester Wilmot noted that the Sicilian invasion progressed so favorably (though it was definitely behind the rough timetable hopes of Eisenhower and his associates) that by July 20 the American members of the Combined Chiefs of Staff approved Eisenhower's plan to invade Italy.

". . . but they still required that after the conquest of Sicily the transfer of air and naval forces from the Mediterranean to other theatres must proceed as planned. Their British colleagues were appalled at this short-sighted policy. It seemed to them that a great victory was within Eisenhower's grasp, but he was being denied the power to seize it." (Chester Wilmot, *The Struggle for Europe*, p. 132.) As Wilmot and others point out, the amphibious craft and shipping available in the Mediterranean were the bottleneck.

79. Montgomery, *op. cit.*, pp. 166, 167.
80. Churchill, *op. cit.*, p. 47.
81. Morison (*op. cit.*, p. 186) comments that "this first air raid on Rome, with the promise of more to come, proved to be the straw that broke the back of Fascism."
82. See William L. Shirer, *The Rise and Fall of the Third Reich*, Ch. 28, p. 995, for details of Mussolini's fall.
83. Admiral Franco Maugeri, *From the Ashes of Disgrace*, p. 121. This book contains details of the plot that led to the coup. See also Churchill, *op. cit.*, pp. 48 ff.; Morison, *op. cit.*, p. 186; and Shirer, *op. cit.*, p. 995.
84. Italian Fascism had never claimed the entire soul of a nation as Nazism had done in Germany. It was more beneficent than the German variety of Fascism because less efficient, and because it was applied to a people who, unlike the Germans, had few martial ambitions and to a nation whose economy was inadequate to the strain of modern war.
85. *The Goebbels Diaries*, July 25, quoted in Bryant, *The Turn of the Tide*, p. 555.

An interesting point of view of the Hitler-Mussolini relationship is given by the German General Heinrich von Vietinghoff (MS No. D-116, "Over-all Situation in the Mediterranean"). Von Vietinghoff writes (p. 1):

The sole significance for Germany of the active entrance of Italy into the war in the Summer of 1940 was a heavy burden. Hitler kept faith with Mussolini as he did with almost no other human being, to the ruin of both men and of their two peoples. To help him, to support him . . . he [Hitler] plunged into the African and Balkan adventure, without following any big over-all plan. Blinded by Mussolini's unquestionably considerable successes in the domestic political field, he did not see—and *did not want* to see—how war-weary the Italian people were after the Abyssinian War, how little value his [Mussolini's] armed forces had, how incompletely equipped they were with all modern means.

86. De Guingand ("Monty's" chief of staff) wrote later that he had "never met in any part of the world such oppressive heat." (Major General Sir Francis de Guingand, *Operation Victory*, p. 299.)
87. Farago, *op. cit.*, p. 318. This book contains a full and objective account of the slapping incidents. See Chapter 16.
88. *Ibid.*, p. 319.
89. See Bradley, *op. cit.*, pp. 152 ff. Flint's name became one to conjure with throughout the U.S. Army in Europe. His 39th Regiment bore, despite regulations, special stencils on their helmets—"AAA-O": "Anything, Anytime, Anywhere—Bar Nothing." Flint rose to fame in Sicily, and died as he would have wished to die—in action with his men in Normandy.
90. *Operations in Sicily and Italy*, p. 19, and Eisenhower, *op. cit.*, p. 176.
91. *Danger Forward*, p. 147.
92. Report of Major Charles Barton Etter, USA (Medical Corps), 93rd Evacuation Hospital, to Surgeon, II Corps (quoted in Farago, *op. cit.*, pp. 330, 331). See also Garland and Smyth, *op. cit.*, pp. 425 ff. The words attributed to Patton differ slightly in form but not in substance.
93. Morison, *op. cit.*, p. 196.
94. Morison (*op. cit.*, p. 199) says it "accomplished little," since the Germans already had commenced to withdraw from the Monte Fratello position.
95. Desmond Flower and James Reeves, eds., *The Taste of Courage*, p. 640, quoted from Douglas Grant, *Commando Landing*.
96. MS No. T-2, *op. cit.*, p. 127.
97. Captain S. W. Roskill, *The War at Sea, 1939–1945*, Vol. III, 1960, pp. 144 ff.
98. Linklater, *op. cit.*, pp. 46–47.
99. Morison, *op. cit.*, pp. 208, 209; Garland and Smyth, *op. cit.*, p. 416.
100. General Marshall later estimated the enemy's losses as 167,000 men, 37,000 of them Germans. (Churchill, *op. cit.*, pp. 40, 41.)
    The obvious discrepancies in these claims, particularly as compared to the German records, speak for themselves. Allied initial claims were highly exaggerated; indeed, Morison points out that the enemy probably lost about 200 planes (in Sicily) during the campaign instead of the 500 to 1,000 variously claimed.
    The actual Italian casualties were 147,000, dead, wounded and captured; the Germans lost 10,000 to 12,000 dead and captured, perhaps another 15,000 to 20,000 wounded.
101. But the Germans, according to Colonel Bonin, replaced their losses with more modern Italian vehicles abandoned by the Italian Army.
102. General Alexander, in a dispatch to Prime Minister Churchill on August 17, put the best light on the statistics of battle. He described Sicily as "heavily fortified" with concrete pillboxes and wire, put the Axis garrison

at nine Italian and four German divisions with a total strength of 315,000 Italians, 90,000 Germans, and estimated that 1,000 enemy aircraft were captured or destroyed, and virtually all Italian units wiped out.

103. The Seventh Army medical personnel processed a total of 20,734 hospital admissions of U.S. personnel during the campaign, 7,714 of them for wounds or injuries, the rest for illness—chiefly malaria and diarrhea. (See Garland and Smyth, *op. cit.*, p. 419.)

Also see Morison, *op. cit.*, pp. 215, 223. Army Air Corps casualties were apparently included for the most part in Army casualties; Royal Air Force figures, small in number, are not broken down. Morison, however, cites Army Air Corps casualties separately as 28 killed, 88 missing, 41 wounded.

There are also discrepancies in various official accounts of U.S. and British casualties in the Seventh and Eighth Armies. Morison gives the figures as: Seventh Army, 2,237 killed, 5,946 wounded, 598 captured; Eighth Army, 2,062 killed, 7,137 wounded, 2,644 missing—a grand total of 20,624 battle casualties. Morison's figures for U.S. casualties are higher than those given in the official Army history (Garland and Smyth, *op. cit.*, p. 417), which gives total casualties as 7,402 for the U.S. Seventh Army, 11,843 for the British Eighth Army. (See also Linklater, *op. cit.*, p. 46.)

104. The higher figure is to be found on p. 21, *Operations in Sicily and Italy;* Morison prefers the lower. I believe Morison is closer to the correct figure. But see also Craven and Cate, *op. cit.*, p. 485, who claim 740 Axis planes destroyed and 1,100 "abandoned."

105. See Roskill, *op. cit.*, pp. 138–139; also Cunningham, *op. cit.*, p. 558, and Morison, *op. cit.*

106. The soldier that Patton slapped in the first incident in the 15th Evacuation Hospital had been with the 1st Division only about 30 days; he had been in the hospital twice before within the prior 20 days. His medical tag noted, "He can't take it at front evidently." However, the soldier involved in the second incident in the 93rd Evacuation Hospital was a veteran of combat in North Africa and Sicily, with creditable service, who started to exhibit "anxiety neurosis" after he received word his wife had given birth to their first child.

Eisenhower received the first report of the incident in the 93rd Evacuation Hospital, not through General Bradley, who pigeonholed the report he received, but through his own Surgeon General on August 17, as Patton was entering Messina. "Ike" immediately started a Top Secret investigation, strictly in the Army family. "If this thing ever gets out," he said, "they'll be howling for Patton's scalp, and that will be the end of Georgie's service in this war. I simply cannot let that happen. Patton is indispensable to the war effort—one of the guarantors of our victory." After the facts about both incidents were verified, Eisenhower wrote a withering letter to Patton and ordered him to make personal apologies to all concerned, including individual units of the Seventh Army. Patton accepted the reprimand in contrite tones and made the apologies. War correspondents with the U.S. forces quickly had most of the facts, but in answer to an appeal from Eisenhower, who pointed out that Patton's "emotional tenseness and his impulsiveness are the very qualities" that made him such a "remarkable leader," they agreed to "kill" the story. After Pearson's garbled exposé, a full statement of the facts was made to the public. For a time many segments of public opinion appeared to be completely outraged, and Patton's head was on the block. But the tide turned, as Eisenhower, Secretary of War Henry Stimson and others defended the General, not for his actions but despite them. As Stimson pointed out in his memoirs (Henry L. Stimson and McGeorge Bundy, *On Active Service in Peace and War*, p. 499), "In the Summer of 1944 (during Patton's sweep across France), Patton became almost overnight the idol of many of the same newspapers and politicians who had most loudly demanded his removal in 1943."

107. General Bradley, then II Corps Commander, in Sicily, is explicit in his book (*A Soldier's Story*, pp. 154 ff.) about the reasons for the relief of Allen and Roosevelt. Patton who also had great misgivings about Allen (to a lesser extent about Roosevelt) and particularly about the 1st Division, approved Bradley's action. Indeed, it was the only possible action to take; division morale was low, discipline "shot" after Troina. Bradley wrote:

> Early in the Sicilian campaign I had made up my mind to relieve Terry Allen at its conclusion. This relief was not to be a reprimand for ineptness or for ineffective command. For in Sicily, as in Tunisia, the 1st Division had set the pace for the ground campaign. . . . Under Allen the 1st Division had become increasingly temperamental, disdainful of both regulations and senior commands. It thought itself exempted from the need for discipline by virtue of its months on the line. And it believed itself to be the only division carrying its fair share of the war. . . . Allen had become too much of an individualist to submerge himself without friction in the group undertakings of war. The . . . division . . . had become too full of self-pity and pride. To save Allen both from himself and from his brilliant record and to save the division from the heady effects of too much success, I decided to separate them. . . . There had also developed in the 1st Division an unintentional rivalry between Terry Allen and Ted Roosevelt, his assistant division commander. . . . Roosevelt's claim to the affections of the 1st Division would present any new commander with an impossible situation from the start. . . . Roosevelt had to go . . . for he, too, had sinned by loving the division too much.

Bradley goes on to describe General Huebner, Allen's successor in command of the "Fighting First" as a "flinty disciplinarian" who had risen from private to general rank and had served in nearly every rank from private to colonel in the division in prior years. Huebner called for a "spit-and-polish" clean-up in the hills of Sicily right after the bloodletting of Troina, organized "a rigid training program which included close-order drill," and right up to the invasion of Normandy bore down heavily on the "prima donnas," administered courts-martial and other punishment to the recalcitrant with a heavy hand and whipped the division into its finest shape for the great adventure in France. Today, more than any other single man, Huebner, hated when he relieved the beloved Allen and Roosevelt in the hills of Sicily, is himself beloved and respected as the "father" of the "Fighting First."

Lieutenant General J. W. Bowen, then commanding the 26th Infantry

Regiment, under both Generals Allen and Huebner, has cast considerable light on the leadership qualities and characteristics of both men in a letter (December 15, 1964) to Major J. L. Rogers, USA, from which I have been given permission to quote extracts.

> Generals Allen and Huebner were such different types that I shall have to deal with them separately. While they both had a fierce pride and abiding interest in the 1st Division, and it was their habit to be out with the troops when action was in progress, their similarities stopped about there.
> General Allen is the type portrayed as the captain of the football team, yet one of the "boys" and players. In tactical situations he spoke in football terms; such as, "We'll send Smith on this off-tackle smash, or around left end.". . . His leadership was by leading rather than beating or driving. . . . His type of personality was not conducive to strict discipline, and the 1st Division often found itself, sometimes unjustly, subject to criticism on disciplinary matters. But every one of his soldiers loved Terry, as they called him, often to his face, and many gave their lives rather than let him down. . . .
> General Huebner was a tough, grinding disciplinarian. Immediately on take-over, he initiated a number of garrison-type measures and buck-up procedures . . . he personally took to account any and every officer and soldier who did not turn out a perfect regulation hand salute. . . . It was his way of starting out tough to show who was boss and disciplinarian. However, through it all he was admired by all for his native intelligence and common sense, his bravery, his past record as a distinguished combat soldier, and his tactical brilliance. . . . In retrospect, he gave the Division a good shaking and re-orientation, which did it a lot of good and enabled it to maintain its already established and enviable record.

Sicily was a school for the soldier. From its battles many leaders who were to become great in Army annals and in military history emerged— such men as Lucian K. Truscott; young "Jim" Gavin, the parachutist; and his commander, "Matt" Ridgway, and many others. It was a school, too, for the Navy; in addition to Hewitt, Rear Admiral Alan Kirk, who was to command U.S. naval forces in the Normandy invasion, Rear Admiral J. L. Hall, Rear Admiral R. L. Conolly and others went on to higher command.

108. The U.S. Seventh Army alone, with supporting troops, approximated more than 200,000 men at the end of the invasion; the Eighth Army was even larger. The maximum German strength at any time was probably never more than 60,000 men, much of the time 40,000 to 50,000, but a grand total of more than 75,000 Germans may have fought at one time or another in Sicily. Personnel and equipment were moving across the Strait of Messina in two-way traffic—replacements and reinforcements moving in, wounded going out—during June, July and August. The figures for input and output do not jibe; indeed, it seems likely to this writer that the total German strength used in Sicily cited in Morison (*op. cit.,* p. 215n., from Kesselring *et al.*) as more than 75,000 is too high, and indeed that the grand total may have approximated only 60,000.

109. Morison, *op. cit.,* p. 209.

110. *Ibid.,* p. 173.

111. Eisenhower in his book (*op. cit.,* pp. 167–168) noted that in May, 1943, during a conference in Algiers with Churchill to try to decide what to do

after the conquest of Sicily, General Sir Alan Brooke, Chief of the Imperial General Staff,

told me that he would be glad to reconsider the cross-Channel project, even to the extent of eliminating that bold concept from accepted Allied strategy. . . .
He said that he favored a policy of applying our naval and air strength toward the blockading of Germany and the destruction of its industry but avoiding great land battles on the main fronts. . . . He wanted to open no larger front than one we could sustain in Italy.

112. Kesselring, after the war, was to write (MS No. B-270, "Questions Regarding General Strategy in the Italian Campaign") that "Italy was of the utmost importance not only to the German but also to the Anglo-American strategy . . . from the viewpoint of air warfare."

To this author, this statement greatly overstresses the actual importance of the Italian air bases.

113. General Truscott in his book (*op. cit.,* p. 553) perhaps summarized as well as anyone, the positive values of the Italian campaign, which he said,

made an important contribution to the Allied victory in World War II.
It eliminated the Axis menace in the Mediterranean; from its inception removed one Axis partner from effective participation in the war; occupied thirty-five or forty divisions which the Germans desperately needed elsewhere; inflicted heavy losses in men and matériel and imposed enormous strains upon an already overburdened economy, and provided bases from which the Allied air forces carried the air war over all of German-held territory from Rumania to Poland.

Truscott noted later (p. 552) that

at the time of the capture of Rome, both General Alexander and General Sir Henry Maitland Wilson [British Commander in Chief, Middle East] recommended to the Combined Chiefs of Staff that troops should not be withdrawn from Italy to invade southern France. They did not believe that an invasion coming so long after the Normandy landing would be of major assistance to "Overlord" [the invasion of Normandy]. They were in favor of shortening the war by utilizing these resources to clear the Germans out of Italy and to thrust into the Balkans toward the Hungarian plains, thus leaving the Allies in a much stronger political position when the war ended. Looking back over the post-war years, there is little doubt that the Western Allies would have profited, politically, had this recommendation been adopted.

Eisenhower (*op. cit.,* p. 190) described the Italian campaign after the capture of the Foggia airfields and of Naples as a "distinctly subsidiary operation, though the results it attained in the actual defeat of Germany were momentous, almost incalculable."

114. Eisenhower, *op. cit.,* p. 164. In his own memoirs Eisenhower defends the Sicilian invasion plan, but there is no doubt that he had afterthoughts. Butcher (*op. cit.,* p. 387) records, under date of August 14, that "Ike now thinks we should have made simultaneous landings on both sides of the Messina Strait, thus cutting off all Sicily and obtaining wholesale sur-

render and saving time and equipment, particularly landing craft, which would have permitted a rapid rush on the mainland itself."

115. Morison, *op. cit.*, p. 20n.

116. Ralph S. Mavrogordato of the Office of the Chief of Military History of the Department of the Army in his chapter on "Hitler's Decision on the Defense of Italy" (*Command Decision*, pp. 233, 234n.) points out in a footnote that General Heinrich von Vietinghoff, who commanded the German Tenth Army in Italy "considered it a costly mistake on the part of the Allies not to have attempted an invasion of Calabria (southern Italy) before the close of the Sicilian campaign." There were only about one and a half German divisions in Calabria at the time. Such a landing would have doomed the approximately 60,000 German troops in Sicily and would thus subsequently have weakened the defense of Italy, for it was upon the troops evacuated from Sicily that a large share of the burden of the defense of southern Italy against Allied attack initially fell.

General von Vietinghoff (MS No. D-116, p. 6) himself wrote after the war that

from the German standpoint it is incomprehensible that the Allies did not seize the Straits of Messina, either at the same time as the landing [in Sicily] or in the course of the initial actions, just as soon as the German troops were contained. On both sides of the Straits—not only in the northeast corner of the island but in southern Calabria as well—this would have been possible without any special difficulty.

But the "special difficulty" the Allies anticipated in any such operation was the establishment of air superiority. Only a few of their fighter planes had enough range to reach the Messina area from bases outside Sicily, whereas an Allied invasion fleet would have been extremely close to Axis air bases. Aircraft carriers were needed, not merely in distant support (the use to which the two British carriers that participated were put) but to mount close support operations for the ground forces and to maintain a combat air patrol over the invasion fleet. Some British light carriers were used for this purpose later in the Salerno invasion.

Admiral Franco Maugeri, Director of Italian Naval Intelligence during a considerable part of World War II, and after the war the Chief of Staff of the Navy, wrote in his memoirs (*op. cit.*, pp. 193–194) that "the entire strategic conception and tactical execution of the war in Europe lacked imagination, daring, boldness and vision after the North African landing. It almost seemed as though the Allied command had exhausted all its inventive genius and courage in that one operation."

Kesselring (and Westphal, MS No. B-270, p. 29) agreed in retrospect that "a secondary landing on Calabria would have turned the landing in Sicily into an annihilating victory" for the Allies.

The German generals as a whole considered the Allied Mediterranean strategy to be cautious, methodical and unimaginative. Kesselring speaks (MS No. T-2-K-1, p. 29) of the exceptionally systematic actions of the Allied forces . . . the slowness of the Allied advance . . . confined to narrow fronts . . . the operational decision not to launch any large-scale landing aimed at capturing the Etna massif; the fact that strong forces had been dispersed to the western part of Sicily which . . . just marched and captured unimportant terrain, instead of fighting at the wing where a major decision had to be reached.

Others referred to the Allied strategic concept as the "safety-first attitude."

In retrospect, the Sicilian operation represented sound but very conservative and cautious strategy—a power play, no razzle-dazzle. A landing around Messina or in Calabria would have risked more to gain much; initial Allied losses—particularly of shipping and landing craft, which were then the bottleneck of all Allied war plans—probably would have been greater, but the ultimate Axis losses might have been much heavier. But the proof of the pudding is in the eating; despite the might-have-beens the Sicilian strategy worked.

117. Garland and Smyth, *op. cit.,* pp. 419, 420.
118. Patton, who became much impressed with the capabilities of sea power, must be given principal credit for these two operations, though Truscott endorsed them. It was Patton's drive and insistence that forced the mounting of the second operation at the time it took place, though both Truscott and Bradley wanted to postpone it. Postponement, it is clear from the German records, would have shut the barn door too late; as it was, neither operation was mounted soon enough, or in great enough force, to really trap any significant number of the enemy. But Patton's tactical instincts were sounder in this instance than Bradley's. Bradley was a generally sound, somewhat conservative commander, who lacked Patton's drive. The two men did not really mix; Bradley, as he was later to show when he was Chairman of the Joint Chiefs of Staff during the Korean War, had no use for the rampant emotionalism, the flamboyance and the histrionics of a MacArthur or a Patton.
119. Cunningham, *op. cit.,* p. 554.
120. Eisenhower, *op. cit.,* p. 160.
121. *Operations in Sicily and Italy,* op. cit., p. 2.
122. Eisenhower, *op. cit.,* p. 159.
123. The Germans evacuated 39,569 men from the eleventh to sixteenth of August, together with 9,605 vehicles, 47 tanks, 94 guns and 17,000 tons of stores. The Italians in a separate, more haphazard, but nonetheless successful operation, which lasted from August 3 to August 16, evacuated 62,000 men, 227 vehicles and 41 guns. Seven of the German craft used in the evacuation were sunk by the Allies, one damaged; eight of the Italian craft were sunk, five damaged and subsequently scuttled. Captain Roskill (*op. cit.,* pp. 149–150) concludes that

the enemy's success was achieved by a skillfully conducted retreat, supported by excellent naval organization. His gun concentration in the Straits successfully inhibited both low-flying air attacks and protracted raids by surface ships . . . it appears that the [Allied] intelligence services were late in drawing the correct conclusions; but even when the enemy's intention was plain, the action taken suffered from lack of inter-service coordination. The naval effort made was weak, and the air effort lacked concentration.

124. The British official naval history (Roskill, *op. cit.*, pp. 144 ff.) notes that the Strait of Messina was covered by four batteries of 280 mm. (11.2-inch) guns, two 152 mm. (6-inch) Italian batteries, four German 170 mm. (6.8-inch) batteries and many mobile 3- to 4-inch guns, a total of perhaps 150 guns. (The official U.S. Army history estimates 500 guns were massed around the Strait.) All the ferries used by the Germans were heavily armed with AA guns; the Siebel ferries, which had been used in the supply of German troops in North Africa, were shallow-draft, nine-knot vessels, which could embark 450 men or 10 vehicles and could be armed with three 88 mm. and many smaller AA weapons. See Roskill for details of the evacuation organization.

125. Craven and Cate (*op. cit.*, p. 473) in the official Air Force history excuse and extenuate the failure of the Allied air forces to prevent or hamper the German evacuation to a greater extent than they did. They also describe the evacuation as a "partially successful withdrawal," which saved "the equivalent of at least one division with equipment"—a gross understatement of what actually occurred. They also cite "claims" of ship sinkings which are far higher, as they are always in combat reports of air claims, than actual Axis losses. There is not much analysis in Craven and Cate about the technical or other reasons for the ineffectiveness of Allied air power at Messina, and, on occasions, in Sicily.

126. Morison (*op. cit.*, p. 22) notes that the "results of depending on Army Air Force tactical support were so disappointing that next time, at Salerno, the Royal Navy managed to produce a few escort carriers." Morison (p. 142) also quotes the report of Rear Admiral Kirk: "No control over fighter patrol was delegated to [his] attack force. No bombers were on call. No fighter protection to spotting planes was provided."

The Allied fighters operated from Malta, Gozo and Pantelleria, but because of the distance from the bases to the assault areas, the many commitments of the fighters (including the protection of heavy bombers) and the limited fighter strength available, the Allied air forces provided continuous fighter cover during daylight hours over only two of the invasion beaches; the others had cover at dawn and dusk and intermittently in daylight hours. (Craven and Cate, *op. cit.*, p. 451.)

Captain Roskill of the Royal Navy, who wrote the official British naval history dealing with the Sicilian operation, presents perhaps the fairest assessment of the achievements and failures of the Allied air forces (Roskill, *op. cit.*, p. 140). He asserts that

some highly-placed Royal Air Force officers later admitted that co-ordination of the air plan with those of the other services was shown by events to have been imperfect, particularly in the matter of close support of the assault forces. . . . The accomplishments of the air forces nonetheless remain impressive . . . Even if fighter protection for the Western Task Force could have been better, [the

Allied air forces] played a big part in gaining the comparative immunity from air attacks which the naval forces enjoyed during the approach and the actual assaults. Losses of ships from bombing were far less than had been expected.

As Admiral Cunningham wrote, it appeared "almost magical that great fleets of ships could remain anchored on the enemy's coast, within forty miles of the main aerodromes with only such slight losses . . . as were incurred."

Roskill's evaluation is the soundest analysis of the Sicilian air operations yet published. Morison overstates the failures and deficiencies of the Allied air forces; Craven and Cate grossly understate them.

127. General James M. Gavin, *Airborne Warfare*, and Ridgway, *op. cit.* For a description of the Sicilian operations as seen by the commanding officer of the 82nd Airborne, see Ridgway, Chapter 5.

128. Department of the Army, *Airborne Operations—A German Appraisal*, p. 25.

129. Roskill, *op. cit.*, p. 115.

130. MS No. D-004, "Specialized Defense Tactics (Sicily) July–August, 1943," p. 3.

131. *Operations in Sicily and Italy, op. cit.*, p. 20.

132. *Ibid.*, p. 22. Kesselring, in his own words (MS No. T-2-K-1, "The Battle of Sicily," p. 13) "believed more and more that the Allies would take advantage of the favorable situation" in the west (of Sicily: the lack of defenses) and would make a secondary landing there, and, unless there was German opposition, would move across the island from Palermo to the east, thus outflanking the German defenders in the east. It was for this reason that he persuaded General Guzzoni to shift, just before the invasion, two-thirds of the 15th Panzer Grenadier Division to the west in the vicinity of Palermo, where it was out of position to react quickly to the Allied invasion in the southeast.

133. Hitler never forbade the evacuation of Sicily, though his original hope was that a stand might be made based on the Etna position. But he apparently never gave positive approval, except by indirection, though he did admit on July 17 that Sicily could not be held.

In view of Hitler's continued indecision, Jodl and Kesselring took it upon themselves to order the last German troops in Sicily to make a fighting withdrawal to the mainland on 17 August. There had been no previous agreement between OKW and the Comando Supremo before this final decision was taken. Remarkably enough even Hitler accepted this strategically significant event in silence and, contrary to all previous practice, bowed to the inevitable. (Warlimont, *op. cit.*, p. 379.

Earlier in the Sicilian fighting, as German units commenced to reinforce Sicily, both Hitler and Mussolini, mistaking belated action for victory, "rapidly reverted to unrealistic ideas," according to General Warlimont.

"Hitler thought that the enemy could be thrown back into the sea and Mussolini telegraphed that: 'both the moral and material effects on the enemy of a defeat at this first attempt to enter Europe would be incalculable.' " (Warlimont, p. 336.)

General Note on the Italian Command System

Mussolini was never interested in the details of battle as was Hitler, but he successfully arrogated to himself the position of supreme Italian commander by making himself, with the King's approval, Marshal of the Empire, and by having the King delegate to him command of all the armed forces. The Armed Forces General Staff, known as the Comando Supremo, expanded, after Marshal Badoglio's ouster in 1941, into a large organization that not only controlled the Italian operational theaters, but also served as a liaison body with the Germans. The service chiefs of staff were subordinate to the chief of the Comando Supremo, who was an appointee of Mussolini. (See Garland and Smyth, *op. cit.*, pp. 29 ff., and other works cited in bibliography.)

Acknowledgments

The Army's official history, *Sicily and the Surrender of Italy*, provides the most detailed, and probably the most accurate, narrative of the Sicilian operations. I have drawn upon it heavily. Morison (*Sicily, Salerno, Anzio*) covers the naval phase of the invasion more thoroughly than any other U.S. published sources, and Roskill (*The War at Sea*, Vol. III) admirably supplements Morison's detail with comprehensive coverage and judicious evaluation. These books in particular provide thorough coverage of the invasion and its consequences. MS No. T-2 is rich in detail from the German point of view.

I have quoted from and paraphrased a part of my own introduction to Colonel Edson D. Raff's book, *We Jumped to Fight*.

Bibliography

Books

BELDEN, JACK, *Still Time to Die*. New York: Harper, 1944
BERNSTEIN, WALTER, "The Taking of Ficarra," *New Yorker Book of War Pieces*. New York: Reynal & Hitchcock, 1947, pp. 235 ff.
BRADLEY, GENERAL OMAR N., *A Soldier's Story*. New York: Holt, 1951
BROWN, JOHN MASON, *To All Hands*. New York: Whittlesey House, 1943
BRYANT, ARTHUR, *The Turn of the Tide*. New York: Doubleday, 1946
BRYANT, ARTHUR, *Triumph in the West*. New York: Doubleday, 1949
BUTCHER, CAPTAIN HARRY C., USNR, *My Three Years with Eisenhower*. New York: Simon & Schuster, 1946
CARTER, ROSS, *Those Devils in Baggy Pants*. New York: Appleton-Century-Crofts, 1951
CHURCHILL, WINSTON S., *The Second World War*, Vol. 5, *Closing the Ring*. Boston: Houghton Mifflin, 1951
CRAVEN, W. F., and CATE, J. L., eds., *The Army Air Forces in World War II*, Vol. 2, *Europe: Torch to Pointblank, August 1942 to December 1943*. Chicago: University of Chicago Press, 1949

CUNNINGHAM, ADMIRAL OF THE FLEET VISCOUNT, *A Sailor's Odyssey*. New York: Dutton, 1951

Department of the Army, *Airborne Operations—A German Appraisal*. Washington: Department of the Army Pamphlet No. 20–232, October, 1951

Department of Military Art and Engineering, *Operations in Sicily and Italy (July 1943 to May 1945)* West Point: U.S. Military Academy, 1945

EISENHOWER, GENERAL DWIGHT D., *Crusade in Europe*. New York: Doubleday, 1948

FARAGO, LADISLAS, *Patton—Ordeal and Triumph*. New York: Obolensky, 1963

FLOWER, DESMOND, and REEVES, JAMES, eds., *The Taste of Courage*. New York: Harper, 1960

GARLAND, LIEUTENANT COLONEL ALBERT N., and SMYTH, HOWARD MCGAW, assisted by BLUMENSON, MARTIN, *Sicily and the Surrender of Italy*. Washington: Office of the Chief of Military History, Department of the Army, 1965

GAVIN, GENERAL JAMES M., *Airborne Warfare*. Washington: Infantry Journal Press, 1947

GOEBBELS, JOSEPH PAUL, *The Goebbels Diaries, 1942–1943*, Louis P. Lochner, ed. New York: Doubleday, 1948

GREENFIELD, KENT ROBERTS, gen. ed., *Command Decisions*. New York: Harcourt Brace, 1959

GUINGAND, MAJOR GENERAL SIR FRANCIS DE, *Operation Victory*. New York: Scribner's, 1947

HALL, WALTER PHELPS, *Iron Out of Calvary*. New York: Appleton-Century, 1946

HART, B. H. LIDDELL, *The Other Side of the Hill*. London: Cassell, 1951

HOWE, GEORGE F., *Northwest Africa—Seizing the Initiative in the West*. Washington: Office of the Chief of Military History, Department of the Army, 1957

ISMAY, GENERAL LORD, *Memoirs*. New York: Viking, 1960

KENNEDY, MAJOR GENERAL SIR JOHN, *The Business of War*. New York: Morrow, 1958

LINKLATER, ERIC, *The Campaign in Italy*. London: His Majesty's Stationery Office, 1951

MATLOFF, MAURICE, *Strategic Planning for Coalition Warfare 1943–1944*. Washington: Office of the Chief of Military History, Department of the Army, 1959

MATLOFF, MAURICE, and SNELL, EDWIN M., *Strategic Planning for Coalition Warfare, 1941–42*. Washington: Office of the Chief of Military History, Department of the Army, 1953

MAUGERI, ADMIRAL FRANCO, *From the Ashes of Disgrace*. New York: Reynal & Hitchcock, 1948

MONTAGU, EWEN, *The Man Who Never Was*. Philadelphia: Lippincott, 1954

MONTGOMERY, FIELD MARSHAL BERNARD LAW, *The Memoirs*. Cleveland, New York: World, 1958

MORISON, SAMUEL ELIOT, *History of United States Naval Operations in World War II*, Vol. IX, *Sicily, Salerno, Anzio, January, 1943–June, 1944*. Boston: Little, Brown, 1954

PATTON, GENERAL GEORGE S., JR., *War As I Knew It*. Boston: Houghton Mifflin, 1947

RAFF, COLONEL EDSON D., *We Jumped to Fight*, with an introduction by Hanson W. Baldwin. New York: Eagle Books, 1944

Report of Major Etter, Charles Barton, USA (Med Corps), to Surgeon, II Corps.

RIDGWAY, GENERAL MATTHEW B., *Soldier: The Memoirs of Matthew B. Ridgway* (as told to Harold H. Martin). New York: Harper, 1956

ROSKILL, CAPTAIN S. W., *The War at Sea, 1939–1945*, Vol. III. London: Her Majesty's Stationery Office, 1960

SHAPIRO, LIONEL S., *They Left the Back Door Open*. Toronto: Ryerson Press, 1944

SHERWOOD, ROBERT E., *Roosevelt and Hopkins*. New York: Harper, 1948

SHIRER, WILLIAM L., *The Rise and Fall of the Third Reich*. New York: Simon & Schuster, 1960

Society of the First Division, *Danger Forward—The Story of the First Division in World War II*. Atlanta: Albert Love, 1947

STIMSON, HENRY L., and BUNDY, MCGEORGE, *On Active Service in Peace and War*. New York: Harper, 1947

TREVOR-ROPER, H. R., *Blitzkrieg to Defeat: Hitler's War Directives, 1939–1945*. New York: Holt, Rinehart & Winston, 1965

TRUSCOTT, LIEUTENANT GENERAL L. K., JR., *Command Missions*. New York: Dutton, 1954

WARLIMONT, GENERAL WALTER, *Inside Hitler's Headquarters, 1939–45*. New York: Praeger, 1964

WILMOT, CHESTER, *The Struggle for Europe*. New York: Harper, 1952

Manuscripts

All Office of the Chief of Military History, Department of the Army, Washington, D.C.

MS-T-2—"The Battle of Sicily"

   T-2-K-1—Kesselring comments, "The Battle of Sicily"

   B-270—Kesselring and Westphal, "Questions Regarding General Strategy in the Italian Campaign"

   D-038—"Commitment of German Air Forces in Sardinia and Corsica"

   D-091—"Evacuation of Sicily and Sardinia in August 1943"

   D-116—"Over-all Situation in the Mediterranean up to the Landing on the Italian Mainland"

   D-089—"Reconnaissance in the Battle of Sicily"

   D-004—"Specialized Defense Tactics (Sicily) July–August, 1943"

CHAPTER 7.   TARAWA

Notes

I am indebted to Colonel C. W. Harrison, in 1958 Head of the Historical Branch, G-3, of the Marine Corps, for the following information:

Adjustments in Marine Corps casualty figures continued to be made until 26 August 1952. At that time the casualty statistics for World War II were closed. Listed below are the final adjusted figures for Marine Corps casualties on Tarawa. Practically all fighting took place on Betio.

	Officers	Enlisted Men
Killed in Action	51	852
Died of Wounds	9	82
Wounded in Action	109	2,125
Missing, Presumed Dead	0	121
Combat Fatigue	1	23
Total	170	3,203

According to Commander Francis D. Fane's *Naked Warriors*—the best history of UDT's in World War II—the statement "frogmen were born from the Battle of Tarawa" is correct. The key word is "from." That is, the object lessons learned at Tarawa, with regard to the requirement for adequate intelligence on underwater conditions and the need for clearance of obstacles, gave impetus to the development of UDT's and their wide use in the remaining campaigns of the Pacific War. The statement is not correct if interpreted to mean that Tarawa was the first operational use of UDT's in a major Pacific operation. The UDT principle was recognized and employed at Tarawa through a hastily put together beach reconnaissance and demolition unit. This outfit was organized too late, however, to take any part in the pre-assault reconnaissance of Tarawa. Its members served on the beach after the landing and did some preliminary coral blasting at Apamama, a job which had to be finished by bulldozers. Formally organized and trained UDT's were first used operationallly in the Pacific at Roi-Namur in the Marshalls, 31 January–1 February 1944.

1. Tarawa to Makin airline distance is 100 miles. Spruance in *Indianapolis* and Turner in *Pennsylvania* were cruising well off Makin.
2. Of the 4,836 Japanese and Korean on Tarawa, 2,619 were first-rate Japanese troops. The exact breakdown, as given by Dr. Stanley L. Falk, in the December, 1962, *Naval Institute Proceedings*, was: 7th Special Naval Landing Force—1,497; 3rd Special Base Force—1,122; 111th Construction Unit—1,247; Fourth Fleet Construction Department Detachment—970; total—4,836. (Fletcher Pratt also lists 400 men of an air base unit and makes the total 5,236.) Only the first two units were fully qualified combat troops, and there were about 1,000 Koreans. The Koreans were rarely armed. The Special Naval Landing Forces were often mistakenly called Japanese "Marines." There were no such units; the Special Naval Landing Forces were the closest equivalent to the U.S. Marine Corps.
3. General David M. Shoup, in a letter to the author (February 12, 1965), points out that the initial position of the transports was the wrong position, and that they had to steam under fire to a new transport area, with the half-laden boats and amtracs following them.
   Tarawa, the official Marine Corps monograph, states (pp. 14–15) that

all three of the assault battalions were delayed while debarking from the transports, due to the movement of the ships from the area where they had first stopped to an area farther north. After the first waves were away from the transports in LCVP's, they had to transfer to the LVT's which would carry them to the beach. Finally, after a great deal of confusion, the troops were loaded in the amphibian tractors and reached the rendezvous area to the northwest of the entrance to the lagoon.

The exact positioning of the transports and the location and marking of the correct landing beaches were one of the problems of amphibious war emphasized by Tarawa. All sorts of devices and expedients to insure precise navigation were developed and utilized in later landings, but the problem remained difficult until the end of the war; at the Normandy landing many waves landed on the wrong beaches.

4. Samuel Eliot Morison, *History of United States Naval Operations in World War II*, Vol. VII, *Aleutians, Gilberts and Marshalls, June 1942–April 1944*, p. 157.
5. Colonel David Shoup, commanding the 2nd Marine Regiment and the assault waves, put three battalion landing teams into the assault and retained one in reserve. Second Battalion, 8th Marines, Major Henry P. Crowe commanding, was to land on Beach Red 3, to the east or left of the long pier which extended from the north shore of Betio. Second Battalion, 2nd Marines, Lieutenant Colonel Herbert Amey commanding, was to land on Beach Red 2 just to the west of the long pier. Third Battalion, 2nd Marines, Major John F. Schoettel commanding, was to land on Beach Red 1 on the western end of the island. First Battalion, 2nd Marines, Major Wood B. Kyle commanding, was in reserve.
6. *Tarawa,* the official Marine Corps monograph on the battle, states (p. 28) that General Julian Smith believed the

Japanese General Shibasaki made his greatest mistake by not counter-attacking the slim Marine beachhead during this [D-day] night. Never again was it so vulnerable. Shibasaki's failure to counter-attack may be traced, probably, to a breakdown in control. Naval gunfire had disrupted his communications, so that he was never able to control his units after early morning of D-day. He was killed on the second day of fighting on Betio.

7. General Shoup, in a terse comment about this description, states that "bull neck [was] swollen from rifle and mortar blast."
8. This remark about Hawkins, credited to Shoup, may have been made by another officer. But it epitomized the general feeling about him.
9. Morison, *op. cit.,* p. 134.
10. Robert Sherrod, *History of Marine Corps Aviation in World War II,* p. 226.
11. General Holland M. Smith and Percy Finch, *Coral and Brass,* pp. 132 ff.
12. Philip A. Crowl and Edmund G. Love, *Seizure of the Gilberts and Marshalls,* p. 156.
13. Louis Morton states in *Strategy and Command—The First Two Years* (p. 573) that "one officer compiled a list of 100 mistakes made during the operation." The Office of the Director of Naval History has not been able to identify the "100 mistakes," but a letter dated December 31, 1943, from the Commander in Chief, U.S. Pacific Fleet and Pacific Ocean Areas, to principal elements of that fleet listed 95 separate "lessons," comments or observations, culled from a "preliminary study of the action reports." Most of the items —all the major ones—are covered in the text.

A far more detailed study, entitled *Secret Information Bulletin No. 15,
Battle Experience—Supporting Operations Before and During the Occupation of the Gilbert Islands, November, 1943 (First Major Stepping Stone
Westward)*, was issued to the Navy by the Commander in Chief, U.S. Fleet,
on July 15, 1944.

This publications states that

land based planes had bombed the island nightly for about one week preceding
D-Day.

On 18 and 19 November, carrier aircraft dropped 184 tons of bombs on the
island. On Nov. 19th Cruiser Division 5 fired about 250 tons of shells onto the
island. On D-Day the island was bombed and strafed by aircraft, and about
3,000 tons of shells were fired by surface vessels at the island. It is believed that
the naval bombardment prior to the landing on D-Day was greater per square
unit of ground than had ever previously been given in preparation of a landing
operation. On practically every square foot of the island pieces of shell fragments
were later found.

The destruction wrought to exposed installations was terrific. Heavy and
anti-aircraft batteries were silenced; radar, searchlights, fire control instruments
were desroyed. Large fires were started on all parts of the island and all
material stored above ground or in open pits was effectively destroyed. . . .
Hundreds of the enemy in open trenches were killed. In contrast to this destruction . . . heavily protected dugouts, pillboxes, machine gun emplacements, and
bombproof shelters, and the personnel in them remained almost unaffected by
this fire.

This same report estimates that in the entire "Galvanic" operation, in
addition to the Marine losses, the United States sustained the loss of the
Liscome Bay (to submarine torpedoes), damage to the *Independence* (CVL)
by an air-launched torpedo, and some 60 aircraft of all types. The Japanese
lost 1 submarine, rammed by the destroyer *Frazier* (three survivors were
picked up), and 1 AK (Naval Cargo Vessel), plus an estimated 110 planes
destroyed, and 4 AK's and 1 submarine damaged.

I am indebted for these reports to Rear Admiral E. M. Eller, USN
(Ret.), Director of Naval History.

14. Jeter A. Isely and Philip A. Crowl, *The U.S. Marines and Amphibious War:
Its Theory and Its Practice in the Pacific*, p. 251.
15. Vice Admiral R. A. Spruance, Fifth Fleet, Action Report.

Acknowledgments and Bibliography

Navy and Marine Corps historical files consulted or quoted include after-
action reports, reports of commanding officers, eyewitness accounts of participants and correspondents, and newspaper and magazine articles. Personal accounts of the Tarawa battle are many since it was the first major action in
which numerous Marine Corps combat correspondents participated.

I am indebted to Brigadier General Samuel P. Griffith, USMC (Ret.), and
to General David M. Shoup, former Commandant of the Marine Corps, at the
time of Tarawa a colonel in command of the 2nd Marines and the assault force,
for reviewing this chapter and for helpful comments.

Robert Sherrod, now an editor of the *Saturday Evening Post,* then a correspondent for *Time,* wrote the most comprehensive and graphic eyewitness accounts of the battle.

I am indebted to Mr. Sherrod for his kindness in reviewing and commenting on this chapter. He recalls in a letter to the author a postwar visit to Tarawa in 1946:

The shocking thing was the loss of many bodies; the Graves Registration people could find only about half of those who died on Tarawa, and only about 265 achieved the dignity of a marked grave. The odd thing was this: men were missing whom I had seen buried in graves marked by wooden crosses with names and serial numbers.

Apparently the Seabees built the airfield over the graves, so the Marines who died there literally paved the way to Tokyo.

The best military analyses of the Battle of Tarawa are to be found in *The U.S. Marines and Amphibious War,* and *History of United States Naval Operations in World War II,* Volume VII.

References and quotations in this chapter are from the documents cited above or from the following works:

CROWL, PHILIP A., and LOVE, EDMUND G., *Seizure of the Gilberts and Marshalls.* Washington: Office of the Chief of Military History, Department of the Army, 1955

HOUGH, MAJOR FRANK O., USMCR, *The Island War: The United States Marine Corps in the Pacific.* Philadelphia: Lippincott, 1947

ISELY, JETER A., and CROWL, PHILIP A., *The U.S. Marines and Amphibious War: Its Theory and Its Practice in the Pacific.* Princeton: Princeton University Press, 1951

JOHNSTON, RICHARD W., *Follow Me! The Story of the Second Marine Division in World War II.* Toronto: Random House of Canada, 1948

KARIG, CAPTAIN WALTER, USNR; HARRIS, LIEUTENANT COMMANDER RUSSELL L., USNR; and MANSON, COMMANDER FRANK A., USN, *Battle Report,* Vol. 4, *The End of an Empire.* New York: Rinehart, 1948

MORISON, SAMUEL ELIOT, *History of United States Naval Operations in World War II,* Vol. VII, *Aleutians, Gilberts and Marshalls, June 1942–April 1944.* Boston: Little, Brown, 1951

MORTON, LOUIS, *Strategy and Command—The First Two Years (U.S. Army in World War II—The War in the Pacific).* Washington: Office of Chief of Military History, Departments of the Army, 1962

PRATT, FLETCHER, *The Marines' War.* New York: Sloane, 1948

SHERROD, ROBERT, *History of Marine Corps Aviation in World War II.* Washington: Combat Forces Press, 1952

SHERROD, ROBERT, *Tarawa: The Story of a Battle.* New York: Duell, Sloan & Pearce, 1944, 1954

SMITH, GENERAL HOLLAND M., USMC (RET.) and FINCH, PERCY, *Coral and Brass.* New York: Scribner's, 1949

STOCKMAN, CAPTAIN JAMES R., USMC, *Tarawa: The Battle for Tarawa.* Historical Section, Division of Public Information, HQ U.S. Marine Corps, 1947

WILSON, CAPTAIN EARL J.; and Marine Combat Correspondents Master Technical

Sergeants LUCAS, JIM G.; SHAFFER, SAMUEL; and Staff Sergeant ZURLINDEN, C. PETER, *Betio Beachhead: U.S. Marines' Own Story of the Battle for Tarawa.* New York: Putnam, 1945

CHAPTER 8. NORMANDY

Notes

1. The armada included 931 ships in the Western Naval Task Force, 1,796 in the Eastern, including a grand total of more than 700 warships. Including the landing craft carried aboard these ships, the total of all ships, vessels, craft and boats reached 5,333.
2. For a graphic account of this incident (and indeed of the entire Normandy invasion), see *The Longest Day* by Cornelius Ryan, pp. 30–34, 96–97.
3. Captain Harry C. Butcher, *My Three Years with Eisenhower,* p. 610.
4. Gordon A. Harrison, *Cross-Channel Attack,* p. 275.
5. Leonard Rapport and Arthur Norwood, Jr., *Rendezvous with Destiny—A History of the 101st Airborne Division,* pp. 79–80.
6. *Ibid.,* p. 80.
7. Butcher, *op. cit.,* p. 566.
8. Harrison, *op. cit.,* pp. 275–276.
9. Rapport and Norwood, *op. cit.,* p. 86.
10. David Howarth, *D-Day: The Sixth of June, 1944,* pp. 36–37.
11. W. F. Craven and J. L. Cate, eds., *The Army Air Forces in World War II,* University of Chicago Press, 1951, Vol. 3, *Europe to V-E Day, January 1944 to May 1945,* p. 195, notes that

A confused mass of German evidence discloses that the GAF on the western front was a negligible force, particularly in respect to fighters. . . . German statements that only twelve fighter-bomber missions were mounted on D-Day, with all save two forced to jettison their bombs and fight before arrival in the battle area, or that the GAF attempted only 250 sorties against the landings become fully credible.

On the other hand, the D-day effort of the U.S. Air Force "was unprecedented in its concentration and phenomenal in its size." The Eighth and Ninth U.S. Air Forces flew 8,722 combat sorties (exclusive of weather and other flights), and lost 71 planes.

Ryan (*op. cit.,* p. 271) note that some accounts reported a raid by eight JU-88's against the invasion beaches on D-day, but he states he could find no record of any attack except one made by two fighters.

12. Samuel Eliot Morison, *The Invasion of France and Germany—1944–1945,* p. 138.
13. *Omaha Beachhead,* p. 71.
14. The Pas-de-Calais, directly across the Strait of Dover from England, was the most direct route, but that coastal area was also more heavily defended.

15. Field Marshal Earl Alexander of Tunis, *The Alexander Memoirs 1940–1945*, ed. by John North, New York, McGraw-Hill, 1963, p. 43.
16. General Mark W. Clark, *Calculated Risk*, pp. 3, 368, 372. It is only fair to point out that many historians feel the southern France invasion had both military and political importance: that Marseilles was a necessary supply port; and that French troops that had been re-equipped and trained in North Africa were part of the spearhead. Hitler did not give an unequivocal order to withdraw from southern France until August 16, the day after the invasion, though a tactical withdrawal had started even *before* the invasion.
17. All casualties are approximate; neither the German nor the British tally permitted anything like chronological accuracy.
18. Harrison, *op. cit.*, p. 448.
19. Chester Wilmot, *The Struggle for Europe*, p. 388.
20. *Ibid.*, p. 247. Martin Blumenson believes that the deception plan ("Fortitude"), which attempted, with considerable initial success, to convince the Germans that the invasion area would be the Pas-de-Calais, was the "big bomb" in achieving tactical surprise in Normandy.
21. Harrison, *op. cit.*, p. 448.
22. *Ibid.*, p. 319. He adds (p. 448):

> Only at Omaha had the fortified coast line proved to be the hard crust that planners had counted on finding everywhere. The 352nd German Infantry Division—a full attack division and not one of the static fortress types—held the Omaha beach area—and though it had been in place for almost three months Allied intelligence had failed to identify it.

Acknowledgments and Bibliography

Martin Blumenson, distinguished historian of the Office of the Chief of Military History, very kindly reviewed this chapter and provided some important comments and criticisms.

Major General John S. Wood, USA (Ret.), World War II commander of the 4th Armored Division, also was kind enough to provide a critical reading.

The documents, source materials and published works, dealing wholly, or in part, with the Normandy invasion are voluminous, and I have quoted from, or drawn upon, many of them.

I am indebted to the Office of the Chief of Military History, Department of the Army, for access to "After Action Reports" of major U.S. units that participated in the invasion. I have quoted from some of these, also from "Combat Interviews" with survivors of the assault recorded soon afterward, and from notes made at the time by participants.

I have also drawn upon my own notes, jotted down at the time aboard the cruiser *Augusta* and, after D-day, on various visits to the invasion beachheads.

The standard American work on the Normandy invasion, and by far the most complete and documented account, is *Cross-Channel Attack* (1951) by Gordon A. Harrison, a volume in the official Army history of the United States Army in World War II. Other important supplementary works are *Omaha Beachhead*, a monograph published in 1945 by the Army's Historical Division, and its companion volume, *Utah Beach to Cherbourg*, both of them publications in the "American Forces in Action" series. All three of these books are published by the Superintendent of Documents, U.S. Government Printing Office.

Samuel Eliot Morison's *The Invasion of France and Germany—1944–1945*, Volume XI of the *History of United States Naval Operations in World War II* (Little, Brown, Boston, 1957), is the best existing naval account of the invasion.

Other volumes which I have quoted or upon which I have leaned heavily include:

BRADLEY, GENERAL OMAR N., *A Soldier's Story*. New York: Holt, 1951

BUTCHER, CAPTAIN HARRY C., USNR, *My Three Years with Eisenhower*. New York: Simon & Schuster, 1946

HOWARTH, DAVID, *D-Day—The Sixth of June, 1944*. New York: McGraw-Hill, 1959

MONTGOMERY, FIELD MARSHAL BERNARD LAW, *The Memoirs*. Cleveland, New York: World, 1958

RAPPORT, LEONARD, and NORTHWOOD, ARTHUR, JR., *Rendezvous with Destiny—A History of the 101st Airborne Division*. Washington: Infantry Journal Press, 1948

RIDGWAY, GENERAL MATTHEW B., *Soldier: The Memoirs of Matthew B. Ridgway (As Told to Harold H. Martin)*. New York: Harper, 1956

RYAN, CORNELIUS, *The Longest Day*. New York: Simon & Schuster, 1959

WILMOT, CHESTER, *The Struggle for Europe*. New York: Harper, 1952
Some of the quotations I have changed to the present tense.

Other volumes consulted include:

AUPHAN, REAR ADMIRAL PAUL, and MORDAL, JACQUES, *The French Navy in World War II*. Annapolis: U.S. Naval Institute, 1959

CHURCHILL, WINSTON S., *The Second World War*, Vol. 5, *Triumph and Tragedy*. New York: Houghton Mifflin, 1953

CLARK, GENERAL MARK W., *Calculated Risk*. New York: Harper, 1950

DETZER, COLONEL KARL, *The Mightiest Army*. Pleasantville, N.Y.: Reader's Digest, 1945

DE GUINGAND, MAJOR GENERAL SIR FRANCIS, *Operation Victory*. New York: Scribner's, 1947

EDWARD, COMMANDER KENNETH, RN, *Operation Neptune*. London: Collins, 1946

EISENHOWER, GENERAL DWIGHT D., *Crusade in Europe*. New York: Doubleday, 1948

First Infantry Division, The Story of. Compiled by the Public Information Office of the Division; printed at Würzburg, Germany

GAVIN, LIEUTENANT GENERAL JAMES M., *War and Peace in the Space Age*. New York: Harper, 1958

JACOBS, BRUCE, *Soldiers*. New York: Norton, 1958

JOHNSON, COLONEL GERDEN F., *History of the Twelfth Infantry Regiment in World War II*. Privately printed, 1947

MARSHALL, S. L. A., *Night Drop*. Boston: Little Brown, 1962

PATTON, GENERAL GEORGE S., JR., *War As I Knew It*. Boston: Houghton Mifflin, 1947

SMITH, GENERAL WALTER BEDELL, *Eisenhower's Six Great Decisions.* New York: Longmans, Green, 1950

SPEIDEL, GENERAL HANS, *Invasion, 1944.* New York: Henry Regnery, 1950

STACEY, COLONEL C. P., *The Canadian Army—An Official Historical Summary.* Ottawa: Ministry of National Defense, 1948

TOBIN, RICHARD L., *Invasion Journal.* New York: Dutton, 1944

V Corps Operations in the E. T. O. 6 Jan. 1942 to 9 May 1945. An official unit history.

VAGTS, DR. ALFRED. *Landing Operations.* Harrisburg and Washington: Military Service Publishing Co., 1946

WILLOUGHBY, LIEUTENANT MALCOLM F., *The U.S. Coast Guard in World War II.* Annapolis: U.S. Naval Institute, 1957

CHAPTER 9.   THE GREATEST SEA FIGHT

Notes

Admiral Robert B. Carney, who was chief of staff to Admiral Halsey at Leyte Gulf, has supplied, in a letter to the author (March 3, 1965) some important comments on the lessons learned and the considerations that influenced Admiral Halsey. His comments follow:

Halsey made a sound point when he pointed out the necessity for a single command in a given naval theater. It is difficult to think of any valid reasoning to the contrary. Had all U.S. naval forces in the area been under a single command, coordinated missions would have been assigned, capabilities of all components would have been understood by the commander, communications plans would have been prescribed and in effect, and the tactics of the battle could have been controlled to fit the grand design.

In the spring of 1944, Halsey had a plan for just such a situation as arose at Leyte. At that time, Halsey proposed to CINCPAC that CINCPAC's submarines be brought into the over-all fleet picture by being disposed across the enemy's line of retreat; this was called the Zoo Plan, the name stemming from animal names given to proposed submarine operating areas. The proposal was not approved.

One impediment to a single command was the MacArthur-Nimitz division of Pacific responsibility.

After the War I spoke to Admiral King to the effect that a chief lesson learned was the fallacy of divided authority and control as exemplified by Leyte. Admiral King was not receptive to my view. . . .

The problem facing Halsey was not one of dividing the entire U.S. naval force vis-à-vis the total Jap forces converging, but rather dividing the Third Fleet in the face of the Jap Center and Northern forces. In the latter context, Halsey decided against dividing.

It is true that Halsey considered the Jap carriers to be the proper target; Flag Plot discussion, prior to the move to the north, took cognizance of the fact that other operations would follow Leyte, and that if Jap carrier air were destroyed the Jap Fleet would never again be a serious threat. His assumptions as to Kinkaid's ammunition situation were in error.

Later, at the time of Lingayen, when General MacArthur expressed concern about

the threat posed by the Jap Fleet, Halsey stated that the Jap Fleet no longer constituted a serious danger, which proved to be correct.

The "third consideration"—Halsey's orders: they did in fact require him to
destroy the Japanese Fleet as his primary objective. You will recall that in October of
1944, east of Formosa, the Third Fleet endeavored to decoy the Jap Fleet to sea, and
would have succeeded in the plan had not a lone Nip scout plane spotted the main
body and got off his contact report before being shot down.

I would emphasize the fact that pilots' damage reports subsequent to the air
attacks on Kurita's force in the Sibuyan Sea played a part in the decision to go north
after Ozawa. Those reports proved to have been too rosy.

One aspect of Kurita's turn-back has received little attention. Jap Fleet tactics
called for individual ship circling maneuvers in the face of air attack. The weak baby
flattops were sending in desperation raids of two or three planes at a time, but
Kurita's ships were circling every time there was a raid however small. This greatly
cut down the speed of advance of Kurita's force—a point that proved to be important
because Kurita was overestimating his speed of advance, and consequently was overestimating the speed of retirement of the carriers in front of him, a retirement speed
that could only have been maintained by the *big* carriers. So, with fuel running short,
and figuring that the Third Fleet was in front of him, he retreated.

Special Notes by
Admiral Thomas C. Kinkaid, USN (Ret.)

The notes are keyed to numerals in the text. Explanatory material in
brackets inserted by author.

1. The invasion armada was "MacArthur's armada" in the sense that it came
   from his area, SWPA [Southwest Pacific Area], and might well be called
   the "great armada from Down Under" [or from MacArthur's area, SWPA].
   McArthur derived his authority from the Combined Chiefs of Staff. He was
   designated "Supreme Commander" in SWPA and was specifically prohibited
   from taking personal command of any of his forces. He was required to
   exercise command through his three major commanders for land, sea, and
   air: Blamey [General Sir Thomas Blamey, Australian Army general commanding land forces], Kinkaid and Kenney [General George C. Kenney, U.S.
   Army Air Forces, commanding air forces].

   From the time we departed from ports in the Admiralties and New
   Guinea to invade the Philippines, I had direct command of the "armada,"
   including the Army forces embarked, until I turned over command of the
   Army forces ashore in Leyte to Krueger [Lieutenant General Walter Krueger,
   commanding Sixth Army]. MacArthur was present as a passenger in his
   capacity as Supreme Commander, Southwest Pacific Area. I exercised direct
   command, as witness the fact that I decided to go ahead with the operation
   without referring to MacArthur when Halsey sent a dispatch, received when
   we were a few hours out from Hollandia, stating that he was concentrating
   his forces to attack the Japanese Fleet and would not be able to give the
   planned support to our landing at Leyte. When MacArthur joined our
   convoy, I sent him a bridge signal: "Welcome to our city." He replied with
   a gracious message referring to the fact that this was the first time he had

sailed under my command and ending with: "Believe it or not we are on our way."

2. Nishimura was due in Leyte one hour before Kurita. He was ahead of schedule without reason—a serious error in a coordinated effort. Kurita was late for good and sufficient reasons.

3. The Seventh Fleet had 18 CVE's [escort carriers]. Two had been sent to Halmahera for replacement planes, and only 16 were present during the action. The Seventh Fleet had a few PBY's, tender-based. Counting the 18 CVE's, the total number of [U.S.] carriers was 34.

4. It is interesting that the *Darter* and *Dace* placed Kurita through the night in Palawan Passage and attacked at dawn—a good job. An extremely important fact, from the operations point of view, is that Kurita was separated from most of his communication personnel in the transfer from *Atago* to *Kishinani* to *Yamato*. Any naval commander will sympathize with him in that situation.

5. Only one strike was made on Nishimura and that only by small search-attack scouting groups. Davison [Rear Admiral Ralph E. Davison, commanding Task Group 38.4 of the Third Fleet] reported that the move to concentrate was taking him out of range of the enemy Southern Force, but Halsey continued the concentration. In the Seventh Fleet we felt well able to take care of the [enemy] Southern Force and had all day to make plans for its reception. I was not informed directly by Halsey that he was leaving Nishimura to me.

6. Halsey had ordered a morning search to northward by the Northern Group, but Jap attacks prevented it from getting off until the afternoon.

7. In the Seventh Fleet we had counted noses carefully and had come to the conclusion that only two BB's [battleships]—*Ise* and *Hyuga*—could be with Ozawa in the [enemy] Northern Force.

8. Halsey had four groups of carriers and had given preparatory orders to form TF [Task Force] 34. "Proceeding north with three groups" is phraseology which failed to give information of vital import not only to me and to Nimitz but to many others. Mitscher [Vice Admiral Marc A. Mitscher, commanding Task Force 38—the four-carrier task groups and their supporting combat ships of the Third Fleet] actually sent instructions for the employment of the two BB's which were to stay with him, that TF 34 would be left behind to guard San Bernardino. It was impossible to believe anything else. The proposed composition of TF 34 was exactly correct in the circumstances.

Even though Halsey banked "too heavily" on the exaggerated claims of his pilots, he knew from the *Independence* night search planes that Kurita was headed for San Bernardino and he should have realized:

a. That the composition of the Seventh Fleet was designed to provide support for the amphibious landing and the troops ashore, not for major combat. The slow speed of the old battleships and a high proportion of high-capacity projectiles in their magazines made them an inadequate adversary for the Japanese Central Force, even if they had been available and were filled with fuel and ammunition.

    b. That the Seventh Fleet would be engaged through the night with surface forces in Surigao Strait and, in any case, could not leave Leyte Gulf unguarded and take station off San Bernardino.

    c. That the three CVE groups of the Seventh Fleet would be on station at daylight 25 October carrying out their mission and would need cover.

    d. That my destroyers would have expended their torpedoes in Surigao Strait and that the battleships would be low in AP ammunition and even in HC [High Capacity, or antipersonnel] ammunition, having rendered gunfire support to forces ashore for several days.

9. Rarely has a commander had all day to stay quietly (except for the antics of Jap planes) in port and prepare without serious interruption for a night action. The tactical dispositions and plans of the Seventh Fleet were checked and counterchecked by all concerned.

10. I believe contact was made about 2215 [10:15 P.M.] a few miles south of Bohol Island. All three PT's of that group were damaged by gunfire and unable to report the contact, but one of them (using his head) managed to make contact with the next PT group to eastward which sent through a message, which was received by Oldendorf about 26 minutes after midnight.

11. Fired by PT 137. The PT fired at a destroyer, missed, but hit and badly damaged the cruiser [*Abukuma*].

12. No, we did not think that the Jap Central Force was west of the Philippines, but we did think that TF 34 was guarding San Bernardino.

    Also, it is of interest that in Leyte Gulf the temporary headquarters of the Army commanders were only a few yards from the water's edge and the beaches were piled high with food and supplies and ammunition for immediate use. Destruction of those supply dumps would have left our forces ashore without food and ammunition. Halsey has said that Kurita could only have "harassed" our forces in Leyte Gulf.

13. I think it should be pointed out that a few words of Nimitz's dispatch were "padding" of the message at the point of origin by the communications officer for code security. The dispatch was first brought to me without padding, as it should have been. Later I was told of the "padding." [Halsey originally took this phrase, "The world wonders," as tacit criticism of him and was irritated. When the message was decoded, the phrase should have been eliminated, as it was in Kinkaid's version, but not in Halsey's.]

14. The attack of the DD's [destroyers] and DE's [destroyer escorts] against the Jap heavy ships was the most courageous and also the most effective incident brought to my attention during the war.

15. Kurita committed a grave error in losing tactical control of his force. He had lost most of his communication personnel. He had been seriously damaged by torpedo hits from Seventh Fleet planes and surface ships and by bomb hits from Seventh Fleet planes, and the upper works of his ships, charthouse, radio, etc., suffered from 5-inch shellfire and from strafing. His ships sheered out of formation to dodge torpedo attacks, real or dummy, made by planes and escort vessels. Soon his individual units became widely separated, which he should not have permitted, and he could not see his forces, or the enemy's, because of the heavy smoke laid by the CVE's and

their escorts. He was confused, and his subordinates did not help him by reporting the nature of the enemy they were attacking. Ozawa had failed to inform him of his success in drawing Halsey away. Also, I have no doubt that Kurita was physically exhausted after three grueling days.

16. McCain sensed what was going on long before Halsey did, and he launched his strike beyond range for a return flight—340 miles.

The following paragraphs constitute my analysis of what occurred: *Halsey had done exactly what the Japs wanted him to do.* He had left San Bernardino unguarded, permitting Kurita to pass through the strait unopposed. Having taken all six of his BB's 300 miles to the north, when two would have been adequate and four were needed at San Bernardino, he belatedly at 11:15 turned south in response to my appeals and to the dispatch from Nimitz, again taking all six BB's with him and leaving Mitscher without any. Mitscher urgently needed two BB's. By that time, 11:15, Mitscher's planes had developed Ozawa's force and the *Ise* and *Hyuga* were known to be with him, but Halsey took all six BB's south. Later Mitscher sent DuBose [Rear Admiral Laurance T. DuBose] to mop up the cripples (with 4 cruisers and 12 destroyers). Ozawa was informed of the actions of DuBose, and sent the *Ise* and *Hyuga* south to look for him. Fortunately, the Jap BB's passed to eastward of our cruisers on their way south and again on their return course to northward.

Halsey informed me that he would arrive off San Bernardino at 0800 26 Oct. Too late! Later, at 1600 [4 P.M.], after fueling, he decided to speed up and took two of his fastest BB's, *Iowa* and *New Jersey,* with three cruisers and eight DD's, south at 28 knots. He missed Kurita entering the strait by two hours. Suppose he had intercepted him? Were two BB's enough?

Suppose Halsey had turned south at top speed immediately upon receipt of my first urgent message at 0825. He would have been about five hours closer to San Bernardino. Actually, he steamed north for two and three-quarters hours at 25 knots—69 miles—whereas if he had steamed south at 28 knots—77 miles—there would have been a total of 146 miles' difference in his 11:15 position.

The net result of all this was that the six strongest battleships in the world—except the *Yamato* and *Musashi*—steamed about 300 miles north and 300 miles south during the "greatest naval battle of the Second World War and the largest engagement ever fought upon the high seas"—and they did not fire a single shot. I can well imagine the feelings of my classmate, Lee [Rear Admiral Willis A. Lee, commanding the battleships of Third Fleet].

Even today (1955) Halsey believes it was not a mistake to take the whole Third Fleet north, and he apparently overlooks the fact that the absence of TF 34 from San Bernardino Strait precluded the total destruction of Kurita's force on the spot, to say nothing of the loss of American lives and ships of the CVE force. The threat to our invasion of the Philippines seems not to have come to his mind. Halsey has stated that I should have sent CVE planes to scout the Sibuyan Sea and San Bernardino Strait during the night of 24-25 Oct. As is evident, I believed that TF 34 was guarding

San Bernardino and that Lee was being kept informed by the night-flying planes from the *Independence*. Actually, I did order a search to the north-ward during the night by PBY's and a search toward San Bernardino at daylight by CVE planes, mostly out of curiosity to find out what was going on.

Even if I had known that San Bernardino was wide open, I did not have the force to meet Kurita. You have quoted me correctly from *Battle Report*. I would not have denuded Leyte Gulf of a defense force. I would have moved the CVE's clear of direct contact with Kurita's surface forces. And, of course, I would have sent planes from the CVE's to keep track of Kurita, although none was equipped or trained for night search.

In that case would Kurita have reached Leyte? It is interesting to speculate. It is very possible. His direct contact with the northern group of CVE's, though painful to us, delayed his progress, seriously damaged his forces and so confused him that he turned back within two hours of his goal.

17. "Divided command" is, of course, not sound procedure. The hard, cold fact is, however, that despite the divided command both Halsey and I had what appeared to me to be clear-cut, definite missions. Had Halsey been mindful of his covering mission when Ozawa beckoned him to come north, he never would have left San Bernardino wide open. Also, he would have told me in a clearly worded dispatch just what he was going to do about it.

The "unwarranted assumption" which you attribute to me probably refers to my assumption that TF 34 was guarding San Bernardino. Perhaps that was unwarranted, but, to my not unprejudiced mind, all logic seemed to point the other way. Halsey's mission included covering our amphibious operation from interruption by the Japanese Fleet. His preparatory order to form TF 34, which I intercepted, set up a plan to guard San Bernardino against the passage of Kurita's forces which was perfect in concept and per-fect in composition of the forces assigned to TF 34. I did not intercept further modifying messages regarding TF 34. Had I done so, I most certainly would not have remained silent.

It was inconceivable that Halsey could have scrapped a perfect plan. His message, "going north with three groups," meant to me that TF 34 plus a carrier group was being left behind—entirely sound. Not only did I and all my staff believe it, and Nimitz and, presumably, his staff believe it, but Mitscher and his staff believed it also. As I have already pointed out, Mitscher actually gave orders for utilization of the two battleships which were to accompany him on the northern trek [four of the Third Fleet's six battleships were to have been left behind in TF 34 to guard San Bernardino; two were to have gone north with Mitscher's carriers after Ozawa]. When Mitscher and his staff found out that TF 34 was not being left to guard the strait, his chief of staff, [Captain] Arleigh Burke, tried to get Mitscher to send a message to Halsey on the subject, but Mitscher declined on the ground that Halsey probably had information not known to him.

Later you point out that I did not specifically ask Halsey whether or not TF 34 was guarding San Bernardino until 0412 25 Oct. That is correct. In the absence of information to the contrary from Halsey, anything else was unthinkable. Early in the morning of 25 Oct. a meeting of the staff was held in my cabin to check for errors of commission or of omission. It broke up about 0400 and my operations officer, Dick Cruzen [Captain Richard H. Cruzen], came back into the cabin and said, "Admiral, I can think of only one other thing. We have never directly asked Halsey if TF 34 is guarding San Bernardino." I told him to send the message.

18. The controversy has not been bitter for the simple and sole reason that I refused to take part in it. I have not publicly stated my side of the case but have kept quiet for ten years. Not so Halsey—he published several articles or interviews in addition to his book endeavoring to justify his actions at Leyte, sometimes at my expense.

19. I believe that the radio on Ozawa's flagship went out with the first bomb hit, but other ships could have sent a message to Kurita for him.

20. Only Halsey's strangely phrased message led to Kurita's surprise of Sprague's carriers.

In the early morning some important messages from me to Halsey were delayed in transmission, and that should not have been.

21. Actually, one or two PBY's took off from a tender in Surigao Strait to make the northern night search. They were ill-equipped for that sort of mission. They had quite a hell of a time because every U.S. ship they came near fired at them. I imagine that their greatest concern was to avoid U.S. ships rather than to find Jap ships.

The dawn search ordered from the CVE's should have gotten off much earlier.

22. Halsey's writings in the *Naval Institute Proceedings* were subjective. If he had been mindful of his covering mission, and had no other distractions, the question of "a single naval command" would be purely academic.

23. Halsey's reasoning regarding the [enemy] Center Force falls short of the mark. His "careful evaluation" of the damage reports was not shared by everyone. Kurita's movements seemed to belie any such evaluation. We knew from our plot that Kurita was approaching San Bernardino at 22 knots. Some plodding! Halsey had a later report from the *Independence* plane which was not forwarded to me. Did he not plot Kurita's progress?

A count of noses by my staff showed that Ozawa's force could not have been as "powerful and dangerous" as Halsey seems to have thought. He took 119 ships north to deal with 19 ships in the [enemy] Northern Force. An intelligent *division* of his forces was in order. In setting up TF 34, he had actually made that intelligent division of forces, but he failed to implement it.

Halsey's decisions (a) and (b) would have been sound if he had had no other obligations. His decision (c) can be described only as erroneous. I doubt if anyone will disagree with the statement that the only reason why Kurita did not reach Leyte Gulf, destroying the CVE's en route, was that he turned back when victory was within his grasp. His [Halsey's] judgment as to the "fatally weakened condition of the [enemy] Center Force" was definitely shown to be in error. Did his "judgment which was happily vindicated" include a forecast that Kurita would break off the action? If so, his crystal ball was certainly in fine working order. Does anyone believe in the "Japs' *inability* to deal with the CVE's and small fry"? They did not deal with them as they could have, but is that "inability"?

24. I am quoted correctly, but I did not have an opportunity to edit my remarks. In the last line "one head would not have altered things" might have been reworded because it meant that "one head would not have produced a better end result if both Halsey and I had carried out our specific missions."

Special Notes by
Fleet Admiral William F. Halsey, USN (Ret.)

The notes are keyed to letters in the text. Explanatory material in brackets inserted by author.

a. I do not remember what Radio Manila was playing. They were usually sending out lying propaganda from "Tokyo Rose" or some other renegade Japanese Nisei. We used Radio Manila as an alarm clock. As soon as we heard the air-raid alarm, we knew our pilots had been sighted.

The change in the American strategy was the direct result of a recommendation sent by me. I recommended that the taking of Yap and Palau be eliminated and that a landing be made in the central Philippines instead of Mindanao. I had once previously recommended that the seizure of Palau be dropped. Admiral Nimitz approved my recommendation, except that about Palau, and immediately forwarded it to the Combined Chiefs of Staff, then sitting in Quebec. General Sutherland, in Hollandia, General MacArthur's chief of staff, in MacArthur's temporary absence, approved the landing in the central Philippines instead of Mindanao. The Combined Chiefs of Staff approved, and it received almost immediate approval from President Roosevelt and Prime Minister Churchill. It was fortunate that the Quebec Conference was on at that time.

The 1st Marine Division had heavy losses on Peleliu (in the Palau group), in many ways comparable to Tarawa. One combat team from the Army 81st (Wildcat) Division also received many losses in the fighting on Peleliu, where they so ably assisted. We constructed airfields on Angaur, captured by the 81st Army Division, and on Peleliu Island, and a partial naval base in Kossol Roads. Kossol Roads was not occupied by the Japanese and we merely had to make arrangement for its defense from the Japanese on Babelthuap Island, the largest island of the Palau Archipelago. I mention these actions and this timing to show that this was not a "Monday quarterback" estimate of the situation on my part. Ulithi was not recommended to be dropped, as I always considered this a necessity as a fleet anchorage. It was occupied without opposition. Peleliu, Angaur and Kossol Roads were a great convenience, but I thought then, and I think now, not a necessity for the further campaign in the Pacific.

The beginning of the end of the war in the Pacific was evident before the Battle of Leyte Gulf. When our fleet obtained freedom of movement, practically anywhere in the Pacific, the Japanese were doomed to defeat.

The *Shō* plan was just another of the many plans the Japs devised. They all failed.

Toyoda [Commander in Chief of the Japanese Combined Fleet] had carriers, but with few planes and half-trained pilots. Now that it is the Monday after the Saturday game, everyone seemed to know this except my staff and me. We bore the responsibility. If the rest of the Navy did not then know it, we, in the Third Fleet, were thoroughly cognizant that the carrier had replaced the battleship, and was potentially the strongest and most dangerous naval weapon our opponents possessed. We had been fighting the Japs for several years. We did not know how many planes the Japs had, but we could not take a chance. We knew the *Princeton* had been attacked, and it was reported they were carrier planes. As we stood northward on the morning of the twenty-sixth, we had a large "bogy" on our screen. We naturally thought they were carrier planes heading toward the Japanese carriers. They finally went off our screen heading toward Luzon. We had been "shuttle-bombed" many times by the Nips, and only once off Guadalcanal had succeeded in reversing this process.

My decision to go north was not based on pilots' reports solely. A possible battle with the Japanese Fleet had long been a matter of discussion and study by us. We had played it frequently on a game board constructed on the deck of the flag quarters. We had long since decided the carriers were potentially the most dangerous ships the Japs had, not only to ourselves but to MacArthur and the Pacific campaign. We named them our primary targets. We knew Kurita's ships had suffered damage from our attacks, particularly to their upper works and probably to their fire-control instruments. This was borne out by their poor shooting against the baby carriers.

b. The "Turkey Shoot" in the Marianas (the Battle of the Philippine Sea) was a magnificent show. That it alone broke the back of Japanese naval aviation, despite its great success, I seriously doubt. I cannot and will not forget the wonderful American pilots in the South Pacific and Southwest Pacific who had knocked out so many Japanese naval air groups and squadrons based on Rabaul. This statement is based on Japanese answers to American interrogations after the war. The fliers who accomplished this were from the U.S. Army Air Force, U.S. Naval and Marine Aviation, the RNZAF and the RAAF. The Japs made their usual mistake of feeding in these groups piecemeal and were thoroughly knocked out.

c. The Japanese Navy had a number of carriers nearing completion in the Inland Sea. I have a fairly good-sized circular plaque, presented to me after the war. In the middle is a U.S. ensign; around the U.S. ensign and near the periphery are the silhouettes of various Japanese ships representing carriers, battleships, a heavy cruiser, light cruisers and submarines. On the periphery it bears the inscription: "Plaque made of metal obtained from these vessels sunk by U.S. Carrier planes, July 1945 at Kure Naval Base, Kure, Japan." The names and numbers are interesting: CV-ASO, CV-AMAGI, CVE-RYUHO, BB-ISE, BB-HYUGA, BB-HARUNA, CA-SETTSU, CL-TONE, CL-OYODO (fleet flagship), CL-AOBA, CL-IZUMA, CL-AWATE and 5 SS (CV: large carrier; CVE: small or jeep carrier; BB: battleship; CA: heavy cruiser; CL: light cruiser; and SS: submarines).

We had orders to get rid of the Japanese Navy so that they could not interfere with the Russians if they decided to invade Japan. I sometimes wonder, in view of present-day events! Of course these ships were sitting ducks, and even high-altitude bombing, with some luck, might have hit them.

There is one Japanese cruiser that I would have felt sorry for, if I could have felt sorry for a Japanese man-of-war in those days. She had escaped from the Battle of Leyte Gulf, sorely wounded. The Japs had brought her into a bay or cove on the west side of Luzon, and heavily camouflaged her and made her almost invisible. They were working night and day to make her seaworthy to return her to the homeland. In the meantime, our fliers were combing every nook and corner, looking for Jap ships. As one of our last flights was about to return, a lucky photograph was taken of this hide-out. Our photographic interpreters made out this cruiser. A heavy strike was made on her the first thing next morning, and that was curtains for this cruiser.

[Admiral Halsey was referring apparently to the heavy cruiser *Kumano*. This ship was struck by a destroyer torpedo during the attack by *Hoel*, *Heermann* and *Johnston* in the battle off Samar on the morning of October 25. She was subsequently struck by a bomb as she was retiring with Kurita's depleted Center Force on October 26. With her bow practically blown off and with only one boiler operable she limped at five knots into Manila Bay, where she got some makeshift repairs. On November 6, while en route back to Japan for permanent repairs, the U.S. submarine *Guitarro*, one of a number patrolling west of Luzon, hit her with another torpedo. Damaged *Kumano* struggled into Dasol Bay, Luzon, where she was finally sunk by air attack from the carrier *Ticonderoga* on November 25.]

d. A "Betty" tried to land among our parked planes on the *Enterprise* during our attack on the Marshall and Gilbert Islands on February 1, 1942 (Eastern Time). Thanks to the masterly ship handling by then Captain, now Admiral (Retired), George D. Murray, U.S. Navy, the "Betty" was forced into a slip while coming up "the groove" and did only minor damage. The "Betty" hit the edge of the flight deck, broke her back and went over the side. She was undoubtedly on fire when she hit us. She cut off a gasoline riser aft and set it on fire. She cut off another gasoline riser forward, but no fire resulted, and cut off the tail of one of our SBD [Douglas two-seat Scout or dive bomber] planes. The fire from the gasoline riser was soon under control, and I remember no further damage, except some slight and easily repairable damage to the flight deck. This was my first encounter with a kamikaze plane; I saw many later. I doubt if this Japanese even knew he was a kamikaze. His plane had dropped all her bombs and fortunately, for us, missed the *Enterprise*. His intentions were very clear. He knew his plane was doomed, and determined to do us as much damage as possible. He tried to land among some 35 or 40 of our planes, lately returned from a strike, refueling and waiting the return of all planes for respotting. The quick thinking of the ship's captain prevented what might have been a catastrophe. I do not mean to detract from Rear Admiral Masabumi Arima's very brave, but very foolhardy, suicide dive. Apparently we fought to live, the Japanese to die.

e. My orders went further than the quoted "to cover and support forces in the Southwest Pacific, in order to assist in the seizure and occupation of objectives in the Central Philippines." This is being written from memory without the advantage of notes, so my overriding orders can only be vaguely quoted. They were that, other conditions notwithstanding, the destruction of the Japanese Fleet was my paramount objective.

f. "Necessary measures for detailed coordination of operations between the [Third Fleet] and the [Seventh Fleet] will be arranged by their commanders." These are just so many words and nothing more. They were impossible of accomplishment. Kinkaid and I had not seen each other since we met in Hollandia, just after the plans for the invasion of the Philippines had been changed. Some key members of my staff and I had flown from Saipan to Hollandia to discuss preliminary arrangements with Kinkaid and his staff and MacArthur's staff. Both Kinkaid and I had been too busily occupied to confer during the Philippine invasion. This illustrates, as nothing else can, the importance of a unified command in the combat zone. Had Kinkaid or I been in Supreme Command at the time of the Battle of Leyte Gulf, I am sure it would have been fought differently. Whether for better or for worse can never be answered.

g. In addition to PBY's, I believe the Seventh Fleet had some PBM's [Martin patrol bombers] under its control at that time.

h. Night snoopers not only scouted the Northern Force but also the Sibuyan Sea and made reports of Kurita turning once again to the eastward, heading toward San Bernardino Strait. A report of this was directed sent to Kinkaid around 2100 or 2130 that night.

i. I had no operational control of submarines, except those specifically assigned to us for some operation. I had no submarines assigned to me at that time.

j. I never thought Kurita's force had been stopped by the day's air attacks. I had received and directed transmittal of a report that his force was again heading toward San Bernardino Strait. I did not bank too heavily on so-called exaggerated claims from pilots. We had rather good evaluation of pilots' reports at this time. I did think Kurita had been rather badly mauled by our pilots, particularly in their upper works, and that their fire control would be poor. Their poor shooting against the CVE's, destroyers and destroyer escorts the next day tended to corroborate this. I did not expect them to be opposed by CVE's, destroyers and destroyer escorts. Their thin skins probably saved them somewhat. After the Battle of Guadalcanal, in which Rear Admiral Callaghan and Rear Admiral Scott lost their lives, there were some thin-skinned ships that were holed by heavy-armor-piercing shells with little damage. I remember one destroyer—I have forgotten her name—that I inspected later. As I remember it, she had 14 14-inch hits from a Jap battleship. Her commanding officer was Commander Coward. Never did a man have a name so inappropriate to fit with his actions in battle.

k. I object to the statement that "on such misunderstandings rest the course of history and the fate of nations." I had no misunderstandings, with the possible exception (if true) that the Jap carriers had no planes. I knew what I was doing at all times, and deliberately took the risks, in order to get rid of the Jap carriers. My estimate that the Seventh Fleet could take care of Kurita's battered forces was amply justified even against the CVE's and small fry during the action of October 26. These brave American ships put up a fight that will be an epic for all time. My hat is off to them.

l. The Battle of Surigao Strait, with Admiral Oldendorf in tactical command, was beautifully conceived and executed. Never has a T been so efficiently capped, and never has a force been so completely defeated and demoralized as was the Jap Surigao force.

m. I am still far from sure that Ozawa's force was intended solely as a lure. The Japs had continuously lied during the war, even to each other. Why believe them implicitly as soon as the war ends? They had plenty of time, before reciting them, to make their stories fit their needs. Despite their "banzai" charges, their "kamikaze" planes, their "foolish bombs" (men-driven), their one- and two-man submarines, built for the purpose of sacrificing their crew, and the many other foolish things they did, it is still difficult for me to believe that they would deliberately use their potentially most dangerous ships as deliberate sacrifices. This is partially borne out by reports from Americans who interviewed Admiral Kurita after the war. When asked why he turned away from Leyte Gulf, he stated that he intended to join forces with Ozawa and attack the Third Fleet.

n. Admiral Nimitz' dispatch to me was "Where is Task Force 34?" The dispatch as quoted is a gross violation of security regulations. [This dispatch has been quoted in its entirety in numerous previous publications. The phrase "the world wonders" after the query "Where is Task Force 34?" was, as Admiral Kinkaid points out, what is known in naval parlance as "padding" for the purposes of code security. Normally, this "padding" should have been removed from the message before it was brought to Halsey, but in this instance the phrase was apparently left in the message as shown to him, and appeared to give it, unintentionally, a critical twist. This allegedly aroused the Admiral's wrath, but also emphasized to him the importance of dispatching aid to Kinkaid. The codes used in the Battle of Leyte Gulf have long since been changed and despite Admiral Halsey's comment, written with some irascibility years after the battle, there is no danger of compromising today's codes.]

o. I note the Seventh Fleet is described as red-eyed from days of shore bombardment and nights of battle. My fleet had been fighting almost continually since early September. When we finally reached Ulithi in late September, for rest and replenishment, we were chased out by a typhoon after a one-night stand. We were almost continually in combat, until some time after the Battle of Leyte Gulf. I wonder what color my splendid pilots' eyes were? I do not know, but I do know they were approaching a stage of exhaustion that kept me on edge. I dared not let up on the Japs when we were running them ragged. This goes for all my officers and men, manning battle stations above and below decks. It was an almost unendurable strain. We fought no battle for Cape Engaño—we fought to do away with the Jap carriers.

p. I knew what force Kinkaid had and believed them capable of taking on Kurita's damaged force. I did not know of Kinkaid's ammunition situation in his old battleships. I have since been told that one of these battleships in the Surigao Strait action did not fire a single shot from her main battery.

In moving north, I took a calculated risk. I figured then, and still believe, that if Kurita arrived at Leyte Gulf he could make nothing but a "hit-and-run bombardment." While in command of the South Pacific, my forces in Guadalcanal had many times been bombarded by Japanese battleships, cruisers and destroyers. The forces ashore caught unmerciful hell, but these bombardments served to delay us no more than a short time. Shipping put to sea, usually, only partly unloaded and moved away from the bombardment area. The troops ashore had to take it in such dugouts as they had. On most occasions I had no heavy fighting ships to oppose them, and they bombarded at their leisure. On one occasion PT boats drove them away. On another, Dan Callaghan and Norm Scott (both rear admirals) made the supreme sacrifice, but with their few ships, cruisers, antiaircraft vessels and destroyers, they routed the Japanese forces consisting of battleships, cruisers and destroyers. Their supreme sacrifice was not in vain. As a result of this action, the Japanese lost the Battleship *Hiyei*—left a derelict and sunk by our planes the next day. During one of their last bombardments, we had been able to fool them and got two of our new battleships near Savo Island, the *South Dakota* and the *Washington*, under command of Rear Admiral, later Vice Admiral, W. A. Lee, Jr., USN. As a result of the night action that followed, the Japs lost various destroyers and one battleship. She [the battleship] was sunk that night.

q. A statement is made that Kurita's intercepted radio traffic convinced him, erroneously, that Leyte airstrips were operational. This was not entirely erroneous. Admiral McCain flew his planes off at such a distance that it was impossible for them to return to their mother carriers. They were directed to land on Leyte airstrips. They did, and for a few days thereafter they operated from these fields until I was directed to return them to Ulithi. This was done, via Palau to Ulithi. Incidentally, I do not remember seeing a report of the damage McCain's fliers inflicted on Kurita's force. It must have been not inconsiderable.

r. I do not fully understand what the author means by unwarranted assumptions by me. Possibly that I placed too much credence in the pilots' reports; I do not believe that I did. These reports were carefully evaluated, and after due consideration a calculated risk was taken. My estimate that the Seventh Fleet could take care of Kurita's battered forces was amply justified. "The proof of the pudding is in the eating." Remember this estimate was "Saturday quarterbacking" and not "Monday quarterbacking."

s. I am in agreement that I made a mistake in bowing to pressure and turning south. I consider this the gravest error I committed during the Battle for Leyte Gulf.

t. I have never stated, to my knowledge and remembrance, that Kinkaid could and should have covered San Bernardino Strait. I have stated that I felt that Kinkaid's force could have taken care of Kurita's battered force, and, furthermore, that Kurita was only capable of a hit-and-run attack if he entered Leyte Gulf. Such an attack, by my experience in the South Pacific, would have little effect on the troops ashore and could cause only a slight delay in the over-all picture.

u. I did not send a preparatory dispatch, but instead a "Battle Plan" addressed only to the Third Fleet. To insure that the Third Fleet did not misunderstand, I sent a further message saying this plan would not be executed until directed by me. As Commander, Task Force 38, Vice Admiral Mitscher should have received both messages.

v. The statement that, had I sent a dispatch to Kinkaid that I was "proceeding north with all my available forces" instead of "proceeding north with three groups," the surprise would not have occurred is purely academic. I did not know that he had intercepted my battle plan and believed it had been executed. A carrier task group was well defined, and every naval commander in the area knew its composition. My dispatch was a correct one. I had notified all interested parties when Admiral McCain's Carrier Task Group started for Ulithi. I am sure no one misconstrued that message.

w. I have explained before that orders requiring "coordination" were mere words and meant nothing. I still stand by what I have written about Leyte Gulf, that "it illustrates the necessity for a single naval command in a combat area, responsible for, and in full control of, all combat units involved."

x. I knew nothing of how the Seventh Fleet was armed. At that time I believe we were rearming the Third Fleet under way. I gave no thought to the Seventh Fleet's armament of shells.

y. I am in agreement with Admiral Kinkaid when he says any errors made were errors of judgment. I am in complete disagreement when he states, "The two areas coming together—the Central Pacific and the Southwest Pacific—posed a difficult problem of command, but one head would not have altered things." As I have previously stated, "Had either Admiral Kinkaid or I been in supreme command, the battle would have been fought quite differently."

z. There is only one word to describe the communications on the American side during this battle, and that word is "rotten." We sent in a long report describing the deficiencies and interference we encountered, also a recommendation for drastic changes. As I remember, our combat circuit was filled with long and relatively unimportant intelligence summaries that could and should have been deferred. Most of these were not Navy reports. As a consequence, there were long and intolerable delays in getting urgent messages through. This should never be permitted again.

These comments have been written almost entirely from memory and without the advantage of any notes or reports. I hope I am not trusting my memory too far; ten and a half years is a long time.

Of special interest is the following message which was written by Halsey at the time of the battle, justifying his actions during the battle. This is an historic message, and I am indebted for it to Admiral Eller, Director of Naval History.

COMMANDER THIRD FLEET

FROM: COM THIRD FLEET   DATE: 25 OCT 44

TO (ACTION):   CINCPAC: CINCSWPA: COM 7TH FLEET: COMINCH

TO (INFO):   *TOP SECRET*

That there be no misunderstanding concerning recent operations of the Third
Fleet I inform you as follows: to obtain information of Jap plans and movements
became vital on twenty three (23) October so three carrier groups were moved
into Philippine coast off Polillo CMA San Bernardino and Surigao to search
as far west as possible. On twenty four (24) October the Third Fleet searches
revealed Jap forces moving east through the Sibuyan and Sulu Seas and both
of those forces were brought under attack by Third Fleet air strikes. The
existence of a Jap plan for coordinated attack was then apparent but the objective was not sure and the expected carrier force was missing from the picture.
Third Fleet carrier searches revealed the presence of the enemy carrier force on
the afternoon of twenty four (24) October completing the picture. To statically
guard San Bernardino Straits until enemy surface and carrier air attacks could be
coordinated would have been childish so three (3) carrier groups were concentrated during the night and started north for a surprise dawn attack on the
enemy carrier fleet. I considered that the enemy force in Sibuyan Sea had been
so badly damaged that they constituted no serious threat to Kinkaid and that
estimate has been borne out by the events of the twenty fifth (25th) off Surigao.
The enemy carrier force was caught off guard there being no air opposition
over target and no air attack against our force. Their air groups were
apparently shore based and arrived too late to land on their carriers or get into
the fight. I had projected surface striking units ahead of our carriers in order
to coordinate surface and air attacks against the enemy. Com Seventh Fleet's
urgent appeals for help came at a time when the enemy force was heavily damaged
and my overwhelming surface striking force was within forty five (45) miles of
the enemy cripples. I had no alternative but to break off from my golden opportunity and head south to support Kinkaid although I was convinced that his force
was adequate to deal with an enemy force that was badly weakened by our
attacks of the twenty fourth (24th)—a conviction justified by later events off
Leyte. I wish to point out that MacArthur and Kinkaid were supported by Able
(A) destruction of twelve hundred (1200) enemy planes between ten (10) and
twenty (20) October plus much shipping, Baker (B) air attacks against Jap forces
in the Sulu Sea, Charlie (C) crippling of enemy force in Sibuyan Sea, Dog (D)
destruction of over one hundred fifty (150) planes on twenty four (24) October
Easy (E) destruction of enemy carrier strength on twenty five (25) October, Fox
(F) carrier attacks on threatening enemy force off Leyte twenty five (25) October,
George (G) surface movements evening twenty five (25) October to cut off enemy
retreat toward San Bernardino.

The back of the Jap Navy has been broken in the course of supporting our
landings at Leyte.   HALSEY

Acknowledgments and Bibliography

I am particularly indebted to Rear Admiral E. M. Eller, USN (Ret.),
Director of Naval History, and to several of his assistants, for reviewing this

chapter. Admiral Robert B. ("Mick") Carney, USN (Ret.), former Chief of Naval Operations, and at the time of Leyte Gulf, chief of staff to Admiral Halsey, very kindly read the final five pages of the chapter, and made some valuable suggestions about the judgments and considerations which influenced Halsey in making his decisions at the time. Vice Admiral John S. McCain, Jr., reviewed the manuscript with a kindly and critical eye.

After-action reports of the Third Fleet and of the USS *Hoel, Heermann, Johnston* and other ships have been consulted for this account.

Samuel Eliot Morison's *Leyte, June 1944–January 1945,* Volume XII of the *History of United States Naval Operations in World War II,* Little, Brown, 1958, represents probably the most complete account yet published of the battle. The Morison volume is not official in that his judgments are his own, but his work was fully supported by the Navy.

In turn, Morison based part of his account on the most comprehensive and detailed study of the battle yet attempted. This account, under the direction of Rear Admiral Richard W. Bates, who was chief of staff to Admiral Oldendorf during the battle, was undertaken at the Naval War College in Newport, and resulted in an extremely lengthy, detailed and technical work—unfortunately still restricted to naval use, and unfortunately, because of the curtailment of government funds, never completed. "Rafe" Bates's work is not available to the general student, though Morison drew upon it.

Books

CANNON, M. HAMLIN, *Leyte—The Return to the Philippines (U.S. Army in World War II—The War in the Pacific).* Washington: Office of Chief of Military History, Department of the Army, 1954

CANT, GILBERT, *The Great Pacific Victory.* New York: John Day, 1945

COMMAGER, HENRY STEELE, ed., *The Story of the Second World War.* Boston: Little, Brown, 1945

CRAVEN, W. F., and CATE, J. L., eds., *The Army Air Force in World War II,* Vol. 5, *The Pacific: Matterhorn to Nagasaki,* June 1944 to August 1945. Chicago: University of Chicago Press, 1953

FIELD, JAMES A., JR., *The Japanese at Leyte Gulf.* Princeton: Princeton University Press, 1947

HALSEY, FLEET ADMIRAL WILLIAM F., USN, and BRYAN, LIEUTENANT COMMANDER J., III, USNR, *Admiral Halsey's Story.* New York: Whittlesey House, 1947

KARIG, CAPTAIN WALTER, USNR; HARRIS, LIEUTENANT COMMANDER RUSSELL L., USNR; and MANSON, LIEUTENANT COMMANDER FRANK A., USN, *Battle Report,* Vol. 4, *The End of An Empire.* New York: Rinehart, 1948

KING, FLEET ADMIRAL ERNEST J., USN, *Official Reports—U.S. Navy at War—1941–1945.* U.S. Navy Department, 1946

Naval Analysis Division, U.S. Strategic Bombing Survey (Pacific). *The Campaigns of the Pacific War.* Washington: U.S. Government Printing Office, 1946

SHERMAN, ADMIRAL FREDERICK C., USN (RET.), *Combat Command.* New York: Dutton, 1950

WILLOUGHBY, MAJOR GENERAL CHARLES A., and CHAMBERLAIN, JOHN, *MacArthur, 1941–1951.* New York: McGraw-Hill, 1954
WOODWARD, C. VANN, *The Battle for Leyte Gulf.* New York: Macmillan, 1947

Magazine

HALSEY, ADMIRAL WILLIAM F., "The Battle for Leyte Gulf," *U.S. Naval Institute Proceedings,* May, 1952
Additional comments by Admiral Halsey, under the special notes, were written specifically for this chapter in 1955.

Admiral Kinkaid, the other principal U.S. naval commander, has not yet published his memoirs, but his reasoning will be found in *Battle Report* and in the special notes to this chapter. I am indebted to him for permission to quote him in his own words.

The surviving Japanese commanders' after-the-war explanations are itemized in Field's *The Japanese at Leyte Gulf.*

CHAPTER 10. THE BATTLE OF THE BULGE

Notes

1. Charles B. MacDonald, *The Siegfried Line Campaign,* p. 612.
2. This order, issued at the CP of the 18 Volksgrenadier Division in Schnee Eifel in November, was later captured by the U.S. 104th Infantry Division. Translation from their intelligence files. From the collection of documents of the author's, gathered during study of the Bulge Battle.
3. MS No. a-876, General der Pzr. Erich Brandenberger, with aid of Major-General Freiherr Rudolf von Gersdorff, *Ardennes Offensive of Seventh Army* (16 Dec. 1944–Jan. 1945).
4. As was usual at this stage of the war, Hitler and his generals differed about the scope of the offensive and its objectives and details. The generals favored a double envelopment offensive to destroy Allied forces in the Liége-Aachen area, or, as an alternative, a more risky single-thrust attack toward Antwerp. Hitler combined them both but earmarked only strength enough for one. See "The German Counteroffensive in the Ardennes" by Charles V. P. von Luttichau, Chapter 17 in *Command Decisions,* Kent Robert Greenfield, ed., N.Y.: Harcourt Brace, 1959, pp. 352–353.

Cole (*The Ardennes: Battle of the Bulge,* pp. 19 ff.) gives a thorough account of this tug of war. He points out that Jodl's section suggested five possible courses of action and recommended the first two, viz., "Operation Holland: a single-thrust attack to be launched from the Venlo area, with Antwerp as the objective. Operation Liége-Aachen: a two-pronged attack with the main effort driving from the northern Luxembourg in a north-westerly direction, subsequently turning due north to meet the secondary attack which would be launched from the sector northwest of Aachen." Hitler himself on October 22 described the attack as "designed to surround and destroy the British and American forces north of the line Bastogne-Brussels-Antwerp. It would be carried out in two phases: the first phase to close the attacking force along the Meuse River and seize bridgeheads; the second phase to culminate in the capture of Antwerp." Cole states there is no evidence of any detailed planning beyond Antwerp. In the event, the Germans never even closed all the way to the Meuse.

5. The 4th Division had also suffered 2,000 noncombat casualties in the Hürtgen Forest. For a graphic, complete account of this "bloodiest battle," see Charles B. MacDonald's *The Battle of the Huertgen Forest,* Philadelphia, Lippincott, 1963.

6. The German order of battle in the Ardennes offensive was, from north to south: Sixth (SS Panzer Army, Colonel General Joseph "Sepp" Dietrich commanding), with three corps; the Fifth Panzer Army (General Hasso von Manteuffel commanding), with two corps, and the Seventh Army (General Erich Brandenberger commanding), with two corps, which held the southern flank. Field Marshal Walther Model, commanding Army Group B, was operational commander of the offensive, under von Rundstedt, who was over-all commander of all German forces in the West. Von Rundstedt had a total—on paper—of about 75 divisions in the West (many of them under strength), approximating 600,000 men. The Fifteenth Army, it was originally contemplated, would join the offensive by covering the north flank of the Sixth Panzer Army, which was to make the main effort. But at the time the attack started the Fifteenth Army was "plugging the gaps" along the Roer front. Though Hitler hoped it would ultimately join the offensive with the aid of reserves, it never did so. The Germans (see Cole, *op. cit.,* pp. 70, 71; 650 ff.) had available 12 infantry and 7 armored divisions in the initial assault, with 5 divisions plus smaller units in immediate reserve, and 5 others in general reserve. About 970 tanks and armored assault guns and 1,900 artillery pieces were used initially. The total force, if the Fifteenth Army was included, was 29 infantry and 12 armored divisions. In the event, by January 2 the Germans had actually used some 28 to 29 divisions.

The Sixth Panzer Army is sometimes described as the Sixth SS Panzer Army, as Hitler originally dubbed it. Its commander, Sepp Dietrich, was an old Nazi party wheel horse, and some of its units and officers were on the rolls of the SS, but the Army itself was never officially called an SS army.

On the actual assault front of about 60 miles, the Germans enjoyed initially a superiority ratio estimated by Cole (p. 650) as three to one in infantry (six to one at "points of concentration"), about two to one in medium tanks, or, if self-propelled guns are included, four to one. In divisions, the U.S. forces in the German assault zone and its flanks (a 104-mile front) numbered on December 16 about four and two-thirds divisions—83,000 men as compared to the German 200,000. By January 2 the U.S. forces mobilized against the German thrust totaled 8 armored, 16 infantry and 2 airborne divisions, plus British forces backstopping the Meuse River line.

7. The exact number of German parachutists used in the Bulge Battle is in doubt. Plans had called for the employment of about 1,000, but apparently only about 300 actually got into action behind U.S. lines. A company and a signal platoon were erroneously dropped just about astride the German front line. Dummies were also dropped. As usual, the paradrop operations caused much wasted motion and undue apprehension in U.S. rear areas,

but the operation was a "shoestring" one—badly planned and executed—and accomplished little.

8. Dwight D. Eisenhower, *Crusade in Europe,* p. 347. The 99th Division, though relatively green to war, did well after initial confusion. Some of its units were overwhelmed by superior numbers, and at Honsfeld there was, as Cole puts it (*op. cit.,* p. 91), a "wild scramble to get out of town," but the division made the Germans pay in blood and for some time denied the German Panzers access to the important Büllingen-Malmédy road.

9. Some 86 Americans were massacred in this incident. *Kampfgruppe Peiper,* a part of the 1st SS Panzer Division, had been responsible for at least two other incidents—one at Honsfeld, when 19 American prisoners were murdered, and one at Büllingen, when 50 were shot.

In all, by December 20 Colonel Joachim Peiper's command had slain about 350 unarmed Americans and 100 Belgian civilians in the "only organized and directed murder of prisoners of war by either side during the Ardennes battle" (Cole, *op cit.,* pp. 261 ff).

The news of the Malmédy massacre spread quickly throughout the American Army, and steeled the bitterness and determination of U.S. troops. Apparently some retributive measures were taken; Cole quotes in a footnote (p. 264) a fragmentary order of the 328th Infantry Regiment, which states that "no SS troops or paratroopers will be taken prisoners but will be shot on sight."

A Congressional investigation and war crimes trials followed after the war.

10. Major Donald P. Boyer, personal report. Major Boyer was S-3, 38th Armored Infantry Battalion, 7th Armored Division. See *7th Armored Division After-Action Report, Battle of Saint-Vith—17–23 December, 1944,* Office of the Chief of Military History, Department of the Army, Washington.

11. *Ibid.*

12. *Ibid.*

13. *Ibid.*

14. Sixth Panzer Army had allowed one day for penetration and breakout; the Meuse was to be reached by the end of the third day and bridgeheads across it secured by the fourth (Cole, *op. cit.,* p. 77)—a wildly optimistic schedule.

15. Actually, a "snafu" had interfered more than the weather. There was bad coordination between U.S. ground and air, and other faults. (See Cole, *op. cit.,* p. 172.)

16. From personal account, Lieutenant Colonel T. Paine Kelly, 589th Field Artillery Battalion, to Colonel Malin Craig, Executive Officer, 106th Division Artillery, p. 3.

17. *Ibid.,* p. 3.

18. Cole (*op. cit.,* p. 170) calls the "Schnee Eifel battle . . . the most serious reverse suffered by American arms during the operations of 1944–45 in the European theatre.

"The Americans would regard this defeat as a blow to Allied prestige. The Germans would see in this victory, won without great superiority in numbers, a dramatic reaffirmation of the Schlieffen-Cannae concept."

19. Diary of Lieutenant Martin Opitz, 1st Company, 295 Volksgrenadier Regiment. Captured by U.S. First Army. Translated copy from U.S. First Army intelligence files, January 25, 1945.

20. Cole, *op. cit.,* p. 258.

21. Brigadier General Bruce C. Clarke, personal report, "Defense of St. Vith—Belgium."

22. Boyer, *op. cit.,* 21 December.

23. *Ibid.*

24. *Ibid.*

25. *7th Armored Division After-Action Report, 1–31 December, 1944.*

26. The proximity or VT fuse, developed in the United States, was first used by the U.S. Navy in antiaircraft shells. It was then used in England against the buzz bombs or V-1's, but, because of fear that the engineering and scientific secret might fall into Germany's hands if an unexploded proximity-fused shell was recovered, it was withheld from land use until the Battle of the Bulge. The Combined (U.S. and British) Chiefs of Staff agreed on October 25, 1944, that it would be released for general use by all services, including the Army, on December 24 or 25. But the use of buzz bombs against Antwerp and the emergency of the Bulge advanced the date. Apparently the fuse was first used in land action against enemy troops in howitzer shells on December 18, or, according to Cole (*op. cit.,* p. 361), on December 21 and thereafter.

According to *Scientists Against Time* by James Phinney Baxter, III (Boston, Little, Brown, 1946, p. 236), it "did deadly service" and "contributed materially to halting the [German] advance and hastening the reduction of the salient. . . . Prisoners of war characterized our artillery fire as the most demoralizing and destructive ever encountered." The electronic or radio fuse, its basic element a photoelectric cell, detonated the shells while still in the air but within just the right proximity to the ground that the burst had a maximum effect even against men in foxholes. (See also *History of Communications-Electronics in the United States Navy* by Captain L. S. Howeth, USN (Ret.), Washington, U.S. Government Printing Office, 1963, p. 500.)

Cole (*op. cit.*) does not agree with the natural exuberance of the scientists, which he calls "grossly exaggerated," and dismisses the fuse as of relatively little importance in the Bulge Battle. This author tends to take a position between these extremes; on a few occasions the fuse was deadly.

27. Saint-Vith, even more than Bastogne, was the bulwark of the Bulge, and, in a sense, its turning point. Bastogne got the publicity; Saint-Vith was even more important as a bastion of defense. The November-December, 1964, issue of *Armor Magazine* (Washington, D.C.) notes in an article by Captain Allen D. Raymond, III, "The Battle of St. Vith," that "St. Vith was at least equally as important as Bastogne."

An editor's note accompanying the article states:

General von Manteuffel has agreed at several joint press conferences that for the German counter-offensive of December, 1944, to be successful at least three things had to happen:

a. The German attack had to be a surprise.

b. The weather to be such as to prevent strikes by allied aircraft on the German columns coming through the Ardennes.

c. The progress of the German main effort through and beyond St. Vith must be rapid and not delayed.

Requirements a. and b. were met. Requirement c. was not met because of the defensive and delaying action of the 7th Armored Division and attached troops in the St. Vith area from 17–23 December 1944.

His timetable called for the capture of St. Vith by 1800 hours on 17 December. He did not capture it until the night of 21 December and did not control the St. Vith area until 23 December when CCB withdrew on order.

On 22 September 1964, at a press conference in Watertown, New York, General von Manteuffel stated, "On the evening of 24 December 1944, I recommended to Hitler's Adjutant that the Germany Army give up the attack and return to the West Wall." He stated that the reason for this recommendation was due to the time lost by his Fifth Panzer Army in the St. Vith area. Hitler did not accept von Manteuffel's recommendation.

Even more important than Saint-Vith to the success of the defensive battle was the tenacious resistance by the 2nd Division, aided after some initial disorganization by the 99th Division, and subsequently reinforced by the 1st Division, of the northern shoulder of the Bulge. The German attempts to widen the salient battered in vain against rocklike defense in the Monschau–Elsenborn Ridge area. The result was that the Nazi attack was canalized and narrowed, and ultimately contained.

28. Messages and citations included in General Hodges' recommendation of the 7th Armored Division for the Presidential Unit Citation.

29. Major General John Shirley Wood, who kindly read and commented on this chapter, points out that "George [Patton] put up this prayer regularly when the weather was bad." (See *Portrait of Patton* by Harry H. Semmes, p. 231.)

30. Montgomery was much of an actor, and a master, as Eisenhower described him, of a "set-piece battle," as well as a colorful, confident leader. His greatest achievement was to provide Britain, nation of beef-eaters, with a hero at the time of her darkest trials, albeit an eccentric one who neither smoked nor drank. His victory at El Alamein was of more major import in the field of British morale than in strategic consequences; it was *not* a decisive battle of the war, not really a battle—given the impending Allied landings in Algeria and Morocco behind Rommel's armies—that Montgomery could have lost. But from El Alamein "Monty" went on, in British opinion and in his own self-evaluation, to greater and greater esteem, and at the time of the Bulge "Monty" had rubbed the Americans the wrong way. There was good reason for this feeling: most military leaders have considerable vanity and *amour-propre,* and neither Bradley, with his deceptive "farmer" appearance, nor any of the other Americans were without great pride in their own achievements and the achievements of American arms. This pride is, of course, an essential element of leadership; it was not an undue pride in most of the American leaders this author knew. With "Monty" it was expressed in egoism and vanity, plus showmanship, qualities also possessed to a high degree by MacArthur and Patton and to a quieter degree by Bradley. These qualities are bearable with achievement, but "Monty's"

NOTES, BIBLIOGRAPHIES AND ACKNOWLEDGMENTS   495

reputation, in American eyes, was, and still is, overinflated. "Monty" was not a great general in the sense that he did much with little; he did much with much; his victories were always based upon a great material superiority to the enemy. To the Americans he appeared to be both cautious and arrogant, and there had been little love lost between him and Bradley and Patton since North Africa. On the other hand Bradley, to the British, and to some Americans, seemed inexperienced and too jealous of his own reputation and independence of command.

When Eisenhower split the command during the Bulge and gave Montgomery (quite logically) command of the northern shoulder, including "Brad's" beloved First Army, Bradley was put out. "Monty's" conduct during the battle did little to pour oil on troubled waters. Chester Wilmot in *The Struggle for Europe* (p. 592) quotes an eyewitness as characterizing "Monty's" first visit to U.S. First Army HQ as follows: "The Field Marshal strode into Hodges' H.Q. like Christ come to cleanse the temple."

Since Normandy there had been an attempt—always suggested somewhat tangentially in official circles, but always supported by the British press—virtually to supersede Eisenhower by appointment of a British ground commander. This intermittent crusade, in the event doomed to disappointment because of the greater American superiority in military power, assumed new force with the setback of the Bulge and "Monty's" appointment to command of the U.S. First as well as the Ninth Army.

When the German drive was halted and in reverse, "Monty," never one to hide his light under a bushel, commanded (he never "called") a press conference, and on January 7, 1945, (in Chester Wilmot's words, *op. cit.,* p. 610) he "surveyed the battle in terms which placed considerable emphasis on his own part in it." "Monty" said his first task had been to "tidy up the battlefield," and he went on to talk about the British role in the battle in a manner which left the impression—at least with the Americans—that the steady British had saved the day.

Eisenhower later wrote in *Crusade in Europe* (p. 356) that "I doubt that Montgomery ever came to realize how deeply resentful some American commanders were [when they heard Monty's press conference broadcast over the British Broadcasting Corporation]. They believed he had belittled them, and they were not slow to voice reciprocal scorn and contempt."

Eisenhower, despite his easygoing, comfortable personality, was one of those American commanders who resented "Monty"; the Britisher, slightly condescending, had been a thorn in the flesh to the Supreme Allied Commander ever since North Africa.

This contretemps almost achieved, out of the soil of human vanity, what the Germans had failed to accomplish.

Bradley felt called upon in a statement on January 9 to answer Montgomery, and the feud, for a time, flared brightly—particularly in the British press, which was campaigning violently, with "Monty's" open or tacit approval, for Montgomery's elevation to ground force commander in the West.

But the issue had already been decided, for Eisenhower had frankly told Montgomery in late December that he would not continue the U.S. First Army under "Monty's" command after the Bulge had been cleaned up, and that he would not consider placing one army group commander (Bradley, Twelfth Army Group) under another army group commander (Montgomery, Twenty-first Army Group). Nor would he consider the intervention of a ground commander between him and his army groups. He hoped, Ike said, there "was not being developed an unbridgeable gulf of convictions between them that would require settlement by the Combined Chiefs" (Butcher, *op. cit.,* p. 736).

This plain talk was effective—in large measure because "Monty" knew Eisenhower had already been assured of backing by General Marshall and President Roosevelt—and it ended, for the duration of World War II, "Monty's" royal pretensions.

These conflicts of personalities would not need laboring if they had not affected the course of the war. But that they did affect it is clear, even though not to a major extent. The clashes influenced more greatly the refighting of the battles after the war—which is still going on in 1966—than they did the actual operations. Neither Montgomery, who appeared to delight in outrageous comments, nor Bradley, who became more acid with age, can take pride in their postwar polemics.

Some observers, among them a distinguished leader of World War II, see the Battle of the Bulge as "the direct result of defects in the character of the top [Allied] command: Eisenhower, the compromiser and conciliator . . . Montgomery, the vainglorious, with his manifest and egregious egotism; Bradley, the plodder, hidebound and dull, mutely vain and resentful."

This is strong criticism, too strong for this author to endorse *in toto,* but nevertheless containing more than a germ of truth. Eisenhower was a compromiser and conciliator; many successful men are, and though these qualities are rarely desirable in great generals, Eisenhower was the right man for the right place in World War II. He was a kind of "general manager" who welded together discordant elements of a fighting team. But this does *not* mean that he would not, as his critics claim, make decisions. He preferred to persuade, but he could, and did, order. Montgomery had, for the British, who had been for so long top dog in the world, a quality of magnetism which symbolized past greatness and invited greater effort; he was also a careful and thorough general. Bradley had a vein of common sense and an understanding of the American character; his leadership, pitched in low key, appealed to a great many Americans.

General James M. Gavin, USA (Ret.), who served under both men, saw Patton and Bradley in these terms:

General Patton was a rambunctious, flamboyant officer with mannerisms intended to impress his troops. He had the wit, as Field Marshal Rommel once expressed it, to make himself distinctive, so that he stood out at all times and was recognized by soldiers wherever he appeared. . . .

Bradley was a sagacious commander, who sought always to balance risk with probable achievement, while at the same time, he held his casualties to a minimum. To Patton, this was sometimes unpardonable conservatism which, he reasoned, in the long run would cost more lives.

("Two Fighting Generals—Patton and MacArthur," by General James M. Gavin, the *Atlantic Monthly,* February, 1965.)

31. Earl F. Ziemke, "Stalingrad to Berlin—The German Campaign in Russia, 1942–1945," unpublished manuscript, Office of the Chief of Military History, Department of the Army, Chapter XVI, p. 10.

32. W. F. Craven and J. L. Cate, eds., *The Army Air Forces in World War II*, Vol. 3, pp. 665 and 672 ff. The editors and authors describe this attack as "stunning" and an "ugly surprise." Some of Germany's carefully hoarded jets—Me-262's—were used.

33. Ziemke, *op. cit.*, Chapter XVI, p. 17.

34. There is considerable disagreement about this point. Charles B. MacDonald, whose judgments are highly respected, believes it may have shortened the war. His reasoning, shared by many other historians, is that the Bulge brought the Germans out into the open and thus exposed them to major casualties. He and others have pointed out that the failure of the Nazi offensive was a subsequent depressant to German morale, and that later in the spring German resistance, weakened by the heavy casualties and disorganization of the Bulge, collapsed sooner than it might have done. On the other hand, Eisenhower retrospectively felt the Bulge had delayed the Allied offensive into Germany by about six weeks but that the battle may have ultimately shortened the war. These are the "if's" of history; this author's feeling is that the Bulge was even more of a moral shock to the U.S. than it was to Germany and that the German collapse may have been slightly, though not long, deferred by it.

35. *Command Decisions*, Chapter 17 (Charles V. P. von Luttichau), pp. 342, 356.

36. Chester Wilmot, *op. cit.*, p. 454.

37. Dwight D. Eisenhower, *op. cit.*, p. 32.

38. Lieutenant Colonel Wilbur E. Showalter, "What Is Calculated Risk?," *Military Review*, May, 1952.

39. Robert E. Merriam, *Dark December*, p. 130.

40. Letter of Dickson to author, May 28, 1952.

41. Volume III of *The Army Air Forces in World War II* points out (p. 673) that Hitler and Göring had promised 3,000 fighters for the Bulge attack. Air Force Command West reported to C-in-C West and to Army Group B on December 2 that its available fighter strength was about 1,700 planes, half of them operational. Actually, on December 16 there was a total of 2,292 German planes of all types in the west, of which 1,376 were operational.

42. Merriam, *op. cit.*, p. 215.

43. *Ibid.*, pp. 92 ff.

44. In a letter to the author of May 28, 1952, Colonel Dickson wrote:

In regard to the OSS we had a fiasco in Tunisia with an OSS party of Asturian dynamiteros who arrived in Tébessa completely without equipment. We outfitted this bunch at the thin end of the supply line and they made an attempt to infiltrate the enemy lines which was stopped by an Italian outpost losing almost all of II Corps weapons and vehicles. In Sicily we had another similar experience with an OSS party.

General Bradley did not want OSS with First Army but it was imposed on us at Bristol [First Army HQ in England, prior to the Normandy invasion] by higher authority. They were very individualistic and would not work with each other. Each OSS section demanded its own individual frequency for radio communications and would not pool their traffic through a common OSS signal unit. Their demands on the lift were extravagant.

Shortly after landing in Normandy we found they were continually bringing over more specialists and were operating without coordination with First Army or among their own sections. One section under Captain Stuyvesant Wainwright doing counterespionage and antisubversive work was excellent. General Bradley retained this OSS section, on my recommendation, and policed the rest.

General Donovan ["Wild Bill" Donovan, head of OSS] did not like this decision. When the Bulge broke he said, "Look what happens to an army without OSS!" General Conrad reminded him that the entire OSS had produced no intelligence indicating von Rundstedt's counterattack which silenced him. . . .

Wainwright's section served with First Army throughout the campaign. Wainwright asked to be transferred to First Army staff in the early months of 1945 and I took him over. Apart from this one section the history of OSS with First Army is rather undistinguished and we were never Donovan's favorite army.

One episode which stung OSS at 12 AG was a very funny parody of a PW interrogation report written in the regular form dealing with a PW who had formerly been Hitler's latrine orderly. Wainwright sent a copy informally to his superior at 12th AG for a laugh, but that character took it seriously and got high brass in an uproar. First Army was ordered to fly the prisoner back to SHAEF. When we requested that the paper be reread as it was obvious farce and had not been transmitted through official channels there was considerable embarrassment among OSS 12th AG. This may have caused them to be willing to let Wainwright transfer to 1st Army.

45. General Wood notes that some front-line units called these literary G-2 efforts from higher headquarters "The Funny Papers" and relied on their own intelligence efforts.
46. Letter to the author, January 2, 1947.
47. *The Army Air Forces in World War II,* Vol. III, p. 68.
48. Showalter, *op. cit.*
49. Major Martin M. Philipsborn, "Summary of Intelligence Operations from July '44 to May '45," May 27, 1945.
50. Cole, *op. cit.,* pp. 57 and 63.

General Notes on the Battle

Hitler's plans for the Battle of the Bulge envisaged anchoring the north flank of the salient on the Vesdre River and by-passing Liége to the south; he did not want his armored elements to get bogged down in fighting in the fortifications and streets of the city. Nevertheless, Sepp Dietrich had planned to send part of the Sixth Panzer Army across the Meuse north of Liége.

Much of the drama of the successful American defense in the Bulge Battle has been focused on Bastogne, and much upon the swashbuckling George Patton and his Third Army. The defenders of Bastogne deserve their fame, and the Third Army commander and staff performed prodigies of planning and logistics in turning the whole army around and attacking the southern flank of the Bulge. But the brunt of the battle was borne by the U.S. First Army, and the holding of the northern shoulder and the defense of Saint-Vith were key factors in ultimate victory.

The main effort of the Sixth Panzer Army was frustrated by the tenacious grip of the 2nd and 99th Divisions on the northern shoulder. When the Germans made a major attack against Saint-Vith several days after the offensive opened, they were checked again.

To the First Army belongs the primary credit—and the primary blame.

The German attempts to sow confusion behind American lines were aided primarily by surprise, second by rumor—some of it deliberately started by the Nazis—only third by the German parachutists (few in number, dispersed in dropping, a failure tactically, but psychologically frightening), and fourth by the German 150th Panzer Brigade (some of its men dressed in U.S. uniforms and equipped with U.S. and British captured tanks and weapons).

A detachment of about 150 English-speaking Germans, dressed in American uniforms, were known as Otto Skorzeny's "Kommandos." A number variously estimated at 28 to 44 managed to get behind U.S. lines, and created fear, rumor and tension disproportionate to their numbers. All but eight safely returned to German lines. The "Kommandos" gathered valuable intelligence, caused confusion, and one, impersonating an American MP, directed a U.S. regiment down the wrong road. But they had no plans, contrary to legend, to assassinate Eisenhower and they made no attempt. (See Merriam's *Dark December,* pp. 126 ff.)

The stunning surprise of the German attack was demonstrated by an ironic incident. Prior to the German assault a "rubber duck" deception operation was planned and executed. The so-called "rubber ducks" were special U.S. intelligence units, equipped with radios and inflatable rubberized fabric replicas of U.S. tanks, artillery and other weapons. These "rubber ducks" were moved into place, inflated by pneumatic pumps and ostentatiously exposed to German eyes. In the Ardennes the "rubber duck" operation behind the VIII Corps was planned, in conjunction with the First Army attack against the Roer River dams, as an "operation" (as Merriam puts it in *Dark December,* p. 87) to "lure German divisions from the Aachen sector to the Ardennes.

"Wags have facetiously and perhaps unfairly suggested that this was the greatest deception in the history of organized warfare—29 German divisions brought down on Middleton's neck to meet one American division which wasn't there."

The Germans were not fooled by the simulated weapons. By the time their offensive started their intelligence estimates had correctly evaluated U.S. strength.

Acknowledgments

I am greatly indebted to Charles B. MacDonald of the Office of the Chief of Military History, USA, and to Major General John Shirley ("P") Wood, USA (Ret.), commander of the 4th Armored Division in the drive across France, for reviewing this manuscript. Mr. MacDonald, who offered many valuable suggestions, feels strongly that there was no "rout" at the Bulge. The eyewitness accounts of panic and confusion referred generally—though not always—to service and support rather than combat units, although some small combat units did "bug out." However, as Mr. MacDonald has pointed out, the First Army as a whole was never in "rout."

The Ardennes: Battle of the Bulge by Hugh M. Cole, a volume in the

Army's official history of World War II, is the definitive work on the battle. I have drawn upon this heavily to check and expand my own account.

For the account of the conference at Twelfth Army Group headquarters, where Eisenhower planned his riposte, and for the remarks of Eisenhower, Bradley, *et al.*, I am indebted to Butcher (*My Three Years with Eisenhower*), Eisenhower (*Crusade in Europe*), John Toland (*Battle—The Story of the Bulge*) and the reminiscences of Bradley and others who were present.

For the shift of command to Field Marshal Montgomery, I am indebted to standard sources and a personal check of all available records by General Eisenhower's staff, with the results summarized in a letter to the author.

I have quoted extensively in the text from intelligence documents, after-action reports of individuals and units, and official papers. These are either identified in the text or in footnotes or listed in the bibliography. Quotations otherwise unidentified in footnotes are drawn either from personal correspondence or interviews with officers mentioned, from personal or unit after-action reports or from captured German documents. Most of these—with the exception of the personal correspondence—are to be found in the files of the Office of the Chief of Military History, Department of the Army, Washington, D.C.

Bibliography

Books

BRADLEY, GENERAL OMAR N., *A Soldier's Story*. New York: Holt, 1951

BUTCHER, HARRY C., *My Three Years with Eisenhower*. New York: Simon & Schuster, 1946

CARPENTER, IRIS, *No Woman's World*. Boston: Houghton Mifflin, 1946

COLE, HUGH M., *The Ardennes: Battle of the Bulge*. Washington: Office of the Chief of Military History, Department of the Army, 1965

CRAVEN, W. F., and CATE, J. L., eds., *The Army Air Forces in World War II*, Vol. 3, *Europe to V-E Day, January 1944 to May 1945*. Chicago: University of Chicago Press, 1951

EISENHOWER, GENERAL DWIGHT D., *Crusade in Europe*. New York: Doubleday, 1948

FOLEY, CHARLES, *Commando Extraordinary*. London: Longmans, Green, 1954

GREENFIELD, KENT ROBERTS, gen. ed., *Command Decisions*. New York: Harcourt Brace, 1959

HART, B. H. LIDDELL, *The Other Side of the Hill*. London: Cassell, 1951

HOWETH, CAPTAIN L. S., *History of Communications-Electronics in the United States Navy*. Washington: Bureau of Ships and Office of Naval History

MACDONALD, CHARLES B., *The Siegfried Line Campaign (U.S. Army in World War II)*. Washington: Office of the Chief of Military History, Department of the Army, 1963

MARSHALL, S. L. A., *Bastogne: The Story of the First Eight Days*. Washington: Infantry Journal Press, 1946

MERRIAM, ROBERT E., *Dark December*. Chicago: Ziff-Davis, 1947

MOOREHEAD, ALAN, *Eclipse*. New York: Coward-McCann, 1945

PATTON, GENERAL GEORGE S., JR., *War As I Knew It*. Boston: Houghton Mifflin, 1957

RIDGWAY, GENERAL MATTHEW B., *Soldier: The Memoirs of Matthew B. Ridgway* (*As Told to Harold H. Martin*). New York: Harper, 1956

SEMMES, HARRY H., *Portrait of Patton*. New York: Appleton-Century-Crofts, 1955

TOLAND, JOHN, *Battle: The Story of the Bulge*. New York: Random House, 1959

WILMOT, CHESTER, *The Struggle for Europe*. New York: Harper, 1952

Magazine

SHOWALTER, LIEUTENANT COLONEL WILBUR E., "What Is Calculated Risk?," *Military Review*, May, 1952

Documents

The documentation for the Battle of the Bulge is voluminous. The war reports of General George C. Marshall, Chief of Staff, U.S. Army ("Biennial Report of C/S, U.S. Army July 1, '44–June 30, '45") and of General Dwight D. Eisenhower, Supreme Commander, Allied Expeditionary Forces, are basic documents. Other and more specific reports include: *First U.S. Army Report of Operations; 1 Aug. 1944–22 Feb. 1945* (particularly pages 99–128) and annexes (privately printed); *V Corps Operations in the E.T.O.; 6 Jan. '42 to 9 May, '45; 7th Armored Division After-Action Report—1–31 Dec. 1944; History of the VII Corps* (privately printed), *After-Action Report, Combat Command B—7th A.D.;* and personal and after-action reports of participating personnel and units. These are supplemented by the intelligence documents of all the units involved.

In addition, I have interviewed and/or corresponded with most of the intelligence officers involved, particularly General Edwin L. Sibert and Colonel B. A. Dickson, both of whom I knew personally, and with the following officers (ranks as of the time): Lieutenant General Courtney Hodges; Major General J. Lawton Collins; Brigadier General W. B. Palmer; Colonel O. C. Troxel, Jr.; Major General W. B. Kean; Colonel R. F. Akers, Jr.; Mr. Shepherd Stone (then an officer assigned to the intelligence section, First Army); Major General Alan Jones; Colonel Malin Craig, Jr.; Brigadier General Bruce C. Clarke; Lieutenant General W. H. Simpson; Major General H. R. Bull; and General Dwight D. Eisenhower. Also Lieutenant Colonel Martin M. Philipsborn, Jr.; Captain William J. Fox; and others. These have supplied me not only with answers to specific questions but also with documents and narratives.

The unpublished manuscript of Earl F. Ziemke, "Stalingrad to Berlin— The German Campaign in Russia, 1942–1945," Office of the Chief of Military History, Department of the Army, also has some ancillary usefulness in strategic background for the Bulge Battle.

CHAPTER 11. THE GREATEST SEA-AIR BATTLE IN HISTORY

Notes

1. About 1,213 of the ships were under Task Force 51, the Joint Expeditionary Force, or the assault forces under Vice Admiral Richmond K. Turner. "The Amphibious Forces, Pacific Fleet Action Report of 25 July, 1945," gives the breakdown and organization as follows:

The *Northern Attack Force* (Task Force 53), comprising an Air Support Control Unit, Two Transport Squadrons, Tractor Flotilla, Control Group, Beach Party Group, Attack Force Screen, Defense and Garrison Group, transported and landed the III Amphibious Corps over the Northern Hagushi Beaches on Okinawa.

The *Southern Attack Force* (Task Force 55) was organized similarly to the Northern Attack Force, with the addition of an LCT and Pontoon Group and Port Director Group. Task Force 55 transported and landed the XXIV Army Corps over the Southern Hagushi Beaches on Okinawa.

The *Western Island Attack Group* (TG 51.1), comprising an Air Support Control Unit, one TransRon, Tractor Flotilla, Assault Tractor Group, Reserve Tractor Group, LSM Group and Control Unit, Beach Party Unit and Screen, transported and landed the 77th Infantry Division on Kerama-Retto, and Field Artillery units on Keise Shima.

Demonstration Group (TG 51.2), consisting of an Air Support Control Unit, One TransRon, Tractor Flotilla, Control Unit and Screen, transported the 2nd Marine Division plus Army Reserves, and after executing diversionary feints on the Southeast coast of Okinawa and landing Army Reserve Units over designated beaches, retired with the 2nd Marine Division to Saipan.

Area Reserve (TG 51.4), consisting of one TransRon, Landing Craft Unit, and Area Reserve Screen, was available and standing by to load, transport and land the 21st Infantry Division, but this division was not released by CINCPAC as it was not necessary to the operation.

Ships employed in the operation. A total of 1,213 ships listed as to type in the table below were employed by Task Force 51. The list includes Assault Shipping and ships from other forces which operated temporarily under Senior Officers Present Afloat at the objective.

SUMMARY OF SHIPS EMPLOYED

Type	No.	Type	No.	Type	No.	Type	No.
AGC	8	ARG	1	CVE	18	LSM	111
AK	1	ARL	3	DD	82	LSV	5
AKA	53	ARS	1	DE	54	LST	187
AKN	4	ATF	6	DM	14	OBB	18
AM	42	ATR	2	DMS	13	PC	16
AN	12	AV	3	IX	1	PCE	7
AP	3	AVD	3	LCI	134	PCS	17
APA	126	AVP	4	LCI(L)	6	PCM	6
APD	36	CA	8	LCS(L)3	42	SC	33
APH	2	CL	4	LCT	67	XAK	7
ARB	1	CM	3	LSD	6	XAP	3
						YMS	40
Total Ships	1,213						

Summary of expeditionary troops engaged. The following table lists the troops employed for Phases I and II of the Operation. Figures include the

2nd Marine Division which was at the objective but did not land during these phases.

SUMMARY OF EXPEDITIONARY TROOPS EMPLOYED

	Assault Troops			Garrison Troops			
	Army	Marine	Navy	Army	Marine	Navy	Total
Landing Force	98,567	81,165	2,380				182,112
Garrison Force				182,137	8,130	79,307	269,754
Net Total Troops Employed	98,567	81,165	2,380	182,137	8,130	79,307	451,866

The Gunfire and Covering Force, consisting chiefly of the older battle-ships, cruisers and destroyers, was organized as Task Force 54, under Rear Admiral M. L. Deyo, in *Tennessee.* Rear Admiral W. H. P. Blandy, in *Estes,* commanded the Amphibious Support Force, Task Force 52, consisting chiefly of escort or support carriers, and destroyers. Task Force 58, the fast carriers, was commanded by Vice Admiral Marc A. Mitscher and included the fleet's newest and fastest battleships (and some cruisers and destroyers) as well as some 15 to 17 carriers.

2. Samuel Eliot Morison, *Victory in the Pacific,* p. 162.

3. *Ibid.,* p. 166.

4. Exact casualty figures on Okinawa and exact Japanese strengths will probably never be known with absolute certainty. On the U.S. side 4,000 naval officers and sailors were killed or missing; a greater number were wounded. Total losses of the Tenth Army (XXIV Army Corps, and III Marine Amphibious Corps, General Simon Bolivar Buckner commanding) were 7,613 soldiers and Marines dead or missing, almost 32,000 wounded, and 26,000 nonbattle casualties, a grand total of about 65,000.

The History of the Medical Department of the United States Navy in World War II—The Statistics of Diseases and Injuries, prepared by the Division of Medical Statistics, Bureau of Medicine and Surgery, Navy Department—Navmed P-1318, Volume 3, Washington, U.S. Government Printing Office, 1950, gives casualty breakdowns for the Navy and Marines as follows:

Killed in action	6,700
Wounded, died subsequently	566
Invalided from service	2,904
Wounded	14,758

It is to be noted that these figures differ somewhat from those given in Morison (*op. cit.,* p. 282) and in Appleman, Burns, Gugeler and Stevens, *Okinawa, The Last Battle* (p. 473), but the Bureau of Medicine and Surgery statistics must be accepted as definitive, as far as the Navy and Marines are concerned. The breakdown follows:

NAVY CASUALTIES ABOARD SHIPS ONLY

Ship Types	Killed in Action		Wounded							
			Total		Died Subsequently		Invalided from Service		Returned to Duty	
	Number	Percent of Total Casualties	Number	Percent of Total	Number	Percent of Wounded	Number	Percent of Wounded	Number	Percent of Wounded
Total, All Ships	3,593	39.3	5,538	60.6	197	3.6	748	13.5	4,593	82.9
Battleships	82	19.9	330	80.1	6	1.8	45	13.6	279	84.5
Heavy Cruisers	46	42.2	63	57.8	2	3.2	10	15.9	51	81.0
Light Cruisers	50	34.7	94	65.3	11	11.7	14	14.9	69	73.4
Carriers (All Types)	461	55.6	368	44.4	17	4.6	58	15.8	293	79.6
Destroyers	1,925	48.3	2,064	51.7	76	3.7	222	10.8	1,766	85.6
Destroyer Escorts	181	38.6	288	61.4	12	4.2	60	20.8	216	75.0
Transports	172	20.3	675	79.7	18	2.7	97	14.4	560	83.0
Mine Craft	357	39.6	544	60.4	26	4.8	97	17.8	421	77.4
Landing Ships and Craft	193	24.5	595	75.5	16	2.7	55	9.2	524	88.1
All Other Type Ships	126	19.6	517	80.4	13	2.5	90	17.4	414	80.1

MARINE CORPS CASUALTIES

Date of Admission			Dead			Wounded, Recovered		
Calendar Date	Relation to D-day	Total	Total	Killed in Action	Wounded, Died Subsequently	Total	Returned to Duty	Invalided from Service
Total campaign	(1,2,45 to 3,31,45)	14,921	3,244	2,899	345	11,677	9,649	2,028
Preceding D-day	(D-day–D + 6)	108	19	15	4	89	73	16
First week	(D + 7–D + 13)	540	132	121	11	408	340	68
Second week	(D + 14–D + 20)	573	137	124	13	436	349	87
Third week	(D + 21–D + 27)	596	117	103	14	479	411	68
Fourth week	(D + 28–D + 34)	171	35	34	1	136	115	21
Fifth week	(D + 35–D + 41)	715	254	233	21	461	377	84
Sixth week	(D + 42–D + 48)	2,018	535	486	49	1,483	1,220	263
Seventh week	(D + 49–D + 55)	2,835	617	544	73	2,218	1,809	409
Eighth week	(D + 56–D + 62)	1,686	292	250	42	1,394	1,149	245
Ninth week	(D + 63–D + 69)	853	148	134	14	705	575	130
Tenth week	(D + 70–D + 76)	1,326	246	212	34	1,080	897	183
Eleventh week	(D + 77–D + 83)	1,443	303	275	28	1,140	974	166
Twelfth week	(D + 84–D + 90)	1,656	356	318	38	1,300	1,074	226
Thirteenth week		222	29	28	1	193	160	33
Fourteenth week and later	(7,1,45 to 8,24,46)	179	24	22	2	155	126	29

The total Japanese strength on the island at the start of the battle has been variously estimated at 89,000 to about 120,000. Some of the discrepancy is due to the fact that Okinawan laborers—numbering possibly 10,000—were included in the total, and some Okinawan civilians (there were some 450,000 on the island) became involved in the fighting. There were probably no more than 90,000 fighting troops, of whom about 83,000 were concentrated in the southern part of the island. All of them were casualties. From 7,400, the number of prisoners captured during the campaign gradually increased, as Japanese in hiding were picked up weeks and months after the campaign ended. By November, 1945 (three months after the war was over) the total number of prisoners had reached 16,346—exclusive of additional unarmed laborers and a few armed Okinawan civilians who had worked with the Japanese forces.

Even long after the war, the exact strength of the Japanese Thirty-second Army, which defended Okinawa, cannot be reconstructed with precision. *Okinawa: The Last Battle* estimates there were 77,199 Japanese fighting men in the Thirty-second Army troop list plus Okinawan reinforcements. (See Appendix B, pp. 483–485.)

A dispatch to the *New York Times* published on June 7, 1964, described the battle scene on Okinawa two decades later and reported that "100,000 Okinawans appear [to have been] killed and 100,000 wounded" in the campaign. These figures are excessive, but civilian deaths *were* high. Monuments to military and civilian dead now dot the battlefield; one, the "Dawn Monument," stands high on "Suicide Cliff" near the entrance to the cave where the Japanese commander and his chief of staff committed suicide. Near the bottom is a memorial to "19 teachers and 307 students from the Okinawa Normal School, who died June 19, 1945, by suicide or suicidal charges against American troops."

5. Morison, *op. cit.*, pp. 200 ff.

6. Appleman, *et al.*, *op. cit.*, p. 97.

7. Morison and the U.S. Strategic Bombing Survey estimate there were ten major kamikaze attacks during the Okinawa campaign. The largest, by far, was the first one on April 6–7, when 355 kamikazes participated (plus conventional aircraft). Some 230 of these were Japanese Navy planes, 125 Army. A total of 185 suiciders attacked on April 12–13; 165 on April 15–16; 115 on April 27–28; 125 on May 3–4; 150 on May 10–11; 165 on May 23–25; 110 on May 27–29; 50 on June 3–7; and 45 on June 21–22. The total number of "suiciders," including individual raids, was about 1,900; 1,050 flown by Japanese Navy pilots and the rest by Army aviators.

The famous struggle at Okinawa between the "men who wished to live and those who wished to die" ended as all such struggles have since time began—in a victory for life. But not without great sacrifice.

According to *The Army Air Forces in World War II* (Craven and Cate), Vol. 5, pp. 632–633, the Japanese flew ten large-scale attacks, totaling 1,465 kamikaze sorties, from Kyushu fields between April 6 and June 22. An additional 185 individual kamikaze sorties from Kyushu were recorded and 250 from Formosa, plus an unknown number—perhaps double the kamikaze total—of conventional enemy air sorties. B-29 and other type aircraft were used repeatedly against enemy fields. The Navy insisted, against objections from the Fifth Air Force, that some of the attacks were coming from Formosa. The Navy apparently overestimated Formosa as the base for the kamikaze suicide missions, but the Army Air Corps underestimated it. Repeated photoreconnaissance missions had been fooled by the extent of Japanese camouflage and dispersion on Formosa; Japanese planes, dismantled, and others, well camouflaged, were parked in scattered villages and towns. At a time when "intelligence officers estimated only eighty-nine [enemy] planes [on Formosa], the Japanese had approximately 700."

8. The Japanese "Sea Raiding Units" or suicide boats had very limited successes during the Okinawa campaign. The U.S. seizure of Kerama-Retto, prior to the Okinawa landing, neutralized one of the principal Japanese bases for these mosquito craft. Some 250 of the boats were discovered, camouflaged and hidden in caves. Each was 18 feet long, manned by one man, and carried two 250-pound depth charges. During the long ordeal off Okinawa, the U.S. Fleet maintained so-called "flycatcher" patrols, which disrupted most of the suicide boat attacks that were attempted. The Japanese did have some successes; on April 9 the destroyer *Charles J. Badger* had both engines put out of commission—for a short time, but with no U.S. casualties—by a suicide boat. Other attempted attacks about the same time, including even swimmers with hand grenades, failed. Large numbers of Japanese suicide craft were captured or destroyed as the conquest of Okinawa continued, but intermittently the Japanese scored against anchored merchant ships or destroyers. The few Japanese submarines that tried to defend Okinawa met strong defenses; as Morison points out (*Victory in the Pacific*, p. 243), most of them were sunk.

9. Appleman *et al., op. cit.*, pp. 470–471.

10. *Ibid.*, p. 473.

11. *Ibid.*

12. U.S. ship losses, by types, were as follows:

	Sunk
Destroyers	17
Landing Craft	10
Supply Ships	3
Mine Sweepers	2
Patrol Craft and Miscellaneous	2
Total	34

The above compilation, although it underscores the ordeal of the destroyers and the "small boys," does not present a comprehensive picture of the kamikaze successes. Many additional ships, including three carriers, the *Enterprise, Bunker Hill* and *Franklin,* and one battleship, the *Maryland,* were so badly damaged that their repairs were not completed until the war had ended.

Acknowledgments and Bibliography

I am indebted to Rear Admiral E. M. Eller, USN (Ret.), Director of Naval History, for his kindness in reviewing, and commenting upon, this chapter.

Personal records, after-action reports, ships' histories, unit and personal diaries, memoirs and letters provide the grist for much of the drama and human interest material detailed in this chapter. Books and other reference material consulted and/or quoted include:

APPLEMAN, BURNS, GUGELER and STEVENS, *Okinawa: The Last Battle (U.S. Army in World War II—The War in the Pacific).* Historical Division, Department of the Army, Washington: Government Printing Office, 1948

CRAVEN, W. F., and CATE, J. L., eds., *The Army Air Forces in World War II,* Vol. 5, *The Pacific: Matterhorn to Nagasaki, June 1944 to August 1945.* Chicago: University of Chicago Press, 1953

HOUGH, MAJOR FRANK O., *The Island War: The United States Marine Corps in the Pacific.* Philadelphia: Lippincott, 1947

INOGUCHI, RIKIHEI; NAKAJIMA, TADASHI; and PINEAU, ROGER, *The Divine Wind.* Annapolis: U.S. Naval Institute, 1958

LOTT, LIEUTENANT COMMANDER ARNOLD S., USN (Ret.), *Brave Ship Brave Men.* Indianapolis: Bobbs-Merrill, 1964

MORISON, SAMUEL ELIOT, *History of the United States Naval Operations in World War II,* Vol. XIV, *Victory in the Pacific, 1945.* Boston: Little Brown, 1960

Parliamentary Debates (Hansard), Vol. 437, No. 104. Wednesday, 14 May, 1947

PRATT, FLETCHER, *The Marines' War.* New York: Sloane, 1948

SCHUON, KARL, ed., *The Leathernecks.* New York: Franklin Watts, 1944

U.S. Strategic Bombing Survey (Pacific), Naval Analysis Division, *The Campaigns of the Pacific War.* Washington: Government Printing Office, 1946

VANDEGRIFT, GENERAL A. A., *Once a Marine: The Memoirs of General A. A. Vandegrift, U.S.M.C.,* as Told to Robert B. Asprey. New York: Norton, 1964

APPENDIX:

CASUALTIES OF WORLD WAR II

The statistics of Armageddon are staggering, but will be forever imprecise.

The human toll of World War II was by far the greatest in history. Total deaths—military and civilian—are variously estimated at from more than 20,000,000 (*Encyclopedia Americana*) to more than 55,000,000 (a German statistical study). The military dead alone totaled more than 16,000,000. About 6,000,000 Jews from all the countries of Europe were murdered by Hitler in his infamous concentration camps or simply disappeared. Millions of other civilians died in air raids, as a result of the great clash of armies, from starvation, malnutrition or deprivation, or in the tremendous ebb and flow of entire peoples that moved back and forth across Europe and Asia in a terrible tide of refugees and displaced persons during the war years.

Russia suffered a greater toll than any other combatant, and in China, teeming with life, millions died. Germany and Japan, on the Axis side, paid most heavily for their attempted conquests and their short-lived glories.

The following pages, which provide a breakdown of casualties by countries, list statistics furnished chiefly from official sources. Some of these, "sicklied o'er with the pale cast" of politics, may be exaggerated; nevertheless, it seems certain that death from war causes claimed a grand total of perhaps 40 million lives in World War II.

BELGIUM

	Number Mobilized	Killed	Wounded	Missing	Imprisoned
Belgian Army (May, 1940)	650,000	9,000	No statistics	No statistics	200,000 (of whom 1,679 died in captivity)
Belgian Army in Exile (1940–1945)	3,500	513	No statistics	No statistics	No statistics
Congo Army in Abyssinian Campaign (1941–1942)	132 Europeans	2	6	5	None
	4,100 Natives	46	86	No statistics	None

SOURCE: *Belgian Embassy, Washington, D.C.*

BRITISH COMMONWEALTH

Country	Killed[a]	Missing	Wounded	POW[b]	Totals
Canada	37,476	1,843	53,174	9,045	101,538
Australia	23,365	6,030	39,803	26,363	95,561
New Zealand	10,033	2,129	19,314	8,453	39,929
South Africa	6,840	1,841	14,363	14,589	37,633
India[c]	24,338	11,754	64,354	79,489[d]	179,935
Colonies	6,877	14,208	6,972	8,115	36,172
Totals	108,929	37,805	197,980	146,054	490,768

[a] *Including those who died of wounds or injuries.*
[b] *Including military internees.*
[c] *Now Pakistan and the Republic of India.*
[d] *Including 20,147 missing but presumed POW.*

SOURCE: *British Information Services.*

BULGARIA

Deaths	10,000 to 20,000

CZECHOSLOVAKIA

Deaths	
Military	160,000
Civilian	215,000

SOURCES: *World Almanac and German statistical service. The military dead probably include many who served with either German or Russian armed forces; the civilians include those killed in the Nazi occupation and in war incidents (viz., the Lidice incident).*

DENMARK

Total Deaths	
(Military and Resistance)	1,400 to 6,300

SOURCES: *Danish Embassy; German sources; World Almanac. The lower figure probably includes only uniformed personnel; the higher one includes merchant seamen, as well as civilian resistance fighters.*

FINLAND

Winter War between Finland and Russia, 1939–40

Total Dead   25,000, of which 23,157 killed in action.
Wounded   45,000, of which 10,000 were permanent invalids.
(Note: Estimated Russian losses, according to Finns: 200,000 killed in action. According to Russian statements, quoted by Finns, the Russians lost 217,500 killed and wounded.)

1941–1944

Killed in Action   60,605
Missing   4,534
Wounded 158,000, of whom 47,500 were permanent invalids.

Grand Totals

(including Winter War, World War II proper, and civilians and seamen)

Dead   86,000
Invalids   57,000[a]

[a] *Includes 7,000 who have since died from wounds; disability of 10,000 of the total is more than 50 percent.*

SOURCE: *Consulate General of Finland, New York.*

FRANCE

	Military (in French or Allied Service)	Civilian	Total
Killed or died	170,000	400,000[a]	570,000
Wounded[b]	230,000	355,000[c]	585,000
Totals	400,000	755,000	1,155,000

[a] *Of this total 250,000 deaths occurred in enemy concentration camps or prisons outside of Metropolitan France.*

[b] *includes only those receiving disability pensions from the government.*

[c] *Of this number 127,000 were wounded in France; the remainder were repatriated from Germany, wounded or ill.*

SOURCES: Cahiers Français d'Information, *January 15, 1949, from statistics furnished by the Direction de la Statistique Générale et le Secrétariat de la Commission Consultatives des Dommages etdes Réparations, 1949.*

GERMANY (INCLUDING AUSTRIA)

Killed in Action[a]	
(Sept. 1, 1939—Jan. 31, 1945 only)	2,001,399
Wounded	4,429,875
Missing and Prisoners	1,902,704
Total	**8,333,978**

[a] *Includes about 191,000 died of disease, accidents, suicides, death sentences, etc.*

Estimated deaths for final three months of war, plus numbers of missing who have not returned to Germany and are believed to have died, chiefly in Russian prison camps, increase estimated total of Germany's Military dead to 4,000,000.

GERMAN COMBAT DEATHS BY SERVICES
TO JANUARY 31, 1945

Army	1,622,561
Navy	48,904
Air Force	138,596

CIVILIAN CASUALTIES (DEAD ONLY)

By air attack or in ground fighting	500,000[b]
Unaccounted for in mass migrations or during flight	2,000,000[b]

[b] *These are approximations only and do not include Jews or Gentiles exterminated in Nazi concentration camps.*

GERMAN JEWS

Killed in concentration camps during war period	About 180,000[c]
Killed prior to war	About 200,000[c]

[c] *German estimates. Others are somewhat higher. Figures do not include Jews of other countries.*

SOURCES: *German Embassy, Washington, D.C., and official documentation,* Losses of the German Wehrmacht, *Bonn.*

GREECE

Losses of Armed Forces World War II, 1940–1944

Officers		Enlisted Men	
Dead	1,126	Dead	15,231
Wounded	1,564	Wounded	48,369
Missing	53	Missing	1,933
Total	2,743	Total	65,533

Communist Guerrilla War, 1944–1949

Officers		Enlisted Men	
Dead	1,198	Dead	14,771
Wounded	2,371	Wounded	35,186
Missing	86	Missing	1,915
Total	3,655	Total	51,872

SOURCE: *Information Service, Royal Greek Embassy, Washington, D.C.*

ESTIMATED TOTAL POPULATION LOSSES OF GREECE IN WORLD WAR II

Deaths	
Greek-Italian War	15,700
Greek-German War	8,000
Executions by Germans and Italians	30,000
Bulgarian Massacres	40,000
Enemy Bombings	3,000
Allied Bombings	4,000
Merchant Marine Casualties	3,500
Guerrilla Warfare	50,000
Estimated Deaths from Hunger (nonviolent deaths in excess of births during period of famine)	260,000
Total	415,300
Hostages	
Hostages to Bulgaria	50,000
Hostages to Germany	30,000
Hostages to Italy	10,000
Jews to Poland	60,000

SOURCE: *Taken from the book* The Sacrifice of Greece in the Second World War, *compiled by a group of experts under the architect K. A. Doxiades, published by the Ministry of Reconstruction, in Athens, 1946.*

HUNGARY

Total Military and Civilian Deaths   420,000

SOURCES: *Hungarian Embassy and* The Geography of Hungary, *Morton Pecsi and Bela Sarfalvi, Budapest, Corvina Press, 1964. Probably more than 100,000 of the total deaths—the* World Almanac *lists 140,000 "battle deaths"—were military personnel.*

ITALY

Dead	309,453
Military Men	162,650
Civilians	146,803
Missing	135,070
Military Men	131,833
Civilians	3,237
Wounded and Crippled	106,054

SOURCE: *Italian Embassy, Washington, D.C.*

THE DEAD AND MISSING OF THE SECOND WORLD WAR
Italy's losses between 1940 and 1945

The Italian Institute of Statistics has recently completed the full data on the men lost by Italy in the Second World War. This inquiry covers both military and civilian losses.*

The statistics refer to the period between June 10, 1940, and December 31, 1945, and have been compiled with the collaboration of the Defense Ministry. The total number of Italians lost through the war were 444,523, including 309,453 dead (263,210 men and 46,243 women) and 135,070 reported missing (134,265 men and 805 women).

JAPAN

Category	Killed and Missing	Wounded	Totals
Army[a]	1,439,101	85,620[c]	1,524,721
Navy[a]	419,710	8,895	428,605
Civilians[b]	658,595	Unknown	?
Totals	2,517,406	?	?

[a] *Includes civilian employees or officials of Army and Navy.*

[b] *Includes 170,000 Japanese who died in Manchuria and China, 165,000 in the Ryuku Islands (Okinawa), and 24,010 found to be missing from their homes after the war. Most of the remainder were killed in the nuclear bombing, fire bombing and conventional bombing of Japan.*

[c] *Rough estimate. Of this number about 20,500 are believed to have died, presumably as a result of wounds, after the war.*

The homes of about 8,750,000 people were destroyed or damaged during the war.

Noteworthy in this table is the small proportion of wounded to killed, and the absence of a prisoner of war category. The Japanese military man was taught to believe that death for the God-Emperor in battle was glorious and would immediately transmute him to a heavenly Paradise. The code of the Bushido and of the Samurai insured a fight-to-the-death, no-quarter struggle; even the wounded, if conscious, tried to kill those who would aid them, and the drowning fought off their rescuers. It was considered a disgrace to be captured, and to the fear of disgrace was added the unwarranted fear of torture. There

DEAD AND MISSING FROM 6-10-1940 TO 12-31-1945 PER LOCALITY

Locality	Prearmistice 6-10-40—9-8-43		Postarmistice 9-9-43—1945		Dead		Missing	
	Dead	Missing	Dead	Missing	Total	Of Which Civilian	Total	Of Which Civilian
Italy	57,321	4,478	151,008	5,582	208,329	142,914	10,060	750
Europe	36,593	79,966	32,309	17,521	68,902	3,734	97,487	2,080
France	814	209	874	220	1,688	51	429	6
Germany and Austria	494	712	22,622	6,428	23,116	3,109	7,140	1,717
Greece and Albania	18,447	8,221	3,379	3,256	21,826	151	11,477	17
Yugoslavia and the Balkans	6,161	4,954	2,664	2,898	8,825	90	7,852	263
U.S.S.R.	10,274	65,703	1,617	4,572	11,891	19	70,275	68
Other Countries	403	167	1,153	147	1,556	314	314	9
Africa	14,983	5,737	1,436	562	16,419	336	6,299	41
North Africa	11,890	4,369	801	355	12,691	168	4,724	15
Egypt	490	190	128	15	618	12	205	2
East Africa	2,236	1,073	221	153	2,457	114	1,226	18
Kenya	65		71		136			
Other Countries	302	105	215	39	517	42	144	6
Asia	272		208		408	23		
India	170		144		314			
Other Countries	102		64		166			
America	36	27	107	24	143	24	51	3
U.S.A. and Canada	27		82		109			
Other Countries	9		25		34			
Australia and New Zealand	16		42		58	4		
At Sea	9,290	15,011	2,553	3,747	11,843	1,922	18,758	241
Not Known	1,793	1,009	1,486	1,406	3,279	539	2,415	536
Total	120,304	106,228	189,149	28,842	309,453	149,496	135,070	3,651

Of the dead, 159,957 were servicemen, 145,996 civilians, 2,693 civilians attached to the services and 807 unknown. Of the missing, 181,419 were servicemen, 2,985 civilians, and 414 civilians attached to the services. In the case of 252 the civil or military status is not known.

* See Italian Institute of Statistics, Morti e dispersi per cause belliche negli anni 1940–1945 (Dead and Missing Owing to the War), Rome, Stabilimento Tipografico Failli, 1957.

were, consequently, few prisoners, and no attempt was made to keep track of them. They simply were crossed out of the life of Japan.

SOURCE: *Press Counselor of the Embassy of Japan, Washington, D.C., from Defense Section, from figures compiled by Japan's Demobilization Agency and Economic Stabilization Board.*

THE NETHERLANDS

Total Number of Dead	250,000
Military	5,200
Merchant Marine	1,200
Jewish citizens	104,000
Hostages	2,700
Citizens who died in German prison camps	20,000
Same, in Dutch prison camps	600
Dead in war actions	21,000
Dead in German labor camps	10,000
Dead in "starvation winter"	15,000
Dead as result of destitution	50,000
Missing	6,500
Prisoners	
Political	35,000
Prisoners of War	9,000
Dead During War in Netherlands East Indies	
Killed in military action	8,500
Citizens killed and deceased in concentration camps	10,500

SOURCE: *The Netherlands Information Service.*

NORWAY

Category	Killed
Military	2,000 (Army, 765; Navy, 923; Air Force, 312)
Merchant Seamen	3,638 (Includes 70 women)
Resistance Movement and Political Prisoners	2,091 (Includes 266 women)
Other Civilians	1,779 (Includes 523 women)
Norwegians in German Army	689
Norwegian "Quislings" Liquidated by Resistance	65
Total	10,262

Average loss for males per 10,000 inhabitants was 12.8, for females 1.2.

SOURCES: *Press Counselor, Norwegian Embassy, Washington, D.C., from official military records, reports of health officers and other Norwegian and German authorities and register of political prisoners compiled by the Department for Social Affairs.*

REPUBLIC OF CHINA (July 7, 1937—August 15, 1945)

Military Casualties	
Killed	1,319,958
Wounded	1,761,335
Missing	130,126
Total	3,211,419

Civilian Casualties: Unknown. Only available estimate by General Ho Ying-chin, then Minister of War: 10,000,000. Other non-Chinese estimates: 6,000,000.

SOURCES: *Statistics from Chinese News Service, from Board of Military Operations, National Military Affairs Council.*

NOTE: *These casualties include those inflicted by the Japanese during their attempted conquest of China, prior to the start of World War II on September 1, 1939.*

RUMANIA

Total Deaths	300,000 to 378,000

RUSSIA

Total Dead (Military and Civilian)	20,000,000[a]
Military Dead	
Killed in Action or Missing	8,500,000
Died of Wounds	2,500,000
Died in Prison Camps	2,600,000
Total	13,600,000[b]
Civilian Dead (about)	7,000,000[b]

[a] *Russian estimate; no breakdown available.*

[b] *German estimates. A German historian, Hans-Adolf Jacobsen, has, however, estimated in testimony at a war crimes trial in Germany that about 4,000,000 Russian prisoners of war died in German prison camps.*

SOURCES: *Novosit Press Agency (APN) through the Press Department of the Soviet Embassy, Washington, D.C., and German estimates through German Embassy.*

Russian casualty statistics are particularly imprecise. There were no graves registration details in the Communist armies and accurate records were not kept.

POLAND

Battle Deaths   320,000 to 644,000[a]
Nonbattle Deaths[b]
    Gassed, murdered or died in concentration or other camps 4,863,000,
        of whom about 3,200,000 were Polish Jews
    Died outside of camps from wounds, malnutrition, etc. 521,000
Estimated Grand Total   5,800,000 to more than 6,000,000[c]

    [a] *Apparently includes both civilians and military personnel killed in battle, by bombing, shellfire, etc. The larger figure is the official Polish figure, the smaller the World Almanac figure. German estimates are that about 100,000 Poles in uniform died in battle.*
    [b] *Estimates only. Apparently includes civilian and military personnel.*
    [c] *The higher figure—6,028,000 Polish citizens—is now used by the present Polish government.*

    SOURCES: *Polish Embassy, Washington, D.C. and Janusz Grukowski and Kazimierz Leszczynski,* Poland under Nazi Occupation, *Warsaw, Polonia Publishing House, 1961.*

UNITED KINGDOM

Total Casualties
(Military, Auxiliary Services, Civilians)

Killed	357,116
Wounded	369,267
Prisoners or Internees	178,332
Missing	46,079
Total	950,794

Military Casualties

Service	Killed	Wounded	Missing	POW	Total
Navy	50,758	14,663	820	7,401	73,642
Army	144,079	239,575	33,771	152,076	569,501
Air Force	69,606	22,839	6,736	13,115	112,296
Totals	264,443	277,077	41,327	172,592	755,439

Of this total, 90,332, or about 12 percent, were incurred in the war against Japan.

Other Casualties

Classification	Total
Civilians	146,777
Merchant Navy and Fishing Fleet	45,329
Home Guard	1,763
Women's Royal Naval Service	124
Auxiliary Territorial Service and Army Nursing Services	751
Women's Auxiliary Air Force	611
Total	195,355

SOURCE: *British Information Services.*

UNITED STATES

Battle Deaths (All Services)	291,557
Other Deaths (Military)	113,842
Wounded	670,846
Total	1,076,244

(Out of a total of 16,112,566 who served in the armed forces)

CASUALTIES BY SERVICES

	Battle Deaths	Other Deaths	Wounded
Army (Including Army Air Forces)	234,874	83,400	565,861
Navy (Including Coast Guard)	36,950	25,664	37,778
Marines	19,733	4,778	67,207
Total	291,557	113,842	670,846

SOURCE: *Department of Defense, Washington, D.C., 1965. The missing are now presumed dead and are included in battle or other deaths. Prisoners of war, long since returned to their homes are not included in current totals.*

UNITED STATES

Military[a]

Deaths[b]	Wounded[c]	Captured[c] or Missing	Total
291,557	670,846	139,709	1,102,112

[a] *Excludes Coast Guard, which serves under the operational control of the Navy in time of war. Excludes Filipinos in Philippine Scouts, Constabulary and Commonwealth Forces.*

[b] *Including killed in action, died of wounds and died while prisoners of war or missing.*

[c] *Excludes deaths.*

U.S. Coast Guard casualties during the war were 244 killed in action; 306 missing in action, presumed dead; 24 died of wounds; a total of 574 battle deaths. Non-battle deaths totaled 1,343, and 432 were wounded in action but recovered.

CIVILIAN

Some U.S. citizens, who were interned by the Japanese in the Philippines and elsewhere in the Orient, when war started, died in internment camps. Some of these deaths were caused by bad treatment, malnutrition and disease, but the number—relatively small—is unavailable. An unknown number of civilian Filipinos (the islands then had a Commonwealth status)—probably thousands—died in Japanese air raids or in combat operations, and other thousands died of malnutrition or disease.

YUGOSLAVIA

Total Deaths	1,706,000[a]
Military Casualties	
Dead	305,000
Wounded	425,000
Prisoners of War	
Deportees, slave laborers, etc.	1,610,000
Grand Total	
Dead, Wounded, Missing,	
Prisoners, etc.	3,741,000

[a] *Civilian and Military.*

SOURCE: *Yugoslav Embassy, Washington, D.C., from booklet,* Compensation of Yugoslav Victims of Nazism *by Nikola D. J. Kosovac, Belgrade, Federation of Yugoslav Journalists, 1964.*

In addition to the casualties of the countries listed—the principal combatants of World War II—there were an unknown number, perhaps varying from thousands to millions, of casualties in such countries as Brazil—which contributed a small expeditionary force to Italy, in what is now Indonesia—the Philippines, Burma, Albania, Egypt and many other countries, some of them colonial dependencies, which were drawn, sometimes only peripherally, into the vortex of war.

INDEX